The Letters of William Lloyd Garrison

EDITED BY

WALTER M. MERRILL AND LOUIS RUCHAMES

PUBLISHER'S NOTE

A word of explanation about the cooperation of the editors on this edition. Some time before 1960, each of the editors, unknown to the other, had embarked on the task of editing Garrison's letters. Each had secured a publisher: Professor Merrill, Harvard University Press; Professor Ruchames, University of Massachusetts Press. On learning accidentally of one another's efforts, the editors decided to cooperate in issuing one edition. The University of Massachusetts Press and Harvard University Press, after mutual discussions, concluded that the latter should assume responsibility for publishing the work.

In arriving at their decision to cooperate, the editors agreed to combine the letters which each had gathered separately as well as to unite in a systematic search for letters that had thus far been overlooked. Repositories of manuscript letters, including libraries, state and local historical societies, and manuscript dealers, in the United States and abroad, were checked. In a number of instances, collections of uncatalogued letters were also searched and additional letters found. During the past two years, several hundred new letters have been discovered and incorporated in the collection. Thus, whereas the original plan called for an edition of four volumes, it appears that ultimately the number will reach six and perhaps eight.

In the allocation of responsibilities, the editors have divided the material by periods as follows:

1822–1835 — Walter M. Merrill	1850–1860 — Louis Ruchames
1836–1840 — Louis Ruchames	1861–1869 — Walter M. Merrill
1841–1849 — Walter M. Merrill	1870–1879 — Louis Ruchames

Each editor assumes complete responsibility for his volumes.

Garrison at thirty

The Letters of
William Lloyd Garrison

Volume I

I
WILL
BE
HEARD!

1822-1835

EDITED BY WALTER M. MERRILL

The Belknap Press of Harvard University Press

Cambridge, Massachusetts   1971

For my wife Adeline

without whom this volume
might never have been completed

PREFACE

I F GARRISON could have looked across the century and witnessed the publication of the first volume of his letters, he would have considered the event propitious. In his nonviolent agitation for the black man he always had an uncanny sense of timing, a serendipitous capacity to guide fortuitous circumstances. And the appearance in print of his early letters at this juncture gives him, in effect, an opportunity to enlist once more in the cause for which he struggled for half a century. Indeed, in these letters he communicates with a wide new audience and states in nineteenth-century terms what in the twentieth century his recently fallen colleague Martin Luther King often insisted, that all men, black as well as white, must be totally free from the bonds of slavery and prejudice, that they must be treated as equals — religiously, socially, politically.

In 1830, at the beginning of his half-century of agitation, Garrison was an unknown printer and sometime editor. By 1833, *The Liberator* having been published for two years, he was to be received in England as an American abolitionist whose voice had been heard — even across the Atlantic. When Garrison appeared at a reception in London, Thomas Fowell Buxton, leader among British abolitionists, greeted him hesitantly: "Have I the pleasure of addressing Mr. Garrison, of Boston, in the United States?" "Yes, sir, . . . I am he; and I am here in accordance with your invitation." Buxton, his bewilderment resolved, extended his hand: "Why, my dear sir, I thought you were a black man! And I have consequently invited this company of ladies and gentlemen to be present to welcome Mr. Garrison, the black advocate of emancipation from the United States of America!" [1] Garrison often retold this story, convinced that Buxton had paid him the highest possible compliment.

By the end of the Civil War Garrison was one of the most famous

1. *Life*, I, 351.

of American citizens. In 1866–1867 the country had an opportunity to express tribute to him in financial terms, and a national fund drive raised for his support a net capital of more than $33,000. The words of a Negro washwoman, who contributed a hard-earned dollar, spoke for many: "If I were a milionare by the God's I would give him $100,000 & make him President of the United States When he dies his destiny is the Heaven of Heavens." [2] Two years later, Samuel J. May commended him in *Some Recollections of Our Antislavery Conflict.* Thomas Wentworth Higginson described Garrison during the postwar years as "contending for the rights of the freed men and of women, as before for those of the slaves." [3]

At Garrison's funeral on May 28, 1879, Wendell Phillips, for many years his friend and for a few his enemy, offered this testimony: "The world suffers its grandest changes not by genius, but by the more potent control of *character*. His was an earnestness that would take no denial, that consumed opposition in the intensity of its convictions, that knew nothing but right." "His was the happiest life I ever saw." "To the day of his death he was as ready as in his boyhood to confront and defy a mad majority. . . . He showed nothing either of the intellectual sluggishness or the timidity of age." [4]

In the decade of the eighties, he was eulogized by his sons, Wendell Phillips Garrison and Francis Jackson Garrison, in their four-volume biography (1885–1889). An anonymous essay review of the book in the *Atlantic Monthly* asserted: "The great personal qualities of Mr. Garrison and his essential leadership in the antislavery enterprise are now generally conceded." [5]

The elegiac mode continued in the twentieth century until 1933 when Gilbert H. Barnes published *The Antislavery Impulse*, which offered a new interpretation of Garrison's role in the antislavery movement. The crusade emanated, Barnes concluded, not from Garrison and New England, but from Theodore D. Weld and New York. Since Barnes's death, his one-time collaborator, Dwight L. Dumond, has reaffirmed the Barnes interpretation in his book, *Antislavery: The Crusade for Freedom in America.* In this book Dumond approves virtually all of the best-known antislavery leaders as great moral giants,

2. This passage is to be found in a letter from Malinda Night [Knight] to Samuel May, Jr., the envelope bearing the postmark November 2 (the year probably being 1867), Merrill Collection of Garrison Papers, Wichita State University Library.
3. "Wendell Phillips," *The Nation,* 38:118 (February 7, 1884).
4. "Remarks of Wendell Phillips," *Tributes to William Lloyd Garrison at the Funeral Services* (Boston, 1879), pp. 43, 47, 48.
5. 57:121 (January 1886), 121.

men inspired in word and act, except for Garrison, whom he considers "*a man of distinctly narrow limitations among the giants of the antislavery movement.*" He was, Dumond says, a man so colossal in conceit as "to claim credit for almost everything that was done in the movement before 1840. He made a contribution. It was neither a large nor an overpowering one, and sometimes it was a negative one." [6]

Although, since the publication of Dumond's book, there has been an occasional restatement of the Barnes-Dumond thesis, there is increasing recognition that that thesis must be challenged. For instance, in 1962 C. Vann Woodward pointed out that "Mr. Dumond's treatment of slavery and the abolitionists admits of no complexities or ambiguities beyond the fixed categories of right and wrong." [7]

The two most recent biographies of Garrison (John L. Thomas, *The Liberator*, and Walter M. Merrill, *Against Wind and Tide*, both published in 1963) disagree regarding the significance of Garrison's contribution to the antislavery movement. The former, using chiefly secondary sources, modifies somewhat the Barnes-Dumond view, whereas the latter seeks to reinterpret Garrison on the basis of the extensive primary materials to be found in public and private collections. With the publication of Garrison's letters many of those materials will be sufficiently available so that the general reader as well as the scholar can observe at close range Garrison the man and Garrison the abolitionist.

In this first volume of his letters Garrison speaks the truth as he sees it: about liberty, about prejudice, about rights, about the eternal verities of human existence. He writes precociously as a teenager to his stern and activist mother (showing her how much he has learned at sixteen and without any formal education). He writes passionately and simply to the woman he loves. He writes gay, bantering letters, full of puns, to his brothers-in-law. He writes enthusiastically and eloquently to innumerable friends and fellow reformers. He writes cynically and indignantly to conservative newspaper editors. He writes pompously and ironically to recalcitrant ministers of God. In his early letters Garrison reveals such contradictory facets of his character that even he is amazed: "Dear Helen, am I not a strange compound? In battling with a whole nation, I am as impetuous, as daring, and as unconquerable, as a lion; but in your presence, I am as timid, and gentle, and submissive, as a dove." [8]

6. (Ann Arbor, 1961), p. 174.
7. C. Vann Woodward, "The Antislavery Myth," *The American Scholar*, 31:320 (Spring 1962).
8. See letter 144, April 24, 1834.

Acknowledgments

It is always difficult for an editor of letters to acknowledge fully his indebtedness to the librarians, colleagues, collectors, autograph dealers, research assistants, societies, and universities without which volumes like the current one could never be completed. In this instance the difficulty is compounded by the fact that the editing of Garrison's letters is the final product (following publication of the journals of James Holley Garrison as well as a biography of William Lloyd Garrison) of more than fifteen years of interest in abolitionist materials. Since it would be difficult to separate the past from the present debt, I wish to express again gratitude for help rendered on the several Garrison projects.

During the years, I have been encouraged and helped by the Garrison family (some of whom, unfortunately, have recently died), who made available manuscripts of letters before they had been deposited in public archives. I am thinking especially of Mr. and Mrs. William Lloyd Garrison, III, Miss Eleanor Garrison, Mr. Frank W. Garrison, Miss Fanny Garrison, Mr. Lloyd K. Garrison, Mrs. Marian K. Chubb (formerly Mrs. Philip McKim Garrison), Mr. Garrison Norton, and Mrs. Lucia Garrison Norton Valentine. I was also helped immeasurably by the work of two of Garrison's sons, Wendell Phillips Garrison and Francis Jackson Garrison, whose four-volume life of their father constituted, in effect, the first selected edition of Garrison's letters.

I want to acknowledge the assistance of Professor Louis Ruchames of the University of Massachusetts (Boston), who is editing alternate volumes of the Garrison letters, for wise advice on innumerable editorial matters, for extensive correspondence in the search for new letters, and for exchanging lists, photocopies, and transcriptions of letters.

Special thanks are due to the following institutions for furnishing photocopies of Garrison autograph letters and for granting permission to print the texts of those letters in this volume: Berea College Library, Boston Public Library, Friends Historical Library of Swarthmore College, Harvard College Library, Haverhill Public Library, Library of Congress, Maine Historical Society, Massachusetts Historical Society, New Hampshire Historical Society, New York Union League Club, Portland (Maine) Public Library, Radcliffe College Library, Rutgers University Library, University College London Library, Wichita State University Library, and Yale University Library. I am grateful also to Mr. John L. Severance of New York City for permission to include a Garrison letter from his collection.

Acknowledgments

In addition, I want to acknowledge the research assistance of librarians at the major repositories of Garrison letters for the period covered by this volume: Mr. John Alden, Keeper of Rare Books, and Miss Ellen M. Oldham, Curator of Printed Books, Boston Public Library; Miss Carolyn E. Jakeman, Houghton Library, Harvard University; and Dr. Stephen T. Riley, Director, Massachusetts Historical Society. Generous research assistance was also provided by the following institutions: American Antiquarian Society (Worcester, Massachusetts); Andover (Massachusetts) Historical Society; Bennington (Vermont) Historical Museum; Connecticut Historical Society; Delaware Historical Society; Groton (Massachusetts) Historical Society; Lowell (Massachusetts) Historical Society; Maine Historical Society; Library of the Society of Friends (London); New-York Historical Society; Newburyport (Massachusetts) Public Library; Old Newbury Historical Society (Newburyport, Massachusetts); Historical Society of Pennsylvania; Pejepscot (Maine) Historical Society; Portland (Maine) Public Library; Rhode Island Historical Society; Smith College Library; and South Carolina Historical Society.

The following friends and colleagues have also assisted in research: Professor Thomas D. S. Bassett, the University of Vermont; Professor Ernest C. Marriner, Colby College; Professor William H. Pease, the University of Maine; Mrs. Dorothy M. Potter, Librarian, Essex Institute (Salem, Massachusetts); Professor John B. Pickard, the University of Florida; and Mrs. Mary Wetmore, Wichita, Kansas.

I am especially indebted to a capable and efficient staff, who have searched for, transcribed, and collated letters, organized files, constructed indexes, identified persons, and the like. Formerly assisting at Wichita were Mrs. Jone L. Butler, Mrs. Joan F. Kornelson, Mrs. Frances J. Majors, Mrs. Virginia C. Griswold, and Mrs. Mary K. Sykes. Most recently at Wichita were Mrs. Greta S. Carroll, Mrs. Barbara A. Ciboski, Mrs. Adeline G. Merrill, Mrs. Wanda K. Sanborn, and Mrs. T. Mildred Wherritt. Working in the Boston area is Mrs. Elizabeth L. Forsythe; assisting in Washington, D.C., is Mrs. Carolyn H. Sung; and in Great Britain, Dr. C. Duncan Rice. The Philadelphia staff, which is helping see the current volume through the press, consists of Dr. Frank M. Laurence, Dr. Alice J. Nearing, Miss Charlotte G. Harp, Mrs. Rebecca McBride, Miss Nancy A. Sahli, and Miss Nancy Zurich.

No amount of help from institutions and individuals would have been fruitful without financial support. The American Council of Learned Societies, earlier so generous in awarding two fellowships, has provided two grants-in-aid of research as has also the American Philosophical Society. More extensive has been the financial assistance

Acknowledgments

received from Wichita State University and during the last six months from Drexel University. The most substantial grant to date, from the National Endowment for the Humanities, was received in the spring of 1970. It is also a pleasure to acknowledge that generous contributions toward the matching funds available under that grant have been received from three members of the Garrison family, Miss Eleanor Garrison, Mr. Robert H. Garrison, and Mrs. Hendon Chubb.

Walter M. Merrill

Philadelphia
September 1, 1970

CONTENTS

Contents

II *GENIUS* AND *LIBERATOR*: 1829–1832 73

Contents

III MISSION TO ENGLAND: 1833   201

Contents

Contents

Contents

V YEAR OF VIOLENCE: 1835   431

Contents

LIST OF ILLUSTRATIONS

Frontispiece

William Lloyd Garrison in 1835, by Manasseh Cutler Torrey; a copy of this painting was made for George Thompson, who took it with him to England. The portrait was also engraved in mezzotint by John Sartain and published in June 1836; a second wood engraving was made for the four-volume life of Garrison. (See *The Words of Garrison*, ed. Wendell Phillips Garrison and Francis Jackson Garrison, Boston and New York, 1905, p. 114.)

Courtesy of the Boston Public Library, photograph by George M. Cushing, Boston.

Following page 32

Garrison in 1825, by William Swain (grandfather of twentieth-century Philadelphia portrait painter Violet Oakley). Painted in Newburyport, Massachusetts, this is the earliest known portrait, the only one showing Garrison with a full head of hair. A wood engraving is reproduced in the four-volume life. (*See The Words of Garrison*, p. 113.)

From the original in the possession of Walter M. Merrill.

Garrison's birthplace, the Farnham house on School Street, Newburyport.

Courtesy of Susan Emery Ricker.

The George Benson home, 64 Angell Street, Providence, Rhode Island. Built about 1796 in the College Hill section of the city, this house was the residence of George Benson and his family until his retirement to Brooklyn, Connecticut, in 1824. (See Providence City Plan Commission, *College Hill*, Providence, 1967, p. 54.)

Photograph courtesy of the Rhode Island Historical Society.

The Benson home, "Friendship Valley," Brooklyn, Connecticut. Although the house was probably built prior to 1795, it was the Benson residence only after the move from Providence in 1824; it remains a private residence today.

Photograph courtesy of Mr. and Mrs. Richard F. Wendel.

The Prudence Crandall house, Canterbury, Connecticut. This house, supposedly built for Elisha Paine about 1800, was acquired by Prudence Crandall in 1832. It was here that she started the controversial school for Negro girls. She moved from the house after her marriage to Calvin Philleo in 1834. The property is currently being developed as a museum.

Photograph courtesy of the Connecticut Development Commission.

List of Illustrations

Following page 118

The first issue of *The Liberator*, January 1, 1831. This simple format was used until April 23, 1831, when it was replaced with a more elaborate design, including at the top of the page an engraving of a slave market.

Photograph courtesy of the New York Public Library.

William Lloyd Garrison to La Roy Sunderland, September 8, 1831 (letter number 53). This letter was in reply to Sunderland's warning that Garrison's life was in danger. Sunderland's letter was promptly printed in *The Liberator*, September 8, 1831. Garrison's reply was sent to the printer of the paper (James Brown Yerrinton) twenty-six years later and printed September 18, 1857.

Photograph courtesy of the Boston Public Library.

Following page 310

William Lloyd Garrison in 1833, painted in New Haven by Nathaniel Jocelyn. The portrait shows Garrison holding *The Liberator* in his hand. Simeon S. Jocelyn, the artist's brother, made a steel engraving from the oil painting. (*See The Words of Garrison*, pp. 113–114.)

Courtesy of Mr. and Mrs. Garrison Norton. Photograph courtesy of the National Portrait Gallery, Smithsonian Institution, Washington, D.C.

Arnold Buffum in 1826, by George Freeman. According to documents preserved in the Buffum family, this water color portrait was painted during the artist's residence in England.

Courtesy of Edith B. Lovell.

Following page 464

Banners used in antislavery celebrations. The first banner here commemorates the emancipation of the slaves in the British West Indies; the other banner reproduces a passage from Garrison's salutatory statement in the first issue of *The Liberator*.

Courtesy of the Massachusetts Historical Society.

William Lloyd Garrison in 1835 or 1836, engraved by Robert M. J. Douglass. Douglass, the brother of Sarah Mapps Douglass, was a Negro artist working in Philadelphia.

Courtesy of the Historical Society of Pennsylvania.

EDITORIAL STATEMENT

THIS VOLUME includes the complete texts of all Garrison's early letters known to the editor (that is, those written between 1822 and 1835). Wherever possible, the text has been established from Garrison's autograph. When the manuscript letter is unavailable, the text has been taken from a copy, either written, typed, or printed, and the exact source is designated in the descriptive notes.

Since many of the early letters have been preserved only in copies printed in newspapers and these versions sometimes vary from the form usual for personal letters, it is occasionally difficult to determine with precision whether a given piece is a letter. The following criteria have been used as guidelines: whether Garrison has himself described the work as a letter, whether the work is addressed to an individual or a specific group, whether there is either a salutation or a name or title in direct address, whether there is a complimentary close, and, finally, whether the content of the work, like that of many letters, is topical or timely. Certain works considered but disqualified are mentioned in pertinent footnotes.

The letters are arranged in chronological periods, the particular groupings being determined by the basic pattern of Garrison's career as well as by the number and nature of letters available in each period. Letters composed during more than one day are placed chronologically according to the initial date. Undated letters are assigned to the end of the periods in which they seem to belong unless conjectural evidence makes it possible to place them more accurately within the period. Prefaced to each of these periods is a brief introductory essay providing the reader with a context for better understanding the letters of that period.

Format of the Text

1. Each letter is numbered according to its chronological position in the entire sequence of letters.

2. Since all the letters are from Garrison, the editor has used a uniform heading, simply printing the name of the recipient in its usual spelling.

3. Each letter is also given a uniform date line using verbatim Garrison's original words, the editor having supplied when necessary additional information in square brackets. In those letters dated by Garrison at the bottom of the text, the date has been supplied twice: in square brackets at the beginning and as intended by Garrison at the end.

Text of the Letters

1. The salutation is uniformly placed but follows Garrison's original wording.

2. The editor has endeavored to supply with scrupulous accuracy the text of each letter as presented in its source. Garrison's misspellings have been followed, his cancellations omitted. Obvious slips, such as the repetition of a word or phrase or the omission of a period following an abbreviation, have been silently corrected.

3. The complimentary close and signature are worded precisely as in the source, but uniformly placed. The punctuation of the signature, when the letter has been printed, follows that of the printed source.

4. Simple postscripts are uniformly placed following Garrison's signature. Marginal notations clearly intended as postscripts are transcribed as such, with notes explaining their position in the manuscript. Marginal notations intended to be read at a particular position in the text are so placed.

5. Certain editorial situations are described by the following symbols:

[. . .] A lacuna in the manuscript or other source. If the lacuna consists of more than a word or two, its extent and nature are explained in the notes.

[   ] Editorial insertion.

[   ] Garrison's brackets.

☞   ☜ Garrison's method of emphasis.

Descriptive Notes

1. The source of the letter is supplied without number immediately following the text, the only abbreviations used being the conventional ALS for "autograph letter signed," AL for "autograph letter" without signature, and ANS for "autograph note signed." When the source is other than an autograph, its nature is described.

2. Known previous publications of the letter, whether in whole or in part, have been indicated.

3. Wherever the manuscript is in such poor condition as to interfere with transcription, that condition is described.

4. Efforts have been made to identify all recipients.

Notes

1. Consecutively numbered notes for each letter are placed immediately following the descriptive notes.

2. The editor has endeavored to identify persons referred to in the texts of the letters, as well as to explain references and allusions not immediately clear in context, the extent of the notes being determined by the importance of the person or the allusion. The editor has also tried to identify Garrison's quotations, but some of the authors quoted are so obscure as to make identification virtually impossible.

3. Quotations from the Bible have been verified or identified in the King James version, which seems to be the only one Garrison used. For quotations from Shakespeare, we have followed the standard concordance: John Bartlett, *A Complete Concordance . . . of Shakespeare* (New York, 1967). This book follows the Globe edition of 1891.

4. The editor has kept abbreviations to a minimum, using only *Life* for the frequent references to Wendell Phillips Garrison and Francis Jackson Garrison, *William Lloyd Garrison* (New York, 1885–1889), four volumes; and "Merrill" for Walter M. Merrill, *Against Wind and Tide, a Biography of Wm. Lloyd Garrison* (Cambridge, Mass., 1963), though the latter, if often used, is seldom cited.

CHRONOLOGY OF GARRISON'S LIFE

1805
December 10 or 12. Birth of William Lloyd Garrison in Newburyport, Massachusetts.

1808
Summer. Death of older sister Caroline Eliza and birth of younger, Maria Elizabeth. Abijah Garrison's desertion of the family.

1814–1817
Childhood in Newburyport, Lynn, and briefly in Haverhill. Apprenticeship to shoemaker and then cabinet-maker. Mother working as nurse in Baltimore.

1818
October. Beginning of apprenticeship to Ephraim W. Allen of the Newburyport *Herald*.

1822
May. Beginning of writing career with letters to Newburyport *Herald*, signed "An Old Bachelor."
September. Death of Maria Elizabeth Garrison.

1823
September 3. Death of mother in Baltimore.

1825
December 10. End of apprenticeship.

1826
March 22–September 21. Editor in Newburyport of the *Free Press*, in which Whittier first published.

1827
Compositor in Boston. Residence with the Rev. William Collier, 30 Federal Street.

Chronology

1828

January 4–July 4. Editor in Boston of the temperance paper, the *National Philanthropist*. Meeting with Benjamin Lundy, March 17.

October 3. Editor in Bennington, Vermont, of the *Journal of the Times*.

1829

March 27. Final issue under his editorship of the *Journal of the Times*.

July 4. In Boston, first public speech against slavery.

September 2. Beginning of collaboration with Benjamin Lundy as editor of the *Genius of Universal Emancipation* in Baltimore.

1830

March. Trial in Baltimore for libel of Francis Todd of Newburyport. Suspension of publication of the *Genius*.

April 17–June 5. Confined in Baltimore jail.

October. Series of lectures on slavery in Boston.

1831

January 1. Publication of the first issue of *The Liberator*, in partnership with Isaac Knapp.

1832

January 6. Founding in Boston of the New-England Anti-Slavery Society.

June 2. Publication of *Thoughts on African Colonization*.

1833

May 2–September 29. First trip to England. Meeting with leading British abolitionists. Campaign against Elliott Cresson and the American Colonization Society.

December. Founding in Philadelphia of the American Anti-Slavery Society.

1834

September 4. Marriage to Helen Eliza Benson.

September 20. Beginning of George Thompson's first American trip.

1835

October 21. Mobbing in Boston.

December 31. Dissolution of partnership with Isaac Knapp.

1836

February 13. Birth of first son, George Thompson Garrison.

1837

August. Controversy with church over "Clerical Appeal."

1838

January 21. Birth of second son, William Lloyd Garrison, Jr.

September. Founding in Boston of the Non-Resistance Society.

Chronology

1839
October. Change of residence from Boston to Cambridgeport.

1840
May. Schism in New York at meeting of the American Anti-Slavery Society, resulting in the formation of a second national organization, the American and Foreign Anti-Slavery Society.
May 22–August 17. Second trip to England, to attend the World's Anti-Slavery Convention.
June 4. Birth of third son, Wendell Phillips Garrison.

1841
August. Tour of White Mountains with Nathaniel P. Rogers.

1842
February. Beginning of disunion policy.
September 9. Birth of fourth son, Charles Follen Garrison.
October 14. Death at Garrison's home of brother, James Holley Garrison.

1843
January. Attack on Constitution.
Autumn. Change of residence from Cambridgeport to 13 Pine Street, Boston.

1844
December 16. Birth of first daughter, Helen Frances (Fanny) Garrison.

1845
January 29. Delegate to Anti-Texas Convention in Boston.

1846
July 16–November 17. Third trip to England.
December 11. Birth of second daughter, Elizabeth Pease Garrison.

1847
August 2–October 28. First western American tour, with Frederick Douglass. Serious illness in Cleveland, Ohio.

1848
April 20. Death of Elizabeth Pease Garrison.
October 29. Birth of fifth son and last child, Francis Jackson Garrison.

1849
April 8. Death of Charles Follen Garrison.
July–September. Controversy with Father Theobald Mathew.

Chronology

1850

May 7. Mobbing at annual meeting of the American Anti-Slavery Society in New York.

October. Woman's Rights Convention in Worcester, Massachusetts. Beginning of George Thompson's second visit to the United States.

1852

February. Publication of *Letter to Louis Kossuth*.

1853

October 3–November 3. Second western tour. Woman's Rights Convention in Cleveland.

December. Visit in Andover, Massachusetts, with Mrs. Harriet Beecher Stowe.

1854

July 4. Burning of the Constitution and the Fugitive Slave Act at Framingham, Massachusetts.

1857

January. Meeting with John Brown at Theodore Parker's house in Boston.

January–July. Participation in various disunion conventions.

1859

October. Sympathy expressed for John Brown after the raid at Harper's Ferry.

1862

January 14. Cooper Union speech in New York, "The Abolitionists and their Relations to the War."

1863

June. Commission for George Thompson Garrison as second lieutenant in colored regiment.

December 29. Helen E. Garrison invalided by stroke.

1864

February. Beginning of George Thompson's third visit to the United States.

June 9. Meeting with Lincoln at the White House.

August. Change of residence to 125 Highland Street, Roxbury, Massachusetts.

1865

April. Trip to Charleston, South Carolina, with George Thompson, Henry Ward Beecher, and others.

May 10. Resignation as president of the American Anti-Slavery Society.

Chronology

August–September. Founding of the American Freedmen's Aid Commission, with Garrison as first vice-president.
November. Lecture tour to the West.
December 6. Marriage of Fanny Garrison to Henry Villard.
December 29. Publication of the last issue of *The Liberator*.

1866
January 25. Withdrawal from the Massachusetts Anti-Slavery Society.
February. Lectures in Philadelphia and Washington.

1867
May 8–November 6. Fourth trip abroad. Delegate from the American Freedmen's Union Commission to the International Anti-Slavery Conference in Paris.

1868
March 10. Presented with a national testimonial of more than $33,000.

1876
January 25. Death of Helen E. Garrison.

1877
May 23–September 4. Fifth and final trip to England.

1879
February. Opposition to Chinese Exclusion policy.
May 24. Death in New York.
May 28. Burial at Forest Hill Cemetery in Boston.

I ANCESTRY AND EARLY YEARS

I ANCESTRY AND EARLY YEARS

ALTHOUGH THE name Garrison can be traced in America back to the early eighteenth century, the first known paternal ancestor of William Lloyd Garrison was Joseph (1734–1783), who, approximately a decade before the Revolution, settled as a farmer on the Jemseg River in what was to become New Brunswick. In 1764 he married Mary Palmer, whose ancestor was supposed to have come to Raleigh, Massachusetts, in 1639. The Garrisons had nine children, of whom the fifth, born in 1773, was Abijah, the father of William Lloyd Garrison. Little is known of Abijah's youth, except that he grew up on the Jemseg River and eventually became a sailing-master in the coastal and West India trade. Toward the close of the century — possibly in 1798 — he married Frances Maria (Fanny) Lloyd.

Fanny Lloyd, the daughter of Andrew and Mary Lawless Lloyd — both Irish by birth — had been born on Deer Island, New Brunswick, in 1776. By the time Abijah Garrison appeared, she had revolted against the Anglican convictions of her parents and become a Baptist; she was ready for marriage and a family of her own. The young couple presumably settled near his family on the Jemseg River. When they moved to Newburyport, Massachusetts, in 1805, there were two surviving children, James Holley (born 1801) and Caroline Eliza (born 1803). In December 1805 (either the tenth or the twelfth), William Lloyd Garrison was born. In 1808 there followed in rapid succession three events destined to destroy the small family. Caroline died, another daughter, Maria Elizabeth, was born, and Abijah deserted the mother and the three remaining children.

Fanny found employment as a nurse, moving restlessly from Newburyport to Lynn and from Lynn to Baltimore. Elizabeth she took with her; but the boys she could not cope with, and soon they were shifting for themselves. James followed the pattern set by his father and went to sea, first in the merchant marine and later in the Navy. He emulated his father, also, in acquiring a taste for alcohol, which developed into an inexorable habit. Lloyd had his own frustrating years and passed from one interrupted apprenticeship to a second before he found printing a trade to his liking.

In the fall of 1818 Lloyd Garrison was bound as an apprentice to the editor of the Newburyport *Herald*. The earliest of Garrison's letters to be preserved date from the period of this apprenticeship. In the spring of 1822 he grew tired of being merely a printer and started writing letters to the *Herald* signed "An Old Bachelor." These letters are the work of an industrious, even precocious, teen-ager, who was acquiring an education of exceptional range and depth, despite past and future misfortunes. The next September his sister died, and the following autumn (September 3, 1823), less than two months after Lloyd's last visit to see her in Baltimore, Fanny herself died.

After 1825, having completed his apprenticeship, Garrison edited three papers of his own before engaging in full-time antislavery agitation. Thanks to a loan from his former master in the spring of 1826, he was able to buy in Newburyport a paper he named the *Free Press* — so called in spite of the marked Federalist bias apparent during his six months' editorship. It was while he was editing this paper that Garrison discovered and several times published the poetry of John Greenleaf Whittier. Then, after a hiatus of a year spent in Boston shifting from one printing job to another, he became the editor of one of the earliest temperance papers, the *National Philanthropist*. Like the *Free Press* this venture lasted only six months, until July 4, 1828. Three months later Garrison was in Bennington, Vermont, editing the weekly *Journal of the Times*. Although in his initial statement to the public he emphasized the independence of the paper, it had in fact been established to promote the reelection of the very man he had considered the poorest candidate for the presidency in January 1825.[1] At any rate, he felt justified in fervently attacking Jackson. He also welcomed the opportunity to express himself on various moral issues, especially slavery. But the pattern earlier established reasserted itself, and in six months he was again without a job.

Although in editing his first three papers Garrison found occasional opportunities to express himself on moral issues, much of his energy was given to political questions — as it was also in his personal letters. Reading his papers and letters, one might have predicted a career as conservative New England politician rather than as radical reformer.

1. In an essay published in the Newburyport *Herald* January 25, 1825, entitled "POLITICAL REFLECTIONS" and signed "A. O. B.," Garrison discussed the relative merits of John Quincy Adams, William H. Crawford, and Andrew Jackson, the candidates from whom Congress must select the President. His own preference was for William H. Crawford. "If a choice *must* be made between Mr. Adams and Gen. Jackson," he said, "give us the latter — he would be the least dangerous man of the two."

1

TO THE EDITOR OF THE NEWBURYPORT *HERALD*

[May 21, 1822.]

The number of cases which have occurred, within a few years, of this breach, are indeed numerous. But I am of opinion, that many of them are decided in favor of the plaintiff, when their proof was insufficient to show that the defendant had *promised* to marry her: and I am more convinced of the fact, by observing in the Herald of the 14th inst. a case which occurred at Boston the first of May. Now I cannot conceive by what justice the Court decided in favor of the plaintiff, at this trial. — "For, (to use the words of the defendant's counsel,) where there is no *promise* there cannot be any breach," and to fine a man for "keeping company," as it is termed, with a lady, who, though having gallanted her for one or two years, yet made no *promise* to marry her, it is, in my opinion, unjust and ridiculous.[1] No doubt, many females are rejoiced in having it in their power to take the property of the man in so easy a manner, who is so unfortunate as to be gulled by them, because policy aids them in this work, as they are the more likely to get husbands.

Doubtless many a female will be angry against me for thus plainly speaking my thoughts, while perusing this communication; but I am one who do not wish to curry favor with them; their anger will be to me as the 'whistling wind.'

I would not, Mr. Editor, be tho't to maintain, that in no case, whatever, the plaintiff should not be remunerated. I profess to be as great a friend to justice as any one; and where there is undoubted *proof* of the marriage promise having been broken, then let the offender be heavily fined, if money will remunerate. But where there is no positive *proof* of the same, it is illegal. A man who could be so base as to desert a virtuous girl, after he has promised to marry her, when her hopes and expectations were thus raised and blasted in a moment, as it were, by him, ought to feel the effects of the law in a heavy degree.

The truth is, however, women in this country are too much idolized and flattered; therefore they are puffed up and inflated with pride and self-conceit. They make the men to crouch, beseech and supplicate, wait upon and do every menial service for them, to gain their favor and approbation: they are, in fact, completely subservient to every whim and caprice of these changeable mortals. — Women generally feel their importance, and they use it without mercy.

For my part, notwithstanding, I am determined to lead the *"single life,"* and not trouble myself about the ladies. I am often asked the question, "Why do you remain single so long? Others of your acquaintance are getting tied by 'Hymen's silken chains,' and it is full time for you also." My answer is, because I see none of the "raptures," "exstacies," "joys," "happiness," "bliss," &c. &c. as is often represented, existing with married persons; — but, on the contrary, "broils," "distrust," "anger," "strife," and "confusion!" — And to be chained to a brawling and contentious woman, would be far worse than to be condemned to the Gallies for life: the roaring of a battery would be much more musical and harmonious than a *scolding wife*.[2] — Besides, were I to think of matrimony, I should wish to be very careful and scrupulous in my choice. But here another difficulty occurs — should I "keep company" with a lady, (which God forbid!) and find her "not much to my liking," I must either wed her, "for better, for worse," or else pay a round sum for a breach of the marriage promise! — This is, I call it, "paying dear for the whistle": — but I am determined, as I said before, to remain *single*, "let the world say what they will."

AN OLD BACHELOR.[3]

Printed: Newburyport *Herald*, May 21, 1822; extract printed in *Life*, I, 43.

The editor of the paper, the man to whom Garrison was apprenticed, was the cautious, frugal, unimaginative Ephraim W. Allen (1779–1846).

1. It was reported in the issue to which Garrison refers that "the learned counsel for the lady pathetically insisted upon it that a *combination* of circumstances proved the promise of marriage, and the jury, in consequence of the defendant being a poor man, adjudged him pay only 750 dollars damages for keeping company two years with a lady, and not offering to marry her during that period!"

2. This letter, Garrison's first published work, sounds almost as though it had been written by his father, Abijah Garrison, who had known what it meant to face the wrath of an angry woman. In the same issue in which Garrison's letter was printed, the editor of the *Herald* made the following comment: "We hope our fair readers will not take offence at the querulous tone and ungallant reflections of our correspondent the 'Old Bachelor.' As he must have undergone some sad disappointment to inspire him with so much aversion for the sex, it would be more generous to pardon him, than to testify resentment for what he says. But truly we cannot but think, with him, that actions for breach of the promise of marriage are beginning to multiply quite alarmingly, when we are compelled to pay heavy damages in cases like that referred to by our correspondent."

3. Garrison used this pen name to sign his early letters and articles, for he doubted that the editor would knowingly publish letters from an apprentice.

2

TO THE EDITOR OF THE NEWBURYPORT *HERALD*

[May 24, 1822.]

Mr. Editor,

As soon as your last Herald came into my Aunt Betty's hands, (who by and bye happens to be an "Old Maid,") and she had perused my communication, fury immediately flashed in her eyes. Clenching her fists, she came directly towards me, *pugnis et calcibus,* and with a voice, I will venture to say, that equalled, if not surpassed, that of Stentor, gave me one of the most terrible lectures I ever had or witnessed. — As for the men, (good Lord deliver us!) they were worse, in my Aunt's opinion, than the vilest of "beasts" — more venomous than "spiders or rattlesnakes" — fit only to dwell with the "swine," &c. But a man who could speak aught against women, — those "heavenly, bewitching, and super-angelic beings," as she *modestly* styled them, — why, he ought to be forever despised, banished from all society, (not even excepting the *beasts,*) and die an outcast: even that she thought too *merciful!* [1]

As for myself, I shall never forget her frightful attitude and overwhelming eloquence; my blood already recoils at the recollection of it; it will, I verily believe, "grow with my growth, and strengthen with my strength"; [2] that is, allowing I do either. Such pathos and sublimity as she uttered would have rivalled even old Lucifer himself! Indeed, so many threatening and overwhelming words were enough to appal a much stouter heart than mine — and I was actually dissolved to a jelly with fears by her tremendous denunciations. — I, who so boldly declared in my former communication, that a woman's anger would be to me as the "whistling wind," was now completely vanquished at the first onset, by this modern Xantippe.

Could you have seen me, Mr. Editor, you would, I am confident, have pitied me from the very bottom of your heart. Jammed up in one corner of the room, while my Aunt Betty entirely blockaded me, with both arms wide expanded in the air, features distorted, and mouth wide open, vociferating vengeance against my poor carcase if ever she caught me again making such "frightful misrepresentations" of her sex; while I, poor I, sat trembling and quaking like an aspen leaf, paler than Hamlet's ghost. — There was no other alternative than to either desert, or else remain and bravely bear the brunt of the battle: the first would have appeared like cowardice — so I resolved to remain where I was; but, instead of cooling her anger, she waxed more wroth. Trembling for my safety, I gladly beat a parley; it was some time, however, before I could make myself heard — on promising my Aunt that I would never write another syllable about the ladies, and a number of other articles, she so far recovered her good-nature, that she left me for the moment; while I, as soon as she had made her exit, gladly scampered to my chamber.

How my Aunt Betty came to know I wrote the communication is more than I can tell — nor could I get a syllable of intelligence from her on that score.·

Why she was never married, is a question I cannot easily solve; but I shrewdly suspect that, being such a "heavenly, bewitching, and super-angelic" creature, and having one of the most pliant and beautiful tempers that ever woman was blessed with, no "vile brute" ever dared offer his hand to such a *desirable* object!

AN OLD BACHELOR.

Printed: Newburyport *Herald*, May 24, 1822.

1. If Garrison's first letter to the *Herald* sounds like his father, the character of Aunt Betty in this one resembles his mother. Incidentally, another letter involving an Aunt Betty and her eccentric ideas about marriage was addressed about this time to Paul Allen, the editor of the Baltimore *Morning Chronicle*, and reprinted in the *Herald* July 19, 1822. But the letter seems unlikely to be Garrison's since the style is unlike his and the signature, "My Aunt's Favorite," is not one he is known to have used.

2. Except for the change of person this is an accurate quotation of Alexander Pope, *An Essay on Man*, Epistle II, line 136.

3

TO THE EDITOR OF THE NEWBURYPORT *HERALD*

[August 6, 1822.]

The late foreign news received, respecting the Ultimatum of the Russians having been agreed to by the Turks, has put the hungry news-mongers, — who have so long been waiting, with uncommon interest and uneasiness, to behold and greet the fulfilment of their most ardent wishes, *War*, — all aback; and they are foaming and venting their spleen against those accounts which have so rudely, so unmannerly deceived them.[1] And who can blame them? — After having had their expectations and hopes raised to almost a certainty as they wished, they are at once laid prostrate by "one fell swoop"[2] of public journalists — and we cannot but heartily sympathize with them at being thus unfortunate in their speculations; besides, having not the least ray of hope left by which to console themselves.

And cruel, cruel Fate! how often dost thou keep thy votaries in torturing suspense! Week after week, nay month after month, have they been waiting for thee to fulfil the numerous prophecies which have already gone forth, from the one end of the continent to the other, respecting the probability of war or peace, and thou deceivest them!

O tempora! O mores! [3] What a changeable world is this which we inhabit! One moment the public newspapers are teeming with "wars and rumors of wars" [4] — then again flat contradictions, and "All's well!" [5] — When we are expecting the next arrivals will bring us the welcome tidings that the sturdy Russians have grappled the furious Turks by their beards, and dragged them over the Hellespont, then do our expectations vanish "like as a puff of empty air," [6] by the unexpected cries of *peace — peace.* — So treacherous and unstable are human expectations!

Such idle rumors not only vex the pericraniums of newsmongers, but are, undoubtedly, of great injury to the trader — who, probably, thinks that all *is* gold which glistens, and that every unfounded report, — manufactured by those persons who have nothing else to do but to excite the attention of the speculator, — must, of course, be wholly correct. For instance — a merchant of Boston,[7] according to a communication in the Centinel of Saturday, has been completely duped, and perhaps ruined, by an unfortunate speculation on Opium, to a large amount, owing to a firm belief of a war betwixt Russia and Turkey being certain!

These are not the only evils, Mr. Editor, which so many false rumors produce — but, sir, I am fearful that if I stop to enumerate them, there will arrive a postscript, fraught with big events, but differing from what has heretofore been received, and thus render this communication "null and void, and of none effect." [8]

In haste, yours, &c.   A. O. B.

Printed: Newburyport *Herald,* August 6, 1822.

1. Garrison's assumption that the war between the Russians and the Turks was about to end was somewhat optimistic since hostilities continued until 1829.
2. Shakespeare, *Macbeth,* IV, iii, 219.
3. Cicero, *In Catilinam,* I, i.
4. Matthew 24:6 or Mark 13:7.
5. Evidently Garrison refers to the title of Shakespeare's play, *All's Well that Ends Well.*
6. Not identified.
7. Not identified.
8. Garrison uses the familiar legal phrase.

4

TO FRANCES MARIA LLOYD GARRISON

Newburyport, May 26th, 1823.

DEAR MOTHER: —

There is something peculiarly gratifying in corresponding frequently with our distant friends, and hearing of their welfare and happiness; — but how much more so is it when we have the invaluable privilege of communicating with one who loveth, not only as a friend, but as an affectionate parent — a tender, affectionate mother! There is a charm in letter writing that interests us unspeakably for those we love, and binds the silken cords of friendship with the most exquisite neatness around our susceptible hearts and affections. It soothes and mitigates the anxious throbbings of the breast, and sheds a refulgent beam of joy around our troubled and solitary hours. It is a healing balm of comfort to the trembling fears and disquietudes of a parent's heart, as well as to their tender offspring. It is a mirror through which we can look, and almost imagine that we can see our long unseen friends, and hear the well-known accents of their interesting voice.

Your letter was alike a source of pleasure and of pain. Of pleasure, because it was pleasing to receive a letter couched in such tender language from an affectionate mother, whose prop of comfort and consolation devolves upon her son, who, should he fail, would bring her in sorrow to the grave. — Of pain, because it brought the intelligence of your having experienced another bleeding at the lungs, which had almost laid you at death's door — but this was mitigated in some degree with the assurance that you had recovered in some measure from the effects of the same.

Since I have received your letter, my time has been swallowed up in turning *author*. — I have written in the Herald three long political pieces, under the caption of *"Our Next Governor"*, and the signature of *"One of the People"* — rather a great signature, to be sure, for such a *small man as myself*.[1] — But vain were the efforts of the friends and disciples of Washington, the true Federal Republicans of Massachusetts — Democracy has finally triumphed over correct principles, and this State may expect to see the scenes of 1811–12 revived in all their blighting influence; — may they be as short lived as they were at that period. You will undoubtedly smile at my turning politician at the age of *eighteen* — but, "true 'tis, and (*perhaps*) pity 'tis 'tis true" — and I cannot but help smiling myself at the thought.[2] — I have likewise published another political communication under the same signature.

10

Besides these, I have written three other communications under the head of "*A Glance at Europe*" — analysing the present state of political affairs between Spain and the Holy Alliance — and which called forth a very handsome notice of the same from Mr. Cushing, the Editor of the Herald.[3] — But I am at last discovered to be the author, notwithstanding my utmost endeavors to let it remain a secret. — It is now but partially known, however, and has created no little sensation in town — so that I have concluded to write no more at present.

Thus you perceive, my dear mother, that my leisure moments have been usefully and wisely employed; — usefully, because it is beneficial in cultivating the seeds of improvement in my breast, and expanding the intellectual powers and faculties of my mind; wisely, because it has kept me from wasting time in that dull, senseless, insipid manner, which generally characterises giddy youths. It is now about one year since I commenced writing for the Herald — and in that time I have written about fifteen communications.[4] — When I peruse them over, I feel absolutely astonished at the different subjects which I have discussed, and the style in which they are written. — Indeed, it is altogether a matter of surprise that I have met with such signal success, seeing I do not understand *one single rule of grammar*, and having a very inferior education.[5] — But enough of my scribblings, in all conscience, for the present, to something that is more important and interesting.

About two months ago, Harriet met with a very distressing accident, which has confined her so that she has been unable to walk or scarcely move almost ever since.[6] She unfortunately run the scissors into her ankle pretty deeply, which probably injured one of the cords, the wound of which was very dangerous and alarming, as it was feared at first that it would cripple her for life — but, fortunately, our fears proved groundless, and she is nearly as well as ever. Uncle and Aunt Farnham[7] are well, as are also Uncle Bartlet's family — all of whom send their kind love to you.[8] — Little James has sailed on an European voyage.[9]

Methinks I hear you say — "What! does he not say one word about my request for him to visit his disconsolate, dying mother once more ere she closes her eyes in death?" — Yes, my dear mother, I have a great deal to say upon that subject — more than I can compress into the narrow compass of a sheet of letter paper; — and the remainder of my letter shall be devoted to it.

You feel, unquestionably, astonished at my long silence, as well as uneasy. — I will tell you the reason of this, and then you can judge whether I am a fit subject for your mercy or otherwise. Your letter was received about the time Mr. Allen calculated to get back from Alabama; — consequently I thought it prudent to defer writing until he did arrive — not doubting but that it would be shortly. One week elapsed, and he came not: — another and another likewise, but in vain — he came not [. . .] You may well suppose that my mind was filled with anxieties on your account — but still I would not write till he returned; — and, not to indulge in prolixity, he did return. — I requested of him a private interview, and informed him of your and my wishes to see you again, if it were only for one week. — He, of course, raised innumerable barriers and obstacles in the way, and converted a mole hill into a mountain, to all which I respectfully answered. — You recollect last fall my intention of visiting you — and which I should inevitably have done had not my ever to be lamented sister's death occurred. — Heaven bless her memory.[10] — It was at this juncture that Mr. Allen promised that, if I would give up the idea then of visiting Baltimore, (as we were very much hurried in printing a book) he would be willing to spare me in the spring. — Spring came, and the boon was again asked. — He now says that I could have gone had he not been absent so long — or, rather, if he had not gone at all — and that therefore his affairs were in confusion, and it would require time to arrange them properly. — Now, all this is a mere pretext, for the purpose of baffling my anxious desires. — His affairs have been regularly and correctly kept by the Editor — and all that is necessary for him to do is to see that all charges have been made correctly.[11] Another obstacle is this: — we are to enlarge the paper the first of June, which will occasion considerable hindrance. Now, he will have to employ a journeyman to accomplish this, for some time; and never could a better opportunity occur than we had one for me to go. — It will, to be sure, cost him a trifle more, and that he ought to be willing to give in a case of emergency like the present; — especially when I have taken the care of the office faithfully upon my shoulders while he was absent — besides he will save about $10 by my board. He finally wished me to write and inform you, that if I came, I could not set out till about the *middle* of June; — and that he would likewise write to you upon the subject immediately. — My dear mother — I can anticipate all the arguments and means which he will employ to represent the state of affairs here — of the impracticability of my going — of his *anxiety* (though feigned) of wishing me to see you, but the situation of affairs renders it extremely difficult, and a thousand other obstacles, alike feeble and fallacious. — You may depend upon it that it is his own interest which lies at the bottom. — He is perfectly willing that I should go, *if I will hire a journeyman in my room!* Wonderful disinterestedness! — Surprising condescension and favor! — He wished to know whether it could not be settled by letter without the *trouble* of visiting you all that was necessary! How cold and sense-less his heart — He knows not the anxious throbbings of a mother's breast to see her affectionate son — nor the bowels of love with which she watches and protects him from evil. — All I have to request of you is that you will answer his letter in a dignified maner — that you will faithfully pourtray to him the feelings of a mother, and the rea-sons for your request — that you will put the case home to his own conscience, and ask him to draw the parallel, what *he* would think were he to be refused in such a case. I beg you will not be wavering in your answer — for if you are, he will take the advantage readily. Ask his request, not merely as a boon, but as a just right which any parent ought to be willing to grant. — But why need I ask any thing further? I am confident you will write EVERY THING that will be necessary for his permission and approbation. ☞ Do not fail of answering both immediately, as every moment will seem an age upon which my destiny hangs. ☜ Write particularly where I shall find you, should I come to B. and how I shall get to your boarding place. — I cannot but exclaim — "Oh! had I the wings of a dove, then would I soar away, and be with you." [12] Excuse this hasty scrawl, as it is now midnight. — Adieu! dear mother, and O may Heaven grant that I shall clasp you again to my throbbing breast. —

W. L. Garrison.

ALS: Garrison Papers, Boston Public Library; printed in *Life*, I, 49–50. Garrison wrote this, the earliest of his extant manuscript letters, to his mother in Baltimore, where she had been trying to support herself and her children as a nurse. She was to die the following September 3.

1. See the Newburyport *Herald* for March 14, April 1, 3, 1823. Although Garrison's exact height is unknown, he was undoubtedly of small stature. His brother, James Holley Garrison, was five feet seven inches.

2. Shakespeare, *Hamlet*, II, ii, 97. At this time in his life Garrison thought that he had been born in December of 1804, whereas he was evidently born a year later, making him seventeen rather than eighteen when he wrote this letter (Merrill, p. 335).

3. See the Newburyport *Herald* for April 22, May 2, 16, 1823. On the editorial page of the issue for April 22 appeared the following unsigned statement: "We invite the attention of our readers to the 'Glance at Europe', in which we recog-nize the hand of a correspondent who at different times has favored us with a number of esteemed and valuable communications." This comment was un-doubtedly made by Caleb Cushing (1800–1879), the brilliant young Newburyport lawyer who is known to have edited the *Herald* in Ephraim W. Allen's absences.

4. Fourteen "communications" have been found, only two of which can be classified as letters for this edition (see letters 1 and 2).

5. It is true that Garrison had only a sporadic formal education, for he was obliged to work from an early age to help support his improverished family.

6. Harriet Farnham, who married Jacob Horton in 1824, was the daughter of Martha Farnham, in whose small house on School Street Garrison had been born, his parents having rented a room or two from the Farnhams. It was also in the Farnham house that Mrs. Garrison had boarded her daughter, Maria Elizabeth, when she went to Baltimore to seek employment.

7. Martha Farnham and her husband, whose name is not known.

8. It was in the family of Deacon Ezekiel Bartlett, a humble sawyer and a pious Baptist, that Garrison lived.

9. Presumably, Garrison refers to a son of Deacon Bartlett.

10. Maria Elizabeth had died in September.

11. Although no name besides Allen's is associated with the editing of the Newburyport *Herald* and his name alone appears on the masthead, Garrison evidently refers to someone else, probably Caleb Cushing.

12. Garrison adapts Psalms 55:6.

5

TO EPHRAIM W. ALLEN

Baltimore, July 7, 1823.

SIR:

I arrived here on Saturday last, after the tedious passage of 14 days — we having had, for the most part of the time, very boisterous weather, and considerable head winds.[1] The evening we sailed from Boston, a very heavy gale of wind tore our foretopsail, maintopsail, and jibs, besides rendering other considerable damage. We were thus obliged to put in at Hyana Heads, for the purpose of repairing our tattered sails, where we remained two days, the winds and the weather conspiring against us. — I felt peculiarly disappointed in not witnessing the celebration of our national independence in Baltimore — having arrived here the next day after.

You must imagine my sensations on beholding a dearly beloved mother, after an absence of *seven* years. — I found her in tears — but, O God, so altered, so emaciated, that I should never have recognized her, had I not known that there were none else in the room. Instead of the tall, robust woman, blooming in health, which I saw last, she is now bent up by "fell disease", pined away to almost a skeleton, and unable to walk. She is under the necessity of being bolstered up in bed, being incompetent to lie down, as it would immediately choke her. A very large swelling has gathered on her right shoulder, which the Physician thinks is a collective mass of deleterious matter, and continues to increase in size. — He says it will be absolutely necessary to have it cut open, for the purpose of drawing the matter off — for that, if it is not done, it will soon break inwardly, and prove fatal. The operation is indeed very critical, and I tremble for the result. If it is fortunate, he thinks it will be the means of restoring her in a great measure to health again, and destroying the inward humors — if *vice versa*, she will not probably survive long. All her friends earnestly wish her to have the operation done — and from the known skill of the physician in surgery, it is believed it will result happily.

I feel very much pleased with Baltimore, and the flattering reception I have had — still I cannot love it as I do the *home of my childhood*.[2] There are here a large number of elegant buildings and monuments, which do credit to the enterprising citizens of Baltimore, and will be lasting mementos of their spirited efforts in beautifying the city. Among the most prominent of these are the Cathedral, Unitarian Church, Exchange, Shot Tower, Washington Monument, a monument for those who were slain at the battle of North Point, with their names inscribed thereon, and a large number of other elegant works, with which I am not acquainted. The Cathedral is the most beautiful building here; and, indeed, it is thought, in the United States. — It has been about 14 years in building, and not yet finished! An enormous sum has been expended on this Church. Contributions have been received from all parts of the world, given by Roman Catholics. Naples, alone, it is said, has contributed over 100,000 dollars. Washington Monument is 160 or 170 feet high, but not yet finished: — is built round, and in the most elegant maner. A bust of Washington is to be brought from Italy, and placed on the top of the same — This has also been several years in building, and is situated in one of the most beautiful spots in Baltimore.

You wished me to call at No. 1, Cornhill, and ask Mr. Carter for some more leads for the paper.[3] — This I intended to have done: but, after wandering about 2 or 3 hours, and enquiring of 20 different persons, (none of whom, however, would take the trouble to show me,) I was forced to give up in despair. — Being totally unacquainted with Boston, and never there before, I got lost several times in my travels — so that all was perplexity. Indeed, I felt truly homesick in being one short day in Boston. — I was sea-sick but about 15 minutes on my passage. I have nothing else particular to write at present.

Yours, respectfully,

Wm. L. Garrison.

ALS: Garrison Papers, Boston Public Library; extract printed in *Life*, I, 52–53.

1. Garrison sailed from Boston June 21 and arrived in Baltimore on July 5.
2. Newburyport.
3. Mr. Carter, who has not been otherwise identified, evidently ran a printing supply house.

6

TO THE EDITOR OF THE SALEM *GAZETTE*

[June 11, 1824.]

The extraordinary interest excited throughout the Union on the publication of this work, and the uncommon eagerness every where evinced to peruse it, are such as might naturally be expected, coming as it did from so distinguished and venerable a man as TIMOTHY PICKERING, and embracing a topic so delicate and important.[1] The ostensible and indeed the only cause for its appearance, and the imperious call which demanded it, are well known to the public, as emanating from the disclosure of that despicable correspondence which existed between Messrs. Adams and Cunningham, which teemed with sentiments alike degrading to both. Those who have perused the *"Cunningham Letters"* are conscious of the bitter animosity there betrayed by Mr. Adams towards Mr. Pickering, and of his gratuitous, ungenerous attack upon his conduct and character, groaning with worthless vituperation and slanderous abuse, which sufficiently illustrated the bad passions and hollow heartedness which have ever been the characteristic traits of the man.

I will not descend to personalities: it is far from my purpose. The general conduct of Mr. Adams, while President, and his subsequent acts, need no labored philippic of mine to stamp them with disgrace: they have already passed the ordeal of the people, and but little else than dross has been gathered from them. Nor would I be thought either as one peculiarly interested in the present discussion, or as wishing to keep alive expiring animosities. In common with every citizen, I feel the same love for justice, and take as deep a solicitude in the welfare of the republic. When injustice is done to great and good men — when they are vilified by the envious or designing — I shall ever deem it a privilege and duty to step forward in their defence, and to use my feeble efforts in vindicating the injured. Mr. Pickering has been abused, not only by Mr. Adams, but by many of the public prints, and he certainly merits an advocate.

Since the publication of the review, various have been the remarks upon it and of different tendency. Some have given it the frank and manly eulogy which its merits deserve: they witness in it a triumphant expose of the greatness of its author, and of the deceit and hypocrisy of his enemies. Others have "damned it with faint praise" and sensitive comments; while others, again, have launched forth into a long strain of vulgar invectives against it, representing

Mr. Pickering as instigated by every feeling of revenge, and hatred, and rage. These last are confined to the partisans of John Q. Adams for the Presidency; they writhe in agony under the lash which has justly been applied to the father, and imagine every blow as castigating the son. Instead of its being a magnified defence from aspersions foul and malignant, they conjure it up into an electioneering rodomontade, circulated for the express purpose of thwarting the views of the Secretary of State, and baffling his election! These wiseacres seem to be wonderfully fearful that the *spotless* character of their idol may be tarnished by the fingers of *truth*; and if one dare question his *consistency*, or be under the *necessity* (as was Mr. P.) of scrutinizing his conduct, let such an one stand prepared to receive the poisoned arrows of malice — let him beware of the hand that covers the dagger destined to stab his reputation and good name — let him shun the snake in the grass, that whets its fangs, and lies coiled in deadly expectation.

Mr. Walsh, the editor of the National Gazette, who, with a great deal of vanity and egotism, unites the talents of a scholar and the prejudices of an *expectant*, and who, moreover, professes to be the standard of criticism in this country — a *fac similie* of one Dr. Johnson — has gratified his readers and the public generally with some half dozen columns of verbose remarks upon Mr. Pickering's Review, which show a puny littleness, a warmth and incongruity, discreditable to his pen as a writer, and unworthy of his candor as a gentleman.[2] If he had perused his own comments with as much attention as he declares to have bestowed upon the subject of them, he would have withheld the greater part of his excited ratiocination from the public eye. His sarcasms partake too much of the return of passion, and his thrusts too much of the bravo. It is evident that he has overlooked and mistaken the object of the work. Being a supporter of J. Q. Adams, he has unwittingly imbibed a share of that unaccountable mania with which the partisans of the Secretary have been seized as respects the *design* of Mr. Pickering's pamphlet. As I have before observed, they wince under the lash that was intended only for the senior Adams. Mr. Walsh has kindly marked out for Mr. Pickering (who, no doubt, as in duty bound, will thank him for his superior discernment) the course which he should have pursued; and very pathetically pourtrays the fatal mistake he has made. It is certainly matter of surprise, if not of amusement, that a man, in the midst of a heated effervescence, should gravely undertake to give advice about a spirit of meekness and forgiveness. Here it follows:

"Mr. Pickering should have added, [after consigning his defence to posterity in a plain, temperate narrative and investigation of facts,

&c.] 'I will and need go no further now — my vindication shall be left behind me in materials for the historian; I cannot consent to pour out the vials of wrath upon the head of a man like Mr. Adams — let him fall into the grave without a propelling blow from me — let not the spectacle be offered to the country, of a revolutionary patriot as I am, who stood so long in high places, endeavoring in his old age to fix opprobrium to the name, AND DRIVE IRONS INTO THE SOUL, of *another* still further advanced in years, and in the very arms of death, with whom I was closely linked in the same elevated career,'" &c.

This is a very affecting episode indeed. A few slight alterations from the answer of *Junius to Sir William Draper* will render a much more appropriate tribute to it than it is possible for me to bestow: — "Sir, an academical education has given you an unlimited command over the most beautiful figures of speech. *Vials of Wrath, propelling blows*, and *irons driven into the soul*, dance through your *criticisms* in all the mazes of metaphorical confusion: the melancholy madness of poetry, without the inspiration." [3]

I would ask Mr. Walsh, what would have been his opinion — what the opinions of the public — if, instead of manfully meeting his opponent and slanderer face to face, Mr. Pickering had remained silent, and transmitted his defence to posterity? Would not duplicity, and cunning, and treachery, have instantly been laid to his charge? Would it not have appeared like conscious guilt? as if waiting till the grave — which can tell no tales, refute no calumnies, nor exact justice — had swallowed up his antagonist, that he might the more easily vilify him? Would not such conduct have been cruel and dastardly in the extreme? This the venerable and magnanimous Pickering well knew: his lofty soul was above it — he scorned an advantage so easily obtained, but rather chose to confront his accuser, sustained by integrity, patriotism and truth. But Mr. Walsh says his defence should be given to posterity "in a plain, temperate narrative, and investigation of facts." Mr. Pickering's publication is replete with all these qualities: it is synonymous with honor, moderation and intelligence. But supposing posterity were the first to have received it in "a round, unvarnished tale" [4] — they nevertheless would at least have doubted the truth of it, and have said: "If the assertions here promulgated are true, and if Mr. Adams were the unworthy person here represented, why did he hesitate to usher them into the world till he who was assailed became incapable of answering them? Why wait to vindicate himself till his cotemporaries, who were more immediately interested in the issue of the contest, and who were more competent to judge the soundness of his reasonings, had disappeared from the stage of life? The book, notwithstanding its apparent candor, bears suspicion upon the face of it." These queries every honest man will say are natural. They are such as would forever leave a vacancy in the minds of the people.

How exactly different was the conduct of Mr. Adams! — and here was the baseness of his conduct. Under the dark and mysterious covert of secrecy, and with the unhallowed feelings of a political assassin, he began the formation of that plot, which was destined to blast the fair fame of Mr. Pickering, and hurl a load of obloquy upon his memory. The correspondence was not to be published till the asperser and aspersed were sleeping in silent dust: farther the secrecy was not binding. How treacherous and unholy was this stipulation! Fortunately the deed was brought to light, and the infamy rests upon him who contracted it.

One more extract from our Philadelphia scrutator [5] will be sufficient. He remarks, after the extract I have copied — "Mr. Pickering's Review implies the reverse of all this — *it is an elaborate, complicate piece of revenge* (!) — he has turned fiercely upon Mr. Adams, displaying himself every kind and degree of the uncharitableness and littleness of which he accuses the chief object of his warfare." I am astonished that a gentleman of Mr. Walsh's erudition should descend to such low bred epithets and assertions: they are the worn out weapons of petty scribblers and weak headed demagogues. Wholesale denunciations of this stamp neither convince nor conciliate — they betray nothing but weakness and passion. The times are singularly altered. *Once* a man's reputation was his own — and he who was most jealous of its integrity and uprightness, he who protected it from the arrows of aspersion and the breath of slander, was looked upon as a patriot and an honest man. *Now* it is *vice versa*. A man's character is at the mercy of every unprincipled pilferer. He may have it tarnished and sullied, abused and misrepresented, but he has no relief. If he endeavor to protect it by a manly display of his wrongs and a spirited castigation of his enemies, the cry of an unhallowed animosity, of an unforgiving temper, of a fiendish malevolence, is immediately heard. Truth is but another name for falsehood, reason is kicked out, and folly enters; unmasking hypocrisy is a crime, and the holding up of a treachery in its true colors is a thankless task. This is no fiction: look where we will we can behold the reality. It is the easiest way imaginable to get rid of arguments and conviction: just represent your antagonist, however high and exalted he may be, as possessed of every vice — that his unanswerable positions are propped up with deceit, and the thing is done.

In conclusion — I did not intend, Mr. Editor, to trespass so long on your patience and time — but the nature of the subject has hurried me onward. If this meet your approbation, I may probably be induced to make some remarks upon certain other affairs that merit a calm discussion, at some future period. Mr. Pickering's pamphlet will stand the test of the critic and the sneers of the prejudiced. It abounds with that sort of information on political affairs which has long been wanting, and is written with a vigor and strength unlooked for at his advanced age. He has accomplished a task which necessity imposed upon him, and covered with disgrace the man who alone deserves it. The name of PICKERING will live when that of Adams will be lost in oblivion.

ARISTIDES.[6]

Printed: Salem *Gazette,* June 11, 1824. This letter is the first of a series of communications to the Salem *Gazette* in 1824 over the signature "Aristides." These pieces can undoubtedly be attributed to Garrison (see *Life,* 1, 54). Another letter signed "Aristides" and printed in the Boston *Courier,* May 16, 1827, has been eliminated from the Garrison canon, since it suggests Garrison only by its signature, and since Garrison is not known to have used that pen name in writing to the *Courier.*

Ferdinand Andrews (1802–1883), cousin of Caleb Cushing and nephew of Thomas C. Cushing, was the editor of the Salem *Gazette.* Thomas C. Cushing had been the proprietor and editor of the paper when Andrews became an apprentice in 1815.

1. Timothy Pickering (1745–1829), staunch Federalist and leading citizen of Salem, Massachusetts, had been George Washington's postmaster general and John Adams' secretary of state. He and Adams had frequently disagreed, and Adams had in a frank series of letters to his distant cousin William Cunningham, Jr., written between 1803 and 1813, attacked Pickering and other associates. In 1823 E. M. Cuningham had published those letters with the hope that the intemperate statements of John Adams might help defeat John Quincy Adams for the presidency. In 1824 Pickering responded with the work to which Garrison refers, *A Review of the Correspondence between the Hon. John Adams . . . and the Late Wm. Cunningham, Esq.,* proving himself no less bitter than Adams.

2. Robert Walsh (1784–1859) was one of the most distinguished editors and journalists of the day, having edited in succession a series of journals and papers including the *American Register* (the first American quarterly), the *American Review of History and Politics,* and the *National Gazette and Literary Register* (a highly successful liberal paper which he was to edit for some fifteen years).

3. Junius was the pen name of one of Garrison's favorite authors, whose invective was an important model for his own. Junius published a series of sixty-nine letters highly critical of George III and his ministers in the London *Public Advertiser* between 1769 and 1772. The identity of Junius has been an intriguing mystery for historians. Dozens of names have been advanced. The most persuasive evidence suggests that he was Sir Philip Francis (1740–1818), a politician and pamphleteer. Garrison adapts the first three sentences of the letter of March 3, 1769 (*The Letters of Junius,* New York, 1821, I, 59), which run as follows:

"An academical education has given to you an unlimited command over the most beautiful figures of speech. Masks, hatchets, racks, and vipers, dance through your letters in all the mazes of metaphorical confusion. These are the gloomy companions of a disturbed imagination; the melancholy madness of poetry, without the inspiration."

4. *Othello,* I, iii, 90.

5. Robert Walsh.

6. The nineteen-year-old Garrison's use of the name of the conservative Athenian general perhaps reveals something of his image of himself.

7

TO THE EDITOR OF THE SALEM *GAZETTE*

[June 29, 1824.]

SIR —

When a man arrogates to himself the office of *critic*, he should first inherit four requisite qualifications — *candor, modesty, good sense,* and *impartiality.* There are those, however, who, professing to be critics, evidently possess good sense without liberality — learned heads overflowing with pedantry — or strong minds with prejudiced imaginations. If interest be in the way, their ebullitions are stamped, either with flattery or low bred scurrility, as the case may be. Nothing will more completely betray the weakness and narrow-mindedness of such, than their feeble, puerile endeavors to attach infamy and every other debasing quality to the characters of unsullied patriots of such men, in short, as Timothy Pickering and other distinguished sages.

It is lamentable to see talents, and prudence, and candor, prostituted by a false zeal, or made the sport of excited passion; especially in one whom we know possesses many amiable and praiseworthy traits. The Editor of the *National Gazette* (whose scholastic abilities are great, and whose writings are *generally* marked with elegance and discretion) in his violent comments upon Colonel PICKERING's Review, seems determined, not only to lower his reputation as a dignified journalist, but also to sacrifice reason and justice, in order to fix a stigma upon the head of a hoary patriot. Whatever effect his inflated sophisms may produce in Pennsylvania, they are nevertheless received in this section of the country with surprise, and coolness, and indignation; and it is but truth to say, that Mr. Walsh has injured himself in the estimation of sound and honest men, and among his admirers, in no trifling degree. Was he aware of the purity of the personage against whom he has hurled his vindictive missiles? then why attempt to sully it? He knew — he *must* have known — that Mr. Pickering was swayed by no other motive, in publishing his defence, than that of shielding his character from a malignant asperser as an upright man, and his integrity as a statesman. He knew that malice, and all the bad passions he has ungenerously laid to his charge, never rankled in this venerable gentleman's heart — for the soil is too immaculate for the growth of such noxious weeds. He knew that it was the respect of his fellow-citizens — a duty which he owed to himself, to his family and friends — a wronged and grieved spirit — and a desire to appeal to the bar of his country for justice — that induced Mr. P., however reluctant and unwilling, to unmask his treacherous enemy, and to vidicate *the truth of history.*

21

And yet Mr. Walsh has hastily (and it is hoped unthinkingly) staked his reputation, as it were, as an impartialist, and his candor as a gentleman, in a pompous *review* of Col. P.'s pamphlet, which teems with nothing but gross libels and unbounded abuse. Let the reader take the following *elegant, unbiassed* extract as a fair sample of the *leven* which pervades the lump of his criticisms: —

"The reader has not yet comprehended or examined what history is, and Tacitus meant and wrote, who can bring into the same line, except in the way of contrast, the mass of egotistical details, gossiping anecdotes, vindictive censures and retorts, opprobrious epithets, gratuitous imputations, sweeping judgments, personal and private resentments, which are huddled together in the same book. Its leven is the restless and implacable animosity of an individual, primarily against two old adversaries, and incidentally against a number of individuals, whose reputations he could not abstain from endeavoring to immolate at the same time."! !

Such a mass of scurrillity and falsehood as is here embodied and *huddled* into the compass of a square — such unfounded assertions and garbled appearances — defy comparison with any thing we have ever seen in the bitter productions of our most inveterate transatlantic reviewers. When a man thus wilfully pollutes his pen and paper — when he thus forgets who and what he is criticising — when he endeavors to cast reproach upon one who, of almost every other man, least deserves it — he becomes an object of pity and compassion — and, were it not that his *name* might carry some influence with it, his violent invectives might pass unnoticed, without comment or perusal. Mr. Walsh says, he was "provoked to animadversion by the *inherent enormities* and general evil tendencies of the book" — and, likewise, that "he has ranked with the friends and well wishers of Mr. P., and has dealt with it [the review] as much in *sorrow* as in anger." Now this is very consistent and uniform, especially when his press has been groaning under the weight of his obloquy — when he has exhausted the whole vocabulary of Billingsgate abuse, and when he seems loth to quit so prolific a subject. Even Mr. Pickering's most hostile foe could not have exceeded Mr. W. in apparent animosity and unnatural hatred against him; and yet it is a *well-wisher* that thus animadverts in so cruel and unmerited a manner! — *Proh Pudor!*

The truth is, Mr. Walsh's love for the Adams family falls little short of devotion; and so affected is he at the extreme age of the ex-President, that he sees nothing but glory and immortality encircling his brows. He sees nothing to condemn in the conduct of the man whose whole life has been marked with weakness and instability; who was the main cause of the downfall of Federal Republicanism, of those political principles which Washington and Hamilton promulgated and adopted. He cannot find cause to censure Mr. A. for his disgraceful, unhallowed efforts to annihilate and blast the spotless fame of Timothy Pickering. Nor does he see aught to reprobate in the life of John Q. Adams, that paragon of pure democracy — the man that was once a violent and unequivocal federalist, who afterwards basely deserted his party, in order to secure the loaves and fishes of office, and who stands a political turncoat — the man who was the most active leader in support of the ridiculous *embargo*, and who would rashly throw away all deliberation when the interests of his country were at stake — the man that ineffectually strove to sully the memory and writings of FISHER AMES, with many other excellent characteristics, has, in Mr. Walsh's view, every thing to boast of, nothing to condemn! [1]

I shall now take my leave of the present discussion — believing that Mr. Pickering needs no adventitious aid to prove his integrity, and that so long as reason is sacrificed by his enemies to animosity, their poisoned arrows will fall harmless at his feet. He stands mailed in innocence and truth; and while our country continues a grateful and free republic, she will enshrine in her bosom the name and services of PICKERING.

ARISTIDES.

Printed: Salem *Gazette*, June 29, 1824.

1. Fisher Ames (1758–1808), Massachusetts lawyer, Federalist member of Congress, and subsequently president of Harvard College, was to Garrison, along with Hamilton, Henry, and Webster, a model of forensic eloquence. In an editorial in *The Liberator* for October 18, 1834, Garrison said: "O, for the thundering, majestic, *prevailing* eloquence of a Hamilton, a Henry, a Webster, or an Ames, that all understandings might be enlightened, and all hearts subdued!"

8

TO ANDREW JACKSON

[July 27, 1824.]

SIR —

Suffer "a plain, unlettered man" to engross your attention for a moment, while he lays before you the language of truth. *Ambition —* a lawless *ambition —* was the downfall of a Caesar and a Napoleon, and there yet remain those who may fall victims to the same inordinate passion. You, sir, profess to be a patriot and friend to your country: I wish not to deprive you of these honorable qualities, nor to detract a tittle from your merits. New Orleans bears an undying testimony of your gallantry in her defence, and your services have met with a glorious reward in the gratitude of a free people. Yet one brave act cannot cancel others which have cast a shade over your character and wither your laurels, or make us overlook the conduct in a false admiration of the man.

Sir, republics are always in danger. Aspiring and designing men can easily and cheaply purchase the tools of action, to consummate their wishes. The views of the people, however pure and upright they may at first be, are nevertheless shuffling and fickle, when these insidious agents are let loose upon the community. Flattery, judiciously disposed, can lull them into the by-paths of error, and prejudice will warp and mislead them. Mankind are too apt to be dazzled with the pomp and trappings of military glory: they are charms, which have proved deadly and dangerous in every age, and by which nations have unconsciously lost their liberties. A love of country compels me to warn my fellow citizens of a delusion that leads to *slavery*; and I do it at this juncture, because it has taken a deep, an amazing hold upon them. It is time that they arouse from their slumbers: it is time that this lethean stupor be shaken off. The crisis is approaching, upon which turns their future peace: a change is shortly to be effected in our cabinet, either for better or for worse — and every one who glories in his liberties must necessarily take a lively interest in the result.

Your friends have imprudently brought you before the public, as an antagonist to cope for the highest office in the gift of the people. But have they calmly considered this premature measure? No, Sir! there is a marked thoughtlessness, a reckless indifference upon the face of it, that proclaim this truth. Are they willing to risk — madly risk — the consequences attending your election? If it be answered in the affirmative, I would ask, *what guarantee have they, that the power which they will thus have placed in your hands, will not be abused*? I wait for a reply.

Sir, the cool, the discerning, and the dispassionate body of your fellow countrymen, perceive your unfitness for the office to which you and so many are aspiring. They look to your conduct while General and Governor as sufficient proof of the fact. They consider, and perhaps rightly, that the man who has trifled with impunity with the laws, in a subordinate station, would, if he reached this pinnacle of power, violate them more grossly, more frequently, and with less compunction: in short, Sir, that the laws with you must be a *dead letter*. These fears are not visionary — they are built upon facts, and upon past actions — they hang suspended in the gloom of futurity — and if the fiery zeal of your friends should accomplish its designs, their truth will undoubtedly be made manifest.

I have said, that the public perceive your *unfitness* to be the Chief Magistrate of the nation. Bred up, as it were, from childhood, in the tented field, you have acquired a savage and domineering spirit, with the requisite qualifications of a soldier. As an experienced *warrior*, there are few from whom you would not bear the palm; and as a *judge*, your sentences are given and executed with unrivalled rapidity. But a man may be brave, and yet completely destitute of every other conspicuous quality — he may wield the sword with success, and face with unshrinking heart the cannon's deadly mouth, and wade through seas of blood with a firm step, or dwell on carnage and slaughter with *philsosphic composure* — he may do all these, and many more, and yet be as disqualified for a civilian as the greatest dunce in Christendom.

Your chance of succeeding to the Presidency is worse than desperate. I will not deny that till within a short period an infatuated admiration of your services rendered your prospects in a flattering view — that your strides to this office were alarmingly rapid — and that your popularity increased with unexampled precedence. But the charm is broken — the mists of prejudice are dispelled, and your case is lost irretrievably. Admiration has given way to astonishment — esteem to disgust — and those who have warmly espoused your cause now stand ready to forsake it. It was not fickleness that effected this instantaneous change in popular opinion: it was not treachery. The timely disclosure of your correspondence with the President raised the first barrier to your advancement, which nothing can overcome. The principles therein contained were not less extraordinary than unexpected. While many of them seemed to come from the heart of a real patriot, (though couched in language cautious and confined) others were stamped with a cold blooded ferocity — a palpable ignorance of our constitution and laws — and a sacrifice of reason and common prudence, which could not otherwise than alarm and astound the nation. The shameless avowal of such glaring inconsistencies was enough to command the attention of every part of the Union: the virtue and intelligence of the people took the alarm at this juncture, in season to preserve their influence and the welfare of the country.

The sentiments expressed in one of your letters to Mr. Monroe, which here follows, roused the slumbering indignation of all upright men: — "I am free to acknowledge, had I commanded the military department where the Hartford Convention sat, if it had been the *last act* of my life, I should have punished *the three principal leaders* of that party.[1] *I am certain* an independent court martial would have condemned them under the 2d section of the act establishing rules and regulations for the government of the army of the United States. *These kind of men*, although called Federalists, are really MONARCHISTS and TRAITORS to the constituted government." [2] If there remain one drop of the blood in our veins which mantled the cheeks of our fathers, it must rush to those of our own at this unhallowed tirade. Even the highminded democrats threw away their badge of party, and condemned it in strong and forcible terms. Nor is there aught to palliate this outrage upon the *rights* of the people. It was not an excited, unmeaning rhodomontade, hastily spoken or written in the heat of passion; it was not penned in thoughtlessness, nor conceived in premature reflection. No, sir! — it was a cool, a determined expose of your real feelings — it was done under the covert of a private correspondence, and addressed to the Chief Magistrate of the nation.

So! it has come to this! — If the wise, the great and the good will not tamely be trampled upon — or will not follow the unholy principles of a Military Prefect in blind submission — or if they constitutionally meet in convention to concert measures for self-defence and protection, in opposition to *his* opinions — they are to be denounced as SPIES and TRAITORS — debarred the privilege of CITIZENSHIP — and their BLOOD must be shed to glut his vengeance and ambition! Horrid doctrine! Smacks this of TYRANNY, Americans?

Sir, you appear to mistake the age in which you live — you betray your ignorance of the materials which compose our country. Believe me, if the above audacious threat had been carried into execution, a BRUTUS would have risen in every son of New-England to avenge the slaughter of his sires; believe me, your life would have been the forfeit.

And who were *these kind of men* upon whom your fury would have been wreaked? I will answer, sir. They were veteren patriots, who had stood by their country from the first hour of the revolution till the present time — many of whom had sacrificed their health, their strength and their fortunes, in maintaining the liberties of their country. They were men of the most exalted patriotism, virtue and honor — whose judgments, collectively, were unerring. They were those, almost individually, who had been placed in the most responsible offices, in the most critical times — whom a majority of the people never found cause to reproach — and who were the firmest pillars of their political fabric. NEW-ENGLAND — the

"*First* to be free, and *last* to be subdued" [3] —

had nothing to fear for her welfare in the hands of her sages — she rested in security.

It is time to close the ungrateful theme. I have spoken fearlessly and candidly, without malice, or hoarded animosity. As a christian, sir, as a patriot, as an upright man, you owe it to yourself, your country, and your admirers, to publicly recant from such ferocious sentiments, and ask forgiveness of an injured people. There are many traits in your character, amiable and honorable — and by curbing the spirit which led a Napoleon to destruction, you may yet live to adorn and exalt mankind, and leave a name behind, which virtue and glory shall love to repeat.

ARISTIDES.

Printed: Salem *Gazette,* July 27, 1824.

Garrison's Federalist convictions prejudiced him against General Jackson. Perhaps because of this, he did accurately appraise Jackson's strength in the forthcoming presidential election; the general won a majority of the popular vote, only to lose to John Quincy Adams in the electoral college.

1. A group of twenty-six Federalist delegates from New England met in secret convention in Hartford, Connecticut, between December 15, 1814, and January 5, 1815. Animated by resentment against commercial restrictions imposed by the federal government during the War of 1812, the delegates discussed the advisability of calling a general convention to revise the Constitution. Leaders among the delegates were Harrison Gray Otis, George Cabot, and Theodore Dwight.

2. Garrison quotes (accurately except for variations in italics and capitalization and the substitution of "sat" for "met") from Jackson's letter to the president-elect of January 6, 1817. This letter had been published in May of 1824, along with other letters exchanged between the two men in 1816 and 1817. Although Federalists tended to react to the passage concerned with the Hartford Convention as Garrison did, Jackson's letters to Monroe were mostly reasonable and moderate and occasionally pro-Federalist. As James Parton said (*Life of Andrew Jackson*, New York, 1860, II, 356), they "won over to his support a large number of Federalists." (For a full discussion of the letters in question see John Spencer Bassett, *The Life of Andrew Jackson*, New York, 1916, pp. 339–344.)

3. Unidentified.

9

TO THE EDITOR OF THE SALEM *GAZETTE*

[August 6, 1824.]

Sɪʀ —

Amid the conflicts of a divided party — of disappointed hopes and parasitical zeal — much may be gathered for the instruction of those, who can be but passive spectators of the Presidential struggle. It is a proud reflection to every Federal Republican of Massachusetts and the Union, that the party, under which he rallies, has, thus far, maintained its high and exalted character; that it has proved itself worthy of its great leader, the immortal Wᴀsʜɪɴɢᴛᴏɴ, and has disseminated its vigor and strength throughout the political fabric of our constitution and government. It is peculiarly gratifying, too, to observe the dignified course pursued generally by the few *sentinels of freedom,* who advocate and uphold those principles, which were promulgated by the Father of his Country, and sanctioned by Jᴀʏ and Hᴀᴍɪʟᴛᴏɴ, and Aᴍᴇs, with a host of other distinguished patriots.[1] But the giant energies of Jᴀʏ are unstrung by age — the magic eloquence and pen of HAMILTON are mute in the grave — the voice of AMES, whose thunders, like the tones of an angel "trumpet tongued," [2] thrilled and astonished our country, has calmly yielded to the slumber of death!

Especially has the Gazette ever been conspicuous for its manly and independent stand as a guardian on freedom's watch-tower — as the fearless minister of justice — as the vehicle of truth and probity. Through all the storms of political excitement, it has held the same honorable and unwavering course, and been a terror to faction — a friend to order.

In discussing a subject which is momently increasing in interest and importance, I shall respectfully solicit the attention of my fellow-citizens — believing that as *facts* are becoming known a powerful reaction is taking place in public opinion. The time has now arrived, when the choice of the people must be fixed upon some one of the candidates for the Presidency; and certainly wisdom, and prudence, and decision, were never more needed. The period has come, likewise, when the questions must be asked and answered by Federalists, unanimously — *To whom shall our suffrages be given, Mr. Crawford* [3] *or Mr. Adams? and which can we consistently support?*

These interrogations demand the serious attention and consideration of the federal party. *Firstly,* because, although in the minority their influence as a body will be powerful — unshaken — decisive. *Secondly,* because, at present, there appears to be a division of sentiment among them, where *union* alone should prevail. Though opposition has almost ceased to act throughout the Union, yet, *at least,* one quarter of our country is federal. Now, if the interests and prosperity of this portion are at stake, and await only its decision — if its simultaneous movements can either check or urge forward what it dislikes or favors — is it not, by every personal consideration, necessary that UNITY should cement the federal ranks?

We are under no *obligations,* it is true, to support either of the present candidates for the Presidency. Reason, however, dictates that we should. A feeble opposition could only be raised, which would answer no desirable end; it would only distract the peace of the Union, and prolong useless warfare. Though we might prefer men of our own principles, yet as their chance of success would be next to impossibility, it would be the climax of folly for us to throw away that influence, which we can now exercise, in order to support a hopeless experiment. Hence policy, if nothing else, plainly shews the necessity, to Federalists, of their preserving their rightful sway by a concentration of feelings and sentiments. Hence if division be suffered to widen the present breach, it will destroy their own power and privileges.

I advocate none of those who are now offered to the public because

I believe them to be the *best* qualified for the station to which they aspire; on the contrary, were I to select my own candidate, they should be a KING, a MARSHALL, a WEBSTER, or a CLINTON.[4] There cannot remain a doubt, if Mr. CLINTON's friends had not foolishly withdrawn from him their support, and New York had properly consulted her own honor and dignity, that he would have easily distanced every competitor, and reached that proud height, which could not honor him but to which he would do honor. But, strange as it may seem, he has not at this term yet been seriously proposed as an antagonist — and a fit opportunity to urge his merits has thus been lost.

In calling the attention of the federal party to this important subject, I wish to escape the charge of egotism, or of untimely intrusion upon their notice. In the present divided state of public opinion, some political pole-star — some beacon of safety — must be pointed out as sure guides to the wavering and inconstant. If the feeble views which I shall offer be deemed prejudiced or inconsistent, or appear to be conceived in error or wilfulness, let them pass, like idle tales, unheeded. But if, on the other hand, they bear the face of honesty, and seem to be couched in decency and truth, let them have their just weight with every unbiased mind. Whatever they may be, I leave the public to decide upon their stability. If I know my heart, nothing but a pure sense of duty and a love of justice incite me to the task; nothing but to unite that party of which I profess to be a humble disciple.

The questions which I have proposed *must* be speedily answered: every moment is big with fate. That the approaching struggle will be only between Messrs. Crawford and Adams the most casual connoisseur of the times must be satisfied; and the only alternative now is, *which* is the most worthy? To me, it appears, that no *consistent*, high minded man can hesitate for a moment to decide between the merits of the two, to whatever sect or order he may belong; and that the choice of the people will be infallibly fixed upon the Hon. WILLIAM H. CRAWFORD. The downfall of Gen. Jackson by his own folly — the few scattered friends (comparatively) of Mr. Clay[5] — and the rapid decline of Mr. Adams's popularity — all render it almost a matter of certainty of Mr. Crawford's election.

The federal presses in Massachusetts, with some few exceptions, have apparently taken no share or interest in the present warfare — and perhaps wisely. The Boston Centinel, the Massachusetts Spy, and the Taunton Reporter, are, I believe, the only ones which have openly supported the claims of Mr. Adams; with what consistency of principle I leave it to Federalists to determine: certain it is they will find but few of their party to coincide with them.

I am a decided opponent to John Quincy Adams, for reasons both just and well founded.[6] Inasmuch as he has cruelly betrayed that body, under whose banners, for a long course of years, he invariably rallied, and has thrown his poisoned arrows and envenomed malice upon his old friends and adherents — inasmuch as, previous to his *miraculous* conversion, he was the most violent enemy to democracy, bestowing upon it, every bitter invective, and using every effort to accomplish its downfall — it does appear to me that NOT ONE honest, genuine member of either party can extend to him that confidence and faith, which he has so basely abused.

ARISTIDES.

Printed: Salem *Gazette*, August 6, 1824.

This letter is the first of *The Crisis* series printed in the *Gazette* between August 6 and October 29. The others have been excluded since it is questionable whether they can be classified as letters.

1. The three aristocratic Federalists, John Jay (1745–1829), Fisher Ames (1758–1808), and Alexander Hamilton (1757–1804), were Garrison's heroes among the founding fathers.

2. Shakespeare, *Macbeth*, I, vii, 19.

3. William H. Crawford (1772–1834), United States senator, cabinet member as well as presidential candidate, and dedicated Georgian, was a curious hero for the future abolitionist.

4. Again Garrison selects for special commendation Federalists dedicated to the protection of financial interests from New England to Virginia: Rufus King (1755–1827), Harvard graduate, lawyer, and minister to Great Britain; John Marshall (1755–1835) of Virginia, chief justice of the United States; Daniel Webster (1782–1852), New England lawyer and United States senator; George Clinton (1739–1812), soldier, seven times governor of New York state, and twice vice-president of the United States, an early advocate of states' rights.

5. Henry Clay (1777–1852) was a congressman, senator, and diplomat, whose influence threw the forthcoming election to John Quincy Adams.

6. Garrison's opposition to Adams is ironic in light of the fact that in 1828 he was to edit the *Journal of the Times*, the *raison d'être* of which was to electioneer for the same Adams.

---

1 0

TO TOBIAS H. MILLER

Newburyport, Oct. 14, 1825.

RESPECTED FRIEND:

I write to you in behalf, not of myself, but of *merits*; you will therefore appreciate the motive. Will you be good enough to extract into the "JOURNAL" — if the remarks coincide with your own sentiments, and you deem them worthy of republishing — the communication in to-day's Herald upon "RESIGNATION," and signed "A. O. B."?[1] — The introductory part is not essential; consequently you can consult your own convenience in regard to it. — [I] should not make this request, were it not [. . .] for the hope of drawing the public attention to this excellent work, and of encouraging *christian genius.* The author, as you are probably aware, belongs to Portsmouth; and as I have heard her express a wish that *some* notice might be taken of "RESIGNATION" in the Journal, and observing none, I have ventured to make this request. Perhaps, however, an *original* article might do better.

☞ You will perceive that poor Henry Stickney has "shuffled off this mortal coil," ² after a career of profligacy, which has brought him to the grave.³ He died, I believe, with the hope of a Savior's pardon.

With sentiments of affection,

  I remain,

    Yours, &c.

[☞ I should be happy   WM. L. GARRISON.
to correspond occasionally.]

ALS: Villard Papers, Harvard College Library.

 Tobias H. Miller (1801–1870), as journeyman printer on the Newburyport *Herald*, had been a considerable influence on Garrison during the years of his apprenticeship; Garrison described him as a patient, cheerful, urbane, philosophical man (see the letter to Frank W. Miller, April 30, 1870, to be published in a subsequent volume, and the reprint of his speech in the Boston *Traveller*, October 15, 1878). After leaving Newburyport, Miller returned to his native Portsmouth, New Hampshire, and was soon one of the proprietors of the *Journal of Literature and Politics.* About 1853 he became one of the editors of the Portsmouth *Daily Chronicle.* Late in life he studied for the ministry and became the pastor of the Congregational church at Kittery Point, Maine, though he subsequently was converted to the Universalist faith.

 1. Garrison's article in the Newburyport *Herald* of October 14, 1825, is a long essay-review of the recently published novel *Resignation* in which he shows a surprising knowledge of nineteenth-century fiction; for he discusses, in addition to Scott and Cooper, Mrs. Radcliffe, Anna Moore, Amelia Opie, and Maria Edgeworth. His criterion of literary excellence here as elsewhere seems to be moral rather than aesthetic. He commends at length the anonymous author of the book, whom he suspects to be the sister of Estwick Evans of Porthmouth, New Hampshire; the young lady was in fact Sarah Ann Evans.

 2. Shakespeare, *Hamlet,* III, i, 67.

 3 Henry Stickney (1793–1825), according to his obituary in the Newburyport *Herald*, October 14, 1825, was a printer — presumably with the *Herald.*

11

TO THE EDITOR OF
HAVERHILL *GAZETTE & ESSEX PATRIOT*

[November 1, 1826.]

DEAR SIR —

In a brief communication, inserted in your last paper, relative to the Free Press, I observed the following sentence:

"The former Editor [of the Free Press,] Mr. Garrison, was no friend to Mr. Cushing, and was displaced." ¹

I hope your correspondent does not imagine, or mean to insinuate, that any man, or any set of men, had the control of the Free Press while I Published it, — as the term "displaced" would seem to imply. For various reasons, I was anxious at the expiration of six months to dispose of the establishment, and fortunately found a ready purchaser.[2] My chief regret, however, in taking leave of the paper at that period, arose from the proximity of the representative election. I had long foreseen that, by the undying bitterness and restless ambition of certain plotting expectants, an antagonist would be arrayed against Mr. Varnum; and, willing to aid the cause of a good man, I could have wished that my subscription term had expired a few weeks later.[3]

The course pursued by the Free Press, at this juncture, gives me neither surprise nor gratification. I think the public have a right to be informed that Mr. Cross, the junior partner of Mr. Cushing, is, the editor of that print; — they will then be able to estimate the true worth of his vituperation against Mr. Varnum, and his gross flattery of Mr. Cushing.[4] The world is censorious; and, in the present case, Mr. Cross must not wonder that his disinterestedness is doubted.

Respectfully yours,

WILLIAM L. GARRISON.

Newburyport, Nov. 1, 1826.

Printed: Haverhill *Gazette & Essex Patriot*, November 4, 1826.

Abijah W. Thayer (1796–1864), from Peterborough, New Hampshire, had edited the *Independent Statesman* in Portland, Maine, between 1821 and 1826, before coming to Haverhill, Massachusetts, to edit the *Gazette*, which he was to purchase the following year, changing the name to the *Essex Gazette*. He became a friend of Whittier's, and the poet boarded in Thayer's house when he attended Haverhill Academy.

1. The full text of the "brief communication" printed in the issue for October 28 is as follows:

"The Newburyport *Free Press* is *Caleb Cushing's* own paper — the trumpet of his own praise. It was chartered for this purpose at the opening of the Electioneering campaign. The former editor, Mr. Garrison, was no friend to Mr. Cushing, and he was displaced. Who turns the crank of that paper, you can all conjecture. The paper is filled with mawkish praise of Cushing, and with his own communications. After the election is over, it has been said the paper will be discontinued. How that may be, a short time will disclose.

GRAMPUS" [unidentified]

2. Garrison had announced in the issue for September 14 that the paper was for sale, "*owing to considerations of importance only to himself*"; a week later he reported the sale to John H. Harris, in whom he seemed to have confidence.

3. John Varnum (1778–1836), a Harvard graduate and lawyer from Haverhill, had been elected to the state senate in 1811 and to Congress in 1824. In 1826 he was again elected to Congress, defeating Caleb Cushing.

4. It is true that Caleb Cushing had a law partner named Robert Cross, but it is not known that he was editing the paper at this time. Certainly it is a fact that *The Free Press* was discontinued the month following Cushing's defeat in the congressional election of 1826.

Garrison in 1825

Garrison's birthplace, Newburyport

George Benson's house, Providence

"Friendship Valley," Brooklyn, Connecticut

Prudence Crandall's house,
Canterbury, Connecticut

1 2

TO THE EDITOR OF THE BOSTON *COURIER*

[December 13, 1826.]

Sɪʀ, —

Although a stranger in this city, and but little acquainted with the manner in which its municipal concerns have been conducted, I cannot refrain from making a few remarks upon the Faneuil Hall caucus of last evening. I went to that meeting, sir, with no political or personal bias. I had supposed that the man, who has so long presided over the city affairs with such lynx-eyed vigilance, untiring industry, and complete success — whose energy and independence are equal to his great genius and talents — and who has been repeatedly elected, as it were, by *acclamation*, to the office of Mayor, — would find but little opposition from the great body of the people, and was deserving of public confidence. I went, therefore, to hear some plausible objections, at least, urged against the re-election of Mr. Quincy.[1] When I entered the hall, a Mr. Davis was flourishing away in a speech, which, for stupidity, egotism and emptiness, merited a more general hiss, and much less applause, than it received.[2] He said that the assertion had been made, that those who oppose Josiah Quincy are virtually opposing John Q. Adams. He would modestly give the lie to this assertion. When he last had the honor to address his fellow citizens in this hall, it was in support of Mr. Adams. Dare any man assert that he had changed his coat, and was now inimical to that distinguished individual? And yet *he* was opposed to Mr. Quincy — *ergo*, the whole Adams party were also — consequently the charge was unfounded! This is a fair specimen of the gentleman's modesty and logic.

When he had concluded, a young man from South Boston next followed in a maiden speech, amidst a tremendous uproar; and, for some time, nothing but hisses and clamorous calls could be heard.[3] But he finally succeeded in his attempts to proceed, and made many smart observations, which elicited no inconsiderable applause. He was, in fact, the only individual who attempted to confine himself to the question under consideration — viz: whether Mr. Quincy had acted properly as Mayor. He said that this gentleman had shot upwards like a *rocket*, but had come down upon Bostonians like a *stick!*

A Mr. Jarvis next mounted the table, and disgorged a mass of political invective upon Mr. Quincy.[4] His language was coarse, and his gestures vehement and ungraceful. He displayed the *sins* of the Mayor (as a politician) in sombre colors, and dwelt upon them with startling minuteness and fluency. His two great damning sins were — a belief that Mr. Jefferson was not immaculate, and that the war was unjust. I was not a little amused with the manner in which Mr. Jarvis threw off his fatal charges. He spit them forth, one by one, with a fierceness which bordered on the ridiculous — seemingly saying by his looks, "There, take *that*, and make the most of it!" — and, indeed, the audience were not slow in accepting the invitation, for they stamped, cheered and hissed most lustily. He lauded Harrison Gray Otis — gave a sugar-plum to every federalist who would swallow the sweet bait — and represented that a majority of the federal party preferred George Blake [5] to Josiah Quincy! His love to democracy was unbounded, &c, &c.

Mr. Dunlap succeeded.[6] He also recapitulated the political sins of Mr. Quincy — said that he (Mr. Q.) abused Jefferson — thought it unbecoming a moral and religious people to rejoice in the successes of the navy — and viewed the war as dishonorable and unjust. When the Constitution returned home in triumph, bringing the Guerriere a captive to her might, did you (said Mr. D. appealing to the audience) then view your war as unjust or dishonorable? [7] When the gallant Perry achieved his memorable victory at Lake Erie, did you believe the war to be dishonorable — unjust? [8] (Tremendous applause.) And thus this logical reasoner went on from one victory to another, to prove the *justness* of our conflict with Great Britain! and the unfitness of Mr. Quincy to be Mayor! I confess, sir, that my indignation was roused at this miserable artifice to touch the passions and to blind the good sense of the audience. After worrying this precious argument to the death, Mr. D. defended and supported Mr. Blake for Mayor — declared his belief that he would be elected and at last concluded.

The above, sir, were some of the strongest reasons adduced, why Mr. Quincy should be ousted from his office. His conduct as Mayor, it is true, was slightly scrutinized; but nothing like argument was given to prove him unworthy of his high trust. Artful insinuations, wholesale assertions, and boisterous exclamations, can never convince, though they may sometimes warp, a sound judgment. But the prejudices of the multitude are easily excited, and he is certainly to be detested, who makes use of them to carry a favorite design. Whatever may be the result of the election, Mr. Quincy may, with great propriety, adopt the language of Junius: — "Professions of patriotism are become stale and ridiculous. For my own part I claim no merit from endeavoring to do a service to my fellow citizens. I have done it to the best of my understanding. Without looking for the approbation of other men, my conscience is satisfied." [9]

A.O.B.

Monday morning.

34

Printed: Boston *Courier*, December 13, 1826.

Joseph T. Buckingham (1779–1861) became the editor of the Boston *Courier* in 1824, supporting during his twenty-four years in that position most of the liberal reforms of the day.

1. Josiah Quincy (1772–1864), an aristocratic Boston Federalist, was by training a Harvard graduate and a lawyer, and by inclination a politician. He was perhaps more effective as a member of the state legislature and as mayor of Boston (1823–1827) than as a member of Congress where his vacillation regarding the government's policy in the War of 1812 limited his usefulness. Although as mayor he had accomplished too many reforms to please everyone, he was safely reelected in 1827. Two years later he was to be elected president of Harvard.

2. Thomas A. Davis (1798–1845) was in the thirties to hold several minor offices in the Boston city government. In 1839 he was to be elected to the House of Representatives where he served one term. The year of his death he was to become mayor of Boston.

3. This passage sounds almost as though Garrison were referring to his own "maiden speech," except that he was at the time living not in South Boston but in Charlestown.

4. William Charles Jarvis (died 1836) was a lawyer and custom house officer who had served in the house of the state legislature since 1821. In 1826–1827 he was active in the free bridge controversy (see letter 15, n. 2).

5. George Blake (1769–1841) was a Boston lawyer who served several terms in the Massachusetts legislature — both the house and the senate.

6. Andrew Dunlap (1794–1835), a Boston lawyer, was among the dissident Federalists who had supported the presidential candidacy of William H. Crawford in 1824 and who were later to form the nucleus of the Democratic party in Massachusetts. Dunlap was to become United States District Attorney for Massachusetts from 1829 until just before his death.

7. The *Constitution*, designed by Joshua Humphreys and launched in 1797, had been victorious in a number of engagements in the War of 1812, most famous of which was the one over the *Guerrière*, a forty-nine-gun British frigate. It was, in fact, this particular victory which persuaded many New Englanders to support the war.

8. Oliver Hazard Perry (1785–1819), older brother of Matthew Calbraith Perry, on September 10, 1813, defeated the British forces in the battle for Lake Erie.

9. Garrison quotes, with a few inaccuracies, from the letter of May 22, 1771, *The Letters of Junius* (New York, 1821), I, 137.

13

TO THE EDITOR OF THE BOSTON *COURIER*

[February 8, 1827.]

SIR, —

I should do injustice to my feelings, were I to suffer the excellent speech of Mr. PICKERING, delivered in the House of Representatives on Monday, upon the lottery bill, to pass without bestowing upon it my entire approbation.[1] To say that it is worth all that has been said upon this subject in the House, partakes neither of flattery nor compliment.

Its sound sense, clear reasoning, and high morality, emanate from a mind whose judgement is at once vigorous and penetrating, and from a character which is impeccable. With grateful feelings, therefore, for this public and timely effort, do I tender the right hand of fellowship to this gentleman.

In connection, sir, with this tribute, I beg leave to remark briefly upon the subject of lotteries. Much effervescence of feeling exists among members of the House, and no little interest in the community, in regard to the fate of the bill now under discussion. As a friend to the poor, as a lover of morality, and an enemy to vice, I hope this bill will not pass. Whatever has a tendency to create an unnatural thirst for gain, or to excite unhallowed appetites and desires, must make men vicious and is injurious to public morals. This position alone is sufficient to determine the dangerous influence of lotteries. If the fatal effects of these snares of vice could be portrayed in proper colors, if the aggregate misery and distress which they occasion could be summed up, if the balance of loss and gain to the public were faithfully struck, the result would be viewed with astonishment. The morally honest but deluded expectant, whose last shilling is wrung from him in this hazardous game, in the moment of desperation may be tempted to commit some crime, in order to obtain means to renew his ill luck, which may bring him to the fate and level of the lowest villain. Nor is this to be sneered at as impossible. When reason gives way to vile and ardent passions, when the fondest expectations of hope are suddenly dashed to the earth, when the purse becomes empty by repeated losses, and industry will not replenish it, the individual thus situated, may without surprise be driven to the worst extremity, and choose rather to be a knave than a reformed simpleton.

I might appeal, sir, with success, even to those who are most interested in the toleration of lotteries. I might ask if, in any other situation, their hearts would not melt to behold the looks and hear the execrations of the miserable and disappointed throng which surround their doors upon the news of the drawing of an important lottery? Age, pinched with poverty and in rags — females, shivering with cold, and scarcely decent in appearance — and children, hungry and barefooted, contribute largely to fill up the group. So high has the frenzy raged to obtain tickets, that I could cite instances, within my own knowledge, where females and others have not only deprived themselves of the necessaries of life, but have actually pawned articles of clothing, furniture, &c. to raise funds for lottery adventures. And yet we are gravely told of the utility and expediency of lotteries!

Some ingenious sophists would fain persuade us, that lotteries do not come under the definition of gambling. But where is the argument?

In what consists the difference, (except in amount,) whether my luck is determined by the toss of a penny, the cast of a die, or by a wheel of fortune? Each act is alike criminal. Men publicly agree to throw in certain sums of money, and then to determine, by pieces of paper called tickets, who shall be winners — and so they also do privately at an ale house and decide their luck by cards or dice. Which is the more criminal?

Again, it is said, that the law against lotteries cannot be carried into execution. This assertion may fall harmless from the lips of an obscure man; but when legislators, men who are set up as guardians of the public morals and public welfare, corroborate and avow the same, it becomes at once dangerous and important. As for myself, sir, my indignation and amazement at this juncture give way to alarm. I perceive that our constitutional walls are no longer steadfast.

Let it be once understood by the people that laws have been enacted, which cannot be executed — let but *one* law be broken, openly, flagrantly, and with impunity — and our halls of legislation, our courts of justice, become places of solemn mockery; they are no longer safe: we may then prepare for the worst deeds of a lawless and turbulent population.

But the assertion of the futility of the law is false. Have the great body of the people, or even individuals, prevented arrests? Have juries refused to convict? No. In what instance has obedience to the laws been resisted by our citizens? I know of none. With these facts, therefore, before him, that legislator who talks of the weakness and inefficacy of the present lottery law, must be blinded by prejudice, and lost to conviction.

All this excitement originates from brokers, lottery ticket vendors, and their agents. They find access to the columns of the public prints, and fill them with declamatory matter about the unconstitutionality of suppressing these pernicious schemes — and they are doubtless well represented in the House. Against such the law should be speedily enforced. Let a few spirited examples be made by those whose duty it is to see that the laws are obeyed, and this clamor will die away. If we cannot wholly exterminate, let us at least restrain the evil.

It is folly to talk of licensing lotteries, that our revenue may be increased. We are not driven to this resort by any consideration; and, if we were, I would exclaim with Mr. Pickering, "Perish the revenue, if it cannot be raised but at the expense of the public morals!"

A. O. B.

Printed: Boston *Courier*, February 8, 1827.

1. Garrison refers to the bill to authorize the use of Jefferson's land for prizes in a lottery to benefit the Jefferson family. Although Timothy Pickering's

speech is not reported in the *Register of Debates in Congress*, the third reading of the bill was ordered on Saturday, February 10; and it was passed on the twelfth. (See Gales and Seaton's *Register of Debates in Congress*, Nineteenth Congress, second session, III, 1053, 1119.)

14

TO THE EDITOR OF THE NEWBURYPORT *HERALD*

Boston, April 21, 1827.

DEAR SIR:

You will perceive by the papers, that the friends of Mr. Adams, in this city, are "taking time by the forelock,"[1] and fully realise the importance of the approaching election for the choice of Representatives.[2] A meeting was held last evening in Faneuil Hall, without distinction of party, to concert measures for forming a union ticket, friendly to the National Administration. Considering the early period at which this meeting was called, it was large and respectable. David L. Child, Esq. first addressed the assembly, and denounced in strong and pungent language, the faction which threatens to disturb the peace, if not destroy the liberty, of our country.[3] He submitted sundry resolutions to the meeting, in favor of the administration of Mr. Adams, &c. which were passed *nem. con.* Mr. Child's delivery is most unhappy — his matter is always better than his manner. His voice is harsh and stubborn, and when exerted, grates painfully upon the ear. He has distinguished himself for his candor, good sense, and sterling independence, as editor of the *Massachusetts Journal*, — a paper which deserves only to be known, to be supported. Mr. C. was a member of the last, and I hope will be of the approaching, legislature.

George Bond, Esq. succeeded Mr. C. in some very pertinent remarks.[4] He stated that he was formerly friendly to the election of Mr. Crawford; but he heartily approved of the course which Mr. Adams had pursued, and was ready to yield him a cordial support. His predilections and convictions were exactly in unison with my own. You know that during the Presidential canvass, my feelings were warmly enlisted in favor of Mr. Crawford; but I do not hesitate to say, that the unseemly and factious conduct of the opposition is sufficient to impel every high-minded antagonist of Mr. Adams to enter into his service. Rely upon it, the phrensied efforts of the Jackson cabal have made more converts to Mr. Adams, throughout the country, than even the enlightened measures of the administration. There has been a wonderful revolution in the feelings of most of the distinguished supporters of Mr. Crawford. They are united in the cause of THE COUNTRY.

Mr. Ebenezer Clough followed Mr. Bond in a plain, homespun

speech, which partook of his usual quaintness and brevity.[5] There is no circumlocution in his remarks — he seeks not to adorn his language with the pinks and posies of rhetoric — but throws off his burden in the shortest manner; and though he often murders "the king's English," he never kills *time*.

My strong desire to see and hear the idol of New England, has been gratified. — Mr. Webster rose after Mr. C. had concluded; and the protracted and deafending applause, which his appearance drew from the audience, was a proud testimony of his great popularity with the people. I can hardly determine whether his figure meets my expectation. He is certainly a finer looking man than I had anticipated. His person is commanding; but has not those colossal dimensions, which I had been led to believe it possessed. His eye would shame an eagle's — it is large, prominent, and restless. His forehead is matchless, and the whole cast of his features of the finest mould. I shall venture to give but a mere sketch of his speech.[6] His language was remarkably plain, without a single ornament. He purposely abstained from all comment upon the measures of the administration, conceiving it to be irrelevant to the time and place. Of Virginia, our ancient friend, he spoke in terms of marked respect. In noticing the liberal support which Massachusetts had shown by her votes for southern Presidents, he mentioned the fact that Virginia had never given a majority of her electoral votes to any candidate for the Presidency who was not a native of that State; and according to present appearances, said he, she never will. He remarked upon the unfairness and injustice which had been exercised towards the administration by its opponents. From the hour of Mr. Adams' election, they had been violent and untiring in their opposition. They did not, said Mr. Webster, wait to "judge the administration by its measures," but proclaimed hostilities from the beginning. Where is our security and strength, if every man, who is disappointed in the success of his favorite candidate, determines to oppose, at all hazards, the Constitutional Magistrate? Our country must be lost. It is highly uncharitable to suppose, that our own candidate is the only person, in these United States, qualified to fill the Presidential Chair. We cannot all be gratified in our wishes, said Mr. W.; and it is our duty as good citizens, to sacrifice our own partialities upon the altar of public good — to judge fairly and candidly of every measure of government — and to suppose that it is adopted with the best intentions, even if it prove a mistaken policy. Much clamor had been raised about a corrupt influence in the election of Mr. Adams by the House of Representatives; but so far as his knowledge and assertion would go, he solemnly believed that the choice was spontaneous, unbiassed, and upright.

Mr. Webster gave a sketch (which he said was not one of fancy) of the management which was resorted to by the opposition at the South and West. They did not sit down and quarrel about old and worn out differences; — but courted alike federalists and democrats, and exhausted their ingenuity to raise a vote against Mr. Adams. Was it politic in the people of this State to waste their strength and influence in obsolete party feuds — to be frightened by the hue and cry of *amalgamation*, — a cry raised by designing men, and senseless in its import? — He recapitulated the principal causes which formerly divided the two great political parties of our country. These causes had long since ceased to live. The treaty of peace banished all contention, and diffused universal joy throughout the Union. It was a point where all could happily unite. The struggle was no longer about measures, but men. The *hearts* of the people, said Mr. W. are united, and the only thing wanting is to join their *hands*. He thought it highly necessary at this juncture, that Massachusetts should give a decided, fair and honest support to the national administration — a support, based upon duty, justice, and merit; and he was willing to lend his humble services in this cause, in conjunction with the State. He cordially approved of the design of the present meeting, and concluded by declaring that he called no man, or body of men, master but the people whom he had the honor to represent.

This is a hasty and most imperfect sketch, but will give you some idea of the wisdom and truth which prompted this truly American speech.

Yours, respectfully,

G.

Printed: Newburyport *Herald*, April 24, 1827. This is the first of a series of letters signed "G." written to the Newburyport *Herald* (Ephraim W. Allen, editor) beginning in 1827. Although attribution of these letters to Garrison cannot be made with certainty on the basis of either style or content (the 1820's being a formative period in the development of Garrison's ideas as well as his expression of them), it seems for a number of reasons highly probably that they are his. The letters were written from Boston, where Garrison was residing at the time. This first letter is introduced with a note from the editor of the *Herald* explaining that it is written by "our Boston friend and correspondent"; and the three letters printed in 1827 are headed "FROM OUR CORRESPONDENT." It is not at all unlikely that the former apprentice would enter into a semiprofessional arrangement with his old paper. Another series of letters signed "G." appeared in the Boston *Courier* (see the issues for July 30, 1827, January 15, 1829, May 24, 1830, October 16, 1830). But these satisfy none of the guidelines for attributing letters to Garrison. Also, two of them were addressed from Boston at a time when Garrison is known to have been elsewhere. Moreover, it seems improbable that he would have used the signature "G." for letters written to the *Courier* at the same period in which he is known to have used several times the signature "G———n."

1. This cliché originates in Spenser, *Amoretti*, LXX, 8.
2. For the state legislature, that is.

3. David Lee Child (1794–1874), was teacher, diplomat, soldier, lawyer, politician, industrialist, and editor. In the thirties he was to become one of the most versatile and capable of Garrison's supporters. Between 1843 and 1844 he was to assist his wife, Lydia Maria Child, in editing the *National Anti-Slavery Standard* in New York.

4. George Bond was a Boston businessman and civic leader as well as a prominent member of the Brattle Street Church.

5. Ebenezer Clough figures in articles about this time in the *American Travel-ler* (see especially the issues for April 27 and May 1, 1827); he is described as "of the Custom House." He may be the same Ebenezer Clough who is listed in the first census of the United States as head of a family in Marblehead, Massachusetts.

6. Garrison's is the only report of this particular speech known to the editor.

15

TO THE EDITOR OF THE NEWBURYPORT *HERALD*

Boston, May 7, 1827.

DEAR SIR:

The election for the choice of Representatives takes place in this city on Thursday next, and a desperate struggle may be anticipated. As the time approaches, the elements of political strife continue to increase in virulence — nor can a correct opinion be hazarded as to the result. The adjourned meeting of the friends of the National and State administration was held last evening in Faneuil Hall, when a union list of candidates was read and accepted. The meeting was then adjourned to Wednesday evening. Previous to adjournment, some little disturbance was made, through the instrumentality of that political nondescript, that satire upon all caucuses, Mr. Emmons.[1] He is a perfect nuisance — and contrives to inflict a mass of unintelligible trumpery, at almost every meeting, upon the patience of the audience. You will recollect the disgraceful but happily abortive attempt which was made last Spring, to place this lunatic in the House; and you would now blush for the dignity, intelligence and spirit of Bostonians, were you to witness the applause which his senseless jargon elicits from the still more senseless multitude. I should state, however, that his supporters are only the rabble.

A *Free Bridge* ticket was likewise formed last evening at Concert Hall.[2] This meeting was little better than an abortion — notwithstanding it was composed of all the discordant and heterogeneous materials in the community. It is wonderful to observe with what adroitness the little, insignificant Jackson cabal turn every variance to their account. Of course, they are, almost to a man, the blustering champions of a free bridge, — full of declamation and fight. They leave

no artifice untried, no falsehood untold, no inflammatory address un-
made, that may forward their designs. Thrown together by selfishness,
and stimulated by the most unhallowed passions, they wickedly appeal to the pockets of the people — to their sordid feelings, and selfishness, and prejudices — and strive to make them lose sight of justice by
blinding their reason. "Hartford Conventionists," "Aristocrats," "Trading Politicians," "Base Monopolists," "Hireling Presses," &c. &c. form
their incantations and enchantments, and find a place in every 6-line
newspaper paragraph. *Furor arma ministrat.*

Since the late administration meeting, the Statesman and Traveller
have deluged their columns with the most unmeasured abuse and
calumny of Mr. Webster — particularly the former.[3] They are quite
wrathful and confounded at the proposal. Still, they make a prodigious
noise; and did not the voice of the ass betray the pseudo lion, it might
possibly terrify some weak-minded persons into their service. It is
vexatious in the extreme, that papers so stinted in their influence and
worthless in their character, should cause so much excitement in the
community. Nine tenths of the electors in this city, unquestionably
prefer Mr. Adams to Gen. Jackson, — but as a large floating mass of
population can always be bound, hand and foot, by their passions, it
is incumbent on the friends of the administration to be watchful that
intrigue, and chicanery, and falsehood, prove not too powerful for a
good cause and good advocates.

The city government, you will perceive, has fixed the number of
Representatives at thirty. It was hoped, by many, that at least ten more
would have been added: but, amidst the many distracting opinions,
interests and parties, which divide the city, it is extremely doubtful if
more than twenty be chosen. We have already four different lists
recommended for our support, viz: The [Broker's] Republican Ticket,
formed at the Exchange; the [mongrel] Republican Ticket, formed at
the old Court House, consisting promiscuously of the friends and
enemies of the national administration and Charleston [4] free bridge; the
Free Bridge Ticket, formed at Concert Hall; and the Union Ticket,
formed at Faneuil Hall. One other ticket may yet be added to the number. It is the great design of the Jackson cabal, and upon which they ex-
haust their ingenuity, to break up and divide the formidable ranks of the
friends of the General Government, by multiplying conflicting lists;
and they will succeed, at least in preventing a choice, unless a cordial
support be given to the UNION TICKET by the friends of good order, of
the old political parties.

I perceive that a hasty expression in my last letter has drawn forth
some characteristic comments from the lynx-eyed editors of the opposition, and been bandied about with much industry. I spoke of Mr.

Webster as being "the *idol* of New-England" — *favorite* would certainly have been a better term. It is hardly necessary to add, that nothing like servility or adoration was intended thereby: it was merely a wandering hyperbole; but it will serve, undoubtedly, for some time to come, as a popgun to discharge at Mr. Webster, at the administration, and at New-England, by the gallant soldiers of General Jackson. I make this apology, not to soothe the delicate nerves and republican sensibility of Mr. Hill and Maj. Noah, but because I dislike the expression myself.[5]

　　Yours, truly,

　　　　　　　　　　　　　　　　　　　　　　　　　　　　C.

Printed: Newburyport *Herald*, May 8, 1827.

　　1. William Emmons (born c. 1792), a Boston printer and Jacksonian politician, had been defeated in running for the state legislature in 1826. He became closely associated with that colorful Kentucky politician Colonel Richard M. Johnson, whose campaign biography he was to write in 1833.

　　2. In this letter Garrison refers to the free bridge controversy which agitated Boston's political and business leaders during 1826–1827. In 1826 a group of real estate speculators (including William C. Jarvis and David Henshaw), interested in developing land in South Boston, sought the right to build a free bridge from Boston to that area. An appropriate bill was passed through the state legislature. Other speculators wanted to build another free bridge to Charlestown. But Bostonians who held toll rights to an older bridge to Charlestown fought the proposed bridges so bitterly that Governor Levi Lincoln refused to sign the legislative bill. Building of free bridges subsequently became a political issue, about which, as Garrison points out, opposing candidates grouped themselves. What Garrison calls the "Union Ticket" was formed by a coalition of conservative interests — especially businessmen and bankers who favored high tariffs and internal improvements and who opposed the building of free bridges.

　　3. The meeting Garrison mentions here was held on March 29. During the period between the meeting and the publication of this letter, the Boston *Daily American Statesman* referred to Webster on seven separate dates (April 5, 17, 23, 24, 28, May 1, 4). All the references were disparaging. Several articles about amalgamation and the free bridge controversy, signed "A VOTER," "TEA PARTY," and "FREE BRIDGE," were printed in the *American Traveller* (April 20, 27, May 1, 1827); but they were only mildly critical of Webster.

　　4. Apparently a misprint for "Charlestown."

　　5. Garrison refers to two staunch Republicans, Isaac Hill (1789–1851) and Mordecai Manual Noah (1785–1851). Hill had by 1827 established himself as editor of an outstanding Republican paper, the *New Hampshire Patriot*, and he had served several terms in the New Hampshire senate. In the thirties he was to move to the United States Senate and to become one of Jackson's "kitchen cabinet"; in 1836 he was to become governor of New Hampshire. Although active in several reforms, he never approved of the methods used by abolitionists. Major Noah (as he was called in Jackson's correspondence) was diplomat, lawyer, playwright, and journalist as well as Jewish patriot. After several years abroad, he settled in New York, becoming editor of the *National Advocate* in 1817 and of the New York *Enquirer* in 1826; the latter paper subsequently merged with the *Morning Courier* and became one of the major supporters of Jackson's first administration.

16

TO THE EDITOR OF THE NEWBURYPORT *HERALD*

BOSTON, *June* 9, 1827.

Dear Sir: —

The statement in your last, relative to Mr. Speaker Jarvis, was premature.[1] His *"near and dear"* friends have NOT relieved him from his unhappy quandary; but, seemingly, are willing to have it understood, that they cannot become vouchers for his integrity as Treasurer of the Commonwealth. The erroneous report which I sent you was deemed to be correct; but as the stage was departing I had no time to ascertain its origin or validity. Mr. Jarvis must now feel but too sensibly, that his best friends are his bitterest enemies. A more humiliating situation cannot well be imagined: and yet, if I mistake not, the public sympathy is not so great but that another candidate would be gladly preferred.

Among the individuals which rumor has named to fill the vacant office, are Alden Bradford, John T. Apthorp, Nathan Appleton, and Minot Thayer, Esq's.[2] Mr. Bradford received the highest number of votes, next to Mr. Jarvis, at the last choice; and will, I hope, on the next trial, be the successful competitor. His mild deportment, unbending integrity, long tried faithfulness, and rich qualifications, strongly recommend him to the suffrages of the legislature. He is, I understand, dependent upon his pen for a support: — in rya [3] pecunia point of view, therefore, the office should be desirable and timely; and scarcely any other than an *honest poor man* should fill it. I do not know that he has requested to be a candidate; but think it probable that the votes which he has already received were altogether unexpected by him. So much the more flattering.

Mr. Webster's majority in the Senate is greater than was anticipated. By his promotion, a pillar of strength has been removed from the House of Representatives; nor am I sure that the cause of Mr. Adams will be benefitted by the transfer. Certainly this depends materially upon the individual who may be chosen to supply the vacancy. The Senate is a more grave and deliberate body than the House, furnishing fewer subjects of debate — not easily excited or convinced — tenacious of its preconceived opinions, stubborn, phlegmatic, and comparatively beyond the arts and subtleties of rhetoric. This follows necessarily from the fewness of its numbers. The influence of a plain, active, business-like member, therefore, is scarcely less than that of a finished orator and scholar. It is the soundness of the vote that gives weight and importance to this body, and deserves the first consideration in selecting its members. On the other hand, the House of Representatives being the larger and more popular branch — constantly vacillating between conflicting opinions, and ready to receive and retain every new impression — looking rather to the judgment and sentiments of its leaders than to its own — less active and vigorous in detecting error — hasty in forming its conclusions and more liable from the buoyancy of its materials to be carried away by every current of popular feeling — derives its efficiency and strength mainly from the vigilance, sagacity, and nervous eloquence of the gigantic debater and affords him a nobler field for action. The influence of a man like *Daniel Webster* over such a body can hardly be exaggerated, or too highly appreciated. When he rises to defend men or measures, his retaliatory blows are terrible his antagonists are buried beneath the ruins of their fortress. Wherever the thunderbolt is aimed, the victim though panoplied in steel, can never escape. The loss of Mr. Webster, then, to the House, must be regretted — not that the people of New England do not rejoice at his elevation — but at this juncture, when the enemies of the administration are coalescing with every interest, inflaming every passion, and exhausting every artifice, to effect their factious designs, Mr. Webster is needed where his services will be great, efficient, and more successful.

The loss of Mr. Webster to the people of Boston will be severely felt. But if, in the approaching election they will act magnanimously, and with a single eye to the honor and interest of the city and of the Commonwealth, they can yet remedy it. In strength of intellect, irresistable eloquence, and more than Roman dignity of manners, Mr. Otis, is the only man who can cope with Mr. Webster, or amply fill his place. My feelings in favor of this great man are intensely fervid; and I earnestly hope, that the highminded, honest, & liberal part of the community, will carry him triumphantly into the House. It is, however, quite problematical with his friends, whether he would consent to become a candidate: still, that he is ever ready to obey the voice of his fellow-citizens there can be no doubt. I never think of the abuse and contumely which have been heaped, like mountains, upon this distinguished individual, without involuntarily repeating the touching declaration of the Prince of Poets:

> "Besides this *Otis*
> Hath borne his faculties so well — hath been
> So clear in his great office, that his virtues
> Do plead like angels, trumpet-tongued, against
> The deep damnation of his taking off." [4]
> Yours, &c.

G.

Printed: Newburyport *Herald*, June 12, 1827.

1. As a brief item in the *Herald* for June 8 indicates, William C. Jarvis' predicament was financial. He had been elected treasurer of the Commonwealth but was obliged to decline the office, owing to his inability "to obtain the necessary 'pecuniary security.'"

2. John T. Apthorp was the president of the Boston Bank. Minot Thayer (1771–1856) was for many years a merchant in Boston and retired about 1813 to his farm in Braintree. Alden Bradford (1765–1843), a descendant of both John Alden and Governor William Bradford, was a man of far-ranging interests and occupations. He had been a minister, a tutor at Harvard, clerk of the court for Lincoln County, the proprietor of an unsuccessful bookselling business, secretary of the Commonwealth of Massachusetts, editor of the Boston *Gazette*, and justice of the peace at New Bedford. He had also found time to advocate many of the leading reforms of the day, to publish historical works of his own and, more important, to publish historical documents. Nathan Appleton (1779–1861) had by the time of this letter already begun the accumulation of what was to become a vast manufacturing and banking fortune. He had also been one of the organizers of the Boston Athenaeum and was active in the Massachusetts Historical Society. In the 1830's as a member of Congress, he became an active advocate of protective tariffs and a national bank. Although always conscientious and interested in reform, Appleton believed slavery to be a local problem. In subsequent years, therefore, after Garrison had become a well-known abolitionist, Appleton grew extremely hostile to him and his methods.

3. Presumably a misprint for *rea*.

4. Garrison adapts Shakespeare, *Macbeth*, I, vii, 16–20.

17

TO THE EDITOR OF THE BOSTON *COURIER*

[July 12, 1827.]

Sir, —

As nature has not made me extemporaneously eloquent, and notes are somewhat troublesome, I must crave your indulgence in occupying the columns of the Courier with a few hasty strictures upon the anomalous proceedings of the late Federal caucus.[1]

The recollection of the unhappy differences on Monday evening, even at this hour, I confess, fills me with indignation and regret. When, sir, has it been known, that a single individual ever presumed to introduce to a political assembly of high-minded, intelligent Federalists, local interests or sectional prejudices? I envy not that man, who could so far forget what was due to the feelings of a highly respectable and intelligent audience — to the character and object of the meeting — and, what outweighs all other considerations, to the magnanimous and extended policy of Federalism. It must console him to learn, that he stood conspicuously alone. The severe but merited rebuke which he received, if properly appreciated, will enlarge his views and liberalize his mind. Of what importance was it to the meeting, whether his individual vote would be given for this or that candidate? Was it proper, was it politic, in him to forestall the opinions of gentlemen present? I am afraid, the gentleman estimates too highly his own influence, if he imagines that his veto will prevent the selection of a candidate, whose views are not precisely in unison with his own. If he will forgive me, I must say, that it was precipitate and indecorous in him, almost at the opening of the meeting, to discard an eminent citizen who was presented, among twenty others, for its consideration and support. It was evident that no previous exertions, no concentration of strength, no canvassing of private opinions, had been made in favor of either of the gentlemen who were named as Representatives. It is true, sir, that in making some remarks upon the importance of the pending election, I viewed Mr. Otis as one who, for his integrity, his talents and experience, stood pre-eminent above all others. We know that he has no competitor — no equal. But in bestowing upon him my feeble panegyric, I also disclaimed any intention to anticipate or bias the feelings of the meeting; I was willing cheerfully to surrender my own predilections, and to support any man whom a majority of the party should nominate; and, sir, if I do not err, this sentiment, with a single exception, was general. A more magnanimous and liberal meeting, so far as public policy was concerned, was never convened in this city. It is not surprising, then, that the tocsin of alarm, which was so unexpectedly sounded in their ears, should have created a strong collision of sentiment, or elicited a warm debate. They were taken by surprise; and the excitement was any thing but unnatural.

Lest, however, the gentleman should misconceive my views, I will state that my feelings are equally strong with his, in favor of commerce, and against an exorbitant tariff. So far as my limited observation extends, I am satisfied that the true source of national wealth arises pre-eminently not from the encouragement of any one branch of industry, but from a fair and liberal support to all — though too many, by their recklessness, seem determined to reverse the position. You may lay heavy restrictions upon commerce — shackle the merchant with extraordinary burdens — to fatten and pamper manufacturing establishments, *and to grow rich*; but the country nevertheless will speedily become bankrupt. You may neglect the manufacturer, and open our ports for the benefit of foreigners, and commerce itself will languish. There is certainly danger to be apprehended that the equilibrium, in this momentous interest, will be lost. If we suffer ourselves to grow delirious with golden visions, a tremendous re-action may restore us to our senses, after we have ruined our estate. The "American System," [2] as it is called, is rapidly strengthening itself, and spreading far and wide — it seeks the obscure and desolate places of nature, and calls villages into being at once — it enables a petty inland parish to spring up and eclipse the seaport — capitalists are every where eagerly investing their property in manufactories — and the natural consequence is, that calls for still further prohibitory duties upon commerce are distinctly audible. Far be it from me to deprecate our present tariff; in some particulars, its amendment would unquestionably be beneficial; but it is sufficiently restrictive, without being partial in its effects. He who contemns the wonderful resources and abilities of this country — who looks with a cold and suspicious eye upon a rational encouragement to home industry and product — neither acts nor feels as an American citizen. Still I must believe, that as manufactures increase beyond a certain ratio, there is reason to fear an aristocracy will imperceptibly spring up with them. The great desideratum therefore is, to find that medium in national policy, which shall whiten every ocean with our canvass, and erect a manufactory by every favorable stream.

But, sir, as a lover of my country, as a federalist and friend to the welfare of this beautiful city — I fervently trust that the approaching election will be conducted without a special reference to either of these growing interests. If men are to be selected to represent merely this or that system of measures, or to be bound hand and foot by a doubtful majority; if they are to be made the political automata of only one portion of the community; the safety of the whole country is endangered, and turbulence, selfishness and disunion will prevail. Every interest will find a premature grave.

I must be excused, sir, for repeating what I have said elsewhere. The decision to be made this evening is one of the highest importance, and requires the utmost caution, candor and unanimity.[3] It involves the interests of this great metropolis, and the reputation of the Commonwealth. It demands a man, who in eloquence is unrivalled, in dignity unsurpassed, in experience complete, in strength of intellect a colossus. The removal of Mr. Webster to the U.S. Senate, has left a blank in the House, which can be *filled* only by an individual who combines all these great requisites in his character. Where shall we look for such a man? — This city, it is true, is opulent in talent — bright minds and strong heads meet us on every side. But who, amidst this congregation of greatness and merit, stands, giant-like, pre-eminent above the rest? Let this evening determine with a voice potential.

It cannot be denied sir, that the federal party in this city embraces the highest talents and the ablest men. No one will presume to deny it. There is now — there has always been, in the other party, a singular paucity in talents and abilities. In making the selection, then, from among federalists, at this interesting crisis, it becomes not a matter of party, but of absolute, unqualified necessity.

Sir, if I could infuse into the breasts of the federal party a portion of the spirit which animates my own, the meeting this evening would be thronged with those who have but one mind and one object. "Our country, *our whole country*" is the only sentiment we can ever acknowledge. PRIVATE PARTIALITIES AND LOCAL INTERESTS MUST BE LEFT BEHIND. The honor and prosperity of the city, and the dignity and stability of federalism, demand, that we should select that man, who embodies the affections of his fellow-citizens — him, who has never betrayed his trust, or slighted the voice of his constituents, or sacrificed the interests of the Commonwealth. Again and again I would say — Federalists of Boston! rally, as one man around your standard this evening — let your wishes be made known — give up any favorite, however dear, to promote union and success — let a voice of encouragement to the friends of good order and good principles, and of dismay to all political trimmers, go forth, nor cease till its echoes are those of victory.

G —— N.

Printed: Boston *Courier*, July 12, 1827.

1. Garrison refers to the caucus held at the Exchange Coffee House in Boston to nominate a candidate for the congressional seat relinquished by Webster, who had gone to the Senate. Garrison had spoken at this caucus on behalf of Harrison Gray Otis (1765–1848), brilliant Boston lawyer, former United States senator, and subsequent mayor of Boston (1829–1831). Garrison's youthful vehemence resulted in the adjournment of the caucus, the offer of the nomination to Otis, who refused to run, and the brief controversy with an unidentified antagonist "S" in the *Courier* (see also the issue for July 13 for S's attack).

2. Called today "high protective tariff."

3. The caucus had been postponed so that Otis could be consulted, but he refused to be nominated.

18

TO THE EDITOR OF THE BOSTON *COURIER*

[July 14, 1827.]

SIR, —

If I am correctly informed, the strictures in your paper of Thursday have excited some attention, and been read with avidity.[1] The Courier of yesterday convinces me that they were not wholly misapplied or unfelt. The spirit, unanimity and decision of the last federal meeting give me so much satisfaction, that I awaken with extreme reluctance the memory of our late unfortunate dissentions. Personal asperity befits not my temperament. I have taken a deep interest in the approaching election; and possibly, in the ardor of my feelings, may have "overstepped the modesty of nature;"[2] but my motives shall not be impeached with impunity.

However ambitious I may feel of becoming known to the public, your correspondent "S" must not flatter himself that I shall go out of my path to seek his applause. There is nothing in his communication which *merits* a reply; [3] but as one may be *expected*, my condescension, in this instance, exceeds even my contempt. If, as the gentleman very spiritedly insinuates, my object be to "write myself into notice," (and surely there is nothing criminal in the motive,) his patronage is unsolicited — I shall neither copy the grossness of his diction, nor degrade my style to the level of his own. I confess, sir, he has chosen his weapons with singular skill and propriety. The insulted dignity of his nature seeks relief in its natural channel. Disdaining the infliction of a manly resentment, he has indulged his irritated feelings in coarse vituperation and vulgar personalities. Let him exult in his imaginary triumph: in my opinion, it is pitiful to the last degree.

I sympathize with the gentleman in the difficulty which he found to learn my cognomination. It is true that my acquaintance in this city is limited — I have sought for none. Let me assure him, however, that if my life be spared, my name shall one day be known to the world — at least, to such an extent that common inquiry shall be unnecessary. This, I know, will be deemed excessive vanity — but time shall prove it prophetic.

It gives me pain, sir, to accuse your correspondent of wilful misrepresentation; but his assertion is too broad to pass unrefuted. I did *not* "take upon myself to make the first nomination to the respectable electors" of Boston. Again and again I disclaimed any intention of biassing their predilections. The eulogy upon Mr. Otis may have been gratuitous, and out of place; this is not for me to determine tho' I am half inclined to coincide with the gentleman; but to the latest hour of my life, I shall rejoice that I was permitted publicly to express my sentiments in favor of a man who has my strongest affections, in unison with those of the whole federal party. So far from believing, however, (for obvious reasons,) that this distinguished individual would be put in nomination, I went to the meeting with an expectation of no such result. *Yet, sir, this belief did injustice to the wishes of a large majority of the electors present* — THEY WANTED MR. OTIS — no other man could have been nominated. Disguise his feelings as he may, it was the strong evidence of this fact — it was the emphatic voice of a whole assembly, *and not my feeble echo* — that alarmed the selfishness and roused the hostility of your querulous correspondent. It was this alone that caused him to lose sight of all decorum in view of his own private interest and occupation; and, sir, I repeat, I do not envy that man who could so far forget his own professions of patriotism and the respect due to the opinions of a liberal, highminded audience, as to thrust upon their attention local interests and sectional prejudices. The deep excitement which instantaneously followed — the murmurs of indignation which were so generally heard — the unfeigned astonishment and surprise of every man present — should teach him a lesson of propriety even in the twilight of life. It shall not be my fault if it be soon forgotten.

The little, paltry sneers at my youth, by your correspondent, have long since become pointless. It is the privileged abuse of old age — the hackneyed allegation of a thousand centuries — the damning *crime* to which all men have been subjected. I leave it to metaphysicians to determine the precise moment when wisdom and experience leap into existence — when, for the first time, the mind distinguishes truth from error, selfishness from patriotism, and passion from reason. It is suffic-ient for me that I am understood. Whatever deficiency "S" has found in my years, I have the vanity to believe he will not complain of the weakness of my strictures. The lash which was applied has cut deeper than he would be willing to acknowledge. His crude and churlish reply betrays the writhings of an excoriated mind, — the strong agita-tions of mortified pride. Though panoplied in all the dignity of wealth and experience, the arrow has pierced his vitals.

If, sir, the gentleman will call on me in person, I will satisfy him that I have "paid taxes" elsewhere, if not for a few months' residence in this city. I admire his industry in searching the books of the Trea-surer — it speaks well for his patriotism; and, to relieve him from fur-ther inquiries I promise to become a legal voter with all commendable haste.

The hours which should be devoted to labor, Mr. Editor, allow me little time to indulge in newspaper essays. Poverty and misfortune are hard masters, and cannot be bribed by the magic of words. However, I am willing to sacrifice one meal, at least, in order that justice may be done to the "tariff and anti-tariff question," which your correspon-dent has submitted to my consideration. It shall be done some time previous to the election.[4] I do not pretend to much information on this subject; but, to my perception, there appears but one great interest to be involved, one straight-forward, liberal policy to be pursued, one cause to be maintained, one generous desire to be gratified.

G———N.

Printed: Boston *Courier*, July 14, 1827; printed partly in *Life*, I, 76–77.

1. Garrison refers to his letter of July 12 (letter 17).
2. Shakespeare, *Hamlet*, III, ii, 21.
3. Garrison refers to S's attack in the paper of the thirteenth. S described the way in which an unknown young man rose at the caucus, "addressed the electors with much verbosity, until his ideas became exhausted, when he had recourse to his hat, which appeared to be well filled with copious notes, from which he drew liberally, to make (for aught I know) his maiden speech. An inquiry went

round the room to know who the speaker was; with some difficulty I found out his name. . . ." It was objected that Garrison's actions were out of order since the nomination had not been "called for." Garrison's critic asserted "that it is revolting to my ideas of propriety, to see a stranger, a man who never paid a tax in our city, and perhaps nowhere else, to possess the impudence to take the lead and nominate a candidate for the electors of Boston."

4. See Garrison's letter (19) to the *Courier*, July 23.

19

TO THE EDITOR OF THE BOSTON *COURIER*

[July 23, 1827.]

SIR:

I find such is the feverish state of the public mind, in relation to the Tariff, that the agitation of this subject, at this juncture, would be most impolitic. Anxious that not a single vote should be scattered this day, by any remarks of mine, I shall abandon my original design, and content myself with making some general reflections upon our situation and prospects.

I cannot find language sufficiently strong to express my regret that any thing should have arisen to divide brethren of the same principle. Heretofore, the federal party in this city has acted in reference only to one great object. It has been reserved for this hour to witness a division in its ranks, narrowed down to one particular interest, and originating solely in individual pursuits. The natural consequences must speedily follow. Humiliating as is the confession, our lessons of wisdom, in a political sense, have all been taught us by our opponents; and instead of profiting by the instruction, we grow foolish by reproof. While we are idly contending about local interests, and wasting that strength which alone gives us vitality — putting a torch to every prejudice, and rousing every selfish feeling — they are actuated but by one sentiment, namely, a determination to triumph as a party.

If the spirit which has been manifested by a portion of the community be the only incentive to action, our worst forebodings may be more than realized. It will be difficult, ere long, to find an eminent individual who has not taken a decided stand in favor of commerce or manufactures — those growing interests of our country, too often represented as rivals, but which, in fact, are merely partners in business. If elected to the National Legislature, he will go there not on the score of merit, but on the avowal of some favorite opinion. Our elections are gradually descending to a *system of pledges*. Men are no longer to be selected for their discernment, experience, and integrity: —

these are qualifications of minor consideration. They are to be the mouth-piece of a selfish and doubtful majority — the representatives of a fraction of the State, and not of the whole. Like the famous Turkish chess-player of Mr. Mælzel, they are to cry "*check*," according as the moves are made and the game won.[1] They may go to Congress — eat, drink, and smoke — pay visits, and even fight duels — and nothing will be required at their hands but to drop a scrap of paper into the ballot-box, with the legible inscription "*No Tariff*," or "*Restrictions upon Commerce.*" Does this partake of caricature? Would to God time may not prove it reality!

The affairs of this country are hastening to a crisis, fraught with the most tremendous results. We are spectators to an opposition to the General Government, as virulent and profligate in its character as the blind and reckless followers of military glory can possibly make it. Foreign divisions having ceased to affect our nation, we are creating artificial ones within our own bosom. The doctrine of internal improvements (those links in the chain of our Union stronger than fetters of brass and lasting as time) has been bitterly opposed by those who profess to be the only correct interpreters of constitutional law, and though the triumph of its friends has been complete, the struggle is not yet ended. A just and liberal support to our manufacturing interests has raised the voice of every commercial interest, which has been responded back by the manufacturer with increased emphasis. The fears and prejudices of the multitude are invoked on either side; and whichsoever way their impressions chance to turn, no arguments or facts, though written with a pencil of light, can restore them to sanity. In Georgia, the smouldering fires of rebellion (that epithet cannot be softened) still remain unquenched; and though, as yet, she has thrown up nothing from her bowels but smoke, the materials for a general conflagration are in readiness, and can be kindled at a moment's warning. The late attempted usurpation of guaranteed rights, by that State, is of a nature so monstrous and alarming, that no man who has carefully watched the "signs of the times," or who pretends to have a moiety of public virtue and patriotism, can view it without amazement and unmingled terror. Never has language so bold, so threatening, so insulting, been used towards the executive of our country, — never has treason dared to stand forth in its brazen deformity, more menacing in its attitude, or more determined in its purpose. As boundless as is my contempt of that political fanatic, Gov. Troup — as little as I care for his thundering epistles and startling defiances — as feeble as I view the arm which has been raised to sever our Union — I cannot consent to view the conduct of Georgia as a subject of merriment, or harmless in its tendency.[2] Such precedents are bad, and full of danger. They serve to encourage opposition, to inflame local resentments, to shield the conspirator from punishment, and to weaken the bonds of our civil compact.

This is the situation of our country, and these are the collisions which are weakening her strength. If there ever was a time when private emolument should be sacrificed to public utility; when our elections should be conducted upon principles of the utmost liberality and fairness; when the represen[ta]tives of the people should be selected solely for their firmness, decision, and integrity; — that time has now come.

"Glory," says Fisher Ames, "was the object of the Roman republic; and gain is of ours." [3] If our pursuit be not the most showy, it is certainly the most profitable. Besides, the harvest of glory which we reaped during the late war should surfeit us for at least ten centuries. We have nothing to do, therefore, but to look after our interests with the anxiety of a parent and the eye of a miser; to hoard up the gold and gems of traffic; to embowel the earth of her treasures; and to make every stream a golden tributary. Unfortunately, after all the advantages which nature has heaped upon us with such reckless prodigality, we must wrangle about the true sources of wealth. We break our eagles into farthings, and then like school-boys scramble for the pieces. We overlook the lessons which history presents upon every page, and grow ignorant with our age. Not content with our own profits, we consider the gain of others as our loss.

Providence has made us as independent in our resources as we are in spirit, — inexhaustible, unconquerable. For my own part, I do not understand that policy or patriotism, which seeks to make us unnecessarily dependent on other nations for a livelihood, and subject to all the changes and embarrassments of foreign markets. I cannot learn why we are to purchase what we do not want. But the argument most frequently used is, that we are unable to compete with Great Britain in the cheapness and quality of her manufactures. In spite of restrictions and prohibitions, in spite of the most liberal support extended to home industry, they have supplanted those of every nation, and penetrated almost as far as British enterprise. An argument may sometimes be very plausible, and very absurd. The encouragement which has been extended by government to our own manufactures has placed them not only on a respectable footing, but rendered them formidable as a rival. They can now be sold cheaper than foreign fabrics; and, with a few exceptions, are equal — in others, superior to any imported. And what hinders? Our water power is immensely greater; our facilities unrivalled. We have the raw materials at our hands; and instead of crossing the Atlantic, we have only to transport them from Louisiana and the Carolinas. Twenty-five years more will place us beyond competition.

But the deplorable state of the manufacturing interest in **Great** Britain is constantly held up, *in terrorem*, before our eyes. We are warned not to make shipwreck of our fortunes upon the same rock. The distresses of the Irish weavers are related with a pathos and minuteness that make us shudder at the recital; and if we do not profit by the tale, the fault will not be found in its daily repetition. In the first place, we can draw no correct parallels between the situation, resources, and burdens of the two governments. Nor will a hasty newspaper essay enable me to consider how far the British system of taxation (which, as Dean Swift [4] has somewhere observed, includes every thing but the air of heaven,) is fatally interwoven with the existence of domestic industry nor what portion of the laborer's scanty pittance is wrung from his grasp to support an aristocracy, whose appetite is equalled only by the grave. Thank heaven, we are free from these evils. Independent of these clogs, however, England has exceeded her abilities, and there lies the fault. She has thrown herself headlong into the tide, and is in danger of being *crushed by the wheels of her manufactories*. The success of manufactures abroad is a death-blow to her prosperity. — Does any man believe, that she would not rejoice to see every loom and shuttle in this country destroyed, and every wheel motionless? No one. This fact, alone, must send conviction to every bosom.

The danger to be apprehended, then, is, of involving ourselves too deeply in manufactures, at the expense of the two great interests of our country, — commerce and agriculture. Of this, we cannot be too apprehensive and watchful. Let us hear what Mr. Ames has said upon this subject: —

"Our own manufactures are growing, and it is a subject of great satisfaction that they are. But it would be wrong to over-rate their capacity to clothe us. The same number of inhabitants require more and more, because wealth increases. Add to this the rapid growth of our numbers, and perhaps it will be correct to estimate the progress of manufactures as only keeping pace with that of our increasing consumption. It follows, that we shall continue to demand in future to the amount of our present importation."

But Mr. Ames did not dream of the wonderful enlargement of this branch of our industry. It has outstripped the conceptions of fancy, and the tide of population. We shall be able, ere long, to supply not only our home consumption, but the wants of the Southern Republics, in defiance of the exertions of England: and here opens a new world of wealth to be gathered by our merchants and manufacturers.

I cannot conclude this essay, without making one more extract from the writings of Mr. Ames. It is pregnant with wisdom and admonition: —

"Let every nation, that is really disposed to extend the liberty of commerce, beware of rash and hasty schemes of prohibition. In the affairs of trade, as in most others, *we make too many laws*. We follow experience too little, and the visions of theorists a great deal too much. Instead of listening to discourses on what the market ought to be, and what the schemes, which always promise much on paper, pretend to make it, let us see what is the actual market for our exports and imports. This will bring vague assertions and sanguine opinions to the test of experience. That rage for theory and system, which would entangle even practical truth in the web of the brain, is the poison of public discussion. One fact is better than two systems."

Whenever, therefore, it can be satisfactorily proved, that we can buy our goods cheaper than we can manufacture them — that commerce and agriculture languish under an unequal and oppressive tariff — that American bottoms find not full employment at home and abroad — that seamen's wages, the price of labor, and freights, are not high — and that the wealth of the country is gradually wasting away — it will be time to rouse from our lethargy, and exert every effort to save the republic. But if, on the other hand, it can be shown, that a fresh impulse has been given to every branch of industry, by manufacturing establishments; if it shall appear that our prosperity, as a nation, was never more visible and certain than at present (divested, it is true, of the unnatural vigor and rankness of former years); if plenty can be found in every lap, and contentment in every bosom, — let us for once indulge the pleasures of reality, and bless God that we are happy. What better policy can we pursue, what single wish remains unsatisfied, what more can we desire, without being guilty of ingratitude?

G———n.

Printed: Boston *Courier*, July 23, 1827.

1. Johann Nepomuk Mælzel (1772–1838) was the German mechanician to the Viennese court, who had invented an automatic chess player as well as a trumpeter, bass fiddler, and speaking figure. For a report of his exhibition in Julien Hall, see the *National Philanthropist*, June 13, 1828.

2. George Michael Troup (1780–1856) had served as the representative of Georgia in both the House and the Senate before being elected governor in 1823 and again in 1825. He was a strong advocate of states' rights, and by defying President Adams and cooperating with his half-breed Indian cousin, William

McIntosh, one of the Creek chiefs, he had arranged to negotiate a treaty for the cession of the Creek lands to the state of Georgia.

3. Except for the omission of one word and a few minor changes in punctuation the quotations from Fisher Ames in this letter are accurate; see Seth Ames, ed., *The Works of Fisher Ames with a Selection from His Speeches and Correspondence* (Boston, 1854), II, 333, 32–33, 12.

4. A rare reference to Jonathan Swift in Garrison's works.

20

TO THE EDITOR OF THE NEWBURYPORT *HERALD*

Boston, *July* 26, 1827.

Dear Sir:

After the collisions of interest, of faction, and of party, which have divided and distracted this city, the result of the election is as unexpected as it is gratifying. If the loss of Mr. Webster be not wholly supplied, it is rendered so trifling by the choice of Mr. Gorham, that it will be scarcely perceptible.[1] — Massachusetts, therefore, will go strongly represented into the next Congress, and the lustre of her delegation be undimmed and permanent. The friends of the National Administration, throughout the country, may rejoice in the acquisition of this gentleman to the House, as he will be found unwavering in his attachment, so long as the same enlightened policy is pursued which has thus far characterised the government. Boston, in this selection, has consulted not only her own reputation and interests, but also those of the State. Mr. Gorham is not trammelled by any committals, nor pledged to any interest, nor under the influence of any local prejudices. He goes into Congress with an honest heart and a clear head, with views that embrace every section of the country; with a mind imbued with the spirit of independence, replete with knowledge, inexhaustible in its resources, — and I am persuaded, that after the petty excitements of the hour shall have passed away, but one feeling of satisfaction will pervade the community at the result.

I hardly know in what terms to speak of the Jackson farce which has been acted in this city — whether to view it as the desperate impulse of despair, in order to test the strength of the party, or as a crafty manœuvre intended to deceive other parts of the country — whether it most betrays the hardihood of faction, or the recklessness of insanity. Whatever was the ruling motive, the beggarly support given to Mr. Henshaw should make the lions of Gen. Jackson "roar gently as a nightingale," [2] and clip them of their terrors.[3] It was no fault of theirs — they beset high-way and by-way to hunt up game — they looked as if the whole herd of opposition were ingloriously

vanquished, and a dainty feast of flesh lay smoking on the field. In
listening to the roarings of their leader, (Mr. Dunlap,) at the late
meeting in the new Court House, I was forcibly reminded of the ludicrous scene in Shakspeare's Midsummer-Night Dream, where "enter
Lion and Moonshine": —

> *Lion.* You ladies, you, whose gentle hearts do fear
>   The smallest monstrous mouse that creeps on floor,
> May now perchance, both quake and tremble here,
>   When lion rough in wildest rage doth roar.
> "Then know, that I, one Snug, the joiner am
> A lion fell, nor else no lion's dam;
> For if I should as lion come in strife
> Into this place, 'twere pity, on my life." [4]

To drop the metaphor. The friends of the Military Chieftain,[5] in
this city, stand forth in their true insignificance, even including their
borrowed strength. They have suffered themselves to be *counted*, and
deception itself can no longer impose upon public credulity. The
whole number of votes for Mr. Henshaw was 459 — of which the
editor of the Massachusetts Journal, from qualifying circumstances,
magnanimously considers 300 to be the disciples of the hotspur of
the South.[6] I am not so charitable. In addition to the Jackson nomination, Mr. H. was the (pseudo) candidate of the "regular Republican
caucus," — and this, to many individuals, was the only governing
principle; he also received unquestionably, many votes from the
enemies of the tariff, and some few by accident, or indifference, or
disappointment. The tickets in favor of Mr. H. were decorated and
embellished with a fair type, and with a flaming ship and eagle; and
as there is something peculiarly attractive to vulgar minds, in a brave
picture, this trick was not without effect. We may suppose too, that
after the formidable "note of preparation" [7] which was sounded in
every nook and corner — after the laborious and unceasing efforts
of the leaders to bring men to the poles — and when the proverbial
watchfulness and alacrity of faction are considered — every man
hostile to the administration found his way to the ballot box, and
gave his vote for Mr. Henshaw. The number of legal voters in this
city is probably upwards of 7000; and we may fairly estimate the
real strength of Gen. Jackson to be something over 200 electors — a
just but "beggarly account." [8] I am certain that even Daniel Webster,
if a candidate for the suffrages of the people, and *avowedly* opposed
to Mr. Adams, could not possibly receive 1000 votes.

To the feelings of Mr. Gorham, the result of the election must
be highly gratifying. The vote was altogether spontaneous — no ef-

fort, besides a mere nomination, was made in his behalf: indeed, not even the common precautions were taken to insure vote distributors and written votes for the different Wards. It is, therefore, a proud testimony to the estimation in which his former services, his rich qualifications, and his unbending integrity and independence are held by his fellow-citizens.

In haste, yours, &c.

G.

Printed: Newburyport *Herald*, July 27, 1827.

1. Benjamin Gorham (1775–1855) was a distinguished Boston lawyer who had just been elected to succeed Daniel Webster in the House of Representatives.
2. Shakespeare, *A Midsummer Night's Dream*, I, ii, 86.
3. David Henshaw (1791–1852) was a banker and the founder of an insurance company. He and others had also established in 1821 the anti-Federalist Boston *Statesman*. In 1826 he had been elected to the state legislature. Along with William C. Jarvis and other real estate speculators he had urged the building of free bridges to link Boston more closely with the surrounding area. Conservative opposition, however, defeated him and his free bridge party in the April 1827 election. Shortly after another defeat, when he ran for Congress in July, Jackson appointed him collector of the port of Boston. By the time of Garrison's letter he was well on his way toward becoming the Democratic party boss of Boston.
4. V, i, 222–229.
5. Andrew Jackson.
6. Presumably Garrison refers to the hot-tempered John Randolph (1773–1833) of Virginia, currently one of the Democratic leaders in the United States Senate, who on April 8, 1826, had fought a duel with Henry Clay.
7. Shakespeare, *Henry V*, IV, Prologue, 14.
8. Shakespeare, *Romeo and Juliet*, V, 1, 45.

21

TO THE EDITOR OF THE NEWBURYPORT *HERALD*

[June 3, 1828.]

MR. EDITOR:

Your correspondent W. seems to be in rather a bad plight.[1] — He has disturbed a hornet's nest and the little spiteful insects seem disposed to make him pay dearly for his daring. But let him not fear, they are but insects, let their buzz be ever so loud — 'though their sting may be rather painful it is not killing.' It is no matter of astonishment to me that the communications of W. have been received with so little friendliness: men do not like to have their religious pursuits interfered with. It is a perilous thing to oppose popular opinion. Of this W. must have been aware and no doubt the justness of his cause and his confidence in his own abilities to support it have induced him to throw down the gauntlet, and I trust that he will not shrink from the contest. I look upon it as being of little importance what Dr. Spring or any other man thinks upon the subject which has employed the pen of W.[2] — He was but a man as well as the rest of us — just as likely to err in judgment — and I am glad to see that in his last piece W. has left him out of the question — instead of authority we want argument. The subject in question is capable of being tried by its own merits, and I look to W. to maintain the ground he has taken. Let him make a full exposition of facts and of the bearing they have on the moral and religious welfare of the community. It is no use to let the matter stop where it is; the ice is broken and W. owes it to himself and the community to come out and make a full exposition of the evils of which he complains: — it is a subject of no ordinary importance — it interests us both as men and as christians. With the dispute I have nothing to do. My sentiments are now and always have been in accordance with those expressed by W. — but the battle is his — and I am satisfied the cause cannot be in abler hands. I admire the temper with which W. has written all his pieces. He has showed himself throughout to be temperate and manful. But it is not so with "A Volunteer" who has crowded himself into the ranks, I presume both unasked and unwished for — and conducted himself in such a manner as to disgrace himself and contaminate the cause which he has exposed. I think the best thing W. can do is to shake himself clear of him as soon as possible — he is a dangerous ally — his enmity is preferable to his friendship. I hold it to be a deadly sin both against truth and good manners to torture our neighbours words into a meaning which he never intended they should have, and to hold him up to scorn as the author of sentiments which none but the most perverse could extort from his language.

This "A Volunteer" has done in his remarks upon the communication of "No snake in the Grass." He puts words into his mouth which he never uttered — he accuses him of calling W. a reprobate, heritic, renegado, and hypocrite; which I defy him to point out in his communication. Let "A Volunteer" rely upon it he will never gain a cause by abusing his antagonist — that the public have more sympathy with the man who is honorable, mild and candid than with him who is petulant, malicious and unjust.

G.

Printed: Newburyport *Herald*, June 3, 1828.

1. Garrison refers to a religious controversy, which began with an article by "W." in the Newburyport *Herald* on May 20. In this article W. was critical of religious meetings in general and of a church conference recently held in Newburyport in particular. He argued for a return to the simplicity and privacy of essential Christianity, deprecating all outward forms and ceremonies. There followed a week later a letter from "No Snake in the Grass," expressing shock

at W.'s position but offering no substantive argument. In the same issue appeared another reply to W., signed "A FRIEND TO CHURCH CONFERENCES," in which he accuses W. of having maligned the late Dr. Spring, whom he had claimed in support of his view; in fact, he suggests that W. must have written in haste and perhaps "under the influence of some unhappy excitement." Also in the issue for May 27 there was printed another statement from W., in which he restates his original position, concluding that "the christian religion was not designed, principally, for the public arena." In the issue for May 30 "A VOLUNTEER" replies to both "NO SNAKE IN THE GRASS" and "A FRIEND TO CHURCH CONFERENCES," extending further W.'s argument: "The multiplication of religious meetings, and church conferences . . . is a very serious evil."

2. Samuel Spring (1746–1819), representative of the extreme Calvinist wing, had been a chaplain to the Continental Army during the Revolution and served after 1777 as pastor of the North Congregational Church in Newburyport. He had been an editor of the *Massachusetts Missionary Magazine* and was the author of some twenty-five publications, mostly collections of sermons.

---

2 2

TO THE EDITOR OF THE *YANKEE* AND BOSTON *LITERARY GAZETTE*

[Boston, July 30, 1828.]

SIR —

You seem to pride yourself upon the excellence of your moral character, *as illustrated since your return from England.* This is a pardonable vanity, if it arise from a consciousness of well-doing. I do not blame you for boasting, merely — nor for endeavoring to repel the charges of your adversaries. A good name, once lost, is seldom reclaimed: repentance and tears may obtain before God, but they cannot always efface the remembrance of vicious deeds from among men. While, however, I grant you the right of self-defence, I am unable to perceive why you should assume a privilege, which belongs to no individual on earth, however high in dignity or low in pollution, — the privilege of abusing and misrepresenting whatsoever and whomsoever you please.

A friend has just placed in my hands the Yankee of last week, which contains the following statement. In your reply to the Portland Argus, you say:

"Most of those who have began a like war with me, are now put aside from their editorial births; and you, the author of this attack on me, will assuredly follow. There's the Philanthropist-man — the Cadet-man — the Saturday-evening-post-man — they are all turned out of office."

I have always supposed, that a strict regard for truth, was a fundamental principle in ethics. Pray, sir, is this your opinion? If it be, your creed and practice libel each other. Or is it one of the prominent beauties of Utilitarianism, that a man may lie roundly, whenever he fancies it may subserve his own or another's interest, or afford him a pitiful and temporary triumph?[1]

Sir, I have mistaken your character. I did not suppose — notwithstanding my knowledge of your vulgarity, your abusiveness, and your brazen arrogance — I did not suppose that you were so imbecile or stupid, as to deliberately misrepresent, where detection and punishment were sure to follow — and follow speedily. I was ever disposed to believe, that, in your various controversies, you were magnanimous to a fault — that you scorned to take an advantage of your antagonist, where it could not be done fairly and manfully — and that, however one might reasonably complain of your abuse, he could not of your candour.

The Yankee of the 23d inst. convinces me, that you combine in your disposition the depravity of falsehood with the meanness of revenge.

You know, sir, that my retirement was voluntary. You were furnished with a copy of the Philanthropist, which contained my resignation; and a more honorable tribute to the value of my labors, or a more sincere expression of regret at my departure, than that which was given by the proprietor, I could not desire. My continuance as editor of the Philanthropist was longer than I at first proposed; for I gave Mr. White distinctly to understand at the commencement, that it would be but temporary, and that I would not obligate myself for a single month.[2] And yet, sir, you have the egregious folly, the egotism, the impudence, and the audacity to say, that I have been turned out of office — because, forsooth, I was foolish enough to deny your infallibility ! ! ! What inflation! You seem to imagine, with one of Shakspeare's characters in Much Ado about Nothing, that "he is now as valiant as a Hercules, that only tells a lie, and swears to it." I think Falstaff, if he were living, would no longer boast of having vanquished "eleven men in buckram."[3] I think your veracity and courage would take the pre-eminence.

I confess, sir, that I am somewhat offended with your freedom in mentioning in the same breath, and placing in the same company, "the Philanthropist-man" with "the Cadet-man" and "the Saturday-evening-post-man." They stand about as high in my estimation as in yours; and I am not ambitious to acknowledge their equality.

This letter is written expressly for private perusal, but you are at liberty to use it as you may think proper. My only desire is, as an act of justice, that you will retract your assertion, as far as it relates to

myself. I have two good reasons for this request. The one is — an unwillingness to have a single reader of the Yankee imagine, that you
were instrumental, in any degree, to my withdrawal from the Philanthropist — *you!* The other — that the public mind may be disabused
of the untruth, that I was ejected from office. It is important to me
that this correction be made. My reputation, trifling as it is, is worth
something: if I lose it, I lose the means whereby I obtain my daily
bread.

With much soberness, I remain yours,

WM. LLOYD GARRISON,
Late editor of the Philanthropist.

Boston, July 30, 1828.

Printed: *Yankee* and Boston *Literary Gazette,* August 13, 1828.

John Neal (1793–1876), the editor of the *Yankee,* had been, by the time of
his altercation with Garrison, a schoolmaster, a lawyer, and a man of letters, both
in the United States and in England. He had written much self-appreciating
literary criticism, numerous novels, and even an elaborate tragedy in verse. In
1827 he had returned to the United States after four years in England, settling
permanently in his native Portland, Maine, where he edited the Portland *Yankee*
(a literary journal subsequently combined with the Boston *Literary Gazette*) and
continued his voluminous literary output. Garrison was often to pay attention to
Neal in the pages of *The Liberator* (see especially the issues for November 12,
1831, July 14, 1832, September 19, 1835, and particularly that for November 3,
1865, where Garrison reported that Neal had admitted that he had been wrong
and Garrison right about colonization and abolition).

1. Neal had been closely associated with Jeremy Bentham during his residence
in England.

2. Nathaniel H. White had shared a room with Garrison at the Reverend
William Collier's boarding house at 30 Federal Street in Boston and had been the
printer of the *National Philanthropist.*

3. Shakespeare, *Much Ado about Nothing,* IV, i, 324; *I Henry IV,* II, iv, 243.
Garrison quotes only the Bible more often than Shakespeare

---

2 3

TO THE EDITOR OF THE BOSTON *COURIER*

[August 11, 1828.]

SIR, —

Agreeably to a notice in the newspapers, the friends of the cause
of slave emancipation held a meeting at the vestry of the Federal-
street meeting house on Thursday evening last, when some propositions for effecting this desirable object were offered by a gentleman * who has distinguished himself, for some years past, by his
zeal and perseverance in favor of the oppressed sons of Africa. As
I did not perceive you were present, and as but a small portion of our

citizens could be accommodated with seats, I beg leave to give you a mere outline of what was elicited on this occasion.

In the course of his remarks, Mr. Lundy detailed, with considerable minuteness, the various measures which had been adopted at the south, and elsewhere, for the abolition of slavery, and explained the views and purposes of those who are foremost in accomplishing this great work. About one hundred and forty anti-slavery societies have been organized, a very large proportion of which are in slave holding states. Though the American Colonization Society has effected much good, and deserves unlimited encouragement, yet to suppose that, single handed and without auxiliaries, it could liberate the blacks in any given period of time, is in the highest degree fallacious. The increase of the slave population during the last year was greater than the diminution which will probably have been effected by this society in half a century. Some other plans, therefore, must be devised to remove the evil.

Mr. Lundy very pertinently observed, that nothing comparatively can be done until the great body of the people are interested in this work. Theirs are the power and the remedy. It is not for legislators, but the people, to dictate laws. The object of these anti-slavery societies is, not to purchase slaves to liberate and transport — for they cannot rightly consider them as lawful property, and it would only tend, in fact, to open a new market to kidnappers and dealers in human flesh — they go upon a broader basis, a more rational system. They seek to unite the moral strength of the country; to enlighten public sentiment by the dissemination of liberal principles; and to warn, advise, and remonstrate, till the shackles of the oppressed are broken by the will, not by the wealth, of the people. This is the only feasible plan; and it requires much patience, immense exertion, and a strong faith in its ultimate accomplishment. New York, New Jersey, and Pennsylvania, have pursued it successfully, and others will follow the example.

Mr. Lundy said he did not hesitate to assert, from a protracted residence at the south and a full knowledge of facts, that a majority of the southern people, and even of the slave-holders, are desirous of seeing the slave system abolished — though they know not how to act, or where to strike the first blow; the spirit of enquiry, however, is rapidly leading them to obvious and definite results. Many fear the danger which threatens their security, though they may not acknowledge the criminality of their conduct. Those who are so vehement in denouncing any interference with their system of bondage, constitute but a small portion of the population. They do not, said Mr. L. go to the bible for proof-texts to support the validity of their practices;

they do not care for the bible; but depend on the strength of their manacles, and the severity of their whips — *on your arms and physical force at the north,* knowing that you are constitutionally bound to protect them in case of insurrection. It is important, therefore, that the people of New England, instead of supinely folding their arms, and imagining that they have no interest in this matter and can effect nothing — it is important that they should let their voice be heard in tones of earnest remonstrance. An opportunity is now presented for acting in a prompt and beneficial manner. At the last session of Congress, a petition, signed by more than one thousand citizens of the highest respectability, and among them *several owners of slaves,* was presented from the District of Columbia, praying that slavery may cease in that district at such time, and with such restrictions, as that body may think proper. In consequence of the Presidential excitement, however, the friends of the abolition did not deem it prudent to urge the consideration of the petition. But a vigorous effort to accomplish this object will be made at the approching session. Petitions are forming in various sections of the Union for this purpose, and it is desirable that Massachusetts should embark with her sister states in the enterprise. The District of Columbia, it is well known, is under the exclusive jurisdiction of Congress; and if success should follow the exertions which are making — even though it do not follow for many succeeding years, it will have an important bearing upon the emancipation of the whole country.

I have not time, this morning, to follow Mr. Lundy in all his remarks. Hereafter, sir, with your permission, I shall interrogate the wisdom of granting the prayer of the petitioners, and at the same time propose that a paper, containing the signatures of our citizens, be forwarded by one of our representatives, praying that the reproach which is affixed to us as a nation may be forever taken away.

I have also something to say to a reverend gentleman, who spoke at the close of the meeting, which I must defer till to-morrow.

A. O. B.

*Benjamin Lundy, Editor of the Genius of Universal Emancipation, Baltimore, Md.[1]

Printed: Boston *Courier*, August 11, 1828; reprinted in the *National Philanthropist*, August 15.

1. Benjamin Lundy (1789–1839), a Quaker abolitionist, was in the midst of a lecture tour to the northern states. During this tour he first met Garrison, whom he subsequently persuaded to join him in Baltimore to co-edit the *Genius*.

2 4

TO THE EDITOR OF THE BOSTON *COURIER*

[August 12, 1828.]

SIR, —

I hope, in the indignant state of my feelings, that nothing unkind or discourteous will escape my pen, in relation to the conduct of the Rev. Gentleman [1] alluded to in my communication of yesterday. He is entitled to the utmost respect, and possesses a liberal portion of my esteem. I am disposed to believe, that his remarks at the meeting on Thursday evening were delivered without premeditation, and do not receive the deliberate sanction of his judgment. It cannot be supposed, that he who professes to have been brought "into the glorious liberty of the sons of God," is inimical to any lawful expedient for meliorating the condition of the African race.

It was evidently the principal desire of Mr. Lundy, to impress upon the minds of his audience, the importance of petitioning for the abolition of slavery in the District of Columbia, in conjunction with the people of the south. For this purpose he recommended a formation of a society, which should pursue this object steadily, until its attainment. One defeat must only animate to more vigorous exertion; the reputation of the nation is involved in the controversy, and upon the result depends the ultimate liberation of every slave in the republic.

After Mr. Lundy had concluded, the Rev. Mr. M——m rose, and among other things strongly insinuated that it was hardly necessary for our citizens to take any proceedings upon Mr. L's proposition, or form any society; that in consequence of the briskness of the slave market in the southern extremities, not only the District of Columbia, but also the states of Maryland and Virginia, had within a few years disposed of a large number of their slaves, and would, ere long unquestionably free themselves in this manner without any adventitious aid; that though there was something revolting to the people of New-England in the idea of trafficking in human flesh, yet upon the whole the practice was not so *very* bad, as it forwarded the work of emancipation quite as fast, perhaps, as could be desirable, &c.&c. If I have mistaken the Rev. Gentleman's meaning, I trust he will make a proper explanation.

Sentiments like these, uttered by a minister of the gospel, you may suppose, Mr. Editor, created a strong effervescence of feeling in the audience, and were received with evident surprise and indignation. I will venture to say; there was not an individual present — man or woman — who did not consider them as unworthy of the occasion.

The gentleman very prudently prevented a reply from any other quarter, by immediately dismissing the assembly. I blame him particularly for this unfair conduct.

Now, throwing aside the paradox, that the slave traffic, as pursued at the south, is desirable under any circumstances, I beg leave to ask the gentleman upon what data he draws his conclusions, that the number of slaves has materially diminished in either of the above named states? upon rumor? upon supposition? They cannot be sustained by the census of 1820; and if a census of the slave population has been taken since that period, I shall be happy if my assertion can thereby be disproved, that no perceptible diminution has since followed south of the Delaware.

I admit that we of the north have no adequate idea of the extent to which this abominable traffic is pursued. The statement of Mr. Lundy, that during one quarter only, the number of slaves registered at the Custom House for transportation from the port of Baltimore to New Orleans, was 199, will throw some light upon the subject. In many counties in Maryland and Virginia, slave labor is not eminently productive; and hence the readiness which is manifested by owners of slaves to speculate upon the flesh and sinews of these miserable beings. But it is erroneous to conclude from this fact, that these states are approximating to a speedy emancipation. While the southern market holds out inducements for the slaveholder to sell, it also urges him to kidnap, smuggle, and purchase again, to meet the demand; and thus a perpetual barter is going on, without the hope or intention of obtaining relief. Indeed, there is a studied policy in all this profligate and inhuman traffic. The Virginian is as careful to have the prolification of his female slaves unobstructed, as he is anxious to improve the condition of his horses for the next race, or his cocks for the next fight. He places his negroes upon the same footing with his cattle, pigs and poultry, and the propagation of each is encouraged in proportion to the value of their productions.

Notwithstanding the rapid diminution of slaves in the District of Columbia — so rapid that it needs no impetus, according to the logic of the Rev. Gentleman — the inhabitants of that district, it seems, are not sanguine of a speedy abolition. As I stated yesterday, they have petitioned Congress, to the number of one thousand and upwards, (among whom, I believe, are all the Judges of the District Court,) to lend a helping hand. It is probable they understand their wants and condition better than any of us — better than Mr. M——m himself. They doubt the morality and justice of freeing themselves at the price of the bodies and souls of the oppressed; and have not complacency enough to apologize for a bad practice merely because it grants a momentary relief. They depend more upon the magnanimity of Congress, and the voice of a contrite people, *than upon the ability of purchasers of slaves.* They are right — and the verdict of every state in the Union will sustain the declaration.

The removal of slaves moreover, from one state to another, does not relieve the country of its Atlantean burden. It only consolidates oppression, and renders the liability of insurrections still more formidable.

Whatever was the intention of the gentleman whose remarks I have so freely canvassed, (and far be it from me to doubt the fervor of his philanthropy or the goodness of his heart,) it is certain that he has been instrumental in rousing the friends of universal emancipation in this city to active exertion, by the apparent perverseness of his argument. The formation of an anti-slavery society is in agitation among some of our citizens, and will be organized shortly.

A. O. B.

Printed: Boston *Courier*, August 12, 1828.

1. Howard Malcom (1799–1879), pastor of the Federal Street Baptist Church.

---

2 5

TO THE EDITOR OF THE *YANKEE* AND BOSTON *LITERARY GAZETTE*

[August 15, 1828.]

You "never read the Philanthropist." Why? Because the Philanthropist never exchanged with the Yankee? Come, sir, be candid, acknowledge that you have perused with considerable interest and promptitude, the few numbers which were forwarded, containing strictures upon you[r] writings and character. You could not so often have quoted my words, if these had been entirely overlooked.

God forbid that I should war with your independence, or despise your influence, or discourage every good and honest purpose of your heart. You have a spirit, which, when governed by wisdom and moderation, is worthy of all imitation; and talents, when not perverted, that deserve the warmest panegyric.

Finally. You declare that you never heard of my name before — that we are entire strangers to each other. But you knew, it appears, my age and origin long ago. (Vide the Yankee of Feb. 27, and March 12.) [1] I have only to repeat, without vanity, what I declared publicly to another opponent [2] — a political one — (and I think he will never forget me,) that, if my life be spared, my name shall one day be known so extensively as to render private enquiry unnecessary; and known, too, in a praiseworthy manner. I speak in the spirit of prophecy, not of vainglory, — with a strong pulse, a flashing eye, and a glow of the heart.

The task may be yours to write my biography.

WM. LLOYD GARRISON.

N.B. I cheerfully apologise for my inadvertence in neglecting to seal my former letter.

Boston, August 15, 1828.

Printed extract: *Yankee* and *Boston Literary Gazette*, August 20, 1828.

1. Garrison's allegation is accurate.
2. The anonymous "S" who had attacked Garrison in the *Courier* following the Federalist caucus in Boston in July 1827.

---

2 6

TO THE EDITOR OF THE BOSTON *COURIER*

[December 13, 1828.]

"And at the town there is a fair kept called Vanity Fair — it beareth the name of vanity fair — because the town where it is kept is lighter than vanity — and also because all that is there sold, or cometh thither, is vanity."

[Pilgrim's Progress.] [1]

MR. EDITOR, —

Some time since I had the misfortune to dream that the trustees of the Athenæum [2] had opened a reading room (being what was then called the conversation room) for the use of the ladies. Thank Heaven, this was *but* a dream. Now, however a greater misfortune threatens me, and into your sympathetic heart I must be allowed to pour out my complaints. Like Lord Byron, I have now "had a dream, which was not all a dream." [3] I thought I was walking in Pearl-street one dark and misty morning, and trying to console myself under the feelings which are apt at times to overcome us during such weather, by looking forward to the beauties of the coming spring and to the picture gallery — and its glories of painting and of company. Each of them, by the way, "works of art." Suddenly a good or evil genius, I do not exactly know which, whispered to me, that I need not wait until the spring for an exhibition: that the trustees had lately granted the gallery to the ladies for the use of some exhibition connected with infant schools. "Ah," said I, in the impatience of my joy, "are we to have a school exhibition of infants, 'mewling and pewking in their nurses arms'?[4] How delighted I shall be. Charming infants — thrice charming nurses." "No," said the genius, "my friend, you quite mistake the matter, as indeed old bachelors are apt to do, when any thing is said about children. This exhibition is to be one of lace, embroidery, needle-work, watch-guards, thread-cases, needle-cases, card-cases, pin-cases, and several other cases not reported in the books, sad cases, some of them I dare say. In addition to this, the ladies themselves are to exhibit — themselves, for a quarter of a dollar, that being the usual price of all exhibitions to any body who can muster the money. After paying for admission, you may look at the wares and buy them, if you see fit." "But, what" said I "has all this to do with infants?" "Much," said the genius, "much. There are infant schools, very good things in their way, to be supported by the proceeds of this exhibition. The ladies to be sure might send their money to the school without letting their left hands know what their right hands were doing,[5] and the Being who sees in secret might reward them openly. But this would not do. In the first place, it would not make fuss enough, and in the next, it would not serve as a pretence for collecting the gentlemen around them as the present plan may, and thus rejoicing their own spirits both by the warmth of their charity, and the approbation of the gentlemen, to gain which a little trouble never comes amiss to them. Besides this, the married ones will be admired — and perhaps the single ones married by it." "Nonsense," said I, "after all it is but a second edition of John Bunyan's VANITY FAIR."

This is my dream, whether I shall ever awake from it, is more than I can say.

Yours,

AN OLD BACHELOR.

Pearl-street.[6]

Printed: Boston *Courier*, December 13, 1828. This letter also appeared in the Newburyport *Herald*, December 16, 1828. Since the texts of the two letters are identical, except for a few typographical errors in the *Herald*, the editor follows the one printed earlier.

1. The brackets appear in the *Courier* but not in the *Herald*. Garrison's quotation of Bunyan's famous passage (see James B. Wharey, ed., Oxford, 1960, p. 88) is accurate except for some variations in punctuation and the omission of the clause "It is kept all the year long" following "called Vanity Fair."
2. The Boston Athenaeum.
3. "Darkness," line 1.
4. Shakespeare, *As You Like It*, II, vii, 144.
5. Garrison alludes to Matthew 6:3.
6. Although this letter is written as if from Pearl Street in Boston, in fact Garrison was at the time in Bennington, Vermont, editing the *Journal of the Times*.

2 7

TO THE EDITOR OF THE BOSTON *COURIER*

[December 16, 1828.]

Mr. Editor, —

The communication which appeared in your paper of Saturday under the title of "Vanity Fair" has been somewhat misunderstood.[1] You will therefore allow me, if you please, a few words of serious explanation. No one has more respect than myself for the character of woman, when she is employed in exerting her proper influence and doing her proper duty. In early life, she is to be the peculiar solace of her parents. She is in truth to pass her *whole* life in softening the character, exciting the affections, and rewarding with a love beyond all price the toils of man. She is to educate her children. She is to develop those powers which as she has taught them to reach forward to good or bad objects, will be a curse or a blessing to the world. Above all, on the mother it depends (as far indeed as such a thing can depend on earthly power) whether her children shall be happy or miserable forever. This is her appropriate sphere of duty, but beside this, she is to be the hand-maiden of charity and of religion. Do I not then think highly enough of woman? I approve too from my heart of infant schools. It remains only to be considered, whether the Fair of the coming week, is the best way of assisting the charity in favor of which it is proposed, and I think it is *not*. The charity of Bostonians has been, and can again be excited without recourse to any such quackery, as I must be allowed to call it. The Boston Female Asylum,[2] is one proof of this. Let the patrons of the infant schools begin and go on as the managers of that excellent charity have, and I will answer for their success. Let them first contribute of their own means, and their fathers, brothers and lovers will assist them. Let them annually enter our churches, and with a matron's affection and a sister's interest bring before the orphan's father and the widow's God, the claims of these children. Our most solemn litanies "for sick persons and young children, for *all* who are desolate and oppressed," [3] shall be said. Our holiest hymns shall be sung for them. The gushing tones of our sweetest singers shall be heard in their behalf. The eloquence of our finest preachers shall derive a new warmth from being employed in such an object. Yes, we will plead together; and if any thing more were wanting to excite the feelings of man or secure the blessing of Heaven, the mute eloquence of these children's smiles might rise and be accepted by Him, who, when on earth suffered little children to come to him, and would not have them forbidden, and who once declared that their guardian angels *always* beheld the face of his Father in Heaven.[4]

AN OLD BACHELOR.

Printed: Boston *Courier,* December 16, 1828.

1. Garrison refers to his own letter, like the current one signed "An Old Bachelor," which appeared December 13 (letter 26).

2. A charitable institution founded in Boston in 1811.

3. Garrison telescopes some lines from a familiar litany in the Book of Common Prayer of the Church of England.

4. Garrison adapts Luke 18:16 and Matthew 18:10.

II *GENIUS AND LIBERATOR*: 1829–1832

II GENIUS AND LIBERATOR: 1829–1832

ARLY IN 1829 Benjamin Lundy, peripatetic editor of the antislavery *Genius of Universal Emancipation*, walked all the way from Baltimore to Bennington, Vermont, hoping to persuade Garrison to become co-editor of his paper. It was a flattering gesture and an attractive offer; Garrison pondered its acceptance. In the spring he moved to Boston, his future still uncertain. But he seemed to have committed himself irrevocably to abolitionism when, on the invitation of the Congregational societies of Boston, he spoke on the Fourth of July at the Park Street Church. A month later he joined Lundy in Baltimore. In the first issue of the new *Genius* (September 2, 1829), Lundy and Garrison explained their editorial arrangement and distinguished between their abolitionist views: Garrison advocated immediate and Lundy gradual emancipation, the plan being that each would sign his own editorials.

For two and a half months as co-editor Garrison was happy, optimistic, good-natured. Then came the most dramatic crisis of his twenty-four years. In several flamboyant editorials he accused a Newburyport merchant of having transported slaves from Baltimore to New Orleans. There followed a civil and then a criminal suit for libel. The paper ceased publication, Garrison was found guilty and, owing to his inability to pay the fine, confined to jail. But his seven weeks of confinement provided the perfect resolution of his crisis, for he had time to think and write and gather support. He had time to develop the kind of strength needed to establish a paper that would endure not for six months but for thirty-five years.

Garrison was released from jail June 5 — thanks to the liberality of New York City philanthropist Arthur Tappan. He first considered publishing a new antislavery paper in Washington, but soon decided on Boston instead. There he sought the support necessary to launch *The Liberator*. Lecturing to large crowds seemed an appropriate initial step. After encountering many difficulties he was finally permitted in October to give a series of three lectures at Julien Hall. Besides reiterating many of the ideas already expressed in the *Genius*, he launched his attack on the American Colonization Society, which he was convinced had failed to solve the problems associated with slavery. Garrison's speeches converted to the cause two who were to be his unwavering supporters during the years ahead, Samuel J. May and his cousin Samuel E. Sewall. Soon Ellis Gray Loring had also joined the Garrisonians. The last weeks of the year Garrison concentrated on organizing associates and friends to build a subscription list. But the list was still painfully small when the first issue of *The Liberator* appeared on January 1, 1831. Although it looked like a mild and colorless sheet compared to the *Genius*, it contained Garrison's manifesto — certainly the most famous and one of the most eloquent passages he was to write: "I *will be* as harsh as truth, and as uncompromising as justice. On this subject I do not wish to think, or speak, or write, with moderation. . . . I am in earnest — I will not equivocate — I will not excuse — I will not retreat a single inch — AND I WILL BE HEARD."

During the first year of *The Liberator* Garrison spoke out on many issues related to slavery and the need for abolition — on boycott of slave-produced goods, on intermarriage, on insurrection. And his language *was* harsh and uncompromising. For he was determined to be heard by five groups: the religious, the philanthropic, the patriotic, the tyrannical, and the free colored. All but the last two groups disappointed him. The ignorant and the tyrannical heard every word he said and reacted violently; the Negroes heard, too, and loved him and subscribed to *The Liberator*. One event in 1831 developed into an incendiary topic — the insurrection of Nat Turner. Although Garrison had had no contact with Turner and was in principle a nonresistant, Southerners considered him and his paper responsible for the uprising. Vigilance associations in Southern states offered rewards for the apprehension of anyone found circulating *The Liberator*. But without such widespread hostility *The Liberator* might not have survived; like Garrison himself it seemed to thrive on opposition — the more violent the better.

Now that *The Liberator* was successfully launched, Garrison concluded that something more than a newspaper was needed for the job at hand. Ever since November 1831 he had been trying to organize the abolitionists in his area to agitate more effectively. Several prior meetings had failed to achieve sufficient agreement, but on January 6 the New England Anti-Slavery Society was officially founded with Garrison in the dominant position of secretary. The goals of the society, as published in *The Liberator* February 18, were opposition to colonization, the improvement of the lot of the free colored, and immediate emancipation.

In the name of the society Garrison spent much of his time during the first six months of 1832 accumulating facts and writing a brief against colonization. On June 2 he published a 238-page pamphlet, *Thoughts on African Colonization*, which was arranged in two sections. The first argued against the Colonization Society, documenting the argument with innumerable passages quoted, although sometimes misrepresenting the meaning of the context, from the society's official publications and from statements of distinguished colonizationists. The second part consisted of testimony about colonization from various Negro organizations. That *Thoughts on African Colonization* was effective and convincing was indicated by the number of readers, like J. Miller McKim, who were converted to abolition, or, like Theodore D. Weld, Nathaniel P. Rogers, and Amos A. Phelps, who forswore the American Colonization Society.

2 8

TO STEPHEN FOSTER

Bennington, March 30, 1829.

My dear Foster:

Although expecting to be in Boston on Saturday evening, I am determined to punish your pocket with a tax of 12½ cents [1] before I leave, not only because you were promised "a *long* letter," but because you have been so urgent with your "write! write!" You must understand, however, that I am mightily pleased with your relentless pertinacity; for it is a perpetual assurance that you value my correspondence. Friend Isaac,[2] it seems, thinks little of my epistles, or he would have answered my last — wherein I told him that the promptness of his reply would evidence his appreciation of my scribblings. To be sure, in this particular he shows decidedly a better taste than yours; but then, yours is the stronger friendship. Of course, I mean now to be very severe upon his neglect — and upon my own; for, shame to tell! I have slighted almost every one of my acquaintance, and have not yet written a line to Newburyport. Well — my apology is, the arduousness of my late labors; and Isaac's will probably be the same.

Ere this arrive, you will have seen my resignation as editor.[3] I am now a gentleman at large, of *very small* fortune, with pockets to let at almost any price. I have been debating how to address you — whether in a strain of affected gaiety, or of real, positive, serious melancholy — whether in a sentimental, semi-jocose, or desponding style. As I feel just in the mood for barking and scratching, methinks I will be both *dog*matical and *categ*orical.[4] Bow-wow-wow-wow! There — that is concise and emphatic. I don't know how to scratch upon paper, except with my pen — as above. Nathless I'll try: [5] — Pshaw, what claws! You can easily suppose a face at either end of them — but neither yours nor mine.

Just twig my friend Knapp's ears, and whisper most dolefully, "This life's a dream." Tell him I have got a barrel of tears bottled off, very salt and brackish.

So! — Mary Cunningham *"paints"* — does she? Never mind, my dear fellow, it shall be at her own expense.[6] I'll make that a *sine qua non* in our articles of marriage. She shall buy her own brushes, *with her own money*; but, if she insist upon it, I'll be the painter — and a rare one I should make! Something, perhaps, after this sort: Hold your head steadily, dearest — so — very still — you shall look in the glass presently — a little more vermilion, a denser flame of health on this cheek — I like to see the *blood*, Mary, mounting up to the very temples, commingling with that lily whiteness — your eyebrows are hardly coal black — a little darker, in order to give a deeper brilliance to your starry eyes, or rather to their light — shut your mouth, and draw back that little saucy tongue, you pretty witch, for I'm going to put a ruby blush upon your twin (not thin) lips, *after I've kissed them* — there — softly — softly — smack goes the brush * * * * *Cetera desunt.*

But a truce to playfulness. A word about Varmaount. I came to this state, you know, with extreme reluctance — against my wishes and expectations: I leave it with *precipitate* delight, caring not whether I again see an inch of its territory, and, I had almost said, any of its inhabitants. You shall have a fine dish of scandal served up when I get home — a queer description of Green Mountain bipeds and quadrupeds. If I can run down one of our gigantic boors, you and the good city of B. shall have the pleasure of seeing the "delicate monster" for nothing — he shall be stuck in one corner of the Atheneum Gallery to draw company.

And speaking of the Gallery, I am reminded that another splendid exhibition will [be] made in May. You and I will be there to inspect the paintings. A fig, however, for canvass faces: there will be fresher, and merrier, and prettier ones, all glowing with life, having most dangerous eyes and bewitching forms, and everything to constitute them angels but the wings. — Oh, the thought is most exhilarating, to one who has been encompassed by ugly mountains for about seven months, and hardly seen a human being, or a *bearable* phiz, all that time — verily, it makes an unnatural disturbance about the heart — it overthrows all my philosophy.

With whom do you think I shook hands on Wednesday last? With none other than our friend Henry Knapp, who was wending his way to Danville in this State.[7] He was in a great hurry, and I had not time to make any inquiries about the Literary Emporium.[8] I parted from him with less regret on knowing that we should shortly see each other in Boston.

My dear F., though I have trifled much on the preceding pages, yet I am truly miserable. I am half resolved never to write an editorial article — never to make another effort to gain either money or applause. My embarrassments are very great. Seven months ago I came to Bennington, poorl[y c]lad, and exceedingly impoverished. Before leaving Boston, Hull loaned me $100.[9] The greater portion of this sum was expended in getting here, and *in purchasing articles for the office.* I have toiled incessantly, night and day — scarcely been absent one hour in the day from labor — and have worked much at the press and case. My wardrobe has not been renewed, neither have I laid out a farthing for clothing. And yet I shall leave this place without any remuneration for my services or sacrifices — $100 in debt — with loss of all my time — and, from present appearances, *in addition to all this*, I shall have to pay my own board here, (70 dollars) with my *subsequent* earnings in Boston!! Indeed I have been treated shamefully. Language is un[ab]le to express the sufferings which I have endured from Hull's abusiveness, meanness, misrepres[en]tations, &c. &c. &c. I would *not* stay with him six months longer for the wealth of the State. I could fellowship the meanest reptile that crawls better than this contemptible puppy. [☞ Let no individual see this till I come — I have a great deal more to say on this head.]

Two or three weeks since, I received an excellent letter from my friend William R. Collier, but was not able to answer it.[10] He dissuaded me from the idea of going to Washington with Lundy, and offered his services to get me employment. I was deeply affected with his generosity. I have but one boon to ask; and that is a journeyman's birth in the office of t[he] Am. Manufacturer. If [he] can grant this, I will be thankful with many tears.

I do not, however, relinquish the hope of ultimately joining Lundy in his great, and glorious, and humane enterprise; but whether I go or stay, the subject of slavery will occupy a great deal of my attention.

My dear Whittier will think me a hollow hypocrite.[11] I will get down on my knees if I cannot otherwise obtain his forgiveness for my shameful neglect. My admiration of his talents and excellent traits of character is unbounded. He should receive a letter now, had I not promised to help Hull get out his next paper. — By the way, Green, the Ed. of the Berkshire American, will probably take my place in the course of a few weeks.[12] (This privately.)

It would please me very much to be kindly noticed in the next Manufacturer.[13] Hull will probably abuse, rather than praise me in Friday's Journal.[14] God forgive him if he do. I have done my duty. I am proud of the paper — it has acquired a quick reputation — its moral character has been pure, its philanthropy active, its principles independent.

Give my love to all Mr. Collier's family, and to all my friends. Possibly, I may be in Boston on Thursday evening — possibly not till next week.

I am deeply indebted to you for all your kindness. May I be able to repay you! I love you with brotherly affection.

In great grief I remain, yours,

Wm. L. Garrison.

☞ You may be surprised to see the following, after reading what I have written about Hull; but Mrs. H. saw only the two first pages.[15] She is a fine girl — too good to be yoked with such a fellow as her husband. She will go to B. when I do.

☞ You may let Whittier, Knapp and Collier read this letter, if they wish — but they must be *mute.* 🖎

ALS: Maine Historical Society. Since the manuscript is stained and slightly torn, it is occasionally difficult to decipher. We are indebted to Dr. Thomas D. S. Bassett of the Department of History of the University of Vermont for help in editing this letter, the text of which is to form part of an article he is writing for *Vermont History.*

Stephen Foster (c. 1807–1831), a printer on the *Massachusetts Journal* in Boston, was at this time one of Garrison's best friends. Two years later, as foreman of the *Christian Examiner,* he was to allow Garrison the use of his type to print the first three issues of *The Liberator.* Stephen Foster should not be confused with Stephen S. Foster, husband of Abby Kelley and Garrison's associate in later years.

1. The postage fee to be paid by the recipient.
2. Isaac Knapp (1804–1843), Garrison's boyhood friend and one of his earliest collaborators, was a printer by trade. When *The Liberator* was first issued in January 1831, he and Garrison were partners in its publication. He also helped found the New England Anti-Slavery Society in 1832.
3. Garrison had resigned after six months as editor of the *Journal of the Times,* a paper dedicated unsuccessfully to the reelection of John Quincy Adams.
4. All his life Garrison was an inveterate punster; these particular puns he developed further in subsequent letters.
5. At this point in the manuscript Garrison drew a crude sketch of a pair of paws with claws extended. Beside them, Mrs. Hull (the former Mary Princeton Browne) inserted an asterisk and, in the margin, commented on his crude draftmanship.
6. Garrison referred to his beloved in the first issue of the *Journal of the Times* under his editorship (October 3, 1828). In that issue he printed one of his own poems, which concluded as follows:

"My bach'lorship I throw aside —
　My haughtiness — my lofty bearing —
Sweet MARY! wilt thou be my bride?
　To thee I bow — thy chains I'm wearing."

Although it is probable that Garrison knew Mary Cunningham before coming to Vermont and that she may have been from Massachusetts, she has not been identified.

7. The Henry Knapp to whom Garrison refers has not been positively identified, but he may be the one listed in the Boston directory for 1829 as a grocer. He was apparently not related to Isaac Knapp.
8. As is clear from other contexts (for example, the letter to Helen Garrison of May 6, 1837, in *The Letters of William Lloyd Garrison,* Louis Ruchames, ed., volume II), Garrison refers to Boston as "the Literary Emporium."
9. Henry S. Hull was the proprietor of the *Journal of the Times.*
10. William R. Collier (1771–1843) was a Baptist missionary who had published the *National Philanthropist* between 1826 and 1828 and was currently publishing the *American Manufacturer,* on which Whittier had his first editorial experience. He was also the proprietor in Boston of a boarding house for printers.

11. Garrison, as editor of *The Free Press* in 1826, had been the first to publish poems by John Greenleaf Whittier; see the issues for June 8, 22, 29, July 6, 13, 20, 27, August 3, 10, 17, 24, and September 7, 14. He continued to publish the young poet's works in the *Journal of the Times* in 1828; see the issues for October 24, November 21, December 5, 12.

12. Asa Greene (1789-c. 1837) — name correctly spelled with a final "e" — was a graduate of Williams College with an M.D. from Brown. He was physician, novelist, and editor (first of the *Berkshire American*, then of the *Socialist*, and, beginning April 8, of the *Journal of the Times*).

13. Whittier did praise Garrison in the *American Manufacturer* for April 2, saying that he was relinquishing his editorship of the *Journal of the Times* to "follow in the path of Howard, Wilberforce and Clarkson." Whittier further testified: "As an editor he has acquired a high reputation. His style of writing is bold, abrupt, and original — just what is wanted to give a new tone to the drowsy, monotonous manner in which too many of our newspapers are conducted."

14. Hull did not abuse Garrison. Instead, in the issue for Wednesday, April 1 — publication day having been changed from Friday to Wednesday — he described him as a man of industry, talent, and integrity, and he expressed "ardent desires for his success" in editing an antislavery "periodical in a neighboring state." Moreover, a week later Asa Greene paid Garrison the following tribute: "In taking upon us the editorial charge of this paper, we succeed to a gentleman of uncommon energy and talent, and one who has gained for the paper a high rank among the journals of the day; and we are aware of the comparison that may be drawn to our disadvantage as his immediate successor."

15. By "the following," Garrison refers to a note added to his letter by Mrs. Hull in which she coyly confesses being unable to resist scribbling on the letter, which she says she found on her table while Garrison and her husband were out walking.

29

TO JACOB HORTON

Boston, Saturday, June 27, 1829.

My dear Jacob:

I am very reluctantly obliged to solicit a favor of you, which, if granted, shall be cancelled in a few weeks.

On Wednesday, the clerk of a militia company, (a poor, worthless scamp,) presented a bill of $4, for failure of appearance on May muster, and at the choice of officers. The fact is, I had been in the city but a fortnight, from my Vermont residence, when the notification came; and, as I expected to leave in a very short time, I neglected to get a certificate of my incapacity to train on account of short-sightedness. Moreover, though I have been repeatedly warned since I first came to the city in 1826, yet never, until now, have I been called upon to pay a fine, or to give any reasons for my non-appearance; and I therefore concluded that I should again be let alone.

I told the fellow the circumstances of the case — that I had never trained — that my sight had always excused me — and that, in fine, I should not pay his bill. He wished me a "good morning," and in the course of the day sent a writ by the hands of a constable, charging me to appear at the Police Court on the 4th of July, and shew cause why I refused to pay the fine! Of course, there is no alternative but to "shell out," or to fee a lawyer to get me clear, which would be no saving in expense.[1]

The writ and fine will be $5 or $6. I have not a farthing by me, and I shall need a trifle for the 4th. Can you make it convenient to loan me $8, for two or three weeks? I am pained to make this request, but my present dilemma is unpleasant.

My address, for the Fourth, is almost completed; and, on the whole, I am tolerably well satisfied with the composition.[2] The delivery will occupy me, probably, a little over an hour — too long, to be sure, for the patience of the audience, but not for the subject. I cannot condense it. Its complexion is sombre, and its animadversions severe. I think it will offend some, though not reasonably. The assembly bids fair to be overwhelming. My very knees knock together at the thought of speaking before so large a concourse. What, then, will be my feelings in the pulpit?

The public expectation, I find, is great. I am certain it will be disappointed; but I shall do my best. You shall know the result.

Rev. Mr. Pierpont honored me with a visit a few days since. He is an accomplished man, and his [fr]iendship worth cultivating.[3] He has promised to [write] an original ode for that day; and says he shall take seat in some corner of Park-street Church to hear the address — a thing that he has not done for many years.

I expect to get a journeyman's berth immediately after the 4th; but, if I do not, I shall take the stage for Newburyport, and *dig on* at the case for Mr. Allen. I am somewhat in a hobble, in a pecuniary point of view, and must work like a tiger. My fingers have not lost their nimbleness, and my pride I have sent on a pilgrimage to Mecca.

By answering this on Tuesday, by the driver, you will confer another obligation on

Yours, with much affection,

Wm. Lloyd Garrison.

☞ Direct to me at No. 30, Federal-st. Boston.

ALS: Garrison Papers, Boston Public Library; printed in *Life*, I, 124–126.

Jacob Horton (c. 1797–1876) was the husband of Garrison's old friend Harriet Farnham.

1. Although by the time of Garrison's letter the effectiveness of the militia system was a subject for discussion (see, for instance, William H. Sumner, *An Inquiry into the Importance of the Militia to a Free Commonwealth . . .*, Boston, 1823), in this case Garrison seems plainly to be in the wrong. According to

the provisions of the various militia acts, state legislatures were permitted to excuse certain persons from service in return for payment of an annual fee. Not until a man was over thirty-five, however, was he entirely exempt.

2. Garrison's speech was published in the *National Philanthropist and Investigator,* July 22, 29, 1829.

3. John Pierpont (1785–1866) was a man of great range, for he was a Unitarian minister, a poet, and a universal reformer; he had graduated from Yale College and Harvard Divinity School. In 1819 he had been ordained as the minister of the Hollis Street Church of Boston, and he was a thoughtful and eloquent minister, though one whose dedication to many reforms (most important of which were abolition and temperance) eventually offended his conservative parishioners, who engaged in a seven years' war to remove him. He won the fight but resigned from the church in 1845. Curiously enough, he was the grandfather of John Pierpont Morgan.

---

3 0

TO THE EDITOR OF THE BOSTON *COURIER*

[July 9, 1829.]

Dear Sir, —

I appreciate the laudable anxiety of the editor of the American Traveller, to give his readers a broad and minute view of all the Addresses which were delivered in this city on the 4th instant; but I do not covet his memory.[1] Either his ears or his understanding were sadly in fault, on that day — for he has made strange patchwork of the fabric of every speaker. Let me (through your columns) gently pull the former, while I endeavor to mend the latter.

I acknowledge, sir, that the gentleman has accurately described my appearance. It was certainly "quite youthful" — the fault was Time's, not mine. My suit (singularly strange as it may seem) was "black," and (still more strange) my shirt-collar was made of "linen." But as the public are probably more interested in the performance than in the performer, it is proper that they should correctly understand its sentiments.

My address was an exposition of the *Dangers of the Nation.* It contained no panegyric. It was plain truth told in a plain manner. From my heart I believe, that the moral and political tendency of this nation is downward; and the cause I trace, among other evils, to that torrent of flattery, artfully sweetened and spiced, which is constantly poured out for the thirsty multitude to swallow. It is that thriftless prodigality of praise, that presumptuous defiance of danger, that treacherous assurance of security, that impudent assumption of ignorance, that pompous declamation of vanity, that lying attestation of falsehood, from the lips of our tumid orators, which are poisoning our life-blood.

We are a vain people, and our love of praise is inordinate. We imagine, and are annually taught to believe, that the republic is immortal; that its flight, like a strong angel's, has been perpetually upward, till it has soared above the impurities of earth, and beyond the farthest star; and, having attained perfection, is forever out of the reach of circumstance and change. An earthquake may rock all Europe, and ingulf empires at a stroke; but it cannot raise an inch of republican territory, nor disturb the composure of a platter on our shelves. The ocean may gather up its forces for a second deluge, and overtop the tallest mountains; but our ark will float securely when the world is drowned.

The editor of the Traveller says, that I accused the people of substituting "profligate persons in office, for men conscientiously religious." These were my words:

"It is an alarming fact, so great is the profligate sensibility of our land, that a religious profession is *the meanest recommendation of a candidate for office*; and still more alarming that humble petitions for *relief*, although emanating from almost every religious sect, are able to conjure up the most horrible spectres and injurious apprehensions. I am not, my friends, advocating a union of Church and State, — that bugbear, which threatens to turn the nation into an insane hospital. But I wish to see men stand up in the dignity of the creatures of God. I wish them to read, compare and judge for themselves, as accountable beings. I wish to see a full ballot-box of unbought, intelligent votes, on every, the most trivial election. *I wish a good moral character to be an indispensable qualification in the selection of candidates for office*, from a Town Clerk to a President of the United States. I wish the "voice of the people" to mean something more than the echo of an evening caucus or a petty committee. The republic does not bear a charmed life: our prescriptions, administered through the medium of the ballot-box, — the mouth of the political body, — may kill or cure, according to the nature of the disease, and our wisdom in applying the remedy."

The editor says, that the burden of my discourse "was in relation to the colonization of the blacks." It is a mistake. My "four positions" contained not a word about colonization.[2]

The editor puts the following ungracious epithet into my mouth: "I *detest* that piety," &c. I give you what I *did* say:

"I suspect the *reality*, and deny the productiveness of that piety, which confines its operations to a particular spot, — if that spot be less than the whole earth, — nor scoops out, in every direction, new channels for the waters of life. Christian charity, while it "begins at home," goes abroad in search of misery. It is as copious as the sun in heaven. It does not, like the Nile, make an occasional inundation, and then withdraw; but it perpetually overflows, and fertilizes every barren spot. It is restricted only by the exact number of God's suffering creatures."

I am made to say, by the editor, without any qualification, that "I could not stand up in a foreign court, and acknowledge myself an American citizen." The following is my entire paragraph:

"Every Fourth of July, our Declaration of Independence is produced, with a sublime indignation, to set forth the tyranny of the mother country, and to challenge the admiration of the world. But what a pitiful detail of grievances does this document present, in comparison with the wrongs which our slaves endure! In the one case, it is hardly the plucking of a hair from the head; in the other, it is the crushing of a live body on the wheel; in this, the vulture, preying upon the quivering entrails — in that, the dove, pecking with angry imbecility at the hand; the stings of the wasp contrasted with the tortures of the inquisition. Before God I must say, that such a glaring contradiction, as exists between our creed and practice, the annals of five thousand years cannot parallel. In view of it, I am ashamed of my country. I am sick of our unmeaning declamations in praise of liberty and equality — of our hypocritical cant about the inalienable rights of man. I could not, for my right hand, stand up before a European assembly, and exult that I am an American citizen, and denounce the usurpations of a kingly government as wicked and unjust; or, should I make the attempt, the recollection of my country's barbarity and despotism would blister my lips, and cover my checks with burning blushes of shame." [3]

Yours respectfully,

WM. LLOYD GARRISON.

No. 30, *Federal street — Tuesday noon.*

Printed: Boston *Courier,* July 9, 1829.

1. Willard Badger (born 1785) and his nephew Royal L. Porter (1802–1844) started the *American Traveller* in Boston in 1825, two years after Porter graduated from Williams College.

2. It is true that Garrison had accepted the invitation to speak on behalf of colonization, and he did recommend "establishing auxiliary colonization societies in every State, county and town." But he discussed primarily the evils of slavery and the necessity for its abolition.

3. Collating of the two extant, though not entirely complete, copies of Garrison's speech (*Selections from the Writings and Speeches of William Lloyd Garrison,* Boston, 1852, pp. 44–61, and the more complete version in the *National Philanthropist and Investigator,* July 22, 29, 1829) with the quotations in this letter establishes the validity of Garrison's contention, that the editor of the *American Traveller* misrepresented him.

3 1

TO EPHRAIM W. ALLEN

[January 29, 1830.]

Mr. ALLEN:

I am quite a short, and small sized man — but I do really love (as I believe is customary among us little ones) to be accommodated, and appear at least as large and important as any person. Now my dear sir, thus situated, and with these feelings, how very considerably must my pride be affected in any public meeting, (for instance at a lecture at the Lyceum,) having arrived at rather a late hour, and poorly accommodated at the extremity of the room, to find my view entirely obstructed by the sudden rising up before me, perhaps at the very moment when something of an interesting nature is attracting the attention of the whole audience, an intolerable number of immensely large, high formed, and fully dressed bonnets. How much more simple, and certainly how much more convenient, and better adapted to the convenience of the assembly (and particularly to us short folks) are head-dresses, or any thing rather than such extremely unaccommodating coverings!

Communicate this, and *possibly* the ladies (dear creatures) will be willing to accommodate

AN OLD BACHELOR.[1]

Printed: Newburyport *Herald*, January 29, 1830.

1. This editorial comment followed the letter: "We hope the ladies will accomodate 'An Old Bachelor:' his case seems truly pitiable. Poor fellows, they are going off one by one, and those who remain should have every indulgence shewn them."

3 2

TO THE EDITORS OF THE LIVERPOOL *TIMES*

[February 16, 1830.]

Gentlemen: —

The Old Bachelors of this country are a grossly calumniated class of his Majesty's subjects. Married people of course rail at them, if it were only to justify the choice made by themselves. Young ladies rail at them, because young ladies are apt to think, in consequence of the notions which they imbibe at home, at school, and from the circulating library, that a single man must be a selfish, useless, and miserable creature. Old maids abuse them, because if there were no old bachelors, there would probably be no old maids; and few elderly spinsters have philosophy enough to despise the foolish laugh which every witling raises against "single blessedness." On the whole, therefore, a bachelor has to maintain through life a kind of running fight against the whole feminine gender, and against all those of his own sex, who feel themselves bound in common consistency to trumpet forth the manifold praises of Hymen, and to depreciate the celibacy which they have relinquished.

Gentlemen, I have myself been grievously miscalled on the *single* score of my old bachelorship. 'Useless animal,' 'cumberer of the ground,' 'human vegetable,' and the like, are the epithets with which I have now and then been saluted, and which I have heard applied without reason or remorse to our whole fraternity. I feel indignant at this treatment by a foolish, marrying world; I have put up with it too long; even the temperate and milky blood of an ancient bachelor is heated at last; and I now conjure you, as you value your character for impartiality, to publish a few observations which I have thrown together on behalf of myself and my ill used brethren.

Consider the old bachelor first as a citizen. It is perfectly well known that he pays (with a very good grace) more taxes than the married man, and consequently does more to swell the revenue and uphold the credit of the nation. While those who traduce him are doing their best to increase the public burthens, he is augmenting the public resources. The fulminations of Malthus touch not him.[1] It is no fault of his that every trade and every profession are so scandalously overstocked, — that the elderly merchant is elbowed by a hundred young merchants out of his place in the commercial world; that mechanics swarm to the utter ruin of each other; that we have twice as many divines as pulpits, and that every revolving year sees a constantly increasing tribe of doctors and lawyers turned loose upon the land, to phlebotomize the persons and pockets of their countrymen. But it is contended that the old bachelor is at best a useless creature. Is he so? What says Lord Bacon upon this head? "Certainly the best works and of greatest merit for the public, have proceeded from the unmarried or childless men; which, both in affection and means, have married and endowed the public." [2] — The great pioneers of science, of art, of literature, of civilization, of liberty, have almost all belonged to the slighted race of bachelors. Observe how much more unshackled the bachelor is than the married man for the performance of all public duties. Is the latter asked to serve his country in Parliament? He talks of a duty to "wife & children," which prevents him. — Does the voice of patriotism call him to the field? — "Wife and children" withhold him, and whisper

in his ear all the ingenious reasoning of the magnanimous Falstaff.*
Is he invited to give up any considerable portion of time, or money,
or labor to the public? The same constant excuse of "wife and children"
is ready at hand. But, fair Sir or Madam who twit the unlucky bachelor
with his celibacy, there is yet another serious charge against the married men. By whom, let me ask, do public abuses chiefly live & thrive?
Why is it a task so Herculean to reform any wide-spreading system of
public corruption — for example, to contract within reasonable bounds
the all pervading influence of the crown, to reduce exorbitant salaries,
to dock sinecures, to pare down the poor rates, the Irish Church, &c.
&c. — why, I say, is this so next to impossible, but because the moment
a statesman opens his mouth upon the subject, he is reminded of the
thousands of amiable wives and innocent little ones whose interests are
bound up with all these nuisances? Yes, yes, it is not to the single men,
but to your loving husbands, that such abuses owe their perpetuity.

Gentlemen, I flatter myself, I have already said enough to show
that in his *public* character, at least, the bachelor is quite as useful, and
often a good deal less mischievous than the married man. I beg now to
add a few words as to the characters which they respectively fill in
private society. And here I doubt not that many of your lady readers
are already triumphing in the anticipated defeat of the old bachelor.
And yet, fair ladies, that same Francis Bacon whom I have already
quoted, assures us that "unmarried men are best friends, best masters,
and best servants," thereby giving them a clear superiority over their
married brethren in three of the most important relations of human life.[3]
I would ask, too, are they not for the most part best sons and best
brothers? They have not that "divided duty," which poor Desdemona
speaks of,[4] nor is there any risk that an unreasonable wife will make
them look with coldness on their earliest and kindest friends. In their
bosoms, the filial and fraternal affections (which are probably the
purest known to our nature) undergo no change. With respect to
friendships out of one's own family, those of the bachelor are unrestricted by any domestic jealousies, while the cooling effect which
marriage so often produces is quite proverbial. Foolish people talk of
the selfishness of the old bachelor, and pretend that the married man,
whose thoughts and cares are almost wholly confined to the narrow
circle of his own hearth, is less obnoxious to this charge than he whose
kindly feelings are under so much less restraint, and expand themselves
over a range so much wider.

But then, quoth some tender hearted damsel, an old bachelor must
be such a *miserable* creature. For my own part I thank the lady for
her sympathy, but I assure her that so far as my own experience goes,
it is quite uncalled for. Whether I am fated, like Benedick,[5] to turn

married man at last, is more than I can say; I only hope that if such is my destiny, I may enjoy half the peace, the liberty, and the comfort which I find in celibacy. But, alas! who can insure me the same freedom to read when I please and what I please, — the same peaceful slumbers, unbroken by scolding wife or squalling brat, — the same liberty of meddling in politics and literature, — the same power to ramble over my own and other lands, — the same unquenched right to see my own friends, to spend my own money, and to remain my own master.

Gentlemen, I have laid before you some of the reasons which induce me to think that the state & character of an Old Bachelor are not altogether to be despised. The ladies, no doubt, and the married men will be indignant at my unpalatable truths, — truths to which the consciences of the latter, if they would but speak out, must bear testimony. I dare say that by publishing this letter I shall be bringing a nest of hornets about my own ears and yours. However, I am content to run this risk, and so I hope for the sake of truth, are you. Mine has been purely a defensive battle: I have been anxious to repel the abominable calumnies heaped upon a long-suffering and unoffending class of the King's subjects; and I trust I have proved that a man may without disgrace subscribe himself

AN OLD BACHELOR.

P.S. I utterly protest against all attempts to reply by unmarried men who have been already asked at Church, or by married men of less than twelve months standing. I expressly deny their competency as witnesses upon the subject.

* "Honor pricks me on. Yea, but how if honor prick me off when I come on? how then! Can honor set a leg?" [6] &c. &c.

Printed: Newburyport *Herald*, February 16, 1830.

In this letter, which is addressed to the editors of the Liverpool *Times*, Garrison changes the nationality of his familiar persona, the Old Bachelor, making him English rather than American.

1. Thomas Robert Malthus (1766–1834) was the distinguished English economist whose *Essay on Population* stated the principle that population tends to increase faster than the available supply of food.

2. Francis Bacon, "Of Marriage and Single Life."

3. Garrison quotes from "Of Marriage and Single Life," supplying a conjunction before "best servants."

4. Shakespeare, *Othello*, I, iii, 181.

5. Of Shakespeare's *Much Ado About Nothing*.

6. Shakespeare, *I Henry IV*, V, i, 131–133.

33

TO HARRIET FARNHAM HORTON

Baltimore Jail, May 12, 1830.

My dear Harriet:

I salute you from the walls of my prison! [1] — So weak is poor human nature, that, commonly, the larger the building it occupies, the more it is puffed up with inordinate pride. I assure you, that, notwithstanding the massive dimensions of this superstructure — its imperishable strength, its redundant passages, its multicapsular apartments — I am as meek as any occupant of a ten-foot building in our great Babel; — which frame of mind, my friends must acknowledge, is very commendable. It is true, I am not the owner of this huge pile, nor the grave lord-keeper of it; but then, I pay no rent — am bound to make no repairs — and enjoy the luxury of independence divested of its cares.

Now, don't look amazed because I am in confinement. I have neither broken any man's head nor picked any man's pocket — neither committed highway robbery nor fired any part of the city — nor done anything worthy of bonds or imprisonment. Yet, true it is, I am in prison, as snug as a robin in his cage; but I sing as often, and quite as well, as I did before my wings were clipped. To change the figure: here I strut the lion of the day, and, of course, attract a great number of visitors, as the exhibition is gratuitous — so that, between the labors of my brain, the conversation of my friends, and the ever changing curiosities of this huge menagerie, time flies away astonishingly swift. Indeed, so perfectly agreeable is my confinement, that I have no occasion to call upon my philosophy or patience. Moreover, this is a capital place to sketch the lights and shadows of human nature. Every day, in the gallery of my imagination, I hang up a fresh picture. I shall have a rare collection at the expiration of my visit.

*   *   *   *   *   *

Playfulness aside. The tyranny of the Court has triumphed over every principle of justice, and even over the law — and here I am in limbo. I shall send Jacob a copy of my trial, by which you will perceive the merits of the whole affair. You upbraid me in your letter, for denouncing the conduct of Mr. Todd. Ah! Harriet, that was not written like a mother. As a New-England man and a fellow-townsman, I am ashamed of Todd. How could he freight his noble vessel with the wretched victims of slavery? Is not the horrible traffic offensive to God, and revolting to humanity? — No, no, I shall never regret that I opposed his wicked conduct.

I shall probably be liberated in the course of next week. My health was never better — my spirits are excessively buoyant — and my prospects tolerable.

Of southern habits, southern doctrines, and southern practices, I am heartily sick. The first are loose; the second disorganising; the last oppressive. There is nothing which the curse of slavery has not tainted. It rests on every herb, and every tree, and every field, and on the people, and on the morals. I am yearning to return again to New-England — that paradise of our fallen world! But I do not expect to see you for many months. Perhaps friend Lundy and I shall resume the weekly publication of the Genius by and by.[2]

I deeply sympathize with you in the loss of your dear little boy.[3] How must your heart be lacerated!

I shall write a long letter to Jacob in a few days, when I shall notice your joint letter more particularly. Tell Aunt F. that she is ever in my thoughts.[4] God preserve her health many years! Kiss little H. many times for Uncle Willy.[5] Love to the whole world.

Good bye — I am in a prodigious hurry to send this by a private conveyance.

Adieu.

Wm. Lloyd Garrison.

Typed transcription from Garrison's manuscript letter provided by Miss Fanny Garrison, February 11, 1952. (The typed transcription in the Villard Papers, Harvard College Library, was not used as the source because the punctuation was at variance from Garrison's usual practice.)

We have not included in this edition the abridged version of the letter to Mrs. Horton which Garrison addressed on the same date to the editor of the Boston *Courier*, since it followed the text herein printed almost precisely. When Joseph T. Buckingham, the editor, printed his letter in the *Courier* of May 24, he described Garrison's editorial career, including the spectacular events in Baltimore, and commended him as "a powerful writer" with "high and honorable motives."

1. Garrison was in jail owing to his inability to pay the fine and costs imposed by the court in a criminal suit for libel committed by him as co-editor of *The Genius of Universal Emancipation*. In the issue of that paper published November 13, 1829, Garrison had revealed that a fellow townsman, Francis Todd (1805–1862), a prosperous and hitherto reputable merchant, had recently transported seventy-five slaves from Baltimore to New Orleans. In the issue for the following week, Garrison had provided further details and suggested that people like Todd should be "SENTENCED TO SOLITARY CONFINEMENT FOR LIFE" and should ultimately *"occupy the lowest depths of perdition."* Early in January Todd instituted a civil suit for libel against Garrison and his co-editor, Benjamin Lundy. A few weeks later (the presentment had been filed on the nineteenth of February) the grand jury in Baltimore found that a libel had been published by Garrison in the November 20 issue of *The Genius* against Francis Todd and his captain, Nicholas Brown. The trial began March 1, and after what Garrison considered a brilliant defense by one Charles Mitchell (died 1831), the court pronounced the verdict of guilty. On April 17 the court imposed a fine of $50 and costs (approximately $100 in all), far more than Garrison was

capable of paying. That same day he was imprisoned. The seven weeks of his confinement, however, were not unproductive. He was able to write a number of sonnets, many letters, and an eight-page pamphlet, *A Brief Sketch of the Trial of William Lloyd Garrison, for an Alleged Libel on Francis Todd, of Massachusetts*, which was published that year in Baltimore, and four years later in Boston. It was this pamphlet which ultimately effected Garrison's release from Prison on June 5, for it was read by New York philanthropist Arthur Tappan, who sent him, by way of Benjamin Lundy, a contribution of $100. In the meantime, the civil action instituted by Francis Todd earlier remained pending, Garrison having refused Todd's offer to drop the suit in return for an apology. In July Garrison was still in Baltimore awaiting trial, but when he heard that it would not come to the court before fall, he left town, "absconded," according to the prosecuting attorney. In October Garrison allowed the case to go by default to the plaintiff; and the court assessed $1000 in damages, a sum never to be collected since Garrison remained outside of the court's jurisdiction. The major sources of information regarding Garrison's trials and imprisonment are, in addition to the pamphlet mentioned above and the letters published herein, articles in the monthly issues of *The Genius* between July and December 1830, and editorials and articles in early issues of *The Liberator*, especially those for January 1 and 8.

2. Garrison was not to be involved again with the publication of *The Genius of Universal Emancipation*; his next editorial venture was *The Liberator*.

3. Charles French Horton had died at the age of eight months, August 30, 1829; he was the second son of that name to die. A third to be so named also died, but a fourth (born in 1834) survived.

4. Garrison refers to Martha Farnham, Harriet's mother.

5. "Little H." was Harriet Elizabeth, born June 11, 1825.

34

TO FRANCIS TODD

[*May* 13, 1830.]

Sir, —

As a New-England man, and a fellow-townsman, I am ashamed of your conduct. How could you suffer your noble ship to be freighted with the wretched victims of slavery? Is not this horrible traffic offensive to God, and revolting to humanity? You have a wife — Do you love her? You have children — if one merchant should kidnap, another sell, and a third transport them to a foreign market, how would you bear this bereavement? What language would be strong enough to denounce the abettor? You would rend the heavens with your lamentations! There is no sacrifice so painful to parents as the loss of their offspring. So cries the voice of nature!

Take another case. Suppose you and your family were seized on execution, and sold at public auction: a New-Orleans planter buys your children — a Georgian, your wife — a South Carolinian, yourself: would one of your townsmen (believing the job to be a profitable one) be blameless for transporting you all thither, though familiar with all these afflicting circumstances?

Sir, I owe you no ill-will. My soul weeps over your error. I denounced your conduct in strong language — but did you not deserve it? Consult your bible and your heart. I am in prison for denouncing slavery in a free country! You, who have assisted in oppressing your fellow-creatures, are permitted to go at large, and to enjoy the fruits of your crime! — *Cui prodest scelus, is fecit.*

You shall hear from me again. In the mean time, with mingled emotions, &c. &c.

WM. LLOYD GARRISON.

Baltimore Jail, May 13, 1830.

Printed: Boston *Courier*, May 24, 1830; printed in *Life*, I, 180–181.

35

TO NICHOLAS BRICE

[*May* 13, 1830.]

YOUR HONOR:

You are a very considerable man. Spare those crimson blushes: it is the office of Judge that raises you to the dignity of my notice, and not your peculiar merit.

At a leisure hour, I propose to dedicate a series of numbers to your Honor, wherein I shall review your conduct as exhibited at my late trial, in a manner that shall secure to you a deathless notoriety.

Even here, barren as is the place, I daily discover new beauties springing up in your official character, which shall certainly embellish my essays. Nay, I will erect your statue even in your lifetime.

Your Honor will not construe my magnanimity into a contempt of Court. I assure you, that I entertain an extraordinary opinion of the merits of the Court! If, however, another action be brought against me, I offer you, gratuitously, this seasonable advice: *Let the indictment embrace that part which is actionable.*

With undying remembrance, I remain, &c. &c.

WM. LLOYD GARRISON.

Baltimore Jail, May 13, 1830.

Printed: *The Genius of Universal Emancipation,* July 1830. This and the two following letters, all dated May 13, are here printed in the order in which they were originally published in the *Genius.*

Nicholas Brice (c. 1770–1851) was chief justice of the Baltimore City Court.

3 6

TO RICHARD W. GILL

[*May* 13, 1830.]

SIR:

I communicated to you, in a note a few days since, the fact that I was preparing a brief sketch of my trial, for the astonishment of all good men, the instruction of the bar, and the consideration of an intelligent public. It is difficult to remember minute objects; but if I do not forget you, perhaps I may generously make you as tall as an ordinary man, with the aid of a block. An elevation or abasement of twenty feet would destroy your visibility.

Your presumptuous, feeble, ridiculous remarks upon the subject of slavery, and the rights of slaveholders, exhausted my patience. A buzzing fly may disturb the equanimity of a sage; but if a pin be stuck through its wings, the insect, Sir, is harmless. Beware of my pen!

WM. LLOYD GARRISON.

Baltimore Jail, May 13, 1830.

Printed: *The Genius of Universal Emancipation,* July 1830.
Richard W. Gill (1793–1852), an Englishman by birth, who had distinguished himself as a lawyer and as a reporter of the Maryland Court of Appeals, was the deputy attorney who prosecuted Garrison.

3 7

TO HENRY THOMPSON

[*May* 13, 1830.]

SIR:

If the severe, pointed, thundering rebuke from my Counsel, before a listening Court, failed to make any impression upon your ample countenance, what condemnation of mine can make it yield? Yet I do not wholly despair. Even bronze is susceptible of change.

The pleasure you derive from my incarceration, I do not grudge. It is a small reward for your disinterested and unremitted exertions in behalf of your employer.[1] I shall charitably give a donation. Be patient. Every day adds compound interest to the principal. Let this evidence that I am, &c. &c.

WM. LLOYD GARRISON.

Baltimore Jail, May 13, 1830.

Printed: *The Genius of Universal Emancipation,* July 1830. Although the identification is not certain, Henry Thompson (1774–1837), the prominent Baltimore merchant, is probably the person Garrison addressed.

1. Thompson acted as the Baltimore agent of Francis Todd.

---

3 8

TO THE EDITOR OF THE BOSTON *COURIER*

[May 13, 1830.]

Mr. Editor, —

At the request of the State of Maryland, (through the medium of Judge Nicholas Brice,) I have removed from my residence in Baltimore-street, to a less central but more imposing tenement. My windows are grated — probably to exclude nocturnal visitants, and to show the singular estimation in which my person is held. The cause of this preferment arises from my opposition to slavery.

I send you a Sonnet which I pencilled upon the wall of my room, the morning after my incarceration. It is a little bulletin showing in what manner I rested during the preceding night.

SONNET TO SLEEP.

Thou art no fawning sycophant, sweet Sleep!
    That turn' st away when fortune 'gins to frown,
Leaving the stricken wretch alone to weep,
    And curse his former opulent renown:
O no! but here — even to this desolate place —
    Thou com'st, as 'twere a palace trimm'd with gold,
Its architecture of Corinthian grace,
    Its gorgeous pageants dazzling to behold: —
No prison walls nor bolts can thee affright —
    Where dwelleth innocence, there thou are found!
How pleasant, how sincere was thou last night!
    What blissful dreams my morning slumber crowned!
Health-giving Sleep! than mine a nobler verse
Must to the world thy matchless worth rehearse.

W.L.G.

Baltimore Jail, May 13, 1830.

Printed: Boston *Courier*, May 24, 1830; printed in *Life*, I, 181. There is also a written copy of this letter in the Garrison Papers of the Boston Public Library.

3 9

TO THE EDITOR OF THE NEWBURYPORT *HERALD*

[June 1, 1830.]

DEAR SIR: —

I thank you for a copy of the Herald, containing a notice of my late trial for an alleged libel on Mr. Francis Todd.[1] Your encomiums I receive with pleasure and humility. The esteem of a good man is always worth possessing; but to him who stands comparatively alone in the world — fatherless, motherless — without wealth, and unassisted by the influence of relatives — and who has just passed the vestibule of manhood, it is invaluable. I have received too many kindnesses at your hands to doubt your friendship; and too many ever to forget the obligations under which I labor.

Yet there are some passages in your review, which seem to require a brief interrogation. You say:

"When carried on by system, for purposes of traffic, the domestic slave trade deserves the reprobation of every man who dares call himself free, or just, or humane."

Surely, sir, you do not mean to justify or palliate the *occasional* transportation of slaves? If the whole system be abhorrent to humanity, can any part of it be venial? If Austin Woolfolk (a slave-exporter of devilish notoriety in Maryland) deserves the withering indignation of a virtuous community, for carrying on the trade *regularly*, does not Francis Todd (or any other merchant) merit reprobation — in a less degree, certainly — for dipping into it *irregularly*?[2] In a case of theft, is it not an orthodox maxim, that "the receiver (i.e. he who knows that the goods are stolen) is as bad as the thief?" Even if a man connives at crime, though he is not the immediate perpetrator thereof, the law does not hold him guiltless; and common sense tells us that it should not.

The above quotation carries a pernicious inference — contrary, I am sure, to your intention. But why not have explicitly declared, that no device should protect the man from public indignation, who assists in any way, or however rarely, in extending and perpetuating the horrible traffic? For myself, neither the terrors of the law, nor the fires of martyrdom,* shall deter me from invoking confiscation and imprisonment upon every such abettor. Pope illustrates the distinction with admirable conciseness:

> "Friend, spare the person, and expose the vice."
> "How! not condemn the *sharper,* but the *dice!*"[3]

Moreover, you remark:

"If, in assailing the traffic, Mr. Garrison steps aside to wound those, *who are not, and would never be, guilty of joining in it,* he is neither to be justified nor commended," — &c. &c. [Certainly not.] "And he who is made the object of the odious charge, if innocent, is not be be browbeaten for taking lawful steps to vindicate his character." [Ditto.] [4]

There is a gratuitous insinuation in these truisms, which is calculated to injure my character with those who are ignorant of the merits of the present case. Have I gone out of my way to attack an *innocent* man? If not, where is the pertinency of your remarks? Now, I substantially proved the truth of my allegations, at my trial — namely, that the Francis carried slaves to New Orleans, and that she was owned by Mr. Todd: nay, that thirteen more were taken than I had represented. Yet you do not apprise your readers of these facts, but leave them to infer that I have slandered the character of this gentleman in the most wilful and unpardonable manner!! Is this suppression commendable? It is true, I did not prove (for I had no time to obtain evidence, as the ship sailed from New-Orleans for Europe) that the slaves were put in close confinement on the voyage. The pilot of the Francis stated, that they were at liberty while he was on board; but it is highly probable, that, after the vessel got out to sea, they were restricted and bound. For if otherwise, I entertain a very poor opinion of Capt. Brown's prudence. But it is incredible that *eighty-eight* negroes, in their degraded condition, were permitted to ramble at pleasure about the ship. Every body (who is familiar with the traffic) knows that chains are inseperable from transportation. Nor, in the eye of the law, is the confinement of slaves a grievance, but a preservative right, indispensable to the safety of the officers, crew and cargo. I have no reason to suppose, that Capt. Brown was excessively rigorous; but I do not believe that his discretion was lost in his humanity.[5]

With regard to my allusion to Mr. Todd's inexplicable success in trade, I did not mean to be understood as insinuating, that this success involved his integrity of character, or was prejudicial thereto; but simply to affirm, (what was popular belief,) that he had always been remarkably lucky — insomuch that his good fortune was occasionally a topic of public conservation. I hinted that the transportation of the slaves, in the Francis, might possibly unravel the enigma — adding the general proposition, that "any man could gather up riches, if he did not care by what means they were obtained."

Again you say:

"That such an one considers it a libel on his reputation, *is a circumstance highly in his favor.* It shows that he himself thinks, with the just and benevolent, that the traffic ought not to be supported."

Now I am inclined to the opinion, that this circumstance proves exactly the reverse of your supposition. *Mr. Todd was deliberately guilty of the charge bro't against him;* and it was his unexpected exposure together with the consciousness of guilt, which made him vindictive. Mr. Thompson, his agent in this city, testified in court, that Mr. Todd sacrificed his conscience for the sake of a little paltry gain — though the witness did not intend, probably, to make so precious a confession.[6] If Mr. Todd had been innocent, he would not have instantaneously kindled into a passion, and presented me as a libeller to a jury whom he suspected of cherishing hostile feelings towards the Genius of Universal Emancipation. Charitably believing that I had been unwittingly led into error, he would have corresponded with me on the subject, and demanded a public apology for the injury inflicted upon his character; and I would have promptly made that apology — yea, upon my bended knees. For I confidently assert, that no individual who knows me personally — not even the accused himself — believes that I was instigated by malice, in the publication of my strictures. *I make no other charge against him.* If I have enemies, I forgive them — I am the enemy of no man. My memory can no more retain the impression of anger, hatred or revenge, than the ocean the track of its monsters.

The admonition of Ganganelli,[7] that *libels and satires make an impression only upon weak and badly organized heads,* ought not to have been lost upon Mr. Todd — especially if his hands were clean and his heart white. Moreover, what if the times *were* hard, freights dull, and money scarce — was he in danger of starvation? And, if so, how much nobler would have been his conduct, if he had adopted the language of the martyred patriot of England — the great Algernon Sidney! —

"I have ever had in my mind, that when God should cast me into such a condition, as that I cannot save my life but by doing an indecent thing, he shews me the time has come wherein I should resign it; *and when I cannot live in my own country but by such means as are worse than dying in it, I think he shews me I ought to keep myself out of it.*"[8]

Finally, you observe:

"We cannot, in such comment as Mr. Garrison desires Editors generally to make on his prosecution, and we cannot, in our real friendship to him, *praise him for any act of rashness and indiscretion.*"

I ask, deserve, and expect the praise of no individuals for my labors; because I am merely endeavoring to perform my duty — and, as I fall far short of that duty, therefore I cannot be meritorious. You misapprehend the nature of the comments that I requested Editors to make upon my trial. It is my solemn belief that a more flagrant infringement upon the liberty of the press, than is presented in the decision of the Court, is hardly to be found in the record of libellous prosecutions in France or Great Britain. I was convicted upon an indictment which was utterly defective, and as innocent as blank paper — evidence failing to prove that I had printed or published, or had any agency in printing or publishing, or had written or caused to be written, or had even seen or known any thing of the obnoxious article!! Here, then, seemed to be an extraordinary procedure, unparalleled for its complexion in this country at least, and dangerous to the freedom of public discussion — deserving, in a special manner, the animadversion of every watchful patriot: — An editor convicted of writing and publishing a "false, wicked and malicious libel," without any authentic evidence of his guilt, and upon the most whimsical pretences!! — I solicited no sympathy for myself: I only requested editors to look at the *law* and the *facts*, and to vindicate their prerogative. "Let it be impressed upon your minds," says Junius, "let it be instilled into your children, that the liberty of the press is the *palladium* of all your civil, political and religious rights." [9]

My "stubbornness" and "dogmaticalness" consist in ardently cherishing, and fearlessly avowing, the following *notions*: — That "all men are born equal, and endowed by their Creator with certain unalienable rights" — consequently, that a slave-holder or a slave-abettor is neither a true patriot, a good citizen, nor an honest man, in all his transactions and relations, and that slavery is a reproach and a curse upon our nation: — That intemperance is a filthy habit and an awful scourge, wholly produced by the moderate, occasional and fashionable use of alcoholic liquors — consequently, that it is sinful to distil, to import, to sell, to drink, or to offer such liquors to our friends or laborers, and that entire abstinence is the duty of every individual: — That war is fruitful in crime, misery, revenge, murder, and every thing abominable and bloody — and, whether offensive or defensive, is contrary to the precepts and example of Jesus Christ, and to the heavenly spirit of the gospel — consequently, that no profession of christianity should march to the battle-field, or murder any of his brethren for the *glory* of his country. These are the first fruits of my *bigotry, fanaticism, rashness* and *folly.*

If I am prompted by *"vanity,"* in pleading for the poor, degraded, miserable Africans, it is at least a harmless, and, I hope, will prove a useful vanity. Would to God it were epidemical! It is a vanity calculated to draw down the curses of the guilty, to elicit the sneers of the malevolent, to excite the suspicion of the cold-hearted, to offend the timidity of the wavering, to disturb the repose of the lethargic; — a vanity that promises to its possessor nothing but neglect, poverty, sorrow, reproach, persecution and imprisonment — *with the approbation of a good conscience, and the smiles of a merciful God.* I think it will last me to the grave.

But why so vehement? so unyielding? so severe? Because the times and the cause demand vehemence. An immense iceberg, larger and more impenetrable than any which floats in the arctic ocean, is to be dissolved, and a little *extra heat* is not only pardonable, but absolutely necessary. Because truth can never be sacrificed, and justice is eternal. Because great crimes and destructive evils ought not to be palliated, nor great sinners applauded. With reasonable men, I will reason; with humane men, I will plead; but to tyrants I will give no quarter, nor waste arguments where they will certainly be lost.

The hearts of some individuals are like ice — congealed by the frigidity of a wintry atmosphere that surrounds, envelopes and obdurates. These may be melted by the rays of humanity, the warmth of expostulation, and the breath of prayer. Others are like adamantine rocks; they require a ponderous sledge and a powerful arm to break them in pieces, or a cask of powder to blow them up. Truth may blaze upon them with mid-day intenseness, but they cannot dissolve.

Every one who comes into the world, should do something to repair its moral desolation, and to restore its pristine loveliness; and he who does not assist, but slumbers away his life in idleness, defeats one great purpose of his creation. But he who, not only refusing to labor himself, endeavors to enlarge and perpetuate the ruin, by discouraging the hearts of the more industrious, and destroying their beautiful works, is a monster and a barbarian, in despite of his human nature and of civilization.

With sentiments of high esteem and ardent affection, I subscribe myself,

Yours, to the grave,

WM. LLOYD GARRISON.

NOTE. I commend Messrs. Beals and Homer of the Boston Commercial Gazette [10] for their frankness, as exhibited in the following commentary:

"Mr. Garrison is to be commiserated for his imprudence; but will any respectable merchant, *who has a proper regard for his own character,* say — after reading the obnoxious article — that that individual DOES NOT RICHLY MERIT THE PUNISHMENT HE IS NOW RECEIVING?"!!!

Let me assure these gentlemen, that there is not a kidnapper or a slave abettor, whether in New-England or out of it, who does not coincide in their opinion. They entertain, certainly, a clear perception of the liberty of the press, and seem to have imbided an extraordinary portion of the spirit of their revolutionary fathers, to say that a person *richly merits punishment* for denouncing the most horrible traffic that ever disgraced humanity! for daring to tell the truth! for asserting the rights of the bondman! — and punished, too, upon such an indictment, without any legal evidence of his guilt! If this be the essence of *Federalism*, I have mistaken its nature, and shall turn my coat. Their "wisdom and experience," their "prudence and judgment," their philanthropy and justice, are indisputably profound, wary and intense.

I have observed, with no little astonishment, that these gentlemen publish, with avidity, almost every thing *in defence of slavery* which emanates from our southern politicians. The raphsodical, incoherent, and vile sentiments of Senator Hayne,[11] and the despicable speculations of Senator Rowan,[12] on this subject, could elicit no objurgatory remarks from their pen, to accompany that correct mass in the columns of the Gazette.

No doubt many merchants in New-England will condemn me, for the significant reason urged by the editors, namely, "a proper regard for their own characters." Why? Because they are guilty, and dread exposure. It is a shameful fact, — and, in private conversation, it is thrown at me repeatedly, — that the transportation of slaves is almost entirely effected in New-England bottoms!!! — The case of Mr. Todd is not a rare one. I was very warmly conversing, the other day, with a slave-owner [13] on the criminality of oppressing the blacks, when he retorted — "Your preaching is fine, but it is more especially needed *at home*. I detest the slave trade — it is cruel and unpardonable: yet your eastern merchants do not scruple to embark in it." "Sir," I replied, "I do not endorse their conduct. The fact, that you state, is humiliating. Am I not confined in prison for exposing one of their number? Let them beware! Every one whom I detect in this nefarious business — merchant or master — shall be advertised to the world."

My "punishment" does not dishearten me. Whether liberated or not, my pen shall not remain idle. My thoughts flow as copiously, my spirit towers as loftily, my soul flames as intensely, in prison, as out of it. The court may shackle the body, but it cannot pinion the mind.

W.L.G.

Baltimore Jail, June 1, 1830.

* A few days since, Judge Brice observed to the Warden of the Jail, that "Mr. Garrison was ambitious of becoming a martyr." "Tell his Honor," I responded, "that if his assertion be true, he is equally ambitious of gathering the faggots, and applying the torch."

Printed: Newburyport *Herald*, June 11, 1830; printed partly in *Life*, I, 185–189.

1. Ephraim W. Allen's comment on the trial of his former apprentice was

printed in the issue for May 25. Although he commended Garrison as "a diligent student" with "an ardent temperament and warm imagination" and "unshaken courage," he also characterized him as sometimes "hasty, stubborn, and dogmatic, rash and unyielding."

2. For his participation in the slave trade Austin Woolfolk had been attacked by Lundy in *The Genius of Universal Emancipation* as early as January of 1827. To this attack Woolfolk had responded by assaulting Lundy on the street; and in turn Lundy had sworn out a writ against Woolfolk, but Judge Brice had fined the assailant only a dollar and expenses on grounds that his provocation was excessive. (See Merton L. Dillon, *Benjamin Lundy and the Struggle for Negro Freedom*, Urbana, 1966.)

3. Garrison misquotes Dialogue II of Pope's "Epiloge to the Satires," lines 12–13. The couplet is as follows:

> "Spare then the person, and expose the vice.
> P. How, Sir! not damn the sharper, but the dice?"

This poem is written in the form of a dialogue between "P" and "F"; Garrison perhaps confused in his memory the two letters, translating "F" into "Friend." He may also unconsciously or otherwise have censored the "damn."

4. Garrison apparently intends to express the same comment as in his other square brackets above.

5. Nicholas Brown (1784–1868) had been known to Garrison before this occasion as a kindly man. It is said, moreover, that Brown did all that he could to make the slaves comfortable during the voyage and that he never again transported human cargo.

6. Garrison seems to be somewhat free in interpreting Thompson's testimony. According to Garrison's sons (*Life*, I, 169–170) Thompson reported in court that he had written Todd that as his agent he had contracted to transport slaves. Todd replied that *"he should have preferred another kind of freight, but as freights were dull, times hard, and money scarce, he was satisfied with the bargain."*

7. Lorenzo Ganganelli (1705–1774), or Pope Clement XIV, was famous for his Brief suppressing the Jesuits.

8. Algernon Sidney (1622–1683), nephew of Sir Philip Sidney, was the republican leader who fought against Charles I and whose moderation alienated him from Cromwell. He was later accused of participating in the Monmouth-Shaftesbury rebellion against Charles II and tried and executed in 1683. Garrison quotes from *The Apology of A. Sidney in the Day of his Death*, using his own italics.

9. Garrison quotes rather inaccurately from the "Dedication to the English Nation," *The Letters of Junius* (New York, 1821), I, vi.

10. William Beals (c. 1786–1870) and James L. Homer are listed in the Boston directory of 1830 as proprietors of the *Gazette and Daily Advertiser*. In 1832 they became part owners of the Boston *Gazette*. Political differences eventually resulted in Beal's transfer to the Boston *Post*.

11. Robert Y. Hayne (1791–1839) was an eloquent South Carolina lawyer and advocate of states' rights, who had served in the United States Senate since 1822.

12. John Rowan (1773–1843) was a distinguished lawyer and, since 1825, United States senator from Louisville, Kentucky.

13. An unidentified person who apparently called at the jail to remonstrate with Garrison.

4 0

TO EBENEZER DOLE

Baltimore, July 14, 1830.

Respected and benevolent Sir:

At the request of my Counsel, and at the desire of my friend Lundy, I visited Boston and Newburyport a few weeks since, in order to get some essential evidence to be used in the civil action which is now pending against me in this city; — and also to see whether any thing could be done towards renewing, and permanently establishing, the weekly publication of the Genius. I left Baltimore without adequate means to carry me home, relying upon Providence to open a door of relief. On my arrival in New-York, I was accidentally introduced to a gentleman named Samuel Leggett, who generously offered me a passage to Rhode-Island, in the splendid steam-boat President, he being a stockholder therein.[1] Thus I was most unexpectedly relieved of my embarrassment, and enabled to reach my place of destination. Mr. L. said that he had read with indignation the proceedings of the court at my late trial, and was glad to have an opportunity of serving me. I gave him many thanks for his kindness.

I found the minds of the people strangely indifferent to the subject of slavery. Their prejudices were invincible — stronger, if possible, than those of slaveholders. Objections were started on every hand; apologies for the abominable system constantly saluted my ears; obstacles were industriously piled up in my path. The cause of this callous state of feeling was owing to their exceeding ignorance of the horrors of slavery. What was yet more discouraging, my best friends — without an exception — besought me to give up the enterprise, and never to return to Baltimore! It was not my duty (they argued) to spend my time, and talents, and services, where persecution, reproach and poverty were the only certain reward. My scheme was visionary — fanatical — unattainable. Why should I make myself an exile from home and all that I held dear on earth, and sojourn in a strange land, among enemies whose hearts were dead to every noble sentiment? — &c. &c. &c. I repeat — *all were against my return.* But I desire to thank God, that he gave me strength to overcome this selfish and pernicious advice. Opposition served only to increase my ardor, and confirm my purpose.

But how was I to return? I had not a dollar in my pocket, and my time was expired. No one understood my circumstances. I was too proud to beg, and ashamed to borrow. My friends were prodigal of pity, but of nothing else. In the extremity of my uneasiness, I went to

the Boston Post Office, and found a letter from my friend Lundy, enclosing a draft for $100, from a stranger — yourself, as a remuneration for my poor, inefficient services in behalf of the slaves! Here Providence had again signally interfered in my behalf. After deducting the expenses of travelling, the remainder of the above named sum was applied in discharging a few of the debts incurred by the unproductiveness of the Genius.

As I lay on my couch one night, in jail, I was led to contrast my situation with that of the poor slave. Ah! dear sir, how wide the difference! In one particular only, (I said,) our conditions are similar. He is confined to the narrow limits of a plantation — I to the narrow limits of a prison-yard. Farther all parallels fail. My food is better and more abundant, as I get a pound of bread and a pound of meat, with a plentiful supply of pure water, *per diem.* I can lie down or rise up, sit or walk, sing or declaim, read or write, as fancy, pleasure or profit dictates. Moreover, I am daily cheered with the presence and conversation of friends; — I am constantly supplied with fresh periodicals from every section of the country, and, consequently, am advertised of every new and interesting occurrence. Occasionally a letter greets me from a distant place, filled with consolatory expressions, tender remembrances, or fine compliments. If it rain, my room is a shelter; if the sun flame too intensely, I can choose a shady retreat; if I am sick, medical aid is at hand. — Besides, I have been charged with a specific offence — have had the privilege of a trial by jury, and the aid of eminent counsel — and am here ostensibly to satisfy the demands of justice. A few months, at the longest, will release me from my captivity.[2]

Now, how is it with the slave? He gets a peck of corn (occasionally a little more) each week, but rarely meat or fish. He must anticipate the sun in rising, or be whipped severely for his somnolency. Rain or shine, he must toil early and late *for the benefit of another.* If he be weary, be cannot rest — for the lash of the driver is flourished over his drooping head, or applied to his naked frame; if sick, he is suspected of laziness, and treated accordingly. For the most trifling or innocent offence, he is felled to the earth, or scourged on his back till it streams with blood. Has he a wife and children, he sees them as cruelly treated as himself. He may be torn from them, or they from him, at any moment, never again to meet on earth. Friends do not visit and console him: *he has no friends.* He knows not what is going on beyond his own narrow boundaries. He can neither read nor write. The letters of the alphabet are caballistical to his eyes. A thick darkness broods over his soul. Even the "glorious gospel of the blessed God," which brings life and immortality to perishing man, is as a sealed

book to his understanding. Nor has his wretched condition been imposed upon him for any criminal offence. He has not been tried by the laws of his country. No one has stepped forth to vindicate *his* rights. He is made an abject slave, simply because God has given him a skin not colored like his master's; and Death, the great Liberator, alone can break his fetters!

Reflections like the foregoing turned my prison into a palace. — Can you wonder, benevolent sir, that I was enabled to sing, — after such an amazing contrast, — with a heart overflowing with gratitude, —

> "When all thy mercies, O my God,
> My rising soul surveys,
> Transported with the view I'm lost
> In wonder, love and praise!"[3]

If the public sympathy is so strongly excited in my behalf, because justice has been denied me in a single instance, how ought it to flame for two millions of as valuable and immortal souls, who are crushed beneath the iron car of despotism? O that my countrymen would look at things in their true light! O that they might feel as keenly for a black skin as for a white one! forgetting me entirely, and thinking only of the poor slave!

Baltimore, July 14, 1830.

$100.

> For value received, I promise to pay Ebenezer Dole, on his order, the sum of *One Hundred Dollars*, with interest, on demand.
> Witness — Isaac Knapp.   Wm. Lloyd Garrison.[4]

Your generosity deeply affects my heart; but as I have done nothing, and can do nothing, in the cause of African emancipation, to merit such a gift, I must receive your donation only *as a loan on interest* — to be repaid as soon as Providence may enable me to do so. At present, I am opulent in nothing but gratitude, though my language is cold and penurious. Be good enough to make my acknowledgements to Mr. J. C. Lovejoy, for his friendly sympathies.[5] Friend Lundy desires to be affectionately remembered. May God bless and prosper you and yours, is the prayer of

Wm. Lloyd Garrison.

Ebenezer Dole,
   Hallowell, Maine.

ALS: New York Union League Club; printed in *Life*, I, 192–195. The bad condition of the manuscript at times makes it difficult to read, though questionable readings can be clarified by reference to a written transcription in the Garrison Papers, Boston Public Library.

Ebenezer Dole (1776–1847), from Newburyport and a distant cousin of

Garrison's, had grown prosperous in Hallowell, Maine. As Garrison's later letters indicate (see especially letter 66, to Dole, June 29, 1832), he continued to be generous to Garrison and the cause.

1. Of Quaker background, Samuel Leggett (1782–1847) was a wealthy New York City merchant who had made his fortune as jobber, auctioneer, and banker. He had been president of the Franklin Bank and the first president of the New York Gas Light Company.

2. In fact, Garrison was confined for seven weeks.

3. Garrison quotes from an eighteenth-century hymn published in the *Spectator* August 9, 1812, which is probably by Joseph Addison.

4. This note signed by Garrison was crossed out, presumably by Ebenezer Dole.

5. Joseph C. Lovejoy (1805–1871), like his two brothers, was both minister and abolitionist. Owen and Joseph were less well known than Elijah P., who was to be martyred by a mob in Alton, Illinois, in 1837.

41

TO GEORGE SHEPARD

Hartford, Ct. Sept. 13, 1830.

Rev. George Shepard:

Your very interesting and important letter of the 18th ult. was duly received; but circumstances have prevented my giving it a suitable reply till the present moment.

Towards the unknown individual,[1] who generously offers a premium of $50 for the best tract on the subject of slavery, I feel an attachment of soul which words cannot express; and for yourself, sir, I beg you to accept my thanks for the sympathy which you express in behalf of the poor slave. Alas! that so few in our land feel an interest in the great cause of emancipation! But let us not despair. The time must come — for the mouth of the Lord of Hosts has spoken it — when all oppression shall cease, and every man shall sit under his own vine and fig tree — there being none to molest or make him afraid.[2] We may not live to see that glorious day, but may hasten it by our prayers, our toils, and our sacrifices; nor shall we lose our reward — for the King of Heaven may peradventure bestow that noblest of panegyrics upon us, "Well done, good and faithful servants!" [3]

At the present day, American slavery is unequalled for cruelty: — antiquity cannot produce its parallel. And yet it is boastingly proclaimed to the world, that this is the land of the free, and the asylum of the oppressed! Was liberty ever so degraded in the eyes of mankind, or justice mocked with such impunity?

For myself, I hold no fellowship with slaveowners. I will not make a truce with them even for a single hour. I blush for them as country-

men — I *know* that they are not *christians*; and the higher they raise
their professions of patriotism or piety, the stronger is my detestation
of their hypocrisy. They are dishonest and cruel — and God, and the
angels, and devils, and the universe know that *they are without excuse.*

> "They hear not — see not — know not; for their eyes
> Are covered with thick mists — they *will not* see:
> The sick earth groans with man's impieties,
> And heaven is tired with man's perversity." [4]

With regard to the outlines of the contemplated tract which you
have given, I think they are highly important — but so broad, that
their discussion could not be easily or efficiently embraced within
twelve duodecimo pages.[5] I would therefore suggest, with deference,
the expediency of confining the object of the tract to one of these two
points — namely, "The Duty of Ministers and Churches, of all denominations, to clear their skirts from the blood of the slaves, and to
make the holding of slaves a barrier to communion and church-member-
ship" — or, secondly, in your own language, "Suggestions as to the
best ways and means to restore the slaves to their unalienable rights,
and elevate them to that standing in society, to which, as brethren of
the human family, and fellow heirs to immortality, they are entitled."

Both of the above points are eminently weighty, and would require separate treatises in their elucidation. I am decidedly in favor of
the one first mentioned; because all plans will be likely to prove
nugatory, as long the church refuses to act on the subject — it must
be purified, as by fire. It must not support, it must not palliate the
horrid system. It seems moral[ly] impossible, that a man can be a
slaveholder and a follower of the Lamb at the same time. A *christian
slaveholder* is as great a solecism as a religious atheist, a sober drunkard, or an honest thief. In 1826, the Synod of Ohio held an animated
discussion on a question which had been before referred to the General
Assembly of the Presbyterian Church, viz. "*Is the holding of slaves
man-stealing?*" in the *affirmative* of which, a large majority concurred.
This is a rational view of the subject; consequently no slaveholder
ought to be embraced within the pale of a christian church.

Is not the fact enough to make one hang his head, that *christian men*
and *christian ministers* (for so they dare to call themselves) are slave
owners? Are there not *Balaams* in our land, who prophesy in the name
of the Lord, but covet the presents of *Balak?* What! shall he who
styles himself an ambassador of Christ — who preaches what angels
sung, "Peace on earth, *good will to man*" [6] — who tells me, Sabbath
after Sabbath, that with God there is no respect of persons — that my

Creator commands me to do unto others as I would that they should do unto me — to love my neighbor as myself — to call no man master — to be meek, and merciful, and blameless — to let my light so shine before men, that they may see my good works, and glorify my Father who is in heaven — to shun every appearance of evil — to rather suffer myself to be defrauded than defraud; — nay, who tells me, as the injunction of my Judge, to love even my enemies, to bless them that curse me, to do good to them that hate me, and to pray for them that despitefully use and persecute me [7] — (alas! how has he needed the prayers and forgiveness of his poor degraded, persecuted slaves!) — I say, shall such a teacher presume to call the creatures of God his *property* — to deal in bones, and sinews, and souls — to whip, and manacle, and brand — merely because his victims differ in complexion from himself, and because the tyrannous laws of a State, and the corrupt usages of society, justify his conduct? Yet so it is. By his example, he sanctifies, in the eyes of ungodly men, a system of blood, and violates every commandment of Jehovah. Horrible state of things!

"For this thing which it cannot bear, the earth is disquieted. The Gospel of Peace and Mercy preached by him who steals, buys or sells the purchase of Messiah's blood! — Rulers of the Church making merchandize of their brethren's souls! — and Christians trading the persons of men! — These are they who are lovers of their own selves — Covetous — Proud — Fierce — Men of corrupt minds, who resist the truth — Having the form of godliness, but denying the power thereof — From su[ch tu]rn away." [8]

I think that an able and faithful tract upon this [point] is greatly needed, and would be the means of incalculable good. — I submit the choice of topics to yourself, and to the benevolent individual who offers the premium.

There is no Society in existence, bearing the title of the "American Abolition Society." I think the tract had better come out to the public, under the auspices of the "Pennsylvania Society for promoting the Abolition of Slavery, — the relief of free Negroes unlawfully held in bondage, — and for improving the Condition of the African Race." Agreeably to your request, I select three members of that Society to decide upon the merits of the various tracts that may be presented — namel[y] the venerable William Rawle, L.L.D. President — and Jonas Preston, M. D. and Thomas Shipley, Vice Presidents of said Society — all thorough-going reformers, and highly intelligent and respectable men, residents of Philadelphia.[9] The premium money may be deposited in the hands of the President, Wm. Rawle.

I am now on an eastern tour for the purpose of delivering public addresses on the subject of slavery, of obtaining subscriptions to my proposed new paper at Washington City, of establishing a National Anti-Slavery Tract Society, &c. &c. I shall leave Hartford for Boston this morning, where I shall probably reside some time, and to which place please to address your next letter as soon as convenient.

Your friend and well-wisher till death,

Wm. Lloyd Garrison.

☞ If Mr. Shepard should not happen to be in Plainfield on the arrival of this letter, E. L. Fuller, Esq. will be kind enough to send it to its proper place of destination, and greatly oblige his grateful servt.[10]

Wm. Lloyd Garrison.

ALS: Garrison Papers, Boston Public Library; printed in *Life*, I, 204–207.

George Shepard (1801–1868), a graduate of Amherst College and Andover Theological Seminary, with a D.D. from Bowdoin College, had since 1828 been the minister of the First Congregational Church of Hallowell, Maine. He had the reputation of being an eloquent speaker and an ardent worker for temperance and abolition.

1. Ebenezer Dole.
2. Garrison freely quotes Micah 4:4.
3. Matthew 25:21, 23. Garrison makes the word "servant" plural.
4. Not identified.
5. The tract to which Garrison refers, if written, was apparently not published.
6. Luke 2:14.
7. A typical Garrisonian pastiche of biblical allusions and quotations, combining passages from Matthew 7:12, Leviticus 19:18, Matthew 5:16, I Corinthians 6:7, and Matthew 5:44.
8. Apparently Garrison quotes again from Shepard's proposal for a tract.
9. Garrison mentions three early abolitionists. William Rawle (1759–1836), a loyalist during the Revolution, was for many years active in the civic and cultural life of Philadelphia and Pennsylvania, as lawyer, as United States attorney for Pennsylvania, and as member of various organizations, including the American Philosophical Society, Benjamin Franklin's Society for Political Inquiries, and the Maryland Society (for "promoting the abolition of slavery"). Jonas Preston (1764–1836) was a distinguished doctor who had a lucrative practice in Chester and later in Philadelphia. He was for some years a member of the state legislature, of the Philadelphia City Council, and a director of the Bank of Pennsylvania. He was also associated with the Pennsylvania Society for Promoting the Abolition of Slavery. Thomas Shipley (1787–1836), a Philadelphia Quaker, was later one of the founders of the American Anti-Slavery Society and a loyal Garrisonian. (See Garrison's eulogy of him in *The Liberator*, October 1, 1836, following his death.)
10. E. L. Fuller was apparently the postmaster of Plainfield, Connecticut. Garrison's letter, which was addressed to Shepard at that town, was forwarded to Shepard at Hallowell, Maine, marked with the following notation: "Free. E. L. Fuller PM."

42

TO THE EDITOR OF THE NEWBURYPORT *HERALD*

[September 30, 1830.]

Sir —

Twice have the inhabitants of this town been deceived, in relation to the delivery of my Addresses on Slavery.[1] Permit me to exonerate myself from blame in this matter. Circumstances, beyond my control, have prevented the fulfilment of my pledges. Toward those who have exerted their influence, with a malignity and success which are discreditable to themselves and the place, in order to seal up my lips on a subject which involves the temporal and eternal condition of millions of our countrymen, I entertain no ill-will, but kindness and compassion. Let them answer to God and posterity for their conduct; for even this communication shall be read by future generations and shall identify the ashes of these enemies of their species.

If I had visited Newburyport to plead the cause of twenty white men in chains, every hall and every meeting-house would have been thrown open, and the fervor of my discourses anticipated and exceeded by my fellow townsmen. The fact, that two millions of colored beings are groaning in bondage, in this land of liberty, excites no interest nor pity!

I leave this morning for Boston. A circumstantial account of my treatment, in this my native place, will probably be given, in a few days, in one of the city papers.

Your grateful servant, and undaunted friend to the cause of universal liberty,

Wm. Lloyd Garrison.

Thursday morning, Sept. 30, 1830.

Printed: Newburyport *Herald*, October 1, 1830; printed in *Life*, I, 209.

1. In two instances trustees of churches in Newburyport had refused Garrison permission to speak, even though the ministers of the churches had already scheduled him; see *Life*, I, 207–209.

43

TO THE EDITOR OF THE BOSTON *EVENING TRANSCRIPT*

[November 6, 1830.]

Sir, —

The Transcript of Monday evening,[1] (which has just been put into my hands,) contains the following paragraph from the Charleston

City Gazette, which you are pleased to style "a fair offset" to an article of mine, published in your paper of Oct. 12th:

"IMPERTINENCE. A MR. GARRISON, who has been lately punished in Baltimore for similar impertinences, presumes to reflect upon this city, in the Boston Transcript, on account of a certain class of our population. Could not this man be provided with some decent honest employment — at the plough or any other vocation which will keep him out of mischief, and prevent him from meddling with the concerns of those about whom he knows nothing, and who are perfectly adequate to the management of their own concerns."

Well, sir, what was the design of the communication which has elicited the foregoing sensible and witty commentary from the Charleston editor, whose politeness exceeds even his humanity? Why, to expose the brazen impudence and abominable hypocrisy of "a certain class" of men at the South, who, while they are riotously exulting at the downfall of the French tyrant [2] — giving dinners, singing songs, drinking toasts, forming processions, discharging cannon, illuminating houses, &c. &c. &c. — are nevertheless holding a large portion of their fellow men in a state of bondage, "*one hour of which,*" to borrow the words of Mr. Jefferson, "*is fraught with more misery, than ages of which our fathers rose in rebellion to oppose.*" [3] Undoubtedly, sir, the note of the Charleston scrutator is "a fair offset" — a sound, courteous, unanswerable rejoinder to my strictures.

Let me say to that unblushing scribbler, that, before he again recommends a particular avocation to *a New-England mechanic who is not ashamed of his trade*, he would be wise to follow his own suggestion, and to urge purse proud, indolent and profligate slaveholders to alter their vile pursuits. Is it "a decent honest employment" to reduce the creatures of God to a level with brutes — to lacerate and brand their bodies with more than savage cruelty — to keep their souls in thick, impenetrable darkness — to tear the mother from her babe, the husband from his wife, the brother from his sister — to steal, day after day, month after month, year after year, the fruits of their unmitigated toil, and give, in return, a little meal and a few herrings — and to kidnap, from their births, the offspring of slave parents, dooming every generation successively to the horrors of slavery? Doubtless this is at least a portion of the employment of the Charleston editor, as it is of a vast number in the southern States — but is it "decent" or "honest"? Does it not deserve the severest execration? When I shall become so mean and dastardly — so lost to every feeling of humanity, every principle of justice, every conviction of conscience — as to fetter and sell my own countrymen, or others, may I receive, (as I ought to receive, if capital punishment be lawful,[)] a just reward for my conduct at the gallows, like any other pirate; may my memory be accursed to the end of time; and may the lightnings of heaven consume my body to ashes. I join with the eloquent and indignant Brougham: — "Tell me not of rights — talk not of the property of the planter in his slaves. *I deny the right — I acknowledge not the property.* The principles, the feelings of our common nature, rise in rebellion against it. Be the appeal made to the understanding or to the heart, the sentence is the same that rejects it. While men despise fraud, and loathe rapine, and abhor blood, they shall reject with indignation the wild and guilty fantasy, that man can hold property in man!" [4]

For myself, I hold no fellowship with slave owners. I will not make a truce with them even for an hour. I blush for them as countrymen — I know not how they are christians; and the higher they raise their professions of patriotism or piety, the stronger is my detestation of their hypocrisy. They are dishonest and cruel, whether they know it or not, whether they believe it or not — and God, and the angels, and devils, and the universe know that they are without excuse. A christian or republican slaveholder is as great a solecism as a religious atheist, a sober drunkard, or an honest thief.

Sir, the people of this country cannot evade the question of negro emancipation. It is in our power, a little longer, to turn from it with indifference; but the hour is at hand — if there be any truth in history, any admonition in experience, any retaliatory spirit in man — when it will be discussed at the point of the bayonet, and recorded in human blood — unless we now *act*, not by threats, nor violence, nor physical force — but by moral suasion, by the energy of an enlightened public opinion, by just, benevolent and constitutional measures.

And now let me give another solemn warning to the owners of slaves at the south. I adopt and modify the prophetic language of Brougham, in relation to British Colonial Slavery: —

In vain you appeal to treaties — to covenants between sovereignties. The covenants of the Almighty, whether the old or the new, denounce such unholy pretensions. To those laws did they of old refer, who maintained the African slave trade: such treaties did they cite. Yet, in despite of law and of treaty, that infernal traffic is now destroyed, and its votaries put to death. How came this change to pass? Not assuredly by Congress leading the way; but the country at length awoke; the indignation of the people was kindled; it descended in thunder, and smote the traffic, and scattered its guilty profits to the winds. Now, then, let the planters beware — let their assemblies beware! the same country is once more awake, — awake to the condition of negro slavery; the same indignation kindles in the bosom of the same people; *the same cloud is gathering that annihilated the slave trade;* and, if it shall descend again, they, on whom its crash shall fall, will not be destroyed before I have warned them; but I pray that their destruction may turn away from us the more terrible judgments of God!

W. L. G.

Saturday Morning, Oct. 6.[5]

Printed: Boston *Evening Transcript*, November 8, 1830. Lynde M. Walter (c. 1799–1842) as editor had founded the *Transcript* only a few weeks before Garrison's letter.

1. November 1.
2. Charles X (1757–1836), who had been overthrown by a liberal revolution in July 1830.
3. Garrison quotes, with slight inaccuracy, from Jefferson's letter to Jean Nicolas Démeunier of June 26, 1786 (Julian P. Boyd, ed., *The Papers of Thomas Jefferson*, Princeton, 1954, X, 63).
4. Henry Peter Brougham, Baron Brougham and Vaux (1778–1868), founder of the Edinburgh *Review* and of London University, was one of the great lawyers, speakers, and politicians of the day. A member of Parliament since 1810, he had recently been triumphantly reelected after having presented the motion against slavery in the British West Indies, which Garrison quotes in part, though he changes a "will" to "shall," uses his own italics, and omits one short and a large part of a long sentence without indicating the omission. (See the records of the House of Commons, Hansard, New Series, 25:1191 [June-July] 1830).
5. This date is in error; it should be "November" rather than "October."

44

TO SAMUEL J. MAY

Boston, Feb. 14, 1831.

Beloved Friend:

If the most unremitted labor had not occupied my time since your departure, I should feel very culpable for my long silence. Without means, and determined to ask the assistance of no individual, — and, indeed, not knowing where to look for it, so unpopular was the cause, — you may suppose that I have been obliged to make severe personal exertions for the establishment of the Liberator. I am ashamed of the meagre aspect which the paper presents in its editorial department; because the public imagine that I have six days each week to cater for it, when, in fact, scarcely six hours are allotted to me, and these at midnight. My worthy partner and I complete the mechanical part; that is to say, we compose and distribute, on every number, one hundred thousand types, besides performing the press-work, mailing the papers to subscribers, &c. &c. In addition to this, a variety of letters, relative to the paper, are constantly accumulating, which require prompt answers. We have just taken a colored apprentice, however, who will shortly be able to alleviate our toil.

I cannot give you a better apprehension of the arduousness of my labors than by stating, that it is more than six weeks since I visited Mr. Coffin — perhaps more properly the Misses Coffin; for, certainly, there is no place in Boston I am disposed to visit so often as in Atkinson-street.[1]

By the editorial fraternity throughout the country, with hardly an exception, the Liberator has been received with acclamation; by the public — the white portion of it — with suspicion or apathy. Upon the colored population in the free states, it has operated like a trumpet-call. They have risen in their hopes and feelings to the perfect stature of men: in this city, every one of them is as tall as a giant. About ninety have subscribed for the paper in Philadelphia, and upwards of thirty in New-York, which number, I am assured, will swell to at least one hundred in a few weeks. This, then, is my consolation: if I cannot do much, in this quarter, toward abolishing slavery, I may be able to elevate our free colored population in the scale of society.

For the success of my exertions, I rely exclusively on the blessing of God. Unless His spirit quicken and sanctify, no eloquence, no argument, that I can use, will be productive. I know that mine is a righteous cause; and, if so, it must ultimately triumph. I am sure that man cannot be the property of man; and, therefore, that every slave has a right to his freedom. Why, then, should I shrink from the contest, or be embarrassed by doubt? I do not shrink — I cherish no doubt. I counted the cost before I went to the battle. I foresaw all that has happened. I knew that my motives would be impeached, my sanity doubted, my warnings mocked; but the clankings of chains broke upon my ear, — I looked up to Heaven for support, — and my resolution was taken.

❖ ❖ ❖

I have a huge volume of matters to write, but neither time nor room. This, you see, is but an apology for a reply. Next time, and very shortly too, I will do better. Our mutual friend Mr. Sewell continues to increase in feeling on the subject of slavery [2] He is a man full of estimable qualities.

Give my affectionate and respectful remembrances to Mrs. May, and kiss your dear little boy for me, again and again.

You have forwarded $2 for the Liberator, but I intended to make you a present of the paper. The business shall be regulated when we meet.

Your first letter was duly received. I shall not be able to visit you in March; but no matter. Your address to the public would be worth a thousand of mine. Let them have it first and then send it on to me for publication.

Your friend and brother,

Wm. Lloyd Garrison.

N.B. I beseech you, most earnestly, to occupy the columns of the Liberator with your essays on any subject, as often as possible.

The noble philanthropist, Ladd, called to see me a few days ago.[3] He spoke of you in exalted terms.

ALS: Garrison Papers, Boston Public Library; printed partly in *Life*, I, 222, 233–234.

Samuel Joseph May (1797–1871) was a Unitarian minister and one of Garrison's most devoted friends and followers. He participated in the founding of the New England Anti-Slavery Society and of the American Anti-Slavery Society, aided Prudence Crandall in her effort to keep a school for Negro girls, served as general agent and secretary of the Massachusetts Anti-Slavery Society in 1835 and 1836, and used his home as a station for Negroes attempting to reach Canada on the Underground Railroad — to name but a few of his activities. He shared with Garrison a concern for woman's rights and supported Lucretia Mott and Angelina Grimké in their crusades. His interest in reform also extended to education, peace, and temperance.

1. Garrison refers to Samuel May's father-in-law, Peter Coffin, and his family. They lived near the office of *The Liberator*.

2. Samuel E. Sewall (1799–1888), whose name Garrison misspells, was a competent attorney and a descendant of the first American abolitionst Judge Samuel Sewall. Like his cousin Samuel J. May, he was a recent convert to Garrison's cause.

3. William Ladd (1778–1841), after graduating from Harvard, became for a time a ship's captain and subsequently a Congregational clergyman. He is known chiefly for having founded the American Peace Society in 1828 and for having agitated for the formation of an international organization, complete with a congress and court of nations.

45

TO ALONZO LEWIS

Boston, March 12, 1831.

My dear Sir:

Pardon me for not acknowledging, ere this, the receipt of your handsome and very valuable present — the History of Lynn.[1] As I am in a great hurry, now, I must take another opportunity (public as well as private) to express my sense of its merits. I did not mean to neglect you, but business —— I am sorry — Forgive.

Do any of the good people of Lynn wish to hear a couple of addresses on slavery? If a Hall can easily and gratuitously be obtained, and if as many will attend as honored friend Lundy with their presence, (20, according to one of your correspondents,) it will give me pleasure to address them, *on Saturday and Sabbath evenings next,* (19th and 20th inst.) at 7 o'clock. I will cheerfully pay for lighting the Hall, &c. The first lecture will be a defence of the doctrine of immediate abolition, and a reply to the popular objections of the day. The other will be an examination of the merits of the American Colonization Society. I am willing to give you a little trouble, because I know **you** will gladly incur it, but you must not be put to the expense of a farthing in procuring a place. On this condition alone can I consent to come.

Supposing a room be got, you will add to my heap of obligations by giving notice of my intention in the next Mirror and Record.[2] I dare say the audience will be respectable in every point of view. I should start for Lynn after dinner on Saturday.

Success to your excellent paper: it is all that any patrons could wish.

Let me receive a note from you as soon as convenient.

In prodigious haste,

Your friend and brother,

Wm. Lloyd Garrison.

N.B. A meeting-house would be aqually acceptable.

ALS: Friends Historical Library, Swarthmore College.
Alonzo Lewis (1794–1861), the "Lynn Bard," wrote verse pleasing to Garrison and other abolitionists. Lewis was also known as teacher (master of six languages), editor, and historian.
1. Lewis had sent Garrison a copy of his own book, *The History of Lynn* (Boston, 1829).
2. Garrison names two Lynn, Massachusetts, weekly newspapers, the *Mirror* (founded in 1825) and the *Record* (founded in 1830); Alonzo Lewis had been involved with the editorial management of both papers. This letter is addressed to him as editor of the *Mirror*.

46

TO EPHRAIM W. ALLEN

[April 29, 1831.]

Mr Allen:

I have examined the columns of the Herald lately, hoping that some of those ladies who are not less skillful in the use of the pen than of the needle, would call the attention of the public to the approaching Fair.[1] Although it is well known that the profits of this fair are to be appropriated to the establishment of two Infant schools, and to the benefit of the Female Asylum, still something more is necessary than a mere advertisement, to excite that interest which is desirable. We need to be reminded of the advantages of these objects, and of the claims which they have upon our charity.

The subject of Infant Schools is not universally understood. The system has some firm adherents who perhaps have been too sanguine in their expectations; if these should be disappointed, it will not prove that the system is not a good one. We have already heard much of its good effects in other places, and have witnessed them in this town. In these schools many children receive instruction that would otherwise be neglected, and that instruction is given in so pleasing a form, that it cannot fail to inspire them with a love of knowledge. Not the least advantage resulting from them is the opportunity they afford to parents, of devoting that time to the maintenance of their children, which they would otherwise be compelled to devote to the care of them.

With regard to the Female Asylum all are prepared to decide. Its good effects are universally known. Here the fatherless — houseless — helpless child finds shelter, receives religious and moral instruction, is fitted to become a useful member of society, and by the blessing of God is prepared for eternal happiness. It not unfrequently happens that she in her turn is able to afford to others that assistance and care which she has so largely received. Many an orphan has thus not only been saved from poverty, suffering, disgrace and death, but has been qualified for the enjoyment of positive happiness.

Who that has known the benefits of parental instruction, that can look back upon the days of his childhood, and call to mind the tender look, the encouraging smile, and the soothing voice of a fond mother, would not freely do all in his power to alleviate the misery of those who enjoy not these blessings? What parent, when he reflects on the mutability of earthly things, and considers that the object of his affection may be left in this helpless state, would not willingly contribute to the support of an institution so benevolent? Surely a very little reflection ought to be sufficient to excite all the kind feelings of our nature in behalf of so praiseworthy an object.

The Fair will afford an opportunity for the exercise of these benevolent feelings — and every person who contributes, will not only have the pleasing consciousness of having promoted the comfort and improvement of some helpless orphan, but will also receive an equivalent for his bounty.

The number, variety, and quality of the articles to be sold are creditable to the industry, ingenuity, taste and judgment of those who have prepared them. No more will be demanded for them than they are worth. If any one should choose to give more than the value, his generosity will neither be refused nor forgotten.

We trust the unremitted exertions of the ladies will be repaid by the liberal purchase of [a]ll the articles exhibited — and that the people of this town, will show that they are not undeserving of that reputation for benevolence which they have so long sustained. —

G.

Printed: Newburyport *Herald*, April 29, 1831.

1. An advertisement in the same issue of the *Herald* indicated that the Fair was to be held in Newburyport at the Town Hall on State Street May 4.

THE LIBERATOR.

VOL. I.]   WILLIAM LLOYD GARRISON AND ISAAC KNAPP, PUBLISHERS.   **[NO. 1.**

BOSTON, MASSACHUSETTS.]   OUR COUNTRY IS THE WORLD—OUR COUNTRYMEN ARE MANKIND.   [SATURDAY, JANUARY 1, 1831.

THE LIBERATOR
IS PUBLISHED WEEKLY
AT NO. 6, MERCHANTS' HALL.
WM. L. GARRISON, EDITOR.

Stephen Foster, Printer.

TERMS.

Two Dollars per annum, payable in advance.

Agents allowed every sixth copy gratis.

No subscription will be received for a shorter period than six months.

All letters and communications must be POST PAID.

THE LIBERATOR

THE SALUTATION.

To date my being from the opening year,
I come, a stranger in this busy sphere,
Where some I meet perchance may pause and ask,
What is my name, my purpose, or my task?

My name is 'LIBERATOR'! I propose
To hurl my shafts at freedom's deadliest foes!
My task is hard—for I am charged to save
Men from his brother!—to redeem the slave!

Ye who may hear, and yet condemn my cause,
Say, shall the best of Nature's holy laws
Be trodden down? and shall her open veins
Flow but for cement to her offspring's chains?

Art thou a parent? shall thy children be
Rent from thy breast, like branches from the tree,
And doom'd to servitude, in helplessness,
On other shores, and thou ask no redress?

Thou, in whose bosom glows the sacred flame
Of filial love, say, if the tyrant came,
To force thy parent shrieking from thy sight,
Would thy heart bleed—*because thy face is white?*

Art thou a brother? shall thy sister twine
Her feeble arm in agony on thine,
And thou not lift the heat, nor aim the blow
At him who bears her off to life-long wo?

Art thou —— sister? will all ——
Awake thy sleeping brother, while thine eye
Beholds the fetters locking on the limb
Stretched out in rest, which hence, must end,
for him?

Art thou a lover?—no! naught e'er was found
In lover's breast, save cords of love, that bound
Man to his kind! then, thy professions save!
Forswear affection, or release thy slave!

Thou who art kneeling at thy Maker's shrine,
Ask if Heaven takes such offerings as thine!
If in thy bonds the son of Afric sighs,
Far higher than thy prayer his groan will rise!

God is a God of mercy, and would see
The prison-doors unbarr'd the bondmen free!
He is a God of truth, with purer eyes
Than to behold the oppressor's sacrifice!

Avarice, thy cry and thine insatiate thirst
Make man consent to see his brother cursed!
Tears, sweat and blood thou drink'st, but in
their turn,
They shall cry 'more!' while vengeance bids
thee burn

The Lord hath said it!—who shall him gainsay?
He says, 'the wicked, they shall go away'—
Who are the wicked?—Contradict who can,
They are the oppressors of their fellow man!

Aid me, NEW ENGLAND! 'tis my hope in you
Which gives me strength my purpose to pursue!
Do you not hear your sister States resound
With Afric's cries to have her sons unbound?

TO THE PUBLIC.

In the month of August, I issued proposals for publishing 'THE LIBERATOR' in Washington city; but the enterprise, though hailed in different sections of the country, was palsied by public indifference. Since that time, the removal of the Genius of Universal Emancipation to the Seat of Government has rendered less imperious the establishment of a similar periodical in that quarter.

During my recent tour for the purpose of exciting the minds of the people by a series of discourses on the subject of slavery, every place that I visited gave fresh evidence of the fact, that a greater revolution in public sentiment was to be effected in the free states—*and particularly in New-England*—than at the south. I found contempt more bitter, opposition more active, detraction more relent-

less, prejudice more stubborn, and apathy more frozen, than among slave owners themselves. Of course, there were individual exceptions to the contrary. This state of things afflicted, but did not dishearten me. I determined at every hazard, to lift up the standard of emancipation in the eyes of the nation, *within sight of Bunker Hill and in the birth place of liberty.* That standard is now unfurled; and long may it float, unhurt by the spoliations of time or the missiles of a desperate foe—yea, till every chain be broken, and every bondman set free! Let southern oppressors tremble—let their secret abettors tremble—let their northern apologists tremble—let all the enemies of the persecuted blacks tremble.

I deem the publication of my original prospectus * unnecessary, as it has obtained a wide circulation. The principles therein inculcated will be steadily pursued in this paper, regarding that I shall not array myself as the political partisan of any man. In defending the great cause of human rights, I wish to derive the assistance of all religions and of all parties.

Assenting to the 'self-evident truth' maintained in the American Declaration of Independence, 'that all men are created equal, and endowed by their Creator with certain inalienable rights—among which are life, liberty and the pursuit of happiness,' I shall strenuously contend for the immediate enfranchisement of our slave population. In Park-street Church, on the Fourth of July, 1829, in an address on slavery, I unreflectingly assented to the popular but pernicious doctrine of *gradual* abolition. I seize this opportunity to make a full and unequivocal recantation, and thus publicly to ask pardon of my God, of my country, and of my brethren the poor slaves, for having uttered a sentiment so full of timidity, injustice and absurdity. A similar recantation, from my pen, was published in the Genius of Universal Emancipation at Baltimore, in September, 1829. My conscience is now satisfied.

I am aware, that many object to the severity of my language; but is there not cause for severity? I *will* be as harsh as truth, and as uncompromising as justice. On this subject, I do not wish to think, or speak, or write, with moderation. No! no! Tell a man whose house is on fire, to give a moderate alarm; tell him to moderately rescue his wife from the hands of the ravisher; tell the mother to gradually extricate her babe from the fire into which it has fallen;—but urge me not to use moderation in a cause like the present. I am in earnest—I will not equivocate—I will not excuse—I will not retreat a single inch—AND I WILL BE HEARD. The apathy of the people is enough to make every statue leap from its pedestal, and to hasten the resurrection of the dead.

It is pretended, that I am retarding the cause of emancipation by the coarseness of my invective, and the precipitancy of my measures. *The charge is not true.* On this question my influence,—humble as it is,—is felt at this moment to a considerable extent, and shall be felt in coming years—not perniciously, but beneficially—not as a curse, but as a blessing; and posterity will bear testimony that I was right. I desire to thank God, that he enables me to disregard 'the fear of man which bringeth a snare,' and to speak his truth in its simplicity and power. And here I close with this fresh dedication:

'Oppression! I have seen thee, face to face,
And met thy cruel eye and cloudy brow;
But thy soul withering glance I fear not now—
For dread to prouder feelings doth give place
Of deep abhorrence! Scorning the disgrace
Of slavish knees that at thy footstool bow,
I also kneel—but with far other vow
Do hail thee and thy lord of hirelings base:—
I swear, while life-blood warms my throbbing veins,
Still to oppose and thwart, with heart and hand,
Thy brutalising sway—till Afric's chains
Are burst, and Freedom rules the rescued land,
Trampling Oppression and his iron rod:
Such is the vow I take—so HELP ME GOD!'

WILLIAM LLOYD GARRISON.

BOSTON, January 1, 1831.

DISTRICT OF COLUMBIA.

'What do many of the professed enemies of slavery mean, by heaping all their reproaches upon the south, and asserting that the crime of oppression is not national? What power but Congress—and Congress by the authority of the American people—has jurisdiction over the District of Columbia? That District is rotten with the plague, and stinks in the nostrils of the world. Though it is the Seat of our National Government,—open to the daily inspection of foreign ambassadors,—and ostensibly opulent with the congregated wisdom, virtue and intelligence of the land,—yet a fouler spot scarcely exists on earth. In it the worst features of slavery are exhibited; and as a mart for slave traders, it is unequalled. These facts are well known to our two or three hundred representatives, but no remedy is proposed; they are known, if not minutely at least generally, to our whole population,—but who calls for redress?

Hitherto, a few straggling petitions, relative to this subject, have gone into Congress; but they have been too few to denote much public anxiety, or to command a deferential notice. It is certainly time that a vigorous and systematic effort should be made, from one end of the country to the other, to pull down that national monument of oppression which towers up in the District. We do hope that the 'earthquake voice' of the people will this session shake the black fabric to its foundation.

The following petition is now circulating in this city, and has obtained several valuable signatures. A copy may be found at the Bookstore of LINCOLN & EDMANDS, No. 59, Washington-street, for a few days longer, where all the friends of the cause are earnestly invited to go and subscribe.

Petition to Congress for the Abolition of Slavery in the District of Columbia.

To the Honorable Senate and House of Representatives of the United States of America in Congress assembled, the petition of the undersigned citizens of Boston, in Massachusetts and its vicinity respectfully represents—

That your petitioners are deeply impressed with the evils arising from the existence of slavery in the District of Columbia. While our Declaration of Independence boldly proclaims as self-evident truths, 'that all men are created equal, that they are endowed by their Creator with certain inalienable rights, that among these are life, liberty, and the pursuit of happiness,'—at the very seat of government human beings are born, almost daily, whom the laws pronounce to be from their birth, not equal to other men, and who are, for life, deprived of *liberty* and the *free pursuit of happiness.* The inconsistency of the conduct of our nation with its political creed, has brought down upon it the just and severe reprehension of foreign nations.

In addition to the other evils flowing from slavery, both moral and political, which it is needless to specify, circumstances have rendered this District a common resort for traders in human flesh, who bring into it their captives in chains, and lodge them in places of confinement, previously to their being carried to the markets of the south and west.

From the small number of slaves in the District of Columbia, and the moderate proportion which they bear to the free population there, the difficulties, which in most of the slaveholding states oppose the restoration of this degraded class of men to their natural rights, do not exist.

Your petitioners therefore pray that Congress will, without delay, take such measures for the immediate and gradual abolition of Slavery in the District of Columbia, and for preventing the bringing of slaves into that District for purposes of traffic, in such mode, as may be thought advisable; and that suitable provision be made for the education of all free blacks and colored children in the District, thus to preserve them from continuing, even as free men, an unenlightened and degraded caste.

If any individual should be unmoved, either by the petition or the introductory remarks, the following article will startle his apathy, unless he be morally dead—dead—dead. Read it—read it! The language of the editor is remarkable for its energy, considering the quarter whence it emanates. After all, we are not the only fanatics in the land!

[From the Washington Spectator, of Dec. 4.]

THE SLAVE TRADE IN THE CAPITAL.

There dies the of father, husband, friend,
All bands of nature in that moment end,
And each volume, while yet he draws his breath,
At once as fatal as the scythe of death.
They lose in tears, the far receding shore,
But not the thought that they must meet no more !

It is well, perhaps, the American people should know, that while we reiterate our boasts of liberty in the cause of the nations, and send back across the Atlantic our shouts of joy at the triumph of liberty in France, we ourselves are busily engaged in the work of oppression. Yes, let it be known to the citizens of America, that at the very time when the procession which contained the President of the United States and his Cabinet was marching in triumph to the Capitol, to celebrate the victory of the French people over their oppressors, another kind of procession was marching another way, and that consisted of colored human beings, handcuffed in pairs and driven along by what had the appearance of a man on a horse! A similar scene was repeated on Saturday last; a drove consisting of males and females chained in couples, starting from Roby's corner on foot, for Alexandria, where, with others, they are to embark on board a slave-ship in waiting to convey them to the South. While we are writing, a colored man enters our room, and begs us to inform him if we can point out any person who will redeem his friend now immured in Alexandria jail, in a state of distress amounting almost to distraction. He has been a faithful servant of a revolutionary officer who recently died—has been sold at auction—parted from affectionate parents—and from decent and mourning friends. Our own servant, who, others, of whom we can speak in commendatory terms, went down to Alexandria to bid him farewell, but they were refused admission to his cell, as was said, 'the sight of his friends made him feel so.' He bears the reputation of a pious man. It is but a few weeks since we saw a ship with her cargo of slaves in the port of Norfolk, Va.; on passing up the river, saw another ship off Alexandria, swarming with the victims of human cupidity. Such are the scenes enacting in the heart of the American nation. Oh patriotism! where is thy indignation? Oh philanthropy! where is thy shame? THE SHAME, WHERE IS THY BLUSH? Well may the generous and noble minded O'Connell say of the American citizen, 'I tell him he is a hypocrite. Look at the stain in your star-spangled standard that was never struck down in battle. I turn from the Declaration of American Independence, and I tell him that he has declared to God and men a lie, and before God and man I arraign him as a hypocrite.' Yes, thou soul of fire, glorious O'Connell, if thou could but witness the spectacles in Washington that made the genius of liberty droop her head in shame, and weep her tears away in deep silence and undissembled sorrow, you would lift your voice even in tones of thunder, but you would make yourself heard. Where is the O'Connell of this republic that will plead for the EMANCIPATION OF THE DISTRICT OF COLUMBIA? These shocking scenes must cease from amongst us, or we must cease to call ourselves free, ay, and we must cease to expect the mercy of God—we must prepare for the coming judgment of Him who, as our charter acknowledges, made all men 'free and equal!'

* At the same time this man was sold, another—a husband—was knocked off. The tears and agonies of his wife made such an impression on the mind of a generous spectator that he bought him back.

When a premium of Fifty Dollars is offered for the best theatrical poem, our newspapers advertise the fact with great unanimity. The following is incomparably more important.

PREMIUM.

A Premium of Fifty Dollars, the Donation of a benevolent individual in the State of Maine, and now deposited with the Treasurer of the Pennsylvania Society for promoting the Abolition of Slavery, &c. is offered to the author of the best Treatise on the following subject: 'The Duties of Ministers and Churches of all denominations to avoid the stain of Slavery, and to make the holding of Slaves a barrier to communion and church membership.'

The composition to be directed (post paid) to either of the subscribers—the name of the author in a separate sealed paper, which will be destroyed if his work shall be rejected.

Six months from this date are allowed for the purpose of receiving the Essays.

The publication and circulation of the preferred Tract will be regulated by the Pennsylvania Society above mentioned.

W. RAWLE,
J. PRESTON, } Committee.
THOMAS SHIPLEY,

Philadelphia, Oct. 11.

First issue of *The Liberator*

Boston, Sept. 8, 1831.

Dear Sir:

I labor under very signal obligations to you for your disclosures, relative to my personal safety. These do not move me from my purpose the breadth of a hair. Desperate wretches exist at the south, no doubt, who would assassinate me for a sixpence. Still, I was aware of this peril when I begun my advocacy of African rights. Slaveholders deem me their enemy; but my aim is simply to benefit and save them, and not to injure them. I value their bodies and souls at a high price, though I abominate their crimes. Moreover, I do not justify the slaves in their rebellion: yet I do not condemn them, and applaud similar conduct in white men. I deny the right of any people to fight for liberty, and so far am a Quaker in principle. Of all men living, however, our slaves have the best reason to assert their rights by violent measures, inasmuch as they are more oppressed than others.

My duty is plain — my path without embarassment. I shall still continue to expose the criminality and danger of slavery, be the consequences what they may to myself. I hold my life at a cheap rate: I know it is in imminent danger: but if the assassin take it away, the Lord will raise up another and better advocate in my stead.

Again thanking you for your friendly letter, I remain, in haste,

Yours, in the best of bonds,

To La Roy Sunderland ~ Wm. Lloyd Garrison.

Letter 53

4 7

TO SIMEON S. JOCELYN

Boston, May 30, 18~~~

Rev. S. S. Jocelyn:

Beloved Coadjutor — I hasten to answer your very important and most interesting letter; [1] and the first thing in my preface shall be an apology for my delay in answering your former epistle. The truth is, I have been purposing, from day to day, ever since its arrival, to send you a long reply; but the cares of business and the deceptive promises of procrastination have defeated my intention.

The proposal to establish a College for our colored population, and the prospect of its being carried into effect, infuse new blood into my veins, and animate my heart. During my residence in Baltimore, the establishment of such an institution, on precisely the same plan as the one suggested in your letter, was an absorbing object of mine, and caused a great deal of conversation among the friends of emancipation. No systematic exertions were made, however, and consequently the scheme miscarried. I have now strong faith in the success of the enterprise: it can be, and *must be*, accomplished.

The offer made by Mr. Tappan is characteristic of his generosity.[2] What a faithful steward of the Lord! His heart is a perpetual fountain of benevolence, which waters the whole land — always flowing, and never diminishing. The way to lay up treasure in heaven is to disburse our earthly possessions in promotion of the cause of humanity and religion.

Although it has not been my privilege to see you, I have frequently heard of your disinterested and unremitted toils in behalf of the colored population of New-Haven. I can imagine the difficulties which must have towered in your path — the indifference, the neglect, the prejudice, which you must necessarily have encountered; but the victory is yours. A higher panegyric than mine awaits you: 'Well done, good and faithful servant — enter thou into the joy of thy Lord.' [3]

All things considered, the Liberator gets along bravely — already enumerating 500 voluntary subscribers. Most of these, however, are colored individuals. Our white people are shy of the paper; or rather they are indifferent to its object. Not more than twenty-five are subscribers in this city! This ill success is partly owing to colonization influence, which is directly and actively opposed to the Liberator.

You may expect me in New-Haven on Saturday, when we will commune with each other by word of mouth instead of the pen.

With high admiration and esteem, I remain,
    Your friend and fellow laborer until death,

Wm. Lloyd Garrison.

ALS: Yale University Library.
    Simeon S. Jocelyn (1799–1879) was, like his older brother, Nathaniel, an engraver by trade, but he was also the minister of a Negro church in New Haven. He and his brother were partners in the firm of N. & S. S. Jocelyn between 1818 and 1843, and subsequently were to be employed by various banknote engraving firms. In 1853, however, S. S. Jocelyn was to relinquish engraving and become secretary of the American Missionary Society and a full-time reformer.
    1. Dated May 28, 1831.
    2. Arthur Tappan (1786–1865) was a successful merchant who gave freely of his wealth to many philanthropic causes. In May of 1830, it was he who sent Garrison $100 to secure his release from prison. In the present instance, he had purchased land for the proposed Negro college. He had also offered to pay Garrison's expenses for the annual Convention of the Colored People of the United States, scheduled for June.
    Although at one time a member of the Colonization Society, by September 1831 he was urging Garrison to argue against that society and was supporting *The Liberator* with financial contributions. In 1833 he participated in the formation of both the New York and the American Anti-Slavery Societies and became the first president of those organizations. Tappan broke with Garrison in 1840 over the issues of woman's rights and political action. He was among those who seceded and formed the American and Foreign Anti-Slavery Society, the so-called New Organization, of which he was elected president. In 1863 he and Garrison were reconciled at a commemorative meeting.
    3. Garrison adapts Matthew 25:23.

48

TO *THE LIBERATOR*

Philadelphia, June 10, 1831.

I spent the Sabbath and a portion of Monday in New-Haven. Of Mr. Jocelyn, it would be difficult to speak in exaggerated terms. As a speaker, he is full of energy and power; his delivery is excellent, and his voice pleasant and sonorous. He has labored for the temporal and spiritual good of the colored people in that city, more than six years, comparatively without fee or reward; and it may now be said, that, as a body, in no place in the Union is their situation so comfortable, or the prejudices of community weaker against them. Sabbath afternoon, twelve colored persons were added to Mr. J's church. The scene was transcendently impressive. These were some of the blessed fruits of that glorious revival which is overspreading the land, and which is working with great power among all classes and denominations in New-Haven. So let it spread, till the kingdoms of this world become the kingdoms of our Lord and of his Christ.[1]

The site, selected for the location of the contemplated College, is one of the most beautiful spots I have ever seen. No other part of New-Haven can compare with it.

Only fifteen delegates, from five states, have assembled together, in consequence of the imperfect and limited notice which was given of the meeting. These delegates are remarkable for their gentlemanly appearance, and conduct their debates with great freedom, urbanity and talent. On Wednesday afternoon, Messrs. Tappan, Jocelyn and myself, addressed the Convention on the subject of the new College. A committee was appointed to consult with us, and to report forthwith to the Convention. Yesterday they reported favorably, and the whole day was consumed in an animated debate upon the report. Suffice it to say, all the delegates but one were in favor of the scheme. Some diversity of sentiment existed, as to the place of location; but a large majority, after hearing our reasons for giving a preference to New-Haven, coincided with us in opinion. The plan agreed to is, for the colored people to raise $10,000, and the whites to raise a similar sum. There are to be seven trustees of the College, (four of them colored) to be chosen by the subscribers to the institution.

Depend upon it, great things are in embryo. The colored people begin to feel their strength and to use it. The proceedings of this Convention, when published, (and I will send them on as soon as may be) will command the attention of the whole country, and operate upon the colored population with the power of electricity.[2] Whether or not the Convention will rise this week, is uncertain.

Printed: *The Liberator*, June 18, 1831. This letter may have been addressed to an individual; it is printed in *The Liberator* as *"Extracts of a letter from the Editor."*

1. Revelation 11:15.
2. The proceedings of this convention were apparently never published in the paper. Moreover, the proposal to found a colored college was rejected at a public meeting of citizens of New Haven; Garrison reported this "EXTRAORDINARY CONDUCT" in *The Liberator* for September 17, 1831.

49

TO EBENEZER DOLE

Boston, July 11, 1831.

Respected Friend:

On my return from Philadelphia, my disappointment was excessive on learning that you had just left our goodly city. To tell you how happy your presence would have made me, requires a higher language than the English tongue. As it is, I can only seize this opportunity to write a few poor, unsatisfactory words on paper, by which to express the hope that I may be enabled to see you in Hallowell, in the course of the ensuing autumn.

My worthy partner, Mr. Knapp, gives me a most exhilarating account of the intensity of your feelings, in regard to the awful condition of the poor slaves. Torn as is your feeling heart by a distant contemplation of their sufferings, how dreadful would be its agony, if you were an eye witness to the horrid scenes which are constantly occurring at the South? The infernal engine of African oppression is in perpetual motion — it has no weekly Sabbath; — and every day, hundreds of new-born victims are thrown under its wheels, and crushed. At times, I dare not gauge its atrocities, nor meditate upon its wickedness. The brain becomes heated with an intense fire, and the heart liquid as water. Yet there are those who can look upon this bloody system with "philosophic composure"! and even professing Christians can coldly talk of its *gradual* abolition! ay, and many of them are busy in denouncing me as a madman and fanatic, because I demand an immediate compliance with the requisitions of justice, and the precepts of our Lord Jesus Christ! — Yet, (to adopt the words of another) the thing I say is true. I speak the truth, though it is most lamentable. I dare not hide it, I dare not palliate it — else the horror with which it covereth me would make me do so. Woe unto such a system! Woe unto the men of this land who have been brought under its operation! It is not felt to be evil, it is not acknowledged to be evil, it is not preached against as evil; and therefore it is only the more inveterate and fearful an evil. *It hath become constitutional.* It is fed from the stream of our life, and it will grow more and more excessive, until it can no longer be endured by God, nor borne with by man.

But, dreadful as is the aspect of slavery in its cruelty to the outward man, it is heightened when we look at its effects upon the inward man. It is the ruin of souls which is most afflictive. The system is one not only of robbery, but of heathenism; for it is full of darkness, ignorance and wo.

I am truly rejoiced to learn that you are no colonizationist. I say rejoiced — because, after the most candid and prayerful investigation, I am persuaded the Colonization Society is based upon wrong principles; and, as for its leading doctrines, my judgment tells me they are abhorrent. Like many other good people, I was, myself, for a time deceived with regard to its character and tendency. I took the scheme upon trust; but my eyes are now open. I find, wherever I go, that thorough-going abolitionists do not support the Society. Great changes are taking place on this subject. The Society is fast losing many of its most worthy supporters; and by and by, I trust, none but slave owners will be found in its support. Among those who have left it, is Arthur Tappan, who is a host in himself.

The contemplated College for colored students, at New Haven, will doubtless receive your approbation. Such an institution, once fairly in operation, will work wonders.

You will be pleased to learn, that an American Anti-Slavery Society is in embryo at Philadelphia. Its objects will be various and energetic.

I find you have laid me under fresh obligations. I stagger beneath the weight of so much kindness, but hope I may be able to square the account.

I take the liberty of sending you two copies of my address, delivered in various cities before the free people of color.[1] May it be productive of good.

Probably, ere this, the Pennsylvania Society has transmitted to you copies of the tract which took your $50 premium. It was written by Evan Lewis, a member of the Society of Friends.[2] It is a very good production, but has not *scriptural pungency* enough. There were only four competitors for the prize. I was not able to be one of them, contrary to my intentions. Perhaps I may write a tract on this subject, as soon as leisure will permit.

I remain, your fellow laborer and debtor,

Wm Lloyd Garrison.

Typed transcript: Garrison Papers, Boston Public Library; extract printed in *Life*, I, 261.

1. In *The Liberator* for July 9, Garrison advertised as just published and for sale for 12½ cents this address which he had delivered in June in Philadelphia, New York, and other cities.

2. Evan Lewis (1782–1834) was the editor of the antislavery *Advocate of Truth*.

50

TO HENRY E. BENSON

Boston, July 30, 1831.

Dear Sir:

At the suggestion of my friend the Rev. Samuel J. May, I ventured to insert your name in the list of Agents for the Liberator; and I would now thank you for your acceptance of the appointment. If your colored population feel a single spark of the enthusiasm which is felt by their brethren elsewhere, in regard to the Liberator, they will subscribe with avidity. The colored people in Hartford, (only 500 in number,) have already subscribed for 50 copies! I am sure that your colored citizens, on learning the design of the paper — that it is to defend their rights and to liberate the slaves — and that it opposes their removal to Africa, will not be outdone in their zeal by those of any other place.

I shall also put Mr. Alfred Niger's name among the Agents, hoping he will consent to serve.[1] Agents are allowed for their trouble, one shilling (or 17 cts.) on every dollar collected. You and Mr. N. will please make your deductions accordingly.

I am anxious to put a copy of my Address to the Free People of Color, into the hands of every colored man, and shall therefore take the liberty to send you, by Tuesday morning's stage, 50 copies of the same.[2] From every copy sold, (at 12½ cts.) deduct 4 cents for yourself.

With a few exceptions, the moving and controlling incentives of the friends of African Colonization may be summed up in a single sentence: *they have an antipathy against the blacks.* They do not wish to admit them to an equality. They can tolerate them only as servants and slaves, but never as brethren and friends. They can love and benefit them four thousand miles off, but not at home. They profess to be, and really believe that they are, actuated by the most philanthropic motives; and yet are cherishing the most unmanly and unchristian prejudices. They tell us that we must always be hostile to the people of color, while they remain in this country. If this be so, then we had better burn our bibles, and our Declaration of Independence, and candidly acknowledge ourselves to be incorrigible tyrants and heathen.

The curse of our age is, men love popularity better than truth, and expediency better than justice. But they are bad calculators, and must ultimately suffer loss. It has always been my maxim — and I believe I have lived up to it — that truth can never conduce to mischief, and is best understood by plain words. I am for hitting the nail on its head; for calling things by their right names; for complying with the requisitions of justice, be the consequence[s] what they may.

Again thanking you for the interest you have manifested in the success of the Liberator, I remain,

                              Yours, truly,

                                                  Wm. Lloyd Garrison.

Henry E. Benson.

ALS: Garrison Papers, Boston Public Library.

Henry E. Benson (1814–1837), Helen's brother, was to become almost indispensable to Garrison not only as agent of *The Liberator* but later as secretary in the antislavery office in Boston. In 1834–1835 he became companion and secretary to British abolitionist George Thompson during his American tour. Henry Benson represented Garrison at many antislavery conventions, including the one in Providence in the subzero January of 1836. He died the following January, his final illness being the aftermath of a cold caught at the convention. Garrison pronounced him a victim on the altar of the antislavery cause.

1. Henry E. Benson's friend Alfred Niger did agree to serve as *The Liberator's* agent in Newport, Rhode Island.

2. Garrison refers to the same address as in letter 49, to Ebenezer Dole, July 11, 1831. In *The Liberator* for July 30, it was announced that the first edition of more than a thousand copies had been sold and a second one printed.

51

TO MESSRS. J. TELEMACHUS HILTON, ROBERT WOOD, AND J. H. HOW, *COMMITTEE*

BOSTON, AUGUST 13, 1831.

GENTLEMEN, —

There are occasions on which language fails to express our feelings, and the heart has no outlet for the tide of its emotions. Such is the present occasion, and such my condition. Sometimes, indeed, gratitude may be eloquent, but it is never loquacious. Conscious of the poverty of words, it has nothing to offer but tears.

For the flattering communication from a number of my colored citizens, politely conveyed to me through your hands as their Committee, you will please to return my most grateful acknowledgments, and to accept, for yourselves, the assurances of my personal esteem.[1]

Professions of disinterestedness and sincerity, in themselves, are worthless; yet, if I am not utterly deceived, I feel that in advocating your cause, I am actuated solely by a desire to achieve your complete emancipation, and to promote the happiness of my country. I trust I do not 'count my life dear unto me,'[2] but am ready, if the Lord require it, to lay it down for your sakes. For those who have committed the keeping of their souls unto a faithful Creator, the dungeon and the rack have no terrors. In the inspiring words of the poet:

'They never fail who die
In a great cause. The block may soak their gore;
Their heads may sodden in the sun; their limbs
Be strung to city gates and castle walls;
But still their spirit walks abroad!'[3]

That spirit cannot be slain. Like the wind, it may indeed be invisible to the eye; but, like the wind, it shall muster its energies from the four quarters of heaven, and overturn the strong towers of despotism, burying their haughty possessors in utter ruin.

'The martyr's blood's the seed of Freedom's tree.'[4]

I am well aware that the path which I am destined to tread, is full of briers and thorns. Foes are on my right hand and on my left. The tongue of detraction is busy against me. I have no communion with the world — the world none with me. The timid, the lukewarm, the base, affect to believe that my brains are disordered, and my words the ravings of a maniac. Even many of my friends — they who have grown up with me from my childhood — are transformed into scoffers and enemies. In view of these things, if sometimes nature groans and my spirits flag, I am instantly strengthened and confirmed in my purpose by the declaration of the Son of God — 'He that loveth father or mother more than me, is not worthy of me; and he that taketh not his cross, and followeth after me, is not worthy of me.' [5]

A communication like yours, gentlemen, (though the encomiums bestowed upon me, I fear, are partial and unmerited,) outweighs in consolation all the abuse which has been heaped upon me. Indeed, my poor services have been already vastly overpaid.

Nothing encourages me more, than to witness the singular unanimity which every where exists among my colored brethren; and to know that they look up to the press as the great instrument, under the blessing of God, of accomplishing their restoration. The liberal donation which they have made in this city, (transmitted by you, gentlemen, as their representatives,) for the support of the Liberator, is the best proof of the deep interest which is felt on this subject. No doubt our enemies are prophesying, and expecting, the downfal of the paper. How great will be their disappointment to find, that it is too permanently fixed in the affections of its patrons to be overthrown! — particularly to see it, (as I trust they will,) on the commencement of the second volume, dressed in a better garb and printed on a larger sheet, at the same price. This will be a triumph, my friends, worthy of our cause.

Let us, on no account, despair of a change in public sentiment. This is the age of great events, and *these are the days of liberty.* Amidst much darkness in our own land, there are many beams of light. Our enemies are growing less confident, and begin to 'hide their diminished heads.' [6] Our friends are multiplying; and if we but persevere and remain true to ourselves, looking to Him who alone is able to give us the victory, we shall soon see the most splendid results.

I am pleased to have an opportunity of bestowing a well-deserved eulogy upon my partner in business. [7] He is willing, for the love of the cause, to go through evil as well as good report; to endure privation, and abuse, and the loss of friends, so that he can put tyrants to shame and break the fetters of the slaves. He has been of essential service to me; and his loss would not be easily made up. He joins with me in returning expressions of gratitude for all the kindnesses bestowed by our colored brethren. We feel pledged to them for life.

It is our desire that the Committee should designate some places of public resort, where copies of the Liberator may be sent, to the amount of the donation. We would also beg them to accept one hundred copies of the Address to the Free People of Color, for distribution where they shall think proper.

Gentlemen, I feel that it is unnecessary for me to enlarge. My conclusion shall be in the words of a quaint writer: — 'Tis the *cause*, and not the *punishment*, that makes the *martyr*. 'Tis not the *what*, but the *why* of a man's suffering, which gives him the credit on 't. The virtue turns chiefly upon the *reason*, not upon the *pain*. He only is the brave man that mortifies upon principle; that chooses rather to suffer than to misbehave himself; and runs through all discouragments upon the score of conscience and honor.[8]

You will please to lay this letter before your constituents; and believe me I shall remain until death,

Your devoted and grateful servant,

WM. LLOYD GARRISON.

Printed: *The Liberator*, August 27, 1831, with an editorial explanation that Garrison is printing this letter at the request of the recipients, even though it was not intended for publication.

John Telemachus Hilton, Robert Wood, and J. H. How were leaders among Garrison's free colored supporters in Boston. The most prominent was Hilton (c. 1803–1865), who had been an active abolitionist as early as 1830, when he was a delegate to the National Negro Convention in Philadelphia. A hairdresser by profession, in 1835 he became president of the Liberator Aiding Association. Robert Wood, according to advertisements in *The Liberator*, opened a boarding house in Boston in 1832. J. H. How is probably the James H. Howe listed in the Boston directory for 1831 as a renovator of human hair.

1 The "flattering communication" was a long letter to *The Liberator*, dated August 7, 1831, grouping Garrison with Clarkson and Wilberforce as champions of the slave. The letter, which Garrison described as containing "a generous and seasonable donation, contributed towards the support of the Liberator," was printed in the issue for August 20.

2. Acts 20:24.

3. Byron, *Marino Faliero*, II, ii, 93–97.

4. Garrison adapts Thomas Campbell's "To the Memory of the Spanish Patriots," line 13, substituting the word "martyr's" for "patriot's."

5. Matthew 10:37–38, with an ellipsis.

6. Milton, *Paradise Lost*, IV, 34.

7. Isaac Knapp.

8. It is difficult to determine the source of the maxims to which Garrison alludes. The "quaint writer" could conceivably be one of the seventeenth-century English divines Thomas Fuller or Samuel Torshell, both of whom express similar maxims. (See the former's *The Hypocrite Discovered*, Part I, chapter 12, and the latter's *Church History of Britain*, Book X, chapter 4.) Or it could be Napoleon's surgeon Barry E. O'Meara, whose *Napoleon in Exile* (containing the same basic maxim) would have been more readily available to Garrison, since it was reprinted in Philadelphia in 1822.

52

TO HENRY E. BENSON

Boston, Aug. 29, 1831.

My Dear Friend:

I have had the pleasure of taking your brother by the hand, and of holding an interesting *tete-a-tete* with him on the subject of slavery.[1] My only regret is, on account of his short tarry, which has prevented me from paying him that attention which would be desirable. He is, I am glad to find, sound in the faith, not having in the least degenerated from his parent stock. Would to Heaven there were a host of such men enlisted in the glorious cause of universal emancipation! But we shall muster an army, by and by. The cause of freedom is onward; and the day is not far distant, I trust, when a black skin will not be merely endurable, but *popular*. For, be assured, favors are to be heaped, in due time, upon our colored countrymen, as thickly as have been sorrow and abuse. I have no despondency — no doubt: the triumph of truth is as sure as the light of heaven.

I wish that the colored people of Providence,[2] if they feel on the subject as their brethren do elsewhere — and I presume they do — would immediately call a public meeting, and express their disapprobation of the colonization scheme. Safety and self-respect require this measure at their hands. Now is the time for the people of color to act — fearlessly, firmly, understandingly.

My principal object, in this hasty epistle, is to give you, or Mr. Niger, a little trouble, which I shall be glad to cancel by incurring double the amount on your own behalf. Every Friday evening — or, rather, Saturday morning — I send a bundle of Liberators to Providence by the stage, directed to the care of "Philip A. Bell, 73, Chamber-street, New-York City."[3] This bundle, I fear, instead of being immediately put on board of the steam-boat, is often delayed a day or more. As it contain[s] papers for all the subscribers in New-York and Philadelphia, a delay of this kind makes them feverish. Now if the steward or one of the colored helps on board of the steam-boat which sails on Saturday, would see that this bundle were regularly put on board, it would confer a great favor. For his trouble, he shall receive a copy of the paper, or whatever recompense he may demand. The bundle, at present, goes with great irregularity.

When shall I have the pleasure of seeing you in Boston? Perhaps I may visit Providence in all September, for the purpose of delivering some addresses on slavery.

This letter has been written in a tremendous hurry, as your brother leaves in a few minutes — so pray excuse it.

I shall be glad to improve every opportunity to assure you how much I appreciate your kindness, and to subscribe myself

Your friend and brother,

Wm. Lloyd Garrison.

ALS: Garrison Papers, Boston Public Library; printed partly in *Life*, I, 274–275.

1. George W. Benson (1808–1879), older brother of Henry E. Benson and Garrison's future brother-in-law, was a Providence wool merchant and partner of William M. Chace. He was to remain Garrison's staunch friend and loyal supporter during the vicissitudes of the antislavery struggle.

2. "Hartford" is written in Garrison's hand, but it has been crossed out and "Providence" supplied above the line in another hand.

3. Philip A. Bell (died c. 1860), a Negro, is listed in New York directories as "Agent" and subsequently as "Intelligence"; his name does not appear after 1860.

53

TO LA ROY SUNDERLAND

Boston, Sept. 8, 1831.

Dear Sir:

I labor under very signal obligations to you for your disclosures, relative to my personal safety. These do not move me from my purpose the breadth of a hair. Desperate wretches exist at the south, no doubt, who would assassinate me for a sixpence. Still, I was aware of this peril when I began my advocacy of African rights. Slaveholders deem me their enemy; but my aim is simply to benefit and save them, and not to injure them. I value their bodies and souls at a high price, though I abominate their crimes. Moreover, I do not justify the slaves in their rebellion: yet I do not condemn *them*, and applaud similar conduct in *white men*. I deny the right of any people to fight for liberty, and so far am a Quaker in principle. Of all men living, however, our slaves have the best reason to assert their rights by violent measures, inasmuch as they are more oppressed than others.

My duty is plain — my path without embarrassment. I shall still continue to expose the criminality and danger of slavery, be the consequences what they may to myself. I hold my life at a cheap rate: I know it is in imminent danger: but if the assassin take it away, the Lord will raise up another and better advocate in my stead.

Again thanking you for your friendly letter, I remain, in haste,

Yours, in the best of bonds,

Wm. Lloyd Garrison.

To La Roy Sunderland

ALS: Garrison Papers, Boston Public Library; printed in *The Liberator*, September 18, 1857.

La Roy Sunderland (1804–1885) was by the date of this letter known as an eloquent revivalist preacher as well as a leading abolitionist. On Monday, September 5, 1831, Garrison received from Sunderland a letter reporting the conversation that he had had with several passengers on the stage from Andover to Boston, to the effect that Garrison's life was in grave danger because it was thought, quite falsely, that he "had contributed in no small degree to" the Nat Turner insurrection of the preceding month. For the text of Sunderland's letter see *The Liberator*, September 10, 1831. Garrison's letter was not made public until 1857, when Sunderland sent it to J. B. Yerrington, then printer of *The Liberator*.

54

TO JOSEPH GALES AND WILLIAM W. SEATON

[c. September 23, 1831.][1]

GENTLEMEN —

The dignity of your station, the extent of your influence, and the established fairness of your characters, give you a claim to my notice, which a multitude of editorial assailants fail to present.

A late number of the National Intelligencer contains a libellous article relative to the Liberator, copied from the Tarborough (N.C.) Free Press, together with the following extract of a letter from 'a gentleman' in Washington City to a Post Master in North Carolina:

'An incendiary paper, "The Liberator," is circulated openly among the free blacks of this city; and if you will search, it is very probable you will find it among the slaves of your county. It is published in Boston or Philadelphia, by a white man, with the avowed purpose of inciting rebellion in the South; and I am informed, is to be carried through your county by secret agents, who are to come amongst you under the pretext of pedling, &c. Keep a sharp look out for these villains, and if you catch them, by all that is sacred, you ought to barbacue them. Diffuse this information among whom it may concern.' [2]

To the above quotation you append some confirmatory remarks, which, I regret to say, breathe the spirit of murder and exhibit the incoherency of madness. Suffer me first to notice the Washington letter writer.

This anonymous traducer is uncertain whether the Liberator is published in Boston or Philadelphia. A most intelligent critic! [3] Probably he has never perused a single number: if otherwise, he is guilty of uttering as black and wanton a falsehood as human depravity can invent. He unblushingly declares, that the '*avowed purpose*' of the paper is to 'incite rebellion in the South.' I appeal to God, whom I fear and serve, and to its patrons, in proof that its *real* and *only* purpose is to *prevent* rebellion, by the application of those preservative principles which breath *peace on earth — good will to men.* I advance nothing more, I stand on no other foundation, than this: 'Whatsoever ye would that men should do to you, *do ye even so to them.*' [4] I urge the immediate abolition of slavery, not only because the slaves possess an inalienable right to liberty, but because the system, to borrow the words of Mr. Randolph, is 'a volcano in full operation;' [5] and, by its continuance, we must expect a national explosion. So far from advocating resistance on the part of the slaves, (though they would be justified in using retaliatory measures more than any people on the face of the earth,) every one, who is familiar with my public or private opinions, knows that I expressly maintain the criminality of war. You, Gentlemen, cannot be ignorant on this point. In the Prospectus of the Liberator, which was published in the columns of the Intelligencer, occurs the following paragraph:

'The cause of PEACE will obtain my zealous and unequivocal support. My creed, as already published to the world, is as follows: — That war is fruitful in crime, misery, revenge, murder, and every thing abominable and bloody — and, whether offensive or *defensive,* is contrary to the precepts and example of Jesus Christ, and to the heavenly spirit of the gospel; consequently, that no professor of Christianity should march to the battle-field, or murder any of his brethren for the glory of his country.' [6]

The charge of the Washington libeller, respecting the circulation of the Liberator by 'secret agents,' is as silly as it is false. The paper courts the light, and not darkness. Every slaveholder ought to become a subscriber to it forthwith: he may thereby learn his duty, and perhaps be induced to follow it. Unfortunately I have not a single subscriber, white or black, *south of the Potomac.*

The recommendation to *'barbacue'* (murder and roast, I suppose) those at the south who are seen with copies of the Liberator, could come only from a cowardly assassin. [7] The author of it, I presume, is steeped to his lips in the blood of his slaves, and cherishes the unquenchable thirst of a cannibal.

And now, Gentlemen, I turn to your 'REMARKS.' [8] You hastily and most unjustly style the Liberator an 'incendiary publication,' 'a diabolical paper, INTENDED BY ITS AUTHOR to lead to precisely such results (as concerns the whites) as the Southampton Tragedy.' [9] You accuse me of being 'the instigator of human butchery,' 'a deluded fanatic or mercenary miscreant,' a cut-throat, &c. &c. To publish and circulate such a paper is, in your view, a 'CRIME AS GREAT AS THAT OF POISON-ING THE WATERS OF LIFE TO A WHOLE COMMUNITY'!!! Sirs, these allegations disclose the spirit of murder in your breasts, (if I understand the meaning of language,) but I pity and forgive you.

It is true, you affect to 'desire not to have me unlawfully dealt with,' *yet represent me in such a fearful light as to point a thousand daggers at my heart,* and *encourage a host of assassins.* If I fall a victim in the glorious cause of emancipation, my blood shall be required at your hands.

Your 'appeal to the worthy Mayor of the City of Boston,' and to 'the intelligent Legislators of Massachusetts,' to interpose their authority, and prevent the publication of the Liberator, is so ineffably ridiculous that I may justly term it *the incoherency of madness.* Sirs, tyrants and slaves may exist at the South, but they are unknown in New-England. *Nullification* is the offspring of despotism. Suppress the paper, forsooth! And why? Because it contends that 'all men are created equal, and endowed by their Creator with certain inalienable rights; among which are life, LIBERTY, and the pursuit of happiness.' Congress, therefore, ought to erase that dangerous clause from the Declaration of Independence. The paper declares that God 'has made of *one blood* all nations of men to dwell on all the face of the earth;' but we must so amend our bibles as to make the passage read, 'God has made of one blood *all southern planters,*' &c. (though the great body of them seem to be enamored of *amalgamation.*)

In my Prospectus which you unhesitatingly published, I assumed as self-evident truths — That no man can have a right over others, unless it be by them granted to him — That that which is not just, is not law; and that which is not law, ought not to be in force — That whosoever grounds his pretensions of right upon usurpation and tyranny, declares himself to be an usurper and a tyrant — that is, an enemy to God and man — and to have no right at all — that that which was unjust in its beginning, can of itself never change its nature — That he who persists in doing injustice, aggravates it, and takes upon himself all the guilt of his predecessors — That there is no safety where there is no strength, no strength without union, no union without justice, no justice where faith and truth are wanting — That the right to be free is a truth planted in the hearts of men, and acknowledged so to be by all who have hearkened to the voice of nature, and denied by none but such as through wickedness, stupidity, or baseness of spirit, seem to have degenerated into the worst of beasts, and to have retained nothing of men but the outward shape, or the ability of doing those mischiefs which they have learnt from their master the devil.

From the foregoing simple, comprehensive, irrefutable principles, the Liberator has never departed. Its objects are to save life, not to destroy it; to overthrow — by moral power, by truth and reason — a system which has no redeeming feature, but is full of blood — the blood of innocent men, women and babes — full of adultery and concupiscence — full of blasphemy, darkness and wo — full of rebellion against God, and treason against the universe — full of wounds and bruises and putrefying sores — full of temporal suffering and eternal damnation — full of wrath, and impurity, and ignorance, and brutality, and awful impiety; to make the slave States as happy and prosperous as the free States; to extract a root of bitterness, which is poisoning the whole nation; to preserve the Union by removing an evil, which, if suffered to grow, must inevitably produce a separation of the States; to elevate and improve the bodies and souls of millions of our fellow beings, who can never be educated while they remain in servitude; to increase the wealth of the South, alleviate its sufferings, remove its fears, increase its population, improve its agriculture, enlighten its ignorance, exalt its piety, and redeem its character! Are not these objects benevolent, praiseworthy, magnanimous? Would 'a mercenary miscreant' sustain them at the imminent risk of his life?

Sirs, the present generation cannot appreciate the purity of my motives or the value of my exertions. I look to posterity for a good reputation. The unborn offspring of those who are now living will reverse the condemnatory decision of my contemporaries. Without presuming to rank myself among them, I do not forget that those reformers who were formerly treated as the 'offscouring of the earth,' [10] are now lauded beyond measure; I do not forget that Christ and his apostles, — harmless, undefiled and prudent as they were, — were buffetted, calumniated and crucified; and therefore my soul is as steady to its pursuit as the needle to the pole. No dangers shall deter me. At the North or the South, at the East or the West, — wherever Providence may call me, — my voice shall be heard in behalf of the perishing slave, and against the claims of his oppressor.

I am for immediate and total abolition. The law of God and the welfare of man require it. This doctrine is at present unpopular in this country; and he who maintains it is ranked among madmen and fanatics. It is otherwise in England. The doctrine is maintained by Wilberforce, and Clarkson, and Brougham, and McCauly, and Buxton, and Lushington, and Stephen, and O'Connell, and a host of other *disorganizers.*[11] Shall I be ashamed of their company? They do not believe, nor do I, that 'moderation in arranging robbery and murder may be very proper and useful.' 'Are we then fanatics, are we enthusiasts, because we cry, *Do not rob! do not murder!*'

If we would not see our land deluged in blood, we must instantly burst asunder the shackles of the slaves — treat them as rational and injured beings — give them lands to cultivate, and the means of employment — and multiply schools for the instruction of themselves and children. We shall then have little to fear. The wildest beasts may be subdued and rendered gentle by kind treatment. Make the slaves free, and every inducement to revolt is taken away. It is only while we are crushing them to the earth, and heaping our curses and our blows upon them, and starving their bodies, and darkening their souls, and selling them as beasts, and goading them to desperation, that we have reason to tremble for our safety, and to feel an unpleasant sensation with regard to our throats.

Tell me not that an evil is cured by covering it up; that it is dangerous to vindicate the rights of the slaves; that if nothing be said, more will be done; and that no adequate remedy can be found. The reasoning is absurd. Is not justice a practical matter? Is humanity, is mercy, a poetic fiction? Is there not a blessed reality in freedom? If every slaveholder would but reform himself, there would be an end of slavery. Great efforts must precede great achievements.

You appeal, Gentlemen, to the people of New-England, to sustain the system of slavery! — 'Dough faces' we have among us, and men lost to every honorable feeling — time-servers, apologists, traitors and cowards; but think not that the great body of the descendants of the Pilgrims sanction southern oppression. Criminal, indeed, they have been in their conduct, and awfully remiss in the discharge of their duty; but a mighty change is taking place in their sentiments. They cherish no hostility to the south; they are ready to give not only their advice but their money towards emancipating the slaves; but they feel that they cannot longer passively remain constitutionally involved in the guilt and danger of slavery. They have a right to be heard: they must and will be heard. If the bodies and souls of millions of rational beings must be sacrificed as the price of the Union, better, far better, that a separation should take place.

I see through the design of the clamor which is raised against the Liberator. It is to prevent public indignation from resting upon the system of slavery, and to concentrate it upon my own head. *That system contains the materials of self-destruction*; yet such is the brazen impudence of its supporters, that they do not hesitate to ascribe the insurrection to a foreign and an impossible cause. What I have published in the Liberator, allow me to repeat here.[12]

Ye patriotic hypocrites! ye panegyrists of Frenchmen, Greeks, and Poles! ye fustian declaimers for liberty! ye valiant sticklers for equal rights among yourselves! ye haters of aristocracy! ye assailants of monarchies! ye republican nullifiers! ye treasonable disunionists! be dumb! Cast no reproach upon the conduct of the slaves, but let your lips and cheeks wear the blisters of condemnation!

Ye accuse the pacific friends of emancipation of instigating the slaves to revolt. Take back the charge as a foul slander. The slaves need no incentives at our hands. They will find them in their stripes — in their emaciated bodies — in their ceaseless toil — in their ignorant minds — in every field, in every valley, on every hill-top and mountain, wherever you and your fathers have fought for liberty — in your speeches, your conversations, your celebrations, your pamphlets, your newspapers — voices in the air, sounds from across the ocean, invitations to resistance above, below, around them! What more do they need? Surrounded by such influences, and smarting under their newly made wounds, is it wonderful that they should rise to contend — as other 'heroes' have contended — for their lost rights? It is *not* wonderful.

What kindled the fire of Seventy-Six? Oppression! What created the bloody scenes at St. Domingo? Oppression! What roused up the Greeks to revenge? Oppression! What caused the recent revolution in France? Oppression! What has driven the Poles to arms? Oppression! What has infuriated the southern slaves? OPPRESSION!

A few queries, and I have done.

Can man justly be the property of man?

What does this mean? — 'All men are created equal, and endowed by their Creator with certain inalienable rights: among which are life, liberty, and the pursuit of happiness?'

Are the Poles justified in fighting for liberty? and why?

By what authority do *you*, Gentlemen, hold your fellow creatures in bondage?

In conclusion, I adopt the frank avowal of the excellent Wilberforce: — 'I can admit of no compromise when the commands of equity and philanthropy are so imperious. I wash my hands of the blood that will be spilled. I protest against the system, as the most flagrant violation of every principle of justice and humanity: I NEVER WILL DESERT THE CAUSE. In my task it is impossible to tire; it fills my mind with complacency and peace. At night I lie down with composure, and rise to it in the morning with alacrity. I never will desist from this blessed work.' [13]

Protracted as is this defence, I trust you will give it a place in your columns; and that those editors who have copied your article, will do me the justice to copy mine. You have (I hope unintentionally) calumniated my character, and put my life in jeopardy. The public has a right to expect my defence, and it ought to be given.

Respectfully, yours, &c. &c.

WM. LLOYD GARRISON.

Printed: *The Liberator*, October 15, 1831; extracts printed in *Life*, I, 238–239.

Although Joseph Gales (1786–1860) and William W. Seaton (1785–1866) were of contrasting backgrounds (Gales being a recent immigrant from England and Seaton of aristocratic Virginia family with seventeenth-century background), they became brothers-in-law and associate editors of the *Daily National Intelligencer*, an outstanding Washington paper. They both distinguished themselves as congressional reporters, Gales specializing in the House and Seaton, the Senate. They edited in some fifty-six volumes the official congressional proceedings and the register of debates. Both men wrote editorials for their paper, expressing a variety of opinions on politics and reform. Both served terms as mayor of Washington. Finally — and most significant from Garrison's point of view — both supported the American Colonization Society. Gales and Seaton did not print Garrison's letter in their paper.

1. The editors of the *National Intelligencer* mentioned in their issue for September 28 that they have just received from Garrison what was evidently this letter. Since in 1831 it took four or five days for mail to travel from Boston to Washington, it would seem likely that Garrison wrote this letter about September 23.

2. Garrison quotes this paragraph from the *National Intelligencer* of September 15; his quotation is accurate except for the change of "amongst" to "among."

3. Garrison was stung by the suggestion that his paper was little known. He said in *The Liberator* of October 8: "The tread of the youthful Liberator already shakes the nation."

4. Matthew 7:12.

5. See Gales and Seaton's *Register of Debates in Congress* (Nineteenth Congress, first session), II, 117. John Randolph, in fact, deplored the institution of slavery, although he was a leading defender of state's rights.

6. Garrison quotes part of a paragraph from "Proposals for Publishing a Weekly Periodical in Washington City, to be Entitled the Public Liberator and Journal of the Times," which he had issued in August 1830. It appeared in the *National Intelligencer*, August 27, 1830.

7. There was at this time a considerable fear that the free circulation of *The Liberator* in the South would encourage insurrection. According to the Charleston (South Carolina) *Mercury* of October 4, 1831, for instance, the Vigilance Association of Columbia offered $1,500 for the conviction of any white man caught circulating that paper or any other seditious publication (see *Life*, I, 240).

8. Garrison refers to the editorial comments printed on September 15 along with the paragraph about *The Liberator* from the Tarborough *Free Press*. In this editorial Gales and Seaton write in general about "the incendiary publications which are *intended by their authors* to lead to precisely such results . . . as the Southampton Tragedy" rather than writing specifically about *The Liberator*. But they do seem to refer to Garrison in the following passage: "We know nothing of the man: we desire not to have him unlawfully dealt with: we can even conceive of his motive being good in his own opinion . . ." They also appeal to Harrison Gray Otis, the mayor of Boston, and especially to public opinion: "Surely, surely, if the Courts of Law have no power, public opinion has, to interfere, until the intelligent Legislators of Massachusetts can provide a durable remedy for this most appalling grievance." Governor James Hamilton of South Carolina also sent an appeal to the mayor. Otis apparently knew little or nothing of *The Liberator* but concluded upon investigation that the paper had few subscribers and little influence.

9. The reference is to the uprising in Southampton County, Virginia, led by a semieducated slave named Nat Turner (1800–1831). On August 21 Turner, who thought himself chosen for a holy mission, led a small band of Negroes against the white population of the county, killing and mutilating more than fifty. Six weeks later Turner and sixteen followers were executed.

10. Perhaps adapted from I Corinthians 4:13.

11. Garrison lists eight of the most distinguished of British abolitionists, of which only Lord Brougham has been identified in a previous note. William Wilberforce (1759–1833) and Thomas Clarkson (1760–1846), both Cambridge men,

both members of Parliament, and both members of an important antislavery committee as early as 1787, were fearless, dedicated, and determined men, who concentrated first on the elimination of the slave trade and then on emancipation. Wilberforce was the man of action, a dynamic and astute politician, who worked closely with the younger William Pitt, and fought assiduously in Parliament for abolition; Clarkson was the scholarly abolitionist, the author of many pamphlets and books influential in the cause.

Zachary Macaulay (1768–1838), whose name Garrison misspells, was the father of the historian and one of the most ardent and unselfish of early reformers. His dedication to abolition was based upon direct experience: he worked on a plantation in Jamaica and was for seven years governor of Sierra Leone. He was the editor of the antislavery *Christian Observer* and was one of the founders of the Anti-Slavery Society in 1823.

Sir Thomas Fowell Buxton (1786–1845) was an English Quaker reformer, who, owing to Wilberforce's ill health, became after 1824 the leading English abolitionist, the one who was to guide the emancipation bill through Parliament.

Stephen Lushington (1782–1873) was one of the most distinguished lawyers and judges of the day. Among his clients were no less personages than Lady Byron and Queen Charlotte. By the time of Garrison's letter, he was judge of the London consistory court, and he was later to become judge of the high court of admiralty as well as a member of the Privy Council. Lushington was also a conscientious reformer, who sought the abolition of capital punishment, of the church rates, and of slavery. As an abolitionist he steadily supported and advised Buxton.

Sir George Stephen (1794–1879) was a successful attorney, whose service for the cause of abolition in the West Indies was rewarded by a knighthood. He was also the author of a number of humorous and popular books and of many impressive speeches, some of which were printed in *The Liberator* (see, for instance, the issue of July 11, 1835).

Daniel O'Connell (1775–1847) was a brilliant lawyer by profession and for years the dominant power in Irish political life. He was a staunch advocate of emancipation of the slaves and of repeal of the union with England.

12. Garrison quotes two paragraphs from an editorial on Nat Turner's insurrection, *The Liberator*, September 3, 1831.

13. Garrison quotes directly from his own quotation of Wilberforce in *Thoughts on African Colonization* (pp. 8 9), using even the same introductory phrase "the frank avowal of the excellent Wilberforce."

55

TO HENRY E. BENSON

Boston, Sept. 26, 1831.

My dear Sir:

I owe you a great debt, and many thanks, for your interesting letter, which was duly received and perused with avidity. Nevertheless, I wish to add to the score of my obligations.

You have had an unexampled riot at Providence — unexampled, at least, in New-England.[1] As it will hardly be possible to obtain the facts from the newspapers as they really occurred, I beg you to favor me, by Wednesday,[2] with replies to the following questions:

Who were the originators of the disturbance — the sailors or the blacks?

Were the sailors seeking an illicit intercourse with the blacks?

What was the *cause* of the riot?

How many houses occupied by colored people have been injured? how many destroyed?

What are the feelings of a majority of the inhabitants towards the blacks?

How many were killed and wounded?

Any additional information will be thankfully received.

These are perilous times, my dear friend, especially for the people of color. So infuriated are the whites against them, since the Virginia and North Carolina insurrections, that the most trifling causes may lead to a war of extermination.[3] Bloody scenes, I fear, are in reserve for our vision; but I pray God that the late events may be overruled for good.

Perhaps the colored people in Providence were entirely to blame — perhaps partially so, or entirely innocent. No doubt they will be deeply implicated, whether innocent or guilty. I wish to know the truth — nothing more. Shall I hear from you on Wednesday?

In great haste, I remain,

Yours, truly,

Wm. Lloyd Garrison.

ALS: Garrison Papers, Boston Public Library.

1. The riot was apparently started by a dozen sailors on the night of Wednesday, September 21, when they cruised through the Negro red-light district looking for excitement. Exchanges of rocks and rifle bullets, between them and the Negro inhabitants, resulted in the death of one white man. The climax came on the twenty-fourth, when the governor called in the militia, and four people in the mob were killed (*The Liberator*, October 8, 1831).

2. September 28.

3. Garrison refers to Nat Turner's insurrection in Virginia and to a supposed massacre in Wilmington, North Carolina. The latter was reported in *The Liberator* September 24 and in the issue for October 1 was described as a fabrication.

56

TO HENRY E. BENSON

Boston, Oct. 19, 1831.

Dear Friend:

Permit me to introduce to you my worthy friend Mr. Joshua Coffin, whom you will find an agreeable and intelligent person.[1] He is a warm friend of the anti-slavery cause, and has correct views relative to the

Colonization Society. He is about opening a school in this city for the instruction of free colored persons, and I have no doubt will be very successful.

I tender you my thanks for your prompt reply to my last letter. As, however, the Committee of your town published a more circumstantial account of the unhappy affair, I deemed it best to give that account an insertion.

The disturbances at the South still continue. The Liberator is causing the most extraordinary movements in the slave States among the whites, as you are doubtless already aware. I am constantly receiving anonymous letters, filled with abominable and bloody sentiments. These trouble me less than the wind. I never was so happy and confident in my mind as at the present time.

The slaveholders are evidently given over to destruction. They are determined to shut out the light — to hear none of the appeals of justice and humanity. I shudder when I contemplate their fate.

Did time permit, I would fill my sheet, but an engagement prevents. Again returning you my acknowledgments for your disinterested acts of kindness, I remain,

Yours, in brotherly bonds,

Wm. Lloyd Garrison.

ALS: Garrison Papers, Boston Public Library; printed partly in *Life*, I, 275.

1. Joshua Coffin (1792–1864) was a fat, good-humored man of forty, the Falstaff of the abolitionists. He was a teacher, an antiquarian, and a historian.

---

5 7

TO HENRY E. BENSON

Boston, Nov. 12, 1831.

My dear Friend:

Your letter of the 1st inst. was very gratifying to my feelings. In the first place, it conveyed to my ears "A Voice from Providence," against the Colonization Society, which I have long been wanting to hear. Secondly, it was a fresh witness of your benevolent zeal in the cause of truth and liberty. Thirdly, it contained something very much to cheer my heart in the statement that a change for the better was taking place in public sentiment at Providence. — Fourthly, it gave me a kind and urgent invitation to visit Providence, and expressed the interest which many of my friends felt to see and hear me.

I am sorry that I can give you in return only a few lines which are destitute of thought and distinguished for bad penmanship, (for I write in haste,) — but so it is. A week's hard labor has just closed, and my mind is too much exhausted for mental effort, and my body too jaded to be serviceable. My correspondence is necessarily extensive and onerous: pen, ink and paper throw me into a kind of intellectual hydrophobia, and so I avoid them as much as possible.

I do exceedingly regret to state, that the pressure of imperious duties will in all probability prevent me visiting your beautiful town the present season. If my health be preserved until the ensuing spring, I shall endeavor to see you without fail.

I have now received from Washington, complete files of the African Repository, and shall for some time be busy in preparing my anti-colonization pamphlet for the press.[1] I am also about to prepare an address to be delivered before the colored people of this city.

You may soon expect to hear of the formation of an anti-slavery Society in this city, on principles steadfast as the pillars of truth. There are some stanch abolitionists here, who are ready for action, and whom no dangers or scoffs can frighten. We can do comparatively little without a concentration of moral strength. With physical force we have, you know, nothing to do.

Be good enough to say to Friend Simeon Brewer, that he may expect to receive a letter from me in the course of all next week.[2] From what I hear of him, he is a sterling reformer, for whom I entertain the warmest attachment. I return him my very grateful thanks for the shelter which he offers me under his hospitable roof.

You will perceive by the Liberator that the people of the slave States are proceeding from one extremity to another. Instead of repenting of their evil doings, their conduct towards the slaves and free people of color grows worse and worse. The Lord have mercy upon our guilty land.

Mr. Knapp and my friend Coffin [3] send their respects to you and your brother. You will both accept the assurances of my regard, ever remaining,

Yours, truly,

Wm. Lloyd Garrison.

ALS: Garrison Papers, Boston Public Library; extract printed in *Life*, I, 223.

1. The *African Repository*, published in Washington, was the official organ of the American Colonization Society.
2. Simeon Brewer (1782–1832), according to Providence directories, had owned a hat store since 1824.
3. Joshua Coffin.

5 8

TO JOHN QUINCY ADAMS

Boston, [January 21, 1832].

SIR —

Perhaps no man has had warmer political friends, or more active political enemies, than yourself. Your signal overthrow, on your second nomination for the Presidency, served to attach the former more closely to your person, and to blunt the animosity of the latter. A great fall may, from its startling fatality, not only assuage the bitterness of party spirit, but even excite its sympathy. Few, it is believed, cherished feelings of regret at your election as a Representative in Congress; the many, among all parties, found in it a proud commentary upon our republican institutions; none doubted the towering ascendency of your abilities. Not only was our vanity gratified by the prospect of being represented on the floor of Congress by an ex-president of the United States, but we felt that our reputation and interest were placed in security. The political sky of the nation, red with fiery portents, warned us to be ready for an extraordinary crisis. We saw cloud after cloud blackening from the horizon to the zenith, and heard the distant roar of the angry thunder. These admonitions were not lost upon us. We felt that the hour had come when the stability of the nation depended upon our suffrages. If we failed to elect our wisest and most inflexible statesmen, we had no reason to suppose that the South or the West would be more jealous of our welfare than ourselves.

It has been your misfortune, Sir, in other years, to be mistrusted by a large portion of your countrymen. Your political conversion, which forms the epoch of your life, was deemed by them to have been effected under circumstances greatly detrimental to your integrity. They believed that it was too precipitate for the reluctant convictions of conscience, and too heady for the monitions of wisdom. They found in you an enemy at a time when they most needed a friend; and they did not hesitate to give your abandonment of the cause the name of apostacy. Perhaps they were uncharitable: they certainly were not fastidious in the choice of epithets. We know that a growing party has power to produce *miraculous* changes in society: like the sun, it pours day-light upon the benighted vision, and confirms a host of irresolute calculators. It is possible a sudden illumination might have removed the scales from your eyes, and you saw at a glance the benefit of immediate repentance. To leave the side of adversity, however, and jump into the stream of popularity, at all times renders the act suspicious, and takes away a full moiety of its merit. I express no opinion in this matter. Political disparagement is not my design in these letters. I simply recapitulate facts, and leave others to make an application.

Notwithstanding these bad opinions of your fidelity, (and they were cherished even to the last hour of your presidential term,) your opponents generously forgave — they could not forget — ancient injuries, and consented to place you in Congress. Do not, Sir, too highly value this singular mark of confidence; for misplaced complacency is always ridiculous. It was the peculiarity of your situation, and not any new discovery of personal integrity, that led them to give you their votes. Had you not been to the topmost round of preferment, they had still left you to rusticate on the family estate at Quincy. Had there been one office calculated to provoke the envy or stimulate the intrigue of an ex-president, in vain would your nomination have been proposed to the high-minded, clear-sighted freemen of Norfolk County. They had some reason to expect that the vulgar ambition of political distinction was sated in your breast. The utter improbability of your ever being called a second time to fill the presidential chair, seemed to leave no occasion for the temptation of your virtue. Of all American citizens, an ex-president of the United States ought to be the least affected by popular clamor, and the best qualified to behave independently. Having ascended to an eminence that embraces the world in its view, and makes him conspicuous to the eyes of all nations, the occupancy of a hillock is beneath the dignity of a struggle. You are, Sir, at the present moment, an object of intense interest to millions of your countrymen. Being the first ex-president who has occupied a seat in the national legislature, your situation has the rareness of novelty. The marked civility which you are receiving from old traducers, and the fixed attention with which you are heard as soon as you mingle in the public discussions, must be flattering to your vanity. It is evidently your desire to conciliate all parties. Beware, Sir, lest this pliant disposition lead you astray from the path of duty. An error of judgment is easily forgiven; but a sacrifice of principle is an offence without mitigation.

The object of these letters is not a political one. The nature of my enterprise unavoidably brings me into a collision with you, as painful as it is unexpected. In presenting to Congress the petitions of sundry inhabitants of Pennsylvania, (members of the Society of Friends,) praying for the abolition of slavery in the District of Columbia, you made an avowal which has shocked the public mind in New-England — I may say in the free States — and astonished even the South. Occupying the station of an advocate for the slaves, the friends of emancipation expect me to interrogate you; and did they not, a sense of duty would force me to the task. Enough for an introduction. Another week, perhaps, may give to the public your 'reasons why you could give no

countenance or support' to the petitions: these reasons may be so conclusive as to establish the propriety of ten millions of freemen holding
six thousand human beings in abject bondage, and to render unnecessary a second letter from my pen. Still distrusting your ability to make
error truth, and fraud equity, and cruelty benevolence, I remain, with
unfeigned respect,

Yours, &c. &c.

W. L. G.

Printed: *The Liberator*, January 21, 1832.

Garrison's admonition to the recently elected member of Congress and his
subsequent silence regarding Adams' reluctance to become involved with the
abolition controversy show unusual restraint. It is almost as though he were convinced that leadership in the cause would eventually be thrust upon Adams, as
indeed it was after 1835.

59

TO SARAH M. DOUGLASS

Boston, March 5, 1832.

Miss Douglass:

I hasten to answer your epistle of the 29th. A copy of the Constitution of the Female Literary Association, which was forwarded to me
some time since, was duly received; but I accidentally mislaid it, and
was thus prevented giving it an *immediate* insertion. It was published,
however, in the Liberator of December 3 (No. 49), with some commendatory remarks from the West Chester Registrar.[1] I regret that I
have not this number of the paper to send you; and the more so, inasmuch as one bundle of the Liberator for subscribers in Philadelphia,
sent by the steam-boat, was lost, containing, I believe, this identical
number. You may assure the members of the Society that the Constitution has been given to the public through the medium of the Liberator. If I can procure a copy of the paper containing it, I will send it
on immediately.

The formation of this Society is a source of unspeakable satisfaction
to my mind. 1st. It is a proof of the appreciation of knowledge by
your sex. 2ndly. It is a concentration of mutual affection, of friendship
and love, of moral influence, of intellectual strength, which, like a
seven-fold cord, cannot easily be broken;[2] and which is capable of
changing the entire aspect of society. 3dly. Its effects upon the members of the association must tend to stir up in each breast not a vain
ambition, but a laudable spirit of emulation, and to perpetuate and
enlarge the desire for improvement. 4thly. It cannot fail to attract the

143

attention and induce the imitation of your sex in other places. 5thly. It puts a new weapon into my hands to use against southern oppressors. Most fervently do I bid you, as a Society, "God speed." Approach in your conduct as near to the angels of heaven as possible, — or rather, be ye perfect even as your heavenly Father is perfect.[3] My hopes for the elevation of your race are mainly centered upon you and others of your sex. To you are committed, if not the destinies of the present, certainly those of the rising generation. You cannot be ignorant of the victorious influence which you possess over the minds of men. You cannot, if you would, be passive; you must either pull down or build up, either corrupt or preserve the morals of the age. There is not a glance of your eye, not a tone of your voice, — however seemingly the look of remonstrance or entreaty be disregarded, or the word of admonition or advice be slighted, — but has a direct connexion with the results of masculine actions and pursuits. Were I not sorely oppressed with business, I would pour out the fulness of my heart before you; but a few brief hints must now suffice. 1st. Do not anticipate great and disproportionate and hasty success. Let your aim be high, but be prepared for discouragements. Do not separate exertion from hope; otherwise hope will grow chimerical and exorbitant, mount so high as to discourage poor exertion, — and thus all will end in dreaming. Hope is the mother of enterprise; — if she gently nurse it, and lead it by the hand, and consult its capacity, it will soon ripen from infancy into manhood, and do wonders; but if she grow weary of the charge, and leave it a foundling at the door of chance, and run away with fancy, it may pine in neglect or perish. Our expectations should never be extravagant; but our endeavors may be always strenuous. 2ndly. Neither let any among you circumscribe her usefulness by deeming herself irresponsible or insignificant. I would not encourage vanity, but self respect; nor excite complacency, but action. To do good, to destroy prejudice, to lift up the helpless, to restore the wandering, in one word to fulfil the design of her creation, this, this must animate her at all times. None of you know what you can accomplish, but you are sure of this, — your influence cannot possibly die, — [must?][4] necessarily, to a great or less degree, pervade the community, — though silently perchance, and yet as sensibly as the atmosphere, it may fall gently upon the white hairs of age, and invigorate his feeble pulse, — upon manhood, and confirm his strength, — upon youth, and cool his feverish brow, — upon infancy, and give it the breath of life; and so, pervading all ranks and ages, it may go down from generation to generation fertilizing the earth, and nursing fruits and flowers, like a stream from its fountain, till it be lost in the great ocean of eternity.

3dly. Let each of you cherish a deep sense of your accountability to

God and of your obligations to your fellow creatures. Shun no labor; rejoice in self-denial; feed your minds with knowledge as regularly as you do your bodies with food. Yes, you have minds capable of wondrous enlargement, made never to expire, fearfully responsible, majestically great.

But I must pause. Sarah, you will excuse my freedom in offering these hasty, undigested hints, and attribute it to the excessive interest which I feel in the welfare of your Society. You write that many are the prayers which are daily offered for the preservation of myself and partner. We are deeply affected in view of our unworthiness, and of the interest which is manifested in our welfare. The Lord has sustained us through many perils, and been our Rock of Defence. Long since we expected to have been cut off by the hand of violence; but, by the help of God, we continue unto this day. We are not afraid nor cast down nor troubled, but courageous, and animated, and joyful.

I hear nothing from my friend Robert; but I trust he continues to progress in his art, meeting with increased notice and encouragement.[5] I send my most affectionate remembrances to your parents, and to all inquiring friends. I hope to see you in June, when the annual Convention meets. The colored ladies of this city have founded an association on a plan somewhat similar to yours.

No, Sarah, ingratitude is not a characteristic trait of your people. Their thoughtfulness flows in upon us without measure.

My partner heartily subscribes to all that I have written. In desire and purpose we are one.

Remember that we have now a Ladies' Department for the Liberator. Pray occupy it as often as possible with your productions, and get others of your Society to do the same.

I am ashamed to send this wretched scrawl, especially when I contrast it with your beautiful penmanship; but I cannot find time to copy it.

With singular respect for your mind and character, I remain ever
Your friend and well wisher,

Wm. Lloyd Garrison.

Typed transcription: Garrison Papers, Boston Public Library.
Sarah Mapps Douglass (1806–1882), unrelated to Frederick Douglass, was from a prominent Negro Quaker family in Philadelphia. For many years a teacher, she was eventually in charge of the Preparatory Department of the Institute for Colored Youth, where she lectured in physiology and hygiene. In 1855 she was to marry the Reverend William Douglass of St. Thomas Protestant Episcopal Church.

1. An account of the founding and the constitution of the Philadelphia association, which had been organized September 20, was printed in a prominent position on the last page of the issue for the date specified.

2. Garrison probably refers to Ecclesiastes 4:12 — "A threefold cord is not quickly broken."

3. Adapted from Matthew 5:48.

4. So transcribed by the typist.

5. Robert M. J. Douglass (1809–1887), a brother of Sarah M. Douglass and a student of Thomas Sully, was a Philadelphia portrait painter of some distinction. At his studio on Seventh Street near the First Presbyterian Church he also made daguerrotypes. He taught painting and French, Spanish, and shorthand. See Anna Bustill Smith, "The Bustill Family," *Journal of Negro History*, 10:638–644 (October 1925).

60

TO ALONZO LEWIS

Boston, March 13, 1832.

My dear Lewis:

At the last meeting of the New-England Anti-Slavery Society, the following resolution was unanimously adopted:

Resolved, That the thanks of the Society be given to the President [1] for his deeply interesting and valuable Address, delivered in Essex-street meeting-house, and that he be requested to deliver the same at Lynn and Lowell, (with such modifications as he shall think proper,) at the expense of the Society, as soon as the necessary arrangements can be made.

As Corresponding Secretary of the Society, I am requested by the President to solicit your cooperation in carrying the above resolution into effect. As your Anti-Slavery Society have done me the honor to invite me to address them on the subject of slavery, and as my engagements are such as to preclude the hope of my soon being able to comply with their request, I would commend Mr. Buffum to them as a worthy substitute. He is, you are aware, a highly esteemed member of the Society of Friends.

Of his Address, the presses in this city have spoken in terms of commendation. I cannot doubt that it will be equally acceptable to the philanthropic and intelligent inhabitants of Lynn.

I know not whether your Society intends to become auxiliary to ours, or to act independently. We should rejoice to have it unite with us, as in union there is strength, and as our Society expressly embraces all New-England in its operations.

A larger congregation could be gathered in a meeting-house, no doubt, to hear Mr. Buffum, than in a hall. He is ready to visit your place as soon as he is informed of the disposition of your people, and the appointment of the time and place for the delivery of his Address.

Please to let me hear from you, in reference to this matter, as soon as convenient.

I hope you will be able to visit Boston at our next monthly meeting, as we shall then have an excellent public address from Mr. Robert B. Hall, a very efficient member of the N. E. Society.[2]

I trust this will find you and your family in good health. My best respects to your lady.

Still holding forth to you the right hand of fellowship, I remain, in haste,

Your friend and admirer,

Wm. Lloyd Garrison.

ALS: Friends Historical Library, Swarthmore College.

1. This was Arnold Buffum (1782–1859), Quaker abolitionist and manufacturer of hats, one of the founders and the first president of the New England Anti-Slavery Society as well as its official lecturing agent.
2. Robert Bernard Hall (1812–1868) was one of the founders of the New England Anti-Slavery Society, but like many other ministers he was in 1839 to defect from the cause of abolition to that of colonization.

61

TO SAMUEL J. MAY

Boston, March 27, 1832.

My dear Sir:

Mr. Webber [1] informs me that he shall leave the city in the course of an hour. I have barely time, therefore, to acknowledge the receipt of your favor, and make confession of regret for my protracted silence. Mr. W., I believe, has satisfactorily arranged matters with regard to his printing materials, paper, &c. I hope your new paper will be instrumental of great moral and spiritual good. You will doubtless contribute liberally to its columns, and therefore I shall expect to see something occasionally on the subject of slavery. Indeed I think every religious paper should have an anti-slavery department.

Several dozen of your addresses [2] have been sold here, and I expect to be able to dispose of some in New-York and Philadelphia. The address is almost universally applauded as a cogent, persuasive and eloquent production.

I hope soon to see you in Boston. I have much to communicate, but must finish here.

I send you fifty copies of your Address, wishing you to accept of them as a present. Should you want any to distribute, you shall have them gratuitously.

In great haste,

    Your true friend and brother,

Wm. Lloyd Garrison.

ALS: Garrison Papers, Boston Public Library.

1. Apparently Charles Webber, May's assistant in publishing the *Christian Monitor* at Brooklyn, Connecticut.

2. *Sermon on Slavery in the United States,* extracts from which are printed in *The Liberator,* June 4, 1831.

---

6 2

TO ROBERT PURVIS

Boston, May 12, 1832.

Dear Sir:

I beg you to accept of my grateful acknowledgements for your interesting letter, the generous sentiments which you express with regard to my feeble efforts in the cause of human freedom, and for your polite invitation to the hospitality of your house, in case I should visit Philadelphia. I exceedingly regret that circumstances will in all probability prevent my attending the Convention in June.[1] The disappointment cannot [be] greater to my friends in P. than it will be to myself. I long to take them by the hand, and renew the expressions of my friendship and gratitude. The Convention, I trust, will be more fully attended than that of last year. The crisis calls for the embodied wisdom and energy of the whole free colored population. A delegate will doubtless be sent from this city.

I shall be happy to correspond with you as often as my numerous avocations will permit.

Make my compliments to your lady, and accept the assurances of my friendship and respect.

    Yours, truly,

Wm. Lloyd Garrison.

ALS: Garrison Papers, Boston Public Library.

Robert Purvis (1810–1898) was born in Charleston, South Carolina, his father a successful cotton-broker and early abolitionist, his mother a native of Morocco who had been kidnapped at the age of twelve and sold into slavery in Charleston, being given her freedom upon the death of her mistress. Educated in Philadelphia and deeply influenced by *The Liberator* and by Garrison himself, Purvis helped to found the American Anti-Slavery Society in Philadelphia in 1833, delivering a eulogy to Garrison on that occasion (*Life,* I, 404–405). He became president of the "Underground Railroad" when it was organized in

Pennsylvania in 1838, and in 1840 he stood loyally by Garrison during the crisis in the abolitionist movement.

1. That is, the General Convention of Colored Delegates; see letter 64, to Henry E. Benson, May 31, 1832.

63

TO ROBERT PURVIS

Boston, May 30, 1832.

My dear Friend:

Contrary to my expectations at the date of my former letter, I am exceedingly happy to inform you that I have arranged my business so as to be able to attend the Convention; consequently, I shall avail myself of your polite invitation, in making your house my home during my tarry. It is probable that I shall arrive in Philadelphia on Saturday evening.

The Convention will be likely to excite the attention of the public in an unusual degree. I am sorry to learn, by a letter from my agent at Cincinnati, that Ohio will not be represented.[1] Such remissness, at a crisis like the present, is hardly excusable. If but few delegates are sent from other places, Philadelphia should enlarge her own number, if nothing in the rules of the Convention prevent.

The Rev. Mr. Jocelyn informs me, by letter, that he intends being present at the Convention. Whether Mr. Tappan will, also, I do not know; but I shall send him a letter this afternoon, urging his attendance.

I would fill this sheet with my poor thoughts, if the hope of seeing you, face to face, did not render the duty unnecessary.

My "Thoughts on African Colonization" have now assumed a tangible shape, and will be ready for sale in this city to-morrow.[2] I make no calculation with regard to their effect upon the public mind; but, hastily as they have been put together, I believe they are calculated to make a salutary impression. I understand that I am very much indebted to you for your efforts, your very successful efforts, to procure subscribers for the same. I shall bring as many copies with me as I can conveniently carry.

My respects and good wishes to your accomplished lady, and to all inquiring friends.

Very sincerely yours,

Wm. Lloyd Garrison.

Robt. Purvis.

ALS: Garrison Papers, Boston Public Library.

1. Garrison gives the name of this agent, George Cary, in the list of letters received within the week in *The Liberator* for May 26. But he has not been otherwise identified.

2. *Thoughts on African Colonization* was first advertised for sale in *The Liberator*, June 2, 1832.

64

TO HENRY E. BENSON

Boston, May 31, 1832.

My dear Benson:

Friend Buffum has doubtless informed you, ere this, that I have requested him to comply with your request, in relation to the colonization controversy in the columns of the American.[1] I would very gladly take up my pen, but the accumulation of duties prevent me. I thank you for a copy of the American, containing your communication and the essay of a friend of the Colonization Society. Your strictures were well-timed and well-written; and I trust you will let no fear of an inability to manage a controversy of this kind on your part, deter you from a trial. Truth is the simplest thing in the universe; and the cause you have espoused is truth's. Drive your quill as often as possible: habit will make the task easy and agreeable. I have no doubt that friend Buffum will do justice to the subject. He promises to furnish a series of numbers. As I do not exchange with the American, you will greatly oblige me by sending me a copy of it whenever any articles, pro or con, relative to the Colonization Society, appear in its pages. The advocate of the Society in the American has uttered some abominable sentiments, and discovered any spirit but that of true philanthropy.[2] Perhaps I may notice him hereafter, in the columns of the Liberator.

On Friday morning, God willing, I start for Philadelphia, to attend the General Convention of Colored Delegates, the proceedings of which will be likely to attract the attention of the nation. May the blessing of Heaven rest upon its deliberations!

I am happy to inform you that my 'Thoughts on Colonization' have now assumed a tangible shape, and will be ready for sale to-morrow.[3] I make no calculation with regard to the reception which the public will give them; but, hastily as they have been put together, I believe they are calculated to make a salutary impression. I am under fresh obligations to you for your efforts, your very successful efforts, to procure subscribers for the same. You may expect a bundle of them on Saturday or Monday. The work is very cheap, considering the amount of reading which is given. I hope my colored friends will feel an interest in its pages.

I shall go to New-York via Norwich, and, consequently, shall not go through Providence. You shall see me on my return.

My own and my partner's respects and good wishes are tendered to your worthy brother and yourself, to friends Brewer, Chace, &c.[4]

In great haste, as usual,

Your truly obliged friend,

Wm. Lloyd Garrison.

☞ Friend May is now in this city. He attended our last anti-slavery meeting, and spoke nobly.

N.B. I conjure my colored brethren in Providence not to fail of being represented in the Convention. A remissness, on their part, to send a delegate at this important crisis, would hardly be excusable. Now is the time for them to act, if ever. Will they not encourage my heart and strengthen my hands by complying with this request?

ALS: Garrison Papers, Boston Public Library.

1. During the early years of *The Liberator* Arnold Buffum was one of the most faithful newspaper correspondents among the Garrisonians. The newspaper here referred to was probably the *Chronicle and American* (published in Providence under various names from 1808 to 1833).

2. The advocate of the American Colonization Society has not been identified.

3. Note how Garrison's "to-morrows" extend themselves; he made the same statement about the sale of *Thoughts* in the preceding letter.

4. Simeon Brewer and William M. Chace (1814–1862). Chace (alternately spelled "Chase") was a Providence wool merchant and abolitionist, the partner of George W. Benson.

65

TO ROBERT PURVIS

Boston, June 22, 1832.

My dear Purvis.

The date of this letter signifies my arrival home. Much as I dislike to wield the pen, I readily seize it to hold correspondence with one to whom I am so deeply indebted, and whose friendship I prize at a high rate. The very generous and unremitted exertions made by yourself and your accomplished lady, to promote my happiness and comfort during my residence in Philadelphia, have left an indelible impression upon my memory, and opened in my breast a fountain of gratitude which only death can close. I know you do not need a profusion of thanks; but when the heart is full, the tongue must speak. May the choicest blessings of Heaven rest upon your heads! May your union be marred by no disappointment or sorrow! You seem formed for each other — happy couple!

Never could I have anticipated such a change as has taken place in my feelings. I have constantly said of Boston, until now, with regard to my affection for it, that every stone in its streets was a magnet of attraction. And now — will you credit the confession? I am — yes, *sighing* to return to the "city of brotherly love." *Must* another long, slow-wasting year pass away before I shall see those dear, confiding, generous friends, who made my recent visit, as it were, a river of delight, in which I daily bathed to the refreshment of body and soul? A year! what may not happen to some of us in its changeful career? Amid the fearful vicissitudes of life, how painful is absence from those we love!

> "Friend after friend departs:
> Who hath not lost a friend?
> There is no union here of hearts,
> That finds not here an end!" [1]

But my strain partakes of sadness. Let me change it to a sprightlier one.

The summer *season* has come in New-England, but it presents an aspect which, if not positively gloomy, is far from exciting pleasurable emotions. To the farmer is promised a blighted harvest — we have had but a few days of summer weather — there is a singular coldness in the atmosphere — the vegetable kingdom looks desolate — and the entire machinery of earth and sky seems to be out of order. There has been no season like this, since the memorable one of 1816. Peradventure we shall have a rapid change for the better; and, instead of sighing for the ardent influences of the sun, we shall cry, in *melting* accents:

> O cooling breeze, from Greenland's frigid zone!
> O thunder-clouds, that black enshroud the sky!
> O winter, who to northern climes hast flown!
> O frost! O ice! whate'er the luxury
> Of cold can bring — come, and resume your reign,
> And never more we promise to complain! [2]

I trust that neither you nor your brother will be deterred from visiting Boston by the description which I have given above. September will doubtless be the most charming month in which to travel. A New-England autumn is worth a voyage from London to witness, and, of course, worth a trip from Philadelphia.

It is possible that I may succeed in making arrangements, by and by, to travel through the free States; for the purpose of vindicating the rights of the free people of color, and forming anti-slavery societies. I am persuaded that I can do more to advance the cause by this method in a few months, than by any other for a series of years. I suggested the enterprise to Arthur Tappan and the Rev. Peter Williams, of New-York city, and they highly approved of it.[3] The only difficulty is, the procurement of means wherewith to defray my travelling expenses. Mr. Williams said he would be responsible for $100, and I presume Mr. Tappan will be disposed to contribute for the same purpose. Mr. Tappan thought I might do a great deal to promote education among colored children and youth, by addressing the people of color, giving them advice and encouragement, examining their schools and endeavoring to establish others, &c. &c. Should I go on such a mission, (and I earnestly desire to prosecute it,) I shall aim first at the great cities, and thus have the pleasure of seeing my Philadelphia friends in the course of a few months. I can leave the Liberator in excellent hands.

I have just received a letter from Mr. Tappan, in which he speaks flatteringly of my "Thoughts on Colonization," and orders *one hundred copies* for gratuitous distribution among clergymen, the colleges, &c. &c. This is a truly liberal subscription.

You shall hear from me again shortly. Grant me, dear P., the favor of a reply. Salute your lady for me, as well as all inquiring friends. My compliments to your brother.

I remain, in weal or wo,

Your very sincere and much obliged friend,

Wm. Lloyd Garrison.

N.B. My friend Cassey [4] will explain to you the cause of the delay of my books on Colonization. I wish you would inform him that I have shipped another box of them, containing about 157 copies, (making, in all, about 400,) this day, on board of the brig Mohawk, Capt. Hawes, which sails this evening.[5] I wrote him, two or three days ago, that I would send enough to allow him to put 200 copies into the hands of Evan Lewis, but as I have no more folded, and as friend Lewis will probably find it difficult to dispose of so large a number, Mr. Cassey may let him have 100 copies, and if he should want more, I will forward them to him. Mr. Cassey will let my friend Lydia White have some copies to keep for sale in her store; [6] but for the six copies which I left in her possession, I do not wish him to receive any money. — Perhaps, through the agency of my friend Robert Henson, he may dispose of some copies in Trenton.[7] Mr. Shadd [8] would also be glad to receive some in Wilmington.

ALS: Garrison Papers, Boston Public Library; extracts from this letter printed in *Life*, I, 284, 313 (misdated on this page "June, 10").

1. James Montgomery, "Friends," stanza 1.
2. This is presumably Garrison's verse.

3. Little is known of Peter Williams (1780–1840), except that he was associated with Arthur Tappan in New York City.

4. Joseph Cassey (c. 1790–1848) was a respected and prosperous Negro who served effectively for a number of years as the first agent for *The Liberator* in Philadelphia. (See his obituary in *The Liberator,* January 28, 1848.)

5. The *Mohawk,* built at Braintree, Massachusetts, in 1831, was engaged in the coastal service. Thomas Howes (not Hawes) was one of her owners as well as her master.

6. Garrison commended Lydia White often for her free-labor dry goods store in Philadelphia. She was also the librarian of the Female Anti-Slavery Society of Philadelphia.

7. It is possible that Robert Henson, who was agent for *The Liberator* at Trenton, New Jersey, was a brother of the more famous Negro minister and antislavery lecturer, Josiah Henson.

8. Possibly the Negro leader Abraham D. Shadd, who was elected president of the. Third Annual National Negro Convention at Philadelphia in June of 1833.

---

6 6

TO EBENEZER DOLE

Boston, June 29, 1832.

Respected Sir:

Permit me to introduce to you the Rev. Moses Thacher of North Wrentham, who is now about to visit your State for the purpose of delivering an address at Augusta on the 4th of July, before the Anti-Masonic State Convention.[1] He is a gentleman of great modesty and worth — great moral courage in every good cause — great perseverance, industry and talent. He is deeply interested in the cause of emancipation, and is one of the Board of Managers of the New England Anti-Slavery Society.

Our little Society is gradually expanding, and begins already to make a perceptible impression upon the public mind. Scarcely has the good seed been buried in the earth, and yet even now it is sending up its shoots in every direction! — While we endeavor to work like good husbandmen, we rely upon God for the increase. Surely, the cause is precious in his sight — and if we repose unfaltering confidence in him, we *cannot* fail of reaping an abundant harvest.

Every Monday evening, an animated discussion is held in this city on the principles and tendency of the American Colonization Society. — The friends of this pernicious combination, having no ground on which to stand, are routed in every debate. They are not conscious of the weakness of their cause until they prepare to defend it — and they come to the contest only to experience an inglorious defeat.

I have had a most delightful visit to Philadelphia, to attend the National Convention of the Free People of Color, — an account of which you will find in the Liberator of to-morrow.[2] The delegates were generally men of large, sound sense and quick discernment — some of them able debaters, and all animated by a kindling, towering spirit of improvement. The people of color now begin to hope for a better state of things: this hope is filling their breasts with motives to exertion — and the consequence is, they are rising fast in moral and literary improvement.

I sincerely wish you had been at the Convention. I wish you had been with me in Philadelphia, to see what I saw, to hear what I heard, and to experience what I felt, in associating with many colored families. There are colored men and women, young men and young ladies, in that city, who have few superiors in refinement, in moral worth, and in all that makes the human character worthy of admiration and praise.

I have forwarded to you, this morning, by the steam-boat, 25 copies of my "Thoughts on Colonization," which I wish you to distribute gratuitously among your friends, (particularly clergymen) who may most need the information it contains, and whom it is most important to convert. These copies absorb but a small part of the money which you have so generously, at various times, given to myself and my partner to promote the cause of bleeding humanity. You shall have as many additional copies to distribute as you desire.

The mockery of mockeries is at hand — the Fourth of July! By many, the day will be spent in rioting and intemperate drinking — by others, in political defamation and partisan heat — by others, in boasting of the freedom of the American people, and unhazardous denunciations of the mother country. The waste of money, and health, and morals, will be immense. Another party will seize the occasion (many of them with the best motives) to extol the merits of the Colonization Society, and increase its funds. Mistaken men! A very small number will spend the day in sadness and supplication, on account of the horrible oppression which is exercised over the bodies and souls of two millions of the rational creatures of God, in this boasted land of liberty.

I have been appointed, by the New-England Anti-Slavery Society, to deliver an address in this city on the 4th of July, on the subject of Slavery. Although the most strenuous exertions have been made by a committee to procure a meeting-house in which to have the address delivered, up to this hour they have not been able to succeed — and probably we must resort to a hall.[3] Tell it not at the South! Publish it not in the capital of Georgia.

I trust this letter will find you and your family in health and prosperity. May the Lord protect and bless you all to a ripe old age, and finally receive you to himself in a world where change and sickness, and decay, and death never come.

Give my respects to the Rev. Mr. Shepard, and accept for yourself the assurances of my high esteem and personal attachment.

Wm. Lloyd Garrison.

N. B. Mr. Knapp sends his grateful remembrances and best wishes to you and yours.

Mr. Ebenezer Dole

    Hallowell, Me.

(Favored by the Rev. Moses Thacher.)

Handwritten transcript: Garrison Papers, Boston Public Library; extract printed in *Life*, I, 284–285.

1. Moses Thacher or "Thatcher," as his name is sometimes spelled (1795–1878), was one of the apostolic dozen who founded the New England Anti-Slavery Society. He was also an enthusiastic temperance worker, and between 1835 and 1836 he edited the *New England Telegraph and Eclectic Review* in North Wrentham, Massachusetts.

2. A full report of the convention, which had been held between January 4 and 15, appeared on schedule, occupying most of the first page of the issue for June 30.

3. Garrison spoke in Boylston Hall.

67

TO GEORGE W. BENSON

Boston, July 7, 1832.

My dear Friend:

I have barely time to make even a scribble; but a line or two, perhaps, will be better than nothing.

I need not say, that I was highly gratified in having a visit from our mutual friend Chace and his associate Congdon.[1] Much to my regret, my engagements have been such as utterly to deny me the pleasure of showing them that attention which I could desire. They have just returned from Lowell, and return to Providence immediately.

At the very hour appointed for the delivery of my address on the 4th inst. a large fire broke out in this city and consumed two or three vessels and some buildings: of course, it deprived me of a great number of hearers, though my audience was quite respectable. $26.20 were collected to promote the objects of our Society.

The Rev. Mr. Danforth held forth on the afternoon of the same day, at the Rev. Dr. Beecher's Church, in behalf of the Colonization Society, to an inconsiderable audience.[2] I cannot learn the amount of his collection. His discourse, I am told, was highly exceptionable. Next week I shall review his discourse, notes of which were taken by a friend of mine.

Our cause is progressing steadily — I may say, rapidly. Friend Buffum has started on his tour through New-England, as Agent for our Society, and I dare say will make a powerful impression upon the public mind. It will require a dozen Danforths to overthrow what he will build up.

I acknowledge the receipt of $7.50 in your letter by friend Chace, on account of certain subscriptions to the Liberator. I sensibly appreciate all your kind and unremitted efforts (as well as those of your brother and other friends) to promote the circulation of the paper and the sale of my work.

The name of our Newport agent shall appear this week. It was omitted accidentally.

I send by Mr. Chace, 50 copies more of my "Thoughts," &c. You will oblige me by forwarding to the agent at Newport as many as you think proper. A commission of one fourth will be allowed on every copy sold.

I sincerely trust that good Dr. Wilson got over his colonization predicament without speaking in favor of the scheme.[3]

I have just received a letter from Miss E. A. Brewer, containing an account of the formation of a Ladies' Anti-Slavery Society in Providence.[4] This is cheering news — I shall give it to the public next week. Hope they will persevere to the end.

My friend Knapp reciprocates your kind remembrances in full.

Make my best respects to all the friends, and accept for yourself a large portion of my esteem.

> Truly yours,
>
> Wm. Lloyd Garrison.

ALS: Garrison Papers, Boston Public Library.

1. This is apparently Joseph Congdon, who was one of the first to be involved with woolen manufacture by power machinery.
2. Joshua N. Danforth (1798–1861) had recently resigned as minister of a church in Washington to become the permanent agent of the American Colonization Society. Danforth appears frequently on editorial pages of *The Liberator* during the period of Garrison's agitation against colonization, as the "pusillanimous pleader" of that society; see, for example, *The Liberator*, February 2, 1834. Lyman Beecher (1775–1863), father of Henry Ward Beecher and Harriet Beecher Stowe, was already well known as a Presbyterian evangelist by 1826, when he was called to the newly established church on Hanover Street in Boston, though by the time of Garrison's letter he was the minister of the Bowdoin Street Church. According to Garrison's sons Lyman Beecher was "Mr. Garrison's pastor if he had any" (*Life*, I, 261). After a volatile six years in Boston, Beecher moved to Cincinnati as first president of Lane Theological Seminary. Although Beecher was an abolitionist, his views — accepting, as they did, the idea of colonization — were too conservative to suit Garrison.
3. The Dr. Wilson referred to here has not been identified. He is not the Reverend James Wilson of letter 68, but more likely is a physician.
4. This is Elizabeth Brewer, according to the list of letters received to be

found in *The Liberator* of July 7, 1832. In the LADIES' DEPARTMENT the following week Garrison said: "It is our privilege, to-day, to record in our columns an account of the formation of the first 'Female Anti-Slavery Society' in New-England. We trust it is the forerunner of a multitude of similar associations, not only in this but in every other part of our country."

---

6 8

TO HENRY E. BENSON

Boston, July 21, 1832.

My dear Friend:

Be not afraid of multiplying your favors too fast — they are a delight to me.

Your description of the enthusiasm with which Mr. Mullarky [1] listened to an account of the efforts of the friends of abolition, is highly gratifying. I would thank you to give him my best respects, and assure him that I hail him as a brother. The cause of Freedom is and always has been the cause of Irishmen. Oppressed themselves, they can appreciate the sufferings of others. They have stout hearts and warm affections, and are true to the cause which they espouse.

I have received several letters from friend Buffum since he started on his great mission, which are full of encouraging facts. He is eminently calculated to make a powerful impression upon individuals and upon public assemblies. To-morrow (Sabbath) evening, he expects to deliver an address in Pawtucket, on the Massachusetts side. May He, who pities the oppressed and is the avenger of innocent blood, give him favor in the eyes of the people, encourage his heart, preserve his health, and through his instrumentality create an influence in New-England which shall ultimately break every fetter!

The letters of Messrs. Prentice and Wyllis, stating their change of views in relation to the Colonization Society, gave me unspeakable satisfaction.[2] I have ventured to lay them before the public, believing that they are calculated to make a most salutary impression at this important crisis. Conversions from colonization to abolition principles are rapidly multiplying in every quarter; and we have reason greatly to rejoice — for I look upon the overthrow of the Colonization Society as the overthrow of slavery itself — they both stand or fall together.

Thus far, my "Thoughts on African Colonization" have been noticed by various newspapers and literary magazines in terms of high approbation; and I am gratified to find that they make a powerful impression wherever they are perused.

Thanks, many thanks, for your very interesting sketch of the Rev.

Mr. Wilson's Address on the Fourth of July. His remarks are eminently candid and fearless, and confer great credit upon his head and heart.[3] I should like to publish your sketch in the Liberator, with the exception of that part of it which relates to myself; provided you think Mr. Wilson would have no objection.[4] However, I will not take this liberty until I hear from you again. You may tell Mr. Wilson, if you please, that I am exceedingly pleased to learn that he delivered so good an address on the 4th inst.

I sent a little bundle to friend Buffum this morning, (directed to the care of Benson and Chace,) containing printed copies of the petition to Congress. If he should not be in P., you or your brother can open it, and take out as many copies as you need. I trust you will succeed in obtaining a large number of signatures. I see that Lord Brougham has lately presented a petition in the House of Commons, for the abolition of slavery in the British Colonies, containing 135,000 signatures!! Let this stimulate us to new exertions.

Start, if you can, an auxiliary Anti-Slavery Society in Providence. And why may you not? There are at least friends Brewer, Chace, your brother and yourself, all seeing, thinking, acting alike. You need no more *to begin with.* Four men may revolutionize the world. Besides, the mere fact that such a society has been formed, will help us here in Boston hugely.

Mr. Danforth and his coadjutors cannot be induced to defend their cause. They affect to belong to the "good-society-folks," and therefore cannot stoop to the *canaille.* Miserable pride! it is destined to have a mighty fall.

I desire to be particularly remembered to all my Providence friends.
Your truly obliged friend,

Wm. Lloyd Garrison.

ALS: Garrison Papers, Boston Public Library.

1. Andrew Mullarky, a trader on Randall Street in Providence.
2. John Prentice (c. 1790–1867) was a merchant tailor by profession and a Congregational preacher by preference. He and his friend James Scott became converts to Swedenborg and the doctrines of the New Jerusalem in 1835 and apparently joined the New Church in Bridgewater, Massachusetts, the following year (see the appendix in William R. Staples, *Annals of the Town of Providence,* Providence, 1843). Wyllis is probably George C. Wyllis, a Negro leader in Providence (see letter 71 below). The letters from Prentice and Wyllis were printed anonymously in *The Liberator* for July 21.
3. James Wilson (1760–1839) had been the minister of the Beneficent Congregational Church in Providence since 1793. He was a popular and beloved pastor, some five revivals occurring during the term of his ministry (one of them in the very year of Garrison's letter). During the years he had also conducted successfully first a public and then a private school.
4. Henry Benson's sketch does not appear in the pages of *The Liberator.*

6 9

TO HENRY BROUGHAM

Boston, August 1, 1832.

To Henry Brougham, &c.

A eulogist has said of our Washington — "His name alone strikes every title dead." [1] Not less aptly may this comprehensive and splendid panegyric be applied to yourself. I omit your titles, not to make a vain and presumptuous show of my republicanism, but because I know you do not need them. In the sincerity of my heart I say, that, of all men living, I esteem you the mightiest. In this country, you are by common consent placed at the head of mankind. What a station! What fame!

But especially is my admiration of your character called forth by your strenuous and noble exertions for the rescue of eight hundred thousand human beings in the British Colonies, from a horrible servitude. Most happy am I to observe, that no elevation can place these unhappy creatures beyond the scope of your vision, or the pale of your compassionate regard. Still contend for their emancipation — for their *immediate* emancipation. Gradual abolition is a cheat — a delusion — an abandonment of the unchangeable principles of justice.

I have dedicated my life to the rescue not of eight hundred thousand slaves merely, but of more than two millions, who groan under an iron yoke of bondage in this self-inflated land of liberty. I am an American citizen, but yet I blush for my country. For the fifty-sixth time we have assembled, by one consent, to declare, before God and the world, that there is nothing which we so utterly abhor as oppression; nothing which we prize at so high a rate as liberty; nothing which so ennobles the character of man as the preference of death to servitude. For the fifty-sixth time we have proclaimed, with a voice that, pealing from every mountain-top and rising from every valley, echoes round the world, that "all men are created equal, and endowed with certain inalienable rights: among which are life, liberty, and the pursuit of happiness; — that when a long train of abuses and usurpations, pursuing invariably the same object, evinces a design to reduce them under absolute despotism, *it is their right*, IT IS THEIR DUTY, to throw off such government, and to provide new guards for their future security."

O, vile hypocrisy! O, solemn, heaven-daring mockery! O, horrible inconsistency! Haters of tyranny, and yet treading upon the necks and spilling the blood of more than two millions of human beings!

Lovers of freedom, and yet buying and selling and brutalizing men, women and children! Heaping imprecations upon the heads of foreign despots, and yet keeping in chains one-sixth portion of our own countrymen! Justifying, ay, even encouraging the bloody resistance of the enslaved of Europe, and yet denouncing those who plead for the immediate liberation of the slaves in this land, as madmen, fanatics and cut-throats! Asserting that all men are born equal, and yet contending that the slaves are the rightful property of the planters!

But, I rejoice to say, the appeal of abolitionists is beginning to be heard and felt in every part of our land. The wrongs of the slaves — the danger of keeping them longer in bondage — the duty of giving them immediate freedom — are the topics of conversa[tion or] discussion in all debating societies, in lyceums, [on] stages and steam-boats, in the pulpit and in periodicals, and between a man and his friend. The current of public sentiment is turning, and soon it will roll a mighty river, sweeping away in its healthful and resistless course all the pollutions of slavery.

I beg you to accept, as a small token of my esteem, a copy of my "Thoughts on African Colonization." It fully exposes the scheme which is now in operation in this country for carrying to the pestilent shores of Africa — nobody can tell when, but sometime between now and the last day — our whole colored population — a scheme, which, for folly, imbecility, violence and presumption, exceeds the wildest ever attempted by men of sane minds in any age — a scheme which directly tends to increase the value of the slaves, to degrade and persecute the free people of color, to quiet the consciences of slaveholders, and to perpetuate the system of slavery — and to promote which scheme, the philanthropists of England have been called to give their money by one Elliott Cresson, the agent of the Colonization Society.[2]

Praying Heaven to prosper your course, preserve your life, and finally to receive you to its bosom, I remain, very respectfully yours,

Wm. Lloyd Garrison.

☞ The book has been directed to the care of the Secretary of the Anti-Slavery Society.[3]

ALS: University College London Library. The manuscript is slightly torn.

1. Not identified.
2. Elliott Cresson (1796–1854) was a Philadelphia Quaker merchant and philanthropist, a man generous to many charities — both in his lifetime and in his will. He was an ardent supporter of the American Colonization Society, and Garrison had begun castigating him in *The Liberator* as early as the issue for October 1, 1831. The opposition to Cresson was to reach its height during the summer of 1833.
3. Garrison uses the full name of the British society.

7 0

TO *THE LIBERATOR*

Worcester, Sept. 7, 1832.

The reasons which have induced me to comply with the unanimous wish of the New-England Anti-Slavery Society, — that I would make a tour to promotė its benevolent objects, — are various and weighty.

The first is — *justice to myself.*

My enemies have had a long indulgence, until they begin to think they are safe from retribution. What libels have they not put forth, what caricatures have they not drawn, what calumnies have they not industriously propagated, from Maine to Missouri, respecting my motives and principles? And their success has been equal to their malignity. They have succeeded in making vast numbers of the people believe, not only that I am a visionary enthusiast, (that is a harmless allegation,) but that it is my desire and object to spill the blood of the planters, excite the fury of the slaves against their masters, and convulse the Union with servile commotions. Even many good men have been so completely deceived by their senseless clamor, as to be wholly indisposed to examine for themselves, whether it be reasonable or unjust. Such phrases as these — 'the madman Garrison,' 'the fanatic Garrison,' 'the incendiary Garrison' — have extensively become as familiar household words. Nothing amuses me more than to witness the unaffected and agreeable surprise which many strangers manifest in their countenances on a personal introduction to myself. They had almost imagined me to be in figure a monster of huge and horrid proportions, but now finding me decently made, *without a single horn,* they take me cordially by the hand, and acknowledge me 'a marvellous proper man.' [1]

I say, then, justice to myself demanded the acceptance of my present trust. I bear no malice toward any living being. My traducers I as freely forgive, as I hope to be forgiven. With the sponge of good nature and pity, I erase all their aspersions from the tablet of my memory; but when they chisel them in marble, as it were, and place them in the streets and highways to excite and deceive the passing multitude, self-defence requires that I should go forth to the people, and, by a simple vindication of my sentiments, induce them to hurl down these lying stones and trample them in the dust.

Another reason is, *justice to the cause of abolition.*

With this cause I am so intimately connected, that prejudices against *me* operate almost as strongly against *it.* If, then, I succeed in removing the misapprehensions of my honest, well-meaning, but hood-winked opponents, in relation to myself, the cause will be proportionably benefitted. Do not think, however, that I cherish the miserable vanity of supposing that I shall easily make converts, and vanquish my assailants. I have carefully counted the cost of this warfare. Indifference, alone, may soon be excited; ignorance, alone, is susceptible of a rapid cultivation; prejudice, alone, may be speedily vanquished; and hate, alone, may need but a short struggle to subdue it; — but when these are combined against light and truth, the contest is indeed arduous. Notwithstanding my efforts, I expect babblers to rail, sophists to throw dust, and the wilful enemies of the colored race to exhibit a spirit of proscription. With men of sound minds, liberal views, tender consciences, and genuine piety, I am confident of success.

A third reason is, *a deep conviction that without the organization of abolitionists into societies,* THE CAUSE WILL BE LOST.

It is time for the friends of bleeding humanity to make a demonstration of their strength. It is idle for them to sigh over the degradation and misery of the slaves, while they neglect to coalesce. To effect this union, agents are indispensable. There are thousands, and tens of thousands, who never peruse the Liberator, or any other anti-slavery publication, through ignorance of its existence, or prejudice based upon a misconception of its principles. These will not hesitate to listen to public discourses on slavery. The same arguments and appeals will answer as well for a multitude as for a single individual; and it is much easier to convince a hundred men in a large audience, than half a dozen by detail. In this manner, I may be able to disarm whole communities of their antipathies, and rally them around the standard which has been lifted up in Boston, who else might remain indifferent or hostile to our cause.

My visit to this place, as you are aware, is not primarily for the purpose of lecturing on slavery. I arrived here on Wednesday morning, and found every hotel literally jammed with strangers who had come either as delegates to the Anti-Masonic State Convention, or as curious spectators.[2] Fortunately, I obtained a place in the private boarding-house of Mr. Flagg[3] — and I seize with pleasure this opportunity to express my *admiration* (the term is not too exalted) of the manner and style in which it is conducted by its worthy occupant and his amiable family. Whether the quietude and order which prevail, — although the house is full, — the pleasantness of accommodation, the quality and variety of the provisions, or the personal attention of the host, be considered, I prefer this house to every other, whether public or private, it has been my lot to patronise. I shall leave it with reluctance.

Since my arrival, my time has been chiefly occupied in the Convention, as a delegate from Suffolk.[4] A more substantial, sober, or intelligent body of men, could not easily be mustered in any Commonwealth — the last to be suspected of sinister motives, or of seeking popular preferment — the last to abandon the ground of principle and equity. I feel proud in being admitted to a seat with them. I go for the immediate, unconditional and total abolition of Free-masonry. Pillar after pillar is falling — the mighty Babel begins to shake — and, ere long, it will be broken into fragments by the American people, and scattered to the winds of heaven.

To the credit of the Convention, there has been no prevalent disposition to *speechify*. Although composed of upwards of three hundred members, we have had but three efforts approaching to the character of *speeches* — namely, by Mr. Walker of Boston, Mr. Jackson of Newton, and the President of the Convention, Pliny Merrick, Esq.[5] Mr. Walker's speech was a successful, in many passages an eloquent delineation of the utter hopelessness of the cause of Henry Clay,[6] and received considerable applause. Mr. Jackson gave a frank and manly account of his conversion to the anti-masonic cause, and bestowed upon the State Committee a just eulogium for their meritorious and indefatigable exertions. The speech of Mr. Merrick was terse, comprehensive and exciting — confident, uncompromising, eloquent. This gentleman is scarcely in the prime of manhood — his personal appearance is handsome and attractive — as a speaker, he is fluent, effective and ardent. As President of the Convention, he deserves great credit for the rapidity with which he has despatched its business, and for the urbanity of his deportment. The Convention rose last evening.

On Wednesday evening, a crowded audience assembled to hear Mr. Hallett's address in reply to the 'twelve hundred masons of Boston and its vicinity.' It was a luminous and masterly effort, divested of all bitterness of spirit, and based upon irrefutable evidence.[7] A copy was requested for the press.

Yesterday, I had the pleasure of seeing and hearing, for the first time, the Hon. John Davis, the distinguished representative in Congress for Worcester County.[8] The cause in which he was engaged was a trivial one, and consequently required no special effort of his genius. There is much apparent sincerity in his manner, but no flourish — no artificial display. His appeals are to the common sense and common honesty of the jury.

Last evening I gave an address on slavery in the Town Hall, which was well filled with ladies and gentlemen, although the notice of the meeting was a very limited one. I trust many hearts were softened in view of the deplorable situation of the slaves, and many judgments enlightened in relation to our duty as a people. Previous to my lecture, I visited the Rev. Mr. M——,[9] to solicit the use of his house. On learning my name, he was exceedingly dogmatical, repulsive and supercillious, uttering sweeping denunciations against abolitionists — did not wish to hear any thing on the subject of slavery — thought I was doing immense mischief — justified southern men-stealers in retaining their victims in fetters — said nobody could enlighten his mind on the subject — asserted that immediate abolition would deluge the land with blood — declared himself to be a thorough-going colonizationist — believed the Colonization Society was doing all that was necessary to be done — and peremptorily refused to open his house. 'But,' said I, 'it is not my design in my address to say aught against the Colonization Society; and I should hope that the friends of that institution would not object to a discourse on slavery.' 'O,' he replied, 'Mr. Danforth [10] has lately given us two excellent addresses, and we do not need any more'!!!

This morning I depart for Providence.
　　　　Adieu,

　　　　　　WM. LLOYD GARRISON.

Printed: *The Liberator*, October 6, 1832.
This letter is the first in a series addressed to the paper in Garrison's absence. Alonzo Lewis was acting as editor.

1. Shakespeare, *Richard III*, I, ii, 255.
2. Garrison arrived in Worcester on September 5, the day the Anti-Masonic State Convention convened. This convention seems to have been concerned with agitation against Masonry rather than the nomination of political candidates. Although Garrison was always opposed to Masonry, the anti-Masonic cause was not one of the reforms that occupied much of his time. In this letter he makes what is in effect his major statement on the issue.
3. Possibly Benjamin or Joel Flagg.
4. Suffolk county, in which Boston is situated.
5. All three speakers were men of some distinction. Amasa Walker (1799–1875), successful Boston businessman, was one of the first enthusiastic advocates of extending railroad transportation. An energetic reformer, he opposed the Masonic movement, slavery, and war. Edmund Jackson (1795–1875), like his better-known brother Francis Jackson, was a prosperous businessman and generous contributor to Garrison's cause. For a record of his gifts on several occasions see *The Liberator* for November 27, 1846; February 2, 1849; February 1, 1850; as well as Garrison's letter to Helen E. Garrison, September 10, 1846. Pliny Merrick (1794–1867), already active in politics as selectman, district attorney, and representative to the legislature, was in 1850 to receive international publicity as the counsel for the notorious Harvard chemistry professor John White Webster in his trial for murder. Ultimately, he was elevated to the Massachusetts Supreme Judicial Court.
6. Probably Clay's tariff ideas, which in 1832 included advocating the reduction of tariff rates on all articles not competing with American products.
7. Benjamin Franklin Hallett (1797–1862) was a lawyer, editor, and politician. Like Garrison he had edited in rapid succession several papers, having come to

Boston in 1831 to edit the anti-Masonic Boston *Daily Advocate*, which soon established him as the leading opponent of Masonry in the state. Hallett's speech was in reply to a declaration signed by twelve hundred Masons of Boston and vicinity, denying the existence of Masonic obligations inconsistent with moral or legal standards. The declaration was printed in the Boston *Evening Transcript*, December 31, 1831, with some five hundred names appended.

8. John Davis (1787–1854) had already served seven years in Congress. Later he was to become governor of Massachusetts and United States senator. Garrison thought him a more than usually effective politician until the spring of 1848 when Davis' stand on antislavery petitions to the Senate brought forth the epithets "treacherous and cowardly" (*The Liberator*, March 3).

9. Howard Malcom.

10. Joshua N. Danforth.

71

TO *THE LIBERATOR*

PROVIDENCE, Sept. 13, 1832.

My Dear L.[1] —

My ride from Worcester to this place was a delightful one — rendered so particularly by the company of an esteemed friend who is deeply interested in the cause of abolition, and by the mode of conveyance — in a chaise. Stage transportation is commonly a stupid and disagreeable affair, requiring an excess of patience and fortitude, and a prodigious sacrifice of bodily ease. Think of it, for a moment! To be incarcerated — wedged — packed — consolidated, (any thing else you please,) with eight others, (a majority, perchance, of extra rotundity,) in a narrow space, (the exact dimensions the coach-maker can give you,) — shut out from the free air and rich sunshine of heaven — covered perchance with dust — assailed and shaken even to soreness every few rods by a troop of belligerous stones or wide-mouthed gullies — now whirling along at an impetuous speed, and then toiling up hill with the gain of an inch at every straggle of the team — the company silent and solitary, though populous, or perhaps superabundantly loquacious about nothing at all, or perhaps never trying their voices except in alternate complaints respecting the road, the carriage, the driver, the horses, the distance, the weather, and the other grievances which cluster as thick as dust about a stage-coach, or perhaps stealthily reconnoitering each other's person for the purpose of discovering 'who and what are you?' or perhaps (having endeavored in vain to avoid a direct encounter of eyes) staring reciprocally at an opposite statue, or perhaps (O, most companionable device! O, happy release from trouble!) dozing felicitously in the arms of Morpheus, and bidding defiance to bad roads, lazy horses, long distances, and speechless associates! Think of all this!

Yankees, you know, are proverbially cautious and wise. I have often been amused in travelling in stages to observe how discreetly sentiments were thrown out on subjects liable to excite a tempest of debate. The fear of unwittingly giving offence, and an irrepressible desire to canvass the opinions of the passengers, often balance the mind so exactly as either wholly to suppress or painfully cramp freedom of speech. The first remark, by way of introduction, is obvious and easy enough — it relates to the weather. This is called 'breaking the ice' — and not inappropriately, for it frequently opens a river of conversation. But how to proceed, is the difficulty. Sometimes one of the company is courageous enough to open a fire on the subject of politics or religion, reckless of consequences, and the battle becomes general and ardent. You may introduce any other theme — the whole circle of physical sciences — and, in ninety-nine cases out of a hundred, you will scarcely be able to provoke and sustain half an hour's conversation. But advance some theological opinions, or proclaim yourself a friend of Wirt,[2] or Clay, or Jackson, and the veriest blockhead instantly grows intelligent and positive — not a tongue is idle — the discomforts of travelling are forgotten, and distance is annihilated — and before the discussion is half consummated, the journey (however protracted) ends, and every man separates from his antagonist inwardly ejaculating, 'If I could ride ten miles farther with you, I'd fix you!'

How shall we account for all this? Is it because the science of politics or of morals is better understood than any other, or requires less investigation? Exactly the reverse: as this is the answer to my first inquiry.

But of all conveyances, give me a chaise, and a free spirited horse, with a beloved friend at my side — a bright sky, an invigorating air and a pleasant landscape — and then my cup of enjoyment is full.

In riding from Worcester to Providence, I had a good opportunity to witness the exceeding fertility and opulence of the soil in Worcester County, and to admire many highly cultivated farms which bore a proud testimony to the value of free labor. Here, every thing intimated independence — happiness — freedom; no driver was seen in the fields with his gang of miserable vassals; the curse of slavery had not blighted the ground; man went forth to his labor, stimulated by the hope of reward for his voluntary toil; and many a school-house and village spire demonstrated that the intellects and souls of the inhabitants were placed at a high value. I could not help sighing, in contrasting the miserable condition of the south with this heart-cheering state of things.

In passing through several villages in Rhode-Island, I was surprised to observe the number of factories which towered up on the right hand and the left. Although I have long since withdrawn from the field of politics, I feel a strong interest in the perpetuity of that system which fosters and protects the industry of the American people; consequently, the unexpected sight of these huge establishments, all alive with power, gave me no inconsiderable pleasure — pleasure, however, mingled with pain — for I fear it will be found, in almost every instance, that an exorbitant exaction of labor and time is required of the operatives; that the education of the children is neglected; and that unnecessarily severe regulations are made for the government of the factories. I am decidedly in favor of the ten-hours-a-day plan: any extension of labor beyond this space of time, without an adequate remuneration, is, I conceive, a pitiful fraud and wretched economy. Ample repose is needed to restore the wasted energies of the body and the buoyancy of the spirit, and to cultivate the mind. Let our rich capitalists beware how they grind the face of the poor; for oppression injures the value of labor, begets resentment, produces tumults, and is hateful in the sight of God.[3]

This is my first *abiding* visit to Providence, and I have enjoyed it perfectly. There is not much regularity about the place; but many of its localities are commanding and beautiful. The Arcade is a costly and spacious structure, decidedly superior to that in New-York, or Philadelphia, or Baltimore, (the last mentioned scarcely deserves remembrance,) and probably unrivalled in this country. And here let me bestow a panegyric (which I should have given last June) upon the new City Hotel, kept by Mr. Wood — a gentleman whose politeness and attention to his visitors add much to the pleasure of their residence, and to whom I have been indebted for a thorough examination of his house from the attic to the cellar.[4] Its internal contrivances are singularly ingenious — there is seemingly not an inch of room wasted or misapplied; it has several large and beautiful rooms for the accommodation of parties or families — a spacious hall capable of holding several hundred people — and numerous well arranged private apartments. Every thing is new, rich, appropriate, without any betrayal of meanness or prodigality. The supplies of the table are abundant and various, served up in a superior style. Altogether, it is decidedly *the best* hotel I have found in any of the cities; and I commend it in an especial manner to the patronage of travellers.

As I came through this city in June, I made a short visit to the venerable Moses Brown, (the patriarch of Friends,) who is now in his ninety-fifth year.[5] I have just returned from a second visit, highly gratified to find that his health continues good and his intellect clear. He is certainly an extraordinary man, and sustains the heavy weight of almost a century in an extraordinary manner. His interest in all the great philanthropic movements of the age rather increases than suffers diminution — especially in the abolition cause. From the commencement of the Colonization Society down to the recent visit of one Joshua N. Danforth, (*'one* Arnold Buffum, a hatter!') [6] he has been frequently annoyed by its agents, who have artfully sought to obtain his approbation of this unholy combination — but in vain. He has met them all promptly, and exposed the folly and wickedness of the African crusade. So intensely, indeed, does he feel on this subject, that he assured me, on my first visit, that, old as he was, he was at times almost tempted to take up his pen, (and he writes vigorously even now,) and oppose the Society! He expressed his surprise and regret that '*The Friend*,' a paper published in New-York, I believe, should admit articles into its columns favorable to the scheme. This truly benevolent and good man has done much to promote the temporal and eternal welfare of the colored population of Providence, and they will cherish his kindness in their memories long after his departure to a better world. He feels much interested in the New-England Anti-Slavery Society, and manifested considerable pleasure on being made acquainted with its steady growth. I left him, this morning, conversing in an animated strain in his carriage with an aged resident six months older than himself, and who is yet active and strong: they had never met before. Each had his store of ancient reminiscences to unfold — extending back 60, 70, and 80 years, or more — and it was curious to see how easily they removed the crusts of time, and revealed the hidden things of oblivion. May Heaven long preserve the life of this venerable man!

During my visit at his dwelling, an individual from New-York was introduced, named ——,[7] (a relative of the patriarch, and a member of the Society of Friends,) whose deportment was somewhat pedantic and lofty — acquired, no doubt, in the school-room, as he was a teacher. The subjects of slavery and colonization being introduced, he instantly avowed himself hostile to immediate abolition, and (of course) friendly to the Colonization Society. He then began (ignorant all the while of my name) in unmeasured terms to denounce 'one *Garrigus*, or Garrison, or some such name — a madman, a fanatic, and a radical, who was calling for the immediate liberation of all the slaves in this country,' &c. &c. This personal assault was exceedingly diverting to all the company, nor could I refrain from laughter. Assuming as much gravity as possible, I asked him whether he knew Mr. Garrison personally? He replied, no. Are you familiar with his sentiments? I again inquired. Yes — he had seen two or three numbers of a paper which he published, called the Liberator. Did you ever see any principles advocated in it by him, which are not held in common by the Society of Friends? O, his memory was not sufficiently tenacious to enable him to cite particular passages. I then inquired, whether he understood the doctrines and principles of the Colonization Society? Yes, he did. Taking up a copy of my 'Thoughts,' which happened to lie on table, I read a few passages from the Reports of the Society, for his edification. These seemed to stagger him, till taking the book from my hands, he discovered on the title page that I was its author — on which he sneeringly remarked, 'O, this is by that radical Garrison! — I don't believe his statements!' — and he was again commencing a tirade against me, when he was checked by friend Brown (who could no longer suppress his pleasant humor) in the following quaint and pithy manner — 'Thee does not know to whom thee has been talking — this is William Lloyd Garrison!' — The effect of this annunciation upon the gentleman was ludicrous in the extreme: he apologised for his plainness of speech, confessed that he had read very few of my writings, and that he had heard many allegations against me which he *supposed* were true, &c. &c. I told him that I hoped he would continue to speak as frankly as he had spoken before the disclosure of my name; that I had taken offence at nothing which he had advanced, except his impeachment of my veracity; and I could easily forgive that, on the supposition that it was hastily made to avoid a defeat. A long and spirited conversation ensued, in which nearly all the company participated; and on parting, I gave him a copy of my 'Thoughts,' for his harmless traducement, — persuaded that our interview had not been altogether unprofitable, and that henceforth the 'madman Garrigus, or Garrison, or some such name,' would not rank quite so low in his estimation.

On Sabbath afternoon, I gave an address to the colored inhabitants of this place, on the motives which should induce them to strive after knowledge, and particularly urging them to be industrious, economical and temperate in their habits. Their meeting house is large and commodious, but unhappily was built in such a manner as to create divisions which prevent the settlement of a minister, and which probably will never be healed until it is owned by a particular denomination. The audience was large, and highly respectable in appearance.

In the evening I delivered an address on slavery in the Rev. Mr. Wilson's [8] meeting house, (which is of startling magnitude,) before a great assembly of people. They gave me a patient and attentive hearing, in a discourse one hour and a half long, which, as far as I could learn, made generally a favorable impression.

On Monday evening, I again addressed the people of color, on the state of the foreign slave trade, the progress of the abolition cause in England and in this country, and on African colonization.

On Tuesday evening, I had the unspeakable satisfaction of assembling with them in their meeting-house, for the purpose of forming a Temperance Society. The chairman of the meeting (Mr. George C. Wyllis) made some very pertinent remarks, expressive of his approbation of the contemplated association, and urging his brethren, by the highest motives that could operate in the human breast, to unite therein as one man. Other colored gentlemen (as also some white friends who were present) addressed the meeting in a hearty and animated manner. They not only advocated total abstinence in health, but would not consent to have in the constitution of the society, the phrase, (which I have long since regarded as a very indefinite and pernicious one,) *except as a medicine.* Between forty and fifty individuals, of both sexes — nearly all who were present — immediately enrolled themselves as members! Many others will undoubtedly follow their example. Thus my colored brethren in Providence have put into my hands another weapon, with which to beat down the enemies of their race: thus, too, do they successfully repel the slanders of the Colonization Society. What a reward is this for all my labors in behalf of this afflicted people! I know that their gratitude far outruns the measure of my deserts, and that they are willing to do me any service; but I ask and desire no other remuneration than this — to see them progressing in virtue and knowledge, and leading quiet and peaceable lives. I have a higher aim than merely to restore them to their proper station in society; for the honors, and offices, and emoluments of this life, are as dust in the balance compared with the favor of God, and the obtainment of eternal happiness.

Last evening I gave an address in the Rev. Mr. Waterman's meeting-house, descriptive of the sufferings endured by our slave population, and answering some of the most popular objections to the course pursued by abolitionists.[9] Some of my remarks evidently offended the fastidious delicacy of a portion of my audience, who left the house. Perhaps the movement was a contrivance of 'the enemy' — indeed, the first individual who retired was a warm colonizationist. I may allude to this occurrence more particularly, on my return. It is proper to state that several of those who went out, came back again in a few minutes, as if ashamed of their conduct.

There is probably no other place in which our cause has more hearty, indefatigable, estimable advocates, than in Providence. I am encouraged to believe that a large and influential anti-slavery society will be organized here in a few weeks, under the most auspicious circumstances.

To-morrow evening you may expect me in Boston. I trust I shall not arrive too late to listen to the discourses of the Rev. George Bourne before our Society.[10]

Yours, truly,

WM. LLOYD GARRISON.

Printed: *The Liberator*, October 13, 1832.

1. Alonzo Lewis, substituting as editor.
2. William Wirt (1772–1834) was a Virginia author and lawyer (counsel for Aaron Burr), and United States attorney general under Monroe and John Quincy Adams.
3. Garrison's compassion for the exploited worker makes this paragraph one of his more liberal statements concerning the labor question.
4. Martin J. Wood is listed in the Providence directory of 1832 as the proprietor of the City Hotel.
5. Moses Brown (1738–1836), of the distinguished Providence family for whom Brown University was named, was a wealthy textile manufacturer and philanthropist. An ardent abolitionist, he was one of Garrison's favorites among his elders.
6. Garrison seems to mock Danforth's snobbery. See letter 68.
7. Unidentified.
8. James Wilson.
9. Henry Waterman (c. 1812–1876) appears to have been of Quaker background.
10. Of English birth, George Bourne (1780–1845) was by 1814 the minister of a Presbyterian church in South River, Virginia, where he soon became convinced of the evil of slavery. In 1816 he advocated immediate emancipation in *The Book and Slavery Irreconcilable*, which became next to the Bible the major influence on Garrison's thought. "The more we read it," he said, "the higher does our admiration of its author rise" (*The Liberator*, March 17, 1832).

72

TO *THE LIBERATOR*

PORTLAND, Sept. 24, 1832.

On Wednesday last, I bade adieu to Boston, for this city, in the Chancellor Livingston, a boat somewhat celebrated in former years for her speed and size, but which is now only a third rate one.[1] Had I selected a day for a sea trip, after a trial of the whole three hundred and sixty-five, I could not have succeeded in obtaining one more to my satisfaction. The air was sweet and mild — the great sun went up in the fullness of his glory, and all day long held a joyous communion with the ocean, which, exhibiting a slight but healthy pulsation, stretched out to the far edge of the horizon in unobstructed amplitude. After slaking the thirst of my curiosity for scenic views beyond the boundaries of Gloucester, I sat down — not feeling in a conversable mood — to the perusal of Article VII, in the North American Review for July, it being an elaborate delineation of the rise, progress, and principles of the American Colonization Society.[2] As its authenticity has been acknowledged in the African Repository, and as it has been commended to the attention of the people in various places by the Rev. Joshua N. Danforth, it assumes an importance far beyond the opinions of an anonymous reviewer. Its author is well known — in our vicinity, at least — to be a young man of some intellectual promise, excusably ambitious to figure in print, and occasionally a writer of verses. The public should understand that this is the same lauder who has attempted a defence of the Society in Buckingham's Review and in the last Christian Examiner — if my informants testify correctly. I cannot doubt the sincerity of his support; but the reward of *one dollar* — perhaps more — for every page of his compilations, (and his papers are little else than compilations,) must naturally stimulate his pen, and enhance his interest in the Society. His Article in the North American Review occupies *forty-seven pages!* for which he may have received *fifty dollars.*

I do not propose, in this Letter, to review this extraordinary paper. I shall now content myself with merely remarking, that it abundantly confirms all the accusations I have brought against the Colonization Society — that it hangs a mill-stone about the neck of this unholy combination, which is sufficient to drown it in the depths of public indignation — that some portions of it are as black as the skin of the native African — that it is disgraceful alike to the North American Review and to our country.

The writer successfully labors to prove (as if the confirmation of the fact were creditable to the Society ! !) that the scheme of African Colonization was conceived and nearly matured by a gang of negro thieves in Virginia, sitting in a legislative capacity, *with closed doors,* on various occasions ! ! I will here make an extract from his essay:

'The earnestness with which the Legislature [of Virginia] prosecuted their design, may be inferred from the fact, that the Executive was requested to adopt measures of the same character with those just mentioned, *at three several times anterior to 1806. But all these,* it should be observed, *were private proceedings;* ☞ and the *injunction of secrecy* HAS NOT BEEN REMOVED, so far as we know, *to this day,* excepting as to the fact that such proceedings took place [! ! !] the first *public* expression of sentiment upon the subject of colonization was also made *by the same* body. This was in December, 1816.'[3]

Thus it is confessed that the *colonization egg* was *hatched in darkness* by a tryrannical legislature, which, from the hour of its conception down to the present time, has annually passed the most atrocious laws with regard to the colored population of Virginia, and at its last session prohibited the instruction of the free people of color, and also their assembling together to worship the God of heaven and earth, under severe penalties ! ! Now, is it possible that these daring transgressors against the laws of God and the rights of man can feel any benevolent regard for our free colored population? Is not their villainy towards their slaves *prima facie* evidence that their object was, from the beginning, to enable themselves to hold their bleeding victims with a more powerful grasp by legally expelling the free blacks from this country, and to throw out a sop to the moral and religious people of the free states in order to divert their attention from the iniquity of man-stealing and reconcile them to the continuance of slavery? They have succeeded in imposing upon the credulity of honest and good men, in all parts of our land, one of the most stupendous frauds ever put forth to deceive mankind. But, detected in their plot, they cannot much longer triumph. In despite of its artifices, and appeals, and desperate efforts, the Colonization Society is becoming more and more abhorrent to the moral sense of community. The veil has been torn from the brow of the monster, and his gorgon features are seen without disguise. He must die! Already he bleeds — he roars — he shakes the earth — his resistance is mighty — but he is doomed to die! The friends of justice and of bleeding humanity are surrounding him, and soon their spears shall reach his vitals. Heaven and earth shall rejoice at his overthrow.

As this is my first visit to Portland, I was exceedingly disappointed in not arriving in season to witness its appearance on approaching the harbor. The murky shades of evening overtook us some time ere we passed Cape Elizabeth, and, of course, the eye could discriminate nothing in the city but dim clusters of stores and dwellings unavailingly designated by a few lamps. My disappointment, however, was partially compensated by the solemn yet pleasurable emotions which I experienced on watching the ignition of the lamps of several lighthouses, some of which, by a constant revolution, would almost imperceptibly fade away into darkness, and then loom up seemingly with more than pristine splendor. A fine emblem, I thought, of the unwasting, imperishable, unextinguishable nature of TRUTH. The billows of time may dash around it — the storms of passion may beat upon it — the darkness of error may shroud it — but neither waves nor winds nor gloom can extinguish its light: it may seem to expire for a time — still it lives to gather new effulgence and burst afresh upon the anxious vision, and to incorporate itself with the beams of the Sun of Righteousness in one eternal day.

Portland, at the first glance, does not compare favorably with

Providence; but it improves rapidly upon acquaintance. On Thursday, — a most lovely day for an excursion, — I was very highly indebted to my friend Mr. Reuben Reuby, (a colored gentleman held in much esteem in this city,) [4] for a protracted ride, during which I obtained various and eminently beautiful views of Portland and the harbor — I am therefore disposed to bestow upon both my best eulogy. The first objects which particularly excite the surprise and pleasure of a stranger are the multitude of islands — necessarily diminutive in size — which gem the bosom of the waters. It is said that, in a clear day, three hundred and sixty-five (as many as there are days in the year) may be counted from the observatory! This stands upon an elevated hill, from which is a pleasant and commanding prospect.

On Saturday, I was invited to a handsome entertainment at the house of Mr. Reuby, and was gratified to meet about twenty colored gentlemen of good intelligence and reputable character. As a mark of their respect for my person and gratitude for my labors, I shall long cherish it in my memory, and I beg them to accept this public acknowledgment of their kindness as some evidence of its appreciation. The interview was a profitable one to myself, and I believe agreeable to all who were present.

The whole number of colored persons in this city is about five hundred. I gave them an address on Friday evening in the Friends' meeting-house, which was very kindly offered for that purpose. A very respectable number of men and women attended, with several Friends, and listened with breathless attention and evident satisfaction. I was surprised to witness so large a collection, as only a few hours had been allowed for the notice, and the evening was very dark and stormy. On Sabbath afternoon I addressed them in the basement story of their own meeting-house. This is a good building, amply large, the second story of which remains to be finished. The room was crowded with attentive listeners, all of whom were dressed in a neat and genteel manner. I am persuaded they will treasure up my advice in their hearts, and carry into effect some of the measures proposed for their benefit. One of these was the immediate formation of a temperance society, in imitation of their brethren and sisters in other places.

Wherever I have been called upon to address an assembly of colored persons, nothing has given me more pleasure than to witness the general air of comfort and gentility which they exhibited in their countenances and persons. On such occasions, I have never failed to remember the scandalous charges put forth against them by the Colonization Society, to wit — 'Free blacks are a greater nuisance than even slaves themselves' — 'They are notoriously ignorant, degraded and miserable, mentally diseased, broken spirited, acted upon by no motives to honorable exertions, *scarcely reached in their debasement by the heavenly light.'* 'Discontented and exciting discontent; scorned by one class, (the whites,) and *foolishly envied by another*' (the slaves ! ! !) — 'Of all the descriptions of our population, and of either portion of the African race, the free people of color are, *by far*, as a class, the most corrupt, depraved and abandoned' — 'The existence, within the very bosom of our country, of an anomalous race of beings, *the most debased upon earth*, who neither enjoy the blessings of freedom, nor are yet in the bonds of slavery, is a great national evil' — 'The class we first seek to remove are neither freemen nor slaves, but between both, and more miserable than either' — 'Freedom confers on them no privilege but the privilege of being more vicious and miserable than slaves can be' ! ! ! — [*Vide* the African Repository.] [5] Monstrous calumnies! — In reply to which I will make but one quotation — 'All liars shall have their part in the lake which burneth with fire and brimstone.' [6]

The Rev. Dr. Tyler is the only clergyman I have visited in the city.[7] His manners are plain and affable — one of the marks of true greatness. He frankly admitted that he had long been disposed to regard the Colonization Society in the light of a benevolent and efficient institution — nor was he yet prepared to abandon it — but his mind had lately been considerably shaken in regard to its merits, in consequence of a more thorough investigation, and was now in a suitable state to weigh evidence impartially. He said he would endeavor to hear my addresses on my return to this city. I think only a little more research and meditation is necessary to induce this good man to rank himself among the opposers of the Society, on its present principles.

To the committee of the Rev. Dr. Nichols's church (a beautiful house, indeed) I beg leave to give my sincere thanks for the readiness with which they opened it last evening, for the delivery of my first address on slavery.[8] It is estimated that two thousand persons were present, whose attention was marked and unbroken to the end. In view of the congregated mass, and of the magnitude of the cause, I felt most painfully my utter insufficiency: still, relying upon Him who has promised to maintain the cause of the afflicted and the right of the poor, I was emboldened to speak the truth plainly and pungently — with what success, time must reveal. Three select hymns, adapted to the occasion, were sung in a skilful and touching manner

* 'Every emigrant to Africa is a ☞ *missionary*, ☜ carrying with him credentials in the holy cause of civilization, religion, and free institutions'!!!! — *Tenth Annual Report.*

by the choir. The Rev. Dr. Nichols was not present, on account of absence from the city.

I am largely indebted to the hospitality of my esteemed friend N—— W———, (one of the most thoroughgoing friends of the abolition cause in our land,) at whose house I have been most agreeably entertained since my arrival.[9] His lady evinces extraordinary sympathy for the poor slaves and admits of no compromise of principle. The children fully imbibe the benevolent spirit of their parents — three of them are promising young ladies. The entire family, indeed, is full of attractions, from which I shall reluctantly break away. I must not forget to number among the rest, a fine, intelligent lady, intimately related to this family, who feels deeply interested in the cause of emancipation, and with whose conversation I have been pleased and edified.[10] She has been an eye-witness to many of the cruelties inflicted upon the slaves at the south.

I must close this letter abruptly. The stage for Hallowell is at the door, and I depart therein — from which place you may expect another epistle. I shall probably extend my visit down as far as Bangor. Farewell!

WM. LLOYD GARRISON.

Printed: *The Liberator*, October 20, 1832.

1. The *Chancellor Livingston*, the last vessel designed by Robert Fulton, was built in New York in 1816.

2. Garrison refers to an anonymous review of two pamphlets: *Fifteenth Report of the American Colonization Society* (Washington, D.C., 1832); and *Letters on the Colonization Society; with a View of its Probable Results; addressed to the Hon. C. F. Mercer* (Philadelphia, 1832), by Mathew Carey (1760–1839). The anonymous reviewer has not been identified.

3. Garrison quotes accurately the author of the review in question, supplying most of the italics, the pointing hand, and the words and punctuation marks in brackets.

4. Not otherwise identified.

5. (For the *African Repository* see letter 57, n. 1.) Evidently, Garrison is quoting in this paragraph not directly from the *African Repository*, as he indicates in brackets, but from his own *Thoughts on African Colonization* (Boston, 1832), pp. 125–127, where he gives long passages from various publications of the American Colonization Society. In his letter, therefore, Garrison telescopes the original source rather violently, quoting passages in the following order from the *African Repository*: II, 328; I, 68; V, 238; VI, 12; and VII, 230. The last two sentences he quotes, however, are not to be found in the *Repository* but in the Society's *Seventh Annual Report*; see *Thoughts on African Colonization* (pp. 126–127), where the same sentences are quoted. Garrison's quotations are accurate except for changes in capitalization, italics, punctuation, spelling, an occasional ellipsis, and twice the supplying of comment in parentheses. Garrison takes liberty especially with capitalization and italics, his use of these devices in *Thoughts* varying from the original about as much as their use in the letter differs from the secondary source.

6. Revelations 21:8.

7. Bennet Tyler (1783–1858) had been a Congregational minister in South Britain, Connecticut, before coming to Portland, Maine, in 1828. He had also

been president of Dartmouth College between 1822 and 1828; and he was to spend his last years as professor of Christian theology at the seminary at East Windham, Connecticut.

8. Ichabod Nichols (1784–1859) was a prominent Unitarian minister.

9. Nathan Winslow (1785–1861) of Portland, Maine, was a prosperous Quaker and a generous contributor to Garrison's cause. In 1836 his daughter Louisa married Samuel E. Sewall; in 1856, six years after Louisa's death, he married her sister, Harriet Winslow List.

10. The "intelligent lady" has not been identified.

73

TO *THE LIBERATOR*

HALLOWELL, Sept. 28, 1832.

Anxious to see as much of this State as possible, during my present visit, I took a seat by the side of the driver from Portland to Hallowell: this enabled me to scan somewhat advantageously several flourishing villages through which we passed, and critically to observe the general features of the country. Maine is emphatically a concatenation of hills — many of which are of an almost mountainous aspect: its distinctive feature, therefore, rather partakes of grandeur than loveliness. Still, in the course of my journey, I discovered several attractive spots, upon which he who prefers the quietude and beauty of Nature to the turbulent society of man might delight to dwell. Having recently left the most fruitful portion of Massachusetts, the soil in this region doubtless suffers from the contrast — for I cannot conceal my disappointment at its meagre appearance. I am told, however, that what I have seen is very far from being a fair specimen of the State — that the lands in the 'back country' — are susceptible of a high cultivation — and that, altogether, Maine has no reason to complain of her resources.

The objects which most attracted my attention on my way thither, were the White Mountains in New-Hampshire —

> 'The palaces of Nature, whose vast walls
> Have pinnacled in clouds their snowy scalps,
> And throned Eternity in icy halls
> Of cold sublimity, where forms and falls
> The avalanche, the thunderbolt of snow!
> All that expands the spirit, yet appals,
> Gathers around their summits — as to show
> How earth may pierce to heaven, yet leave vain man below!' [1]

'The avalanche, *the thunderbolt of snow!*' — a singular conception indeed, but formidably expressive. This line recalls to the mind the destructive slide from the Notch of one of these mountains, which took place a few years since. Although about one hundred miles distant, they were distinctly visible. I had much rather look at these tremendous excrescences than ascend them. My journey over the Green Mountains in the spring of 1829 effectually clipped the wings of my ambition to soar above the Alps, and ever since I have fallen in love with every level plain. There is, however, a moral elevation to which my soul aspires, high as Heaven; and though rough and difficult the ascent, may my courage and faith carry me upward to its summit, and be crowned with eternal victory!

Hallowell is a very considerable village, advantageously located on the side of the Kennebec, and almost blending with Gardiner on the south, and Augusta on the north. Its political weight, I believe, ranks next to that of Portland, and is almost entirely thrown into the scale of the opposition to the national and state administrations. It has an intelligent, clear-headed and industrious population, whom it is not easy to mislead by any political impostures, and who are fully aware that the protection of American industry is the life-blood of the nation. This is the chosen residence of the Hon. Peleg Sprague, the distinguished representative in Congress from Maine — a gentleman who in many particulars resembles our Webster, possessing the same irreproachable character, as exalted in patriotism, as conspicuous for political integrity, and as highly beloved by his constituents.[2] He is now absent from this place, and consequently I cannot acknowledge the honor of a personal introduction to him. No man regards the slavery of his species with more unmingled execration than himself; but he is, I regret to learn, favorably disposed toward the Colonization Society, although in no sense of the term a partisan. It is not probable that he has critically examined this subject, amid the ever-multitudinous avocations of his profession. Like many other great and good men, similarly situated, he has — we may charitably suppose   taken upon trust the utility and benevolence of this powerful combination.

The first individual in Hallowell upon whom, as in duty bound, I called, was Mr. Ebenezer Dole, a philanthropist whose name is familiar to the readers of the Liberator — the first life-member of the New-England Anti-Slavery Society — the friend of the poor and needy, and supporter of the various benevolent operations of the times — whose interest in the abolition cause is unsurpassed — and to whom I labor under very onerous obligations. Our meeting was a cordial one. I received from him the cheering information that an attempt by the Rev. Cyril Pearl, (one of the Rev. Mr. Danforth's sub-agents for New-England,) at the Annual Kennebec County Conference, held on the 19th inst. to obtain a passage through that body of a resolution approving of the American Colonization Society, was promptly frustrated by a motion to lay the resolution on the table, which was carried without debate.[3] This expression of sentiment, by such an association, speaks well for the progress of light and sound information, and is ominous of the speedy abandonment of the colonization crusade by all the churches in New-England.

I have found a worthy and decided friend to our cause in the Rev. Mr. Shepard, and another sterling advocate in the venerable person of Dea. James Gow, who was formerly a supporter of the Colonization Society, honestly supposing it to be a benevolent institution, but who now on all suitable occasions bears a noble testimony against it.[4] As a proof of his long-cherished hostility to African slavery, it is only necessary to state that for forty years he has abstained from the consumption of sugar! May he live to see the day when every slave in our land shall be set free, and every fetter broken, and every heavy burden undone!

My addresses in this place have been listened to by respectable audiences, and their sentiments apparently received with much cordiality. Hitherto the subject of slavery has not dwelt sensibly upon the minds of the inhabitants, but we may now hope in a short time to see many of them rallying around the standard of the New-England Anti-Slavery Society, in an auxiliary association. It is not improbable, moreover, that the ladies will form a similar society. Indeed, here are all the *materials* for a noble combination — kind and liberal dispositions, unprejudiced minds, and sympathetic souls.

Yesterday I happened to find on the table in the Eagle Hotel where I abide, (kept by Messrs. G. & S. W. Eustis [5] — very pleasant and attentive gentlemen, by the way,) a small pamphlet of 16 pages, purporting on its title page to be 'A Poem delivered on the anniversary of the Literary Fraternity of Waterville College, July 26, 1831 — by Richard Hampton Vose'.[6] I perused it with much pleasure. As a specimen of its spirit and easy versification, I take the following stirring extract:

> 'Is Freedom safe, when men may wear the chain
> On her own soil, and cry for help in vain?
> When ye can hear the oft repeated tale
> Of Afric's wrongs, with cheeks no longer pale?
> As though it were some idle, fond conceit,
> Contrived to frighten those it could not cheat!
> Shame to the land, whose motto ought to be,
> All men are equal, by their nature free —
> And cannot wear the fetter, nor resign
> This best of gifts, this treasure all divine.
> What! chain thy brother, born of kindred clay,

And justify the deed in open day?
And say, he eats, and drinks, and sleeps, (perchance as well
As other brutes!) Heard ye the funeral knell,
When the poor negro crossed the stormy wave,
Bought as thy property, to live thy slave?

But not by chains and fetters are confined
The mighty workings of the human mind —
A few short years, his pilgrimage shall cease,
Then, deathless spirit, thou shalt find release:
In other climes beyond the tyrant's rod,
There shalt thou dwell, companion with thy God.'

My attention has just been called to a paragraph in the New York Evening Post, extracted from the letter of 'A Tobacco Planter of Virginia,'[7] residing in Bloomsbury, Halifax County, to the editors of that paper. I copy it as a specimen of political profligacy and southern audacity. Here it is!

'I am no office seeker or office holder, (nor will I ever be either) but I am a tobacco planter, [a negro thief,] and thank God [solemn mockery!] I make a plenty of it. All the land, ☞ NEGROES, ☜ tobacco, cotton, wheat, hemp and corn in the State of Virginia *will be staked that* Andrew Jackson will be elected in November the President of the United States — at least, you are authorized to say *all I have will be staked,* amounting to about 70 or $80,000. ! ! !

This is political swaggering by wholesale, put forth by an anonymous kidnapper to influence public opinion! He must surely be superior to Mr. Ritchie of the Richmond Enquirer, or John Randolph, thus to be able to stake the State of Virginia, with half a million of slaves, upon the re-election of Andrew Jackson.[8] If, however, no one is disposed to bet the value of the Ancient Dominion in the negative, this *honest man*, by way of accommodation, is willing to stake all he possesses — 'negroes, tobacco,' &c. Ought we not to be proud of our country, that in a large portion of it, human beings may be reckoned with wheat, hemp and corn, and staked on the result of a game of whist, a horse race, or a presidential election? This sort of gambling is common at the south, and is another striking illustration of the atrocity of negro slavery.

A word in relation to Article VII in the July number of the American Review, alluded to in my last letter.[9]

An extract of a letter is given by the author of that paper from the Rev. Robert Finley, to whom 'the operations which gave existence to the American Colonization Society are to be mainly attributed,' written about the commencement of the year 1815.[10] Alluding to the free people of color, Mr. F. says:

'Every thing connected with their condition, *including their color,* is against them; ☞ NOR IS THERE MUCH PROSPECT THAT THEIR STATE CAN EVER BE GREATLY AMELIORATED, *while they shall continue among us.*'

I wish the reader of this letter to peruse the foregoing extract once more, and very deliberately. It reveals a spirit of prejudice and infidelity, which has since given vitality and strength to the Colonization Society; *a spirit of prejudice,* because if Mr. Finley had cherished no repugnance to color, he would have seen no insuperable difficulty in others to overcome their hostility — and *a spirit of infidelity,* because it assents to the abominable doctrine which has since been preached in all parts of our land, that it is beyond the power of Christianity to raise our colored population from their low estate. 'Nor is there much prospect that their state can ever be greatly ameliorated, while they shall continue among us' — how complimentary to us as a people ! ! An echo to this is found in the last Report of the Board of Managers of the Colonization Society, in which it is proclaimed that the blacks must remain 'for ever a SEPARATE and DESPISED *class in community!* — Christianity cannot do for them here, what it will do for them in Africa! — This is not the fault of the colored man, *nor of the white man,* nor of Christianity; but AN ORDINATION OF PROVIDENCE, *and no more to be changed than the laws of Nature' ! ! !*

One more extract shall suffice. Elias B. Caldwell was another of the founders of the Colonization Society, and its first Secretary.[11] In a speech delivered at its formation, he not only indirectly but explicitly dissuaded from any attempt to educate the people of color in this country, in the following style:

'The more you improve the condition of these people, the more you cultivate their minds, the more *miserable* you make them in their present state. You give them a higher relish for those privileges *which they can never attain,* and turn what you intend for a blessing into *a curse.* — No, if they must remain in their present situation, *keep them in the lowest state of ignorance and degradation.* The nearer you bring them to the condition of *brutes,* the better chance do you give them of possessing their apathy.' [12]

Such sentiments are to be held in utter detestation by all who aspire to be men or christians.

I must close abruptly, as my sheet is full. My next letter will probably be written at Bangor.

WILLIAM LLOYD GARRISON.

Printed: *The Liberator,* October 20, 1832.

1. Byron, *Childe Harold's Pilgrimage,* Canto III, Stanza 62; Garrison quotes accurately, omitting only the first line of the stanza.
2. Peleg Sprague (1793–1880) later moved to Boston and became a distin-

guished United States district judge. Although Sprague considered slavery a political and a moral evil, Garrison never forgave him for putting legalistic above ethical considerations. He attacked Sprague repeatedly in *The Liberator,* sometimes featuring his statements in the pro-slavery section of the paper, "The Refuge of Oppression." See Garrison's letter (209) to Sprague, September 5, 1835.

3. Cyril Pearl (born 1805), of Bolton, Connecticut, traveled through Maine as Joshua N. Danforth's representative, in the same year as Garrison's visit.

4. James Gow (1766–1842) was a deacon of the Old South (Congregational) Church in Hallowell, Maine, and sometime poet.

5. Possibly, the Maine-born Eustis brothers; G. Eustis died in Cincinnati in 1844.

6. Richard Hampton Vose (1803–1864), of Augusta, Maine, was both lawyer and poet.

7. Unidentified.

8. Garrison's single-minded dedication to abolition colored his appraisal of men whose convictions differed from his. Among these were Thomas Ritchie (1778–1854) and John Randolph, who has been identified in an earlier note. Ritchie, who in 1804 had founded the Richmond *Enquirer,* which he published until his death, was one of the leading Southern editors and journalists. He dedicated his paper to serious discussion of the major issues of the day. Although he attacked the abolitionists, he also urged gradual emancipation. Randolph, by the time of Garrison's letter, had become so eccentric as to be considered insane; in fact, the will written that year was contested after his death. Garrison followed the litigation over the will with no little interest. When, in 1845, an earlier will freeing all the Randolph slaves was declared valid, Garrison reprinted the document (*The Liberator,* August 25, 1837) and spoke favorably of Randolph's character.

9. Letter 72, September 24.

10. Robert Finley (1772–1817) graduated from the College of New Jersey (later Princeton) when only sixteen, became clothier to the American army, and later distinguished himself as teacher, as minister, and — a few months before his death — as the chief founder of the American Colonization Society. He was the author of *Thoughts on the Colonization of Free Blacks* (Washington, D.C., 1816), from which Garrison quotes,

11. Elias B. Caldwell (c. 1776–1825), from Washington, D.C., and a brother-in-law of Finley, organized the colonization society in the South.

12. Garrison's source for this passage is a quotation by Jesse Torrey, Jr., in *A Portraiture of Domestic Slavery in the United States* (Philadelphia, 1817). Garrison had used the same quotation from Torrey in *Thoughts on African Colonization* (p. 149). In the fall of 1833 William Leete Stone, editor of the New York *Commercial Advertiser,* accused Garrison of misrepresenting Caldwell's meaning by quoting him out of context. Stone supplied from Torrey the two sentences following the passage quoted by Garrison: "Surely, Americans ought to be the last people on earth, to advocate such slavish doctrines, to cry peace and contentment to those who are deprived of the privileges of civil liberty. They who have so largely partaken of its blessings — who know so well how to estimate its value, ought to be among the foremost to extend it to others." Garrison replied to Stone's charge in two and a half vituperative columns in *The Liberator* of November 2, 1833, saying that he had not been aware of the context of Caldwell's speech until he read it a few months before in the English edition of Torrey's work. Then he went on to insist that his omission had not misrepresented Caldwell's meaning. "In other words," he paraphrased Caldwell, "it is perfectly right and eminently humane to keep the slaves ignorant 'in their present situation,' and as long as they remain in that situation; but shame on him who would advocate their perpetual degradation and servitude! Let us gradually rid ourselves of this direful necessity, by removing them out of the country!" In his last paragraph Garrison turned again on Stone: "When the viper of the New-York Com-

mercial Advertiser shall have eaten and digested this file, I will give him another upon which to try his teeth." Garrison's bitter outburst betrays the fact that he did misrepresent Caldwell's meaning since in fact both editions of the speech contain the sentences Stone supplied and Garrison deleted.

7 4

TO *THE LIBERATOR*

BANGOR, Oct. 2, 1832.

My dear L.[1] —

Faithful to my original determination, to see all that is to be seen in a new and hasty journey, I mounted the driver's seat from Hallowell to this place, and thus had an unobstructed view of 'field and forest, rock and river.'[2] Some portions of the route were full of scenic entertainment; but as you leave Augusta, the road becomes monstrously inflated, and exhibits more protuberances than the back of the sea serpent. Up and down — up, up, *up*, — down, down, *'way* down,' as we sometimes say in New England — how delightful is such a state of alternate exaltation and depression! We may, however, extract a moral from it, that may enable us to encounter the vicissitudes of life with a philosophical spirit. The 'Dixmont Hills' are as famous and formidable to travellers on this route, as is Point Judith to tourists from Providence to N. York: they are piled upon my memory in all their massive stability, and I fear it will take that indefatigable laborer, Time, a weary space to remove them with his plough, and shovel, and pickaxe.

Bangor hardly realises my expectations, with regard to its size and consolidation; but it has the bones and cartilages of a giant, and only needs a few years to give it the lusty perfection of manhood. It has a more business-like appearance than any place I have yet visited in this state — the inhabitants speak of its ultimate greatness with a tone of confidence and sincerity. It looks as if it had been built up in a prodigious hurry — as if the increase of population outran their ability to provide habitations. There has not been time for improvement, or an exhibition of taste in the location of the houses and arrangement of the streets. A rapidly growing people require first of all a shelter from the weather, and are often necessitated to sacrifice elegance and taste to convenience and utility. Bangor is unquestionably destined soon to rank next to Portland: many indeed, are sanguine enough to affirm that it will take precedence of all other towns in the State. The Exchange Coffee House, kept by C. Hayes, (every

inch a gentleman,) is a noble building, with whose internal arrangements I have been highly pleased; every thing is conducted on the
most liberal scale.[3] There is a very extensive block of brick buildings,
nearly completed, which would confer credit upon Boston or New-
York.

Ever since my arrival, it has rained — rained — rained — almost in-
cessantly. The streets are beds of clay, and the walking intolerable.
I gave my first address to the people on Sabbath evening in the Rev.
Mr. Pomroy's meeting-house; [4] and I confess I went to the meeting
in a dispirited mood, not expecting to see even an apology for an
audience, in consequence of the rain; but, to my surprise and pleasure,
there was a large collection of persons present, and they gave earnest
heed to those things which were spoken. May the impression which
was then made be deep and permanent, and excite a spirit of benevolent activity in the cause of abolition! The house is constructed in
the gothic style, and is quite an ornament to the place.

Last evening I delivered another address in the Rev. Mr. Huntoon's meeting-house to a very respectable and somewhat numerous
audience; this, also, is a fine building.[5] The number collected together
on this occasion was a source of greater surprise to me than that of
Sabbath evening — for the evening was yet more unpropitious — dark
and stormy, and the roads were indescribably bad.

My interviews with the Rev. Mr. Pomroy and the Rev. Mr. Huntoon
have been very agreeable: they are men of urbane deportment, fine
intellects and benevolent souls. They may unhesitatingly be reckoned
among the friends of immediate abolition, and of the New-England
Anti-Slavery Society — consequently, opposed to the Colonization Society. Mr. Pomroy has recently given up this combination, in consequence of a solemn conviction of its abandonment of the grounds of
justice, and its utter inefficiency. He is another important acquisition to our cause. We have also an estimable advocate in the person
of Mr. J. C. L. who presents to our Society $5.00 for the promotion
of its great objects.[6] An auxiliary society may, ere long, be formed in
this place.

I am sorry that the inclemency of the weather has been so severe
as to deter me from visiting Orono, or Old Town, as it is called, the
Indian settlement, some twelve miles distant. There are several hundreds of these children of the forest, congregated together — some of
them tolerably well off, but the mass, I learn, are in poor circumstances, morally and physically. They are all Papists, and have a small
mass-house in which a priest occasionally officiates. I have met several
in the streets here, of both sexes, and looked upon them with feelings
of compassion and curiosity. It is somewhat difficult for one who is

not familiar with their mode of dress to distinguish the women from the men; for they wear nearly the same habiliments, which hide all distinguishing personal marks, and complete the deception by covering their heads with hats. Is it not owing to the prejudice and neglect of Protestant christians that these benighted creatures have fallen a prey to the superstition and idolatry of Popery? Can no systematic measures be formed to rescue them or their children from this thraldom?

We cannot expect, *at present*, to increase the funds of the Anti-Slavery Society by public contributions. In the first place, the frequency with which these petty exactions have been made, for a multitude of purposes, has become almost a nuisance to the people. Again, those whose confidence and generosity have once been abused — as in the African colonization crusade, for instance — will not be disposed readily to patronise a new project. And lastly, the principles and objects of the Anti-Slavery Society are not sufficiently understood; and even after making a full development of them to an audience, it is not to be expected that they will be instantly and implicitly received. Men of intelligence and philanthropy wish first to weigh evidence, and examine principles, before they contribute to an object. To present boxes to an assembly soliciting contributions in aid of a cause which is new and imperfectly understood, is, I am more and more persuaded, almost a sure method to destroy the interest which may have been created, and to lead to suspicions of selfish purposes. We do not wish to take even an apparent advantage of ignorance and unenlightened faith — we do not wish the aid given to our cause to outrun discretion and intelligence. We court a national scrutiny, and are confident that our views and feelings and intentions need only to be fairly understood to receive the liberal co-operation of all good men.

But what is to be done? The abolition cause cannot progress to its triumph without funds — a large amount of funds: The New England Anti-Slavery Society, if destitute of support, can neither send forth agents, nor print and gratuitously circulate tracts or petitions, nor form auxiliary associations. It is undeniably true that there is no cause which has such strong claims upon the prayers, sympathies and charities of good men and good women as this — whether we consider its relation to ourselves, to others, to our country, to the world, or to God — to the temporal or spiritual welfare of millions of our suffering men. To whom, then, must the Anti-Slavery Society look for nourishment and protection, in its infancy? I answer —

First — To that numerous class *in* and *out* of New England, who are in truth the enemies of slavery — uncompromising abolitionists — and

whose generous sympathy far exceeds their ability to contribute largely to the funds of our Society. The only request we make of those,
who are not in good circumstances, is, to enrol themselves immediately
as members of the Anti-Slavery Society, and pay an annual subscription of *two dollars*. This little sum they can easily spare — will they
withhold it, and give us nothing but sighs, and good wishes, and empty
declamation? No — I am persuaded that this paragraph will be perused
by a thousand individuals of both sexes, who are ready and willing
to comply with this invitation. By so doing, they may in the space
of a month raise the sum of two thousand dollars, and thus give a
mighty impetus to the cause of emancipation.

Secondly — To those who adopt the principles and cherish the objects of our Society, and who are surrounded with the comforts of
life. Wherever they reside, let them immediately transmit the sum of
fifteen dollars which will constitute them life members. In this manner, also, a very considerable amount may easily be raised and expended in the promotion of a cause which is second to none ever
agitated since the creation of man. The third article of our Constitution is as follows: — 'Any person by signing the Constitution, [or,
of course, authorising his name to be affixed thereto,] and paying to
the Treasurer fifteen dollars as a life subscription, or two dollars annually, shall be considered a member of the Society, and entitled to
a voice and a vote in all its meetings, and to a copy of any publications
or communications which may be distributed among its members.'

Thirdly — To the friends of abolition in the various towns and
cities. We wish them to be active in forming auxiliary societies. If
there are not more than five or six such persons in a place, it is im-
material — the number is sufficient to make an experiment. The life
and usefulness of the Parent Society must depend mainly upon the
number and efficiency of its auxiliaries. These, by their regular contributions to the general fund, furnish the life-blood that gives vitality to the whole system.

Fourthly — To opulent philanthropists, who are abundantly able
to contribute at least $100 annually, and never miss their money.
And,

Lastly — To the pastors of churches, who, agreeing with us in
sentiment, are constantly favored with opportunities which may be
improved in commending our Society to the patronage of their flocks.
They can take up at least one collection annually, in aid of our funds.

These hints, I trust, will be cordially adopted by the various classes
for whom they are intended.

I shall close this hasty epistle with an advertisement which I copy
from the National Intelligencer [7] of the 25th ultimo:

'FIFTY DOLLARS REWARD!!

Ranaway from the Subscriber, living in Prince George's county, Md. on Thursday morning, September 13th, negro man Harry, calling himself Harry or Henry Lowe. He is very black, between 25 and 30 years of age — about five feet ten inches in height, square, well and strongly made — speaks quickly, and with some impediment when agitated. *There are two particular* MARKS *by which he may be easily recognized,* VIZ. THE LOSS OF ONE OF HIS TOES, on which foot it is not remembered — and A CONSPICUOUS MARK, or *prominent excrescence* ACROSS HIS BREAST, which has the appearance of *an old burn* or *scar,* FROM THE STROKE OF A WHIP. His clothes are such as are commonly worn by the negroes of Maryland. The above slave was purchased from the estate of Walter H. Hillary, of Prince George's county, Md. in which neighborhood he may now be loitering.

The above reward will be given, if taken out of the county; and $20, if taken in the county, and brought home to me, or delivered in any jail, so that I may get him again.

WALTER BOURIE,[8]
Forest of Prince George's county.'

Comment is unnecessary. O, how humanely the slaves are treated at the south! Strange, indeed, that they are so prone to run away from their *philanthropic* masters!

You may expect my next letter from Waterville.

Yours, ever,

WM. LLOYD GARRISON.

Printed: *The Liberator,* October 27, 1832.

1. Alonzo Lewis.
2. Unidentified.
3. Charles Hayes (c. 1799–1839) is listed in the Bangor city directory as the innkeeper of the Penobscot Exchange.
4. Garrison mistakes the spelling of the name of Swan L. Pomeroy (1799–1869), who had been the minister of the First Congregational Church in Bangor since 1825; after twenty-three years of service he became secretary of the American Board of Commissioners for Foreign Missions.
5. Benjamin Huntoon (1792–1864), born in New Hampshire and trained in Massachusetts, settled in Bangor, Maine, as minister of the new Unitarian church in 1829 or shortly thereafter. In subsequent years he moved from parish to parish, serving mostly in Massachusetts but also as far west as Cincinnati, Ohio, and Peoria, Illinois.
6. Joseph C. Lovejoy.
7. A conservative and, as Garrison thought, pro-slavery paper published in Washington, D.C.
8. According to the State of Maryland Hall of Records, Harry or Henry Lowe belonged to Walter Hillary or Hilleary, who died about 1824. A few months later Harry Lowe, along with other property, was sold to Stephen H. Tyng, an Episcopal minister with a church in Prince George's county. Whether Harry ran away from Tyng, or was sold to Walter Bourie is not known; nor can Bourie be identified. It is possible that Tyng, being a minister, would not want to advertise the fact that his slave had run away.

75

TO *THE LIBERATOR*

WATERVILLE, Oct. 8, 1832.

A pretty, quiet, attractive village, this! — I almost positively decided at Bangor, not to visit it on my return, on account of a multiplicity of engagements elsewhere; but happily — I think providentially — my determination was overruled, by the advice of several friends, and now I sit down to thank them and to congratulate our cause in view of the results of this journey.

A word as to the weather: at Bangor, it was inexpressibly dreary, as you have been already apprized — but here, what a bright and exhilarating change! O, for a suitable panegyric upon the sun — the gorgeous, world-enlightening sun! My feelings burst out into song whenever he shows his majestic countenance; and particularly at this season of the year does my attachment acquire a strength proportionate to the intensity of his beams. But I have a two-fold source of pleasure — for three evenings has the moon put on her best attire, and exhibited the perfection of beauty. I have been standing upon the fragments of a noble bridge which was shattered and vanquished by a tremendous freshet early in the spring, and listening to the sonorous voice of an ambitious waterfall, and watching the rapid current of the Kennebec as it went joyfully onward to the ocean, flashing and foaming in the light of the moon. The scene was worth a trip from Boston to Waterville.

I was politely requested by the students belonging to the College,[1] to address them on Saturday on the subject of African Colonization. I declined making a formal discourse, but gave them, as briefly and clearly as I could, my views of the delusive character and dangerous tendency of the American Colonization Society. I also exhibited the principles and purposes of the New-England Anti-Slavery Society, satisfying the students that the two societies could never co-operate with each other. At the close of my remarks, I requested any individuals who were friendly to the colonization scheme to propound their objections to my doctrines, and to sustain their own sentiments. Two or three of the students asked several very pertinent questions, and started some difficulties, which I endeavored to answer and remove. A glow of enthusiasm seemed to pervade the entire audience, which was dismissed under the most cheering circumstances. I beseech the students, individually and collectively, to accept the assurances of my high regard, and my thanks for their politeness and attention. Their enlistment in the cause of abolition is of great importance, as they are destined to exert a wide and powerful influence upon society.

Through the kindness of the Rev. Mr. Green, a highly esteemed Baptist clergyman, I was permitted to occupy his pulpit on Saturday and Sabbath evenings, to very excellent audiences.[2] We may confidently anticipate the formation of an Anti-Slavery Society in this place, in a short time.

I have inflicted upon the readers of the Liberator some very long epistles, and now offer this brief scrawl by way of expiation. Yet I cannot close without acknowledging my obligations to President Chaplin and his interesting family, for their urbanity and hospitality to my person.[3]

In the greatest hurry I remain, as ever,

Yours, &c.

WM. LLOYD GARRISON

Printed: *The Liberator*, November 10, 1832.

1. Waterville College, subsequently to become Colby College.
2. Henry K. Greene (correct spelling) became the minister of the First Baptist Church in 1831. In his two years as pastor he acquired the reputation of being an ardent evangelist, for he presided at several of the protracted meetings which became increasingly common in the state in the 1830's.
3. Jeremiah Chaplin (1776–1841), after fourteen years as minister of the Baptist Church in Danvers, Massachusetts, came in 1817 to Waterville to run the college. He and his wife, later found to be a distant relative of Garrison's, had ten children. In 1833 the Reverend Chaplin resigned as president of the college, owing to a conflict with the students. He preached out his years in Massachusetts, Connecticut, and New York state.

---

7 6

TO SAMUEL J. MAY

BOSTON, NOV. 30, 1832.

DEAR SIR:

THE NEW-ENGLAND ANTI-SLAVERY SOCIETY will hold its *First Annual Meeting* in this city on the second Wednesday of January next.[1] It unanimously invites you — among other friends of God and man, of religion and humanity, of immediate and universal justice — to be present on that occasion, and to speak to a Resolution expressive of the evils and criminality of slavery, in a moral and religious point of view.

It is earnestly hoped, for the sake of millions of perishing souls, that you will be able to comply with this invitation; that you will, at a crisis so important and on an occasion so interesting, lend your influence and exert your talents to promote a cause that is paramount to any other which now attracts the attention and commands the support of wise and good men. The principles and designs of the Anti-Slavery Society, it is presumed, are fully understood by you. By immediately signifying whether you deem it probable that circumstances will enable you to be present at its anniversary, and whether you should be willing to speak on the subject above suggested, (or on any other topic more congenial to your feelings, appertaining to the welfare of the free colored and slave population of this country,) you will oblige the Society. You are requested to put the Resolution in such words as you may deem best, and send a copy of it in your reply — which may be directed to

Yours, respectfully,

WM. LLOYD GARRISON.
Corresponding Secretary.

Rev. Samuel J. May.

Printed: Garrison Papers, Boston Public Library.

This is a printed form letter of which two copies are known. A typed transcript of the second copy, of the same date and addressed to General Samuel Fessenden (see letter 77), is preserved in the Merrill Collection of Garrison Papers, Wichita State University Library. In the letter to May the day of the month is supplied in Garrison's hand as well as the name of the recipient and the final sentence of the first paragraph, following "expressive of." Another hand has written at the bottom of the page this statement: "Resolved — that the principles of the Anti Slavery do not impinge the rights of any of our fellow citizens, nor endanger the peace & happiness of our country." In the letter to Fessenden there is at the end of the first paragraph the following: "the political evils of southern slavery — as tending directly to distract and divide the Union, and putting into the hands of slaveholders a dangerous and unjust privilege at the polls, they being now permitted to vote in behalf of three-fifths of their slaves."

1. Garrison refers to the meeting at which the New-England Anti-Slavery Society was to be founded, which was called in the invitation "the First Annual Meeting."

---

7 7

TO SAMUEL FESSENDEN

Nov. 30, 1832.

My dear Sir:

I do sincerely hope that you will honor our annual meeting with your presence, according to the printed invitation contained in this sheet. As the Legislature will be in session at that time, we shall probably have a large portion of its six hundred members present on that occasion. Hence it is important that we should then make a demonstration of talent and strength.

By a letter from my friend Winslow,[1] I learn that you have generously contributed $10 towards sustaining the Liberator in its perilous warfare against the enemies of justice, humanity and righteousness. That sum entitles you to two dozen copies of my "Thoughts on African Colonization," which I presume you can obtain of Mr. Winslow, as I have recently forwarded to him, at his request, seven dozen.

I have just received the most cheering letters from England, relative to the triumphant progress of the abolition cause in that country. The British philanthropists are also rejoicing to learn that we have organized an Anti-Slavery Society, and bid us God speed.

Be pleased to communicate my respectful remembrances to your excellent lady — express to your dear little children my affection for them — and accept for yourself the esteem, friendship and admiration, as well as gratitude, of

Your humble coadjutor,

Wm. Lloyd Garrison.

Samuel Fessenden, Esq.
Portland, Me.

Typed transcript: Merrill Collection of Garrison Papers, Wichita State University Library. Accompanying this letter was a printed form letter of the same date; see letter 76.

Samuel Fessenden (1784–1869), holding the rank of general in the militia, was one of the most distinguished lawyers in the state of Maine. General Fessenden helped to found a state antislavery society the following spring. Originally a colonizationist, he was by the time of this letter a Garrisonian.

1. Nathan Winslow.

78

TO SAMUEL J. MAY

Boston, Dec. 4, 1832.

Beloved Brother:

At the time of our annual meeting, there will be in this city at least six hundred members of the Legislature, a large portion of whom we shall probably secure as auditors: hence it is highly important that we should make a demonstration of strength and talent on that occasion.

Our cause goes on prosperously. Indeed, when I consider the brevity of the period in which we have been engaged, and the nature and number of the obstacles which towered in our path, I am surprised to observe the impression we have made upon the nation.

Our coadjutors in England are fighting most manfully, with spiritual weapons against sin and cruelty. I have just received from them a large bundle of anti-slavery pamphlets, tracts, circulars, &c. &c. the perusal of which is almost too much for my poor nerves. The British abolitionists waste no ammunition — every shot tells — *they write in earnest* — they call, as did old John Knox, a fig a fig, and a spade a spade.[1] When I see what they are doing, and read what they write, I blush to think of my own past apathy, and mourn in view of my poverty of thought and language.

By all means come at our annual meeting, if possible.

This letter, I trust, will find you and your lady, as it leaves me, in the enjoyment of good health.

Your steadfast friend,

Wm. Lloyd Garrison.

ALS: Garrison Papers, Boston Public Library; printed partly in *Life*, I, 314.

Enclosed with this letter was a printed form letter, which, since it was dated November 30, has been placed in the appropriate chronological position.

1. John Knox (1505–1572) was the leader of the Protestant Reformation and the founder of the Presbyterian church in Scotland.

79

TO JOHN B. VASHON

Boston, Dec. 8, 1832.

My noble friend:

With the most grateful emotions I hasten to acknowledge the receipt of your favor of the 1st instant, containing a 50 dollar Note of the U.S. Bank. The promptitude with which you have responded to our Circular, demands our most thankful acknowledgments. The loan will prove highly serviceable to us at this juncture, and shall be liquidated whenever you desire it. Since we made our appeal to the friends of the Liberator, nearly all our "Thoughts on Colonization" have been spoken for, on the terms proposed in our Circular.

Since my last epistle to you, you have sent me some most cheering letters, in relation to the change of sentiment on the subject of Colonization among highly reputable men in Pittsburgh. I read them to many individuals on my late tour in the State of Maine, and they produced a capital effect. Truly, we have reason to be encouraged in our cause, when it is espoused by such men as the Rev. Dr. Bruce and Judge Pentler.[1] Every week I receive information of the abandonment of the Colonization Society by some of its warmest supporters.

The signs of the times cannot be mistaken. It is apparent that a generous compassion and a liberal feeling are extending among the whites for the people of color. If South Carolina should withdraw from the Union, the abolition of slavery in that State must be inevitable; and if she still keep within the circle of the Union, she, with every other slave State, is destined to feel the force of a public sentiment that shall break every servile fetter.

I am struck to observe how strongly the fire of moral indignation burns in the bosoms of those who, discovering that they have been shamefully duped by the colonization scheme, are led to contemplate the features of the monster Slavery. I am more and more convinced, that the permanency of the bloody system depends upon the stability of the Colonization Society. The union between them is perfect — the overthrow of one must be the destruction of the other.

Nothing encourages me more than to witness such unanimity, and efforts for mutual improvement, among my free colored brethren. True, they have not yet fully aroused to the importance of aiming at high intellectual and moral attainments; but they have accomplished much in a short time, and are evidently making rapid strides to respectability and knowledge.

I trust my life may be spared many years — not because I am not desirous to depart and be with Christ, for I rejoice in my mortality — but because I wish to do something for the emancipation of my suffering countrymen, far beyond any of my past exertions. Time is rapidly flying — much remains to be done — O, may my zeal and activity in this great cause increase.

Accept my best wishes for your success in all your laudable enterprises. My partner wishes to be understood as cherishing the same respect and friendship for your person, as does

　　　　Your steadfast friend,

　　　　　　　　　　　　　　　　Wm. Lloyd Garrison.

Mr. John B. Vashon,
Pittsburgh, Pa.

Typed transcription: Villard Papers, Harvard College Library.

John B. Vashon (died 1854), a prosperous Negro barber and subsequently proprietor of the City Baths of Pittsburgh, Pennsylvania, was active in the cause of abolition as early as 1831 when as chairman of a group of Negro citizens he wrote a series of resolutions opposing the American Colonization Society (*The Liberator*, September 17, 1831). He was for many years Garrison's close friend and was, in fact, to be entertained in the Garrison home on October 21, 1835, the day of the famous Boston mob. It was he who visited the imprisoned abolitionist the morning after the riot, presenting him with a new hat to replace the one destroyed by the mob. (See *The Liberator*, December 19, 1835, October 29, 1836, and, for his obituary, January 20, 1854.)

1. Robert Bruce (1778–1846) was born in Scotland and sent by the Asso-

ciate Synod of that country as a missionary to the United States in 1806. Since 1813 he had served as the minister of the Associate (Presbyterian) Church in the thriving town of Pittsburgh. Beginning in 1820 he served also as the principal of the Western University of Pennsylvania. In the last years of his life he was to be instrumental in founding Duquesne College, a short-lived institution organized by dissenting faculty and students from the Western University (not to be confused with the present-day university). Judge Pentler has not been identified.

---

8 0

TO ROBERT PURVIS

Boston, Dec. 10, 1832.

My dear Purvis:

Heaven, it seems, has given you and your lady a fine boy. Blessings on his infancy! may he prove one of the best of his persecuted race! — Both of you can now, doubtless, feel yet more intensely for those unhappy parents who are pining in hopeless bondage. Till now, you could only sympathise in imagination; but you have a precious infant to make your hearts recoil, as they have never recoiled before, at the thought of a ruthless separation of the ties of Nature. What would induce you to sell that child as a slave? — Money? You would spurn a thousand argosies, freighted with gold and gems. Threats of torture? You would sooner perish than give it up. *It is yours* — the God of Heaven has deposited it with you for safe keeping — no one on earth has a right to take it from you. How liberal, how blissful, how sacred is the trust! — You will, if its life should be spared, "train it up in the way it should go"[1] — and thus it shall be an ornament to society, and finally sit with multitudes in glory.

It was with much delicacy of feeling, and a strong reluctance, that we addressed our Circular to some of our Philadelphia friends, conscious how much they had done to give stability to the Liberator. But we had but this hard alternative — either to suffer the paper to die, or make known the embarrassments into which the publication of our "Thoughts" had unavoidably plunged us.[2] The idea of the suppression of the Liberator was to us as dreadful almost as the cutting off a right hand, or plucking out a right eye. How would southern kidnappers and their apologists shout! What a prodigious shock would be given to the lively sensibilities of the friends of humanity in every part of the nation! What extensive injury would be done to the abolition cause! With what exultation would its overthrow be hailed by the colonization leaders!

I am happy to inform you that the appeal we put forth to our friends will not be in vain. — Already we are enabled to assure you that there is no cause for apprehension in regard to the continuance of the Liberator. The extraordinary purchase of so large a number of copies of our "Thoughts" in Philadelphia as has been ordered by our friends Cassey, Forten and yourself, has given us material assistance;[3] and the response in other places is beginning to come back in a very encouraging manner. The entire edition will probably soon be taken up, the distribution of which, I am confident, will, more than any thing else, put an end to the colonization mania.

You will please to convey to your noble father-in-law, for me and my partner, all that hearts filled with gratitude, and keenly susceptible, may be supposed to utter.

This is my twenty-eighth birth-day![4] — I am startled at the hurricane-speed of time. My life seems to me to have been a blank. The older I grow, the less do I seem to accomplish. Days and weeks vanish like flashes of light upon a sombre sky, and seem to diminish to the duration of moments. I am twenty-eight! — Infancy passed away unheedingly — passively; childhood in frolic and sport, in smiles and tears; boyhood in the school-room, and abroad in the fields, and in venturesome but forbidden excursions upon the river; youth in mec[hanica]l toil, assisted by dreams of future happiness and cheered by the phantom Hope; — and now — what! has it come to this? — yes, *now* I have struck deep into manhood! — Well, then, manhood shall be my most serviceable stage; and being so, the happiest of the whole!

Your hint respecting Mr. Cæsar shall be improved in the Liberator. You shall there find shortly, not *"Cæsar's Commentaries,"* but commentaries upon Cæsar, not in Latin, but in good plain English.[5]

Of course, I wish to include in this hasty epistle, my best respects to your lady, to Mr. Forten, his lady and family, your brother, Mr. Hinton,[6] and other friends — in which my partner heartily joins. A letter from you will always be thankfully received.

Yours, unreservedly,

Wm. Lloyd Garrison.

ALS: Garrison Papers, Boston Public Library; printed partly in *Life*, I, 311–312, 314.

1. Garrison alludes to Proverbs 22:6.
2. Garrison and Knapp's frequent financial embarrassment was due not only to the publication of expensive pamphlets like *Thoughts on African Colonization* but also to the printing of many other tracts, addresses, and circulars. Moreover, Garrison was having difficulty collecting money due from subscribers, as the many duns in *The Liberator* would indicate; see the issues for October 13, November 24, and December 1, 1832.
3. Joseph Cassey. James E. Forten (1766–1842) was a prosperous Philadel-

phia sailmaker and leader in the large Negro community. As an early and determined opponent of colonization, he greatly influenced Garrison's thought. Forten was the father-in-law of Robert Purvis.

4. Actually, Garrison was twenty-seven rather than twenty-eight. See letter 4, to Frances Lloyd Garrison, May 26, 1823.

5. According to Charles W. Dennison, editor of the *Emancipator*, the Reverend Caesar was sent out by the Episcopal church as a missionary to Liberia. There he was found engaging in politics, petty lawsuits, and selling rum; see *The Liberator*, May 18, 1833. Garrison protested "this mode of spiritualizing Africa" in *The Liberator*, December 15, 1832.

6. Frederick A. Hinton, perfumer and hairdresser, one of the leaders of the Philadelphia antislavery movement and probably a *Liberator* agent in that city.

81

TO GEORGE W. BENSON

Boston, Dec. 10, 1832.

My dear friend:

It gives me pleasure to acknowledge the receipt of yours of the 7th inst., as also two or three from your attentive and estimable brother. It was with extreme delicacy and reluctance that I sent a copy of our Circular [1] to you and him, seeing we were already so deeply indebted to you both; and, moreover, knowing the disproportionate liberality of your minds to your limited means, I feared you would make some large sacrifices to serve us in our exigency. The promptness with which the Circular was answered, and the very generous engagement of 200 copies more of our "Thoughts," [2] demand from us the strongest expressions of thankfulness. The only recompense we can make, (and we know you require no other,) is, to be yet more diligent and faithful in promoting that cause which lies so near your hearts, and which, in importance, is paramount to all others.

I am sure it will give you true satisfaction to be informed that the prospects of the Liberator, which, three weeks ago, were dark and discouraging, are now bright and cheering! — The appeal which we put forth to our friends, in various places, has been answered in a manner that shows a deep attachment for the Liberator. There is now a fair prospect that we shall dispose of the whole of the remaining copies of our "Thoughts" — and thus we shall be disenthralled from those pecuniary embarrassments which were unavoidably incurred in publishing the work. The distribution of these copies cannot fail to open the eyes of many good people, who through ignorance are giving their influence and money to aid the Colonization Society. The death-like silence which has reigned among the leaders of the crusade since the appearance of the work, very plainly shows that they are unable to disprove its allegations. Surely six months furnish a space amply sufficient to make a reply; — and I know if they could, by any possibility, put me down, they would do so. The book, then, being a just exposition of colonization principles, it behooves every lover of truth, every friend of humanity, every disciple of Jesus Christ, to read it carefully, and understand the nature and design of the Colonization Society. You will have seen, by the last Liberator, the weak and beggarly manner in which R. R. Gurley attempts to invalidate the work.[3] I will not leave him till I have shown that every position he has assumed is utterly untenable.

I have lately received a letter from the distinguished Friend in Liverpool, James Cropper, in which he denounces the Colonization Society as "a diabolical scheme to perpetuate slavery."[4] You will see the letter in the next Liberator. It will make a salutary impression upon the minds of many in the Society of Friends in this country.

Happy am I to learn that you contemplate, in the course of the present week, to lift up the Banner of Emancipation in the city of Providence, and that my dearly beloved brother Jocelyn[5] is to be present with you. — It is undoubtedly true, as you candidly intimate, that, owing to the numerous prejudices which unhappily, and I think undeservedly, exist against us, friend Buffum and myself could be of no service to you were we present. We shall be with you in spirit — you shall have our best wishes and most fervent aspirations to Heaven for the success of your noble enterprise. You will find a strong advocate in brother Jocelyn, whose eloquent app[eal] can scarcely fail to disarm prejudice, rebuke slothfulness, stimulate zeal, and secure many converts. Go forward, boldly — fear nothing — the Lord of Hosts is with you.

My friend Knapp regrets that he cannot be present at your meeting, but sends to you and Henry his grateful acknowledgments for your manifold kindnesses.

Your hint, respecting a letter from the Anti-Slavery Society to be addressed to members of the Society of Friends, shall be duly attended to. It strikes me very favorably.

Be particular in giving the strongest assurances of my regard to our mutual friend Mr. Prentice.[6] I hope soon to be able to send him a letter.

Much love to your brother, your partner in trade, friends Brown, Brewer, Scott, Potter, Chase, &c. &c. &c.[7]

Assuredly yours to the grave,

Wm. Lloyd Garrison.

ALS: Garrison Papers, Boston Public Library; printed partly in *Life*, I, 312–313.

1. Urging financial support of *The Liberator*.

2. *Thoughts on African Colonization.*

3. Ralph Randolph Gurley (1797–1872), a Yale graduate settled in Washington, where he worked assiduously for the American Colonization Society as agent, secretary, vice president, life director, and editor of the society's official organ, the *African Repository.* Among many of his contemporaries he gained the reputation of being the champion of poor Negroes in Washington and one of the most dedicated of philanthropists.

4. James Cropper (1773–1840), a wealthy Quaker merchant, was dedicated to the abolition of slavery in the West Indies; he was one of the first English abolitionists to oppose the American Colonization Society.

5. Simeon S. Jocelyn.

6. John Prentice.

7. Garrison lists Rhode Island friends Moses Brown, Simeon Brewer, James Scott, Anson Potter, and William M. Chace (or Chase), of whom all but Scott and Potter have been identified in previous notes. James Scott (1788–1862), son of a Quaker minister and first cousin of Henry Anthony, Charlotte Benson's husband, was prominent among Providence abolitionists. Anson Potter, of Cranston, Rhode Island, a close friend of Scott's, had been converted from deism to the doctrines of the New Jerusalem. About 1835 the two men moved to the New Church in Bridgewater, Massachusetts. (See the appendix of William R. Staples, *Annals of the Town of Providence from its First Settlement to the Organization of the City Government in June, 1832*, Providence, 1843.)

III   MISSION TO ENGLAND: 1833

III MISSION TO ENGLAND: 1833

Y THE SPRING of 1833 Garrison and the New England Anti-Slavery Society had decided to emphasize as their major objective the improvement of the free colored. Following the lead of Arthur and Lewis Tappan of New York City, who had been interested in such a project as early as the summer of 1831, they decided to promote manual-labor education by founding a school where indigent Negroes could be inexpensively educated by working part time. It was thought that money available in this country could be substantially augmented by a fund-raising mission to England. Garrison was quite willing to undertake the mission. In *The Liberator* for March 9 the New England Anti-Slavery Society announced the plan for a mission to England "for the purpose of procuring funds to aid in the establishment of the proposed MANUAL LABOR SCHOOL FOR COLORED YOUTH, and of disseminating in that country the truth in relation to American Slavery, and its ally, the American Colonization Society." Sufficient money was raised to pay Garrison's passage to England and most of his expenses there. Oliver Johnson was persuaded to edit *The Liberator* in Garrison's absence.

Before sailing from New York on May 1, Garrison indulged in a ceremonial farewell tour complete with a series of addresses in Boston, Providence, and New York. He landed in Liverpool on May 22 and soon found himself in London, completely at home with English abolitionists, who were all discussing immediate emancipation and awaiting the passage through Parliament of the abolition bill.

It was an exciting time for an American abolitionist to be in London, but it seemed hardly appropriate to plead for support of a manual-labor school in the United States, especially with all the poverty visible in England. Garrison decided that he was needed in England for the alternate purpose announced in *The Liberator* of presenting the truth about American slavery and colonization. It happened that Elliott Cresson, a Quaker philanthropist from Philadelphia, was in

England on behalf of the American Colonization Society. Garrison felt that he was confronted with a personal as well as an ideological challenge. The conflict between the two men is described fully in Garrison's letters. What those letters do not explain, however, is that Garrison pursued Cresson so relentlessly that he attacked not only Cresson but the United States as well.

By the time he reached New York City early in October, Garrison's enemies had spread the word that he was disloyal, a traitor to his country. Stirred up by publicity to this effect in several papers, a mob disrupted an antislavery meeting planned by the Tappans to found a New York City society. Garrison, unrecognized, watched calmly from the sidelines. In Boston there was also adverse publicity and a riotous homecoming.

The year 1833 was marked by another signal event. Since the spring of 1831 Garrison had been urging the formation of a national antislavery organization, and his observation of the success of the British movement strengthened his resolve. The Tappans also had wanted a national society, but the riots in New York and Boston convinced them that it must be postponed. Garrison argued that the new society must be founded while the British precedent was vividly remembered, and he succeeded in having a convention gathered in Philadelphia on December 3. At the convention there was no disagreement about the necessity for having a national society, but there was a struggle for power between Garrison and his New England associates on the one hand and Lewis Tappan and the New York group on the other. The New Yorkers being more numerous, the absent Arthur Tappan was put up for president and Garrison was relegated to the relatively unimportant post of secretary of foreign correspondence, though he was also given the honor of writing the Declaration of Sentiments for the new organization.

82

TO BENJAMIN FERRIS

Boston, Feb. 16, 1833.

Respected Friend:

I presume the enclosed plan, for the establishment and government of the Manual Labor School for Colored Youth, will be acceptable to you and your benevolent friend.[1] The Managers of the Anti-Slavery Society deem it unnecessary to urge upon either of you the importance and need of the contemplated school. It is desirable that whatever is done, should be done speedily. Subscriptions have been commenced, in this quarter, under very favorable circumstances. Your friend, we trust, will add his name to the list of donors.

We are cheered in view of the progress of the anti-slavery cause in this country. The example, so long given by the Society of Friends, is beginning to have its legitimate influence.

Your humble friend,

Wm. Lloyd Garrison.

Benjamin Ferris.

ALS: Philip D. Sang Slavery Collection, Rutgers State University Library.

Benjamin Ferris (1780–1867), Wilmington, Delaware, had been first a watchmaker and then a conveyancer; he became sufficiently successful to be able to retire relatively young and devote his energies to historical, religious, and reform interests. During 1821–1822, Ferris engaged in a religious controversy with the Reverend Dr. Paul Gilbert, subsequently to be published under the title *Letters of Paul and Amicus*; in 1846 he was to publish *A History of the Original Settlements on the Delaware*. (*Biographical and Genealogical History of the State of Delaware*, Chambersburg, Pa., 1899, I, 108.)

1. Not identified.

83

TO THE EDITOR OF THE *ESSEX REGISTER*

Boston, Feb. 23, 1833.

Sir, —

To obviate any misapprehensions which may arise in the minds of individuals, in relation to the occurrence that took place between the Rev. Dr. Flint and myself, on Friday evening, permit me to state that when I replied to him, I was ignorant of his name and profession — consequently, I intended no *personal* disrespect or impeachment; that I understood him to represent, *as a matter of fact*, or to stamp this impression upon the minds of the audience, that the free colored inhabitants of Baltimore were a miserable and worthless class, and the slaves exactly the reverse; — that, thus construing his statement, I pronounced it to be untrue, from my own personal knowledge, having resided several months in that city; and that I did not mean to charge him with making a wilful misrepresentation. Whether he was a good or a bad man — a lover of truth or falsehood — a friend of liberty or slavery — I knew not, on rising to answer him. My object was, simply, to vindicate the free colored Baltimoreans from the reproach cast upon them — whether purposely or ignorantly cast, I could not tell, until the name of the gentleman was communicated to me. On ascertaining it, I was immediately satisfied of his integrity, and great moral worth. An explanation was promptly given to the meeting.[1]

By inserting this note in the Register, you will greatly oblige

Yours, respectfully,

WM. LLOYD GARRISON.

Printed: *Essex Register*, February 28, 1833; reprinted here from the text Garrison must have revised slightly for publication in *The Liberator*, March 2, 1833.

Warwick Palfray, Jr. (1787–1838), a fair-minded, self-educated man, had edited the *Essex Register* in Salem since 1807.

1. Although it is unusual for Garrison to admit being in the wrong, he apologizes in this letter for "a short collision [that] took place between the Rev. Dr. Flint and the Editor of the Liberator" in Salem on the occasion of a debate between the Reverend Joshua N. Danforth, agent of the American Colonization Society, and Arnold Buffum, Garrison supporter (*The Liberator*, March 2, 1833). Garrison's opponent was James Flint (1779–1855), who had been installed as minister of the East Meeting House in 1821 (Harriet S. Tapley, *Salem Imprints, 1768–1825*, Salem, Massachusetts, 1927, p. 462). He was a man of scholarly inclinations and had the reputation of being a good writer and an excellent preacher; he was a man universally respected in the Salem community.

84

TO HARRIOTT PLUMMER

Boston, March 4, 1833.

❋   ❋   ❋   ❋

My soul trembles in view of the magnitude of the cause in which I have embarked. I stand, as it were, on an eminence, commanding a sight of Africa, — the Niobe of nations, — and watch the flames of a thousand burning villages fearfully reddening the wide heavens, and hear the shrieks and groans of her enslaved and dying children — and a voice from Heaven cries, — *"Plead for the oppressed!"* The troublous ocean throws aside its blue curtain, and reveals to my vision an African golgotha, — the bodies of the dead, men, women and babes, tracking the paths of the slave ships, and numerous as the waves that chant their requiem. A sickly sensation passes over my frame, as if their blood was drenching my garments; and again I hear that voice from Heaven, saying, — "*Plead for the oppressed!*" The cries of the suffocating victims in the holds of the ships, who, stolen to glut European and American avarice, are destined either to be the prey of sharks, or, what is far worse, to be sold and used for life like cattle, are borne to my ears by every breeze from the ocean; and still I hear that voice from Heaven, saying, — "*Plead for the oppressed!*" Around me throng the two millions of slaves in this guilty land, — debased, weary, famishing, bleeding and bound, — and they wound my ears with their sighs and shrieks, and melt my heart by their agonizing appeals; and they point to the graves of the millions of their kindred who have perished in their chains; and I see unborn generations of victims stalking like apparitions before me; and once more I hear that voice from Heaven, saying, in a tone awful and loud, and with increasing earnestness, — "*Plead for the oppressed!*"

And shall I disobey that voice? If so, will my advisers give me acquital in the day of judgment? If I put out my eyes and stop my ears, and petrify my heart, and become insensible as a marble statue, to please the community, will the community rescue me from the charge of inhumanity, selfishness and cruelty toward my suffering fellow creatures, which will be preferred against me at the bar of God? I am anxious to please the people; but if, in order to do so, I must violate the plainest precepts of the gospel, and disregard the most solemn obligations, will the people see that my name is written in the Book of Life, and that my sins are blotted out of the Book of Remembrance? If they cannot, I must obey the voice from Heaven, whether men will hear or whether they will forbear.

This, then, is the extent of my fanaticism. I mean to perform my duty to God and my fellow men — to love Him supremely, and them as myself.

There does not breathe a human being whom I would injure for worlds. All my enemies I freely pardon, and under the strongest provocations to resentment which they can give me, can use the language of the expiring Son of God — "*Father, forgive them: they know not what they do.*" [1] As I have said elsewhere: [2] my memory can no more retain the impression of anger, hatred or revenge, than the ocean the track of its monsters. To the slave-holder I address myself in the language of the apostle: "Am I therefore your enemy because I tell you the truth?" [3] He is a robber — a great robber — a robber of God and man — and he should be made to see and feel his guilt, if he be not given over to hardness of heart and blindness of mind. I will not plaster over his conscience with anything like this: "You are very unfortunate! You cannot do otherwise, at present! The evil of slavery was entailed upon you! It would be dangerous and cruel to liberate your slaves now! How much better they are off than free persons of color! Do not emancipate until you can send them to Liberia!" &c., &c. Unfortunate thieves! merciful oppressors! — Sober drunkards! religious atheists! believing infidels!

❀   ❀   ❀   ❀

You ask: "How much is it expedient for members of society, uninfluential as ourselves, to think of the subject of slavery?"

Perhaps no truer criterion can be given than this: the golden rule of our Savior. It is my constant endeavor to place myself, in imagination, in the situation of the slaves; and thus I never fail to plead earnestly. We must meditate much, to feel and act properly. The danger is not, I think, that we shall suffer our thoughts to dwell too much upon the cruel slave-system, but that our ardor may expire with the novelty of the subject.

"*Uninfluential* as ourselves"! Whose influence is so potent as Woman's? Who has a form, an eye, a voice like hers? Whose sceptre is so imperial as her own? Whose benevolent heroism, or moral excellence, or tender sensibility, or deep devotion, is comparable to hers? "Uninfluential"! You have infused new hope and courage into one heart at least — into my own; and if I exert any influence upon public sentiment, a portion of the merit will hereafter belong to you. Your letters reveal a talent, a spirit, a sympathy, which, if actively exerted, are sufficient to save our country. You may set an example which shall not be powerless beyond the limits of your village: it shall go forth like a universal blessing. The destiny of the slaves is in the hands of the American women, and complete emancipation can never take place without their co-operation.[4] See what the females of Great Britain have accomplished by uniting together in this labor of love. Many years ago, a distinguished lady in England was so deeply affected in reading Ramsey's View of Slavery in the British Colonies, that she resolved to devote her time, and wealth, and talents, to the abolition of slavery.[5] She soon succeeded in forming among her acquaintance an Anti-Slavery Society; and from that little association has proceeded an influence which has regenerated public sentiment, and to which, undoubtedly, in a great measure, we shall owe the speedy emancipation of eight hundred thousand British slaves. — The ladies of this country may do as much as those of Great Britain have done, in this good cause. Fully comprehending the horrible situation of the female slaves, how can they rest quietly upon their beds at night, or feel indifferent to the deliverance of those in bonds? Oh, if the shrieks could reach our ears which are constantly rising to heaven from the bosom of some bleeding wife or ruined daughter at the South, we should shudder and turn pale, and make new resolutions to seek their deliverance. Women of New England — mothers and daughters! if I fail to awake your sympathies, and secure your aid, I may well despair of gaining the hearts and support of men. If my heart bleeds over the degraded and insufferable condition of a large portion of your sex, how ought you, whose sensibility is more susceptible than the wind-harp, to weep, and speak, and act, in their behalf?

> "Shall we behold, unheeding,
>   Life's holiest feelings crushed?
> When woman's heart is bleeding,
>   Shall woman's voice be hushed?
>
> Oh, by every blessing,
>   That Heaven to thee may lend,
> Forget not their oppression —
>   Remember, sister, friend!" [6]

No — no! you will not, must not, cannot forget. But then you fear lest this cause may exclude other good objects from your attention. It may, indeed, to some extent, but not culpably so. My interest in the cause of Temperance, Peace, Missions, &c., &c., suffers no abatement from my devotion to the cause of emancipation: on the contrary, it rises daily in all the moral enterprises of the age. It is true, I cannot give them all the same attention and assistance — nor does duty require such a division of my time and energy — but I can do something for them all. Besides, all of them, except the anti-slavery cause, are supported by a powerful host: hence we may be permitted to labor chiefly for the promotion of that one cause. Am I right? In reference to the absorbing interest which you feel in this cause, you say, "Tell us, then, how we may prevent the supremacy of these feelings." No, indeed, ladies, I would not, on any account, put down that supremacy.

      ✻   ✻   ✻   ✻

You excite my curiosity and interest still more, by informing me that my dearly beloved Whittier is a *friend* and townsman of yours. Can we not induce him to devote his brilliant genius more to the advancement of our cause, and kindred enterprises, and less to the creations of romance and fancy, and the disturbing incidents of political strife?

      ✻   ✻   ✻   ✻

The worthy pastor who says that distributing the Liberator in the southern states is like throwing fire-brands into a magazine of powder, should remember that truth is revolutionary in its tendency. Does he never inflame the minds of sinners by his faithful admonitions? What incendiaries were the apostles! So cut to the heart were the guilty Jews by the preaching of Stephen, that "they cried out with a loud voice, and stopped their ears, and ran upon him with one accord, and cast him out of the city, and stoned him." [7] It is my object to blow the slave system into fragments, that upon its ruins may be erected a splendid edifice of Freedom.

Typed transcript of extracts: Garrison Papers, Boston Public Library; extract printed in *Life*, I, 331. The asterisks are in the typescript. Names of recipients in this series of letters are provided in parentheses at the end of each letter, the information apparently having been taken from the addresses on the envelopes.

Garrison had received letters from three young ladies from Haverhill, Massachusetts, who were schoolmates at Derry, New Hampshire; they called themselves "Inquirers after Truth." These letters, according to the interpretation of Garrison's sons years later (*Life*, I, 330–331), "caused a lively emotion in an always susceptible bosom." In fact, they read their father's statement in *The Liberator* of March 16, 1833, evoked in the course of his attack on a Massachusetts law forbidding intermarriage between the races ("We declare that our heart is neither affected *by*, nor pledged *to*, any lady, white or black, bond or free.") as a form of courtship of the girls. At any rate, late in the month Garrison did make a trip to Haverhill to speak and to meet the young ladies, whose identity, in the meantime, he had discovered. They were Judge Stephen Minot's daughter Harriet (1815–1888), who subsequently married Isaac Pitman and lived in Somerville, Massachusetts; Harriott Plummer (born c. 1813), daughter of Hiram Plummer, who married Charles L. Bartlett and became the mother of General William F. Bartlett; and Elizabeth E. Parrott (1817–1895), who married George Hughes of Boston.

1. Luke 23:34. Garrison omits the conjunction "for."
2. See Garrison's letter (39) to the editor of the Newburyport *Herald*, June 1, 1830.
3. Garrison quotes Galatians 4:16, omitting "become" after "therefore."
4. Garrison is determined to involve the recipients of his letter in the cause just as he was shortly determined to involve Helen Benson; see especially letter (120) to her, January 18, 1834.
5. James Ramsay (1733–1789), as his name is usually spelled, was a surgeon and clergyman. While serving as surgeon aboard the *Arundel*, of which Sir Charles Middleton (later Lord Barham) was captain, Ramsay had an opportunity to observe some of the horrors of slavery. Later, as minister of a church in the West Indies, he became an ardent abolitionist. Eventually he returned to England and became Vicar of Teston, a living controlled by Middleton. Sir Charles and especially Lady Margaret Middleton (died 1792) were converted to the cause by Ramsay's writings against slavery. The most influential of these was *An Essay on the Treatment and Conversion of African Slaves in the British Sugar Colonies* (London, 1784), which may be the pamphlet to which Garrison refers by a mistaken title. Garrison's appraisal of Lady Middleton's influence on the abolition cause seems to be valid, for it is thought that she helped persuade Wilberforce to fight for the emancipation of British slaves (see Robert Isaac and Samuel Wilberforce, *The Life of William Wilberforce*, Philadelphia, 1841, I, 76).
6. Elizabeth Margaret Chandler, "Patriotism and Sympathy," stanzas 4 and

5, the whole of which is printed in Maria W. Chapman, ed., *Songs of the Free, and Hymns of Christian Freedom* (Boston, 1836).

7. Acts 7:57–58.

---

8 5

TO GEORGE BOURNE

Boston, March 7, 1833.

My dear Coadjutor:

The Board of Managers of the New-England Anti-Slavery Society have determined that I shall go on a mission to England, forthwith, to procure funds for our Manual Labor School for Colored Youth, and to put down the colonization impostor Elliott Cresson. They wish me to depart by the 1st of April, if possible, or by the 15th, at farthest. The grand difficulty is, — Who shall supply my place as Editor of the Liberator? Perhaps it is in your power to remove it. Resolve me these queries:

1st. Can you arrange matters so as to fill my editorial chair by a residence in Boston?

2d. If so, how speedily?

3d. If so, on what terms?

I shall be gone at least six months, and probably a year.

Perhaps you might make arrangements to preach in this quarter, occasionally if not statedly.

You will understand, of course, what duties are embraced in an editorial situation. There will be some considerable correspondence, &c.

If you cannot leave New-York for this purpose, my friend Johnson, of the Christian Soldier, is willing to buckle on the armor, and give battle to that double-headed monster — Slavery and Colonization.[1]

A prompt answer will oblige your friend,

Wm. Lloyd Garrison.

ALS: William L. Garrison Collection, Massachusetts Historical Society.

The name of the recipient is inserted immediately following the text in what appears to be the hand of Francis Jackson Garrison.

1. Between January 1831, and November 1833, Oliver Johnson (1809–1889) used *The Liberator* press to publish the anti-Universalist *Christian Soldier*. Having become acquainted with Garrison's point of view in 1828 by reading his *Journal of the Times*, Johnson was in agreement with Garrison on abolition and political matters. He was among the founders of the New England Anti-Slavery Society and was substitute editor of *The Liberator* during several of Garrison's absences. He subsequently held a number of editing positions, many of them on antislavery papers. Like Garrison, he was active in many reform movements, including woman's rights and peace. He wrote several books, among them the biography, *William Lloyd Garrison and His Times* (Boston, 1879).

8 6

TO GEORGE W. BENSON

Boston, March 8, 1833.

My dear Friend:

Although distracted with cares, I *must* seize my pen to express my admiration of your generous and prompt defence of Miss Crandall from her pitiful assailants.[1] In view of their outrageous conduct, my indignation kindles intensely. What will be the result? If possible, Miss C. must be sustained at all hazards. If we suffer the school to be put down in Canterbury, other places will partake of the panic, and also prevent its introduction in their vicinity. We may as well, "first as last," meet this proscriptive spirit, *and conquer it*. We — i.e. all true friends of the cause — must make this a common concern. The New-Haven excitement has furnished a bad precedent — a second must not be given, or I know not what we can do, to raise up the colored population in a manner which their intellectual and moral necessities demand. In Boston, we are all excited at the Canterbury affair. Colonizationists are rejoicing, and abolitionists looking sternly.

The result of the meeting to be held in C. to-morrow, will be waited for by us with great anxiety. Our brother May deserves much credit for venturing to expostulate with the conspirators. If any one can make them ashamed of their conduct, he is the man. May the Lord give him courage, wisdom and success!

Ours is truly a great and arduous cause, my brother; but it is also a holy and benevolent cause, and it is one day to be a popular and triumphant cause. Your labors shall not be forgotten. Did I think it necessary, I would say to you — Be not cast down[;] glory in the name of an abolitionist; speak always confidently of success; remember that the heavier the cross, the brighter the crown. But you need nothing like this. A spirit like yours cannot droop: like a fixed star, "it looks on tempests, and is never shaken."[2]

It is determined that I shall depart on a mission to England, forthwith! — The Liberator of to-morrow breaks the information to the public. The enterprise will give dignity to the abolition cause in this country, and, I trust, will secure to that cause the patronage and applause of the abolitionists in Great Britain. I feel wholly inadequate to the task assigned me, but the Lord of hosts must be my stay.

My desire is, to start by the 1st of April. This I can do, if the funds necessary for the mission should be promptly obtained — and I think they will be. The probability is, that I shall be detained till the 15th. In a few weeks, then, (Providence permitting,) I shall have the pleasure of greeting you, on my way to New-York.

It is with great self-denial I tear myself away from the Liberator; but, having a talented coadjutor to supply my place, I venture to leave it for a time. — My mission will occupy six, probably twelve months.

When I pass through Providence, I shall desire to give a farewell address to the people of color.

At present, I am afflicted with a severe cold, but expect to throw it off without difficulty.

Happy am I to have another opportunity to subscribe myself
            Your friend and brother,
Geo. W. Benson.   Wm. Lloyd Garrison.

ALS: Garrison Papers, Boston Public Library; printed partly in *Life*, I, 320.

1. Prudence Crandall (1803–1889) was the victim of a conservative community's opposition to her attempt to integrate the races in a girls' school she had founded in Canterbury, Connecticut. In response to the protest against the admission of a Negro girl, she had resolved to limit future enrollment to "young ladies of color." This time the reaction took the form of filling her well with refuse, forbidding her to enter church, attacking her house, and breaking the windows. Ultimately a bill was forced through the state legislature prohibiting colored schools for out-of-state students without prior approval of the selectmen of the town. Although a decision against her in the lower court was reversed in the upper court, Miss Crandall became convinced that she could never successfully run her school in Connecticut. Following her marriage to Calvin Philleo, she moved to Illinois; and after her husband's death in 1874, she moved to Kansas.

2. Shakespeare, Sonnet CXVI, line 6. Garrison changes "that" to "it."

---

8 7

TO HENRY E. BENSON

[March 8, 1833.] [1]

My dear friend Henry:

As I have not time conveniently to fill a sheet, and as you and George are one, in spirit, in zeal, and in action, I venture to devote this page to you.

On the present occasion especially, — expecting soon to leave my native land, — it is incumbent on me to renew, in behalf of my partner and myself, the expressions of our gratitude for the multitude of favors you have bestowed upon us. As an agent for the Liberator, your services have been rendered with a disinterestedness, a promptitude and an efficiency, which merit a nobler acknowledgment than we can make. We know that you do not desire even the smallest declaration of thankfulness; b[ut] we should betray a hardened and selfish spirit not to make so small a return as this.

If you happen to see my much respected friend James Scott, tell him I am truly obliged to him for sending the pieces written by several members of the Female Anti-Slavery Society. They shall be published without fail, although they may be delayed awhile.

Give my friendly and grateful remembrances to Mr. Prentice. He ranks high on my list of friends. Also to Messrs. Brewer, Chace, Potter, &c.

Mr. Ladd,[2] on his return from Providence, told me of his interview with you and George. He is a good-natured man, but somewhat superficial.

In a great hurry, I remain,
Yours, faithfully,

Wm. Lloyd Garrison.

ALS: Garrison Papers, Boston Public Library.

1. The date is supplied at the bottom of the page in the hand, I believe, of Wendell Phillips Garrison. This letter was presumably written on the same sheet as the one to George (letter 86).
2. William Ladd.

---

8 8

TO HARRIOTT PLUMMER

Boston, March 18, 1833.

✿   ✿   ✿   ✿

You think my influence will prevail with my dear Whittier more than yours. I think otherwise. If he has not already blotted my name from the tablet of his memory, it is because his magnanimity is superior to neglect. We have had no correspondence whatever, for more than a year, with each other! Does this look like friendship between us? And yet I take the blame all to myself. He is not a debtor to me — I owe him many letters. My only excuse is, an almost unconquerable aversion to pen, ink and paper, (as well he knows,) and the numerous obligations which rest upon me, growing out of my connection with the cause of emancipation. Pray secure his forgiveness, and tell him that my love to him is as strong as was that of David to Jonathan. Soon I hope to send him a contrite epistle; and I know he will return a generous pardon.

Typed transcript of extract: Garrison Papers, Boston Public Library; printed in *Life*, I, 331. The asterisks are in the typescript.

Although Garrison's sons describe this extract as addressed to "Inquirers after Truth" (*Life*, I, 331), it has been labeled here as to Harriott Plummer since that information is part of the typed source.

8 9

TO HARRIET MINOT

Boston, March 19, 1833.

❖   ❖   ❖   ❖

In the course of a few weeks, I expect to leave my native land on an important mission to England, in behalf of the great and glorious cause of African emancipation. This mission will occupy six months — perhaps a year. What my reception will be in that country, — should I be wafted safely across the deep, — I cannot doubt. There, I shall breathe freely — there, my sentiments and language on the subject of slavery, will receive the acclamations of the people — there, my spirit will be elevated and strengthened in the presence of Clarkson, and Wilberforce, and Brougham, and Buxton, and O'Connell, and their noble coadjutors — there, I can tell the story of the black man's wrongs, in this land of liberty and light, to hearts that will melt with pity, and devise liberally for his rescue — there, I shall doubtless be permitted to address those of your own sex who are animated with a zeal for the overthrow of slavery which many waters cannot quench. Delightful anticipation!

❖   ❖   ❖   ❖

A thought has just occurred to me. Suppose I should visit Haverhill, previous to my departure for England: is it probable that I could obtain a meeting-house, in which to address the inhabitants on the subject of slavery? — (probably I should deem it expedient to say nothing derogatory to the Colonization Society.) If I can be *sure* of a house, I will try to come Sabbath after next. I will consult my friend Whittier, and see what can be done.

Typed transcription of extracts: Garrison Papers, Boston Public Library; printed partly in *Life*, I, 331–332. The asterisks are in the typescript.

9 0

TO HARRIET MINOT

Boston, March 26, 1833.

❖   ❖   ❖   ❖

I have written to Whittier respecting my visit to Haverhill, but have heard nothing from him. Nevertheless, I shall visit your beautiful village on Saturday next, even should no arrangements be made for the delivery of an address.

Typed transcript of extract: Garrison Papers, Boston Public Library; printed in *Life*, I, 332. The asterisks are in the typescript.

91

TO HARRIET MINOT

Boston, April 3, 1833.

Although it is midnight, and in a few hours I expect to bid adieu to Boston, yet I cannot consent to woo "Tired Nature's sweet restorer, balmy sleep," [1] until I express to you — very imperfectly, indeed — the pleasure which I received from my recent visit to Haverhill. Beautiful village! it has almost stolen my heart. Already do I sigh at the separation, like a faithful lover absent from the mistress of his affections. Must months elapse ere I again behold it? The thought is grievous.

During my brief sojourn in H., my spirit was as elastic as the breeze, and, like the lark, soared steadily upward to the gate of heaven, carolling its notes of joy. How invigorating was the atmosphere! how bright the sun! how cheerful each field and hill! how magnificent the landscape! What have I not lost by a residence in this "populous solitude," — this city of bustle, dust and bricks!

But, pleasant as it is to behold the face of Nature, it has no beauty like the countenance of a beloved friend. Sweet is the song of birds, but sweeter the voices of those we love. To see my dear Whittier, once more, full of health and manly beauty, was pleasurable indeed. Other friends I saw whom I esteem and admire. Could I, then, but enjoy my visit?

❉   ❉   ❉   ❉

Typed transcript of extract: Garrison Papers, Boston Public Library; printed partly in *Life*, I, 332. The asterisks are in the typescript.

1. Edward Young, *Night Thoughts*, "Night I," line 1.

92

To Messrs. S. Snowden, P. Hall, G. Putnam, P. Howard, C. Caples, W. Brown, J. B. Pero, J. T. Hilton, G. W. Thompson, J. Silver, L. York, J. Lennox, Watertown, F. Standing, T. Cole, C. L. Remond, Salem, E. F. B. Mundrucu, and H. Thacker.

BOSTON, April 4, 1833.

Gentlemen —

Just as I am on the eve of departing for New-York, a Committee, delegated by your body, (consisting of Messrs. Pero, Brown and Hilton,) present me, on your and their behalf, with a beautiful silver cup, in commemoration of our farewell interview at the hospitable home of Mr. George Putman,[1] and as a pledge of your friendship and appreciation of my labors in that noblest of all enterprises, the rescue of the whole colored race from servitude and degradation.

Gentlemen, I thank you for this liberal expression of your sentiments. It was not needed to convince me of your friendship for my person; for I had already received the most unequivocal marks of confidence and esteem from you all. Gratitude shall engrave your names upon the tablet of my memory, more deeply than they are engraved upon this cup. Deeply conscious that you place far too high an estimate upon my services, I will endeavor to be more worthy of your regard.

My colored brethren, in this city, have bound me to them by so many ties, that a separation from them fills me with grief and disquietude. But I leave them, to promote their best interests; and this consoles me. — I shall labor more abundantly, and I trust more successfully, in their behalf, while absent in body, than if I continued with them.

The spirit of brotherly love, the laudable ambition, the gentlemanly behaviour, the generous confidence, the noble magnanimity, which characterise your actions, fill my heart with joy, and nerve my arms with strength.

Be ever thus actuated, one toward another. 'United, we stand — divided, we fall'[2] — is the motto you have placed upon the cup. Having chosen this, never lose sight of it: follow it as your polestar, and neither the winds nor waves of persecution or reproach shall separate you.

Take my heart, and divide it equally among you. As you have presented me with a silver cup as a testimonial of your affection, so may each of you, and every descendant of Africa, soon receive a better cup from the Father of mercies — the cup of joy and salvation, running over.

I tender each of you my personal regards, and beg you collectively to accept my grateful acknowledgments for your goodness.

Your unflinching advocate,

WM. LLOYD GARRISON.

Printed: *The Liberator*, April 13, 1833.
Garrison explained in a note that he was printing this letter at the request of

the recipients. All these men are Negroes who are in most cases too obscure to be more than sketchily identified, through the Boston directories. They were not, except for Snowden, sufficiently prominent to have been delegates to national Negro meetings, such as those at Philadelphia reported in *The Liberator,* October 22, 1831, and June 30, 1832. Samuel Snowden (1765–1850) was a Methodist minister and an abolitionist, active especially in aiding runaway slaves. P. Hall was Primus Hall (c. 1753–1842), a soapmaker and a veteran of the Revolution. G. Putnam may refer to George Putnam, who was a Boston perfumer and hairdresser. P. Howard was Peter Howard, listed in the directory as "hairdresser and music." W. Brown was probably William Brown, clothes cleaner. J. B. Pero is John B. Pero, a hairdresser, who according to advertisements in *The Liberator* also sold merchandise in a small way. J. T. Hilton is the John Telemachus Hilton identified in an earlier note. G. W. Thompson is listed as a hairdresser. J. Silver was either Joseph A. or John D., both listed as mariners. L. York is Lewis York, a waiter. F. Standing is probably Francis Standin, a clothes cleaner. Thomas Cole was a member of the Massachusetts General Colored Association, a hairdresser by profession, who served in 1840 on a Negro committee formed to aid *The Liberator.* Charles Lenox Remond (1810–1873) was an outstanding abolitionist orator and writer. In 1840 he was closely associated with Garrison as a delegate to the World's Anti-Slavery Convention in London. E. F. B. Mundrucu was Emiliano Mundrucu, "clothing." H. Thacker was Henry Thacker, a bootblack. C. Caples and J. Lennox have not been identified.

1. Presumably a typographical error for "Putnam" (see *Life,* I, 330).
2. It is not known exactly when this expression — perhaps originally from the Aesop fable "The Four Oxen and the Lion" — gained currency as a motto. It was adopted as the motto of the state of Kentucky in 1792.

---

9 3

TO HARRIET MINOT

Hartford, April 9, 1833.

❈　　❈　　❈　　❈

Since I left Haverhill, an ocean of conflicting emotions has been dashing upon the shore of my affections — emotions of gratitude and regret. On Tuesday evening last, I bade farewell to my colored friends of Boston, in a public address, and on Friday evening to the people of color in Providence.[1] On both occasions, the highest interest and most intense feeling were felt and exhibited by the audience. They wept freely — they clustered around me in throngs, each one eager to receive the pressure of my hand and implore Heaven's choicest blessings upon my head. You cannot imagine the scene, and my pen is wholly inadequate to describe it. As I stood before them, and reflected it might be the last time I should behold them together on earth, — the last time I should be permitted to administer advice and consolation to their minds, — the last time I should have an opportunity to pour out my gratitude before them for the numerous manifestations of their confidence in my integrity, and appreciation of my humble services in their cause, — I could not but feel a strong depression of mind. The separation of friends, — especially if it is to be a long and hazardous one, — is a painful event indeed.

❖   ❖   ❖

But a separation like that, was to me, and I believe to the people of color themselves, one of no ordinary occurrence. Their condition has long attracted my attention, secured my efforts, and awakened in my bosom a flame of sympathy, which neither the winds nor waves of opposition can ever extinguish. It is the lowness of their estate, in the estimation of the world, which exalts them in my eyes. It is the distance which separates them from the blessings and privileges of society, which brings them so closely to my affections. It is the un-merited scorn, reproach and persecution of their persons, by those whose complexion *is* colored like my own, that command for them my sympathy and respect. It is the fewness of their friends and the great number of their enemies, that induce me to stand forth in their defence, and enables me, I trust, to exhibit to the world the purity of my motives.

On their part, do I not know how deep and intense is their affection for me? Have they not multiplied, as individuals and as societies, their expressions and tokens of regard, until my obligations assume a mountainous height? Have I more steadfast and grateful friends, in this hostile world, than themselves? Not that I deserve so much at their hands — not that the value of my labors bears any proportion to the rich recompense of their unbounded confidence and love — not that I am qualified in all things to instruct them; — yet they have shown, in a thousand ways, that the course I have pursued has secured their entire approbation — that the language I have uttered has been the language of their own hearts, — that the advice I have given has been treasured up in their hearts, like good seed sown in good ground, and is now producing fruit, ten, thirty, sixty, and even a hundred fold.[2]

Why should my parting from them be an occasion of sadness? I go, not to escape from toil, but to labor more abundantly in their cause. If I may do something for their good at home, I hope to do more abroad. Is not the heaven over their heads, which has so long been clothed in sackcloth, beginning to disclose its starry principalities, and illumine their pathway? Is not the storm, which has been so long pouring its rage upon their heads, breaking away, and a bow of promise, as glorious as that which succeeded the ancient deluge, spanning the sky, — a token that, to the end of time, the billows of pre-judice and oppression shall no more cover the earth, to the destruction

— for it rained heavily. I arrived in Hartford late that evening, and the next morning thought of starting for New Haven; but at the urgent solicitations of the colored friends, I gave them an address in the evening in their church. They collected four dollars. On Wednesday morning, I took the stage for New Haven. On passing through Middletown, I saw the Rev. J. C. Beman and a few other colored friends, and it was with as much difficulty as reluctance I tore myself from their company.[3] I was disappointed in not seeing friend Jocelyn in New-Haven, as he had gone to New-York; but his brother gave me a welcome, and commenced upon my portrait.[4] To-day noon, (Friday,) I start for New-York, but shall pass on to Philadelphia without delay. I must return to New Haven again, to address the colored people, and have my portrait completed. Friend Robert B. Hall has been very attentive.

Philadelphia, April 17, 1833.

Dear K. —

This letter was begun in New-Haven, and must now be completed in this city. No doubt you are all scolding about me heartily. I arrived here on Saturday and found friend Sharpless and his family in good health.[5] Last evening, I gave an address to the colored people. The audience was pretty large, but the colored Philadelphians, as a body, do not evince that interest and warmth of attachment which characterise my Boston friends — nor is it to be expected, as I have associated with scarcely a dozen of their number. I have not, as yet, made any call upon them for pecuniary assistance in aid of my mission, but shall consult to-day or to-morrow with friends Forten, Cassey, Hinton, Purvis, &c. I am glad to find that the mission meets with a general approval. At the request of Mr. Purvis, I have been sitting for my portrait, and the artist (Brewster) has succeeded pretty well.[6] On Friday morning, I start for New-York, where I shall tarry until Monday morning, and then go to New-Haven, in company with the Rev. Mr. Bourne. I shall sail in the packet for Liverpool for May 1st, provided the necessary funds be raised, and my enemies do not throw any hindrances in my path. — I saw brother Jocelyn in New-York. He shewed me a letter which he had just received from Miss Crandall, in which she states that I had not left Brooklyn more than half an hour before a sheriff from Canterbury drove up to the door of Mr. Benson at full speed, having five writs against me from Andrew T. Judson and company;[7] and finding that I had gone he pursued after me for several miles, but had to give up the chase. No doubt the colonization party will resort to some base measures to prevent, if possible, my departure for England.

Mr. Hinton wishes me to say that the gentlemen on whom he sent an order to you for the payment of a sum of money, belongs to the Navy Yard at Charlestown.

The subscribers to the Abolitionist [8] are complaining here that they have not received their April number. Some of them have received only the first — some, none at all.

I wish the Board of Managers to give me a letter of introduction to James Cropper.

I shall write again to-morrow.

Yours, ever,

Wm. Lloyd Garrison.

ALS: Garrison Papers, Boston Public Library; printed partly in *Life*, I, 340–342.

1. Not otherwise identified.
2. Almira Crandall.
3. J. C. Beman was serving as a missionary to the Negroes in Middletown, Connecticut. He had been accused of trying to divert the church-going public from established churches to his mission meetings; see the anonymous letter in *The Liberator*, July 28, 1832.
4. It was Simeon S. Jocelyn, the active abolitionist and Garrison's closer friend of the two brothers, who had gone to New York, and Nathaniel who began to paint the portrait.
5. Joseph Sharpless (c. 1771–1849) was one of the founders of the American Anti-Slavery Society.
6. Edmund Brewster (active 1818–1839) was a landscape and portrait painter as well as engraver who worked both in Philadelphia and in New Orleans.
7. Andrew T. Judson (1784–1853), a lawyer with political ambitions, was Prudence Crandall's neighbor and principal opponent in 1833 when she opened a school for Negro girls. Garrison rose to Miss Crandall's defense and selected Judson for attacks that were to bring forth the libel suit referred to in letter (124) to Henry E. Benson, February 26, 1834. It seemed to Garrison altogether fitting that Judson should be defeated when he ran for the state legislature in the spring of the same year; see *The Liberator*, April 19, 1834. (For other reactions to Judson's role in the Prudence Crandall case see *The Liberator*, March 16, July 20, November 2, 1833.)
8. The *Abolitionist* was published in Boston as the official monthly magazine of the New England Anti-Slavery Society between January and December 1833.

95

TO HARRIET MINOT

Philadelphia, April 22, 1833.

On Friday afternoon I arrived in New York from this city, and had the pleasure of receiving your favor of the 9th inst. I was immediately told that the enemies of the abolition cause had formed a conspiracy to seize my body by legal writs on some false pretenses, with the sole intention to convey me South, and deliver me up to the authorities of

Georgia, — or, in other words, to abduct and destroy me. The agent, who was to carry this murderous design into operation, had been in New York several days, waiting my appearance. As a packet was to sail the next day for Liverpool from Philadelphia, my friends advised me to start early the next morning for this city, in the steam-boat, hoping I might arrive in season to take passage therein, and thus baffle the vigilance of the enemy, — but the ship sailed in the morning, and I did not get here till the afternoon, — consequently, I failed to accomplish my purpose. My only alternative, therefore, is to return again to New York to-morrow evening, and stealthily get away, if possible, in the Liverpool packet that sails the next morning.[1] Probably I shall not start in the ship, but go down the river in a pilot boat, and overtake her.

My friends are full of apprehension and disquietude, but I *cannot* know fear. I feel that it is impossible for danger to awe me. I tremble at nothing but my own delinquencies, as one who is bound to be perfect, even as my heavenly Father is perfect.[2]

❖   ❖   ❖   ❖

Typed transcription of extract: Garrison Papers, Boston Public Library; printed in *Life*, I, 342–343. The asterisks are in the typescript.

1. Garrison returned to New York the next time by a different route. Robert Purvis drove him by fast horse (thirty miles in three hours) to Trenton, New Jersey. The unruly horse proved more dangerous than Garrison's southern enemies, for he and Purvis nearly had a serious accident.
2. Garrison alludes to Matthew 5:48.

96

TO ROBERT PURVIS

New-York, April 30, 1833.

My dear friend:

Since I left Trenton, I have been spending my time principally in New-Haven, and am happy to inform you that Mr. N. Jocelyn has completed what is deemed a good likeness of the madman Garrison.

He who bears this hasty note to you is one of whom you have heard much, and to whom we are all deeply indebted — Arnold Buffum, the able advocate of the colored race. May he find his visit an agreeable one — indeed, it cannot be otherwise.

I sail in the packet ship Hibernia in the morning, for Liverpool.[1]

Mrs. Purvis, and the dear little one, I trust are in good health.

Grateful for the many kindnesses you have shown to me, I remain,

AL: Garrison Papers, Boston Public Library.

Although this manuscript is in Garrison's hand, both the complimentary close and the signature are lacking.

1. The *Hibernia* was built in New York in 1830 and served first as a packet on the Black Ball Line and later as a whaleship out of New London, Connecticut.

---

9 7

TO SIMEON S. JOCELYN

New York, May 1, 1833.

My dear Brother:

In a few minutes, I leave this port for Liverpool, in the packet ship Hibernia; consequently I have scarcely time to scrawl my name. The package sent by Mr. Merwin [1] was promptly delivered. I had considerable conversation with Mr. Tappan,[2] respecting you as an Agent for the N.E. Anti-Slavery Society. His only doubts seemed to be whether you could arrange your business and whether your compensation could be secured, as the funds of the Society were nearly exhausted. I think he regards such an agency favorably. — I wish you would correspond with Samuel E. Sewell, Esq. the Corr. Sec. of the Society, and state to him, confidentially but explicitly, your views and situation.

The Lord be your strength and wisdom is the prayer of
Your unworthy brother,

Wm. Lloyd Garrison.

ALS: Historical Manuscripts, Yale University Library.

1. Not identified.
2. Arthur Tappan.

---

9 8

TO HARRIET MINOT

Below the Harbor of New York,
May 1, 1833.

I am now fairly embarked for Liverpool, on board the ship Hibernia, Capt. Maxwell.[1] We lie about ten miles below the city, at anchor, and here we must remain twenty-four hours. * * * *

Since the transmission of my last letter, I have been journeying from place to place, rather for the purpose of defeating the designs of my enemies than from choice. I expected to have sailed in the packet of the 24th ult., but applied too late, as every berth had been previously engaged. I do not now regret the detention, as it enabled the artist at New Haven to complete my portrait; and I think he has succeeded in making a very tolerable likeness.[2] To be sure, those who imagine that I am a monster, on seeing it will doubt or deny its accuracy, seeing no horns about the head; but my friends, I think, will recognize it easily.

This, then, is May Day! How happy I should be were I in the woods, singing like the birds (as most assuredly I should be singing, were I there,) and roaming free as the air of heaven.

* * * * How can one help singing? I do not mean by this that all must be familiar with the science of music, — but how natural it is to sing! My friend Whittier must not see this little rhapsody, — else he will be very severe upon me. But then I can retort upon him. A strange creature is he who really prefers the quack of a duck, or the scream of a goose, to the song of a robin!

Last evening I had a large audience of colored persons in the Methodist African Church in New York, who came to hear my fare-well address. Alas! that the value of my labors in their behalf bears so small a proportion to their unbounded gratitude and love. Mr. Finley, the General Agent of the Colonization Society, was present, and wit-nessed a tremendous assault upon his darling scheme.

Typed transcript of extract: Garrison Papers, Boston Public Library; printed part-ly in *Life*, I, 344–345. The asterisks are in the typescript.

1. George Maxwell had served as a master in the Navy between 1812 and 1813 and with the Black Ball Line since 1818.
2. The opinion here expressed of the Nathaniel Jocelyn portrait is more fa-vorable than his subsequent opinion of the engraving made from that portrait by Simeon S. Jocelyn; see the letters (145, 147) to Helen Benson of April 25 and May 1, 1834.

99

TO THE EDITOR OF THE *MORAL DAILY ADVERTISER*

[May 2, 1833.]

DEAR SIR —

Your city rapidly recedes from my view. We have been wind-bound in the harbor twenty-four hours, but a favorable breeze is now springing up, and bearing us away on its ethereal pinions. Steady and swift be our flight, until we arrive at Liverpool! Adieu, my much be-loved yet guilty country! Adieu, the place of my adoption — the queen of cities — the home most pleasant of all the world beside! Adieu, friends the truest, hearts the warmest, patrons the most gener-ous! Adieu, courageous advocates of freedom, whom no opposition can vanquish, nor persecution appal! Adieu, poor bleeding, fettered, perishing slaves! still do you occupy my thoughts, and excite my sympathies, and elicit my prayers.

It is natural I should feel great anxiety of mind, respecting the future progress of the cause of abolition. I pray that there may be no diminution of zeal or effort, on the part of its supporters, but an increase at least equal to the growth of oppression. If the single fact, that two hundred infants are *daily* born and doomed to a life of ignominious servitude in our land, be not sufficient to melt the hardest heart and arouse to benevolent activity the most sluggish spirit, it is because he who possesses it is beyond repentance — beyond the influence of mercy, and allied to brutality.

The grand point now to be aimed at is the formation of a National Anti-Slavery Society — after which, auxiliary associations may be multiplied without difficulty. Let, then, the standard of emancipation be lifted up forthwith! Give its broad folds to the breeze, and let a rallying cry go over the land, loud as a thousand thunders. The dead shall arise — the deaf hear — the blind see.[1]

I am admonished that the pilot will leave the ship immediately — else I would fill up my sheet. Below are appended a few poetical lines which have been composed in great haste.

SONNET.

Unto the winds and waves I now commit
　　My body, subject to the will of Heaven;
Its resting place may be the watery pit —
　　'Tis His alone to take who life has given,
But, O ye elements! the deathless soul,
　　Impalpable, outsoaring time and space,
Submits not to your mightiest control,
　　Nor meanly dwells in any earthly place.
Ocean may bleach, earth crumble, worms devour,
　　Beyond identity, its wondrous frame;
Decay wilts not the spiritual flower,
　　Nor age suppresses the ethereal flame; —
Thus thy dread sting, O DEATH! I dare to brave —
Thus do I take from thee the victory, O GRAVE!

I remain, in all great and good enterprises, your faithful friend and unflinching fellow laborer,

WM. LLOYD GARRISON.

On board the ship Hibernia,
　May 2, 1833.

ALS: Berea College Library.

William Goodell (1792–1878), a self-educated businessman and an ardent abolitionist following his defection from the American Colonization Society in 1832, was currently editing the *Moral Daily Advertiser* in New York City. An active supporter of the temperance movement and the author of several books and articles on slavery, he had edited various reform papers in eastern cities, among them the *Investigator* at Providence, a paper which reflected his Calvinist views. As reformers he and Garrison were in close agreement until the mid 1840's, when they differed on the constitutional question.

1. Garrison adapts Luke 7:22.

100

TO *THE LIBERATOR*

LIVERPOOL, May 23, 1833.

You may advertise my arrival at this port, in tolerable health and spirits, after a passage of twenty-one days — a passage which, though extremely favorable in point of time, has been inexpressibly wearisome both to my flesh and spirit. Commend me for tone and integrity of stomach, against the all-disturbing influences of wind and water! Before I left New-York, I generously conceded to myself two days for sea sickness — deeming it probable, however, that I should wholly escape this most annoying of all illnesses. Shame on me! — yet some credit for the confession — I was assailed and vanquished even within sight of the Hook, although the sun exhibited a fine countenance, and there prevailed but a petty tumult among the waves! Nay, what was worse — I was the first victim on board, by many hours. There is some dignity in falling after a host of stout bodies; but to be cast down when delicate females and bird-like children bear up bravely against the enemy, is weak indeed! In vain did the inward argue with the outward man: all its remonstrances and entreaties, strong and pathetic as they were, wrought nothing but consummate disobedience. My system refused nourishment of almost every kind for the first week; nor has it yet recovered its wonted vigor.

Although in a strange land, and for the first time a foreigner, I cannot but feel myself at home among a people whose cry is for universal freedom, who never speak in the cause of suffering humanity but with authority, who are doing so much in behalf of African emancipation, and whose voices have cheered my spirit even on the other side of the Atlantic.

My principal object in visiting England is, to obtain funds for the establishment of a manual labor school for the education of the colored youth of our country. This is a humiliating yet necessary task; humiliating, because there is no lack of opulence in the United States — necessary, inasmuch as the charities of the rich among us are frequently showered upon every enterprise except that which aims to exalt and improve the colored race. In England there is much wealth, but also much suffering and poverty. Undoubtedly the calls upon the liberality of her philanthropists are loud and frequent. Could I believe that the amount I may accumulate here will be just so much withdrawn from the fund for the relief of the poor and oppressed in this country and in the Colonies, I would not solicit a farthing, although the cause is a common one all over the globe. As Burns says —

'A man's a man, for a' that.' [1]

But I have no such apprehension. The seeds of charity, wherever sown, bring forth a harvest which is common stock. A fine poet has wisely told us that

' — scattered truth is never, never wasted' [2] — it is just as true of universal benevolence. Causes may operate, however, at the present time, to prevent successful appeals for pecuniary aid; and should this be the case, my tarry in England will not be long. It is true, now that I am on this side of the Atlantic, I should be pleased to see (though not to be seen,) as much as possible — all that is beautiful, vast or sublime — all that is ancient or curious — had I a less important cause to manage; but neither time, nor inclination, nor duty, will allow me to act the mere tourist. I cannot travel for amusement, nor even for relaxation: of course, you may expect little from my pen that is foreign to the subject of emancipation.

Having as yet seen no English newspaper, I cannot send you a syllable of intelligence, respecting the progress of the Emancipation Bill through Parliament. I am as anxious as you can be, to learn its fate. There is a report that it has passed to a third reading, one feature of which is the unconditional emancipation of all children who may hereafter be born of slave parents, and also of those who are now under six years of age. This is an approximation to justice, but it will not suffice. My next letter will be more intelligent and authoritative on this point.

Be sure to apprise me early, and minutely, of all the anti-slavery and pro-slavery movements in the United States. Still make the Liberator *a forty-two pounder* for the discharge of solid arguments, accompanied by some flashes of declamation. Starve not your epithets against slavery, through fear or parsimony: let them be heavy, robust and powerful. It is a waste of politeness to be courteous to the devil; and to think of beating down his strongholds with straws is sheer insanity. The language of reform is always severe — unavoidably severe; and simply because crime has grown monstrous, and endurance has passed its bounds.[3] But after the reform has been effected, then all agree that no terms can be too strong against the corruption or oppression which has been put down.

In conducting this controversy, we certainly need great prudence, great courage, great perseverance, great integrity. If we are actuated by mere animal enthusiasm, it will soon burn out; if by a reliance for victory upon our own strength, we shall utterly fail; if by personal or sectional animosities, we deserve more than our enemies have yet heaped upon our heads.

It is with reluctance I bid you adieu, but with much affection I subscribe myself, in weal and in wo,

Your faithful friend,

WM. LLOYD GARRISON.

Printed: *The Liberator*, July 6, 1833. This is the first of a series of letters from England.

1. Burns, "For A' That and A' That," line 12. This, one of his favorite poems, Garrison used as the basis for antislavery versions of his own verse.

2. Not identified.

3. From his earliest antislavery days Garrison was on the defensive against the charge that his language was too severe; see, for instance, editorials in *The Liberator* for January 8, March 26, October 15, November 12, 1831; February 9, June 8, 1833.

101

TO *THE LIBERATOR*

LIVERPOOL, May 24, 1833.

The Silas Richards sails this morning for New-York.[1] I seize the opportunity to communicate to you the result of my last evening's reading. The intelligence, it is true, is some days old, and may have been anticipated by you.

Whatever English newspaper I take up, the abolition of slavery in the Colonies forms its prominent topic. As in our own country, there are various and opposite views presented, but it is universally conceded that slavery has received its death-blow. Abolitionists are divided on the question of compensation to the planters — to what extent divided, I am at present ignorant. Those who are willing to purchase the slaves are generally actuated by a hope that they shall thereby remove the only obstacle to immediate abolition, rather than a conviction that the claims of the masters are just — that is, expediency in this instance seems to promise so well, they consent to abandon principle. Such fanatics and unjust men as ourselves will view this as an unconditional surrender of the whole ground of controversy. Nothing can be more absurd than to contend that man cannot hold property in man, and that all men are born free and equal — and upon this ground to assail the slave system as iniquitous; and yet to acknowledge, or in any way sanction, the compensation claim set up by the oppressor. My indignation kindles at such a base proposition — I will not listen to it for a moment. For those who have been, for a long course of years, whipping, starving, plundering, brutalizing and trafficking their own species, to come forward and demand a handsome remuneration if they cease from these atrocious practices, argues a hardihood of mind unsurpassed in the annals of villany; and for the public to listen to this demand with complacency, and even with a serious determination to grant it, evinces extraordinary obliquity of moral vision, or something worse. Compensation! it should be such as only felons receive — punishment proportionate to their crimes. What! hang a man who buys or steals men, women and children on the coast of Africa; and pay another in solid specie if he will not buy or steal them in a British colony, or in 'the land of the free and the home of the brave!' Oh! equitable legislation! O! sapient distinction! The slaves, and the slaves only, are entitled to remuneration; but the wealth of the world cannot balance the account between them and their task-masters. Let me briefly illustrate this point. I have the Liverpool Times of the 21st before me, in which almost the first paragraph that caught my eye was the following, in a speech recently delivered in Parliament:

'In 1830 the number of slaves in Demarara [2] had decreased from 60,599 to 59,547, while the number of recorded punishments had increased from 17,359 to 18,324, and the number of lashes inflicted in that year was no less than 194,744. In 1831, the population had still further decreased to 58,404, but the punishments had increased to 21,656, and the number of lashes amounted to 199,207.'

These, be it observed, are only the *recorded* punishments and lashes: how many are left unrecorded, except in the Book of Remembrance, none on earth can disclose. To whom, then, does compensation justly belong — to the slaves or their masters? And this is only a partial view of the evils of slavery.

Now, with such facts before our eyes, and worse that might be recapitulated, what shall we say *of* those, and *to* those, who insist that they must be paid for becoming honest men? Let this compensation heresy obtain no root in the United States, at least in the soil of abolition.

But I am digressing. In the House of Commons on Tuesday the 14th inst. Mr. Stanley brought forward the Ministerial plan for abolishing slavery in the Colonies, which he supported in a long and elaborate speech, some parts of which were argumentative and eloquent.[3] This plan is embraced in the following resolutions:

'1. That it is the opinion of this Committee that immediate and effectual measures be taken for the entire abolition of slavery throughout the Colonies, under such provisions for regulating the condition of the negroes as may combine their welfare with the interests of the proprietors.

2. That it is expedient that all children born after the passing of any act, or who shall be under the age of six years at the time of passing any act of Parliament for this purpose, be declared free — subject, nevertheless, to such temporary restrictions as may be deemed necessary for their support and maintenance.

3. That all persons now slaves be entitled to be registered as apprenticed laborers, and to acquire thereby all the rights and privileges of freemen, subject to the restriction of laboring under conditions and for a time to be fixed by Parliament, for their present owners.

4. That to provide against the risk of loss which proprietors in his Majesty's colonial possessions might sustain by the abolition of slavery, his Majesty be enabled to advance, by way of loan, to be raised from time to time, a sum not exceeding in the whole £15,000,000, to be repaid in such manner, and at such rate of interest, as shall be prescribed by Parliament.

5. That his Majesty be enabled to defray any such expense as he may incur in establishing an efficient stipendiary magistracy in the colonies, and in aiding the local legislatures in providing for the religious and moral education of the negro population to be emancipated.'

This plan is a kind of *go-between* the planters and the abolition party, and, of course, gives satisfaction to neither. I have not time to examine Mr. Stanley's arguments in its support. In answer to a question from Sir R. Peel,[4] he said the power of punishing the slaves was to be taken from the masters, and vested in stipendiary magistrates.

Lord Howick opposed the scheme in a short but sensible speech, in which he confessed that his opinions upon the subject of slavery had lately undergone a very great change.[5] He was now ashamed to think how lightly he had imbibed the notion that it was all a delusion to talk of the evils of slavery, and that the slave was not to be pitied, &c. &c. The conclusion to which he had been irresistibly led was, that there were only two possible courses to be adopted — *we must recognise perfect slavery or perfect freedom* — the present scheme was neither. The safest course was by fixing a date, at the earliest possible period, for the absolute and entire termination of slavery.

Mr. Buxton observed that it would be very desirable to know who was to pay the sum proposed (the £15,000,000) — the country or the slave laborer; because if it were to be imposed on the latter, he should decidedly object to such an arrangement, except some better reasons were urged in its favor than he had yet heard.

The debate on the resolutions was then adjourned till the 30th instant.

Petitions are crowding into Parliament *by thousands* from every part of the United Kingdom, praying for the abolition of slavery — Lord Suffield [6] alone presented 201 on Tuesday in the House of Lords — one of which was of amazing size, 'which, closely packed as it was, seemed to rival the woolsack itself in its dimensions.' It was signed by EIGHT HUNDRED THOUSAND ladies!!! Its presentation excited considerable sensation and some merriment. In the House of Commons, on the same day, Mr. Buxton presented 300 petitions, among them one containing 187,000 female signatures, which required four members to lay it on the table. At the head of it stood the name of the celebrated Amelia Opie, and next to hers that of Priscilla Buxton.[7] Cheers for the Ladies of Great Britain!

Most truly yours,

WM. LLOYD GARRISON.

Printed: *The Liberator*, July 13, 1833.

1. The *Silas Richards*, built in New York in 1824, a packet in the Liverpool Blue Swallowtail Line, served briefly in the China trade until 1841 when she sailed out of Sag Harbor and New Bedford as a whaler. The ship was lost in the South Pacific in 1854.

2. One of the three counties of the colony of British Guiana.

3. Edward George Geoffrey Smith Stanley (1799–1869) — subsequently Lord Stanley and Earl of Derby — had served as under-secretary for Ireland and been transferred, a few weeks before Garrison's arrival in England, to the Colonial Department, where he espoused the moderate position expressed in the resolutions Garrison quotes.

4. Sir Robert Peel (1788–1850), conservative, skillful politician, had been active in public life since first seated in Parliament in 1809, held many offices, and effected many reforms.

5. Charles Grey, Viscount Howick and Earl Grey (1764–1845), was the high-minded, conscientious, though sometimes narrow, nobleman who in the current issue was more than usually liberal.

6. Edward Harbord, Baron Suffield (1781–1835), after a long and successful political career, became a radical reformer, dedicated chiefly to the abolition of the slave trade, which he advocated persistently in the House of Lords

7. Of the two ladies so much admired by Garrison, one was famous and the other little known. Mrs. Amelia Opie (1769–1853) was the widow of painter John Opie and herself an extremely popular and prolific writer of poetry and fiction, though her literary output decreased sharply after 1825, when she became a Quaker and her interests shifted to charity and reform. Priscilla Buxton was the daughter of Sir Thomas Fowell Buxton, who was to help her brother Charles compile the Buxton biography.

102

TO AN UNKNOWN RECIPIENT

Liverpool, May 27, 1833.

The population of Liverpool, including its suburbs, is about as large as that of New-York. I have had but a cursory view of the place, and shall therefore avoid entering into the minute in my descriptions. Let this suffice: it is bustling, prosperous and great. I would not, however, choose it as a place of residence. It wears strictly a commercial aspect; and you well know there is nothing of trade or barter in my disposition. Indeed, nothing surprises me so much on approaching Boston, after a short exile from it, (and I am always in exile when absent,) as a glimpse at its shipping; for I generally feel as little inclined to visit its wharves, as to make a pilgrimage to Mecca. My instinct and taste prefer hills and valleys, and trees and flowers, to bales and boxes of merchandize; and tiny cataracts and gentle streams, to sublime water-spouts and the great ocean. Hence, another place for me than Liverpool; and such a place I could easily find, in almost any direction, within a few miles of it — that is to say, if I were friendly to colonization. My excellent friend James Cropper has a delightful retreat, called *Dingle Bank*, which nature and art have embellished in the most attractive manner. This great and good man is now in London, but there has been no lack of hospitality toward me on the part of those whom he has left behind. I have also been very kindly entertained by James Riley, a worthy and much respected member of the Society of Friends. My obligations to Thomas Thorneley, Esq. and Dr. Hancock, (the former, late the Parliamentary candidate of the friends of emancipation, and the latter, a consistent advocate of the cause of Peace,) likewise deserve a public acknowledgment.[1]

ALS: Garrison Papers, Boston Public Library.

This fragment of a letter was probably addressed either to Isaac Knapp or to *The Liberator*.

1. Garrison refers to three English abolitionists. James Riley (1768–1845) — more commonly spelled "Ryley" — was a prosperous Liverpool sailmaker and the husband of Margaret Cropper. Thomas Thorneley, a merchant and reformer, was twice defeated in Liverpool in his candidacy for Parliament; in 1835, he was elected from Wolverhampton. Thomas Hancock (1783–1849) wrote extensively on Quakerism and on medical subjects such as epidemics, quarantine, and pestilence. A great admirer of John Locke, he edited some of Locke's essays.

103

TO ELLIOTT CRESSON

[*June* 4, 1833.]

SIR —

I affirm that the American Colonization Society, of which you are an Agent, is utterly corrupt and proscriptive in its principles; that its tendency is to embarrass the freedom and diminish the happiness of the colored population of the United States, and, consequently, that you are abusing the confidence and generosity of the philanthropists of Great Britain. As an American citizen, and the accredited Agent of the New-England Anti-Slavery Society, I invite you to meet me in public debate in this city, to discuss the following

PROPOSITIONS.

1. The American Colonization Society was conceived, perfected, and is principally managed by those who retain a portion of their own countrymen as slaves and property.

2. Its avowed and exclusive object is, the colonization of the *free* people of color, in Africa, *or some other place.*

3. It is the active, inveterate, uncompromising enemy of immediate abolition, and deprecates the liberation of the slaves, except on condition of their being simultaneously transported to Africa.

4. It maintains that possessors of slaves, in the southern States, are not such from *choice* but *necessity*; and that, of course, they are not, under present circumstances, blameworthy for holding millions of human beings in servile bondage.

5. Its tendency is, to increase the value of the slaves, to confirm the power of the oppressors, and to injure the free colored population, by whom it is held in abhorrence, wherever they possess liberty of speech and the means of intelligence.

6. It is influenced by fear, selfishness, and prejudice, and neither calls for any change of conduct on the part of the nation, nor has in itself any principle of reform.

7. Its mode of civilizing and christianizing Africa is preposterous and cruel, and calculated rather to retard than promote the moral and spiritual improvement of her benighted children.

These charges, Sir, are grave and vital. I dare you to attempt their refutation. Let them be taken up in their present order, and each discussed and decided upon separately.[1] And may God prosper the right!

Yours, &c.

WM. LLOYD GARRISON.

18, *Addle-street, Aldermanbury*,[2] June 4, 1833.

Printed: *Second Annual Report of the Board of Managers of the New-England Anti-Slavery Society* (Boston, 1834), p. 36; printed in *Life*, I, 352–353.

1. Although Cresson answered this letter (see the reference to the reply in letter 104, to Joseph Price and Thomas Hodgkin, June 7), he was unwilling to accept the challenge.

2. The address of the Anti-Slavery Rooms in London. Aldermanbury is a street near Guildhall, and Addle-street runs between Aldermanbury and Wood Street.

104

TO JOSEPH PRICE AND THOMAS HODGKIN

London, June 7, 1833.

Gentlemen —

I have received, this morning, a note from Mr. Elliott Cresson, acknowledging the receipt of my letter to him of the 4th instant; in which he informs me 'that having agreed to follow the course which J. T. Price and Dr. Hodgkin should recommend as to a private or public discussion of the merits of the American Colonization Society, with reference to slavery in the United States and the slave trade in Africa, E. C. awaits their recommendation for the government of his conduct on the occasion.'

I wait to learn the course which you may recommend Mr. Cresson to adopt, as to my proposition to him for a public discussion.[1] An answer this day, as so much time has already elapsed in this negociation, will much oblige

Yours, respectfully,

WM. LLOYD GARRISON.

Printed: *Second Annual Report of the Board of Managers of the New-England Anti-Slavery Society* (Boston, 1834), p. 37.

Joseph T. Price (1784–1854) was a defender of the American Colonization Society and a delegate for Swansea at the international antislavery convention of 1840. Thomas Hodgkin (1798–1866), also a defender of colonization, was a distinguished surgeon and one of the most eminent anatomists of his day. He was also an ardent philanthropist and a founder of the Aborigines' Rights' Protection Society, conservative English analogue to the American Colonization Society.

1. Price and Hodgkin recommended a small private meeting with a few friends (*Second Annual Report . . . of the New-England Anti-Slavery Society*, p. 38).

105

TO THE BOARD OF MANAGERS OF THE NEW ENGLAND ANTI-SLAVERY SOCIETY

LONDON, June 20, 1833.

GENTLEMEN, —

My arrival in England, at this great crisis, I consider not only in the highest degree providential, but all the great leading abolitionists deem it a matter of sincere congratulation. A large number of delegates, from various anti-slavery Societies throughout the kingdom, are now in this city, watching the progress of the ministerial plan of emancipation through Parliament. It has been my privilege, for several days past, to take breakfast with them at the Guildhall Coffee House, where the interchange of opinions in relation to the state of affairs, has been open and free. After the cloth is removed, about two hours are usually spent in the communication of any facts which may have been obtained since the preceding morning, and in devising ways and means to ensure the termination of the struggle during the present session. The assembly then adjourn to the rooms at Aldermanbury, for the purpose of discussing more fully any questions that may arise. Some of the debates have been highly piquant, talented and eloquent — all of them pregnant with interest. Among the speakers are Lord Suffield, Buxton, Macaulay, Cropper, Stephen, Gurney and Thompson.[1] Perfect unanimity of sentiment, as to the wisest course to be pursued, is not to be expected in so large a body; but whatever differences exist, in regard to the government plan, all are agreed upon these two fundamental points, — namely, that the right of property in the slaves shall 'instantly cease, and that, whatever relief or compensation may be granted to the planters, no part of it shall be paid by the slaves.'

The resolutions which have almost unanimously passed the House of Commons are substantially these — that the emancipation of the slaves shall be immediate, so that they can neither be bought nor sold; that they shall serve as apprentices for a term not exceeding twelve years; that a compensatory sum of twenty millions shall be given to the planters; and that there shall be no hindrance to the unrestricted exercise of religious freedom. There is scarcely a doubt that these resolutions will be adopted by the House of Lords, without any material variation. It is generally believed that the plan of apprenticeship (which gives great offence) will not work a single year; indeed, many of the West Indians themselves declare, that there must be complete and instantaneous freedom given both to the masters and the slaves. The payment of £20,000,000 by way of compensation, excites

237

universal reprobation among the people, and is justly viewed not only as money bestowed where no loss can be proved, but as an abandonment of the high ground of justice.

I have had frequent consultations with our abolition friends, as to the objects of my mission. The plan and object of our School excite their admiration; and as soon as the question relative to colonial slavery is finally settled in this country, they promise to give us liberal and constant assistance. It is their purpose to organize societies for the abolition of slavery throughout the world.

Mr. Elliott Cresson, the agent of the American Colonization Society, is now in this city. I have repeatedly invited him to meet me in public, and defend his cause; he has been publicly and privately advised to accept my challenge, or to leave the country; but, up to this moment, he shrinks from the contest. He is conscious that he has dealt falsely with the British people, and that the Colonization Society is wholly indefensible in a land where prejudice against color is unknown, and where the principles of justice and love govern the actions of the friends of the colored race.

On Monday evening last, I gave a lecture upon the scheme of African Colonization, in the Rev. T. Price's meeting-house, Devonshire-square.[2] James Cropper, Esq. of Liverpool, took the chair. Mr. Cresson, with one or two of his partizans, was in attendance; and, at the close of my address, George Thompson, Esq. (the eloquent lecturer,) gave him a most terrible castigation for his duplicity and misrepresentations. The meeting was adjourned to the next evening, at which time I completed my examination of the principles and measures of the Colonization Society. Addresses were then made by several gentlemen, (among them was my excellent friend, the Rev. Nathaniel Paul, from Upper Canada,) all expressive of the utmost abhorrence of the Society.[3] The Rev. Mr. Price, (who has been unanimously invited to occupy the pulpit of the celebrated Robert Hall,[4]) in rising to offer some resolutions for the adoption of the assembly, stated that he, among others, had been led by the deceptive statements of Mr. Cresson to regard the Colonization Society as a wise, benificent and christian association; but since he had investigated its claims, and particularly since he had heard the expositions of the lecturer, he was convinced of its wickedness and cruelty. His resolutions (declaring that all my charges had been sustained by indubitable evidence, and expressing thanks for my lectures) were passed unanimously, *with a single exception.* You will see a report of the meetings in the London Patriot.

I have seen Mr. Wilberforce.[5] He has repudiated his views of the Colonization Society, and regards its principles and purposes with disapprobation. This fact you may publish to the country. Cresson may succeed a little longer in deceiving a few lords and dukes, but his career has ended among the friends of abolition and the religious community. Charles Stuart, Esq. has done much to obstruct his progress; and we cannot be too thankful to this eminently pious and indefatigable philanthropist for his labors of love.[6]

With sentiments of esteem, I remain,

Your obedient servant,

WM. LLOYD GARRISON.

Printed: *The Liberator*, August 31, 1833; extract printed in *Life*, I, 351.

1. Garrison names leading British abolitionists, of whom George Thompson (1804–1878) was perhaps the most important, at least in terms of subsequent association with Garrison. From their first meeting the two men formed an immediate attachment which was to lead to a lifetime of cooperative effort in the abolitionist movement. On Garrison's invitation, Thompson was to visit the United States from September 1834 to December 1835, lecturing at many anti-slavery meetings. Having enraged many citizens with his doctrine of uncompromising abolition, he was to experience physical danger and to find it necessary to flee the country. He was to make two other trips to America, one in 1850 and another in 1864.

The only other person who has not been identified in previous notes is Samuel Gurney (1786–1856), a wealthy Quaker banker who gave generously to further the cause of abolition.

2. Thomas L. Price (died c. 1854), the minister of the most prominent Baptist church in London, supported the abolition movement throughout the thirties. He was a close friend of Joseph Sturge and the editor of the *Eclectic Review* (1837–1850) and of various narratives concerned with slavery in the West Indies.

3. Nathaniel Paul (died 1839, "in . . . the prime of life," according to Garrison) was formerly a Baptist minister in Albany, New York, currently from the Wilberforce Settlement in Upper Canada (the southern part of what is now Ontario), where the British colonial government offered a refuge to free Negroes and fugitive slaves. In 1832 the settlement sent him to England to raise funds. During Garrison's own trip to Britain the following year, Paul was his almost constant companion; they appeared together on innumerable lecture platforms. Eventually, Garrison borrowed money from Paul for his return passage, money which may never have been repaid. The two men did not meet again after 1833.

4. Robert Hall (1764–1831) was a prolific author and the celebrated evangelical minister of the Broadmead Chapel in Bristol, the call to which pulpit Thomas L. Price had resisted.

5. Although Wilberforce had long since retired, Garrison sought him out in order to discuss the American Colonization Society; for a report of the visit see the reprint from the *Christian Keepsake* in *The Liberator*, January 9, 1836.

6. Charles Stuart (1783–1865), a bachelor captain retired from the East India Service, was one of the English abolitionists Garrison admired chiefly for his early disapproval of the colonization scheme, though Garrison was later to repudiate Stuart when he adopted views on woman's rights and nonresistance in opposition to Garrison's.

106

TO ELLIOTT CRESSON

[June 27, 1833.]

Sir, —

With a zeal and industry worthy of a better cause, you have for a long period pressed the American Colonization Society upon the attention of the British public, and you have collected considerable sums in furtherance of its views, although its wickedness and cruelty have been again and again demonstrated.

You have refused to comply with my private invitation to meet me before an audience in this metropolis in defence of your principles and proceedings, notwithstanding you have been repeatedly admonished by those whose opinions are entitled to great consideration, that you must either vindicate the society of which you are the representative in the manner proposed by me, or leave the country. I now publicly renew my challenge to you, in reference to this momentous question. Will you shrink from this offer also? I beg leave to propound the following questions: —

1. Does not the American Colonization Society stand pledged to the pursuit of one object exclusively — namely, the colonization of free persons of colour in Africa or some other place?

2. Does not that Society recommend the expulsion of the slaves from the United States as the condition of their emancipation?

3. Does not that Society maintain that the whites and blacks can never amalgamate and live in harmony together, owing to causes which are beyond the control of the human will?

4. Does not that Society contend that the coloured population of the United States must for ever remain a separate, degraded, and miserable population in their native country?

5. Does not that Society represent the free people of colour of the United States (the only class which it seeks to remove to Africa, for her moral and spiritual improvement) as constituting, with few exceptions, the vilest portion of the human race?

6. Does not that Society array itself as the opponent of those who are exerting themselves to procure the speedy emancipation of the slaves in the United States?

7. Does not that Society refuse to assail, first, the prejudices of the people of the United States against colour; secondly, the laws which proscribe and degrade the coloured population; and, thirdly, the conduct of American slave-owners?

8. Does not that Society receive the general reprobation of the free people of colour?

9. Does not that Society admit that fear, selfishness, and prejudice control its operations?

10. Does not that Society proclaim that it is supported by the almost unanimous voice of the American people?

I maintain, Sir, that the affirmative is true in every instance, and I challenge you to take the negative of either or all of the above questions before a public audience in London.

The last (June) number of the *Baptist Magazine* contains a letter addressed by you to Edmund Clarke, Esq., in which you thus speak apparently of me: —

"Indeed, thus fiercely to assault a system adopted by the most judicious and pious men of every Christian body in our land, after deep and earnest investigation, with the advantage of personal observation of its practical operation, and merely on the testimony of a violent pamphleteer, *who often sacrifices truth to the support of his mistaken views, and whose very quotations are so garbled as entirely to pervert the real meaning of the speaker,* can only create bitterness between nations whose duty and interest it is to love one another." [1]

I challenge you to meet me in public discussion, and to prove the charges which I have put in italic. The meeting shall decide between us; and if the decision be in your favour, I hereby promise to pay 20 guineas into the hands of the Mayor of New York, in aid of the education of the coloured children of that city.[2]

Respectfully yours, &c.,

WILLIAM LLOYD GARRISON,

Agent of the New England Anti-Slavery Society.
18, Addle-street, Aldermanbury, June 27.

Printed: *The* (London) *Times,* June 28, 1833, at an expense to Garrison of £6 6s.

1. Garrison's quotation from Cresson's letter (*Baptist Magazine,* 25:277 [1833]) is accurate except for the italics, which are his own. Cresson identifies Edmund Clarke as an English Baptist minister.

2. Cresson never responded to Garrison's challenge, though he did hold a meeting on July 3, at which the Duke of Sussex presided, and which Garrison attended. At that meeting there were testimonials for the cause of colonization, and the abolitionists were allowed to speak only briefly. Garrison and his group, however, were able to make full statements concerning the iniquity of colonization at a meeting at Exeter Hall on the thirteenth, though Cresson failed to attend.

107

TO PRINCE AUGUSTUS FREDERICK, THE DUKE OF SUSSEX

[June 28, 1833.]

MAY IT PLEASE YOUR GRACE —

I perceive by the Times of yesterday morning, that you are expected to preside at a meeting which is to be held at the Hanover Square Rooms, on Wednesday next, the 3d of July, the object of which is to give currency to the scheme of the American Colonization Society. I am sure that your Lordship is actuated by pure and benevolent motives, in thus consenting to occupy the chair on the occasion above alluded to; and just as sure that, if you can be satisfied that the Agent of that Society is imposing not only upon your generous confidence, but upon the British community, you will give no countenance to the proposed meeting. I affirm that Mr. Elliott Cresson is a deceiver; I have challenged him, in private and public, (vide the 'Times' of this morning,) to meet me before a British assembly, in order to vindicate his own cause, and the Society of which he is the Agent. I further affirm that the American Colonization Society is corrupt in its principles, proscriptive in its measures, and the worst enemy of the free colored and slave population of the United States; and as an American citizen — as the accredited Agent of the New-England Anti-Slavery Society, I hold myself in readiness to convince your Lordship of the truth of these charges, from the official documents of the American Colonization Society, if your Lordship will grant me the privilege of conferring with you a single hour between the receipt of this letter and Wednesday evening. As an individual whose life is dedicated to the cause of negro emancipation in the United States, and who has suffered much in its prosecution; and as the representative of the abolitionists of that country, I beseech your Lordship to grant me a private interview; or, at least, to make some further inquiries into the merits of the African Colonization enterprise, before you appear publicly in its support. Permit me to recommend T. F. Buxton, Z. Macaulay, and James Cropper, (who rank among the best friends of the colored race,) as gentlemen who will satisfy you of my official character, and of the design and tendency of the American Colonization Society. I have the honor to be, with great respect,

Your Grace's obd't serv't,

WILLIAM LLOYD GARRISON.

18, Aldermanbury, June 28, 1834.[1]

Printed: *Second Annual Report of the Board of Managers of the New-England Anti-Slavery Society* (Boston, 1834), p. 42.

Prince Augustus Frederick, Duke of Sussex (1773–1843), sixth son of George III, had offended his father by supporting many liberal causes, including the elimination of the slave trade. He had also been active in the Royal Society, serving as its president between 1830 and 1838. At the time of Garrison's letter the duke was acting as sponsor to Elliott Cresson.

1. The letter is misdated; it was written in 1833, during Garrison's visit to England.

108

TO THE BOARD OF MANAGERS OF THE NEW ENGLAND ANTI-SLAVERY SOCIETY

LONDON, July 1, 1833.

GENTLEMEN, —

A vessel sails to-morrow for Boston, and I gladly embrace the opportunity to send you another communication.

I think the results of my mission, (brief as it will prove,) may be summed up in the following items: — 1st, Awakening a general interest among the friends of emancipation in this country, and securing their efficient co-operation with us, in the abolition of slavery in the United States. 2d, Dispelling the mists with which the Agent of the American Colonization Society has blinded the eyes of benevolent men, in relation to the design and tendency of that Society. 3d, Enlisting able and eloquent advocates to plead our cause. 4th, Inducing editors of periodicals and able writers, to give us the weight of their influence. 5th, exciting a spirit of emulation, in the redemption of our slave population, among the numerous female anti-slavery societies. 6th, Procuring a large collection of anti-slavery documents, tracts, pamphlets and volumes, which will furnish us with an inexhaustible supply of ammunition.

There is now great certainty that Parliament will complete the scheme of emancipation this session, as the House of Lords has adopted, without any amendment, the resolutions of the House of Commons. To-night, the Bill, containing the details of the measure, will be read a first time in the latter House. It is now highly probable that the term of apprenticeship will be reduced from twelve years to one or two, and perhaps swept entirely away. Remonstrances are pouring into Parliament, from various parts of the kingdom, against the grant of £20,000,000 to the planters, but I fear they will prove ineffectual.

Mr. Elliott Cresson continues to skulk from a public controversy. In the leading city paper, the 'Times,' of the 28th ultimo, I inserted a challenge to him, in which I stated ten Propositions, which I offered to maintain against the American Colonization Society.[1] I also promised that if he would prove, to the satisfaction of a majority of the audience, the following charge against me in a letter which he published in the Baptist Magazine for June — namely, 'a violent pamphleteer, who often sacrifices truth to the support of his mistaken views, *and whose very quotations are so garbled as entirely to pervert the real meaning of the speaker,*' I would pay *twenty guineas* into the hands of the Mayor of New-York, in aid of the education of the colored children of that city. The insertion of this article in the Times, although making less than three squares, cost me £6, 6s., that is, about *thirty dollars!!* This is the usual advertising rate in that paper. Cresson's effrontery is truly surprising; for, notwithstanding these repeated challenges, he has advertised a meeting of his own, to be held on Wednesday next, at the Hanover Rooms, at which the Duke of Sussex is expected to preside! I have no hesitation in prophesying that it will be a complete failure: of course, I shall endeavor to be present, as I anticipate some amusing collisions on the occasion, if not between me and the speaker, at least between him and some sturdy abolitionists. As an off-set to this meeting, I propose to hold one next week, which many of the noblest friends of liberty in England will probably attend. The arrangements, however, have not yet been made; and perhaps another, and even more effectual course may be adopted.

In my first public lecture in this city,[2] at which Mr. Cresson was present, I said among other things to the audience —

'Suppose the Legislature of Jamaica, after having brooded upon it in secret session at various periods, for more than sixteen years, should now come out with a scheme for colonizing all the free people of color in the colonies; suppose a public meeting should thereupon be immediately held in Jamaica, by the most distinguished planters; suppose they should, in conjunction with a few well-meaning gradualists from England, form a society for the purpose of removing the free people of color to Africa — at the same time denouncing this class as a nuisance, and as rendering the slave system insecure by their presence among the slaves, and yet pretending to cherish the highest regard for their temporal and spiritual welfare; suppose they should lay it down, as a fundamental rule, that no slave ought to be liberated except on condition of expulsion from the colonies; suppose the number of slaves, instead of diminishing as at present, was increasing at the rate of 70,000 annually, and that the whole number was 2,200,000 instead of 800,000; suppose that this Society should begin to denounce every abolitionist as a madman and an incendiary, and should say, "We protest, most solemnly protest, against the adoption of your views, as alike destructive of the ends of justice, of policy, and of humanity;" * and suppose that this Society should assume the whole ground of emancipation, and oppose every other plan to abolish slavery: — what would you say of such a Society, originating with such men, holding forth such a scheme, and propagating such doctrines? I know what you would say! I know what you would do! No matter how many good men you might see unwarily entangled in the base conspiracy; no matter how fanciful and glowing might be the descriptions respecting the condition of the African exiles; you would say, as the noblest advocates of the colored race — "O, cursed combination, full of all subtlety! more to be feared than slavery itself! the contemner of justice and mercy! the mocker of God and man! the complication of all evil! the masterpiece of all the contrivances of the devil!" You would view it as the wall that surrounded Babylon the great! You would carry it by storm — you would not leave one stone upon another. And if any agent should come before you, and ask you for means to assist in carrying into effect this diabolical scheme, or ask you in any way to support it, your moral indignation would kindle into a flame. He might plead his respectability — his good intentions — his personal sacrifices — his association with great and good men. In vain! in vain! You might pity his delusion; you might possibly excuse his ignorance, if you saw no cause to doubt his sincerity. But if you detected him in circulating monstrous fabrications and wilful misrepresentations, you would order him back to his negro-stealing employers without delay, and bid him be thankful *that you did not arrest him on a charge of collecting money upon fraudulent pretexts.* This is a true picture of the American Colonization Society and its Agent in this country," &c.

G. Pilkington, Esq. (a lecturer on peace and abolition,) [3] then rose and observed with great animation, — 'After what has dropped from the lecturer, that Mr. Cresson may be accused, and is liable to be accused, of obtaining money under false pretences, — before this Christian assembly has that charge escaped, — it is his (Mr. C's) duty to meet it. The truth will shine in spite of the devil; and let Mr. Cresson's friends tell him if he values his character to come forward, and stand up like a man, and tell the people of this country whether or not he has raised money under false pretences, and whether he is not employed by slaveholders.'

The Rev. Mr. Price also said — 'If Mr. Cresson is at all anxious to receive any more money from the English public, let him meet the challenge at once; for he may depend upon it that if John Bull hears he has refused it, every pocket will be shut against him.'

And yet, under all these circumstances, and with this serious charge

* African Repository, vol. vii. p. 101.

recorded publicly against him, Mr. Cresson refuses to defend either his own conduct or the Colonization Society in a public controversy!

I remain sincerely yours,

WM. LLOYD GARRISON.

Printed: *The Liberator*, September 7, 1833; printed partly in *Life*, I, 366–367.

1. See letter 106, to Cresson, June 27.
2. At Wesleyan Chapel, Devonshire Square, June 10, 1833.
3. George Pilkington, a rather insignificant lecturer for the Agency Committee, was apparently to emigrate to Brazil in 1839.

109

TO PRINCE AUGUSTUS FREDERICK, THE DUKE OF SUSSEX

18, Aldermanbury, July 13, 1833.

May it please your Royal Highness:

The enclosed Circular and Ticket will inform you that a meeting is to be held to-morrow, at 12 o'clock, at Exeter Hall, for the purpose of exposing the real character and object of the American Colonization Society. Although your Royal Highness generously declared, at the meeting in the Hanover Square Rooms, that you regarded the Agent of that Society as a gentleman who was above attack; yet, with the utmost deference to the opinion of your Royal Highness, it is possible that he may not be impeccable. Many great and good men, who, a few months since, were captivated by his fanciful and false statements, are now led, by a careful investigation of the subject, to regard him as a public deceiver. Surely, there is no one more disposed to weigh evidence and examine facts than your Royal Highness; especially in a case so momentous as the present. If your Royal Highness could make it convenient to honor the meeting to-morrow with your presence, I should not only regard the act as exceedingly magnanimous, but it would unquestionably be a source of sincere pleasure to the auditors.

In my note of the 29th ultimo, I addressed your Royal Highness by the title of 'Your Grace.' [1] As the error, though trivial in itself, might seem to imply intentional disrespect, I must here apologize for the same. An American citizen, in Europe, is ever liable to err, through ignorance, in the application of hereditary titles, as they do not obtain in his own country.

I am confident that your Royal Highness will most cheerfully pardon the blunder.

With sentiments of the highest respect for the benevolence and goodness of your character, I am

Your Obed't Serv't,

(Signed) WM. LLOYD GARRISON,
Representative of the New-England Anti-Slavery Society.

Printed: *Second Annual Report of the Board of Managers of the New-England Anti-Slavery Society* (Boston, 1834), p. 44; extract printed in *Life,* I, 368.

1. Garrison refers to letter 107.

110

TO THE EDITOR OF THE LONDON *PATRIOT*

[July 22, 1833.]

SIR, —

By publishing in the *Patriot* the following letters which have been addressed to me by two eminent advocates of negro emancipation, I do not doubt that you will not only hasten the liberation of more than two millions of slaves in the United States, and the downfall of that brazen hand-maid of slavery, the American Colonization Society, but also prevent many a benevolent and confiding person from giving his money to the agent of that Society.[1] For notwithstanding he stands publicly charged, by the leading abolitionists in this country, with having misrepresented the character and objects of the Colonization Society, and notwithstanding he has pusillanimously shrunk from the offer of a public discussion in this metropolis, to my astonishment I learn that Mr. Cresson, in company with an Irish female partisan, has either departed, or is about to depart, for Ireland, in order to obtain new charities for a scheme which is "full of all deceivableness of unrighteousness."[2] Happily, the imposture is now generally understood; and the speech of the eloquent O'Connell, at Exeter Hall, on the 13th instant, in opposition to the Society, will anticipate the arrival of Mr. Cresson in Dublin.[3]

Your much obliged servant,

WILLIAM LLOYD GARRISON,

18, Aldermanbury, July 22, 1833.

Printed: London *Patriot*, July 24, 1833; here reprinted from *The Liberator*, October 26, 1833.

Josiah Conder (1789–1855) was a bookseller, popular poet, and the author of *On Protestant Nonconformity*, as well as the editor of the nonconformist *Patriot*.

1. Garrison enclosed two letters written in opposition to the American Coloniz-

ation Society, one by Zachary Macaulay, dated July 14, and one by English Quaker William Allen (1770–1843), dated July 15.

2. II Thessalonians 2:10.

3. O'Connell criticized slavery in general and the American Colonization Society in particular, calling it "the most ludicrous Society that ever yet was dreamed of." He moved a resolution that its fundamental principle was ever the colonization of free people of color, "and abolition never the object, but on the contrary the security of slave property." (See *The Liberator*, November 23, 1833.)

111

TO THE EDITOR OF THE LONDON *PATRIOT*

[August 6, 1833.]

SIR, — The *Patriot* of Wednesday last [1] contains a communication from Mr. Elliott Cresson, purporting to be a reply to some inquiries which I addressed to him in the *Times*, a few weeks since, in relation to the principles and measures of the American Colonization Society. I have no ambition to gratify in a contest with Mr. Cresson. Personally, he would escape my notice, detached from the agency of a Society, which alone elevates him to a point of visibility. Regarding him as an imposter, who has succeeded largely in duping that generous, confiding, unexampled spirit of abolition which pervades the breasts of the British people, — sympathy for the enslaved millions of my own countrymen, — obedience to the instructions of those whose commission I bear, — justice to the friends of negro emancipation in this country, — and duty to God, require that I should tear the mask from his own face, and expose the Colonization Society in all its naked deformity.

Mr. Cresson commences his reply with a learned display of constitutional knowledge. He has discovered (*mirabile dictu!*) that "Great Britain has the power to abolish slavery," but "the general Government [of the United States] has no jurisdiction within these [State] limits, and has no power as regards slavery." Now, the position which has been maintained *ab origine* by the West India planters, against any interference on the part of the mother country, is, that "Great Britain has *not* the power to abolish slavery," and that it "has no jurisdiction" on that subject. But how the relative powers of the American Congress and the British Parliament affect the principles of an independent, self-constituted Society, I cannot perceive. This is not a constitutional controversy, but one affecting conscience, justice, righteousness, and brotherly love. It does not relate to the legal authority of a legislative assembly, but to the doctrines and tendencies of the American Colonization Society. I am not disposed, therefore, to deny the assertion of

Mr. Cresson, that of the twenty-four independent States of America, "each State possesses sovereign power within its own limits;" and yet I maintain that the guilt of slavery is national, its danger is national, and the obligation to remove it is national. I affirm that Pennsylvania is as really a slave-holding State as Georgia — that the free States are as criminal as the slave-holding States — and that the latter are merely the agents of the former. Hence, the people of the United States (not of one portion of territory merely) are wholly responsible, and altogether inexcusable, for the present existence of slavery in that country.[2]

I know that there is much declamation about the sacredness of the compact which was formed between the free and the slave States, on the adoption of the national Constitution. A sacred compact, forsooth! I pronounce it the most bloody and heaven-daring arrangement ever made by men for the continuance and protection of a system of the most atrocious villany ever exhibited on earth. Yes, I recognise the compact, but with feelings of shame and indignation; and it will be held in everlasting infamy by the friends of justice and humanity throughout the world. It was a compact formed at the sacrifice of the bodies and souls of millions of our race, for the sake of achieving a political object — an unblushing and monstrous coalition to do "evil that good might come." [3] Such a compact was, in the nature of things, and according to the law of God, null and void from the beginning. No body of men ever had the right to guarantee the holding of human beings in bondage. Who or what were the framers of the American Government, that they should dare confirm and authorize such high-handed villany — such a flagrant robbery of the inalienable rights of man — such a glaring violation of all the precepts and injunctions of the Gospel — such a savage war upon a sixth part of their whole population? They were men, like ourselves — as fallible, as sinful, as weak, as ourselves. By the infamous bargain which they made between themselves, they virtually dethroned the Most High God, and trampled beneath their feet their own solemn and heaven-attested declaration, that all men are created equal, and endowed by their Creator with certain inalienable rights — among which are life, liberty, and the pursuit of happiness. They had no lawful power to bind themselves, or their posterity, for one hour — for one moment — by such an unholy alliance. It was not valid then — it is not valid now. Still they persisted in maintaining it — and still do their successors, the people of New England, and of the twelve free States, persist in maintaining it. A sacred compact! a sacred compact! What, then, is wicked and ignominious?

This, then, is the relation in which the people of the free States

stand to the holders of slaves at the south, and this is virtually their language toward them — "Go on, most worthy associates, from day to day, from month to month, from year to year, from generation to generation, plundering two millions of human beings of their liberty and the fruits of their toil — driving them into the fields like cattle — starving and lacerating their bodies — selling the husband from his wife, the wife from her husband, and children from their parents — spilling their blood — withholding the Bible from their hands and all knowledge from their minds — and kidnapping annually one hundred thousand infants, the offspring of pollution and shame! Go on in these practices — we do not wish nor mean to interfere for the rescue of your victims, even by expostulation or warning — we like your company too well to offend you by denouncing your conduct — 'although we know that by every principle of law which does not utterly disgrace us by assimilating us to pirates, they have as good and as true a right to the equal protection of the law as we have; and, although we ourselves stand prepared to die, rather than submit even to a fragment of the intolerable load of oppression to which we are subjecting them — yet never mind — let that be — they have grown old in suffering and we in iniquity — and we have nothing to do now but to speak peace, peace, to one another in our sins. We are too wicked ever to love them as God commands us to do — we are so resolute in our wickedness as not even to desire to do so — and we are so proud in our iniquity that we will hate and revile whoever disturbs us in it. We want, like the devils of old, to be let alone in our sin. We are unalterably determined, and neither God nor man shall move us from this resolution, that our coloured subjects never shall be free or happy in their native land.' *
Go on, from bad to worse — add link to link to the chains upon the bodies of your victims — add constantly to the intolerable burdens under which they groan; and if, goaded to desperation by your cruelties, they should rise to assert their rights and redress their wrongs, fear nothing — we are pledged, by a sacred compact, [sacred!!] to shoot them like dogs, and deliver you from their vengeance! Go on — we never will forsake you, for 'there is honour among thieves' [4] — our swords are ready to leap from their scabbards, and our muskets to pour forth deadly volleys as soon as you are in danger. We pledge you our physical strength by the sacredness of the national compact — a compact by which we have enabled you already to plunder, persecute, and destroy two millions of slaves, who now lie beneath the sod; and by which we now give you the same piratical license to prey upon a much larger number of victims and all their posterity. Go on — and by this sacred instrument, the Constitution of the United States, drip-

* Circular of Charles Stuart, Esq.

ping as it is with human blood, we solemnly pledge our lives, our fortunes, and our sacred honour, that we will stand by you to the last."

In the First Annual Report of the Society which I have the honour to represent, "the managers solemnly protest against the doctrine that slavery concerns the south alone, and that the people of the free States have no right to demand its removal. They regard it as politically and morally false, calculated to paralyze the consciences and efforts of the people, and to give perpetuity to the system. It is true that the people of New England cannot legislate for the Southern States; that the national compact was so framed as to guarantee the legal possession of slaves; and that physical interference would be a violation of Chris tian principles. But, so long as slaves are held in the district of Co- lumbia, and in the Territories of the United States (over which Con- gress has exclusive jurisdiction); † so long as ours is a representative Government, subject to the will of the people; so long as no efforts are made to modify or repeal the present compact, by those who have both the right and the power thus to do; so long as the interests of the non-slave-holding States are jeoparded by the twenty-five slave votes in Congress; ‡ so long as moral influence, widely and wisely dissemi- nated, is productive of beneficial results; so long as public opinion is the lever of national reform; so long as the people of New England are liable to be called upon to put down slave insurrections at the south; § so long as there is neither liberty of speech nor of the press, on the subject of oppression, in a large portion of our country; * so long as Southern States deprive the coloured citizens of New England, who may visit them, of their liberty and the rights of citizenship guaranteed

---

† Yet Mr. Cresson declares that "the general Government has no power as regards slavery!"

‡ The slave-holders are permitted to vote for three-fifths of all their slaves as property; *i.e.* five slaves are equal to three freemen. Thus, a planter possessing five hundred slaves can, in addition to his own suffrage, cast three hundred votes into the ballot-box for those who will faithfully guard and represent his property upon the floor of Congress, and for a President and Vice-President of the United States; while the northern citizen, who may be worth twice as much in personal and real estate, can only give one vote!! And this is permitted by the free States, to the destruction of their own interests, and to the enslavement of millions of human beings! And yet Mr. Cresson would fain lead the British public to imagine that the Northern States are not chargeable with the perpetuity of slavery.

§ During the insurrection of the slaves in Virginia in 1831, troops were drafted from the harbour of Boston, and sent against the revolters. A standing army is supported by the nation in the slave States, principally to suppress the spirit of insubordination among the slaves, and to make it easy and safe to hold them in servitude. Slaves eloping into the free States are seized and sent back to their tyrannical masters. Still, according to Mr. Cresson, these States are innocent of any participation in the guilt of southern oppression!!

* If an orator or an editor should dare to expound the principles recognised in the declaration of American independence at the South, and apply them to negro slavery, he would be compelled to fly for his life.

to them by the Constitution of the United States; † so long as slavery mars the harmony, divides the policy, retards the prosperity, and fearfully threatens the existence of the nation; ‡ so long as the commands of Jesus remain binding upon all men, — 'Whatsoever ye would that men should do to you, do ye even so to them' [5] — 'Thou shalt love thy neighbour as thyself;' [6] so long as there remains any flesh in our hearts, any physical or moral affinity between us and our enslaved brethren, any love to God or man in our souls, — just so long it never can be true that the people of New England are not bound to use their moral and political power to overthrow slavery in the United States." [7]

These sentiments form a lofty contrast to the pusillanimous, corrupt, and proscriptive principles and doctrines of the American Colonization Society.

Mr. Cresson's assertion, that "nearly one-half" of the emigrants to Liberia have been emancipated through the instrumentality of the Colonization Society, is flagrant mendacity.[8] Rather less than one-fourth of the whole number of colonists have been liberated slaves — including a few intelligent and industrious persons, with a large proportion of those whom the Governor of Liberia styles, "the lowest and most abandoned of their class," who "have never, when in the United States, voluntarily laboured for their own support, and now, when the stimulus of the overseer's lash is removed, cannot be induced to exert themselves sufficiently to procure even a scanty subsistence!" § The Colonization Society opens an excellent drain by which the planters may rid themselves of their turbulent, vicious, and worn-out slaves, and at the same time be lauded for their generous sacrifices in the cause of philanthropy!!

But, allowing that instead of one-fourth, all who have been trans-

---

† Coloured men, who go as seamen or stewards in vessels from the Northern to the Southern States, are seized on their arrival, and thrust into prison until the sailing of the ships! If any coloured traveller from the free States ventures to step upon Southern territory, he is liable to be imprisoned on suspicion of being a runaway slave, or for being there contrary to law; and if he cannot prove his title to freedom, or pay the fine and prison fees, he is sold at public vendue as a slave! Although the outrage is as great a violation of the Constitution, as if the most distinguished white citizen was treated in the same manner, yet the free States make no remonstrance, simply because the victim has a tawny or black skin!

‡ Nearly all the troubles and excitements in the United States spring from slavery, and there can be no end to collisions until that root of bitterness be taken away. How is it possible for Congress to legislate satisfactorily and equally on any question of national policy, which is intended alike for free labourers and slaves? That which gives a healthy impulse to Northern industry must inevitably enfeeble slave labour at the South, and *vice versa*. There are no difficulties or heart-burnings between the free States; they do not threaten each other, or talk of a separation one from another. The longer slavery is tolerated, the more probable is a dismemberment of the American Union.

§ Vide Governor Mechlin's Letter, *African Repository* for December last.[9]

ported to the American slave-holders' Botany Bay [10] (about 3,000) were thereby released from servitude, the direct and inevitable effect of their banishment is to augment the power of the oppressors, and to raise the value of the slaves in the United States (so far as it really has any effect), by reducing the surplus population! It has done nothing to destroy, but something to perpetuate slavery. At least two hundred thousand slaves could be spared and sent to Liberia (such is their excessive increase "beyond the occasions of profitable employment"), much to the pecuniary advantage of the South, and to the vigorous maintenance of the slave system.[11]

About seven hundred slaves have been sent to Liberia since the organization of the Colonization Society in December, 1816. Since that period the slave population of the United States has increased more than six hundred thousand! and the rate of manumissions, as compared with former years, has decreased from seven to three per cent. per annum! Thus, owing to the withering influences of the Colonization Society upon the cause of abolition, nearly three hundred thousand victims are now pining in ruthless bondage, who else might have been freemen! The managers of this Society in their address to its auxiliaries (vide *African Repository*, No. 10, vol. vii.),[12] positively declare that "they determined to avoid the question of slavery," and that "the emancipation of slaves, or the amelioration of their condition, with the moral, intellectual, and political improvement of people of colour within the United States, are subjects foreign to the powers of this Society. To mingle them with the great and exclusive end of the Colonization Society [the transportation of free persons of colour], would be destructive to it." Its most distinguished champion, the Hon. Henry Clay, asserts that "from its origin, and throughout the whole period of its existence, it has constantly disclaimed all intention whatever of interfering, in the smallest degree, with the rights of property, or the object of emancipation, gradual or immediate." — *African Repository*, vol. vi. p. 13. Again it is affirmed, in an elaborate vindication of the Society in the same work (vol. iii. p. 197) — "It is no abolition Society; it addresses as yet arguments to no master, and disavows with horror the idea of offering temptations to any slaves; it denies the design of attempting emancipation, either partial or general." Again, the organ of the Society affirms (vol. iv. p. 145), "It has no intention to open the door to universal liberty, but only to cut out a channel where the merciful providence of God(!) may cause those dark waters [the free coloured and surplus slave population] to flow off." Again it avers, in the same volume, p. 306, "The Colonization Society, as such, have renounced wholly the name and the characteristics of abolitionists. On this point, they have been unjustly and injuriously slandered.

Into their accounts the subject of emancipation does not enter at all."
Notwithstanding these, and a hundred other similar authorities and
unequivocal statements, Mr. Cresson has had the dishonesty and
hardihood to publish in this country the statement that the great and
primary object of the Society is "the final and entire abolition of
slavery!!" [13] According to the organ of the Society which he represents,
he is, therefore, a slanderer.

To my interrogation, whether the Colonization Society does not
recommend the expulsion of the slaves from the United States as the
condition of their emancipation, Mr. Cresson replies, "Certainly not."
He then "quotes its own words," disavowing and reprobating every
coercive measure.[14] Against this solitary extract I array the following
proof: — "We would say, liberate them only on condition of their going
to Africa or to Hayti." — *African Repository*, vol. iii. p. 26. "Any scheme
of emancipation without colonization, they know, and see, and feel to
be productive of nothing but evil." — *Idem*, vol. iv. p. 300. "All emancipation, to however small an extent, which permits the emancipated
to remain in this country, is an evil which must increase with the
increase of the operation." — First Annual Report, Appendix.[15] "They
will annex the condition that the emancipated shall leave the country."
— Second ditto, App. "Emancipation, with the liberty to remain on this
side of the Atlantic, is but an act of dreamy madness." — Thirteenth
ditto, App.[16] "The Society maintains that no slave ought to receive his
liberty, except on condition of being excluded, not merely from the
State which sets him loose, but from the whole country; that is, of being
colonized." — *North American Review* for July, 1832. If these extracts
are not explicit and numerous enough to prove that expulsion is the
only condition of freedom, I will add to their number. Even Mr.
Cresson will not have the hardihood to deny that those slaves, who
have been sent to Liberia, had no alternative but to leave the country,
or remain in bondage; although their masters might have removed
them to the free States at a very trifling expense. Against this doctrine
of suspending emancipation upon the contingency or condition of expatriation, the abolitionists of the United States feel bound to protest —
because they believe that every man has a right to reside in his native
country, if he chooses, and that every man's native country is the
country in which he was born. That no man's right to freedom is
suspended upon, or taken away by, his desire to remain in his native
country; that to make a removal from one's native country a *sine qua
non* of setting him free, when held in involuntary bondage, is the
climax of moral absurdity; because, it is an offer to restore an inalienable right, on condition of being permitted to restrain the exercise of
that right, in one of its most fundamental and essential particulars. It

offers freedom, on condition that freedom of choice shall not exist; that the person made free shall not remain where he chooses, and reside where he pleases. It offers to discharge a duty by the perpetration of an act of injustice; to make restitution by a new aggression; to do right, with a reservation of the privilege of doing wrong.

I must defer other strictures upon Mr. Cresson's communication until another opportunity.[17]   One word, however, as to the Rev. Leonard Bacon, whom Mr. C. eulogizes as "a distinguished divine, a firm friend of negro emancipation and education, and, consequently(!!), of the American Colonization and African Education Societies." [18] Mr. Bacon, in a feeble and self-confuted review of my "Thoughts on African Colonization," says, "This author not only misconstrues, but he garbles, mutilates, and interpolates false explanations, to make his misconstructions more effectual." [19] The charge is utterly groundless. He has taxed his ingenuity to the utmost in order to substantiate it, but he has succeeded in proving only his own deceitfulness and corruption.   I have already offered Mr. Cresson twenty guineas if he will fairly convict me of misconstruing, garbling, mutilating, or interpolating false explanations in my work; and with all the light which the "distinguished divine" has poured upon his vision, I renew my offer. Nearly a year has elapsed, probably, since my work came into Mr. C.'s possession. As he has also all the documents and publications of the Colonization Society, from which I have taken my quotations chiefly, he can easily convict me of falsehood and calumny, if I have been guilty of such wickedness. Why has he not long since exposed me to public scorn, or publicly referred to the page and paragraph in which I had invented a fiction or committed a forgery? True, I find it stated in a report of a discussion which he held with Mr. Impey,[20] at Scarborough, before my arrival in England, — "He (Mr. Cresson) then turned to a passage (what passage?) which had been quoted from Mr. Garrison, as copied from the *African Repository,* but which, instead of being found in the number and page alluded to, could not be discovered at all. This, he contended, completely overturned the validity of Mr. Garrison's testimony"(!) At the same meeting, the Rev. B. Evans [21] is reported to have said — "He had also read C.'s book, and he found a quotation from it in the *Eclectic Review,* a reference to a number and page of the *African Repository,* where he could find neither the words nor the sentiments; and he must confess, when he saw a man had not the moral honesty to quote correctly, he could not value his evidence highly." Surely, this exultation is premature — this condemnation is unjust. To my belief and knowledge, every extract purporting to be from the *African Repository* is contained in that work; and yet it is probable that in such a multitude of quotations as I have brought together, a wrong figure or numeral has been used, in a few instances. I have discovered but one error of this kind — there may be others. If, in ninety-nine cases out of a hundred, I have correctly given the No. and page of my authority, is a single error of the proof-reader or printer to convict me of wilful forgery? Knowing how critically and severely it would be examined, and how much I had staked upon its integrity, it was my object and watchful endeavour to make the work as fair in its quotations, and as correct in its typography, as possible. Still, a few typographical errors escaped my vigilance; and according to the triumphant decision of Mr. Cresson, they "completely overturn the validity of Mr. G.'s testimony"! — and in the sagacious opinion of his reverend friend, it proves that I am destitute of "moral honesty"!! Really, I must have been as destitute of discernment and wisdom as my censors, — had my object been to impose upon the public, — in falsely referring to a particular No. and page, where detection was certain. The reference itself is indubitable evidence of my sincerity and honesty. The same clerical critic also said, — "He could not consider that evidence," (I will endeavour to "quote correctly,") "where one sentence was taken from page ——, and another from page ——, and both were united together *for the purpose of putting a different construction on the sentiments, to what was intended*" — (the italics are mine.) This is a bold allegation, but there is not a syllable of truth in it. The *onus probandi* rests upon the accuser.

But I return to that "distinguished divine, the firm friend of negro emancipation and education," the Rev. Leonard Bacon, of New Haven. No writer in the United States, no slave-holder in the south, has uttered or published more excusatory, corrupt, and blasphemous sentiments as regards slavery, than this individual. Take a few specimens, drawn from his papers in defence of the Colonization Society:

"Among the twelve millions who make up our census, two millions are Africans — separated from the possessors of the soil by birth, by the brand of indelible ignominy, by prejudices, mutual, deep, incurable, by an irreconcilable diversity of interests. Whatever may be effected for elevating the mass of the nation in the scale of happiness or of intellectual and moral character, their degradation is the same, — dark, and deep, and hopeless."

"He [the humane and conscientious oppressor!] looks around him, and sees that the condition of the great mass of emancipated Africans is one in comparison with which the condition of his slaves is enviable"! — "Hundreds of humane and Christian slave-holders [pious robbers] retain their fellow-men in bondage, because they are convinced that they can do no better"! — "It is a well established point, that the public safety forbids either the emancipation or general instruction of the slaves."

"Leaving slavery and its subjects for the moment entirely out of view, there are in the United States 238,000 blacks denominated free, but whose freedom confers on them, we might say, no privilege but the privilege of being more vicious and miserable than slaves can be." [Atrocious calumny.]

"Would you set before him [the free man of colour] the importance of a good character? But of how much value is character to him who stands now, and must always stand, in the lowest order of society?[!!] It is this degradation of the condition of our free coloured population which ensures their degradation of character, and their degradation of character reacts to make their condition still more degraded. They constitute a class by themselves, — a class out of which no individual can be elevated, and below which none can be depressed. And this is the difficulty, the invariable and insuperable difficulty, in the way of every scheme for their benefit. Much can be done for them — much has been done; but still they are, and, in this country, always must be, a depressed and abject race." "A population which, even if it were not literally enslaved, must for ever remain in a state of degradation no better than bondage."

"We are ready even to grant, for our present purpose, that, so far as mere animal existence is concerned, the slaves have no reason to complain, and the friends of humanity have no reason to complain for them." "For the *existence* of slavery in the United States, those, and those only,[!!] are accountable who bore a part in originating such a constitution of society."

"The Bible contains no explicit prohibition of slavery. There is neither chapter nor verse of Holy Writ, which lends any countenance to the fulminating spirit of universal emancipation, of which some exhibitions may be seen in some of the newspapers."

"In every part of the United States, there is a broad and impassable line of demarcation between every man who has one drop of African blood in his veins, and every other class in the community. The habits, the feelings, all the prejudices of society — prejudices which neither refinement, nor argument, nor education, nor religion itself can subdue — mark the people of colour, whether bond or free, as the subjects of a degradation, inevitable and incurable. The African in this country belongs by birth to the very lowest station in society; and from that station he can never rise, be his talents, his enterprise, his virtues what they may."

These horrible sentiments of Mr. Cresson's Magnus Apollo [22] are copied into the official publications of the Colonization Society, and declared to be "admirable," [vide *African Repository* for June, 1828,* the Appendix to the Seventh Annual Report, and the *Christian Spectator* for September, 1830, published in New Haven.] [23] "This able Address," [24] says the *Repository*, "we understand has been widely circulated in Connecticut, and we sincerely wish it may be republished in every State of the Union. The spirit of liberality and candour, and the convincing argument and eloquence which pervade it throughout, must recommend it to the notice of all those whose good opinion merits regard"!!! So much for the "Rev. Leonard Bacon, of the Presbyterian church, the distinguished divine, the firm friend of negro emancipation and education, and consequently, of the American Colonization and African Education Societies"!!

Mr. Editor, in behalf of the perishing slaves, of the persecuted free blacks, and of the abolitionists of the United States, I beg you to accept my grateful acknowledgments for the readiness with which you have opened your columns for the discussion of this most momentous subject. I know not how you can more effectually open the eyes of the British people to the Colonization imposture, than by publishing the following Protest, (duplicates of which have been signed,) on the part of the most distinguished abolitionists in this country. I had no agency in getting it up, and never saw it until it was sent to me by those whose signatures are appended to it. Mr. Wilberforce signed it about a week or ten days before his death: his autograph is remarkably firm and plain. His testimony is almost like a voice from the grave, and in giving it, he has made the last act of his life as useful and important in the destruction of prejudice and slavery, as any other single act in his noble career of philanthropy.

Yours, respectfully,

WM. LLOYD GARRISON,
Agent of the New England Anti-Slavery Society.
18, Aldermanbury, Aug. 6, 1833.

* "An address to the Public by the Managers of the Colonization Society of Connecticut," written by the Rev. Mr. Bacon.

Printed: London *Patriot*, August 21, 1833; partly printed in *The Liberator*, December 21, 1833.

When Garrison edited this letter for publication in his paper, he omitted approximately half of the text and all the footnotes as originally printed in the *Patriot*, eliminating in the process many of the passages most critical of the "compact" between the northern and southern states.

In order to avoid the multiplication of asterisks as used in the *Patriot* to designate the footnotes, the editor has arbitrarily changed some of the conventional printer's symbols.

1. July 21.
2. The next four paragraphs and their footnotes are omitted in *The Liberator*.
3. Romans 3:8.

4. Garrison quotes a maxim of Roman origin, which was used frequently by nineteenth-century writers.

5. Matthew 7:12.

6. Matthew 19:19.

7. Garrison quotes from the *First Annual Report of the . . . New-England Anti-Slavery Society* (Boston, 1833, pp. 21–22) a long passage probably composed by himself, making a few changes in punctuation, adding parenthetical comment, and supplying the footnotes.

8. The *Liberator* text resumes with this paragraph. It is virtually impossible to determine which estimate, Garrison's or Cresson's, is more accurate, owing to the confused state of the statistics concerning the settlement at Liberia. It is known that prior to 1827 most of the emigrants transported were free Negroes. Following that date an increasing number of the emigrants were freed by their masters for the purposes of colonization. But the reports of the Colonization Society are not clear. (See Early Lee Fox, *The American Colonization Society, 1870–1840*, Baltimore, 1919, p. 211.] Certainly Garrison is unfair in branding Cresson's assertion as "flagrant mendacity."

9. Mechlin's letter to Rev. Ralph R. Gurley, secretary of the Colonization Society, *African Repository*, 8:298–302 (December 1832). Dr. Joseph Mechlin had gone to Liberia in 1828 as a physician and assistant agent of the Colonization Society. The following year he was appointed government agent, which, strictly speaking, was his title — not governor, as Garrison says.

10. An allusion to the infamous Australian penal colony.

11. In *The Liberator*, the next two paragraphs and the first sentence of the one following are omitted.

12. The passage quoted by Garrison is to be found in the December 1831 issue (pp. 191–192). Garrison's subsequent quotations from the *African Repository*, except for minor alterations in punctuation, are accurate, as are the page references.

13. The source of this quotation which Garrison attributes to Cresson has not been identified.

14. Garrison refers to Cresson's letter of July 21 to the editor of the *Patriot*.

15. Garrison abridges a passage from a letter of Robert G. Harper to the secretary of the colonization society, Elias B. Caldwell, printed in the *First Annual Report of the American Society for Colonizing the Free People of Colour of the United States* (Washington, D.C., 1818), p. 19. Harper (1765–1825), an early member of the American Colonization Society, was the one who had named the African colony Liberia and its capital, Monrovia.

16. Garrison's citations to both the second and the thirteenth annual reports appear to be inaccurate. The quotation alleged to be from the second can be found neither in the report itself nor in the appendix, and the other quotation (from an address by playwright George Washington Parke Custis) is not from the appendix but from the "Proceedings" of the thirteenth report (p. viii), Garrison, moreover, misquotes Custis, substituting "liberty" for "liberated" — an error also to be found in Garrison's quotation of the passage in *Thoughts on African Colonization* (p. 113), where the quotation supposed to be from the second report is also found.

17. The *Liberator* text resumes with the next sentence.

18. Leonard Bacon (1802–1881), the distinguished theologian and minister of the First Church of New Haven (Congregational), was a leader among moderate abolitionists, who had begun writing on the slavery problem as early as 1823 (a report *On the Black Population of the United States*) while a student at the Andover Theological Seminary. In New Haven he edited between 1826 and 1838 the *Christian Spectator* in which he supported the colonizationists and opposed the Garrisonians; he was also instrumental in organizing a society for the improvement of Negroes in New Haven.

19. Bacon's review was printed in the *Christian Quarterly Spectator*, 5:145–157 (March 1833); Garrison quotes accurately from page 153.

20. Possibly Walter J. Impey, who published *A Series of Questions on the Practice of the Courts of King's Bench and Common Pleas* (London, 1835).

21. Apparently a Baptist minister at Scarborough, who is known to the editor by a letter preserved at the library of Rhodes House, Oxford.

22. Presumably Leonard Bacon.

23. These quotations are scattered throughout the three sources Garrison cites. The patchwork arrangement is confusing, but the quotations are accurate.

24. The Address to the Public cited in Garrison's footnote.

112

TO THE EDITOR OF THE LONDON *CHRISTIAN ADVOCATE*

[August 10, 1833.]

Sir, —

The cause of bleeding humanity in the United States is deeply indebted to you, for your early and frequent exposures of the guilt and hypocrisy of the American Colonization Society. I am happy in believing that British abolitionists are now too well acquainted with the corrupt principles, the proscriptive measures, and the destructive tendencies of that association, to be misled by the deceptive statements of its agent. The buyers and sellers of human flesh, the enslavers of their fellow-creatures, ay, and of their own children — the plunderers of the helpless and needy — as well as all those whose prejudices are fiercely demanding a foreign separation of the white and colored races in the United States — applaud, defend, and patronize the Colonization Society. Mr. Cresson may now successfully seek the charities of the pro-slavery party in England; for, according to the *North American Review* for July, 1832, — 'nothing is requisite to make them (slaveholders and their apologists) *universally* the warmest patrons of the Colonization policy, but a fair understanding of its principles' !! [1]

Convicted of duplicity and fraud in this country — the execrations of the American coloured population resting upon his head — and repudiated by all the friends of immediate emancipation, who are multiplying rapidly in the United States — for him to remain here, or return home, is an alternative full of distress and mortification.

By inserting the following Protest, which has been kindly sent to me within a few days, in the columns of the *Christian Advocate*, you will hang a millstone about the neck of the American Colonization Society, sufficiently weighty to drown it in an ocean of public indignation.[2]

Respectfully yours,

         WM. LLOYD GARRISON.

18, Aldermanbury, Aug. 10, 1833.

Printed: London *Christian Advocate,* August 12, 1833; here reprinted from *The Liberator,* October 12, 1833.

1. Garrison quotes — accurately except for the italics, the words within the parentheses, and the terminal exclamation points — from an anonymous review of the *Fifteenth Report of the American Colonization Society* (see *North American Review,* 35:138, July 1832).

2. The protest, which was signed by leading British abolitionists, including Buxton, O'Connell, Wilberforce, and even Macaulay himself, was printed, along with Garrison's letter, in the *Christian Advocate* for the twelfth. Macaulay had edited this paper, which was dedicated to the abolition of the slave trade, between 1802 and 1816.

113

TO NATHANIEL PAUL

London, August 17th, 1833.

ESTEEMED FRIEND AND BROTHER IN CHRIST JESUS,

As I am now on the eve of embarking for the United States, my heart is moved within me to give you a testimonial, which I trust the God of mercy will bless to the advancement of your Mission, and to the relief of "a people scattered and peeled, meted out and trodden under foot." [1]

If there be any Settlement, at the present time, which is peculiarly interesting in its origin and progress, or in its relation to Slavery in the United States; or if there be a people eminently deserving of the sympathies, prayers and charities of the followers of Him "who went about *doing good,*" [2] it is the Wilberforce Colony in Upper Canada — it is the little band of sufferers who constitute its population, of whom you are the faithful and worthy representative. Founded, as it was, in consequence of a brutal and exterminating prejudice against a colored complexion in the United States. — watered with the tears of the afflicted exiles, — and struggling under many difficulties and deprivations, — and, moreover, steadily advancing in despite of all opposition, — it presents all that is sublime in human fortitude, or heroic in human action, or affecting in human suffering, or meritorious in human virtue, for the admiration, encouragement, and commiseration of every philanthropist and lover of his species.

Its bearing upon Slavery in the United States is a consideration which greatly magnifies its importance, and entitles it to peculiar regard. As it increases in population, intelligence, and power, it will render the prolongation of that accursed and bloody system more and more insecure, and increase more and more the necessity of abolishing it altogether, and without delay. Already the American men-stealers regard it with dismay; for nothing weakens their hands and endangers their despotic rule so much, perhaps, as the presence or location of large bodies of independent free colored persons near their miserable victims: hence, their cruel scheme of banishing them to the coast of Africa, where they can neither sympathize with their afflicted brethren, nor afford them any relief. I need not say to you that the pillars of the American Colonization Society are falsehood, fear, selfishness, and hatred; for you, in common with the rest of your people, have felt its tyrannous power.

As an asylum for runaway Slaves, and for those free coloured persons who are so persecuted and trodden down in the Slave States as to be compelled to fly somewhere, life being insupportable as many of them are now situated, its contiguity renders it easy of access. It has already secured freedom to some, and, if timely assistance be given to it, it will be instrumental of breaking many a fetter and liberating many a captive in time to come. Thus, it presents, in this single particular, an unspeakably important claim to encouragement and support.

In regard to the American Colonization Society, and the Colony of Liberia, there is but one sentiment entertained by the Abolitionists and free people of Color of the United States. To both, they have strong, growing, insuperable objections, and would just as soon patronize Slavery or the Foreign Slave Trade. The same unanimity prevails among them in favor of the Wilberforce Colony, and they cordially bid it 'God speed!' [3]

It is a noble example of philanthropy and liberality, on the part of the British Government, in welcoming those unhappy exiles who have been excluded from a land which audaciously and hypocritically pretends to be "the freest of the free," — the asylum of the hunted and oppressed of all nations, — to a local habitation upon its colonial territory. It will mightily redound still more to the benevolence and honor of the British people, to assist, improve and elevate these unoffending outcasts, as well as to grant them an abiding place. What they can do, what they intend to do, let it be done quickly; for "hope deferred maketh the heart sick?" [4] Why should there be any delay or difficulty in raising the amount of funds you need?

With great pleasure do I bear witness to your spotless integrity and moral worth, my dearly beloved brother. And may that God, to whom belong the gold and silver, and the cattle upon a thousand hills, and who turns the hearts of men as the rivers of water are turned, protect, bless, and abundantly prosper you and your mission, and at last return you in safety to your friends, is the ardent desire and sincere prayer of your brother, and the advocate of the perishing slave, in stripes, in imprisonment, in peril, in life and in death.[5]

WILLIAM LLOYD GARRISON.

Printed form letter: William L. Garrison Collection, Massachusetts Historical Society; printed in *The Liberator*, November 23, 1833.

Written on the remaining space of the single page folio leaflet on which the letter was originally printed is a letter from Nathaniel Paul to George Thompson, dated September 13, describing Garrison's departure and his own "*collecting* tour" for the Wilberforce Colony, which would shortly bring him to Scotland.

1. Isaiah 18:7. Garrison's quotation is accurate except for the omission of a long phrase following "peeled."
2. Acts 10:30.
3. The Wilberforce Colony was the only project for settlement of Negroes outside the United States approved by Garrison.
4. Proverbs 13·12.
5. In the biblical pastiche in the first part of this sentence, Garrison seems to allude to Genesis 13:2, Psalms 50:10, and 1:3.

114

TO THE PATRONS OF *THE LIBERATOR* AND
THE FRIENDS OF ABOLITION

[October 11, 1833.]

RESPECTED CO-WORKERS:

Once more upon my native soil do I greet you! The God of the oppressed has graciously preserved my life, and abundantly prospered my mission: to Him let us ascribe the honor, and render thanksgiving and praise.

My arrival in England was at a period in the highest degree interesting, and signally providential. I was received by the friends of emancipation with great kindness and hospitality: no better treatment should any man receive, or could any man deserve. Their claims upon my gratitude — rather let me say upon *our* gratitude, (for it was your approbation which secured me theirs,) are large and weighty: we can discharge them only by increasing our activity, faithfulness and zeal, in behalf of the perishing slaves in the United States.

The great object of my mission, — namely, the exposure of the real character and object of the American Colonization Society, — has been accomplished, expeditiously, comprehensively, and effectually.[1] The philanthropists of Great Britain now see clearly the deformity and foulness of that Society, and their detestation of it is equalled only by their indignation at having been so basely deceived, and so extensively defrauded, by its corrupt and pusillanimous 'representative.'

My interviews with WILBERFORCE and CLARKSON were full of interest and satisfaction — the particulars of which shall be recorded hereafter. In another column will be found the signature of the former, appended to a strong and unequivocal 'PROTEST' against the Colonization

Society, in which it is declared 'that the professions made by the Society of promoting the abolition of slavery are altogether delusive' — that 'to the destruction of slavery *throughout the world,* the Society is believed *to be an obstruction*' — and that the Society is 'not deserving of the countenance of the British public.' CLARKSON's name is not affixed to the 'PROTEST,' not because he is any longer the advocate of the Colonization Society, but because, having many months since resolved that he would henceforth occupy neutral ground, he thought a departure from the course he had marked out would be a just impeachment of his integrity.[2]

The career of Elliott Cresson in England has been marked by running, duplicity and cowardice. His overthrow has been complete. Not even the aid of a Royal Duke [3] could save him! — Unhappy man! 'if his bed be a bed of thorns, he has made it himself,' and must suffer penance upon it.[4]

I regret to say that the Bill for the abolition of slavery throughout the West India Colonies, which passed through both houses of Parliament before I left England, is a complete triumph of colonial chicanery over the philanthropy of the British people. It is not an example for us to imitate, but a precedent for us to shun. It is as base in its principles, as it is impracticable in its requirements. It pleases neither the West Indian slave proprietors nor the abolitionists of England — although the former have cause for great exultation, and the latter for great lamentation. As soon as convenient, I shall publish the Bill in the Liberator, with some of the numerous protestations which have been made against it in various parts of the kingdom. Let us, however, console ourselves with the certainty of the complete emancipation of all the slaves in the British Colonies within seven years.[5]

The progress of the abolition cause in this country, during my absence, has outrun my anticipations. We have ceased to be insignificant in numbers — in devotion and courage we are unsurpassed — our moral strength is mighty — daily additions are made to our ranks. Ours is no longer the meagre victory of a skirmish, but the splendid triumph of a general engagement. Our banner is floating over many a citadel, in various States — much territory has been conquered, and nothing lost. The southern kidnappers and their northern allies have lost much of their courage, but none of their malignity. They hate us with a perfect hatred, and they fear us more than they affect to despise us. That great blasphemer, the colonization monster, cannot long survive: his present terrific struggles are but the throes of death.

One important measure remains to be effected — *a national organization of our strength.* A Circular, I am happy to perceive, has been laid before you, in which it is stated that a meeting will be held in Philadelphia for the purpose of forming a National Anti-Slavery Society, and a general invitation to the friends of immediate abolition is given, to assemble for that purpose. In the next Liberator, it is probable the day of the meeting will be designated.[6]

Conscious that we are aiming to advance as much the happiness and interests of the planters as of the slaves — that we are actuated by love, and not by malice — that we desire to promote the welfare, and exalt the reputation, and perpetuate the existence of our country — and that the Prince of Peace is the Captain of our Salvation, let us not falter nor tire in this glorious strife of truth and justice, but remain faithful unto death. 'For God hath not given us the spirit of fear; but of power, and of love and of a sound mind.' Let us ever remember that 'if a man also strive for masteries, yet he is not crowned, except he strive lawfully.' Let us 'take pleasure in infirmities, in reproaches, in necessities, in persecutions, in distresses for Christ's sake.' Truly, I can adopt the language of the apostle — 'Great is my boldness of speech toward you, great is my glorying of you: I am filled with comfort, I am exceeding joyful in all our tribulation.'[7]

The success of my mission seems to have driven 'the enemies of slavery *in the abstract*' to the verge of madness. They who cannot wield the pen against us, resort to *tar and feathers, and clubs!* Miserable wretches! 'they know not what they do.'[8] Far more culpable are their instigators — men who have more intelligence but less virtue, more ferocity but less courage.

I confidently look to you, beloved friends, not only for a continuance but an enlargement of your patronage to the Liberator. This paper has, from its commencement, struggled under many embarrassments, and its permanency and efficiency mainly depend upon your support. In the course of three or four weeks, I expect to resume my editorial labors uninterruptedly. It gives me pleasure to perceive that the Liberator has been conducted with ability and spirit during my absence.

                          WM. LLOYD GARRISON,

Boston, Oct. 11, 1833.

Printed: *The Liberator*, October 12, 1833.
    This work is included because it completes a series of letters concerned with Garrison's trip, even though it does not comply with some of the guidelines described in the Editorial Statement.

    1. Garrison does not mention in this letter the original objective of the mission — to raise funds to found a manual labor school for Negroes.
    2. Garrison, along with Nathaniel Paul, called on Clarkson at his country place. But, as Garrison explained in the *Second Annual Report of the Board of Managers of the New-England Anti-Slavery Society*, four hours of discussion (during which Garrison admitted, "I was awed into silence") were insufficient to persuade Clarkson to relinquish his neutral position regarding colonization. Garrison blamed Clarkson's infirm old age (he was to live thirteen more years) and the influence

of an English friend and supporter of Cresson's. (The annual report referred to above was partly reprinted in *Life*, I, 362–365.)

3. Prince Augustus Frederick, Duke of Sussex.

4. Garrison possibly telescopes one of several biblical passages involving a "crown of thorns" and the familiar maxim about lying in the bed one has made.

5. In *The Liberator* for October 19 Garrison makes clear the reason for his opposition to the British bill for emancipation — that the document speaks favorably of colonization. "It is thus," Garrison commented, "that the American Colonization Society is putting arguments into the mouths of the defenders of West Indian slavery, and obstructing the emancipation of the enslaved Africans throughout the world!"

6. In *The Liberator* for the nineteenth it was announced that the meeting which was to have been held in Philadelphia had been postponed; in fact, the meeting began December 3.

7. Garrison accurately quotes a series of passages from the New Testament: II Timothy 1:7, 2:5; II Corinthians 12:10, 7:4.

8. Luke 23:34.

115

TO LEWIS F. LAINE

[November 1, 1833.]

Please to lay this before the members of your Society, and send as many delegates as possible, or, at least, send a spirit-stirring epistle. I have some valuable anti-slavery books for you, presented by some English friends. Will you send for them?

Wm. Lloyd Garrison.

ANS: Friends Historical Library, Swarthmore College.

This note, a postscript to a printed form letter dated October 29, 1833, was probably written November 1, a date inscribed in someone else's hand on the addressed side of the sheet. The form letter was signed by Arthur Tappan, Joshua Leavitt, and Elizur Wright, Jr., who urged the prompt formation of a national antislavery society. The entire letter was addressed in Garrison's hand to Lewis F. Laine (1806–1891), a graduate of Dartmouth and currently a student at the theological seminary in Andover, where he was also secretary of the antislavery society. He was to be the minister and at times the home missionary in various communities from Ohio to Maine to New York state.

116

TO GEORGE W. BENSON

Boston, Nov. 2, 1833.

My dear friend:

Here is the warrant for our national meeting. Show it among the genuine friends of our cause as extensively as possible, and urge them to be fully represented in the Convention.

My mind is crowded with pleasing remembrances of my late visit to Canterbury and Brooklyn. How deeply am I indebted to you, to your brother, and all the members of your venerable father's household! And above all, how infinite are my obligations to that Almighty Being who has given me such dear friends, whose shield has protected me from the arrows of my bitter persecutors, and whose arm is made bare for my deliverance! Truly, "b[lessed] is he that considereth the poor: the Lord will deliver him in time of trouble."

I am more and more impressed with the importance of "working whilst the day lasts." If "we all do fade as a leaf" — if we are "as the sparks that fly upwards" — if the billows of time are swiftly removing the sandy foundation of our life — what we intend to do for the captive, and for our country, and for the subjugation of a hostile world, must be done quickly. Happily, "our light afflictions are but for a moment." [1]

Show a bold front at the annual meeting of your Society. I shall be with you in spirit, though not bodily.

Among your numerous friends, remember there is none more attached to you than

Wm. Lloyd Garrison.

ALS: Garrison Papers, Boston Public Library; printed in *Life*, I, 393.

1. This assemblage of biblical allusions and quotations (Psalms 41:1, Isaiah 64:6, Job 5:7, II Corinthians 4:17) is not uncharacteristic of Garrison. Except for two slips the quotations are accurate.

117

TO JOHN B. VASHON

Boston, Nov. 5, 1833.

My dear Friend·

To see your hand-writing once more, is almost like seeing yourself; and to see you would give me the highest pleasure. Absence from this city must be my apology for not answering your letter sooner, as well as a multiplicity of engagements.

First of all, it is my duty to express my grateful obligations to you for the generous presentation of your Note for sixty dollars as a gift to my partner and myself. Still, we trust you will consider it only as an extension of the loan, and permit us to liquidate it whenever we possess the means. At the present time, indeed, we are struggling under great embarrassments. During my absence to England, there seems to have been little interest taken in the Liberator on the part of subscribers, and our subscription list is gradually diminishing instead of growing larger. This, no doubt, is partly owing to the establishment of the Emancipator at New York, a paper which is well conducted, and which I am happy to see is prospering.[1] Whether we shall be able to continue the Liberator much longer is certainly doubtful; although its extinction would be a heavy blow to our great and glorious cause, and would deeply afflict my own heart, and greatly rejoice our enemies all over the land. One reason why we are embarrassed in our pecuniary means is, that in our anxiety to hasten the redemption of the slaves, to enlighten the public mind, and to crush the Colonization Society, we have printed beyond our means — that is, we have published larger quantities of circulars, addresses, tracts, books, etc., for gratuitous distribution — and our reward has been not in money, but in an increase of the friends of justice, humanity, and equal rights.

You have seen, doubtless, how I have been treated since my return from England — especially by the leaders in the colonization crusade.[2] They have basely accused me of having slandered my country abroad, and thus have been enabled to stir up the fury of a senseless mob. It is now literally the club against truth — tar and feathers against common humanity and justice. The contest is unequal: — a good argument is more than a match for the cudgel. Moral influence cannot be struck down even by the club of Hercules. Hence, the victory is ours, to a moral certainty. It is true, it may cost some of us our lives; but it is also true that

> "The martyr's blood's the seed of
> freedom's tree,"

and that

> "There is a victory in dying well
> For freedom — and we shall not die in vain." [3]

Besides all this, we are assured that "blessed is he that considereth the poor: the Lord will deliver him in time of trouble".[4]

We cannot fear, therefore, as to the issue of this warfare. We shall not tire or faint — our march is onward, right onward, to victory.

So far are we from being disheartened by the clamors and threats of our enemies, that we shall organize a National Anti-Slavery Society on the 4th of next month at Philadelphia! That will be a standard worth looking at!

My mission to England will prove of great service to our cause. The Protest against the American Colonization Society which was signed by Wilberforce and other distinguished champions of the colored race, is worth thousands of dollars to our cause.

My health is perfectly good, my spirit lofty as the Alps, my zeal unabated, my faith unshaken, my courage unsubdued. My enemies will find out, by and by, that I am storm-proof.

Be assured, my dear friend, that I shall rejoice to hear from you as often as possible; and that you have the good wishes, blessings, and gratitude of

Your untiring advocate,

Wm. Lloyd Garrison.

Mr. John B. Vashon.

Typed transcription: Villard Papers, Harvard College Library.

1. The *Emancipator* had this year been founded as the official organ of the American Anti-Slavery Society.

2. Garrison's return to New York coincided with the founding of a city anti-slavery society. Hostile publicity aroused a mob that broke up the meeting and might have killed Garrison and his friends.

3. Garrison adapts Thomas Campbell's "To the Memory of the Spanish Patriots," lines 13 and 3–4.

4. Psalms 41:1.

118

TO ELLIOTT CRESSON

[November 16, 1833.]

Sɪʀ —

I perceive by Poulson's Daily Advertiser [1] that at a meeting of the friends of that ungodly combination, the Colonization Society, recently held in Philadelphia, 'a handsome piece of plate, with a suitable inscription,' was voted to be presented to you for the '*dignified*, (!) FIRM (!!) and SPIRITED (!!!) manner in which the rights and objects of the Society were advocated by you before the British people'!! — This, I suppose, is intended to make the contrast between our receptions at home as broadly as possible, and also to resuscitate the petty vanity of your mind which was so wofully humbled in England. Now, I have no doubt that the present will be a valuable one; but I would not give, in exchange for it, the expression of sentiment by the New-York rioters, in relation to my mission and the abolition cause, unless I could dispose of the plate for something like a hundred thousand dollars; for with that sum there may be moral machinery put into operation of sufficient power to emancipate every slave in the United States within seven years. The uproar at New-York is worth to our side more than you collected for the Colonization Society in three years of chicanery and imposture in England.

Let me remind you that a splendid presentation of plate was made to PETER BORTHWICK, — the audacious defender of West Indian slavery, and a most infamous creature, — by certain admirers in Bath, England, 'for the dignified, firm and spirited manner in which he defended the rights' of the colonial kidnappers, against the *fanatical* attacks of the Rev. Mr. Knibb, Rev. Mr. Price, Rev. Mr. Dewdney, and that most eloquent and fearless champion of liberty, George Thompson, Esq.[2] The backers of Peter Borthwick were not unlike your own, in many particulars: they hypocritically confessed that slavery was a great evil — that it was injurious to the pecuniary interests of the planters — that these kidnappers were anxiously desiring its abolition as soon as it could be done with safety to themselves, and benefit to the slaves; and they also maintained that 'were the very spirit of angelic charity to pervade and fill the hearts of all the slaveholders, it would by no means require that all the slaves should be instantaneously liberated' — that the free people of color were 'in every form a curse; and if the system, so long contended for by the uncompromising abolitionist, could prevail, its effect would be to spread discord and devastation from one end of the *colonies* to the other' — that 'it was not right that men should be free when their freedom would prove injurious to themselves and others' — that 'it was a well established point, that the public safety forbade either the emancipation or the general instruction of the slaves' — that 'to set them loose would be an evil more intolerable than slavery itself' — that 'the condition of the great mass of emancipated Africans was one in comparison with which the condition of the slaves was enviable' — that abolitionists 'confounded the misfortunes of one generation with the crimes of another, and would sacrifice both individual and public good to an unsubstantial theory of the rights of man' — and that property in slaves was as 'SACRED' as any other. [See African Repository.] Accordingly, they gave their champion, Peter Borthwick, 'handsome pieces of plate, with a suitable inscription.' But, on the whole, Mr. Cresson, I like them better than I do your persecuting, men-stealing constituents; for, with all their cant, and sophistry, and silliness, and lying contradiction, they were not so base or cruel as to say, 'liberate the slaves only on condition of their going to Africa,' or so chimerical in their schemes or desperate in their views as to 'require that the whole mass of free persons of color should be progressively removed' to that benighted continent. And, sir, the career of Peter Borthwick, in England, was more honorable than your own. It is true, he stood higher upon the stilts of his effrontery than you did upon yours; but he was no coward — *you was*. He did not skulk away from an antagonist — *you did*. His slander and abuse were all done in public — *yours in private*. He was a bold, audacious, *tangible* opponent, 'open as a mountain, gross and palpable,' and commended himself for the towering conspicuity of his wickedness. Deception was inseparable from every thing which you uttered or published — the thin drapery with which you vainly attempted to cover the hideous deformity of your idol. You are to receive a single piece of plate — he obtained several pieces — each getting *quantum meruit*.

But 'a suitable inscription' is to be engraven upon the 'handsome plate.' I submit the following — it is laconic and expressive; — 'To ELLIOTT CRESSON — *"Instinct is a great matter — I was a coward upon instinct."* [3] Presented by,' &c.

Those gentlemen, by whom the plate is to be presented, are perhaps 'respectable.' I urge nothing against them but their support of a Society which is a disgrace to this country, and their panegyric of an individual so unworthy as yourself.

They compliment you for 'the *dignified, firm* and *spirited* manner in which the rights and objects of the Colonization Society' were advocated by you before the British people. Excellent! They could not have used language more cutting to your feelings. Truly, you have reason to exclaim, '*Save me from my friends!*' The eulogy will excite the smiles of all England.

WM. LLOYD GARRISON.

Printed: *The Liberator*, November 16, 1833.

1. *Poulson's American Daily Advertiser*, a Whig journal published by Zachariah Poulson (1761–1844), editor, treasurer, and director of the Philadelphia Library Company, as well as general reformer.

2. Garrison groups together Britons of various persuasion. Peter Borthwick (1804–1852) was a Scot who, after a pro-slavery speech in 1832, became so popular in conservative circles that he was rewarded with silver services, plates, and cups and, eventually, with a political career (to be elected to Parliament in 1835). William Knibb (1803–1845), a Baptist missionary returned from the West Indies, had been occupied during the previous three years as an antislavery lecturer. After the emancipation of the British West Indies, he returned to Jamaica to continue his missionary work In 1840, as a delegate to the World's Anti-Slavery Convention in London, he became known as "the O'Connell of Jamaica." Joseph T. Price has been identified in a previous note. Edmund Dewdney was a Baptist minister apparently with a church at Portsea, Hampshire.

3. Garrison adapts Shakespeare's *1 Henry IV*, II, iv, 299–300.

119

TO GEORGE W. BENSON

Boston, Nov. 25, 1833.

My good friend:

Do you wish to take by the hand as courageous, as devoted, as uncompromising an abolitionist (not excepting ourselves) as lives in our despotic land? Then give a hearty welcome to the bearer of this — David T. Kimball of the Andover Theological Seminary, and President

of the Anti-Slavery Society in that hot-bed of Colonization.[1] His father
is a clergyman residing in Ipswich, and as zealously affected in our
cause as himself. He is accompanied by another worthy abolitionist,
named Jewett, also a student at Andover.[2] Now to illustrate their readiness to make sacrifices in our most holy cause, I need only to state that,
as their means are very limited, they have resolved to go on foot, say
as far as New-Haven, in order that they may thus be enabled to get
to the Convention in Philadelphia![3] This morning they start for Providence — from thence they propose going to Canterbury — and from
thence to New-Haven, where they will take the steam-boat for New-
York. They will probably tarry one day in Providence, and I dare presume that between you and brother Prentice,[4] and the rest of the dear
friends, they will be entertained without much cost to themselves. I
think you cannot fail to be pleased with the modesty and worth of
these good "fanatics."

Probably you will have scarcely perused this scrawl, ere I shall constitute one in your midst. I expect to take the stage to-morrow for P.,
and arrive there in the evening. Be good enough, if you can conveniently, to call at the City Hotel at the hour of 7, and see if the madman G. has come. Perhaps I may not get away from this city till
Wednesday.

Many thanks to you and my generous creditor Henry for your kind
letters.

What news from Canterbury? I long to get there once more — but
more particularly under the hospitable roof of your father. I confess,
in addition to the other delightful attractions which are there found,
the soft blue eyes and pleasant countenance of Miss Ellen are by no
means impotent or unattractive.[5] — But this is episodical.

The Young Men's Anti-Slavery Association of Boston are driving
ahead with even a better spirit than that of '76. They have now upwards of 90 members! Their example cannot be lost.

I trust our Boston delegation to the Convention will not be less
than eight.[6] Whether we shall get any from the State of Maine is uncertain.

How do you like O'Connell's speech? Is it not just the thing? "Let
the galled jade wince — *our* withers are unwrung."[7]

Poor Elliott Cresson! he is not the only apologist of slavery who has
good and sufficient reasons for writhing under the lash of

Your devoted friend, and the friend of all good men, and the advocate of the enslaved,

                                                Wm. Lloyd Garrison.

Mr. George W. Benson.

N. B. I congratulate you on the favorable result of your annual meeting. Our good friend Bourne [8] gave us a powerful dose of cayenne pepper at Boyleston Hall. What sort of a dish did he give you in P——————?

ALS: Garrison Papers, Boston Public Library; printed partly in *Life*, I, 394–395.

1. David Tenney Kimball (1808–1886) was a graduate of Middlebury College and at the time of Garrison's letter a student at the Andover Theological Seminary. He was to be one of the original members of the American Anti-Slavery Society. After a two-year ministry in Hartford, Connecticut (1835–1837), he became ill and spent the rest of his life going from one occupation to another. (Leonard Allison Morrison and Stephen Paschall Sharples, *History of the Kimball Family in America from 1634 to 1897*, Boston, 1897, I).

2. Daniel Emerson Jewett (1804–1844), a Dartmouth man, was to graduate from Andover in 1834; he subsequently moved to Philadelphia.

3. The convention was for the purpose of founding the American Anti-Slavery Society.

4. John Prentice.

5. Garrison refers to Helen E. Benson, having mistaken her name.

6. In fact, there were to be six delegates: James G. Barbadoes, Arnold Buffum, Joshua Coffin, Amos A. Phelps, and Nathaniel Southard, in addition to Garrison.

7. Shakespeare, *Hamlet*, III, ii, 253.

8. George Bourne.

IV COURTSHIP AND MARRIAGE: 1834

IV COURTSHIP AND MARRIAGE: 1834

EORGE W. AND HENRY E. BENSON were among Garrison's closest friends and supporters by the time he came to Providence to speak the evening of April 5, 1833. In the audience that night were other members of the closely knit Benson family. There was the father, George Benson (1752–1836), successful Providence merchant retired to Brooklyn, Connecticut, and dedicating his last years to abolition. Possibly present was his wife, Sarah Thurber Benson (1770–1844), a modest, self-denying, shy woman, an excellent housekeeper and a devoted wife and mother. Probably on hand and looking like drab Quakers were their unmarried older daughters — all of them innocent, conscientious, and diffident: Mary (1797–1842), Sarah Thurber (1799–1850), and Anna Elizabeth (1801–1843). Mary was eventually to make her home with the Garrisons. Anna, herself a dedicated abolitionist, was to be Garrison's closest friend among the sisters-in-law. (Probably not present was another daughter, Charlotte, 1803–1886, who had in 1826 married Providence businessman Henry Anthony. Still another daughter, Frances, born in 1794, had died in 1832.) But the Benson whom Garrison especially noticed that night was the bright, blushingly attractive Helen Eliza (1811–1876), the family's youngest daughter, looking like a jewel surrounded by pebbles.

Lloyd talked briefly with Helen that evening, and he saw her again the next morning at her brother's store "If it was not 'love at first sight,'" he later testified, "it was something very like it — a magnetic influence being exerted which became irresistible on further acquaintance."[1] Proof of the love was not proclaimed at once in letters. It was ten months, in fact, before Garrison committed what he called "the first offense, in an epistolary shape" against his future wife. But once the flow had begun, there was no ebb: letters were exchanged at regular intervals during the eight months before their

1. *Helen Eliza Garrison, A Memorial* (Cambridge, Massachusetts, 1876), p. 18.

wedding on September 4, 1834. Thirty-three of his letters and most of her answers have been preserved.

These love letters show, besides the fondness and self-conscious rapture to be expected, a mutual concern for reforms: especially for temperance, for abolition, and for peace. Lloyd and Helen shared, also, a personal concern for one particular social problem. Prudence Crandall opened a school for Negro girls in Canterbury, Connecticut; the community was outraged. A cat was crucified on her gate, her well was filled with refuse, and her house was set on fire. Lloyd and Helen stood by the persecuted Prudence, defended her against the malice of the town, and preached against prejudice.

In her letters Helen shows herself as the modest and devoted young lady the aggressive Garrison needed for a wife. On April 3, 1834, she writes: "And is so much happiness in reserve for me, thought I! Indeed, I can never feel sufficiently grateful to you, for having caused my heart to beat high with such joyful anticipations. How little do I merit so much affection from so noble a being; but as it is offered in sincerity, I will accept it all, and confide in your kind and gentle love." Garrison basked in the warmth of such a relationship.

As the time of their wedding approached, Helen expressed some sadness at leaving her family and friends — those with whom she had spent so many years of "uninterrupted happiness." But since they were all enthusiastic about Lloyd and the marriage, she concludes in a letter of July 31, 1834, that her earthly happiness is complete. "How rapidly the time approaches when I shall surrender myself to you, with a holy pledge to endeavor to live always, so as to secure your approbation and love, and above all, to approximate nearer His throne, who is infinitely lovely & worthy our highest adoration and praise." And on August 13, having discussed the plans for the marriage, she declares, "I see nothing wanting to add to our happiness."

If ever a woman knew what her competition was to be, Helen Benson did. But if ever a woman accepted a man's preoccupation with a cause, Helen Benson was that woman. She and her large family brought to Garrison's life the relaxation and security which he needed, the haven from which he could emerge to confront the hostile world.

120

TO HELEN E. BENSON

Freedom's Cottage,[1]
Roxbury, Jan. 18, 1834.

Miss Helen:

This is a day which even the delicate Spring would not disown —
a day expressly for a cottage residence in the woods! — The sun is
refulgent — the air balmy — the sky serene. Yesterday, my feelings
were as rigid as the weather — to-day, they are gushing forth like an
unsealed fountain. My spirit is perfectly bird-like — not merely hop-
ping from twig to twig, and tree to tree, but soaring upward and onward with a stronger flight and with better pinions than an eagle's.
Where has it not been? It has flown to Providence, and been refreshed with a smile from you, and with the gratulations of George,
and Henry, and all the dear friends: — to Brooklyn and Canterbury,[2]
and gathered strength from the interview: — to New-York and Philadelphia, and held sweet converse with those whose companionship
is better than the riches of the earth. From thence it has darted more
swiftly than the winds across the Atlantic, and stood in the midst of
the friends of the drooping slaves. Best of all, it has taken a flight to
the heaven of heavens, and communed with Him whose name is Love,
with angels, and with the spirits of the just made perfect. Thus I have
felt what it is to run, and not be weary; to walk, and not faint.[3]

When the bees are among the flowers, and the birds are on the
wing; when the golden fruit hangs in clusters upon the opulent
boughs, and a glorious embellishment is given to field and forest, hill
and valley; how sombre and sterilizing are our anticipations of winter! — O, for the perpetuity of Spring, or Summer, or Autumn, we
cry — any thing but Winter! — But the earth, wisely heedless of our
fickle wishes, continues its revolutions, and time pursues its steady
flight. Decay touches one flower after another, and the race fall as
imperceptibly as that of man. With great subtlety comes the northern
destroyer, Cold, causing the trees to decline into "the sear and yel-
low leaf," [4] and the verdure to change its color and perish. Gentle and
merciful are thy changes, O Nature! — solid and various thy enjoyments, O, Winter! — Instructive are the lessons which ye teach, and
he is ungrateful who does not give heed to them.

Do you wish to know, Helen, what is a strong token of my esteem
for a friend? *It is an epistle.* I am covetous of my letters — that is, I
have a great repugnance to quill-driving — and therefore necessity
must press very hard, or my friendship must be very ardent, to in-

duce me to take up the pen. "How fortunate" — you may reasonably exclaim — "how fortunate it is for your absent acquaintance, that you cherish such an aversion to writing! — Otherwise, your scribblings would be past endurance! — It is too bad to impose a tax upon their patience and upon their purse."

This is the first offence, in an epistolary shape at least, that I have committed against you; therefore, Helen, be merciful. In order to obtain your forgiveness, must I promise never to trespass again, in like manner? — Indeed, I cannot! — Pray, make some other condition.

I shall look to you for the formation of a Female Anti-Slavery Society in Providence. You know, or must know, that I rely upon female influence to break the shackles of the bleeding slave. Two or three days since, I was cheered beyond measure to learn that 70 females in the little village of Amesbury had organized themselves into an anti-slavery society, and that a similar organization had been made among the ladies of Portland. Let these encourage you to seek such an association in Providence.

I have heard nothing recently from Brooklyn or Canterbury. If you have information that may prove interesting to me, do communicate it. Be assured that I feel the obligations which I owe to your father and mother, and to all the members of the family, for their unmerited kindness to me.

Make the most winning expressions of my esteem to George and his lady [5] — to my dear Henry, &c.

I am an hour older than when I commenced this rambling epistle; but it has been well spent in writing to one so highly deserving of the respect of

Your friend and well-wisher,

Wm. Lloyd Garrison.

Miss Helen Benson.

ALS: Villard Papers, Harvard College Library.

1. Garrison called the house in Roxbury in which he roomed "Freedom's Cottage."

2. Brooklyn, Connecticut, was a small town to which the senior Bensons had moved when they left Providence; Canterbury, the adjacent town, was to become famous as the locale for Prudence Crandall's school.

3. Garrison adapts Isaiah 40:31.

4. Shakespeare, *Macbeth*, V, iii, 23.

5. Catharine Knapp Stetson Benson (born in 1808), whose name Garrison often spells "Catherine," was the daughter of Benjamin and Mary Alexander Stetson (see John S. Barry, *A Genealogical and Biographical Sketch on The Name and Family of Stetson, 1634–1847*, Boston, 1847).

121

TO WILLIAM ELLERY CHANNING

Boston, Jan. 20, 1834.

Rev. and dear Sir:

I have taken the liberty to send you a few anti-slavery publications, the perusal of which, by you, I shall esteem a noble recompense. Let me invite your attention particularly to the Lectures of the Rev. Mr. Phelps, which cover the whole ground of controversy, and which I deem unanswerable.[1]

Guilty as it is, there is yet hope for this nation. There are more than seven thousand men who have not bowed the knee to Baal. The slumber of half a century has been broken up, and henceforth there is to be no repose until the monster SLAVERY be slain. The deaf begin to hear, and the blind to see. The weak are made valiant, and the timid strengthened through faith in the promises of Him who is pledged to "maintain the cause of the afflicted and the right of the poor." [2] The noise of the conflict is already like the voice of many waters. Truth is going on from conquering to conquer. The mystery of iniquity, alias the American Colonization Society, is now stripped of its guise, and seen in its naked deformity. *There is hope for the nation.*

It is true, not many mighty have as yet been called to this sacred strife. Like every other great reform, it has been commenced by obscure and ignorant men. It is God's mode, commonly, to choose the foolish things of the world to confound the wise; because his foolishness is wiser than men, and his weakness stronger than men. In having entered early into this great cause, I arrogate not to myself any superior wisdom or goodness. Some providential circumstances turned my attention to it; and humble as I was, I feared my God too much, and hated the base plunderers of my species too cordially, and pitied the poor bleeding slaves too sincerely, to shrink even single-handed from a conflict with the enemies of justice and humanity. I then told the American slaveholders that they should hear me, of me, and from me, in a tone and with a frequency that should make them tremble — not that I was the enemy of their happiness or safety, but that I detested their crimes. How faithful I have been in the performance of my pledge, a quickened, an astonished, and a repenting nation may testify. Ridiculed, reviled, threatened, persecuted and imprisoned, still God has wonderfully blessed my humble labors. I give him all the glory — I sink myself into nothingness.

In a cause like this, there are two things to be remembered — 1st, that a tremendous responsibility rests upon him who perverts his influence; and 2nd, that an equally fearful responsibility *rests upon him who withholds his influence.* Why should a Christian, however distinguished, wait for the movements of a concurrent populace, before he espouse the side of the outraged and guiltless slaves? That which claims the sympathy and attention of Jehovah of hosts, is not beneath the dignity of his creatures. That which has elicited the best efforts of a Wilberforce, a Clarkson, a Pitt, a Fox, a Brougham, and a Buxton, is neither trivial nor despicable.

I thought of beseeching you, in this letter, to exert your victorious influence for the deliverance of this country from impending ruin. But if the slaughter of two millions of victims who have gone down to the grave with their chains around them; if the cries of more than that number of tortured slaves now living; if a soil red with innocent blood; if a desecrated Sabbath; if a vast system of adultery, and pollution, and robbery; if perpetuated ignorance and legalized barbarity; if the invasion of the dearest rights of man, and a disruption of the holiest ties of life; — and, above all, if the clear and imperious injunctions of the most high God, fail to stimulate you to plead for the suffering and the dumb, it is scarcely possible that any appeal can succeed from

Yours, most affectionately and respectfully,

Wm. Lloyd Garrison.

Rev. Dr. Channing.

Handwritten transcription: Garrison Papers, Boston Public Library; printed in *Life*, I, 464–465.

William Ellery Channing (1780–1842), the leading Unitarian clergyman of the day, had been since 1803 the minister of the Federal Street Church in Boston, a position he held until his death. Although Channing had for many years been opposed to slavery, he did not officially express himself on abolition until 1835, when he published a small book entitled *Slavery.* According to Samuel J. May, Garrison's letter was not his first appeal to Channing since he had written him in 1830 (*Some Recollections of Our Antislavery Conflict*, Boston, 1869, p. 20).

1. Amos A. Phelps (1804–1847) was at this time pastor of the Pine-Street (Trinitarian) Church. Having been influenced by Garrison's *Thoughts on African Colonization* to leave the Colonization Society, Phelps became an ardent abolitionist. He was, however, to part with Garrison over such issues as religion and woman's rights. The lectures recommended here are a version published by the New England Anti-Slavery Society (Boston, 1834) entitled *Lectures on Slavery and Its Remedy.*

2. Psalms 140:12.

122

TO HELEN E. BENSON

Freedom's Cottage,
Roxbury, Feb. 18, 1834.

[Miss] Helen:

My letter contained nothing worthy of a reply; but you have sent one — an admirable one — and I thank you. With all sincerity I say, I am delighted with it. *I love its frankness*. There is no affectation in your personal demeanor, and I felt sure that there would be none in your epistolary correspondence. *I love its contemplative spirit*: it is exactly in unison with my own. You are perfectly right, philosophically and religiously, in your estimate of the comparative advantages of the city and country, for calm reflection and spiritual enjoyment. One may almost liken the soul of a good man in the city, to the dove which went forth from the ark, "but found no rest for the sole of her foot." [1] It is surrounded with such a deluge of wor[l]dliness — the current of fashion, of folly, and of temptation, runs so impetuously — the billows of party and polemical strife rage so furiously — there is, in short, such a collision of all the grosser elements of life — that it often sighs for "a lodge in some vast wilderness," [2] and even acquires new eagerness to enjoy the repose and purity of that blissful abode, "where the wicked cease from troubling, and the weary are at rest." [3]

Further — I am pleased with [. . .] the good sense, and the talent, exhibited [. . .] letter — with every line and every word, indeed [. . .] the sentence in which you disparage yourself [. . .] exalt me.

I appreciate the difficulties which seem [to] obstruct your progress, in the formation of a Female Anti-Slavery Society; but you must not despond. The pleasure of success is in proportion to the toil of attaining it. [4]

So! — I am still under the ban of the ladies of Providence! — Really, in this instance, "I am a man more sinned against than sinning." [5] Why are they so inexorable? Why will they cherish such a false delicacy? Should I happen to encounter one of them, I might say to her, peradventure — "Madam," or "Miss," (as the case might be,) "you are very angry with me, because I was so *immodest* as to allude, as delicately and guardedly as possible, to the awful situation in which a million of your sex are placed, who groan in bondage, and who have no protection whatever from the licentiousness of their tyrannical masters; but if a remote and imperfect reference to this horrible state of morals be a crime of so deep a dye, tell me how you feel in view of the conduct of the base libertines themselves? Does this

[. . .] [e]motion in your bosom? Is my offense so great [. . .] theirs from your view? If so, your modesty is [. . .] — it is rank prudery, which would surrender to [the] first temptation."

Indeed, Miss Helen, I am grieved and surprised to learn the prevalence of this heartless refinement. Mark my words: you will find that those females who are loudest in their denunciations of my unfortunate address, neither cherish nor evince any real sympathy for their poor enslaved sisters, nor any holy indignation at the conduct of those libidinous monsters who rob their victims of that which is infinitely more precious than life.

O, the persecuted, the dauntless, the heroic Prudence Crandall! What severe trials now are hers! what ecstatic joys shall be hers hereafter! She has my sympathy, my admiration, my prayers. I trust that the firing of her house will yet prove to have been accidental.

You ask, whether she has rightly designated your lovely dwelling in Brooklyn, as "THE ASYLUM OF THE OPPRESSED." With my whole soul I respond — YES! — Ah! how great are my own obligations to your father and mother — to your brothers and sisters — and to you — for your united friendship, hospitality and aid! What am I that I should thus be treated? May He who is the great proprietor of the universe reward you all, in a manner and to an extent beyond the power of languish to describe!

I am delighted that the time is [. . .] [at] hand for me to visit Brooklyn once more: [. . .] very reluctant to trespass upon that hospitality [. . .] I am already so largely indebted; but I know it is [. . .] in sincerity, and therefore I accept it gratefully. Esp[ecially] am I pleased to learn that you will be at home. [I] [. . .] however, go and come like an arrow.

Did not the date of my other epistle puzzle you exceedingly? It was unintentionally delayed some time after it was written, so that its rhapsody on the spring-like weather was entirely out of place on its receipt.[6]

I shall ascertain your name, by and by! — I used to call you Ellen, but you rectified the error. Now I perceive by your signature that you have a middle name.

Much affection I send to George and his lady — to Henry, &c. &c. Take for yourself as much as you will from
 Your sincere friend,

         Wm. Lloyd Garrison.

ALS: Villard Papers, Harvard College Library. A substantial portion of one corner of the folded sheet of the manuscript is missing; as a result there is a hiatus in the text of each of the four pages of the letter.

 1. Garrison adapts Genesis 8:9.

2. William Cowper, *The Task*, Book II, line 1.
3. Garrison adapts Job 3:17.
4. In reply to Garrison's suggestion that she organize a female antislavery society in Providence, Helen had said that "you are not aware how extremely limited my influence is, and how inefficient my efforts would be in such a cause. There are only two families in the large circle of my acquaintance where I can feel the liberty of introducing the subject of slavery. . . ."
5. Shakespeare, *King Lear*, III, ii. 59–60.
6. In fact, Garrison had mislaid the letter for a period of several weeks.

123

TO SAMUEL J. MAY

Boston, Feb. 18, 1834.

My dear friend:

I find that love does not come to maturity at once, but is progressive in its growth, and infinite in its expansion. Two years ago you were *very* dear to me; but the further we travel together through this earthly wilderness to the heavenly Jerusalem, the dearer you become. Thus I trust it will be through all eternity. Thus will every redeemed soul go on "from glory to glory," getting higher and nobler views of Jehovah, and deriving new and better enjoyments. The wants, the desires, the abilities of the human soul are amazing, and cannot be supplied with any thing short of the infinite fulness of its Creator, and the unutterable and inconceivable blessedness of heaven.

Two things trouble me abundantly. The first is, "a heart deceitful above all things, and desperately wicked" [1] — yet, I trust, in some degree sanctified, and made subject to the law of God. — The other is, the rapid flight — more truly, the lightning flight of time, and the imperfect manner in which I improve it. I interrogate myself closely: How is it that I accomplish so little, either for my own edification, or the advancement of the happiness of my fellow creatures? Day after day, week after week, month after month, rolls away with alarming swiftness, and yet — O, what a beggarly show of deeds is mine! And yet I seem to be — nay, I am, constantly immersed in labor, from morning till noon, and from noon till evening — visiting no where, and being as miserly of my minutes as the niggard is of his dollars. I toil much, and produce little. I am dissatisfied with almost every thing that I perform. When I reflect how much there is to be done to redeem this fallen world from the thraldom of him who goeth about like a roaring lion, seeking whom he may devour, — and then how far short I have come of my duty in all things, — I am troubled in spirit, and deplore my supineness, my ingratitude, and my folly. Not that I expect to win heaven by my own merits, for "there is none righteous — no, not one," and "all our righteousness are as filthy rags, and we all do fade as a leaf" — but I wish to accomplish more for God, and more for man. Happy is it for us that "we have an Advocate with the Father!" [2]

No where does my body or spirit go more joyfully, on earth, than to Brooklyn. My visits hitherto have been signally refreshing to my spirit, and replete with pleasure. But, great as is my desire to see you — impatient as I am to be sheltered once more under the hospitable roof of my venerated friend and benefactor George Benson — strongly as I wish to see the noble christian heroine, Prudence Crandall, and her interesting pupils — still, I am so surrounded with obligations and duties at home, which are exceedingly imperious, and my constant presence is so much needed here, that I have been cherishing the hope that it would not be necessary for me to visit Brooklyn, on account of my case at Court in March. By your letter, however, and another received from Esq. Parrish, it seems that I must personally be in your midst; and therefore you may look for me in due season, health and life permitting.[3] My visit must be as short as possible: this I regret, because I should like to spend some time among friends who are so dear to my heart. I will thank you to mention to Esq. Parrish that his letter was duly received. It seems that if the trial be postponed, special bail will be required. To obtain that, I must rely upon the kindness of those on the spot who are friendly to the cause of justice and humanity.

You will rejoice at the downfal of the colonization Babel. Almost every hour brings some tidings of victory. What an almost incredible change in public sentiment has been effected within the last three years! — But I cannot enlarge.

Tender my friendly remembrances to your lady, to Mr. and Mrs. Gray, to Mr. Benson and family, to Mr. Burleigh, &c. &c.[4]

If you can read this hasty scrawl, you will deserve a better one at the hands of

Your much attached friend,

Wm. Lloyd Garrison.

ALS: Garrison Papers, Boston Public Library.

1. Jeremiah 17:9.
2. Romans 3:10; Isaiah 64:6; I John 2:1.
3. Garrison refers to John Parrish (spelled "Parish" in *Life*, I, 392), his legal counsel in a libel suit brought by five men whom he had accused of a physical assault on Prudence Crandall's school. Little is known about Parrish except that he was a friend of the Bensons, that Garrison later bought him a box of types, and that at the time of Garrison's last reference to him he was seriously ill and probably dying (see letter 238, to Samuel J. May, December 26, 1835).
4. Garrison sends remembrances to several Brooklyn friends. Mr. and Mrs.

John Gray, who are often mentioned in Garrison's letters of this period, were close friends and apparently contemporaries of the senior George Bensons. Charles C. Burleigh (1810–1878), an attorney and lecturer with strong abolitionist convictions, was currently editing the short-lived Brooklyn *Unionist* and doing everything possible to defend Prudence Crandall against the attacks of her detractors.

124

TO HENRY E. BENSON

Boston, Feb. 26, 1834.

My dear Henry:

Two letters from you, with a bundle, were safely delivered at my office last evening by Mr. Farrar, with whom I was pleased, both for the modesty of his manners, and for the growing interest which he manifests in that great cause, which is so dear to our hearts.[1]

The object of this very hasty scrawl is to answer your inquiry, as to the time I propose to be in Brooklyn. None of my Providence friends need any assurance from me, that it would give me unspeakable pleasure to visit them on this occasion; but I am so crowded and crushed by my home-duties, and so pinched for time, that I cannot take a circuitous route, but must go direct from this city to Brooklyn, and return with all possible rapidity. It is my purpose, therefore, to start on Monday morning next, at 4 o'clock, in the stage, which will carry me to B. before sunset.

I have had an invitation from the Pawtucket Anti-Slavery Society to deliver an address in that village, on my way to Brooklyn. It grieves me to disappoint them, but I *must* decline, for the present at least, making public addresses.

Happy, very happy, shall I be to see you in Brooklyn; but I hope you are not going up with the expectation that my case will be tried at the approaching term. I shall baffle my persecutors as long as possible, by taking every just advantage of the law in postponing my trial, &c.[2]

Almost every day brings some intelligence highly favorable to our cause. The beacon-fires of Liberty are now blazing all over New-England, and a hundred standards are now proudly floating in the breeze of heaven. The abolition trumpet is giving a *certain* sound, and awakening, inspiring, and combining a host of good men, for the rescue of our beloved country from ruin, and the deliverance of those who groan in bondage. Such a mustering of choice spirits, such an enlistment of pure hearts, such a tide of moral power, such an affinity of human affection, our country has never before seen. Ought they not to strengthen our hands, and encourage our hearts? Does not the mighty spectacle repay us for all the toils and sacrifices we have made in the cause of bleeding humanity? Truly, it becomes us to say with the apostle, "Thanks be to GOD, who giveth us the victory!"[3] Yes, He shall be glorified; for we owe our success, even instrumentally, to his truth and love.

My dear friend, I need some other language, higher and better than our own, to express my thanks to your parents, to your brother and sisters, and to you, for your unmerited kindness and hospitality; but I am conscious that a profusion of words is no evidence of gratitude, and therefore I will be silent.

The New-England Anti-Slavery Society held a meeting on Monday evening for the choice of officers. Your venerable father was unanimously re-elected its President. I submitted a resolution, which was adopted, requesting the Board of Managers to call, as soon as practicable, a Convention of Delegates from all the Anti-Slavery Societies in New-England, to be held in this city. Our grand aim should now be to effect a complete concentration of all the anti-slavery strength we can muster, that division may not weaken our efforts, and that we may all see eye to eye. I trust the call will be sustained by our abolition friends. The object is not to make the various societies auxiliary to the N. E. Society, but to devise ways and means for the promotion of our glorious cause.

Proffer my best regards to your noble brother and his lady, to Miss Helen, to Messrs. Chace, Prentice, Robinson,[4] and other dear friends. Accept for yourself the assurance of my growing esteem.

Hastily, but steadfastly yours,

Wm. Lloyd Garrison.

Mr. H. E. Benson.

ALS: Garrison Papers, Boston Public Library.

1. Mr. Farrar has not been identified.

2. A suit for libel had been brought against Garrison for statements he had made in the case of Prudence Crandall. The trial, originally set for December 1833 at the Windham County (Connecticut) Court, had been continued until the March 1834 term. But the date was to be postponed again until the January 1835 term, and slightly before that date the suit was dropped on condition that "neither party shall receive cost of the other."

3. I Corinthians 15:57.

4. Probably Martin Robinson, a Providence stationer.

125

TO HELEN E. BENSON

Freedom's Cottage,
Roxbury, March 8, 1834.

Miss Helen:

You see I am once more in my dear little cottage; and although I am very tired, and almost appalled by the numerous claims upon my pen, yet gratitude, affection and duty lead me at once to send you a hasty note in which I wish to embody my whole heart, that you may divide it among all the members of that most estimable family residing in "Friendship's Vale." [1] Nay, I forget myself — how can I send to you that which I left in Brooklyn? All of you have got possession of my heart, and I doubt whether I should be able to recover it by making another trip to B. You kindly presented to me a pretty little gift, bearing on one side the inscription, "Liberty is the *Watchword*," and on the other my name, which I estimate very highly; but — do not, I pray you, consider me captious, or covetous, or ungracious — you will remember, doubtless, that it was in a *circular* shape. Have you any thing to give me *in the shape of a heart*, Helen? Just examine carefully, if agreeable, and let me know hereafter. [2]

My ride from Brooklyn to Providence afforded me some amusement. At one of our halting places, we took in a person who evidently rejected the doctrine of total abstinence, for he found it extremely difficult to speak coherently. I presume he did not know me; but he immediately began to ask me what I thought of the "nigger school" in Canterbury, [3] stating that he "did not believe in it." Much to the amusement of the good lady who came from Brooklyn, and who sat by my side, I put a few satirical shafts into him which made him feel very uncomfortable, as he could not pull them out again. The poor fellow was horrified at the thought of intermarriages between the whites and blacks — it seemed to haunt him like a guilty conscience. Mrs. M. [4] gave him a capital thrust by saying that, if she had to choose *either* for a husband, she would greatly prefer a virtuous and sober colored man to an intemperate white man!

At another tavern, two young and dissipated pedestrians joined our company, and again the "nigger school" was brought up for condemnation by the same anti-temperance man. They, however, were for letting the school "go ahead," if any persons were willing to back it up; but as for the whites and blacks marrying together, that would never answer. One of them declared that if he had a sister who should marry a *nigger*, he would put a ball into his (the nigger's) heart in a moment. They were somewhat afflicted because efforts were making to prevent the niggers from going to *Siberia*! — thus evincing the accuracy of their geographical knowledge. Next, they ran to religion, and became exceedingly impious and garrulous. They believed in every thing and nothing — in the Bible and Tom Paine — in punishment for sin and no punishment. But enough of their nonsense — I have referred to them simply to show what so[rt o]f creatures cluster around the Colonizatio[n Socie]ty, and oppose the education of our colore[d] population.

In Providence I saw George and his lady, Henry, and your accomplished sister Mary. I also made a hasty visit to friend Moses Brown, who I found in good health. I had the pleasure of seeing and conversing with Mrs. Jenkins at his house.[5] She manifested considerable interest in the anti-slavery movements of the day.

Mr. Anthony rode with me from Providence to Boston.[6]

I feel extremely anxious to learn the result of Mr. Olney's trial.[7] Will you write soon?

Remember me most cordially to your venerable father and mother, to Miss Sarah and Miss Ann, to Mr. May, &c. &c. If not literally, I am at least in the ties of friendship,

Yours, ever,

Wm. Lloyd Garrison.

Miss H. E. Benson.

ALS: Villard Papers, Harvard College Library.

1. This is the family name for the Benson home in Brooklyn, Connecticut.

2. Judging from subsequent letters written by Garrison and Helen, the second half of this paragraph was intended as a cryptic proposal of marriage.

3. Prudence Crandall's school for young ladies of color.

4. Mrs. Samuel J. May.

5. Garrison apparently refers to Anna Jenkins (Mrs. William). The Jenkinses are described in some detail in Garrison's letter to Helen (162), July 15, 1834.

6. Henry Anthony (c. 1801–1879) — not to be confused with his better-known cousin, Henry Bowen Anthony, subsequently a governor of Rhode Island — was married to Helen's sister Charlotte. Anthony's name seldom appears in the Garrison papers since he and the abolitionist were not in agreement regarding reform.

7. Mr. Olney was a Negro accused of setting fire to Miss Crandall's school but subsequently acquitted.

126

TO HELEN E. BENSON

Boston, March 12, 1834.

Miss Helen:

The sun rolled a torrent of golden light into my room this morning, at an early hour, and, in spite of my soft attachment to my couch, roused me up as if by an electrical shock. As, for some time past, he has been setting me a good example of early rising, — getting up himself more early every morning, — I blushed to think that he had caught me napping. But I did not hesitate to rise, and pour forth the joy and gratitude of my soul — exclaiming, in the language of Milton, —

"Thou Sun, of this great world both eye and soul,
Acknowledge Him thy greater; sound His praise
In thy eternal course, both when thou climb'st,
And when high noon hast gained, and when thou fall'st.
Him first, him last, him midst, and without end!"

It was indeed a glorious morning — I cannot describe it — I seemed to live months of bliss in moments — the zenith of the sky was so majestic and vast — not a cloud to sully its face — and then such melodious warbling from the forest birds!

"Join voices, all ye living souls! Ye birds,
That singing up to heaven's gate ascend,
Bear in your wings, and in your notes, His praise!" [1]

Could I refrain from lending my voice to the general song? I gave it utterance, to the relief of my swelling heart and tearful eyes.

We have in our family a dear little boy, three or four years of age; and so I spent half an hour in frolicking with him on the piazza, causing his little heart to beat high with joyful excitement, and a brighter flush to paint his rosy cheeks.[2] Not only do I love children, but I love to be a child. How is it that time has borne me along so swiftly? How is it that I have been so imperceptibly carried over the threshold of manhood? I am willing to "put away childish things," [3] but I am resolved to be a child still in my feelings! Neither years, nor the conflicts of life, have at all indurated my heart — I weep as easily as a babe, am as sensitive as a flower, and as aerial as a bird. But mine are not the tears of misanthropy, nor is my exquisite sensitiveness allied to criminal timidity, nor my airiness to folly. And yet what a terrible, hard-hearted, blood-thirsty monster I am, in the estimation of many people! Why, I am so cruel, and so wicked, as to contend that all the slaves in our land ought at once to be set free!

After I had done sporting with the child, I took a book and strolled into the woods. I thought of you, and of our ramble up that precipitous hill which bears so unpoetical a name; and I also felt rebuked that I was so lethargic as to suffer you to anticipate me in rising, and take your morning walk alone. "If Helen was here," I mentally exclaimed, "her delight would equal the tenderness of her soul, and I am sure that her presence would add to that of my own."

Pursuant to adjournment, the New-England Anti-Slavery Society held a public meeting at the Temple in this city, on a Monday evening.[4] The rush of spectators was prodigious — overwhelming; perhaps not less than one thousand were compelled to go away, the spacious hall not being able to contain them! — and this, too, notwithstanding that the annual meeting of the Massachusetts Colonization Society was held at Park-street meeting-house on the same evening. At our meeting, addresses were made by Professor Follen of Cambridge University, the Rev. Mr. Grosvenor of Salem, and the Rev. Mr. Grew, formerly of Hartford — these were all very eloquent and impressive.[5] I also made a short speech. An account of the proceedings you will see in the Liberator of Saturday.[6] The Rev. Dr. Channing would have been present, and probably made some remarks, had not sickness prevented him.

As I cannot see *you*, favor me with a sight of that which is next most agreeable to see — viz. *your hand-writing.* I am afraid that I shall afflict you with a multiplicity of letters; but if they thicken too fast, or become too tedious, be faithful with me, and I will reform.

All that is tender in affection, or expressive in gratitude, or commanding in respect, I send to your excellent parents and amiable sisters. Remember me kindly to that worthy blind female, and your other domestic.[7]

To you, is offered the whole heart of
Yours, with increasing esteem,

Wm. Lloyd Garrison.

Miss H. E. Benson.

ALS: Villard Papers, Harvard College Library.

1. Garrison quotes, accurately except for slight variations in capitalization and punctuation, *Paradise Lost*, Book V, lines 171–174, 165, 197–199, though he does misplace line 165, putting it after line 174.

2. Garrison refers to the family with whom he is boarding in Roxbury; they have not been identified.

3. I Corinthians 13:11.

4. The meeting was held at the Masonic Temple on Tremont Street on March 10.

5. Garrison praises three men who have not been mentioned earlier in his letters. Charles Follen (1796–1840), a brilliant German refugee, was at the time of Garrison's letter professor of German literature at Harvard College (which Garrison calls "Cambridge University"), and he had also taught ethics and history at the Divinity School and lectured on jurisprudence to lawyers in Boston. Already an abolitionist before the appearance of the first issue of *The Liberator*, he had joined the New England Anti-Slavery Society in 1834. A year later his professorship was terminated as a result of his antislavery "Address to the People of the United States." His wife, Eliza Lee Cabot, was also an ardent abolitionist. Unfortunately, Follen died in a fire aboard the steamer *Lexington* in 1840. (See Garrison's letter to Richard D. Webb, February 28, 1843.) Cyrus P. Grosvenor was a liberal Baptist minister of Salem, Massachusetts. In 1835 he was to be appointed a general agent for the Massachusetts Anti-Slavery Society (successor to the New England Anti-Slavery Society). His letters were occasionally printed in *The Liberator*; see the issues for April 4, May 23, 1835. Henry Grew (1781–1862)

was a relatively conservative Philadelphia minister and abolitionist, who differed from Garrison particularly on the issue of woman's rights. The difference became quite obvious in 1840 at the World's Anti-Slavery Convention in London, to which, incidentally, his daughter Mary was a delegate. For Henry Grew's full expression on the issue of woman's rights see *The Liberator*, January 4, 1850, and January 3, 1851.

6. A report of the meeting, including Garrison's speech, was printed in *The Liberator*, March 15.

7. Garrison mentions servants in the Benson household: Eunice, who was blind, and Mary Burnet, to whom he later refers in several ways, including "M. Burnett" and "M. Burton."

127

TO GEORGE W. BENSON

Boston, March 13, 1834.

My inestimable friend:

Our Board of Managers have not yet been called together, to act upon the proposition for calling a Convention of anti-slavery Delegates in this city; but, as my advice will probably be followed, whenever they shall meet, I have concluded to say to you, in reference to your meeting to-morrow evening, that it will be premature for your Society to appoint any representatives, for the present. It is now my opinion that our Convention will *tell* more powerfully, if delayed until summer; because the time, between now and the middle or last of April, to notify the various anti-slavery societies, is too limited; and because, as these societies are now rapidly multiplying, by a little delay we shall be able to muster a strong delegation, which cannot be obtained at the present time. Moreover, as there will probably be a great desire among our prominent anti-slavery friends to attend the national meeting in New-York, in May, they will scarcely be able to incur the expense and the loss of time in attending a meeting in this city, in April. For these and other reasons, I shall advocate a postponement of the Convention until June or July next.

The adjourned meeting of the N. E. Anti-Slavery Society at the Temple, on Monday evening, was the grandest we have ever held in Boston. An *immense* concourse of people attended, and though the hall accommodates about 1500, it is believed that not less than 1000 went away, unable to gain admission! — I made a few remarks, which, though strong and ardent, were well received. Professor Follen, of Cambridge University, followed me in an excellent speech — next followed the Rev. Mr. Grosvenor of Salem, in a spirited and impressive speech — and then the Rev. Mr. Grew, formerly of Hartford, whose appeals were truly pathetic and powerful.

On the same evening, the Massachusetts Colonization Society held its annual meeting in Park-street meeting-house. It was an abortive effort, and they were wholly indebted to us for their audience — as it consisted of those who could not get into the Temple to hear our appeals.

Say to our esteemed abolition friends in Providence, that Boston is now fairly redeemed from the thraldom of colonization corruption, and that the prospect of the complete and speedy regeneration of New-England is truly animating. Vermont is coming up to the work nobly — I have just heard of several new anti-slavery societies in that State, to one of which (in Peacham) there are about 300 members!

Sickness prevented the Rev. Dr. Channing from being present at our meeting; otherwise, we should in all probability have had a speech from him. I understand he fully agrees with us on the great question of *immediate* emancipation.

Letters, just received from England, speak cheeringly as to the interest and sympathy which are felt and expanding in the breasts of the philanthropists in that country, in relation to the anti-slavery contest in the U.S. We shall receive much assistance from them. The fruits of my mission will soon be seen in all their richness and abundance.

My best regards to Miss Mary, your lady, Henry, Mr. Chace, Mr. Prentice, &c. &c.

Most affectionately and indissolubly yours,

Wm. Lloyd Garrison.

Mr. Geo. W. Benson.

ALS: Garrison Papers, Boston Public Library.

128

TO CHARLES FOLLEN

Boston, March 18, 1834.

Dear Sir:

I presume you have received a letter from a Committee of the Salem Anti-Slavery Society, inviting you to be present at their annual meeting, which is to be holden on Monday evening, 24th inst. In addition to their direct invitation to you, such is their anxiety to see and *hear* you on that occasion, that they have requested me to send you an epistle, urging you, if practicable, to honor them with your presence. I am sure that you need no solicitation from any one to seize every suitable occasion to plead the cause of those who are pining in servitude; and that, if you can make your arrangements accordingly, you will be ready not only to gratify, but also to enlighten the inhabitants of Salem. Next to Boston, of all the towns in the Commonwealth, Salem ranks deservedly, — in population, in wealth, in intelligence, and in respectability. It is immensely important, therefore, that the massive weight of her moral influence should be thrown into the scales of justice and humanity. Now is a most propitious moment to turn the balance in favor of emancipation. Already three hundred members are enrolled on the list of the Salem Anti-Slavery Society. The spirit of inquiry, on the subject of slavery, powerfully pervades that community; and the cry for "Light!" increases in earnestness and pathos.

Go, then, dear Sir, if possible. Your name alone will ensure a large, respectable, and truly intellectual audience. Some great and glorious truth, uttered by you, may be the means of giving a victorious impulse to a mass of mind, that shall result in the entire renovation of a corrupt public sentiment.

Invitations from the same Society have also been given to the Rev. Mr. Phelps, Rev. E. M. P. Wells, David Lee Child, Esq., Mr. Sewall, and myself.[1] We shall all probably comply with the same. We shall take a carriage, on Monday afternoon, and return the same night.

I have no language to express my admiration of the moral courage which you have displayed, in thus connecting yourself with a cause which is at present so unpopular. May an infinite reward be yours!

Respectfully yours,

Wm. Lloyd Garrison.

Prof. C. Follen.

ALS: Villard Papers, Harvard College Library.

1. Of the four Boston abolitionists here listed by Garrison, only E. M. P. Wells (1793–1878) has not been previously identified. He was an Episcopal clergyman and former vice-president of the Massachusetts Anti-Slavery Society, and was the principal of the Boston Asylum and Farm School. In 1840 he was to join Phelps and other conservative clergymen in splitting away from the Garrisonians on the issue of woman's rights.

129

TO HELEN E. BENSON

Boston, March 19, 1834.

Miss Helen:

I know not why, — but a cloud of melancholy has been impendent over my breast within the last few days. Your letter came like a gleam of sunshine, and I thank you sincerely for it.

In this letter it is proper for me to premise — first, that I shall not expect to be answered letter for letter, because I have no claim upon your time or attention; although it will gratify me exceedingly to receive as many epistolary favors as you can bestow; — and secondly, that my communications will contain nothing which may not be revealed freely to your parents, sisters and brothers. The only objection which I feel to their being read by others, arises from the haste with which they have hitherto been, and probably will be hereafter, written.

You seem to think that as I become more intimately acquainted with you, I shall place a lower estimate upon your merit. It may be so — but this opinion of yours rather tends to exalt you in my own.

The acquittal of Olney relieves my mind of much anxiety. As he was taken up simply for being *in* Miss Crandall's house at the time of the fire, suppose we have Andrew T. Judson arrested, as he lives in the dwelling next to her own.

You did well to deal frankly with Miss C., in relation to her contemplated marriage.[1]

I often revert with real pleasure, in my imagination, to my journey across the Atlantic. How many inestimable friends it secured to me in England, whom I now pant to see, but shall probably never again behold on earth! — During my absence from the United States, I was cheered and strengthened, in the midst of my perils and labors, by an assurance that I had left behind me thousands of devoted and affectionate friends, whose kind wishes and fervent prayers for my safety and success were constantly ascending up to the throne of mercy. But even then, a tear would frequently start unbidden to my eye, from a melancholy consciousness that, among them all, there was not *one* who cherished toward me aught beyond "friendship's affection." I could not say with Byron —

> "There is a mystic thread of life,
>   So dearly wreathed with mine alone,
> That Destiny's relentless knife
>   At once must sever both or none" — [2]

Nor with Moore —

> "There's one, whose smile shines out alone,
> Amidst a world, the only one!
> Whose light, among so many lights,
> Is like that star, on starry nights,
> The seaman singles from the sky,
> To steer his bark forever by!" [3]

And therefore I wept in sadness and in solitude. Is it ever thus to be? Alas! all may be mated but me — I have no attractions to enkindle or secure love — there is none in the wide world whose heart I am authorised to claim — none, into whose bosom I can pour the wealth of my affections.

"O, melancholy Love! amid thy fears,
Thy darkness, thy despair, there runs a vein
Of pleasure, like a smile midst many tears —
The pride of sorrow that will not complain —
The exultation that, *in after years,*
The loved one will discover — and in vain,
How much the heart silently in its cell
Did suffer till it broke, yet nothing tell." [4]

I am admonished by my favorite, Mrs. Hemans, that

"We endow
Those whom we love, in our fond, passionate blindness,
With power upon our souls, too absolute
To be a mortal's trust! Within their hands
We lay the flaming sword, whose stroke alone
Can reach our hearts; and they are merciful,
As they are strong, that wield it no[t to pierce us!"] [5]

You will be weary of this [. . .] from it. Human ties are frail as gossame[r . . . so]journ here is but for a moment. Whether we [. . .] died hearts to whom we may be united, or live in [. . .]sion, let us never forget supremely to adore that glor[. . .] who has so loved the world as to give his only Son to redee[m . . .] Him who is "the chief among ten thousand, and the one [. . . lo]vely," [6] possess the best and strongest affections of [. . .]

[. . .] have written to Whittier for the Album. — [. . .]ment is truly gratifying, in as much as I [. . .] deal in flattery.

[   ] remembrances to your parents, and all the [. . .] will immediately burn this epistle, you [. . .] a better one from

Your admiring friend,

Wm. Lloyd Garrison.

N.B. I beseech you not to make any apologies for the manner in which your letters are written — they require none.

Let me urge you to a frequent perusal of "The Daughter's Own Book" — it is stored with golden treasures. [7]

The healthful example which you and Miss Anna set me, in the use of that best and purest of all beverages — water — is fresh in my memory whenever I sit down to take bodily refreshments.

When I was in Brooklyn, I think I [. . .] the solitude of my little cottage in the woods. [. . .] rested upon the following verse of Cowper:

> "I praise the Frenchman, his rem[ark was shrewd, —]
> How sweet, how passing sweet[, is solitude!]
> But grant me still a friend in [my retreat,]
> Whom I may whisper — solitude [is sweet.] [8]

What think you — is Cowp[er . . .]
say with Byron —

> "There is society where *none* [intrudes,] [9]

ALS: Villard Papers, Harvard College Library. Since the manuscript of this letter is torn in places, it cannot all be deciphered.

1. Both Helen and Garrison were concerned that Prudence Crandall was considering marriage to the Rev. Calvin Philleo from Ithaca, New York, a peculiar Baptist minister of questionable probity.
2. "Stanzas to Jessy," lines 1–4. This poem, though attributed to Byron, was not acknowledged by him.
3. Garrison slightly adapts Thomas Moore, *Lallah Rookh*, Part VI, "Story of the Sultana Nourmahal" (or "The Light of the Haram"), lines 530–535.
4. Not identified.
5. "The Siege of Valencia," Scene ii. Felicia Dorothea Hemans (1793–1835) was the minor English poet best known for *Casabianca*.
6. Garrison adapts and combines Song of Solomon 5:10 and 5:16.
7. *The Daughter's Own Book; or, Practical Hints from a Father to His Daughter* (Boston, 1833) is a collection of moralistic essays on such subjects as "Early Friendships," "Forming Religious Sentiments," and "Independence of Mind."
8. William Cowper, "Retirement," lines 739–742.
9. *Childe Harold's Pilgrimage*, Canto IV, stanza 178, line 1596.

130

TO JOHN B. VASHON

Boston, March 22, 1834.

My dear friend:

I stand before the public as an editor; but, the truth is, my epistolary duties absorb much more of my time than my editorial. You may easily suppose that the pressure upon my shoulders is immense, and that it becomes heavier as our great and glorious cause advances in our land. This is the reason I have not been more prompt in answering your affectionate letters. My correspondence is so extensive, that I am really weary of the pen; and yet my pleasure is always great in writing to those whom I esteem as I do you.

You refer to the state of things in our country two or three years ago, when I was laboring as it were single-handed to destroy those two great monsters — Slavery and the American Colonization Society;

and you refer with pride and pleasure to the wonderful change which has since taken place in public sentiment. The retrospect is indeed animating; but I think I can truly say that it does not lift me up, but rather humbles me, and magnifies the truths of "the glorious gospel of the blessed God." [1] Instrumentally, I have indeed been crowned with success, and my heart is glad, because it encourages me to press onward in this sacred strife, and still to fasten my hopes upon those promises which are sure of being strictly fulfilled; but let Jehovah have *all* the glory.

Having now effectually crippled the Colonization Society, and measurably overthrown that wall of partition which has so long protected slaveholders and slavery from the shafts of truth and the blows of justice, there is a fair prospect that the chains of every bondman will soon fall to the earth, and every captive be set free. And when that event shall happen, the song of the angels shall again be renewed — "Glory to God in the highest — peace on earth, good will to men!" [2] In that delightful song, the penitent master and the grateful freedman shall unite — and from the east to the west, from the north to the south, there shall go up to heaven the cry, in thunder tones of praise, "Alleluia! for the Lord God omnipotent reigneth!" [3]

Our cause has been retarded, not so much by prejudice and wickedness, as by ignorance and misconception. Just as fast as we get light among the people, and make ourselves heard, and our principles and purposes known, we make converts. Rely upon it, my dear brother, with all their failings, the great mass of the people of this country are *really* the enemies of slavery — really the friends of emancipation. But appeals have been made to their fears — the truth has been kept back from them — those who are striving to deliver our land from its deadliest curse have been made hideous by caricatures — and hence so much opposition has prevailed to that which is holy, just and good.

It is delightful to hear that the British Colonies are giving complete freedom to their slaves. Now we shall see whether the emancipated will destroy their masters, or do any acts of violence, in return for their enfranchisement. Only give the slaveholders guineas enough for their victims, and they are perfectly willing to risk being slaughtered, or robbed of their goods.

I trust my colored brethren in Pittsburgh are virtuously striving to get knowledge, to improve their minds, their manners, and their morals, and to secure the pearl of great price.[4] Great would be my happiness to visit them, and cheer them by my counsels and my presence; but they are so remote from Boston, as to discourage the hope of my visiting them at present. I rejoice that you are among them, benefitting them alike by your example and efforts. Be ye all of good courage — for in due time ye shall reap a rich harvest, if ye faint not.[5]

If my much esteemed friend Mr. Loughhead is in Pittsburgh, give my warmest regards to him.[6] He is a good soldier, with whom I gladly enlist.

You perceive that anti-slavery societies are multiplying all over our land. This is the way to reform, consolidate and enlighten the moral power of the nation, and to overthrow iniquity and oppression.

In great haste, but with deliberate regard and strong affection, I remain

Yours ever,

          Wm. Lloyd Garrison.

Mr. J. B. Vashon.

Typed transcript: Villard Papers, Harvard College Library.

1. I Timothy 1:11.
2. Luke 2:14, adapted.
3. Revelation 19:6.
4. Matthew 13:46.
5. Garrison adapts Numbers 13:20 and Galatians 6:9.
6. Garrison probably refers to James Loughead, Jr. (1764–1839), the postmaster of Danville, Pennsylvania. His father, Lieutenant Colonel Loughead, had been one of George Washington's aides.

131

TO HELEN E. BENSON

Freedom's Cottage,
Roxbury, March 25, 1834.

Miss Helen:

You perceive that I am very vain and very presumptuous: vain, in supposing that my letters can either amuse or interest you — presumptuous, in thrusting them so frequently upon your notice. I confess my weaknesses, but look to the goodness of your disposition for my pardon. I do not send you these hasty productions of my brain on account of their value, but merely as some slight tokens of my friendship. If I am intrusive, deal frankly with me: indeed, I am sure that you will — for your abhorrence of dissimulation is as great as my own.

A lady has just communicated to me a most encouraging fact. She said that while I was addressing the crowded audience at our late great anti-slavery meeting in this city,[1] the whisper ran all round her from the spectators — "Who is that speaking?" "That is Mr. Garrison." "Is that Mr. Garrison? Why, I thought he was — *an old man!*" Now, is not such a remark encouraging, Helen? Is it not equivalent to saying that I am a young man? Why, I *do* begin to feel a little less ancient, and somewhat more modern! — See what a compliment can effect!

I believe I commenced one of my letters (for I do not keep a copy of them) with a brilliant rhapsody upon the sun, in consequence of his pouring a golden flood into my cottage windows, and bathing me with his lustrous streams. Of course, that description had reference to the morning —

"————— Day's glowing herald
Came dancing from the orient, and led
The meek eyed Morning, like a blushing bride,
Who brought her wonted tribute from the meads
Of golden Hesperus, and threw her store
Of freshest roses 'long her gladsome path."

It is now evening — most beautiful and bright:

"————— the Moon amid the host
Of constellations, like some fairy boat,
Glides o'er the waveless sea; then as a bride
She hides her cheek behind a fleecy veil,
Timid and fair; or, bright in regal robes,
Dost bid her full-orb'd chariot proudly roll,
Sweeping with silent reign the starry path
Up to the highest node." [2]

You have, I suppose, been exchanging bright glances with her, and mutually gazing in admiration upon each other's fair and placid countenance. Allow me to compliment you both.

In contemplating the heavens this evening, my thoughts have strangely taken an aristocratic turn. For instance — if I were now called upon to vindicate a form of government like that of England, I should say, peradventure, that it is clearly sanctioned by the analogy of creation — thus: The sun shows forth the majesty and glory of a monarch. Nay, he is properly styled a King —

"But yonder comes the powerful King of Day,
Rejoicing in the East" — [3]

and though he often seems to expire, yet he never dies. And to prove that Woman should occasionally exercise royal supremacy, it is only necessary to refer to the

"Fair Queen of Silence, silver Moon!" [4]

Then, only look at the stars, to see the aristocracy pervading their ranks! — There are Dukes and Duchesses, Earls and Lords, and all the subordinate grades down to the "common people of the skies." [5] Have I not made out my case? — Nevertheless, I cry at the top of my lungs, — "Down with monarchy! Up with republicanism! Liberty and Equality forever!" [6]

On Sabbath evening, I went out to Waltham, with my excellent friend the Rev. Mr. Phelps, who delivered a thrilling discourse on the horrors of slavery; at the conclusion of which, he took me by surprise, by calling upon me to offer some remarks to the assembly. I did so, and was listened to most respectfully and attentively. After I had finished, the Rev. Mr. Whitman arose, and made an admirable address, in which he fully coincided with all that had been previously said, and. said that he would unite all his energies to overthrow the cruel system of slavery.[7] The meeting-house was crowded to excess, and many could gain no admittance. A large number of persons added their names to the Waltham Anti-Slavery Society. The ladies are about organizing a Society by themselves.

The Managers of our Society have voted to request Miss Crandall to have her portrait taken in Boston by one of our most distinguished artists. I shall apprise her of the fact in a few days. It is done at my suggestion.

Of course, you will remember me faithfully and affectionately, to all the members of the family — and believe me

Your admiring friend, in weal and in wo,

Wm. Lloyd Garrison.

Miss H. E. Benson.

ALS: Villard Papers, Harvard College Library.

1. The second annual meeting of the New England Anti-Slavery Society, held on March 10 in the Temple on Tremont Street.
2. Not identified.
3. James Thomson, *The Seasons*, "Summer," lines 81–82.
4. Not identified.
5. Sir Henry Wotton, "On his Mistress, the Queen of Bohemia," line 4.
6. Garrison seems to refer to the French Revolution.
7. Bernard Whitman (1796–1834), after graduating from Phillips Exeter Academy and being dismissed from Harvard, opened a school in Billerica, Massachusetts. In 1826 he became the minister of the Second Religious Society in Waltham and in 1833 the General Secretary of the American Unitarian Association. As an abolitionist, he advocated a moderate position.

132

TO HELEN E. BENSON

Freedom's Cottage,
Roxbury, March 26, 1834.

Dearest Helen:

For such you will allow me to call you now. How happy I am to dismiss the formal and distant appellation "Miss," and adopt, in its place, one that in some degree expresses the nature of my affection for you!

Yesterday, I put into the Post Office another hasty epistle, addressed to you; and to-day I have received yours of the 21st. You desire a speedy reply; but my heart is so full in reading it, and its contents are so *delightfully* oppressive to my feelings, that I fear I have not sufficient composure to endite a coherent answer.[1]

I was indeed depressed by your former letter; for, although it contained the avowal of a more generous and sincere *friendship*, on your part, than I merited, yet it was simply "friendship" — and I was led to interpret its truly modest and delicate sentiments, in a manner that filled my heart with melancholy. I then felt as if I might justly exclaim, in the sorrowful and pathetic language of the poet —

> "Oh! ever thus, from childhood's hour,
> I've seen my fondest hopes decay;
> I never loved a tree or flower,
> But 'twas the first to fade away.
> I never nursed a dear gazelle,
> To glad me with its soft black eye,
> But when it came to know me well,
> And love me, it was sure to die!"[2]

Oh! generous, confiding, excellent girl! do you then reciprocate my *love*? Yes, my fears are dispelled — my hopes are confirmed — and I can shed delicious tears of joy! Those tender, affectionate, ardent confessions of yours! — they are all that I could desire, and inestimably more than I ever could have anticipated, or can ever deserve. No, dear Helen, I never, for a moment, imagined that you "possessed a most unfeeling, ungrateful heart" — strange that you will thus reproach yourself; but, I confess, (although I cherished a hope that I was not wholly indifferent to you,) I did not dare to presume that you regarded me with so much esteem. You say, in the most simple and touching language "I have opened my heart to you! perhaps have expressed too much, and have now erred on the other side. But do accept the right — the wrong forgive." I see nothing wrong — nothing to forgive — but every thing to accept. You may confide in my fidelity — in the singleness and devotedness of my heart — in the purity and holiness of my love.

And now let me say, that the first time I ever saw you, I was favorably and deeply impressed by your sweet countenance and pleasant conversation. You were in my thoughts while I was riding upon the billowy Atlantic, and during my sojourn in England; and all the way with me on my return. Each subsequent interview deepened the impression, and raised you higher in my regard.

———————— "Love went on,
Day after day expanding, like the flower
That closes with the darkness, and awakes
When the new morn awakens. So my love
Caught new life from each blissful interview,
And opened and grew riper." [3]

This is poetry, but it is also the truth; and I quote it because it so accurately describes the rise and progress of my affection for you, and because you will thus perceive that I have not been precipitate in my conduct.

Much as I am pleased with your person, it is not that upon which my esteem is based:

"No — beaming with light as thy mild features are,
There's a light round thy heart which is lovelier far!
It is not that cheek — *'tis the soul dawning clear*
Through its innocent blush makes thy beauty so dear:
As the sky we look up to, though glorious and fair,
It looked up to the more, because heaven is there!" [4]

During our pleasant ride to Canterbury, I wished to disclose some of my feelings to you; but my tongue was tied, and my heart timorous, and so I was dumb. I thought, moreover, that it would be taking you by surprise, and thus placing you in a delicate position; and that it would be more deliberate, and far more proper, to write to you; and, in case of receiving a refusal, the embarrassment and pain felt by each would be mitigated, although not removed.

You express much anxiety on the score of your "deficiences," for which state of mind I must gently chide you. It is for me to be uneasy on account of my unworthiness, and to crave your indulgence. Be assured, Helen, that I write thus with seriousness and sincerity, and not for the purpose of eliciting any compliment: — nay, I beg you will hereafter discard all panegyric upon my humble self. To assure me, from time to time, that I am dear to you, will be praise and pleasure enough; but I trust there is One whom we love and admire more than we do each other — *and only one.* Oh! he is infinitely lovely!

I have just been down to Salem with Professor Follen, Rev. Mr. Wells,[5] Rev. Mr. Phelps, S. E. Sewall, Esq., &c. &c. to attend an anti-slavery meeting in the Rev. Mr. Grosvenor's meeting-house. The concourse of people was immense — hundreds could obtain no seats — and probably not less than 2000 were present. We all made addresses, which appeared to produce a salutary and stirring impression.

As a little more than a year ago, I had an unfortunate collision with the Rev. Dr. Flint in Salem, during the discussion between

Friend Buffum and Mr. Danforth, I did not know how I should be received on rising to address the audience; but they gave me *four* tremendous rounds of applause before I opened my lips, and applauded me excessively throughout my extempore speech!

Dear Helen, my sheet is full, but it seems to me that I can never be tired while addressing you. Let me hear from you often, for I shall seize every opportunity to tell you how dear you are to

Your affectionate lover,

Wm. Lloyd Garrison.

N.B. No — I will not insist upon your burning any of my letters. They are yours — do with them as you shall deem proper.

☞ Please to write "Private" on the outside of your letters, at one corner.

ALS: Villard Papers, Harvard College Library.

1. In her letter of March 21 Helen replied to what she considered his melancholy one of March 19: "I am *grieved*, exceedingly *grieved* to think my letter conveyed to your mind, such unpleasant reflections; for I surely did not intend it, and thought I said sufficient to convince you that I felt *deeply interested* in your welfare." She assured him that she returned his affections and that the only thing standing between them was her own inferiority. "But as you seem inclined to overlook my many deficiencies; and pass them by — I see not why, I may not gratefully, acknowledge your attention in confessing so high an obligation upon me, and I sincerely respond to every tender expression of feeling, which you have manifested throughout your letters." This letter Garrison interpreted as an acceptance of the proposal he had expressed so cryptically in his letter of March 8.

2. Thomas Moore, *Lalla Rookh*, Part V, "The Fire-worshippers," lines 279–286.
3. Not identified.
4. Thomas Moore, *Irish Melodies*, "They Know Not My Heart," lines 7–12.
5. E. M. P. Wells.

133

TO GEORGE W. BENSON

[☞ *Private.*]

Boston, March 29, 1834.

My dear friend.

This very hasty letter will be handed to you, I trust, by my beloved partner,[1] who is on a visit to our friends in New-York and Philadelphia. I am delighted that he has at last consented to make a journey; for he certainly needs some recreation, and I think it will advance his health as well as relieve his mind. He will be exceedingly happy to see you and the rest of the goodly company of abolitionists in Providence; and I am sure that he will receive a hearty welcome at your hands.

You have expressed, my dear G., on various occasions, a warm attachment for me, and invariably treated me with respect and affection. I have endeavored to manifest a similar regard for you, although I am still much in your debt. Will you love me any less, or will the ardor of your friendship abate, after hearing what I am about to disclose to you? My heart would be sad, indeed, if I could believe that this will be the result of my communication. Do not, I pray you, now disown me, but let me be dearer to you than ever — as you certainly are to me.

The case, then, is briefly this. From the first moment I ever saw your gentle sister Helen, and had the pleasure of enjoying her society, I was most favorably impressed, in relation to her personal, mental, and moral worth. Her image was with me constantly, during my absence from the country — and it was with joy I saw her on my return. At each successive interview, I felt a growing attachment, but I disclosed my feelings and predilections to no one. — My recent visit to Brooklyn was peculiarly satisfactory and delightful, and I wished then to say to Helen all that I felt — but my lips refused, or rather my heart was too timid, to make a confession. It seemed to me proper to wait till my return home. I did not wish to take her by surprise, or, if she could not reciprocate my affection, to put her under the painful necessity of refusing my offer to my face. Accordingly, I sent a letter to her, in which I revealed the state of my heart, if not in the plainest language and most direct method, still in a manner to leave no doubt of my attachment. How anxiously did I wait to receive a reply! You have been placed in a similar situation, and therefore can realise its hopes and fears. A reply came — it was modest, kind, *very* kind, and interesting — and yet I construed it as, if not absolutely rejecting, still discouraging my suit, and it gave me much unhappiness. In my next letter, I disclosed the sorrowful emotions of my heart, but felt deterred from pressing my suit. The dear girl promptly answered this, in an epistle full of tenderness and affection — declaring that I had misinterpreted her language, and that she was willing to be mine, but diffidently expressing her fears that she was not worthy of my choice. I have forwarded a reply, expressive of joy and thankfulness, and pledging her my whole heart. Thus, our faith is plighted, and our love made reciprocal.

I have felt it my duty to seize the first opportunity to relate these circumstances to you; but, for the present, I beg you will not divulge the contents of this letter to any but your lady and your sisters. Indeed, I suppose the latter, together with your parents and Henry, are now fully aware of the fact. My friend Knapp mistrusts something, but I shall not tell him all at once — pray don't you.

To have won the heart of my dear Helen, (for so I must now be allowed to call her,) is truly gratifying to my feelings; but they will be still more exquisitely delightful, if I can only have the cordial approbation of your venerable father and mother, Mary, Anna, Sarah, Henry, yourself — all, in short, connected with the family. Until this be granted to me, my happiness will not be complete. I shall write to your parents on the subject within a few days.

A signer of the Declaration has gone — a standard bearer in our cause has fallen! — I have just received the melancholy tidings, that our esteemed friend Evan Lewis is no more! His loss will be severely felt. I have no room for particulars.

If you can, I wish you would answer this letter immediately, and deal with me frankly. Mark *"Private"* on the envelope of your letter. Henry, I presume, is in Brooklyn. My best remembrances to your lady, Miss Mary, Mr. & Mrs. Anthony, Mr. Chase, Mr. Prentice, &c. &c.

If you will not allow me to subscribe myself your affectionate brother, you will permit me to assure you that

I am your much attached friend,

Wm. Lloyd Garrison.

Mr. G. W. Benson.

ALS: Villard Papers, Harvard College Library.

1. Isaac Knapp.

134

TO AMOS FARNSWORTH

Boston March 31, 1834.

Dear Sir,

You may readily suppose that my heart is cheered whenever and wherever tidings are brought to me of the advancement of the sacred cause of emancipation. Especially am I pleased to learn by your favor of the 27th instant, that the spirit of freedom is stirring in your patriotic town and that you are soon to organize an antislavery society. Public sentiment enlightened and consolidated, may as easily abolish slavery as intemperance or any other prevalent evil; and as, in order easily to lift a heavy load men must unite their physical strength — so they must bring their moral influence together in associations for the removal of the incubus of slavery which is crushing us to the earth. In all cases of reform, the difficulty lies not in the magnitude of the evil to be overcome, but in the hostility, or ignorance or lukewarmness of the people. As soon as the people of England resolved that slavery should be abolished in the Colonies, the work was achieved, and the slaves are now rejoicing in freedom.

The antislavery cause in this country has been caricatured and made hideous by its enemies; and, consequently many excellent people, who are yet ignorant of its principles oppose it as something very terrible. All that they need is correct information to make them its most strenuous friends, for their hearts are really full of sympathy for the oppressed.

I regret that I can give you no encouragement of my being able to comply with your kind invitation to deliver an address in Groton. My editorial duties and my extensive correspondence consume so much of my time, and are increasing so oppressively, as to make my absence from Boston a matter of extreme difficulty and much perplexity. Invitations are crowding upon me from various quarters; but I shall be necessitated to decline every one of them. I must either give up lecturing, or get some one to supply my place as editor of the Liberator. Perhaps some arrangement of this kind may be made hereafter. All that I can promise now is, that I will endeavor to visit you the first convenient opportunity.

I presume Mr. Child gave you a forcible Address.

Begging you to convey my thanks to the gentlemen in whose behalf you write, and tendering my best acknowledgments to you, I remain,

Yours, respectfully

Wm. Lloyd Garrison.

Dr. Amos Farnsworth.

Handwritten transcription: Garrison Papers, Boston Public Library.

Dr. Amos Farnsworth (1788–1861) of Groton, Massachusetts, was a member of the Groton Anti-Slavery Society and a loyal supporter of the Massachusetts Anti-Slavery Society.

135

TO HELEN E. BENSON

Freedom's Cottage,
Roxbury, April 1, 1834.

My dear Helen:

My last letter, acknowledging more fully my affection for you, was written with a heart full of thrilling emotions; but I fear lest, in endeavoring to write with calmness, I may have seemed reserved, and almost frigid in my feelings. And yet I strived hard, by the use of forcible terms, to tell you how entirely I was yours, and how gratefully I felt for your generous return of my love.

Since your precious confession, dear girl, I have felt an undefinable, but truly exquisite state of mind — at first, slightly tumultuous, but gradually becoming placid, and permanently blissful. How it becomes me to strive earnestly to be worthy of you! How can I manifest my interest in your welfare, in the most pleasing and signal manner? Hide nothing from me; and remember that I shall at all times obey your commands with alacrity.

Till very recently, time has flown away with the swiftness of an eagle; but now the hours move tardily, and the days seem protracted to the duration of weeks, while I am waiting to receive an epistle from you. It is true, I ought not to expect to receive a reply so soon; but hope deferred has made me feverish, and morning, noon, and night, I go to the Post Office in vain — no letter arrives, and I go away with a sigh.

This forenoon, I sent a letter by mail to our respected friend Prudence Crandall, urging her to come to this city, immediately if practicable, in order to have her portrait taken, according to a vote of the Managers of the New-England Anti-Slavery Society. — It had scarcely been gone two hours, before she arrived in Boston! — Of course, I hastened to greet her, and was glad to find her in excellent health and good spirits. "Did you stop at our dear friend Benson's?" said I, somewhat eagerly. "O, yes — certainly," was the reply, "and kindly and cordially was I received — the family are all well." "But have you no letters for me?" I inquired, despondingly. "Yes — here are two." I took them eagerly, and saw at a glance that one was from Mr. May, and the other from — not Helen, but my dear Henry. Now, Henry must forgive me if I say, that, although his letters always give me pleasure, yet in this instance I should have preferred a letter from — you know who — one who is even dearer to me than himself. — But I will break the seal, and see what he says — it is broken, and my wishes are realised! — the writing is yours! This was truly an ingenious surprise, and a most felicitous disappointment. — But what do I see? A chill is given to my ardor at once — for the letter commences, not "Dear William," but thus — "Mr. Garrison"! How formal, after such an epistle as your last! — True, the next line reads — "My dear friend" — and this is somewhat consolatory. On reading your favor, how great was my regret to learn that my last letter had not been received by you, although it was promptly written and mailed on the receipt of yours! — You acknowledge the receipt of my letter written on the previous day, and naturally express surprise and solicitude that it contained no acknowledgment of your epistle. I know not how to account for the delay, except in the irregularity of the mail; for, aware that you would be anxious to receive an immediate reply, I wrote one without delay, which I hope you have now received. Oh! that it may prove acceptable!

Your letters are read by no one but myself. I have not communicated the secret even to my dear companion Knapp — although I opine that he suspects *something,* but he says nothing. Nevertheless, I have deemed it my duty to make full confession to your venerable father, and to George. I hope the former will show you my letter to him — but, O, if he should refuse to grant his approbation — and also your dear mother, and sisters! I will try to wait calmly till I ascertain their views and feelings. Have I been too hasty in revealing to them the state of our affections? If so, forgive me. It seemed to me that honor and honesty demanded such a step.

Prudence will probably be detained in this city at least one week. When she returns, you may expect another letter from me.

April comes in to-day in the most repulsive form. It rains and blows very rudely, and her voice is loud and turbulent. My Sonnet to her in the last paper [1] is at present unmerited. But *you* deserve and command the admiration and love of

Yours, until death,

Wm. Lloyd Garrison.

Miss H. E. Benson.

N.B. In my last, I had so much to say *of* you, and *to* you, that I had no room left to send my compliments to the cat. Your attention to her I esteem a compliment to myself — it pleases me exceedingly.

I am proud to hear that I am in the "good graces" of Eunice and your other domestic — always give my best salutations to them, and to all the family.

It really makes me blush to send you letters so hastily and so imperfectly written; but I cannot get time to copy them. You say they are perused by you with avidity — how many times have I read yours!

I expect to see my dear friend May to-morrow. — When shall I see you?

Whittier has not yet sent me the Album — I shall have to chide him again severely for his criminal negligence.

☞ Remember that I shall always be famishing for a letter — therefore *do* write *frequently,* even if you send but five lines. Two things I would *seriously* enjoin — do not ever begin another letter with the distant address, "Mr. Garrison" — say "William," or "Lloyd," or any thing else — and pay no postage on your letters.

ALS: Villard Papers, Harvard College Library.

1. It was not uncommon for Garrison to publish sonnets in *The Liberator.* This one appeared in the issue for March 29, 1834.

Garrison in 1833

Arnold Buffum

136

TO HELEN E. BENSON

Freedom's Cottage,
Roxbury, April 5, 1834.

Dear Helen:

You have made me fall in love, not only with you, but also with my pen — that is, whenever it is to convey to you the sentiments of my heart.

Our mutual friend Miss Prudence is enabled to return sooner than was anticipated, and therefore she will leave to-day, at one o'clock, for Providence. Although it is only three days since I sent you a letter, you would scarcely pardon me, — at least, I am sure that I could not forgive myself, — if I should let this favorable opportunity slip, without sending you a few lines.

I am happy to say that the artist has been very successful in taking the portrait of Miss Crandall; but the story of her persecution will outlive the canvass. One thing she must guard against — namely, being exalted in her mind by the abundant panegyric of her friends. Certainly, she deserves the sympathy, the affection, and the praise of all those who feel for the suffering and the dumb — for what disgrace and opposition she has voluntarily encountered! what indignities have been cast upon her! what perils have beset her path! and then, how steadfast has been her purpose! how untiring her perseverance! how calm and gentle her deportment! how resolute her courage! Still, (and I am aware that these remarks are strictly applicable to me as to her,) she must be careful lest she be "exalted above measure." [1] We should meekly bend like the reed to the breath of eulogy, but be lofty and unyielding as the oak when the tempest of an unrighteous persecution is raging around us. How contemptible, how foolish, how disgusting is personal egotism!

These remarks have not been elicited in consequence of the appearance of any thing vain, either in the language or conduct of our dear friend; for I am charmed with the simplicity and meekness of her manners; — but a situation like hers calls for sleepless vigilance.

Perhaps I may be interrogated by some one — "If praise be thus dangerous, why do you speak and print so highly in her behalf?" I answer, first, because she is a meritorious woman — secondly, the excessive abuse of her enemies requires the ardent approbation of her friends — and, thirdly, in vindicating her conduct, we advance the cause of the entire colored population of the United States.

She will tell you, I presume, that her visit to this city has proved a very agreeable one to herself and her white and colored friends. There are hundreds yearning to see her, who cannot get an opportunity. When an engraved copy of her portrait is struck off, I will send it to you.

Yesterday, new gladness was infused into my heart, on the receipt of a brief but touching epistle from your venerable parent, the conclusion of which ran as follows: — "I now add the consent of myself and wife to your proposal of the most endearing union with our dear daughter Helen, and ardently implore the divine blessing upon both of you." This consummates my happiness. The obtainment of your own consent was indeed of primary importance, but the sanction of your parents was essential to the quietude and full enjoyment of my mind. Oh! may they never have cause to regret that they were induced to give it! Realising the greatness of the sacrifice they have made, and the value of the favor they have conferred, I will do all that in me lies to cheer and sustain their declining days.

And now, my dear Helen, what shall I say to you? My heart is full, and liquid as water; but though I pour it out so freely, the fountain suffers no diminution. We have given to each other the pledge of a deathless affection — we hope to be united in the bonds of a blissful union, which only death can sever — we are looking forward to years of mutual happiness, and fancy is busy in picturing scenes of domestic enjoyment. What may be our joys, or what our sorrows, He only knows who sees the end from the beginning. Come what may, however, if we have given first the supreme homage of our hearts to Him, and then their pure affections to each other, we cannot but be happy. It is sinful to be presumptuously confident of enjoying a pleasant life, but we are not forbidden meekly and submissively to cherish this soul-inspiring hope. I cannot doubt that a wedded life, if there be a union of hearts as well as of hands, is usually preferable to a single one — "marriage is honorable in all." [2] I am sure that I do not lack the will or the desire to make you perfectly happy.

Dear girl, a pensiveness steals over my mind, which needs only a letter from you to remove. I have received no answer to my two last epistles — and I fear that the first at least, has miscarried, which was peculiarly important. The sincerity and strength of my affection for you must apologize for my importunity. Distance separates us, and yet we may freely converse together, as it were face to face, through an epistolary medium. Each letter from you is a mirror which reveals to me your sweet countenance, and I am never weary of contemplating it.

Give for me a thousand good wishes and blessings to your parents, and to all the members of the family — and keep for yourself that which is now in your possession — the heart of

Your faithful admirer,

Wm. Lloyd Garrison.

H. E. Benson.

☞ I believe I told you in my last, that my partner Mr. Knapp was ignorant of our contemplated union. Yesterday, however, (not dreaming of its contents,) he took your father's letter out of the Post Office, read it, and thus became possessed of the secret. He gave it to me smilingly, and evinced his gratification in his countenance. Proud of being favored with your affection, I can have no objection to the whole world being apprised of the fact. Still, you had better mark "private" on your letters, as possibly they may otherwise be opened and read by others.

The family with whom I board will leave "Freedom's Cottage" on the 20th of May, and move to "Mount Pleasant." I shall either hire the cottage myself, or return to the city. If Prudence had had time, she would have come out and spent a few hours here. The probability now is, that I shall take the cottage.

April still remains sullen and cold. In this vicinity, the influenza begins to prevail, but my health is, as usual, excellent. — Be careful of your own, and avoid exposure to the chilling dews at night.

You see, dear Helen, that the fault is not mine that my letter is so brief, but the paper-maker's.

ALS: Villard Papers, Harvard College Library.

1. II Corinthians 12:7.
2. Hebrews 13:4.

137

TO HELEN E. BENSON

Boston, April 7, 1834.

My sweet Helen:

What a burden you have removed from my breast! — Your delightful favor of April 3d and 4th is before me, and joyful am I to learn that my letters have all safely arrived in "Friendship's Valley." As our dear friend Prudence has delayed going until this morning, I *must* devote a few moments in heaping my thanks and blessings upon you. Excuse that which is hasty, and overlook that which is imperfect.

Your letter is sparkling and flashing with the rarest gems of affection. It is a fountain of feeling — a treasury of love. Let me try to do my best, I shall be dissatisfied with my reply; because my pen can never be so eloquent and fervent as my heart. Noble girl! do not accuse me of *affecting* humility, while I again seriously and tenderly beseech you not so highly to exalt an erring child of the dust. And yet I cannot say that there is one sentence in your letter I would alter or erase. Yes — I must avow it — your praise is delightful to me: — and yet I will strive to be truly humble. — The highest panegyric which it is in my power to pass upon your virtues and excellencies, I have already bestowed — in making you an offer of my hand and heart: — and the best tribute I could receive in return, is your acceptance of that offer. Certainly, we cannot now be justly accused of dealing in flattery — our expressions may be ardent, but not more ardent than sincere. Our thoughts, our feelings, our purposes, are one

———

> "Are we not one? are we not joined by heaven?
> Each interwoven with the other's fate?
> Are we not mix'd like streams of meeting rivers,
> Whose blended waters are no more distinguished,
> But roll into the sea one common flood?" [1]

The inducements which you hold out to me, to write often to you, are irresistible. You inspire my pen —

1st. Because you have captivated my heart.

2d. Because your replies are invaluable.

3d. Because you assure me that my letters are not wholly destitute of interest — and to please you is my highest ambition, next to the rendering of that supreme homage which I owe my heavenly Father.

By the statement in your letter, it would seem as if our hearts were mutually attracted toward each other at our first interview, before my departure for England. — I well remember greeting you at your brother's store, and the reluctance I felt in separating from you. George will remember, perhaps, that I complimented you highly, for I was forcibly struck with your winning appearance.

How is it that you, dear H., see aught in me to admire? Do I not come short in all things? I have no personal attractions; and as for the qualities of my mind, how many there are whose minds are incomparably superior! — But, to *you* I will apply the descriptive language of Moore — (I quote from memory) —

> "As streams that run o'er golden mines,
>   Yet humbly, calmly glide,
> Nor seem to know the wealth that shines
>   Within their gentle tide;

So, veil'd beneath the simplest guise,
  Thy radiant merit beams,
And that which charms all other eyes,
  Seems worthless in thy own." [2]

You see I have spoilt the rhyme, but exalted the sentiment, by using the present tense instead of the past, and by applying the words to one who has not had, and has not now, a superior.

You inquire, "What time do you leave Boston for Roxbury?" Commonly, about half past five; and if the weather is fine, a delightful tour I make of it. By the time I reach my pretty cottage, the sun is going down in an ocean of radiant splendor; —

"Until on yonder western mountain's top
Lingering, he rests at last, and leaves a look
More beautiful than e'er he shed before." [3]

In my morning and evening walks, your image constantly attends me, and I am led almost involuntarily to exclaim — "Helen — *dear* Helen!" To the birds that warble around me I call your name, and bid them repeat it as being far sweeter than their songs.

Tell your beautiful Anna that I gladly accept of her love — as a sister. Will she accept of mine — as a brother? I offer as much to Miss Sarah, for whom I cherish a high regard.

So! you are quietly listening to the numerous and contradictory statements which are made in the conversations of those who neither know me personally, nor are aware of our attachment for each other. Of a truth, you must often be diverted — but pray do not attempt to take my part.

In addition to the consent of your parents, I have received a letter from my dear friend George, in which he cordially assents to our union, together with Miss Mary, Mr. Anthony, and his lady. How fortunate I am thus to have secured the esteem and confidence of all! and how ardently I desire the consummation of our wishes, according to the forms of law! — But more hereafter.

Your faithful admirer,

Wm. Lloyd Garrison.

Miss H. F. Benson.

☞ Am happy to inform you that Prudence has wholly given up Mr. Phillio.[4]

☞ Write often, dear H.

ALS: Villard Papers, Harvard College Library.

1. This verse has not been identified.
2. Garrison quotes the second stanza of one of Thomas Moore's *Irish Melodies*, "I saw thy form in youthful prime." Following is an accurate version:
"As streams that run o'er golden mines,

Yet humbly, calmly glide.
Nor seem to know the wealth that shines
   Within their gentle tide, Mary!
So veil'd beneath the simplest guise,
   Thy radiant genius shone,
And that which charm'd all other eyes,
   Seem'd worthless in thy own, Mary!"

3. These three lines have not been identified.
4. Garrison misspells the name of Calvin Philleo.

138

TO HELEN E. BENSON

Freedom's Cottage,
Roxbury, April 12, 1834.

My Chosen One:

How the most trivial circumstance will sometimes affect us in the most extraordinary manner! — Let me give you an example. A day or two since, as I was wending my way to my cottage, the Providence stage came rolling by, in which was a female form, who seemed to follow me with her eye as if she recognised my person. "If that was only my dear Helen!" I exclaimed. Of course, I knew it must be otherwise; but the mere ideal supposition that it was you, made my blood flush to my temples, and caused my heart to flutter like a startled bird around its nest. If my feelings are thus easily affected when separated from you, shall I be able to meet you composedly? I will try to assume an air of — indifference? — oh, no! never — of calmness and self-possession.

Your solitary love for me is dearer to me than the multitudinous friendships of all my admirers. Not that I undervalue those friendships, for they are very precious; but your love is a part of my being, and deprived of it I should droop and sicken. If it were in my power, I would make some new combinations of language to express to you the affections of my soul, and my gratitude for your reciprocal attachment.

I am struck with the nobleness of your spirit, in condescending to bestow your heart upon one who has so little to recommend him, who is so extensively ridiculed and reviled, whose enemies are so numerous and implacable, whose situation is so adverse to quietude and ease, and whose path is so beset with perils. But, sweet girl, I trust these are the darkest hours of my life. It is not present defamation, but future panegyric, that afflicts me. I am sure that the renown of my philanthropy will be far greater than its actual merits. I shall be honored and applauded, long after the defenders of slavery are cast into oblivion. This is the fruit of benevolence.

In none of my epistles have I said any thing to you respecting the time of our union. It might, perhaps, be hasty and premature to come instantly to a decision upon this point. I will frankly avow, however, that it is my desire to make you mine, according to the forms of law, as soon as I can satisfactorily arrange my business; but I wish, most submissively and implicitly, to obey your wishes, and fulfil your appointment, in relation to this matter. *Your* convenience and disposition I shall most scrupulously consult and follow. Yet, allow me to express the hope, that at least *in all this year* our hands may be joined together in wedlock.

Hitherto, — having had none to care or provide for but myself, — I have felt contented in getting merely my daily bread. But duty to myself and to you requires that I should make such arrangements with the Liberator as shall afford me, if a moderate, at least a sure income. I am therefore resolved no longer to be shackled by the pecuniary responsibilities of the paper, but to have *a stipulated salary for my services.* This salary ought to be not less than one thousand dollars a year, for my editorial abilities will readily command more than that sum if devoted to politics or literature: still, I shall be satisfied with $800, for the present. In order to make this new arrangement, I shall be induced to visit New-York and Philadelphia in the course of a fortnight.[1] Shall I go by the way of Brooklyn or Providence? Will *you* decide? *I* have decided already — how? — My presence at the door of your pleasant dwelling shall answer!

I shall endeavor to have my income fixed at $1000. Indeed, I can now get that sum by abandoning the Liberator, and acting as a general agent for the National Society; but how can I give up my paper? When we meet, I will explain my purposes to you more fully.

I addressed two letters to you, by Miss Prudence. In your last, you mentioned that you intended to send a few lines by Mr. Gray, of this city, by the middle of this week.[2] It is now Saturday, but no letter has come. I live upon expectation from hour to hour, and solace myself by a frequent perusal of those invaluable favors which have already been received from you.

Did Miss C. tell you that in the room of the artist who took her portrait, there was a likeness which closely resembled you? and, consequently, that I gazed upon it, and referred to it, with frequency and delight? I did not tell her of our engagement — but love, as well as murder, "will out," and I am inclined to think her suspicions were awakened, and that she pleasantly interrogated you upon this "delicate subject," as the slaveholders say of slavery. Pray let me into the secret of her inquiries.

Whittier has written me a letter, apologizing for his long detention of your Album, and acknowledging that he is without excuse. He informs me that he has sent it to me — probably by the stage-driver — but I have not yet received it. I hope to get it in season to take it with me to Brooklyn.

The news of the infamous Judson's political overthrow has reached our city, as well as the complete regeneration of Connecticut, and excited universal joy. Let us now cherish the hope that the *black* laws of the State will be repealed by the new Legislature.[3] Cheers for Miss Crandall!

The Spring is progressing slowly. Beautiful as she is, in her best estate, your charms are incomparably superior in the eyes of

Your obedient and constant lover,

Wm. Lloyd Garrison.

Miss H. E. Benson.

Dear Helen, I need not add, — *write soon,* — because you know my desires.

I thank you for banishing from your epistolary territory that frightful creature "*Mr.*"! You have substituted a familiar and an affectionate appellation, which is truly pleasing to me.

It is scarcely necessary for me to say, that in all my letters I desire to be affectionately remembered to your parents, and to *all* residing under their roof. I wrote to your father on Thursday, acknowledging the receipt of his confirmatory letter.

Say to my dear Henry, that I miss his friendly correspondence. Now that he has a little leisure, will he not favor me with a letter? I am sure that there is no abatement of his regard for me. Is it otherwise? Will he not personally write to me, and say — "My dear friend, I approve of your own and my sister's choice"?

Watch over your health — your simple regime will be its best safeguard. You deserve all praise for your abstinence.

The sun is now going down in all his glory. I will now go into the woods, and watch his expiring rays, and learn yet more tenderly to love its great Author. Farewell, Helen!

☞ Perhaps it may be advisable to postpone our marriage until after my trial in October.[4] The expenses of that trial will be borne by my friends in various places.

P. S. Yours is received.

ALS: Villard Papers, Harvard College Library; extract printed in *Life*, I, 429.

1. The financial crisis of *The Liberator*, like Garrison's optimism, was perennial.

The trip to New York and Philadelphia produced no instant solution and certainly no guaranteed salary for the editor.

2. According to Helen (letter to Garrison, dated April 9, 1834) this is Frederick Gray, who boarded at Tremont Place in Boston and who visited in Brooklyn — his parents presumably being the John Grays. Since, like Helen, he was engaged to a Bostonian (Elizabeth Chapman), he and Helen frequented the Brooklyn post office looking for letters and exchanged condolences or congratulations depending on their luck.

3. The only law restricting Negroes in Connecticut at this time was that forbidding the establishment of schools for the instruction of Negroes not residents of Connecticut without the consent in writing of the civil authority. This legislation was the direct result of the establishment of Prudence Crandall's school for Negroes.

4. See letter 124, to Henry E. Benson, February 26, 1834.

139

TO ANNA E. BENSON

Freedom's Cottage,
Roxbury, April 14, 1834.

My much esteemed Friend:

Your beautifully executed and most affectionate note, enclosed in a letter from my dear Helen, came duly to hand; and I hasten to acknowledge my obligations to you. — You will get a poor return, because whenever I am most oppressed by a sense of the unmerited favors of my friends, I am then the most unskilful in the use of words. My heart always vanquishes my pen. To say, "I thank you," is a return so common and cheap, that, unless you attach to these words, in this instance, (and I beg you to do so,) something incomparably better than is found in their usual acceptation, you will have no just conception of my gratitude.

I use the term *gratitude*, not only because you have honored me with a note, which in itself should prompt this feeling, but because you say, in reference to dear H. and myself, — "I have no fears in consigning the lovely plant to thy care, knowing thou wilt assuredly watch over it for good."

Yes, my lovely friend, — unworthy as I am to receive so precious a trust, — it shall be my constant care and pride to cherish that plant with the utmost tenderness and assiduity. I am sure that the love which I bear for her whom I have chosen, is based upon imperishable worth; that it is not a transient flash of passion, but an undying attachment of the soul; and that, although time may give it maturity and greater expansion, yet it cannot diminish nor destroy the principle. There are so many fine traits in Helen's character, that they will always be entwined like golden cords around my affections. — How much do I admire the goodness of her heart, the simplicity of her manners, and the innocence and purity of her mind!

You speak of the joy which fills and gathers around my heart. Yes, I am indeed happy — exquisitely happy. Why should I not be? I might be sad, if Helen were making me a cold and formal return for my love; but she perfects and enlarges my happiness, by pouring out the affections of her soul, without measure, and in the most endearing manner. I can weep delicious tears, in the abundance of my bliss. Heaven has beneficently supplied a void in my breast, and I am happy. There is one who cherishes for me feelings which soar above the common sympathies of the world — which are stronger and holier than those of friendship merely — and I reciprocate those feelings, in all their intensity.

You know, dear friend, that in the estimation of thousands, I am, both physically and morally, a very terrible monster. How little do they know me! — Why, I feel more and more child-like, as time hurries me on to the maturity of manhood. My mind is as susceptible as it was in my infancy — it is a fountain of tenderness. It is not usual for men to indulge in tears; yet how freely do I weep! Not that I am unhappy when I weep — not that I am subject to painful depressions of spirits — not that there is the least degree of misanthropy in my disposition: exactly the reverse of all this is true. A kind word, a fine thought, a lovely scene, a tone of music, will easily bring a tear to my eye; and yet I doubt if any personal injury or outrage could extort a drop, however aggravated the attack or keen the anguish. In endurance of martyrdom, I am all adamant — I *know* that I possess an Indian fortitude, which the fires of persecution can never subdue — a hostile world cannot move me from the path of duty; — and yet I am a very woman in the gentleness of my disposition. This may seem paradoxical to some — but not to one so inflexible in the storm, and so dove-like in the sun-shine, as yourself.

I am happy to have this opportunity to tell you how greatly I have admired that generous devotion and dauntless courage, as well as sterling friendship and lively sympathy, which you exhibited in going into a dreary prison, and resolutely staying with her who has been so cruelly treated by the enemies of an outcast and guiltless race.[1] Your conduct was full of angelic heroism and majesty. I love to recur to it, inasmuch as you are ordinarily so like a lily of the valley; and I praise you because you deserve not only this, but a better tribute. I speak admiringly, as a brother to a sister. My amiable friend May has frequently spoken of you to me in the most exalted terms of commendation.

It is pleasing to hear that there is some prospect of your having a Female Anti-Slavery Society in Brooklyn. — O! the poor victims of tyranny — is there one in this land who feels and strives in their behalf, strongly and perseveringly enough? I fear not — at least, I am sure that in this, as in all other respects, *I* come far short of my duty.

For the liberal — altogether too liberal supply of nut-cakes and apples, sent by you and my sweet H., I beg you to accept a whole ream of thanks.

It is not improbable that I may be in Brooklyn a week from this evening, on my way to Philadelphia. Still, there is no certainty of it. If I am preserved in health, you may certainly expect my arrival in all next week.

Your kind wishes and fervent aspirations duly affect my heart. I beseech you and Helen not to forget me in your supplications to our heavenly Benefactor.

Remember how I am crushed under the weight of duties, and excuse every defect in this imperfect epistle.

Love to Helen and all the family. I can only add that I am

Yours, most affectionately,

Wm. Lloyd Garrison.

Miss Anna E. Benson.

N.B. I sent a letter to your father last week; but I wish him to feel under no obligation to answer it, although I shall always be glad to hear from him. I remember the number of his years, and would not impose the slightest burden upon him.

Tell Miss Sarah that she may ultimately expect a letter from me. One from her will be truly acceptable.

ALS: Garrison Papers, Boston Public Library.

1. Prudence Crandall.

140

TO AN UNKNOWN RECIPIENT

Boston, April 15, 1834.

My dear sir:

Knowing that you have long felt, not only a deep interest in the prosperity of the Liberator, but also a personal friendship for me, which not all the calumnies of the enemies of freedom have been able to shake, I feel emboldened to put the accompanying appeal into your hands, to be used discreetly and confidentially among those.

who in your opinion, may be disposed to unite for the support of the paper. If this were strictly in behalf of myself, I should feel extremely mortified, and would not on any account make it; but it does not so much concern me, or my partner, as it does an immense multitude of victims upon whom are rivetted the galling fetters of tyranny, and four hundred thousand persons who are nominally free, and yet deprived of almost every privilege that makes life pleasant and serviceable. Will you endeavor to ascertain how many individuals, within the immediate circle of your acquaintance, are willing to assist in raising the sum proposed on the following page, by taking shares at the specified rate? By sending the paper to no subscribers hereafter, who do not pay in advance, its circulation will probably be diminished, but to its benefit rather than to its injury; for then we shall be sure of two things — first, of getting all our dues, and secondly, of losing a heavy burden growing out of the delinquencies of those who *patronise* us by never paying a farthing for the paper. I am sure that our friends every where, — and especially our colored friends, — will say, and make good their declaration, that the expenses of printing and editing the Liberator, at a suitable compensation, shall be guaranteed and paid.

Yours Respectfully,

WILLIAM LLOYD GARRISON.

Printed form letter: Garrison Papers, Boston Public Library.

This form letter accompanied a fuller statement of the financial difficulties of *The Liberator*, which can be summarized: 500 of the paper's 2,000 subscribers have not paid the annual $2 fee, resulting in a deficit of $1,700, $700 of which figure should be for the support of the editor. The solution proposed is that the circulation be extended, that subscriptions be paid in advance, and that a fund be raised by selling 100 shares at $10 per share.

141

TO HELEN E. BENSON

Freedom's Cottage,
Roxbury, April 16, 1834.

My Love:

So! my observant friend May has caught me in the act of gallanting a lady through the streets of Boston, and has advertised you of my infidelity! — Well, — (now do not start, for you have assured me that you are not of a jealous disposition,) I must plead *guilty* to the charge.

It is but fair, however, that you should know the name of that lady — it being none other than Prudence Crandall.

It is now evening — the sky is gorgeously bedecked, like a bride sparkling with jewels. The moon, I believe, completes its first quarter to-night. I am sighing to enjoy these pleasant hours by your side. Shall I give you a Sonnet?

> Girl of my choice! though forc'd awhile to part,
> And days and weeks do sadly intervene,
> Yet hope illumes the darkness of the scene,
> And gives to love its aliment. Thou art
> The radiant cynosure of my fond heart.
> O! who can gaze upon thy brow serene —
> Thy winning graces — gentleness of mien —
> And not in tremulous confusion start?
> Or catch the tender glances of thine eyes,
> Nor feel the influence of their mellow light?
> O! thou art ever present to my sight,
> An angel who hath failed in thy disguise!
> And in my wakeful hours, and dreams by night,
> I dwell upon thy charms with glad surprise.

There, dear Helen, if I have sprinkled the above with a little hyperbole, receive it for what it is really worth. Poets are authorised to take extraordinary licenses; but as I am a mere rhymer, it is unfair for me to trespass upon their ground. I do not mean to say, however, that the above lines are not a true transcript of my feelings toward you.

Instead of living upon bread and water, I am faring sumptuously every day! — Some weeks since, friend Simeon Brewer's family (formerly of Providence) sent me a large basket filled with various pies and cakes, all sweetened with free sugar. A little anterior to that, my noble friend George and his lady left a huge loaf of wedding cake at my office; and last week I received another entire loaf, upon which were ingeniously formed the initials of my name, from an esteemed female friend in Philadelphia. Next came your present of nut-cakes and apples, by the hands of Mr. Gray, for which I will not attempt to remunerate you with words. Instead of regretting that you could not transmit a larger box, you ought not to have been so generous. Finally, I was persuaded, a few evenings since, to mix with a large company of ladies and gentlemen, as the "lion" of the occasion; and when the cake was handed about the room, I observed strips of letter-paper affixed to each slice, upon which were written various poetical mottos upon the subject of slavery. This was an unexpected, and a very delicate compliment. On opening the neatly folded paper which was pinned to my slice of cake, I was greeted with the following Acrostic, written (as I afterwards ascertained) by a young lady whose abolitionism is of the first quality, whatever may be the merits of her poetry.

> "Goodness and mercy shall attend thy way;
> Around thy path shall brightest angels stand,
> Ready to urge thee on to noble deeds,
> Remembering thy Redeemer's blest command.
> Imprisonment, nor fear of death, hath yet
> Subdued the ardor of thy *glorious* mind!
> Oh, no! thy soul still cries, — "Give liberty!"
> Never, no, never here to be resigned." [1]

I have copied it exactly, because I suppose it will not be wholly uninteresting to you. Such tributes are pleasing to a certain extent, but here the panegyric is excessive.

Thus you perceive how bountiful are my supplies — and I have disclosed but a small part of them. Truly, it behooves me to be on my guard against dyspepsia: but it shall not have power over me, if there be any virtue in cold water.

My letter of Saturday was sealed before I received yours by Mr. Gray. Thanks without number for your invaluable favor — it fills my bosom with joy. I am reading it constantly, and feel reluctant to come to its termination. Your good opinion of me is inexpressibly delightful, because I am sure that all your expressions are sincere. O, fortunate lover that I am! to be so tenderly regarded! to possess the affections of so amiable a being! to excite so much admiration and pleasure!

I did not disclose our engagement to Mr. May, inasmuch as I had no convenient opportunity. He seems, by your letter, to have enjoyed the discovery of it on his return.

I agree with you in your estimate of the exalted worth of Mrs. May, and am proud to hear that I possess her esteem.

Mr. Gray is personally a stranger to me. He put your letter into the Post Office on his arrival, and thus prevented an introduction. He is highly regarded in Boston. I must send him a note, to thank him for bringing the box.

It amuses me to learn that your quiet village is curiously excited by the frequency of my letters to you, and of yours to me, and by a knowledge that we have plighted to each other our affections. Like every new phenomenon, it will create conversation for a time, and then become obsolete. I have no doubt, the exclamation will be made, — "How could she make such a choice! she is too good for him." But none will be able to accuse me of having chosen wrong.

The pleasant bantering between you and Mr. Gray excited a smile upon my countenance. I wish I could have been behind the door!

On Monday I sent a letter to Anna, in reply to her admirably written note. In it I transmitted (as I do in this) my best regards to your parents, and Sarah and Henry — and to you my love.

I remain, purely, steadfastly, and obediently yours,

Wm. Lloyd Garrison.

Miss H. E. Benson.

☞ I felt alarmed at my boldness in sending you such a salutation upon the cheek by Miss Prudence, but am happy to be assured that it gave you no offence but rather pleasure.

My amiable partner, Mr. Knapp, reciprocates your friendship in full. He feels mortified, however, that at the time of your visit, he was so circumstanced as to be unable to pay you that respect and attention which you ought ever to command.

☞ Do not apologize for your handwriting. If you labor hereafter to make it better, I shall be sorry. It is perfectly plain and legible.

P.S. Just as I am folding this, I am greeted with your favor of Monday evening. Every word of it is precious. You are kind, very kind, in being so prompt to answer my poor letters. Although the word "private" was not written upon the preceding one, yet my friend Knapp very properly refused to open it, on taking it out of the Post Office. *No person sees your epistles but myself.* I keep them as secret and choice as the miser does his gold.

It is very probable that I shall be in Brooklyn on Monday evening, although I may be detained until Wednesday noon. I am not yet decided whether to go direct, or via Providence. You had better not write until you hear from me again. You will afflict me by making any special preparation to receive me.

☞ Of course, my Sonnet was intended for you.

ALS: Villard Papers, Harvard College Library.

1. The young female author of this verse has not been identified. Garrison's opinion of its quality is not sufficiently high for it to be by Elizabeth Margaret Chandler, his favorite among young ladies who wrote antislavery verse.

142

TO EDMUND B. DEARBORN

Boston, April 18, 1834.

Mr. E. B. Dearborn,

Dear Sir — This will be handed you by Mr. Beckwith from Western Reserve College, Hudson, Ohio, an ardent friend to the glorious cause of immediate emancipation.[1] He is in pursuit of an opportunity for a fishing voyage for the benefit of his health.

Any facilities you can bestow upon him, in furtherance of his object, will confer obligations upon us which will be cheerfully reciprocated whenever you will afford us opportunity.

Garrison & Knapp.

ALS: Collection of John L. Severance of New York City. This letter is in the hand of Isaac Knapp.

Edmund Batchelder Dearborn (1806–1886), from New Hampshire, was teaching school in Marblehead, Massachusetts. Later in life he moved to Boston, where he became the librarian of the Historic-Genealogical Society.

1. Little is known of Elijah Beckwith except that he was enrolled in the class of 1836 at Western Reserve University, then located in Hudson rather than Cleveland.

143

TO GEORGE W. BENSON

Brooklyn, April 23, 1834.

My dear George:

You see, by the date of my letter, where I am — in the place which is now the dearest spot to me on earth. But, here at the outset, let me caution you not to expect a regular epistle. I have seized my pen merely to send you a little token of my good will and friendship; for necessity compels me to be brief, inasmuch as the bearer of this, (our good friend Rev. Thomas Williams,) leaves here immediately for Providence, via Pomfret.[1]

This, you are aware, is "Friendship's Valley" to our excellent friend Prudence Crandall; but I need a dearer appellation — not that I esteem *friendship* less, but *love* more. Here centre all the affections of my heart; here is the object, who, of all others on the face of the earth, is the chief and the most precious to me; and here I am received in a manner too kind, and too indulgent, for one so unworthy as myself. Of course — aside from the painful consciousness that I do not deserve half of the kindnesses I am receiving — I am exquisitely happy. Dear Helen is in excellent health and spirits, and manifests a truly tender and sincere attachment for me; and the more I see and associate with her, the more closely does she entwine herself around my heart. I trust that the ardor of my affection for her is not less sincere and apparent. My pleasure is so delightful, that I am almost afraid to move, lest, perchance, I awake, and find that it is merely the illusion of a dream.

To-morrow, I shall go away sighing — probably to Norwich and Essex Ferry, from thence to New-York, and then to Philadelphia, in which city I shall tarry till a day or two before the national meeting in New-York. My anticipations are highly raised in regard to that meeting — but I know not whether I shall be able to prepare a speech for the occasion. I believe it is expected that Judge Jay,[2] Pres. Green,[3] Rev. Mr. Phelps, and Rev. Mr. May, will then deliver addresses. These are all strong men — good speakers — and truly respectable citizens.

I have just received my portrait as engraved by my dear friend Jocelyn,[4] and am sorry to say that all who have seen it agree with me in the opinion that it is a total failure. I am truly surprised, that, familiar as he is with my features, he has erred so widely in his attempt to delineate them. On his own account, too, I am sorry — for he will fail to make such a sale of the picture as will remunerate him for his labor — at least, I presume this will be the fact.

——— But here I must stop — abruptly. Helen and the rest of the family send their love to you.

Your true friend and devoted brother,

Wm. Lloyd Garrison.

Mr. G. W. Benson.

ALS: Garrison Papers, Boston Public Library; extract printed in *Life*, I, 344.

1. Thomas Williams (1779–1876), a Yale graduate and Congregational minister later familiarly known as Father Williams, was sufficiently dynamic and eccentric in person, dress, and style to draw large audiences in Providence.
2. William Jay (1789–1858), son of Justice John Jay, graduate of Yale, judge of the court of Westchester County, New York, and an active champion of abolition.
3. Beriah Green (1795–1874), liberal Presbyterian, and then Congregationalist minister and abolitionist, since 1833 president of Oneida Institute at Whitesboro, New York.
4. Simeon Jocelyn.

144

TO HELEN E. BENSON

Hartford, Thursday Evening,
8 o'clock, April 24, 1834.

Dearest, sweetest, kindest, best!

I am no longer William Lloyd Garrison, but Helen Eliza Benson. There is such a fine and perfect affinity of souls between us, that I have lost my identity, and am now completely engrossed in your person. You are now in "Friendship's Vale" — so am I — all of me, except the physical man and the material matter. Would that they were there also!

Last evening, at this hour, I was sitting by your side, with an eloquent heart but barren lips — almost rendered miserable by an overwhelming pressure of bliss! Excessive happiness carried me to the verge of unhappiness!

This morning, at eight o'clock, we parted, sighing and kissing — with no hope of seeing each other's face again under a lapse of three weeks; but we solaced ourselves with the promise, mutually made, to send epistolary favors, and hold communion through the medium of the pen and letter-paper.

This evening I am some forty or fifty miles from you — that is, in a *bodily* sense; and having just arrived, and eaten a hasty supper, I seize the first moment allowed me to send you a few lines, which I am sure will be received with pleasure; *and to increase your pleasure is henceforth to be the governing object of my life.*

It is scarcely necessary for me to say that I had an agreeable ride with my dear Henry, and that I parted from him with regret. For about twenty-five miles, I had not a single companion in the coach, but was "monarch of all I surveyed." [1] Ah! I forget myself — *you* were with me in all your loveliness. I gazed intently upon your features — I pressed you to my bosom — I felt the warm glow of your soft cheek kindling my own in contact — I poured into your ear the tenderest expressions of attachment, and received [them] back again clothed in a more endearing form — I held you by the hand, as if no inducement could tear me from your presence — I besought you to pardon the ardor of my love, and to indulge its manifestation as far as purity of thought and propriety of action would allow. In short, I dwelt upon all your movements, your words, your looks, your tokens of affection, until I almost fancied that you were indeed before me. The spell was broken by the introduction of two middle-aged ladies into the coach, whom I succeeded in drawing into a conversation on the subject of slavery and colonization. They were highly intelligent, and devotedly pious; but had both been friendly to the American Colonization Society, although now disposed to give it up. One of them whispered something to the other, who said to me inquiringly, "Is this Mr. Garrison from Boston?" "Yes, madam, I am that terrible fanatic," was my answer. They were evidently pleased at the discovery, and desired me to give them all the information that I could, in reference to the great controversy now going on between the friends of freedom and the upholders of oppression. I did so, and believe all that I said will be carefully treasured up in their memories, and ultimately bring forth good fruit.

Dear Helen, am I not a strange compound? In battling with a whole nation, I am as impetuous, as daring, and as unconquerable, as a lion; but in your presence, I am as timid, and gentle, and submissive, as a dove.

I cannot express to you how great was my satisfaction, on arriving at your house, to meet you dressed in the same simple manner in which in all my preceding visits I had seen you. It was a fine proof of your good sense and sterling integrity, in rejecting all tawdry ornaments and artificial aids to the embellishment of your person. How lovely this single circumstance made you appear in my eyes! — Truly, not one young lady out of ten thousand, in a first interview with her lover, but would have endeavored falsely to heighten her charms, and allure by outward attractions.

"Beauty, when unadorned, 's adorned the most." [2]

I begin to tremble at the power of my love for you: but I will strive to keep it within those limits which duty to God and my country requires. O, how indescribably blissful were our recent interviews!

"Hours of bliss, too quickly vanished,
When will aught like ye return?" [3]

To-morrow morning I start at an early hour for New-Haven, and shall probably be greeted on the road by the carol of some gladsome bird; but I shall then mournfully repeat the lines which I recited to you when standing by your side —

"These ears, alas! for other notes repine,
A different object do these eyes require!"
"I fruitless mourn to her who cannot hear,
And weep the more, because I weep in vain." [4]

Probably, as soon as this reaches you, George's lady and Miss Chace will have arrived in Brooklyn.[5] I hope to see them on my return, for I "desire their better acquaintance." Be sure to give them my kind remembrances.

Don't forget the poetical effusion, commencing —

"A letter my love, O, send to me!" [6]

Remember me at Philadelphia in an epistle, as well as at New-York, and you will unseal a new fountain of gratitude.

Tell the gentle Anne that I tenderly desire her to cover both of your fair cheeks with sweet kisses for me, and I will settle the account on my return. I rely upon receiving an epistle from her by Mr. May.

This wretched scrawl requires many apologies for its ill-looking, ill-written, and ill-composed appearance; but I do assure you it has been prepared with a great effort, and in very great haste, in the midst of tavern company. I must retire to rest my weary limbs — so, good night! good night! May Heaven watch over us both for good! I remain,

Yours, in the dearest bonds,

Wm. Lloyd Garrison.

Miss H. E. Benson.

ALS: Villard Papers, Harvard College Library; extract printed in Walter M. Merrill, "A Passionate Attachment: William Lloyd Garrison's Courtship of Helen Eliza Benson," *The New England Quarterly,* 29:190 (June 1956).

1. William Cowper, "Verses Supposed to Be Written by Alexander Selkirk," line 1.
2. Garrison slightly adapts James Thomson, *The Seasons,* "Autumn," line 206.
3. Unidentified.
4. Garrison slightly adapts Thomas Gray, "Sonnet: On the Death of Richard West," lines 5–6, 13–14.
5. Eliza Chace (*c.* 1809–1840), Helen's best friend, was the sister of George W. Benson's partner, William M. Chace. She subsequently married Thomas Davis, a member of Congress.
6. Not identified.

145

TO HELEN E. BENSON

[☞ For dear Helen.]

New Haven, April 25, 1834.

My stately Queen:

I arrived this afternoon in this beautiful town from Hartford; and having the good fortune to ride in company with one of the best members of the famous Hartford Convention, I passed my time very entertainingly, without experiencing any fatigue.[1] — We discussed, in the most amicable manner, a great variety of topics, appertaining to slavery, politics, morals, &c. &c.

The weather is cold and lowering, and rather sensibly affects my body. But although gloom is without, sunshine is within my breast — here all is calm, blissful and changeless.

I have just taken from my trunk the precious lock of hair which you kindly gave to me at our separation. It is prettily braided, and tastefully bound. I have pressed it to my lips, and shall treasure it up as a choice token of your esteem.

Unquestionably, I shall have frequent occasion to praise you; but you have too much genuine modesty, and too clear a conviction of your own demerits, to let it inflate your vanity. It is lawful for you to be happy, in knowing that you are so dear to my heart; but you will deem it weak and criminal to suffer any panegyric to blind your own judgment, and destroy your natural humility. My praise of you shall ever be the unaffected language of my heart: — its object shall be to cheer and strengthen you, — not to create or excite any vain feelings.

We are now trustingly looking forward to a period of exquisite bliss, subsequent to our contemplated marriage. If the future be full of hope, it is also full of uncertainty. Appointment is as closely allied to disappointment, as life is to death. Let us remember our own mortality — that "we all do fade as a leaf" — [2] that here the cup of joy often contains a bitter ingredient — that all things wear the marks of change and decay — and that the dispensations of Providence are not infrequently dark and afflictive. Let us not build for time but eternity.

It is truly delightful to know that we possess each other's affections, in all their purity and strength; — but, oh! how incomparably more precious is that assurance, which I trust we both cherish, leading us to believe that we are loved by our heavenly Father, and that we love Him supremely! — Dear Helen, in our morning and evening devotions, when bowing in our hearts at the mercy-seat, let us pray that we may be kept from all sin — from the temptations and snares of an evil world — from idolatry — from slothfulness and folly — and that we may be continually replenished with heavenly wisdom, purity, goodness and truth. It is a wonderful favor to be a dutiful child of God — an obedient disciple of the meek and lowly Jesus.

The deeper I get in my moral researches, the more does my soul sicken at the depravity of the times. As a nation, we are "full of wounds, and bruises, and putrefying sores." [3] Men are profane — impure — vicious — rebellious. The leprosy of corruption covers society, and the cancer of selfishness is preying upon its vitals. As a people, we are by no means backward in our professions of christianity and republicanism; but it is certain that we draw nigh unto God with our lips, while our hearts are far from him — else we should bring forth the peaceable fruits of righteousness.

I cannot yet determine, whether I shall attempt to make a speech at the anniversary in New-York. [4] This will depend upon many contingencies. Unless I am pretty sure of doing justice to myself, as well as to the cause of human rights, I shall be dumb, and let another occupy my place. But I have a strong desire to improve that extraordinary occasion, in vindicating the doctrine of immediate emancipation, and in depicting the odious features of slavery in all their frightfulness. Pray for me that I may receive wisdom and strength from above, equal to my necessities.

I shall depart from this place at 4 o'clock in the morning, and probably be in New-York about three o'clock in the afternoon.

This morning I put a letter for you into the Post Office at Hartford.

You see how much you are in my thoughts, by my writing another this evening. I shall direct this to Henry, as I must leave it with the bar-keeper to put it into the mail for me, as the Post-Office is now closed.

By turning to one of my letters, you will see that I prohibited your paying the postage upon your letters to me — but you still continue to do so. Do oblige and gratify me, my sweet Helen, by discontinuing that practice. Will you?

To-day I have been rummaging my trunk to find the bundle of letters from you, that I might peruse them with new delight — but I cannot find them! — I must have left them inadvertently in Brooklyn. If you have found them, keep them as carefully as you would my life. How much do I regret that I have them not with me!

My friend, the Rev. Mr. Jocelyn, is in New-York — but I have seen his brother, and candidly told him what my friends think of the engraved portrait. He thinks himself that it is defective, but that it may be materially improved.

☞ Do not forget Philadelphia. You can scarcely imagine how much joy a letter from you in that city will give me. I hope to be there on Monday afternoon, and remain in it all next week.

You see I am growing negligent in my chirography — but you will kindly excuse it, as it is *readible,* and as you know I *can* write better.

I freight this letter with all sorts of precious tokens of attachment for Anne, Sarah, Henry, your parents, Mr. and Mrs. May — &c. &c. I have nothing to give *you,* which you do not already possess.

Your faithful lover,

Wm. Lloyd Garrison.

Miss H. E. Benson.

ALS: Villard Papers, Harvard College Library.

1. The Hartford Convention (December 15, 1814–January 4, 1815) brought together twenty-six New England Federalists for a series of secret meetings. The Federalists were animated by opposition to the War of 1812 and wished to revise the Constitution and reassert state and regional rights. The most prominent figure at the convention was Garrison's old idol, Harrison Gray Otis.

2. Isaiah 64:6.

3. Garrison adapts Isaiah 1:6.

4. Garrison refers to the first anniversary of the founding of the New York City Anti-Slavery Society, to take place in May.

146

TO HELEN E. BENSON

New-York City, April 27, [1834].
Sabbath Morning.

My dear Helen:

What loveliness, and purity, and benevolence, and holiness, cluster around the Sabbath-day! — Even limiting its utility to the renovation of those bodily powers which a week of unmitigated toil has prostrated, how good is it for man and beast! But this is not its limitation. The Sabbath was made as well for the soul as the body of man. It is a beautiful, though imperfect, type of heavenly rest. It is a rich and special provision for those who hunger and thirst after righteousness. Shall we not remember to keep it holy? [1]

Yesterday was a dark, cold and turbulent day; but how fine a contrast does this morning present! The sun is rising splendidly — the wings of the wind are folded to repose — the sky is of a clear blue color — and a holy quietude has taken possession of the earth. How emblematical of the superior excellence of this sacred day over every other!

When I awoke to consciousness, my thoughts went heavenward, borne on the pinions of gratitude and devotion. I felt unusual tenderness of spirit, in view of my own vileness, and the ravishing perfection of my Savior. On retiring to rest last night, I felt chilled and fatigued in body, and somewhat depressed in mind; but on waking this morning, the chill, and fatigue, and depression, were gone, and in their place had come a genial glow, a buoyant elasticity, and a strong assurance.

"When all thy mercies, O my God,
    My rising soul surveys,
Transported with the view, I'm lost
    In wonder, love, and praise." [2]

On a day like this, I love to repeat the following verse from De Rancy:

"Dear is the hallowed morn to me,
    When village bells awake the day,
And by their sacred minstrelsy,
    Call me from earthly cares away." [3]

It has ever been the grand device of Satan to vitiate the Sabbath, and destroy its sanctity. Let him succeed in blotting it out, and he will hold complete dominion over the universe. Infidels hate it as they hate its great Author. France has shown us the horrors which must ensue upon its extinction. In her atheistical fury, she annihilated the Sabbath by express statute, and thereby became "a reeking hell." [4] Unspeakably dreadful, yet inestimably salutary, is the lesson she has taught a rebellious world, how fearful a thing it is to depart from the living God.

That the Sabbath has imperative and abiding claims to universal obedience is as certain as that it is sinful to steal or covet, or take the name of God in vain, or have any other God before him. When was the fourth commandment revoked? Dare any to be so presumptuous as to erase it from the ten? Why not strike out the first — the third — the fifth — the seventh? Why not repeal the whole decalogue?

You, my sweet Helen, are too familiar with the liberality of my mind to suppose that I am contending for a bigotted observance of this holy day. Bigotry is a monster, ferocious, sightless, bloody. I abhor it to the full measure of my mental and spiritual powers. No one is less tenacious of devotional forms than myself, or more desirous that every man should worship God according to the dictates of *his own* conscience. Indeed, there is so much of the *form* of godliness, and so little of its *power*, in our land, that I am compelled to take refuge in silent meditation and secret prayer, more frequently than in outward exhibitions of worship. The most hypocritical and superstitious are the most punctilious and rigid in all religious ceremonies, and the most unsparing in their invective towards those who pay more attention to the spirit than to the letter of the law. These proud pharisees are described in the following graphic manner, by Him who searches the heart and tries the reins: — "Yet they seek me daily, and delight to know my ways, as a nation that did righteousness, and forsook not the ordinance of their God: they ask of me the ordinances of justice; they take delight in approaching to God. Wherefore have we fasted, say they, and thou seest not? wherefore have we afflicted our soul, and thou takest no knowledge?"

What is the reply of Jehovah? — "Behold, in the day of your fast ye find pleasure, and exact all your labors. Behold, ye fast for strife and debate, and to smite with the first of wickedness." [5] The hypocrites!

The noblest moral phenomenon — the sublimest spectacle on earth, is the return of the Sabbath. What a tide of worldliness was yesterday pouring through every avenue and section of this mighty city! The thunder of clashing interests broke out in deafening peals. The streets were crowded with men and beasts, and merchandize and wares. Eternity, in the minds of the busy populace, had seemingly dwindled to a point, and Time expanded to the dimension of Eternity. But the morn of the holy Sabbath has come, and the proud waves of selfishness are stayed. The noise of a boisterous trade is scarcely as audible as the whisper of the passing breeze. The dwellers in the city no longer throng at the Exchange, or infest the streets. God reigns in awful majesty to-day. To-day, is taken an accurate measurement of time and eternity. To-day, Satan's empire totters to its foundations; and to-day, Christ is the power of God, and the wisdom of God, unto salvation and eternal life, in all who repent and believe.

We all need the weekly purification, assistance and rest of the Sabbath. It is but a small portion of our time that God requires us specially and exclusively to dedicate to his worship — only one day in seven! Our souls, in spite of all our watchfulness, become so soiled and tainted by the dust and corruption of six days' servile labor, as to render indispensable, for their preservation, the purifying and life-giving influences of a day like this.

This, dear Helen, is rather an essay than a letter. I have written it, because I think it will be acceptable to your pure mind, and because "it is lawful *to do well* on the Sabbath-day" [6] — and I know not that I could have spent an hour more profitably.

With the most ardent attachment, I remain,

Yours, unceasingly,

Wm. Lloyd Garrison.

Miss H. E. Benson.

Sabbath Evening.

Although the morning was so placid and beautiful, yet the day has proved *excessively* cold and stormy. For an hour or two, *snow* fell quite briskly! So much for April, and my unmerited sonnet upon it!

To-day I have heard two excellent sermons from the Rev. Mr. Williams and Rev. Mr. Cornish, colored preachers — and have taken by the hand many of my colored friends, who were overjoyed to see me.[7]

To-morrow evening I shall meet some of the leading colored gentlemen, in relation to the future concerns of the Liberator, and on Tuesday morning start for Philadelphia, where I shall probably remain until Saturday. A week from that time, I hope to be sitting by your side in Brooklyn.

Tell my dear friend May that he is calculated upon to speak at the anniversary of the American Anti-Slavery Society, by the Board of Managers. They need some thunder and lightning here. Judge Jay will be absent from the city at the time of the meeting, and therefore will make no speech. My best regards to all.

ALS: Villard Papers, Harvard College Library.

1. In light of his later views, Garrison's attitude here and in his letter to Helen (194), May 4, 1835, seems surprisingly conservative.
2. Garrison quotes from a hymn by Joseph Addison.
3. John W. Cunningham, "De Rancé, a Poem" — also sung as a hymn.
4. Unidentified.
5. Isaiah 58:2, 3, 4.
6. Matthew 12:12.

7. Garrison refers to two Negroes who were both ministers and editors. Ransom G. Williams was the publishing agent of the American Anti-Slavery Society and on the staff of the society's official organ, the *Emancipator*. Samuel E. Cornish became in 1837 the editor of the *Colored American*, in which he criticized Boston Negroes for siding with Garrison in his conflict with the orthodox clergy. For Garrison's surprisingly restrained response see his editorials in *The Liberator* for October 6, 13, 20, and November 3, 1837.

147

TO HELEN E. BENSON

Philadelphia, May 1, 1834.

Gentle One:

Do I love you too much? Do I think of you too often? Do I devote too much time in writing to you? This I know — that our separation is truly painful to my heart; that you occupy my thoughts more than any other human being; that in addressing myself to you so often, I am not only permitted to cherish the pleasing assurance that I am contributing to your happiness, but enabled to pour out the tender emotions of my breast; and that I might as well attempt to forget my own unworthiness, as one so dear and meritorious as my own sweet Helen.

How wearily Time pursues his flight! And yet so slothfully and imperfectly do I improve the moments which indulgent Heaven is bestowing upon me, that, tardily as they now seem to move, I ought to desire their detention, rather than their more rapid passage.

Still, I sigh for your presence. Happily, your tenderly expressive and most affectionate letter of the 28th ultimo was received this morning, and melancholy now gives place to delight. Oh, my chosen one! to think I am so dear to you! to receive such renewed and ardent expressions of your love! to be favored so promptly with this fresh token of your attachment! why should I not be happy?

The flight of Rumor surpasses in speed that of Time, and is surpassed only by the lightning rapidity of Thought. I had scarcely interchanged the usual salutations with the family of my friend Joseph Sharpless in this city, on my arrival, before Mary,[1] with a laughing countenance, said — "What is her name, William? They say it is Helen Benson, a sister of George — I wish thee much joy!" — "You are quizzical, Mary," said I, "and there is some meaning to such language, if one could only find it out." So, after a little humorous evasion, I was forced to make confession of our attachment for each other. My Sonnets to you seem to have awakened suspicion universally, and caused much speculation among my male and female friends as to the chosen one.[2] Many thought it must be Prudence, whom I intended to take, "for better, for worse" — while others surmised a number of females out of whom I had selected a future *cara sposa*.

For some time to come, our names will be coupled [. . .] and uttered by thousands; and, doubtless, it would greatly amuse us both if we could hear all that is said about us. "I hope she is a good abolitionist," says a young female friend, "else I *will* not love her." "And do you think, for one moment," I pleasantly retort, "that I would chose any other than a good abolitionist?"

Well, dear Helen, let a curious and talkative world gossip. No matter whether it approves or disapproves of our choice — no matter whether it praises or disparages us — no matter whether it smiles or frowns upon us — no matter whether it prophesies good or evil; — happy in ourselves — conscious of a oneness of souls between us — rejoicing in each other's fervent love — resolving with all fidelity to make good the pledges of our affection — and feeling ourselves united together by the most sacred ties — what need we care? Let us beware of flattery, and trample calumny beneath our feet. Our happiness measurably depends upon ourselves, not upon others. I am certain that nothing will be wanting, on your part, to strow my path through life with flowers; and, if I know my own heart, there is no sacrifice, consistent with my allegiance to the King of kings, too great for me to make, to perfect and secure your bliss upon earth. In consenting to be mine, you have manifested great condescension, surprising sympathy, a generous devotion, and a proud contempt for worldly splendor and opulence. Much do I mourn that I have so little to give you; but I am comforted in knowing the humility and contentment of your mind, and how heartily you despise the gilded trappings of a fashionable world. Engaged in the noblest cause of benevolence which has ever received the approbation of God, or the countenance of man, I am necessarily precluded from heaping up treasures upon earth. But little do I covet those treasures — I trust I am laying up those which shall never perish, "where neither moth nor rust shall corrupt, nor thieves break through and steal."[3] But I shall not lack a full supply of earthly comforts. — All the aid that I shall need, will be liberally extended to me. If my enemies are bitter and numerous, my friends are proportionably kind and steadfast. The prospect is truly encouraging.

I have not yet written a syllable of my speech for the annual meeting in New-York! — In this city, I have so many friends and acquaintance as to deprive me of rest. Hundreds are grieved because it is out of my power to visit them.

You express some anxiety on the score of my health, in your letter. My *bodily* health, I think, was never better — it approaches closely to perfection. It is true, when I was about bidding you farewell, my *heart* was sick — I felt sad and faint, as at times I now do — but I am not ill from any disease. May Heaven vouchsafe to you a continuance of that bloom and beauty which mantled and adorned your countenance when I was sitting by your side, and which are the best signs of a well-regulated appetite and a contented disposition. The wise man has truly said that "a sound heart is *the life of the flesh.*" [4] Possessing such a heart, and following such a diet as you do, you need not be apprehensive on the score of health.

I do not wonder that you could discover no resemblance [. . .] in my portrait, and was forced to turn away, "sick at heart." It is indeed an excellent engraving, but a most unfortunate caricature. — My friend Jocelyn has sent on to this city what he calls an improved copy of it, but all who have seen it pronounce it an utter failure.[5] It is wholly inexplicable to me how he can imagine it to be a good likeness. He has given me a face as broad as that of a Dutch burgher — "there is no speculation in those eyes" [6] — he has copied neither my nose nor my mouth — the forehead is too low and too retreating — and he has advanced my looks some ten or twenty years! — I regret the failure, not so much on my own account, nor even on that of my friends, but on Mr. Jocelyn's, as he has spent so much time, labor and skill to make the portrait a good one.

I am getting to be quite in demand among artists. One of them has got out a large lithographic portrait of me, in handsome style, which is a much better likeness than Mr. Jocelyn's; but it is not the thing. Another has published a smaller one — but that also is a failure. Another has been sketching my face to-day, with tolerable success; and another earnestly desires me to sit to him before I leave — but I shall not be able to comply with his request.[7] I will bring with me to Brooklyn specimens of these several attempts. Is there any thing in my countenance that cannot be painted?

You think I shall be surprised to receive an epistle [from] you in Philadelphia. No, my love, far otherwise — I have been anticipating confidently your favor which was received to-day, and should have wept if disappointment had been my lot. This makes my fourth letter to you since we parted — one written at Hartford, another at New-Haven, a third at New-York — all which I hope are now in your possession, excepting the present.[8] It is not probable that I shall write again until after the annual meeting — and perhaps conclude to pay you first a visit in person.

☞ When our wedding takes place, I hope we shall see among the guests "blind Eunice" and "M. Burnet," the latter of whom seems so anxious to witness so imposing and important a ceremony.

☞ You urge me to burn up your letter, and forget you for the time being! O, no — no — no! I *cannot* do either.

I am feasting upon the expectation of receiving letters from you and my dear Anna by Mr. May, on Monday next.

I send you a thousand kisses. More may be expected on the return of

Your dutiful and affectionate lover,

Wm. Lloyd Garrison.

Miss H. E. Benson.

ALS: Villard Papers, Harvard College Library.

1. Presumably the wife of Joseph Sharpless.
2. Garrison printed sonnets addressed to Helen in *The Liberator* for April 12 and 19.
3. Matthew 6:20.
4. Proverbs 14:30.
5. Garrison refers to the steel engraving made by Simeon S. Jocelyn from the oil portrait by his brother Nathaniel Jocelyn.
6. Shakespeare, *Macbeth*, III, iv, 95.
7. Unfortunately diligent search in various libraries and museums has not revealed the identity of the several artists besides Jocelyn referred to in this paragraph, though the "large lithographic portrait" is apparently the same as the unsigned one in the collections of the New-York Historical Society.
8. See the letters dated April 24, 25, 27 (144, 145, 146).

148

TO HELEN E. BENSON

Boston, May 16, 1834.

My sweet Flower of Friendship Valley:

This wintry weather is making fearful havoc among the buds, and blossoms, and flowers of Spring, and causing every thing beautiful and frail to droop. Yesterday was as cold as January: we had an abundance of ice, and in the morning a smart snow-storm! This is worthy of being chronicled. To-day the temperature is severe; and the genial sun, instead of dispensing his usual heat, seems really to need a huge Lehigh fire [1] to keep himself warm! Happily, it is not in the power of all the elements to lessen the ardor of my affection for you.

I have been home but two days; and yet, so completely do you hold the mastery over my heart, I cannot delay any longer in sending you a new token of my love. You know I told you to expect a letter once in six weeks; but, when I am absent from you, two days are quite as long as six weeks spent by your side.

My dear Helen, I mourn our separation. Your kind endearments, during my late visit, have bound you yet more closely to my heart, and make your absence a source of poignant regret. I confess, I am very deeply affected in recalling to mind the tenderness of your manner, the warmth of your affection, and the charming innocence of your behaviour. If, in my endeavors to manifest something of that high regard which I cherish for you, I said or did aught which was unworthy of me, you will attribute it to my passionate attachment, and so pardon me. But I remember nothing with which to upbraid myself; for I love you with a pure heart, and would not for worlds behave unseemly in your sight. O, those blissful hours which we spent together! O, those tender glances which you bestowed upon me! O, those choice expressions which flowed from your ruby lips! Truly, "I am sick of love." "Sweet is thy voice; thou hast doves' eyes; thy countenance is comely." [2]

If Heaven permit, in the course of six months "we twain shall be one." That time will soon pass away. It exhilarates me to think of seeing you morning, noon, and night. 1 am sure that you will make a good wife — I will try to be a good husband.

My ride to Providence was exceedingly uncomfortable, in consequence of the severity of the weather. The coach was so crowded that I chose to ride with the driver; and I therefore had not the privilege of enjoying the company of Miss Lee.[3] After hastily partaking of a supper at the hotel, I went to College-street, and spent the evening with my excellent friends Mary and George, who received me with a brotherly and sisterly regard.[4] The more I see of the former, the more highly do I appreciate her worth. She has a first-rate mind, a clearness and copiousness of thought, and very fine manners. I must certainly secure her as a correspondent. As for the latter, it is as unnecessary, as it would be impracticable, for me to say how much I esteem him.

On taking the coach the next morning for Boston, I had no alternative but to ride wedged up between solid masses of human flesh, (and not very desirable flesh, I assure you,) or sit with the driver. Of the two evils, I chose the latter, but suffered much by my exposure — for it was almost a freezing day. My cold was somewhat aggravated, and is not yet removed; but it is now beginning to yield. Be not the least uneasy on my account, for I am habitually watchful over my health. I am anxious, however, in regard to your cough. Remember that this is winter, instead of spring, and do not unnecessarily expose yourself to the chilling influences of this most extraordinary season.

Now, my pretty dove, shall I tell you something to make you jealous? I think I see a smile on your countenance, and hear you say pleasantly, "O, to be sure!"

Judge of my surprise and consternation, on opening a letter put into my hands by Mr. Knapp, to find proposals from a handsome female acquaintance of mine, (a member of the Society of Friends,) for uniting herself to me in marriage![5] She commences her letter quite lovingly — thus: "Dear William — I venture to give thee this sweet ap-

pellation. I have latterly thought that my peace of mind, and usefulness in society, will depend on a union with thee. I have had a slight
fancy for many who have been ready to make pretensions, but one
only has captured my heart — my hand and heart are thine. If the
union, dear William, should take place, and if thee thinks well of it, I
would like that in whatever manner it is to be accomplished, it may be
performed in a public meeting, appointed for the purpose, and our
friends be invited. * * * I expect to be disowned from our meeting,
but I would rather be disowned than to encourage superstitious
bigotry" — &c. &c. &c.

This is rather a serious matter, my dear Helen, and therefore it
would be wrong for me to indulge in any levity. Indeed, I am pained
by the occurrence. I have sent a reply to the young lady, in which I
fully disclosed the obligations which bind us together, and stated that
I had long since given my heart to Helen Eliza Benson, whom I loved
beyond any other human being, and to whom I fondly expected to be
united, in the course of a few months. It must be a sad thing to love,
and get nothing in return but bitter disappointment. But the fault is
not mine. Pray, keep this a secret in the family. When I see your sweet
face again, I will show you the entire letter from which I have made
the above extract.

I forgot to leave some money with Henry, to defray the expense of
bringing my portrait [6] from Norwich to Brooklyn, but I will remunerate him when we meet. I hope the portrait came safely to hand
— not on account of its being a good likeness, but because the artist is
desirous of receiving it again.

I am anticipating a rich treat at our Convention.[7] There will unquestionably be a large number of delegates, and a strong array of
talent. May the Almighty smile upon our exertion, and crown them
with success. Day after day the victims of tyranny are multiplying, and
the necessity for active and laborious effort to redeem them becomes
more and more imperious. O, shame upon my stupidity!

This is Friday noon. I wish my letter could reach you to-morrow, but
you will not receive it until Monday at 12 o'clock. Shall we not complain to the Postmaster General at Washington, and request him to
establish a daily mail between Brooklyn and Boston, not only for our
accommodation, but also for that of other lovers who may be similarly
situated?

Do not fail to write by my well-beloved brother May, even if you
send but six lines. You must be conscious that I shall be sighing to
hear from you. Pity and relieve me.

Say to my dear friend Anna, who grows continually upon my esteem,
that I shall actively strive to send her an epistle next week. What an

angel she is! My very cordial and grateful regards to your dear parents, whom I long to call *my* parents, and also to Sarah and Henry. "Blind Eunice and M. Burton" are both in my memory. To my pleasant and highly estimable friend Mr. Gray, I beg you to offer my thanks for his many kindnesses shown to me. Do not forget to make my compliments to Mrs. May, and kiss her dear little Charlotte many times for me. Ah, that you were here to receive the kisses of

Your happy lover,

Wm. Lloyd Garrison.

Miss H. E. Benson.

ALS: Villard Papers, Harvard College Library; extract printed in Walter M. Merrill, "A Passionate Attachment: William Lloyd Garrison's Courtship of Helen Eliza Benson," *The New England Quarterly*, 29:193–194 (June 1956).

1. Apparently a fire built of Lehigh coal.
2. Garrison telescopes three passages from Song of Solomon 2:5, 14, and 4:1.
3. Miss Lee is unidentified except that her brother was soon to be employed in Garrison's office; see letter 172, to Helen, August 23, 1834.
4. Garrison refers to the second oldest of Helen's five sisters and to her brother George W. Benson.
5. It would seem that the letter in question reached Garrison's office during his absence from Boston some time between Monday, April 21, and Saturday, April 26, though he did not receive it until his return and shortly before writing this letter. (The date of arrival can be established by the fact that the correspondent's name is listed in *The Liberator* of April 27 among those whose letters had been received at the office since the last issue of the paper.) Garrison identifies the writer of the letter in his to Helen of May 30 (152). She is Leah Fell (1798–1891), the thirty-six-year-old daughter of Benjamin and Jane Fell of East Land, Lancaster County, Pennsylvania. According to the family genealogy (Sarah M. Fell, *Genealogy of the Fell Family in America* . . . , Philadelphia, 1887, p. 138), she was a gifted woman who had some reputation as a teacher, but whose mind became clouded in later years.
6. Supposedly the one by Nathaniel Jocelyn.
7. Garrison refers to the convention of delegates from various antislavery societies throughout New England to be held in Boylston Hall in Boston the last week of the month.

149
TO ROBERT PURVIS

Boston, May 20, 1834.

My dear Purvis:

Since my return, I have been so disturbed and distracted by conflicting engagements and duties, as to be unable to send you half as many letters to my dear friends in England, as I contemplated when I saw you. You will be disappointed, and I am sorry; but I dare not delay any longer. Should you fail to go immediately, (and I know not how you can be spared from this country,) I wish you would put the accompanying letters into the Liverpool and London mail-bags, erasing the lines at the bottom referring to yourself.

The persons whom I meant to introduce you to by letter, are — James Ryley and Dr. Hancock, Liverpool; Joseph Sturge, Birmingham; Arthur West, Bath; Elizabeth and Mary Dudley, Peckham, near London; William Allen, Richard Barrett, Joseph Phillips, Danl. O'Connell, Dr. Lushington, George Stephen, Joseph and Emanuel Cooper, John Scoble, &c. &c.[1] I hope you will become acquainted with all these.

You will be able to communicate many interesting facts to our English brethren. Be sure to take out with you our latest anti-slavery publications. Mr. Bell [2] will give you copies of the Liberator.

If practicable, let me hear from you on your arrival in England.

I know not how to bid you farewell. May Heaven, my dear friend, bless, prosper, and preserve you — grant you a swift and pleasant passage — and return you in safety to the bosom of your family and the arms of your friends. You are very dear to my heart. I honor and esteem you beyond the power of speech to tell.

Remember me in a very special manner to my dear friend, the Rev. Nathl. Paul, and also to his estimable lady.

I write and conclude in great haste, but am ever

Your affectionate friend,

Wm. Lloyd Garrison.

Mr. Robt Purvis.

ALS: Weston Papers, Boston Public Library; a handwritten transcription of the same letter is in the Garrison Papers, Boston Public Library.

1. Among this list of Garrison's British associates James Ryley, Thomas Hancock, Daniel O'Connell, Stephen Lushington, and Sir George Stephen have been identified in previous notes. Joseph Sturge (1793–1859) was a member of the Anti-Slavery Society in England and one who, through his travels to the West Indies, was to provide the cause with detailed information contributing toward full emancipation. Sturge worked also for complete suffrage, peace, temperance, and other reforms. Arthur West has not been identified. The sisters Elizabeth (1779–1849) and Mary Dudley (1782–1847) were Friends, originally from Ireland, who settled in London in 1810; they were involved in various reforms. Elizabeth was prominent in the Quaker ministry, being at one time clerk of the London Women's Yearly Meeting. She edited *The Life of Mary Dudley* (London, 1825). Mary was the author of several works, including *An Extempore Discourse, Spoken at a Public Meeting . . . at Epping . . .* (London, 1823). William Allen (1770–1843), a scientist by profession, was an ardent Quaker and an energetic reformer. Among the abolitionists he was unique in the range of his friendships, for he knew well not only Wilberforce and Clarkson but also many of the leading nobles and statesmen of Europe, including even Czar Alexander I. Richard Barrett (1784–1855), a London Friend and a partner in a brass-founding business, was involved in many reforms, including abolition, peace, temperance, and circulation of the Scriptures. Joseph Phillips (1793–1880), a Friend from Manchester, was probably a publisher and bookseller as well as a supporter of the abolition movement. Joseph Cooper (c. 1800–1881) and his brother Emanuel Cooper (c. 1795–1851), both business-

men, were, along with Sir George Stephen, leading figures in the Agency Committee, the radical British antislavery organization. John Scoble (born c. 1810) was an independent clergyman and an active abolitionist, a man greatly admired by Garrison during the thirties. Later he became secretary of the British and Foreign Anti-Slavery Society and aggressively opposed Garrison's views. In fact, after 1840 he became the chief British rival to George Thompson. Garrisonians were relieved when late in 1852 he emigrated to Canada, where he had a frustrated political career.

2. Evidently Philip A. Bell.

150

TO ANNA E. BENSON

Boston, May 20, 1834.

My sweet Friend:

I have been at home exactly six days, and yet — to say nothing of other labors — I have written *seventeen* letters since my return, several of them very long and elaborate, and am now commencing my eighteenth.[1] Do you wonder that I grow weary of the pen? But I seize it with delight to write to one whom I esteem and admire so much as yourself. Indeed, your epistle, sent to me at New-York, is so affectionate in its spirit, and so choice in its composition, that you deserve from me, in return, a whole ream of letters. These you should have, if my avocations would permit. It is with extreme difficulty I can send you even this hasty scrawl.

You tenderly allude to "the tie which in prospect is to unite us in a nearer connexion with each other." My dear Anna, I will not wait until Helen and myself shall have gone through the forms of law, to regard you as a sister. The weight of your friendship overpowers me. The language which you use is as sweet as the tones of a harp to my ears. I am glad that you can thus freely communicate the sentiments of your heart through an epistolary medium; and I hope, when I visit Brooklyn again, that you will entirely lose that diffidence of mind, which, in direct opposition to your feelings, has hitherto awed you into silence. You must recollect that I am, essentially, your affectionate brother. Talk to me, then, as freely as you do to Henry or Helen. Why should you shrink or hesitate? Is there — has there been, any thing cold or repulsive in my manner? I confess, your diffidence has made *me* somewhat diffident. Let us both endeavor to be more voluble at our next interview.

Pure, disinterested friendship, in this jarring world, is as rare as the gold of Ophir. Why is it so? The inimitable Young solves the enigma thus:

> "———— Pride repress! nor hope to find

A friend, but what has found a friend in thee:
All like the purchase; few the price will pay;
And this makes friends such miracles below." [2]

My list of bosom friends is not a long one, but the names recorded upon it are very precious to my heart. The circle of friendship is necessarily a charmed one, within which none may hope to enter whose happiness is not enlarged by the happiness of others. There are few, indeed, with whom we may commune unreservedly; and wherever they are found, they are above all price.

But, alas! the ties which bind us together on earth are almost as frail as the flowers of the field. Alas, too, that every cup of human bliss has its alloy! My soul leaps at the prospect of its being ultimately released from its brittle tenement of clay, and the body itself contemplates its final dissolution with delight. I am willing patiently to wait "all the days of my appointed time," [3] until my Master in heaven deem my services below no longer needed. Soul-enrapturing is the thought of heaven! What peace, and joy, and safety, and love, reign there!

"Go, wing thy flight from star to star,
From world to luminous world, as far
    As the universe spreads its flaming wall;
Take all the pleasures of all the spheres,
And multiply each through endless years,
    One minute of Heaven is worth them all!" [4]

* * * *

He who holds a large share of my love stands before me — my noble, generous, gentle Samuel J. May! Pleasant is the sight of his countenance to my soul — charming the tones of his voice to my ear. He proffers me a letter from the beloved one — Helen, dear Helen; and in her name imprints upon my lips a tender kiss. Sadness has been resting like a cloud upon my spirits, ever since I left Brooklyn; but the sunshine of joy now bursts forth, and I am as happy as a freed bird. Say to my chosen one that her favor is a cordial to my heart; that my cold is almost wholly subdued; and that all she discloses in regard to the pangs of a separation has been keenly felt in my breast. She says — "It was not my intention to write you till next week Tuesday — but Anna said I must." Ten thousand thanks, dear friend, for urging her thus to send me an early epistle. Had I not received one at the hands of Mr. May, I should have been heart-sick. How could my precious H. think of delaying so long? And yet I am too unreasonable. It is only a week since I was in Brooklyn. Ah! there is nothing so impatient, nothing so craving, nothing so hard to control as love! And well may I yearn to be once more by the side of her who is so dear to my heart, and surrounded by those who, next to her, are uppermost in my affections. To leave you all was almost like tearing out the fibres of my soul. Many a sigh shall I heave until I stand again in your midst. When will that be? I hope sometime in June; and yet I fear I shall not be able to make my contemplated arrangement with Capt. Stuart. Should he visit Brooklyn, you will receive him as if he were myself; and urge him, I pray you, to take charge of the Liberator awhile, that I may visit you shortly, and make my tour to Philadelphia and other places.

I am sorry, dear Anna, that haste compels me to send you so dull and incoherent a letter; but it may prove acceptable, nevertheless. I am sure I shall do better on another occasion. Although I am now deeply in your debt, yet I should be extremely happy to receive another epistle from you. Beseech my esteemed friend Sarah to bestow a similar favor upon me.

In giving my high regards to your father and mother, use for me the most fervent language of a grateful heart. Henry shares largely in my remembrances. If Helen has my heart, what can I send to her? All that is precious in sacred friendship is transmitted for you by
 Yours, affectionately,

          Wm. Lloyd Garrison.

Miss Anna E. Benson.

ALS: Garrison Papers, Boston Public Library.
 1. Apparently only three of the eighteen letters have been preserved.
 2. Edward Young, *Night Thoughts*, "Night II," lines 555–558.
 3. Job 14:14.
 4. Thomas Moore, *Lalla Rookh*, Part IV, "Paradise and the Peri," lines 22–27.

151

TO HELEN E. BENSON

Boston, May 23, 1834.

My blooming Rose:

Mr. May gave me your precious letter, and a sweet kiss from you, and added, in his peculiarly significant and pleasant manner, "I left your wife and my wife busily conversing together." *Your wife!* — I could not but sigh at the expression, wishing it were literally true. But, whether his flight be slow or swift, in our imagination, Time is steadily on the wing; and soon, my love, the period which we contemplate for our union will come round. Meanwhile, — carefully refraining from borrowing too much bliss from the future, lest disap-

pointment be our lot, owing to causes over which no human power
has any control, — let us sedulously endeavor to make the passing
hours fly pleasantly, by a frequent interchange of thoughts through
the medium of the post. O, what magic there is in a genuine love-
letter! How the bosom heaves, how the heart throbs, how the pulse
leaps, how the hand trembles, on the receipt of it! First, the outward
superscription fixes the eye — then the sacred seal, which hides the
mysterious contents, is eagerly broken — and then every word, and
syllable, and letter, that is revealed, operates for a moment like a
spell. Then impatient love goes over the pages, like a young race-
horse over the course, eager to arrive at the goal of victory. Or, peradventure, covetous of every sentence, and loath to arrive at the conclusion of that which is so precious, it reads slowly and deliberately
to the end, in despite of its strong desires. Dear Helen, is not this a
true picture?

I beseech your pardon, for having given you so much uneasiness
on account of my riding on the outside of the coach to Providence
and Boston. My reasons for doing so were stated in my last letter.
You will be glad to hear that I have entirely recovered from the effects
of my cold. How is yours? When I see you again, pray scold me heartily — I will be very submissive and penitent. I did wrong to disobey
your commands, and must hereafter be more obedient. Agreeably to
your desire, I promise you that I will not neglect my health.

So, my dear girl, your spirits began to droop immediately after
I bade you farewell. Truly it seems to me that we were created for each
other. Your love invigorates my soul, and mine, it delights me to
perceive, is fully appreciated by you. I am happy, *very* happy, too,
to know from you that all the dear friends whom I left behind in
Brooklyn "love me dearly."

In reading that part of your letter, in which you state that in
endeavoring to be mirthful, you were forced to give vent to your
feelings in tears, the fountain of my heart was touched, and I too
found relief in tears. You have said, in some of your other letters,
that I can never know the strength of your attachment for me; and
truly that language I can use in regard to my affection for you. The
tongue is a wretched interpreter of the dialect of the soul. Actions,
it is justly said, speak louder than words; but there are feelings and
emotions belonging to the soul, which neither actions nor words are
competent to reveal.

There is a fine comparison by Moore:

> "As slow our ship her foamy track
> Against the wind was cleaving,
> Her trembling pennant still look'd back

To that dear isle 'twas leaving; —
So loath we part from all we love,
From all the links that bind us;
So turn our hearts, where'er we rove,
To those we've left behind us!" [1]

Last evening, Mr. May delivered an anti-slavery address in Roxbury. The audience was small, in consequence of a limited notice having been given, but very respectable and very attentive. He acquitted himself uncommonly well. The evening was resplendent in the highest degree. I walked into the city with my friend Sewall, and time and space seemed to be annihilated. The heavens were cloudless — and the moon — O, if I were a poet, if I had any imagination, I would try to describe her noble countenance; but you must have seen and enjoyed it, and therefore I will not make the attempt. — Much did I long to have the strong wings of an angel, that I might fly to you, and enjoy by your side full communion of soul. These beautiful evenings make a separation from you doubly insupportable, and almost force me again into the Brooklyn coach. When I visit you again — (ah! *when?*) — I hope the moon will revolve seasonably, and appear as bright and beautiful as she now does. And yet, if she refuse to show her face, I shall not mark her absence, while enjoying your sweet company. The light of your eyes is better than her lustrous effulgence.

This evening I am called to South Reading to plead in a public discourse for my sable brethren. I have nothing specially prepared for the occasion; but as out of the abundance of the heart the mouth speaketh, I do not fear that I shall lack either thoughts or words. And I ought to plead more earnestly and more eloquently now than ever, because I can realize how dreadful a thing it is for lover to be torn away from lover, and husband from wife, and parents from children. The thought of a separation from you, even for a few months, would fill my bosom with distress. How could I bear the thought of a separation for life? O, *we* can, and *we* will, sympathize with the poor slaves, dear Helen, let others scoff as they please.

You are right in supposing me surrounded with newspapers and letters. They necessarily occupy much of my time, but furnish me with a mass of interesting matter.

Capt. Stuart, I hope, is with you in Brooklyn. I cannot promise you a visit in June. Do throw away that unsightly hat-box. Has my portrait arrived from Norwich? If so, in what condition? and what do you think of it?

Public expectation stands on tip-toe, in relation to our Anti-Slavery Convention next week. I wish you could be present, to witness its proceedings; but as you deemed the visit impracticable, I shall despair of seeing you. Happily, I anticipate the pleasure of beholding George and Henry, and of receiving another choice epistle from you by the latter.

I am determined to disobey you once more, and not to oblige you! — You desire me to *burn* your letter ! ! — Is that a reasonable request? O, no! — Then, of course, I ought not to comply with it.

Tell dear Anna that your "carelessness" in writing needs neither censure nor apology. I am afraid you will bestow too much pains upon the composition of your letters, and thus make it irksome to you. I hope you will do no such thing. Whenever you take up your pen to honor and delight me with an epistle, imagine me to be sitting at your elbow, and then write as familiarly as you would talk to me. Of all letters, those passing between lovers should be the least studied, and the least carefully written, so far as penmanship is concerned.

My dear friend May has just dropped in, and says, "I have just written home — but tell *your* wife to take good care of *my* wife until my return." Be true to your trust, and give my best compliments to Mrs. May. Kiss the little ones many times for me.

I trust the health of your dear father continues to improve, and that this will find you all well. May constant peace, and joy, and happiness be yours. Farewell!

Yours, with boundless affection,

Wm. Lloyd Garrison.

Miss H. E. Benson.

ALS: Villard Papers, Harvard College Library.

1. With slight modification, Thomas Moore, "As Slow Our Ship," lines 1–8.

152

TO HELEN E. BENSON

Boston, May 30, 1834.

Helen — dearest!

O, what a week has the present been to my soul! such fulness of bliss! such ardor of love! such thankfulness of heart! — I am staggering under a load of gratitude to God — to many dear advocates of the bleeding, dying slave — to you. I am filled with joy unspeakable.

First, came those noble youths — dear George and Henry. The light of their countenances was pleasant to my sight; the sound of their voices was music to my ears; the echo of their footsteps was as the falling of a gentle rain. The latter gave me that, which, you are aware, I prize next to your own soul-enlivening presence — viz. a letter from you. *It was worthy of you*: what can I say more in its praise? Not the least interesting portion of it was that which related to your views respecting plainness of deportment in "Garrison's wife." Your humility charms me, and your good sense and wise judgment greatly redound to your credit. Our views, on this point, are perfectly in unison. I love simplicity of dress, of manners, and of mind — of course, I love you. This I told you long ago, but I can never say those words, "I love you," too often.

I regret to say that it is too true that a passion for gaudy finery is too prevalent among our colored population; but this is naturally created and inflamed by their degraded situation, which leads them to imitate and surpass in folly those who are on a higher level than themselves. This is another reason why prejudice should expire, and slavery be abolished; for as soon as they are enlightened, and made virtuous, they will despise that in which they now take the most delight.

You express some astonishment at the proposal of marriage by the young lady at Philadelphia, and think it must be a device of the enemy. It was made, dear Helen, I assure you, in good earnest — in all soberness of mind. I could wish it were an imposition — but it is true. Since I sent you my last, I have received another letter from her — not in answer to mine, for she had not at the time of writing received it — in which she humbly apologizes for the course she had pursued, hopes I will erase the memory of it from my mind, and expresses her regret that she had not previously known that I was engaged to another. She writes as if her mind was in a state of painful confusion, in consequence of the discovery she had made.

You ask, "Cannot you gratify me by giving me her name?" Certainly, my love — I will not hide it from you, especially as you "would not expose her for the world." Her name, then, is Leah Fell. In her first letter to me, containing her matrimonial proposition, she gives me a detailed account of her parents, brothers, sisters, &c. and intimates that she believes the union would be very agreeable to them as well as to her! She is a pretty, artless, simple-minded girl; but, from my acquaintance with her, I am inclined to hope that she will soon recover from the shock occasioned by the disappointment.

It seems, then, my portrait that came via Norwich to Brooklyn, bears, in your opinion, of all others, "the faintest resemblance to the dear original" — which, in other words, is to say, it is any body's face but mine.[1] Happily, it is not my fault, but the artist's, that I am not more successful in pleasing the ladies.

I send you by Henry an improved copy of Mr. Jocelyn's engraving — but it is still sadly deficient as a likeness.[2] The anatomy of the head is wrong — the face is certainly too old and too grave, if my glass and my friends do not declare falsely — the whole expression is sleepy and insipid — in fine, it is a failure, and I am sorry for it. Nevertheless, as it is decidedly better than the one you have, keep *this*, and destroy *that* — i.e. if you please; for your choice is my choice, and what displeases you will displease me. Try, and see if *you* cannot sketch my features. I know you do not paint — your fair cheeks; but can't you paint mine?

[. . .] ³

Our dear friend Capt. Stuart, it seems, has not had the pleasure yet of visiting either Brooklyn or Canterbury. Say to Prudence that he hopes to be enabled to visit her shortly. He has left in my charge a variety of elegant and valuable presents to her and her pupils from the ladies of Birmingham, Liverpool, &c. which I shall transmit almost immediately. You will be amused and pleased to see them.

I have just taken leave of George and Henry; but as the latter does not expect to be in Brooklyn until Tuesday, I have concluded to anticipate [his] arrival one day by sending this by mail — as I know how long a day seems to those who are separated from the loved and loving one.

Our Convention has been eminently interesting, and triumphantly successful. Henry must tell you all about it. I made no speech, but from choice gave way to others.

In five minutes, the mail closes. I have written this in a distracted state of mind, surrounded by a troop of talkative abolitionists, and scarcely know what I have written. I grieve to say that Capt. Stuart will not be able to stop in Boston; but, if my life and health be spared, I will strive to visit you in all July.

A thousand blessings upon you and Anna, your dear parents, and all. I thank you for your other precious epistle by Mr. Williams.⁴ Adieu — you shall hear again in a few days from

　　Yours, ever,

　　　　　　　　　　　　Wm. Lloyd Garrison

ALS: Villard Papers, Harvard College Library.

1. In her letter of May 22, from which Garrison quotes, Helen explained that she considered the portrait so poor a likeness that she "would not have it exposed to the public gaze." Presumably she refers to one of the two lithographic portraits that Garrison mentioned in his letter of May 1, both of which he considered failures. Although he said in that same letter that he would bring specimens of the several recent portraits with him when he came to Brooklyn, he may have changed his mind and sent one of them to her.

2. Simeon S. Jocelyn attempted several improvements upon his original engraving of Garrison. Although the exact history of this series is not known, perhaps Garrison refers to the second version.

3. A portion of the page, apparently containing one paragraph, is torn off the manuscript.

4. Presumably this is the Herbert Williams who owned a farm in the vicinity of Brooklyn.

153

TO GEORGE BENSON

Boston, May 31, 1834.

Dearly beloved Sir:

If my admiration of your benevolent labors, and esteem for your character, were exalted before that relation was formed which now so closely unites me to you and yours; certainly, I cannot feel less respect and attachment since I gave my affections to one of your amiable children, and received hers in return. Were it not for the multitude of my engagements, nothing would delight me more than to send you an epistle as often at least as once a week; — you will not, therefore, construe my silence into indifference or neglect.

Never shall I forget the emotions which arose in my bosom, on bidding you farewell at the close of my visit in March last. Your house was then thronged with colored pupils from Miss Crandall's school, who were summoned as witnesses at Mr. Olney's [1] trial, and who had no other place in Brooklyn "where to lay their heads," [2] than your hospitable dwelling. They were kindly received by you all; and although in number sufficient to overwhelm a quiet family like yours, yet your dear wife and daughters were as composed as if not one of them had been present. Some families, under such circumstances, would have been thrown into utter confusion — and bustle, bustle, nothing but bustle, and running to and fro, would have been the consequence. I was forcibly struck by the quietude of spirit manifested by you all, and by that domestic order which reigned paramount; but more especially by that benevolent condescension, which is as rare as it is godlike, and that disinterested philanthropy which led you cheerfully to entertain and accommodate so many of those who are generally treated in society as the offscouring of the earth. In riding to Providence, my thoughts constantly reverted back to the scene which I had just left, and my heart grew liquid as water. "Heavenly Father!" I inwardly ejaculated, "let thy choicest blessings fall upon the head of that very dear and venerable philanthropist, and upon his dear wife, and all their children, for thus compassionating the condition of an injured and helpless race."

I can scarcely dare hope that this letter will find you in vigorous health; but I trust it will not find you ill. My constant prayer is, that you may be spared to the cause of bleeding humanity many years to come; for an example like yours is trumpet-tongued,[3] and pleads with the oppressors of the human race like an angel. But He whose wisdom and goodness are infinite — who has "beautifully mingled life and death" [4] — who sees the end from the beginning — will decide as to the best period for the termination of your earthly pilgrimage. Who would live always in this miserable, sin-polluted world? O, the thought must be agony to the soul which longs to lose its earthly clogs, and be with Christ, "which is far better." [5] I presume the grave presents no terrors to you. What is the grave? Is it the despository of the soul — the despoiler of the inward man? If so — if it annihilates that which gives motion, feeling, action to the body — then we may dread the grave. But it has no power over the soul — blessed be God that it has not! — It only receives a body of dust — a tenement of clay. In the language of an eloquent writer — "Man does not die, though the forms of popular speech thus announce his exit. He does not die. We bury, not our friend, but only the form, the vehicle, in which, for a time, our friend lived. It is the dust only that descends to dust. The grave! — let us break its awful spell, its dread dominion. It is the place where man lays down his weakness, his infirmity, his diseases and sorrows, that he may rise up to a new and glorious life. It is the place where man ceases — in all that is frail and decaying — ceases to be man, that he may be, in glory and blessedness, an angel of light! Say, ye aged and infirm, is it the greatest of evils to die? Say, ye children of care and toil! say, afflicted and tempted! is it the greatest of evils to die?" [6]

Oh! no. Come the last hour, in God's own time! and a good life and a glorious hope shall make it welcome. Come the hour of release! — and affliction shall make it welcome. Come the hour of re-union with the loved and lost on earth! — and the passionate yearnings of affection, and the strong aspirations of faith, shall bear us to their blessed land. Come death to this body — this burdened, tempted, frail, failing, dying body! — and to the soul, come freedom, light and joy unceasing! come the immortal life! — "He that liveth," — saith the conqueror over the Devil, — "he that liveth and believeth in me, shall never die." [7]

> "Sure the last end
> Of the good man is peace. How calm his exit!
> Night dews fall not more gently to the ground,
> Nor weary, worn-out winds expire so soft." [8]

Henry will tell you many cheering things in regard to our great Anti-Slavery Convention in this city, which has just terminated. [9] Could you have been present, gladness would have possessed your soul. There is now hope for the poor slaves — hope for the free men of color — hope for our whole country — hope for the world.

I hope this letter will be handed to you by my much respected friend Mr. James G. Barbadoes,[10] who is a delegate to the General Colored Convention in New-York.

In great haste I remain,

Yours, with much affection and respect,

Wm. Lloyd Garrison.

Please remember me affectionately to Mrs. Benson and all the members of your family.

ALS: Garrison Papers, Boston Public Library; printed partly in *Life*, I, 424.

1. See Garrison's letter (125) to Helen E. Benson, March 8, 1834.
2. Matthew 8:20.
3. Shakespeare, *Macbeth*, I, vii, 19.
4. Not identified.
5. Philippians 1:23.
6. Not identified.
7. John 11:26.
8. Robert Blair, "The Grave," lines 712–715.
9. Garrison refers to the New England Anti-Slavery Convention held in Boylston Hall, Boston, May 27–28, to which various antislavery societies in the region sent delegates. In *The Liberator* for May 31 Garrison reported that it was "the most interesting and important convocation ever held in the United States, in relation to the momentous subject of slavery — excepting, perhaps, the Convention at Philadelphia in December last."
10. James G. Barbadoes (died 1841), an outstanding leader among Boston Negroes, was a dependable supporter and admirer of Garrison, for whom he named a son. He was a member of the Massachusetts General Colored Association, formed in Boston in 1826, a founder of the American Anti-Slavery Society as well as a member of its Board of Managers.

154

TO HELEN E. BENSON

Boston, June 2, 1834.

Star of my heart:

An esteemed colored friend, Mr. James G. Barbadoes of this city, goes this morning to attend the General Colored Convention at New-York; and as he takes Brooklyn in his route, how can I suffer him to go, without sending a few lines to my beautiful and intensely beloved Helen? Would you forgive me for such an omission? Could I pardon myself?

To-day, at 12 o'clock, you will receive a letter from me by the mail, which I put into the Post Office on Friday evening. It was written in full gallop, and requires an apology. This, I suppose, will be put into your hands before sunset. Pray let it atone for the other.

Amid all the distractions of business, the image of her to whom

I have plighted my faith is ever before me. I see you, and hear you, wherever I go — at all times, and under all circumstances. In truth, you are a generous, lovely, devoted girl — worthy of all admiration — too deserving to be mated to one like me. — I delight to praise you; and I rejoice that I can do so without offending you, inasmuch as I am yours in all sincerity and fervency of soul. When I think of the happy hours that we have spent together, it is no marvel that I weep at our separation. O, if Brooklyn were only as contiguous to Boston as Roxbury, how frequently, and eagerly, and fondly, would I rush into your presence, and clasp you to my breast! Alas! a distance of seventy miles intervenes — and were it not for the joys arising from a fruitful correspondence with you, I should be filled with so much unhappiness as to be measurably incapacitated to pursue the great and glorious cause in which I am enlisted.

A few days since, Mr. May kindly permitted me to read an admirably written letter from his accomplished lady, which evinced great affection for him, and which seemed to delight him exceedingly. I was scarcely less pleased than himself; for it contained a fine panegyric upon my dear Helen, declaring her to be just such a one as I needed for my wife, and complimenting me upon my fortunate selection. Convey to her my thanks, and my best wishes for her permanent happiness.

I have just been perusing and reperusing your excellent favors, sent by Henry and Mr. Williams.[1] There is a sentence in one of them which has awakened a train of reflections in my mind, of a novel character. It is this:

"Never was I more astonished than to hear of the proposal of marriage made by that female acquaintance of yours. I cannot believe that one of my sex would venture thus far."

I do not wonder at your incredulity and astonishment, dear one, because a case like this is certainly a rare occurrence. But the question has occurred to me, — Why should not females as freely communicate their love as the other sex? Perhaps this question surprises you — but reflect upon the subject, for one moment. Is it reasonable that overtures should always be made on the part of men? True, custom so decides it; but ought custom to rule in so exclusive and despotic a manner? Will it be said that delicacy ought to deter a woman from first avowing her love? Is not this tantamount to saying that there is something indelicate in a marriage proposal? Why, then, should the other sex be called upon to make it? Tenderly loving you, my dear H., — yet ignorant as to the state of your own heart, — I made bold to throw myself at your feet, and avow my passion. Happily for my peace of mind, you did not reject me, but, on the contrary, confessed a kindred attachment. — Suppose that *I* had remained silent, and your love had gone on increasing until it had become insupportable — would you not, or, rather, ought you not to have made me acquainted with the state of your heart, and endeavored to ascertain whether I could reciprocate your affection? Ah! how many lovely females have gone down to the grave broken-hearted, in consequence of having studiously refrained from acknowledging their attachment! How pathetically does Shakespeare describe one in this situation!

> "She never told her love,
> But let concealment, like a worm i' the bud,
> Feed on her damask cheek: she pin'd in thought;
> And, with a green and yellow melancholy,
> She sat, like Patience on a monument,
> Smiling at grief." [2]

I am not acquainted with anything more affecting in description than the above.

In my letter to you of Friday evening, I mentioned that I had received an apologetical letter from Miss Fell of Philadelphia. She writes thus:

"I felt a little surprised to hear that thee was engaged. I wish all to be erased from thy memory. My sympathy, when excited, is, I think, naturally strong, and my affections of an immoveable nature; yet I am rather surprised that, after having been guarded in youth, and still feeling conscious of being in possession of an innocent heart, (unless it is to effect my own humiliation,) I have been left to myself, and thus allowed insensibly to err." — "If thee should hear from me again, I think it will be in a very different style. Shall I be vain enough to tell thee, that in my youth I had many admirers, and have several at present; but in myself I see a fading plant, but I trust not without a root yet to bud and to bloom in eternity" — &c. &c.

Be not uneasy, my love, on account of this unfortunate affair. When I see you, I can make such explanations as fully to relieve your mind.

Our contemplated union, I am happy to find, gives universal satisfaction among my friends, both white and colored. Of course, they are extremely anxious to see you; and should this letter be delivered to you in person by Mr. Barbadoes, you may expect to receive a pretty rigid scrutiny. He is so attached to me that I am confident he would surrender his life in a moment to save my own.

You are affectionately holding out inducements for me to make another visit to Brooklyn. You say — "You would scarcely realize the change there is already in the forest trees. They hang full of foliage on Mount Gray. When you were here, the buds had scarcely begun to swell." I need no other attraction than yourself to draw me to your pleasant village; but it is not probable that I shall be able to visit you before the last of July. Rely upon it, I shall shorten this period, if practicable; and when I come again, I will make my arrangements so as to spend at least one week in your society.

My health is good, despite this dreary, *horrible* weather. Where is summer? Are you well? For a whole week, the sun has revealed his countenance scarcely for a moment. His fickleness shall never be imitated by

Yours, with all fidelity of soul, and with unutterable love, to the close of life,

Wm. Lloyd Garrison.

☞ Remember that "next to the pleasure of hearing you, is the pleasure of hearing from you — next to the pleasure of seeing you, is the pleasure of seeing your hand-writing." [3]

I am happy to learn that my letter to dear Anna was received with pleasure. I think I have promised to send one to my esteemed friend Miss Sarah: she shall get it soon.

It seems to me that Mr. Philio [4] is somewhat tardy in coming to Canterbury. My best regards to Prudence and Almira — they were both remembered in a resolution passed by our Convention.

☞ I am not yet fully satisfied in my own mind, whether it will be most desirable, all things considered, to board out after our marriage, or take a cottage *per se*. When I was in England, I told George Thompson that Roxbury would be the most agreeable situation for his family in this country; and I expect he will make it his place of residence. Should he do so, perhaps it will be agreeable to us all to live together. He has a very amiable lady and one child. I think he would like such an arrangement exceedingly well; but we can talk of this on his arrival. I send you ten thousand kisses. Adieu, sweet girl!

ALS: Villard Papers, Harvard College Library.

1. Probably Herbert Williams.

2. Garrison quotes accurately from *Twelfth Night*, II, iv, 113–118. He used the same passage in *The Liberator* for July 19, 1834.

3. Garrison quotes accurately, except for a couple of redundant words, Richard West's letter to Thomas Gray, dated November 14, 1735; see Paget Toynbee and Leonard Whibley, *Correspondence of Thomas Gray* (Oxford, 1935), I, 33.

4. Garrison misspells the name of Calvin Philleo.

155

TO HELEN E. BENSON

Boston, June 6, 1834.

My charming Conqueror:

You perceive that I make a very submissive, and even loyal prisoner, and am well pleased with my captivity. I am not anxious to have one of my fetters broken; for to serve and obey you is henceforth to be the pleasing duty of my life. "Perfect love casteth out fear:"[1] I can therefore safely trust my liberty with you, assured that your commands will be reasonable, and your government humane.

One thing delights me — that there is nothing either affected in our love, or constrained in our intercourse with each other. When we meet, we mingle like kindred drops, and pour forth our affections with the freedom and fulness of a fountain. We have nothing to conceal — we throw our hearts open — our lips express the sentiments which we cherish. This is just as it should be — it is the simplicity of nature — it is the honesty of truth.

O! how tedious and painful is a *mechanical* courtship! — I have known a couple, who have plighted to each other their faith, so restrict their intercourse, through fear or coyness or diffidence, for months and months; they were so excessively formal, and so polite, and so dainty, and so bound by the rules of an unnatural etiquette, and so shy in communicating their thoughts and feelings; that they constantly marred their own happiness, and kept at a distance as lovers, which would be inexcusably remote as friends. I hate such icy frigidity — there is no soul in it: it looks insincere — it looks suspicious. Not that I approve of an unseemly familiarity of conduct — a reckless disregard of all rules of propriety. There is a happy medium between these extremes, which I think we have found. When you generously accepted of the offer of my heart, I felt that we were no longer twain, but one flesh. I know that to be legally one, the law properly requires us to go through a certain process; but we are now really and truly one. Whether, then, in our correspondence or personal interviews with each other, let us write or converse with all that freedom which is inalienably allied to genuine love, and let there be nothing artificial or repulsive in our actions.

Only think of it, dear Helen! — for more than a week, you and Anna were all alone — Sarah being in Providence, and Henry in Boston. I have been sighing to-day at the thought of what I have lost. If I could have spent that week with you, how exquisite would have been my happiness — shall I not say, *our* happiness? When I think how evanescent is human life — how quickly youth passes away — how fast days and months revolve — I am impatient for our union, and covetous of every moment that bears witness to our separation. Perhaps I anticipate too much — and yet I think otherwise.

> "I never draw a radiant scene,
>   But thou mak'st all its happiness;
> And dark and cold my life had been,
>   Hadst thou not promised it to bless.
> The world in its domain holds naught,
>   Which could requite thy loss to me;
> Whole months have been one long   long thought —
>   One deep expressive dream of thee.
> Thine image from the first hath dwelt
>   Within my breast, as in a shrine,
> Before which my young heart hath knelt
>   With faith that ne'er can know decline." [2]

Why did I not become acquainted with you at an earlier period? How much I have lost — and yet how much have I gained!

You think, then, that in every instance, professions of love should be made by my sex to yours, and not *vice versa*. You say, moreover, that however strong might have been your attachment for me, you would never have revealed it to me, had I not first offered myself to you. Well — I cannot but admire that high sense of decorum which governs your actions; but still I believe there may be cases in which it would be no real breach of modesty, or the rules of decorum, for a lady to reveal the love which she cherishes towards him who has captivated her heart.

As for Miss F——,[3] I doubt whether the disappointment will affect her so deeply as it would one of your keen susceptibilities. I have heard, and hope I shall hear, nothing further from her on the subject. Her last two letters remain unanswered. My engagement to you will certainly show her the hopelessness of her passion.

My beloved friend Knapp's health is in rather a precarious state. His constitution is habitually consumptive. For some weeks he has had a severe cold upon his lungs, attended with a slight cough. He is now gradually recovering. I have been endeavoring to get him to make a visit to Providence and Brooklyn, as I think the jaunt would revive him; but he declines the journey, although he would be extremely happy to see you all.

I return my thanks to my lively friend Mrs. May, *in black and white*, for the feline gift which she is disposed to send me. As I am opposed to colonization, let the little sable animal remain until I visit B. I may possibly volunteer a sonnet upon it, by and by — es-

pecially if a *cat*-astrophe overtake it, so that I may say of it, "Resquies-
cat in pace!" in conveying its mortal remains to the *cat*-acombs.

My friend Barbadoes must have been disappointed in not seeing
"Garrison's wife." Should he fail to get a glimpse of her in Brooklyn
on his return, I hope he will ultimately behold her in Boston.

Your letter, which reached me on Wednesday noon, was as pleasant as sun-light after a storm. You are extremely kind in taxing
yourself so much, in order to augment my happiness. I ought not
to expect you to write so often, or such long letters; and yet I should
despond to have a longer interval elapse between your favors. Shall
I be permitted to cherish the hope that I shall hear from you by the
next Wednesday's mail?

In your next, I shall expect to hear the particulars of Mr. Philleo's
visit to Canterbury. I am troubled in spirit lest our dear friend Prudence marry ill. The step which she is about to take will seal her
earthly destiny, either for good or evil. Let her seriously weigh the
consequences. Is not the thought of being indissolubly allied to a
worthless person insupportable? To marry, or not to marry, is a most
serious question for man or woman to consider, and ought not to be
settled hastily. Tell Prudence that she has my fervent prayers and
best wishes for her happiness. Also convey my compliments to Miss
Almira.

I am, as usual, overburdened with duties; but while I have health,
and the means of putting my thoughts on paper, I can let nothing
interfere to prevent my frequently assuring you that

I am, in weal and in wo,

Your lover now, and your loving husband in prospect,

Wm. Lloyd Garrison.

Miss H. E. Benson.

N.B. Excellent, my love! — "I do think that if a woman was allowed to choose a husband for herself, her choice would generally
be the most judicious one." [4] Ought she not, then, whenever practicable, to choose for herself? And does this not prove that it may be
proper, in some cases at least, for her to disclose her love first?

I am pleased to hear that my hasty scrawl to your venerable father
was very acceptable. I hope he will not attempt to answer it while
his health remains so infirm. Your dear mother — I long to say, *my*
dear mother — shall receive a letter from me as soon as I can command the time to write it. Give my cordial remembrances to both
of them.

I am happy to say that it is probable the Managers of the New-
England Anti-Slavery Society will determine, to-morrow afternoon,

to take all the pecuniary liabilities of the Liberator hereafter, and give me a regular salary for editing it, and friend Knapp a fair price for printing it. My salary will not be less than $800 per annum, and perhaps it will be fixed at $1000.[5] The former sum will enable us, my love, to live very comfortably; but if the latter be allowed, I shall be able to do more for the cause of bleeding humanity than I have yet done. The new arrangement will go into effect on the 1st of July.

I hope to see Mr. May at Salem on Wednesday next. You declare you mean to *scold* him on his return. *You* scold! I wish I could hear you. But you had better begin with him, as I shall often need a good scolding myself.

Adieu!

ALS: Villard Papers, Harvard College Library.

1. I John 4:18.
2. Not identified.
3. Leah Fell.
4. Garrison quotes from Helen's letter of June 2, 1834.
5. Garrison's financial problems were not so easily solved as he had hoped. In *The Liberator* for November 1, 1834, he is still dunning his patrons, blaming them for thinking him bodiless and ethereal, "requiring neither food nor raiment." Also, on January 12, 1835 (letter 184), he writes his father-in-law that it is doubtful whether there is support sufficient for *The Liberator* to be continued.

156

TO HELEN E. BENSON

Boston, June 14, 1834.

My dear Girl:

Agreeably to my hopes, your letter arrived in Boston on Wednesday noon; but I did not receive it until yesterday, (Friday,) on returning from the Essex County Anti-Slavery Convention at Salem. You must get my dear friends May and Stuart, who started yesterday for Brooklyn, to give you some account of the proceedings of the Convention. As you have regularly received a letter from me every Monday, I hope this will not fail to arrive seasonably. Hitherto, I have put my letters into the Post Office on Fridays; but it was out of my power to write this yesterday.

I have read your sketch of Mr. Philio's visit to B. with considerable care, and feel as much perplexed in relation to the real character of the man, as you do.[1] If he is an innocent man, he is certainly an injured man; and he had better be both than a bad man. Let us hope for the best. I think if Prudence marries him, she will act wisely in giving up her school.

"Love is blind," you have admonished me repeatedly. Sometimes, undoubtedly — not always; for instance, not when the selection of W. L. G. fell upon so excellent and gentle a creature as Helen Eliza Benson. O, surely love was not blind then! But you shall not decide in this case. I appeal to my dear sister Anna.

In a city, summer brings out as many belles, as butterflies in the country. Every fair day, our Washington-street is swarming with them; but a single glance at you would be preferred to the steadfast gaze of a month at them. I attend a variety of public meetings, and see crowds of "the gentler sex" — but my dear Helen is not among them, and I turn away with a sigh. Am I childish? Will you blame me for loving you so tenderly? If Prudence cherishes half the attachment for Mr. P. which I bear toward you, you need not wonder that she clings to him so dutifully.

I may be very selfish in wishing you w[ould arrive] in Boston — and yet I am sure I would not wish so, if I did not believe that your stock of happiness, as well as my own, would be materially increased by the visit. As I make my morning promenade around our beautiful Common, I want your arm locked in my own to perfect my happiness. Summer is now arrayed in all its glory. It seems to me as if an unusual beauty pervaded earth and sky. It is soul-refreshing to look at the trees, dressed out in their gorgeous robes, and lifting up their stately heads unto the clouds. And then, our evenings — how incomparably fine! — O, there is nothing equal to our clear blue sky, arching the high and eternal ramparts of Nature — the hills, the majestic, glorious hills! And, moreover, such stars! so large, so gorgeous, so soul-overpowering! painting the heavens so richly, and illuminating it with such resplendent fires! It is a beautiful world that we inhabit, dearest — at least, all that the Creator has made is, in the brief but expressive language of scripture, "very good" — but, oh! how is it marred by the selfishness, the lust, the cruelty, the oppression, the hatred and revenge of man!

I wish you were here, too, for another reason. The Atheneum Gallery of Paintings is now open for the examination of the lovers of the fine arts. It is an attractive exhibition, and thousands annually crowd to witness it. Doubtless many of these go to see, not merely the painted canvass, but the *living pictures* which adorn the spacious gallery. Here friend meets friend — and the lover the mistress of his affections. Here the rogue Cupid is busy with his darts, and many a heart he has pierced through and through. Here Fashion displays its variable colors and forms, and Beauty heightens its palpable charms; and here, too, indisputably, there is no lack of scandal and folly. Nevertheless, the exhibition is worth seeing. Are you fond of paintings, Helen? I am acquiring a passion for them.

Ever since our New-England Anti-Slavery Convention, my thoughts, feelings, and purposes, have been confusedly blended together — partly in consequence of having so much to do, and especially in consequence of being so frequently visited and over-visited by troops of anti-slavery converts. I cannot write in the city, as I could in Roxbury — (this is proved by the barrenness of my recent letters to you.) If I sit down at my editorial desk, either to write for the public eye or for private inspection, I am constantly interrupted, and my thoughts scattered like a flock of birds by a volley of musketry. Peradventure, next week will find me located in Roxbury once more; after which, you may expect something less tedious in my letters than you will find in this.

The fourth of July is rapidly approaching — and many a mighty voice will be lifted up in behalf of the perishing slaves on that day. In all quarters, applications are made to me to deliver an address on that occasion. Two came to-day — one from dear George. He wishes me to hold forth in Providence, with some other anti-slavery friends, on the approaching anniversary — but I must decline. Others will do more good there than myself — others against whom there is less prejudice. The Pawtucket Anti-Slavery Society have also invited me to make an oration in that town, and I have concluded to accept of the invitation on the Fourth. Should the meeting in Providence be held at a different hour on that day, of course I mean to attend it.

I meant to have given my friend May several choice kisses for you — but in the hurry of departure, it was forgotten. Have you *scolded* him since his return, agreeably to your promise? Well — be merciful to him, and tell Mrs. May she must freely grant him absolution for all his domestic transgressions. He has been on a holy errand — a sacred and glorious mission — and faithfully and successfully has he performed it. He has really done immense good to our noble cause since he left Brooklyn. His addresses have been attended with a victorious p [. . .] he has won the hearts of thousands by his generous appeals an[d] stirring eloquence — therefore, let him be rebuked *very* mildly by you all. Be assured, it was exceedingly painful to him to be absent from home, sweet home, so long. He frequently expressed to me the longing desires of his soul to be with his beloved wife and children; and he returned yesterday with a heart full of joy. He doats upon Mrs. May, and declares that marriage is happier than courtship. There — you and Mrs. M. will forgive him now — won't you?

Capt. Stuart, I hope, will not fail to stop at your house. You know how much I love him. His labors have already been invaluable, since his arrival in this country.

Poor Eunice had a narrow escape — I congratulate her that she was not seriously injured by her fall.

Mr. Knapp's health is miserable — he will go home to Newbury-port next week: then I shall "have my hands full."

With intense affection,

Yours, unreservedly,

Wm. Lloyd Garrison.

Miss H. E. Benson.

ALS: Villard Papers, Harvard College Library.

1. On June 9 Helen wrote to Garrison at length about the visit to Brooklyn and the Benson house of Calvin Philleo (or "Philio" as she spelled his name). She explained that she had heard "so many intimations of his ill behavior," that she found herself hopelessly prejudiced against him, so prejudiced that she even refused to hear him preach. Prudence Crandall she considered so blind in her love that Philleo could persuade her "*black* was *white* if he chose." Helen's suspicions have been confirmed by the report handed down to collateral descendants in the Crandall family, that Calvin Philleo proved to be impecunious, inconsiderate, and dishonest.

157

TO GEORGE W. BENSON

Boston, June 16, 1834.

My dear Friend:

I am covered with applications for my services as an anti-slavery orator on the Fourth of July. — To whom shall I give the preference? I should be very happy to comply with your invitation, if I were not satisfied in my own mind that there is too much prejudice against me in Providence for me to encounter it successfully at present, and that you will be able to obtain a more acceptable person in my stead. Nevertheless, I thank your Society for their kind remembrance of me.

It is not probable that you will be able to secure either Mr. May or Capt. Stuart. The former told me that he must *positively* decline the invitation, and stay at home. The latter has gone to New-York, and I know not when he will be again in this quarter.

Do not wholly despair. George Thompson may arrive in season to make his *debut* on the 4th, in Providence; and should he, you will have no occasion to regret the absence of others.

The same mail that brought me your favor, also brought me a letter from my lion-hearted and estimable friend Rev. Ray Potter, in which I am invited, in behalf of the Pawtucket Anti-Slavery Society, to deliver an address in that "fanatical" village on the approaching anniversary.[1] I shall write to him this evening, accepting the offer;

so that, if no unforeseen hindrance prevent, we shall be pretty near each other on that day; and, indeed, if your meeting be held at a different hour from the one in Pawtucket, I will endeavor to attend it.[2]

The Minutes of the Anti-Slavery Convention will not be issued short of three or four weeks. We are waiting for the completion of sundry reports and addresses.[3]

The Convention at Salem, last week, was very interesting, though hardly equal to ours in Boston.[4] The speeches of Messrs. May and Phelps were well received by the Salemites. I have never heard them do better. Mr. May is a gallant conqueror of hearts — men and women alike yield to his fascinating powers.

Let us not deceive ourselves. Although our cause is *certainly* advancing with a mighty stride, yet the opposition still to be encountered is truly formidable. This is no time for repose; and if we exult, it must be with our weapons in our hands, ready to meet the combined powers of earth and hell. Happily, the Lord God of hosts is our strength and shield — else we should surely be overthrown. As it is, he will put our faith and courage to a severe test. Let us walk in his light, and we shall not stumble.

I have just received a letter from Prudence, in which she expresses much joy at the arrival of the Rev. Mr. Phillio, and bestows a very high eulogy upon his character. Helen tells me that "Love is blind," and perhaps this confirms her declaration. However, I will not condemn Mr. Phillio, for I have never heard any special and vital allegations brought against him. Prudence tells me he is for continuing the school in Canterbury, and increasing the number of its scholars, if possible, to one hundred. In my opinion, however, she had better take advantage of her marriage,[5] and move off with flying colors; especially as the Legislature of Connecticut — to its everlasting disgrace — has adjourned, without repealing the odious law against her school.

I regret to learn that my esteemed friend Mr. Prentice has recently lost one of his children. May an abundance of heavenly grace be given him to sustain his spirits, and also those of his dear family, under this heavy bereavement. Assure them that they have my condolence.

My friend Knapp's health is in a very precarious state. He has a severe cough, is very weak, and I almost tremble for the issue. I shall try to induce him to go to Newburyport, and spend a few weeks.

My own health continues good. I grieve to learn by a letter from my dear Helen, that your father's continues very feeble. You will caution him to be careful how he exposes himself.

Remember me deferentially and affectionately to friends Moses Brown, Anson Potter, Jas. Scott, Mr. Prentice, Mr. Chace, &c. &c. and to your lady.

Yours, faithfully,

Wm. Lloyd Garrison.

ALS: Garrison Papers, Boston Public Library.

1. Ray Potter (1795–1858) was a Baptist minister of Pawtucket, Rhode Island, whom Garrison later eulogized (*The Liberator*, January 30, 1836) as "one of the first ministers who espoused our cause" and renounced colonization.

2. Garrison did speak in Pawtucket, Rhode Island, on the fourth; the speech was reported in *The Liberator* on the twelfth.

3. Garrison refers to the New England Anti-Slavery Convention described in letter 153, to George Benson, May 31, 1834 (see n. 9).

4. In *The Liberator* for June 14 Garrison explains that he has just returned from the Essex County Anti-Slavery Convention in Salem.

5. Which was to occur August 12.

158

TO THE EDITOR OF THE BOSTON *COURIER*

[June 19, 1834.]

Sir, —

A communication, professedly in defence of the Anti-Slavery cause, appeared in your columns yesterday, from a correspondent at Cambridge, which I deem worthy of animadversion, inasmuch as it contains one statement at least, at variance with impartial truth, and calculated to mislead the public. The writer says:

"It must have been apparent to all, conversant at all with the anti-slavery writings or proceedings, that a MAJORITY of its friends, especially of late, are fully sensible of the unhappy condition of the slaveholders, and of all the *circumstances which palliate the guilt of slaveholding.* They so far *regard the* RIGHT *of property,* as to bring forward a measure publicly, to *remunerate,* in some measure, those who liberate their slaves. *This measure is popular among the most influential men of the Society.*"

The confidence with which the above statement is made surprizes me, not merely because its author declares that he is "not a member of the Anti-Slavery Society, and does not approve all its measures," but because it is wholly erroneous. I repel it as an aspersion. That abolitionists "are fully sensible of the unhappy condition of slaveholders," no one can doubt, after witnessing their efforts to alter and improve that condition. As to the "circumstances," which, in their opinion, "*palliate* the guilt of slaveholding," I, as a humble advocate of emancipation, profess to be ignorant of them. It seems to me, Sir, that the peculiar "circumstances" of southern oppressors *aggravate* their guilt. They are famous lovers of freedom; they maintain, as a self-evident truth, that all men are born free and equal; they live in "a land of liberty;" and they are supplied with the Bible. No apology can save them from the condemnation of Jehovah, or the execration of mankind. They are without excuse.

To say that abolitionists regard at all the slaveholder's *"right of property"* in the bones, and sinews, and souls of his victims, is to insult their understanding and impeach their morality. With Lord Brougham, "they deny the right — they acknowledge not the property" [1] — and they never will consent to purchase the villany of the south, either in the mass or by piece-meal. On this subject, their views are clearly and unitedly expressed in the following extract from the "DECLARATION" of the National Anti-Slavery Convention:

"We maintain that no compensation should be given to the planters emancipating their slaves —
Because it would be a surrender of the great fundamental principle that man cannot hold property in man;
Because SLAVERY IS A CRIME, AND THEREFORE IT IS NOT AN ARTICLE TO BE SOLD;
Because the holders of slaves are not the just proprietors of what they claim; — freeing the slaves is not depriving them of property, but restoring it to the right owner; — it is not wronging the master, but righting the slave — restoring him to himself;
Because immediate and general emancipation would only destroy nominal, not real property: it would not amputate a limb or break a bone of the slaves, but by infusing motives into their breasts, would make them doubly valuable to the masters as free laborers; and
Because if compensation is to be given at all, it should be given to the outraged and guiltless slaves, and not to those who have plundered and abused them." [2]

So much for the assertion of your correspondent, that "this measure [remuneration] is popular among the most influential men" in the anti-slavery ranks! Who are meant by "the most influential men," I know not; but this I know, that all genuine abolitionists will scout any proposition to pay the thief for becoming an honest man, and the oppressor for ceasing to trample upon his fellow-creatures.

It is seldom, sir, that I am induced to notice anonymous writers; but in this instance, I deem a correction necessary. My object is not controversy; and I therefore believe you will permit this brief vindication of anti-slavery principles to appear in the Courier.

Respectfully yours,

WM. LLOYD GARRISON.

Printed: Boston *Courier*, June 19, 1834; reprinted in *The Liberator*, June 21, 1834.

1. This is one of Garrison's favorite passages, the motion against slavery pre-

sented to Parliament in 1830 (Hansard, New Series, 25:1191, June–July 1830). For a fuller quotation of the same passage see letter 43, to the editor of the Boston *Evening Transcript*, November 6, 1830.

2. Garrison quotes from the Declaration of Sentiments he wrote for the American Anti-Slavery Society in December of 1833. The full text of this document was published in *The Liberator*, December 14, 1833.

159

TO HELEN E. BENSON

Boston, June 21, 1834.

Very dear Helen:

How gratifying, — how touching, — how filial, — how eminently worthy of yourself, — was your letter of Wednesday! — It made me womanish, and I wept. You have never sent me one which I appreciate more highly, always excepting that precious epistle in which you first avowed your love for me. Beautiful mistress of my heart! Affectionate daughter of transcendantly worthy parents! How shall I express, in adequate language, my admiration of your innate modesty, your moral worth, your dutiful affection? Well do you write thus — "You, dear Lloyd, who know how ardently I am attached to you, will not love me the less because I am sometimes melancholy at the thought of parting with the dear ones around me." No — if I should, it would be conclusive evidence that I was a miserably selfish being, altogether unworthy of one so generous, so pure, and so lovely as yourself. *I* love you "the less"! — Exactly the reverse — I love you the more for this fine developement of your mind. Yes, dear girl, you may indeed weep — freely weep. Nature must have way. You speak of "a mother's love," and ask, "what love is comparable to hers?"[1] An allusion like this dissolves my heart, and causes it to grow liquid as water. I had a mother once, who cared for me with such a passionate regard, who loved me so intensely, that no language can describe the yearnings of her soul — no instrument measure the circumference of her maternal spirit. As to her person, I sum up my panegyric of it in the following original verse:

> She was the masterpiece of womankind —
> In shape and height majestically fine;
> Her cheeks the lily and the rose combined;
> Her lips — more opulently red than wine;
> Her raven locks hung tastefully entwined;
> Her aspect fair as Nature could design:
> And then her eyes! so cloquently bright!
> An eagle would recoil before their light.

But she was not remarkable for her personal attractions merely. Her mind was of the first order — clear, vigorous, creative, and lustrous, and sanctified by an ever-glowing piety. How often did she watch over me — weep over me — and pray over me! (I hope, not in vain.) She has been dead almost eleven years; but my grief at her loss is as fresh and poignant now, as it was at that period. "O that my mother were living!" is often the exclamation of my heart. Alas! she cannot come to me. But why do I say "alas!" Would I, even if I could, call her away from the joys and glories of a better world, to this transient, polluted, dying state of existence? Oh, no! Rest in heaven, dear mother! I would go to thee, but not have thee come to me. The thought of that perfect happiness which thou art enjoying, in the presence of the angels of God and the spirits of the just made perfect, enlarges my own happiness below. Thy dutiful, penitent, affectionate child hopes to spend with thee a blissful eternity! [2]

☼   ☼   ☼   ☼   ☼

In your letter (which I cannot peruse too often) you remark — "I tremble for fear of my utter incapacity to serve you as I ought." A great poet, dear Helen, assures us that "the dread of death is most in apprehension" [3] — and I trust you will find all your fears to have been premature. Let not disquietude fill your mind. Be assured that nothing arduous, or excessive, or difficult, will be required of you as the wife of W. L. G. I am a plain man — at least, I mean to be; my habits are, like yours, very simple and abstemious; I am fond of solitude rather than much company; my *visiting* acquaintance is extremely limited; and I shall aim to be very domestic. We shall live without any parade, in a quiet manner, at a convenient distance from this bustling city. So, my love, dismiss your fears, and be of a cheerful spirit. It is for me to cherish a dutiful solicitude. I am almost afraid to receive you, lest I shall fail in making you happy. Can I fill that void in your heart which a separation from your beautiful home — your father, mother, brother, and sisters — is to create? I will try to do so. You shall find that my love is ardent, pure and steadfast; that it will be my aim to soothe every sorrow that may arise in your breast, and to strow your path with flowers. Perfect happiness we must not expect in our pilgrimage on earth, but still we may find great delight, and ripen together for a nobler, a brighter, a more blissful state of existence.

Perhaps it will not be premature to allude to our wedding. What shall I say, in relation to it? First, as to the time. I have thought it best to take place early in October, or sooner, or later, — just as you shall decide. Indeed, I wish you *would* decide; for I am sure that your time will suit me, but I am *not* sure that I shall be judicious myself in making an appointment. Then, as to the wedding itself. I shall invite my Aunt, who resides in Lowell, and two or three friends. [4]

Of course, you will invite as large a circle as you think proper. I hope no wine will be used on the occasion, and no *wedding-cake*. I object to wine, because it is impure and intoxicating, and I wish to brand it as a poison. As to the cake, I will not be strenuous for its banishment; but, I confess, it would please me to have our marriage distinguished for simplicity. *How* we were married, will of course be widely tol[d,] especially among the colored population. It is for us, therefore, to avoid extravagance on the one hand, and eccentricity on the other. When I speak of the propriety of banishing *wedding cake*, I allude of course to that rich and showy kind which is commonly resorted to on similar occasions. Perhaps it will be well to have a plain substitute; but having expressed my desire, I leave it with you to decide, assuring you that I shall cheerfully acquiescence in any arrangement or provision you shall make, except in the use of wine; and I know you will not desire either to poison me, or yourself, or your dear parents, or brothers and sisters, or friends and acquaintance.

You express a hope that, as I shall go to Pawtucket and Providence on the 4th of July, you may have the pleasure of beholding me in Brooklyn. Eager as I am to clasp you in my arms, I shall not — such are my engagements — be able to gratify your desire; but I shall certainly endeavor to be with you when Miss Crandall's trial takes place. I understand that comes on the last of July. Then I hope to spend a week or ten days with you.

Rev. Mr. Philleo is now in this city, and called upon me last evening and to-day. He leaves on Monday morning. He certainly appears to be a good man, and I sincerely hope that "he is a man more sinned against than sinning." [5]

The mail closes in five minutes. The Post Office is closed, and I must send this without being able to pay the postage.

My best regards to all.

Yours, wholly and ardently,

Wm. Lloyd Garrison.

ALS: Villard Papers, Harvard College Library; printed partly in *Life*, I, 34.

1. Garrison quotes from Helen's letter of June 16. Two changes of phraseology suggest that he may be quoting from memory.
2. As this letter indicates, Garrison tended to idealize his mother and their relationship in absence and after death.
3. Garrison adapts *Measure for Measure*, III, i, 78: "The sense of death is most in apprehension."
4. Charlotte Lloyd Newell, who died in Garrison's house after an extended illness in 1857, was apparently at this time a widow; it was she who was to accompany Garrison and Helen on their wedding trip.
5. In Shakespeare's *King Lear* (III, ii, 59–60) the passage reads:

"I am a man

More sinn'd against than sinning."

160

TO HELEN E. BENSON

Boston, June 25, 1834.

Dear Helen:

I sincerely pity you, if you deplore my absence as much as I do yours. My heart almost dies within me daily, at our separation. Friends — dear, ardent, admiring friends, cluster around me as usual, and are constantly multiplying; but I feel as if I had but one friend in the world — your own dear self. Nothing can atone for the bereavement which your absence creates. I am depressed — the hours move tardily along — I try to borrow consolation from the future; but my heart still repines, and refuses to be comforted.

The beautiful lock of hair that you gave me is unspeakably precious. I gaze upon it with exquisite delight, and almost fancy that you are really in my presence. How often do I press it to my lips, with all the fervor and sincerity of a faithful lover! I have also kissed your charming letters many, many times, and felt a thrill of pleasure rushing through every vein. Think not, dear Helen, that I am indulging in a mere rhapsody: it is the language of my soul.

I am not exactly in a poetical mood, but I will try to weave an acrostic upon your name. So, here it is:

How beautiful is morn upon the hills!
E'en so art thou whose sight my bosom thrills:
Love kindles in my heart its vestal flame, —
Electrifies and runs through all my frame;
Nor would I from this soft captivity
Enfranchisement desire, away from thee.
Let Heaven bear witness to the pledge I give —
In weal or wo, to love thee while I live;
Zealous to strow thy path with fadeless flowers,
And gild with rapture's rays the flying hours.

*　　☆　　✿　　❁

Beautiful girl! my chosen one! my pride!
Elect as mistress — soon to be my bride —
Not all the strong attractions of the earth
Shall draw my heart like thy magnetic worth:
Obedient — constant — kind, I'll ever be,
Nor doubt to meet a sweet return from thee.

The above is too tame — too inexpressive. I hope to give you a better one when I get more leisure.

*   *   *   *

2 o'clock.

I had written thus far, when Mr. Knapp put your favor of Monday afternoon into my hand. I hardly dared to anticipate it, especially as my last letter was put into the Post Office at so late an hour, that I was afraid it would not arrive on Monday. Your kindness in answering my poor scrawls so promptly, and so exactly, deeply affects my heart, and shows the liberality and goodness of your disposition.

I am glad that you have seen and heard my estimable friend Charles Stuart, and that you esteem him so highly. He is exceedingly affectionate in his manner, watchful in his behaviour, and devout in his feelings; but, as you remark, also exceedingly eccentric in his appearance. — However, if the inward man be clothed in the robes of heaven, it is of little consequence as to the color, or shape, or quality, of the habiliments which cover the outward man. Still, I wish he had more taste and neatness about his person, for it is worthy of some regard.

I thank you for sending me his friendly advice as to "the severity of my language." My conscience acquits me of the charge. The strength of my speech bears no proportion to the enormity of the conduct of the scourgers of helpless women, and the robbers of my species.

He, and my dear brother May, and yourself — all extol me above my merits, but I will try to be more worthy of so much affection and regard.

You will be happy to hear that the health of my friend Knapp is improving. He begs to return his thanks for your kind inquiries, and promises to make a visit to "Friendship Vale" shortly, and in your presence get some of the *elixir vitae.* He has just remarked to me — "Tell Miss Helen that she has not yet asked my consent to let her come into the firm"! — You will find no difficulty in getting it; for he is almost as much pleased at the prospect of my union with you, as if he was about taking unto himself a wife.

Our marriage, then, shall be in September, if you please, and as early as you please in the month. I am anxious to hasten the time, because I know not why much delay is necessary, nor why we should not enjoy each other's society as early and as long as possible. Suppose we decide upon the first week, or, if more agreeable, the first day of September. Recollect, *you* must decide — therefore do so without any hesitancy.

As to my trial, I did at first think it might be well to wait until it took place; but as it is somewhat uncertain whether it will come on in October, and how long it may be postponed — and, as you justly observe, September is a warmer and pleasanter month — I now think it is not worth while to pay any regard to the petty and foolish prosecution. My friend Knapp would even prefer August to September for our wedding.

I knew you would readily agree to banish wine from our marriage ceremony. As to the cake, do just as you think best: if you should have any, let it be very plain — not like common wedding cake. I hope my dear May will not fail to unite us together. While he is breaking so many fetters, he may be excused for occasionally putting a couple into bondage "with their own consent."

Convey my most affectionate regards to your dear parents, and to all the household.

Your affectionate lover,

Wm. Lloyd Garrison.

Miss Helen E. Benson.

N.B. Tell Mr. May that I have no doubt Hingham is a beautiful village, but Roxbury is prettier. The former is certainly too remote from Boston. You say truly, "if you had a home, you would prefer to come to dinner" — which I could not do if that home were in Hingham.

My aunt, who resides in Lowell, is my mother's youngest sister, and the only relation I have in this vicinity. All my relations, or nearly all, reside in New-Brunswick, (British dominions,) and they constitute together a numerous collection.

☞ What will you say, dearest, *if you should see me in Brooklyn on Monday afternoon?* I have not yet got my address prepared for the 4th of July at Pawtucket, and it is pretty certain that I shall not be able to complete it if I stay in Boston. Now, friend Knapp proposes that I should go to "Friendship Vale," and there write it, and go from thence to Pawtucket. *I think I shall do so,* although you must not *positively* expect me. Still, *it is my purpose to come,* and so not visit you the last of July, as I contemplated. I will spend the evenings with you, and shut myself up in the day time till I finish my address. Will you agree to this? If I should not arrive in Monday's stage, of course I shall not see you till the close of July.

ALS: Villard Papers, Harvard College Library.

161

TO GEORGE W. BENSON

Brooklyn, July 10, 1834.

My dear George:

I dare not make a *positive* promise, as to the delivery of an address to my colored brethren in Providence, on Sabbath evening next; for my physical and intellectual energies are unstrung, and there is nothing special that impresses itself upon my mind, as worthy of being communicated to them. You need not, therefore, circulate any notice until my arrival. Perhaps we shall deem it best to make some other arrangement; and if not, by giving notice of my intention in the forenoon and afternoon, at the close of the services in the colored meeting-house, we shall doubtless be enabled to collect an audience. My address, if delivered, will be extemporaneous — and, of course, very simple and plain.

You may expect me on Saturday evening; and, fearing lest I shall offend you if I do otherwise, I shall comply with your kind invitation to stop at your dwelling — although I am afraid of really incommoding you. One thing quiets me — you know I am a plain man, and the more simple the treatment I receive, the better I am pleased. Receive me, then, not as a guest — not even as a friend — but as a brother.

Every thing in Brooklyn, at the present time, conspires to make my bliss as abundant and perfect, as it is ever the lot of erring and perishing man to receive. The garniture of the fields and hills is beautifully luxuriant — the perfume of the flowers is wafted upon every breeze — and every tree is decorated most gorgeously. — Every morning and evening, ten thousand birds, (I may exaggerate the number, but their multitudinous collection surprises me,) of various plumage and note, greet me with their fine voices, and pour forth a tide of melody almost overpoweringly. But there is one source of delight — one object of love, dearer to me than all those I have named above. You need no explanation.

This afternoon, we think of making a visit to Rowland Green.[1] Yesterday, his son spent an hour with us, and I was pleased with his deportment and conversation. As I have not yet visited Prudence, we shall journey to Plainfield, via Canterbury. The Canterburians lately killed a cat, cut her throat, and hung her by the neck to Prudence's gate. We may say to the victim, Requies-*cat* in pace — and to the perpetrators of the murderous deed, "You have added another black act to the long *cat*-alogue of your offences." The *cat*-astrophe will be duly chronicled, not *dog*-matically but *cat*-egorically.[2]

All the members of the family are well. Helen desires to be specially and most affectionately remembered to you. Henry, we presume, will come home to-morrow. His absence makes quite a void.

With the utmost affection,

Your admiring brother,

Wm. Lloyd Garrison

Mr. Geo. W. Benson

ALS: Garrison Papers, Boston Public Library.

1. The date of birth of Dr. Rowland W. Greene (the correct spelling of his name) is uncertain since there is an error in the *Vital Record of Rhode Island, 1636–1850*, Providence, 1895, where his date of birth is given as 1779, which would make him thirteen years old at the time his first son was born. He was probably born about 1769 and he did die in 1859. Dr. Greene ran a small Quaker school in Plainfield, Connecticut. The son to whom Garrison refers cannot be positively identified since Rowland and Susannah Greene had in 1834 six sons ranging in age from twenty-five to forty-two.

2. Garrison's fondness for puns is well illustrated in this passage, the fullest development of the "cat" and "dog" puns he had used before and would use again.

162

TO HELEN E. BENSON

Providence, July 15, 1834.

My dear Wife — *prospectively:*

On my arrival in this city, on Saturday evening, a tide of emotions was called up in my breast by the appalling intelligence from New-York, respecting the riotous proceedings of the mob against our abolition brethren in that city.[1] On the Sabbath, the news was still more afflicting. To think that we who venture to remonstrate against the utter debasement and cruel oppression of a large portion of our countrymen, are branded by the daily press as outlaws, and declared to be unworthy of the least protection from the murderous designs of a lawless mob! — to think that religious meetings may be disturbed with impunity, and forcibly broken up! — to think that our temples, dedicated to the worship of Almighty God, may be razed to the earth, and their contents burnt in the streets! — to think that ministers must fly from the city into the country to escape martyrdom! — to think that the sacred privacy of home may be invaded, and private property scattered to the winds of heaven, in the broad blaze of day as well as in the darkness of night! — to think of scenes like these, not in Hindostan, not in Burmah, not in Rome, not in Paris, but in a land boasting of its liberty and laws — is it not enough to overwhelm the soul with horror and amazement? And this is not the worst of it.

There are hundreds and thousands, in this region, calling themselves honorable and high-minded men, — patriots, — *christians* even, — who either openly applaud, or covertly justify, all that has been committed by as licentious and desperate a mob as were ever rallied together in any country to do the vile work of their great master the Devil.

In view of all these things, dear Helen, you may be anxious to know the state of my mind. Truly can I affirm, that it is full of sweet tranquillity. I can no more doubt that this shameful riot will ultimately advance the cause of the enslaved in our land, than I can doubt that a storm of thunder and lightning will purify a vitiated atmosphere. Therefore, I rejoice in hope. But I pity and weep over those poor misguided, ignorant creatures who have actually committed the violence, and who have been made the tools of intelligent and influential, but base and cowardly men. I pray God to forgive them, as I most cheerfully do, and as I hope to be forgiven. Perilous times have come — but our trust is in the Lord of hosts, and our souls are unmoved — we cannot be driven back.

I found all the family in good health. Mr. and Mrs. Anthony did not return from Taunton until Monday noon. George smilingly alludes to your compliment respecting his flourishing appearance and fine bodily health, and says that it induced him to get weighed, and he found that he had gained just nothing at all, but had lost several pounds of flesh! — So I have some hope that as you supposed I grew thinner in Brooklyn, it may turn out that I *gained* something in body, as well as much in mind.

Sabbath forenoon and afternoon, I attended the Rev. Mr. Waterman's [2] church, in company with George, and heard two solemn, faithful, powerful sermons from the text, "Perilous times shall come." They had direct reference to the New-York mobs, and produced a most salutary impression.

On Monday forenoon, I called with George to see William and Anna Jenkins. William Almy went out at the back door as we went in at the front, and so we lost him.[3] We found Mrs. Jonathan Backhouse and some other friends present, who had to leave us in a few minutes to take the steam-boat for New-York.[4] William Jenkins was very much agitated, and began to *denounce* my *denunciations* against slaveholders, and to oppose the doctrine of immediate emancipation — all the while hurriedly moving about the room, like a man struggling with a strong but naughty conscience. In a few minutes, by applying Quaker principles to his reasoning, I wound him up in a manner so simple and comprehensive, that he was evidently rejoiced to find an excuse for leaving the room, in seeing Mrs. Backhouse into the carriage. He did not return again into the room. I am sure that I treated him in the most pleasant and respectful manner. I forgot to say that among those in the room, was providentially our venerable friend Moses Brown, who listened silently but with much apparent satisfaction to my rejoinders to Jenkins. I had considerable conversation with Mrs. Jenkins, and found her in a calm and sweet frame of mind, and clearly in favor of the sentiments I uttered. Undoubtedly, she is mortified at the perverseness of her husband. I did not expect to find him so irritable in his temper, but this is an evidence that he has little peace of mind.

Friend Brown took George and myself into his carriage, and drove home. We took dinner with him, and had an exceedingly interesting and profitable interview. His mind seemed to be as clear and lucid as the sun. He pleasantly quizzed me about Brooklyn, and said he understood I had found a certain attraction in that place, which would probably call me there frequently. He inquired with much particularity after your dear father, and expressed a hope that his health would soon enable him to visit Providence.

Monday (yesterday) afternoon, I took my leave of Providence for Pawtucket and Boston. I had a pleasant interview with Rev. Mr. Blain, Elder Potter, Samuel Foster, Joseph Healy, and other abolition friends.[5] The evening was a glorious one. The moon was highly effulgent, and the stars put on their best attire. I wandered down to the falls, where the water was rushing and dashing with vast power and beautiful effect. Every thing bordered upon romance, and was full of enchantment. Amid that whirl of waters and thunder of contending waves, and that shower of moon-light, and that high romance of vision, where were my thoughts? — where, but in Brooklyn, in Friendship's Vale, clustering about your own dear self, and the rest of your delightful companions? Truly, "where our treasure is, there are our hearts also."[6] I had no doubt that you were thinking of me — that at the same hour you too were looking at the same bright luminaries, and lamenting with me that we could not enjoy the soul-enrapturing scene in each other's company.

This evening I expected to have been in Boston; but the stage neglected to call for me in Pawtucket, and, consequently, I lost my passage. I came over this afternoon to Providence, in order to seize this opportunity to send you a *very* hasty, and I fear an almost illegible scrawl — purposing to-morrow morning to depart for Boston without fail.

Of course, I am with my dear brother George, who, with his sweet lady, sends all the love that can be crowded into a letter-sheet. I am already sadly home-sick — that is to say, pining to return to

Brooklyn: how, then, shall I be able to endure a separation of six or seven weeks? You will pity me in my solitude, and cheer me with an epistle as often as once a week. Surely, dear Helen, I am

Yours, with intense affection,

Wm. Lloyd Garrison.

Miss H. E. Benson.

ALS: Villard Papers, Harvard College Library.

1. Riots against abolitionists began at an antislavery meeting on July 4, recommenced on the seventh and continued sporadically for three days. It was reported that there was considerable damage to the Chatham Chapel, where the antislavery meeting had been held, and to the houses of leading abolitionists Lewis Tappan and Reverend Dr. Samuel H. Cox. According to reports and editorials in *The Liberator* for July 12 and 19 the following were to be blamed: a man named Wilder, who had led similar riots in his native Jamaica, the editors of the New York *Courier and Enquirer* and the New York *Commercial Advertiser*, and colonizationists in general.

2. Henry Waterman's.

3. William Almy (1761–1836) was a Quaker and an abolitionist of many years' standing; he was the son-in-law of Moses Brown, and, with a brother-in-law, ran the Brown textile business, the name of the firm becoming Almy, Brown, and Slater.

4. Hannah Chapman Backhouse (1787–1850), a niece of John Gurner and the wife of banker-businessman Jonathan Backhouse (1774–1842), was a leader among the Orthodox Quakers and a dedicated abolitionist.

5. Of the abolitionist friends mentioned, only Ray Potter has previously been identified. John Blain (1795–1879), originally from New York state, was a Baptist minister and evangelist who had since 1819 preached extensively in New York state, Connecticut, Massachusetts, and Rhode Island. At the time of Garrison's letter he was apparently situated either in Pawtucket or in Providence. (See *Biographical Cyclopedia of Representative Men of Rhode Island*, Providence, 1881.) Samuel Foster (1803–1901) was a successful Providence businessman, with substantial investments in retail and wholesale grocery and in the manufacture of cotton goods. (See *Rhode Island Historical Society Proceedings*, 1901–1902, p. 65.) Joseph Healy cannot be identified with certainty, but he may have been the one who was born in East Greenwich about 1774 and who was listed in the Providence directory for 1836 as a teacher.

6. Matthew 6:21, adapted.

163

TO HELEN E. BENSON

Boston, July 21, 1834.

Dear Girl:

Your letter reached me in season to save me from utter despondency — just as my feelings were sinking to the very lowest ebb. I feel revived, like the thirsty Arabian traveller by the side of a well-spring.

Since my return, I have been as busy as one of those little squirrels which we saw turning the cage so briskly, at Mr. Phillips's,[1] on our return from Providence. My tongue, however, and not my pen, has been active. Loquacity I hate — but talk I must, for people come to me for information, and they will have it from my lips, and not merely from the documents which I put into their hands. So long as I remain in my office in Boston, I despair of doing much *on paper* for the cause of liberty. Happily, there are now so many powerful minds at work, producing some of the best specimens of eloquent and valuable composition in our language, that I may suffer my quill to rest awhile, without any detriment to myself or others. Happily, too, in the course of seven weeks, I hope to be in a snug retreat in Roxbury, where I shall be enabled to pour out my soul in torrents of holy indignation against the slave system, — inspired by your presence, as well as by the subject itself.

You are a good girl for not letting my absence prey too keenly upon your spirits. Industry is an excellent panacea for sorrow — not always infallible, but generally successful. Make your needle a weapon, and I will my pen, against the despondency of love, and I dare say we shall come off victorious.

O, but love is a naughty thing! How it becomes a part of our person, following us like our shadow, wherever we move, over hill and dale, in tumult and in solitude, by day and by night! It has got into the citadel of my heart, and there it remains invulnerable.

Now for the cottages in Roxbury. I have been looking at them, as I always do, with great pleasure; but they are as much in demand, as the madman Garrison is in the southern States. After all, I find none that pleases me so much, both in regard to retirement and beauty of scenery, as the one at which I boarded last winter. It has recently been enlarged and materially improved, and is now to let or sell. — It has six commodious chambers, and one small one — a cellar kitchen and an upper one — two fine parlors and a sitting room, &c. &c. The cottage is admirably contrived, and at the present time looks delightfully, in consequence of the opulent beauty of Nature round about it. It is about three miles and a quarter from the centre of this city — about 50 minutes walk, or 10 minutes to the place where the omnibusses pass every half hour, which carry one into Boston very quickly. I have not yet engaged it, but have offered $150 rent per year for it. The owner wishes to get $200, but I am not willing to give it, nor do I think he will get it from any one at this late period in the season, although he would perhaps be able to, if it were now April instead of the close of July. I am confident of obtaining it, and shall know to a certainty within a few days. In the back cellar is one of the finest wells of water I have ever seen — the water is conducted into the kitchen, so that it is not necessary to go out of the house for it. This will doubtless be an agreeable piece of information to you, as you are such a famous patron of cold water. I am somewhat afraid that you will deem it too secluded — but it is very little more so than your dwelling in Friendship Vale; and then it is so easy to get into the midst of the town of Roxbury, or into this bustling city, that you never need be lonesome, or lead a monotonous life.

To-day I have been round to some of our Furniture Stores, in order to make a selection of such articles as we shall need. There is a great variety in the prices and patterns of the various articles; and I am puzzled in coming to a choice. I have wished you were here, forty times; but I hope (with the assistance of some friends) to be tasteful and judicious in my selection. As yet, I have engaged nothing, and shall not until I hear from you. — Some purchases may be left until your arrival. I propose to buy now, (if agreeable to you,) a bureau, a sofa, two neat dining tables, (to match,) two and a half dozen chairs, three common tables, one toilet table, washstands, looking-glasses, clock, &c. &c.; besides all the paraphernalia of the kitchen. Whatever else is needed on your arrival, can be obtained at any moment. As to the carpets, I shall do nothing about them until you come. Let me know if the above list is agreeable to you, and what alteration, or addition, if any, you desire. Should you prefer a secretary to a bureau, or shall we need both?

Let me know how many beds you have in contemplation, and whether single or double. I think we may do with three double ones, and two single. My friend Knapp, and our servant girl, will only require a single one each. A double bed will require about 35 lbs. of feathers — these can be obtained from 30 to 50 cents per lb. I am advised by my married friends not to get any mattresses to put under the feather beds, first, as they are somewhat expensive, and secondly, as straw-beds answer the purpose equally well. What do you say? I wish you would send on your bed-ticks and bedding as soon as convenient, that I may be getting things ready with all convenient despatch. I wish to get the cottage in as good trim as possible, before your arrival *home*.

Perhaps you did not mean to have any mattresses to put *under* the feather beds, but only to be substituted for them. If so, inform me.

I am flattered to find that I am so much in the good graces of my worthy and grateful friend M. Burnett. Give my best compliments to her, and remember me to dear blind Eunice, whom I unwittingly neglected to bid farewell on my departure from Brooklyn. To your father and mother, Henry, Mary, Anne and Sarah, Miss Eliza, Mr.

May and lady, &c. give my best wishes and most pleasing remembrances.

I am yours indissolubly,

Wm. Lloyd Garrison.

☞ Write soon.

ALS: Villard Papers, Harvard College Library.

1. Presumably a resident of Brooklyn, possibly the owner of a pet shop.

164

TO SAMUEL J. MAY

Boston, July 23, 1834.

Beloved Friend:

A young man, such as you need at Brooklyn to take charge of the Unionist, cannot easily be found.[1] — Journeymen printers are generally of little worth, and those who aspire to be editors are commonly but little better. I shall be sorry — very sorry, to see the Unionist go down — for many reasons, but especially on account of its unwavering adherence to our most unpopular cause, and of its advocacy of the Canterbury school. It will be a fresh scandal to Connecticut to let such a paper die, and such a vile sheet as the Advertiser live.[2] Should such a catastrophe happen, a general shout from the base slaves of the devil may be expected as far as they shall gain information of the fact. The editor of the N.Y. Commercial Advertiser will throw a *Stone*; the ruffian of the Courier and Enquirer will weave a new *Webb*; and a *Holbrook* of pollution will sweep over you in Brooklyn.[3] If you hate puns and punsters as heartily as did Dr. Johnson, you will give no quarter to me or mine. But pray excuse me. The names of this infamous trio seemed to be so expressive in this connexion, that I could not refrain from using them up.

I will make further inquiry, and if I can find a suitable printer for your meridian, you shall be informed of the fact without delay.

So, it seems, you are almost vexed with me for putting in that advertisement for a colored wife.[4] Young Dr. Atlee, of Philadelphia, has sent me a chiding letter on this point.[5] There is also much fluttering among abolitionists generally. The enemy, of course, is largely commenting upon the advertisement. O, imprudent Mr. Garrison! obstinate Mr. Garrison! in view of these things, art thou not sorry for what thou hast done? No, indeed, my friend, I am not sorry. I weighed the matter deliberately before I advertised, and see no cause now to regret the decision which I made. We will canvass the subject at large when we meet again.

"When are you going to be married?" is your inquiry. If Providence permit, and it be agreeable to Helen, I propose to make the following arrangements. On Monday morning, September 1, I shall start from Boston in a barouche, accompanied by my Aunt [6] and friend Knapp, and go to Providence that day. On Tuesday, 2d, I shall endeavor to reach Brooklyn in the afternoon. On Wednesday, 3d, arrangements may be made for the wedding. On Thursday morning, 4th, you will be called upon to tie the nuptial knot, and make Helen and myself no more twain, but one. As soon as the ceremony is over, we shall take our departure with all decent despatch, and calculate to reach Worcester on Thursday evening. On Friday afternoon, I hope we shall be in our cottage in Roxbury; so that on Saturday, all household affairs, as far as practicable, may be "put to rights." And then, you know, follows a day of rest.

If any alteration be made in these arrangements, you shall be informed thereof without delay. Every thing is so unstable in this fleeting world, that it seems almost like presumption or mockery to make any calculations for the future.

I am anxious to learn whether you have come to a fixed determination as to an agency for the American Anti-Slavery Society. You know that, independent of our most holy cause, I do not consider Brooklyn a suitable place for a mind, and talents, like yours. Say to Mrs. May that "there's no place like —— Roxbury." If she will come and occupy a part of our cottage, and thus be a companion for dear Helen, she shall be accommodated in the most ample manner. She can have a parlour, a kitchen, chambers, &c. — i.e. provided I succeed (as I expect to) in getting the one I have in view; which is the same, materially enlarged and improved, as I occupied as a boarder last winter. It is about three miles from Boston; but as our omnibuses are running constantly to and from Roxbury, every few minutes, the distance is almost annihilated.

What tidings have been received from New-York since we parted! — Our country is in an awful condition. There is cause for alarm and lamentation, not that our cause is really in danger, (for it towers up more majestically and strongly than ever,) but on account of the general disposition in community, on the part of many who call themselves honorable men, patriots and christians, to excuse the outrages committed by the mob, and destroy the character of such men as Arthur Tappan, Dr. Cox, and other devoted philanthropists.[7] Stone I have long since branded as "a murderous hypocrite," and few will now hesitate to say that the description is unjust. Had it not been for his paper, there is no probability that the mob could have taken place. If any man ever deserved to be sent to the Penitentiary or State Prison for life, Stone is that man. Webb has not been less active and venomous; but every body knows that he is a ruffian who glories in his shame, and makes no pretensions to virtue and religion.

At this great crisis it behooves all abolitionists to be "watchful unto prayer," and to put unlimited confidence in the Lord of hosts. We shall be called, my brother, to pass through many perils; but if the love of God reign supremely in our hearts, we shall encounter them victoriously.

Do you intend to observe the 1st of August in Brooklyn? David L. Child, Esq. will deliver an address on that day in South Reading. Our Board of Managers deem it unwise to hold a *public* meeting in this city, in the present inflammable state of the public mind; but we shall convene a special private meeting at our anti-slavery rooms, and commemorate the day with religious services.

See that Helen behaves like a good girl till I come — and give my respects to your estimable lady, and as many kisses to your dear children for me as a fond parent can bestow. I am neither a husband nor a father, but

Your much attached and admiring friend,

Wm. Lloyd Garrison.

Rev. S. J. May.

ALS: Garrison Papers, Boston Public Library.

1. Charles C. Burleigh edited the Brooklyn *Unionist*, founded in 1833, for about two years.
2. Garrison considered the Boston *Advertiser* an unconscionably conservative newspaper. It was this paper, incidentally, that was to defend the mob that attacked Garrison on October 21, 1835.
3. Garrison lists three editors he considers notoriously reprehensible for not supporting the abolitionist movement. William Leete Stone (1792–1844) had been associated with several papers — notably the Cooperstown *Federalist* and the Federalist *Herkimer American* — before becoming one of the proprietors of the New York *Commercial Advertiser*. James Watson Webb (1802–1884) was one of the most influential and vitriolic of nineteenth-century journalists. In 1827 he acquired the *Morning Courier*, which merged to become the *Morning Courier and New-York Enquirer* in 1829. Josiah Holbrook (1788–1854) was the founder of the lyceum movement in 1826 which sponsored a series of local lectures. It was a fact that lyceum lecturers remained silent on the issue of slavery. In 1832 Holbrook had published a weekly newspaper, the *Family Lyceum*.
4. The advertisement to which Garrison refers appeared in *The Liberator* for June 28, 1834. Headed, "A Wife Wanted," the advertisement asserted that the subscriber wished to demonstrate his lack of prejudice by marrying a suitable Negro woman. "Information would be thankfully received," he said, "of any young, respectable, and intelligent Colored Woman, . . . who would be willing to endure the insults and reproaches that would be heaped upon her for being the partner of a white man, . . ."
5. Edwin P. Atlee (died 1836) of Philadelphia had been an early friend of

Garrison's, a founder of the American Anti-Slavery Society, and the chairman of the committee on the Declaration of Sentiments, though Garrison was the author of that famous document.

6. Charlotte Lloyd Newell.

7. Samuel Hanson Cox (1793–1880), although of Quaker ancestry, was a convert to the Presbyterian church, in which he became one of the leading ministers in a theological controversy which split the church in the late 1830's. He was one of the few ministers with genuinely radical antislavery convictions — convictions that resulted in his being hanged in effigy along with Garrison in 1835. He was also a staunch temperance man, objecting violently to the use of both alcohol and tobacco. His brother was Abraham Liddon Cox.

165

TO SAMUEL J. MAY

Boston, July 28, 1834.

Dear Friend:

In reply to your favor of the 24th, my partner joins with me in consenting to print an edition of Miss Crandall's, as large as the one proposed by you, at our own risk. As to the profits that may arise from the sale of the pamphlet, we do not expect to make any: on the contrary, we shall probably suffer some loss, in consequence of the difficulty of disposing of any publication, however interesting or valuable in itself. But a trial so important as Miss C's — involving such momentous consequences to a large portion of our countrymen — implicating so deeply the character of this great nation — ought not to go unpublished, and *shall* not while we have the necessary materials for printing it.[1] Ellsworth, it seems, has by his plea exalted his own reputation, but I fear he will not be able to redeem the reputation of Connecticut.[2] The friends of the colored population — and the colored population themselves — are largely indebted to that fearless advocate of impartial liberty, for his manly efforts to rescue a feeble but deeply injured race from the fangs of prejudice and the jaws of oppression.

I regret to perceive by the newspapers, that Mr. Ellsworth is soon to retire from Congress. It is rather unfortunate, and somewhat remarkable, that the only man upon whom we could depend for any co-operation in overthrowing slavery in the District of Columbia, upon the floor of Congress, declines a re-election.

A correspondent of the New-York Journal of Commerce speaks in handsome terms of the manner in which Messrs. Ellsworth and Goddard[3] acquitted themselves.

Send me the report of the trial with all convenient despatch, and we will put it to press immediately.

Messrs. Robert J. Breckinridge, John Breckinridge, and Leonard Bacon, and Rev. Mr. M'Kenney, Agent of the Maryland Colonization Society; are now in this city, with two African Princes.[4] They have come *en masse*, to make a grand attack upon us, but will be defeated, according to present appearances. On Saturday, our city papers contained a bold and showy advertisement, stating that a meeting would be held by these gentlemen at the Bromfield-street (Methodist) Church on Sabbath evening, to urge the claims of the Maryland Colonization Society; and that other meetings for the same object would be held successively during the same week. Of course, this created much animation in our ranks. Brother Phelps was just on the eve of embarking for Portland, but concluded to tarry and encounter the shock of these potent antagonists. However, the evening papers of Saturday contained a notice, that the contemplated meetings would be postponed until further notice, which you may read, "postponed indefinitely." It is said that they received a visit from the Mayor, who urged them not to hold their meetings at this juncture — stating, among other things, that the mob would not be likely to discriminate between colonizationists and abolitionists, but would readily seize any pretext to create a disturbance. It is said, moreover, that the trustees of the church reconsidered their vote, granting these gentlemen the use of their house. Thus matters stand at present.

A rumor reaches us from Providence, that they attempted to get a hearing in that city, but could not succeed! — Truly, colonization seems to be poor stock in the market of humanity and morality in New-England.

On Friday evening, I called upon the Rev. John Breckinridge, in company with brother Phelps. The interview lasted till between 11 and 12 o'clock. The first half hour was spent in an amicable and argumentative discussion, respecting the duty of immediate emancipation. Brother Phelps left me to manage the case, only now and then thrusting in a keen, pithy and pertinent remark. Mr. B., I am sorry to say, soon lost his temper and overwhelmed us poor abolitionists with a tempest of epithets. His nervous system is extremely sensitive, and when it is excited, he almost becomes frantic. His language towards me was really abusive, and unworthy of a christian minister. Notwithstanding the provocations which he gave me, I endeavored — and I trust not without success — to preserve my equanimity. I said to him — "Mr. Breckinridge, we are both aware that the best men in our land are divided on the question of African colonization, and they need and are calling for more light. They wish to hear both sides of the question. Will you discuss it with me before the citizens of Boston?" "No," said he — "I do not consider you my equal. You are too debased and degraded in community for me — occupying the station that I do — to hold a controversy with you." "This," I replied, "is a convenient mode of escape. Will you encounter my brother Phelps?" "No." "Will you discuss the subject with any abolitionist?" "No." He was much excited when we separated, and intimated that he did not desire to have me call upon him again. I went home, lamenting that our interview had not been more placid, but feeling no unkindness, but rather much pity, toward him. I fell down on my knees, and besought the Lord to forgive him for all his accusations against me, to open his eyes if he were in error, and to grant that no ill-will should be left to rankle in our hearts. I also earnestly besought forgiveness for myself, if I had said or done aught amiss. My mind was very tranquil.

Say to my dear Helen, that I am anxious to comply with the *spirit* as well as the *letter* of your Connecticut marriage law; and therefore I wish you to give due notice to the community of Brooklyn, of our intended union. I leave the case with you and her. You shall have the necessary fees on my arrival in B. We were published in this city on Thursday last, for the first time.

Make my compliments to your lady — kiss the babe for me — and believe me

Ever yours,

Wm. Lloyd Garrison.

☞ Mr. Bacon wishes those numbers of the Unionist which are sent to the New-England Anti-Slavery Society, to be directed to him, and not to the Liberator office.[5] Will you be kind enough to see that the alteration is made?

ALS: Garrison Papers, Boston Public Library; printed partly in *Life*, I, 448–449, 431–432.

1. In *The Liberator*, November 8, 1834, the *Report of the Arguments of Counsel, in the Case of Prudence Crandall*, was advertised as just published and for sale at the rates of 16 cents each, $1.20 per dozen, or $10.00 per hundred.

2. William Wolcott Ellsworth (1791–1868), the son of Oliver Ellsworth, chief justice of the United States, was himself a distinguished lawyer and Whig congressman from Connecticut. In 1838 he was to be elected governor of the state and in 1847 to be appointed associate judge of the state supreme court.

3. Calvin Goddard, Prudence Crandall's defense attorney.

4. The brothers Robert Jefferson (1800–1871) and John Breckinridge (1797–1841) of Kentucky were Presbyterian ministers active in the various disputes concerning church dogma. Both were men of real distinction. John, an intense though not robust man, won honors at Princeton — both the college and the theological seminary — became chaplain of Congress and later minister of churches in Lexington and in Baltimore. After filling various offices in the Presbyterian church, he became in 1836 professor of pastoral theology in Princeton Seminary. At the time of his death he was president-elect of Oglethorpe University. Robert J. Breckinridge, after studying law and serving in the state legislature, entered the ministry and be-

came pastor of the Second Presbyterian Church in Baltimore. Later in life he was superintendent of public instruction in Kentucky and a professor at Danville Theological Seminary. A great controversialist, he supported many reforms, including temperance and colonization. During the Civil War he was Lincoln's chief adviser in Kentucky. William McKenney (1790–1857) was a chaplain of the United States Navy from 1841 to 1857 and was also secretary and treasurer of the Society for the Colonization of Liberia with American Negroes. Less important were the two native African princes, if one may judge by Garrison's report of their Boston meeting in *The Liberator* for August 2; indeed, they were evidently imposters (see letter 169, to George W. Benson, August 11, 1834).

5. This is Benjamin C. Bacon (1803–1874), a founder of the New England Anti-Slavery Society and Garrison's office agent and secretary of the Anti-Slavery Depository — that is, in charge of the books sold by Garrison and Knapp. He continued to serve the cause after moving to Philadelphia. (See Garrison's letter to Oliver Johnson, dated February 24, 1874.)

166

TO HELEN E. BENSON

Boston, July 28, 1834.

My own dear Girl:

If no accident betide me, nor obstacle interfere, in five weeks from to-day, I expect to be on my journey toward Brooklyn. In spite of my anxiety to see your sweet countenance again, and to have those legal ceremonies performed which are necessary to constitute us one flesh, time moves along with amazing speed. What are five weeks in his interminable calendar? Five drops in the great ocean — five stars in the firmament above — five grains of sand upon the sea-shore. They will pass away like the shadows of morning, as though they had not been: and thus it is with years, and thus with centuries. I dare say your dear parents, so true and vivid is Memory to things that have long since transpired, can retrace the long career of wedded life they have run, and make the period of their union as seemingly to be dated from yesterday. Surely, the soul was made for eternity. Time can no more fill its desires, than a particle of dust the universe.

There is but one epoch, and two eras, in our lives. Our birth — existence itself, constitutes the first; our marriage and death, the two last. Other events are collateral and incidental, not worthy of comparison. To us, dear Helen, the first era is rapidly approaching. We have staked much for time, and perhaps more for eternity, upon it. It is to be regarded with thrilling emotions, not with indifference or levity. I cannot doubt, for a moment, that our union will be the consummation of our earthly bliss. But, as the poet solemnly inquires, who can tell

"Through what new scenes and changes must we pass?" [1] It is well that none can solve the enigma. The hidden events of time are swift enough in their revelations. Those that transpire in a single day, are as much as we can bear in a single day, whether they be good or evil. If we resolve to do well to-day, we can let to-morrow take care of itself. Hence, I learn to be content, and to chasten and restrict my roving fancy. Of the future, I am resolved to borrow no trouble — nor have I any right to borrow too much happiness. In the midst of perils, I will not fear; in darkness, I will not despond; in prosperity, I will be lowly; in honor, I will be abased.

For the space of three days, we have had [weather] more intense than an African climate in Boston. The hea[t has] been excessive. Vegetation has marvelously enjoyed its ripening influences; but as for man and beast — for mind and body — these have not ceased to groan, "being burdened." However, I do not refer to the ardent temperature of the weather by way of complaint. If the wind blow east, it is well — if west, it is well — if north or south, it is well. If the sun flames like a universal conflagration, or muffles up his countenance, or puts out his fires, still it is well. Whatever infinite wisdom does, must be infinitely for the best. And yet the complaints of ungrateful, restless, fickle mortals about the weather are "as the sands upon the sea-shore innumerable." [2] It is a topic of discourse or complaint, at once exhaustless and everlasting. It is too hot — too cold — too dry — too wet — too tempestuous — too calm. All this is absurd and false; but it generally runs from the tongue as water from a fountain, without effort and without premeditation. It is true, the weather is a subject worthy of remark and of observation. We may say, it is cold to-day — or, it is very warm — or, it is very changeable — and yet make no complaint. I am only censuring that repining, querulous spirit, which is so generally manifested in society upon this subject.

I have engaged the cottage from the 1st of August until the 1st of next May — after which time, I am to have the refusal of it. If we should not find it agreeable, we can then seek a better elsewhere. As a summer residence, it is very picturesque; and during the last winter, I found it scarcely less agreeable. Its retirement delights me, and I feel very much attached to the spot. I could wish, for your sake, that it were now April or May, that we might enjoy the spring and summer together in the cottage; but I remember that, in one of your letters, you say that you prefer autumn to spring — and therefore I am happy in believing that we shall pass our time together very agreeably. I shall begin immediately to put the rooms in order.

I thought you would need two bureaus, and shall [ge]t them accordingly. A secretary is a convenient article, but it may be well to postpone the purchase of one for the present. When I suggested the expediency of getting two *dining* tables, I was in error: I meant two *parlor* tables, to match in cases of emergency. These are neat and pretty, and almost square, occupying but little space, and each accommodating six or eight persons. One of these would answer for the front, and the other for the back parlor. Our cottage is not calculated for large dining tables: the parlor tables answer a double purpose, and are extremely convenient. Perhaps, however, they are not such as you desire: if so, I will make no purchase until you come.

Your arrangements as to the beds are very liberal and judicious.

When George Thompson arrives, I have no doubt that he will gladly hire a part of our cottage for his lady, whom you will find to be an excellent young lady, of amiable manners and good intelligence. In this manner we shall get a social little circle.

I have invited my friend Knapp to request his sister Abigail,[3] who now resides in Newburyport, to spend a portion of her time with us, as a companion for you and Miss Eliza. He thinks she will; and her presence will serve to enliven him greatly, as well as us. She is an excellent girl — one of the very best in existence, both as to her head and heart. You cannot fail to be pleased with her. And, moreover, she understands all the machinery of household affairs.

I have not yet obtained a servant woman, but expect to succeed in my inquiries in a few days.

I trust their journey to Providence will renovate the health of your father and mother. Be careful of your own.

My love to dear Anna, and Sarah, and Mary, and Henry. Remember me to Eunice and Mary Burnett.

Most affectionately yours,

Wm. Lloyd Garrison.

ALS: Villard Papers, Harvard College Library. A small portion of the corner of the folded sheet on which the letter is written is torn off.

1. Not identified.
2. Garrison abridges slightly a passage from Hebrews 11:12.
3. Abigail Knapp (1800–1872) — or "Knap" as the name is spelled in the Newburyport vital records — was the sister of Isaac Knapp.

167

TO HELEN E. BENSON

Boston, August 4, 1834.

My dear Helen:

Time seems to be almost as anxious as ourselves to see us united in the holy bands of wedlock. He has reduced the term of our separation another week since my last letter; and while I am writing, is rushing onward with impetuous speed to the 4th of September, as if that day were the goal of his as well as of our happiness.

I have risen with the lark (O, that I could sing as sweetly! and soar as buoyantly!) this morning, to send you a few hasty lines — this being the only opportunity I shall have to-day; for duties and engagements crowd upon me beyond my ability to meet them. Should you fail to receive a letter from me on Wednesday, I am admonished by your last epistle (which was duly received, and for which I thank you) that you would feel disconsolate, and ready to "weep bitterly." This, I trust, will arrive seasonably.

On Saturday, I was very busy at the cottage in getting the chambers and entries carpeted — and to-day I shall go out to see that the work is completed. The front parlors I shall leave until you come, that you may select such carpeting for it as suits your taste, and is most appropriate. That which I have used for the chambers is straw carpeting, a nice, clean, neatly wrought article, which is now very generally used in preference to all other kinds, especially in warm weather. It is at present very cheap, in consequence of an unusual supply being in our market. I gave 23 cents a yard for it, — yard wide.

Stepping into Mr. Allen's Auction Room [1] on Saturday, friend Knapp and myself were captivated by a very beautiful pair of card tables, of the best mahogany and finest workmanship, but which were admirably adapted by their construction for dining as well as evening tables. They belonged to a gentleman who was about leaving the city, and cost him seventy-five dollars! They were sold on Saturday for less than one-third their cost — Mr. Knapp bid them off for me at $23. They please me much better than any I have seen, and are better adapted to our rooms — although (cheap as they are) they cost rather more than I had intended for our dining tables.

You express great satisfaction that your dear parents are perfectly willing to consign you to my care. I am not less happy, in ascertaining this delightful fact. You will remember, dear Helen, how anxious I was, after learning from your lips that I was the object of your love, to secure the approbation and blessing of your parents upon our union.

May I never cease to appreciate the sacrifice which you and they have made, to increase and perpetuate my happiness!

On Thursday last, we had one of those extraordinary exhibitions which even startle not merely a city, but a far-spread community, and call forth a great multitude of anxious observers. Mr. Durant made a grand ascension in his balloon from our beautiful Common, in the presence of perhaps thirty or forty thousand people.[2] Among all the attractions our city has ever presented, I know of none that has ever drawn out such prodigious crowds. It tells well for us to affirm — as I can truly — that there was not *the least* disturbance or tumult, nor any sign of intoxication. It was really gratifying to see such a mighty throng, all respectful and orderly in their deportment, and nearly all in neat and handsome attire. Such a population, it is not boasting to say, cannot be found in any other part of the world. The afternoon was remarkably fine. At 6 o'clock, the intrepid aeronaut stepped into his car — the cords that bound him to the earth were cut — and up he rode heavenward, waving his hat and the star-spangled banner most gracefully, amid the roar of cannon and the acclamations of the people. In the course of half an hour, his balloon was reduced in appearance to the size of a sparrow, and was finally lost to view. It seems that in descending, a current of wind blew him into the ocean, and he narrowly escaped a watery grave. He has returned to this city, and will probably make another journey to the skies in the course of two or three weeks. Shall I beseech him to wait until after our wedding, that you may get a view of his ascension? Perhaps if you will consent to go up with him, (and several ladies in this city have had the courage to offer to go up,) he will consent to postpone his flight. I saw two men riding sublimely in a balloon over the great city of London: it was the finest sight I ever saw.

❋   ❋   ❋   ❋   ❋

It is now evening. We have had a sultry day, — one of our warmest this season. How soothing is the breeze of evening! — After breakfast, I had to go out to my little cottage in Roxbury, to complete carpeting the rooms. They are all now finished, and look very neatly. To-morrow I hope to get out some of the furniture, so that friend Knapp and myself may speedily keep "Bachelor's Hall" in good earnest. I took a ramble in the fields to-day for about an hour, and gathered a fine lot of blackberries and some mulberries. The prospect from the cottage is now extremely beautiful. It will be somewhat less beautiful in September, but by no means uninviting. I am becoming more and more attached to the spot; and when you come to be my partner, and to participate in the pleasures it affords, my affection for it will be increased a thousand fold.

We have had, this afternoon, a colonization meeting at the Brom-field-street Church, at which the B[reck]inridges from Baltimore and Philadelphia have [been] dealing in words which were "full of sound and fury, [si]gnifying nothing." [3] Nothing? I err — they revealed much, to the downfal of their own detestable scheme, and the advancement of the abolition cause. I shall try to pick them to pieces in the Liberator of Saturday.

It seems, by your letter, dear Helen, that your breast is still disquieted, as to your ability to meet the duties and responsibilities that may devolve upon you after our marriage. What can I say more to relieve you than I have repeatedly said to you? Be not uneasy, my love.

I am happy, and grateful to God, in saying, that I am in the enjoyment of perfect health. My mind and body are alike sound and vigorous.

Make my best compliments to all. They know how dearly I love them.

Darkness is beginning to put out the light of day — but nothing shall be able to extinguish the affection of

Your devoted lover,

Wm. Lloyd Garrison.

Miss H. E. Benson.

ALS: Villard Papers, Harvard College Library. Part of the sheet around the stamp has been torn away.

1. The firm of J. M. Allen and Company, Auctioneers and Commission Merchants, was located at the corner of Milk and Congress Streets in Boston.
2. Charles Ferson Durant (1805–1873) made a balloon flight as early as 1830; he was the first American to make a profession of aeronautics.
3. Shakespeare, *Macbeth*, V, v, 27–28.

168

TO HELEN E. BENSON

Freedom's Cottage,⎱
Roxbury, August 11, 1834.⎰

Dear Helen:

You perceive, by the date of this letter, that I am once more located in my much loved cottage. O, sacred retreat from the tumult and confusion of a city residence! The tide of human life no longer swells and rushes around me. The pomp of power — the parade of wealth — the vanity of fashion — are absent. I hear nothing of the din of human voices — I see nothing of human ingenuity and skill.

It seems like getting into another state of existence. But though away from the great multitude, I am neither solitary nor lonely. Every thing around me is cheerful with joy, and alive with pleasurable animation. The honey-bee, as he flies from flower to flower, hums a pleasant tune to lessen the burden of industry. A distant bird calls to his mate in tones that betoken the solicitude of affection, and is answered by a gush of melody that only love can make. A gentle breeze is toying with the leaves of the apple, the peach, the walnut and the elm, which lift their wings with exceeding gracefulness, as if meditating a flight to those ethereal regions where no blight comes to the fair and beautiful. The day is one of a thousand — full of enchantment to the eye, of perfume to the smell, of elasticity to the spirit, and of purity to the soul. Indeed, for a month past, the weather has been uncommonly fine — warm at times to excess, but constantly serene and lovely. I have rarely known so many bright and balmy days in succession.

You may readily suppose that I am at this moment very happy — but not so happy as if you were seated by my side on the sofa. Why should my feelings be otherwise than pleasant? It was here, in this parlor, that I first made an avowal of my attachment to you, and put it into an epistle that brought me a return of affection which is to be prized above the gold of Golconda.[1] Here it was that many of your letters came to me like messengers of mercy, giving to winter the beauty of spring, causing gladness to flow in my bosom like a fountain, and invigorating the strength of my youth. Here, too, meditation has done much to quicken the devotion of my soul, and prepare me for all the vicissitudes of time and the scenes of eternity. — Beautiful cottage! thou art indeed worthy of all praise. Thou shalt have a place in my memory until with me "time is no longer."[2]

I cannot but regret that you are not [. . .] the luxury of the season. Wherever I turn my eyes, there is a [, . .] greenness and an excessive verdure. But there is soon to be a [change.] Even now, death is among the flowers. One kind of fruit after another has ripened, and been gathered, and the last is soon to arrive at maturity and disappear. In September, there will be less brilliancy and affluence than there is now; but Nature, in her dying moments, presents a more touching and tender aspect than when arrayed in all the bloom of life. As autumn is your favorite season, you will find much in the vicinage of the cottage to awaken reflection and extort admiration.

But I must put a check upon my imagination, and discourse upon matters more practical, and certainly, at this interesting crisis, more important. * * * *

I was highly gratified, last week, on receiving a letter from my Aunt at Lowell, in reply to one that I sent to her, inviting her to be present at our wedding. She promises to accompany me — and very kindly adds — "Your letter contained a subject which was rather unexpected to my mind, but not uninteresting nor unpleasant. I was happy to learn that you had selected a friend, in whom you could confide, — one who was lovely and amiable, and whose counsels and sympathies will no doubt, if needed, be such as will guide in the hour of uncertainty, and cheer and console in the dark night of adversity. It will be my greatest pleasure to accompany you to that spot on which are located all your hopes for future domestic happiness. May God, in his overruling providence, so order it hereafter, that you shall have occasion to bless Him for that hour in which you learned the name of Helen Eliza Benson!"

I propose to make some alterations in the arrangement of my visit to Brooklyn. My friend Knapp and his sister will go in one chaise, and my Aunt and myself in another. — Returning, I shall of course substitute *my wife* for *my aunt*, and friend K. will accompany us with his sister, via Worcester. As the Brooklyn stage goes to Providence on the day of our wedding, perhaps it will be agreeable to my aunt and our dear friend Eliza Chace to go in it, and tarry at P. till the next day, and so arrive in Boston by the stage a few hours after us. I am not at all particular in this arrangement. If it will be more agreeable [. . .] Eliza to return together, let me know in your next, [and I] will procure a carriage that will accommodate all six of us. [Be] particular in expressing your wishes in this case, as either mode of conveyance will be perfectly agreeable to me.

George transmitted your boxes promptly and safely. In taking out the crockery, &c. I accidentally broke one of your tumblers — so you must scold me a little for my carelessness.

I perceive you have purchased a china tea-sett. I meant to have told you that when I was in London, I bought a beautiful sett (for coffee and tea) with various plates, &c. containing various striking representations of slavery. However, we can keep the latter more for show than use.

I hope you have made no ticks for the straw-beds, as I have purchased four excellent beds just filled, which come at a very reasonable price. Two of them are of a superior [kind,] and all of them will be highly serviceable.

The quantity of things sent in the boxes surprises me. Certainly, you have all been very industrious with your needle, and deserve a high panegyric. I shall let the things remain in the boxes until you come.

House-keeping is a much more formidable enterpri[se] than I had anticipated, in consequence of the multiplicity of articles (most of them very petty in themselves) necessary to complete the stock. I shall endeavor to get nothing superfluous, and yet to have every thing convenient. As far as I can anticipate what is wanted, I shall procure it previous to your arrival.

I have fortunately secured, as a domestic, the sister of Mr. Barbadoes,[3] who visited Brooklyn a few weeks since. She is very highly recommended — indeed, as the best among the best — is modest in her deportment and genteel in her appearance — is an excellent cook who needs no instruction — is a professor of religion and a member of the Baptist church in Boston — in short, she is just such a person as we need, and we are extremely fortunate in getting her. Your mind will now be relieved of much anxiety.

I am sorry to find that *all* the shells (and many of them were very beautiful) that were sent to me from Port-au-Prince, have been given away to divers persons — so that I have none for "little Amelia Williams."[4] I have no particular fondness for shells myself; but for her sake I regret that mine have been put into other hands.

The account of the meeting of the Ladies' [Anti-Slavery] Society gave me real pleasure.[5] The contribution was truly [. . .]. There is no zeal, no liberality, no devotion, like Woman's!

The eventful hour swiftly aproaches! — Is it possible that three weeks, from to-day, will find me on my way to Brooklyn, to procure a partner for life? Dear one, I will not attempt to describe how much I desire to see you, and to be in *form*, as well as in *plighted faith*, yours indissolubly. Judge of my feelings by your own. Can I refer you to a truer gauge?

Mr. and Mrs. Alcott are now in this city from Philadelphia.[6] He has called to see me several times, and I have *promised* to call and see his noble lady, but have not yet found time.

My dear friend May keeps *count* very accurately. He will soon put a stop to our correspondence, by making us two *one*. Well, he will stand a better chance to get a letter now and then from one who feels as if he had slighted him — *almost* — not intentionally.

Anna sent me a beautiful letter last week. She probably received my answer to it on Monday. Love to all.

Ever yours devotedly,

Wm. Lloyd Garrison.

Miss H. E. Benson.

ALS: Villard Papers, Harvard College Library. A corner of the folded sheet on which this letter was written has been torn off.

1. Golconda was an ancient city, the ruins of which are near the capital city

of Hyderabad in India. Once the capital of a powerful Mohammedan kingdom, it was renowned for its wealth and diamond cutting.

2. Garrison adapts Revelation 10:6.

3. The sister of James G. Barbadoes has not been identified.

4. Amelia Williams is perhaps the daughter of Herbert Williams.

5. Garrison refers to the organizational meeting of the Female Anti-Slavery Society of Brooklyn and vicinity on the fifth which he reported in *The Liberator* of the sixteenth.

6. A. Bronson Alcott (1799–1888) and Samuel J. May's sister Abigail May Alcott (1800–1877) were both extraordinary persons — reformers and also intellectuals. Alcott was a transcendental philosopher, a man brilliant and imaginative, but impractical. A teacher by profession, he had organized a series of progressive schools in Connecticut, in Massachusetts, and in the Philadelphia area. Each school had failed in turn because it was too advanced for the time and because Alcott self-righteously refused to modify any of his ideas. He was shortly to open in Boston his famous Temple School. In later years he was to run schools in Concord, Massachusetts, and to found Fruitlands (1843–1844), one of the best known of experimental communities. Alcott could hardly have survived at all without his remarkable wife, who like her husband was imaginative, brilliant, and dedicated; unlike him she was also practical. She and later their daughter Louisa May Alcott gave the family balance and eventually prosperity. The Alcotts were, of course, reformers, involved with abolition, temperance, peace, and woman's rights.

169

TO GEORGE W. BENSON

Freedom's Cottage, ⎱
Roxbury, August 11, 1834. ⎰

My dear George:

Here I am perched in my snug little cottage, all up in the woods, like a bird in its nest — whistling and singing to as bright and beautiful a day as ever smiled upon the earth. I should like now to take a ramble with you around these precincts for about twenty or thirty minutes, over hedge and field, just to give you a taste of *the country*. Avaunt, ye brick houses, and towering domes, and noisy populace, that crowd the neighboring city! Welcome, ye verdant hills, ye teeming fields, ye majestic trees! All that man achieves is petty — is laborious — is imitative — is worthless — i.e. all that pertains to his physical efforts. All that the great Creator executes is spontaneous — original — beautiful or grand — and incomparably excellent. Here is his handiwork before me, bathed in a flood of sun-light. Here is beauty in full perfection — here is arrangement in exquisite taste — here is magnificence in regal display — and here is sublimity in all its vastness; for wherever the heavens are seen, there is seen the best specimen of sublimity.

There is a small grove of trees close by me, and the birds, by the liquid torrents of melody which they are pouring forth, seem to be aware that I have an ear for music, and am one of their admirers. I'll give them a tune to balance accounts directly, and what is lacking in quality shall be made up in quantity. My voice is more sonorous than theirs, and yet any one of their number will make himself heard with his tiny pipe much farther than I can "at the top of my lungs." What a vile contest there is between man, bird and beast, to see who will make the most noise in the world! I have done with it. Henceforth you shall hear me "roar as gently as a nightingale." [1]

But a truce to romance. The balloon of my imagination is much nearer the stars than was Durant's the other day, and I must let out the gas, and throw out all the ballast, if I wish to attend to any matters concerning this little paltry ball called earth. Here, then, I alight.

The three boxes transmitted by you came safely to hand. They are a presage of matrimony, most indisputably. The hour for perpetrating that deed is rushing on like a young hurricane. Ten chances to one, but I shall be run over by it, before the words "Jack Robinson" can escape from my lips. [2] However, I hail its approach with unfeigned joy, and care not how fast it speeds. Nearly all things are in readiness in the cottage: the key-stone of the arch is a wife, and dear Helen will make a capital one.

I trust events will be so ordered as to enable you to be at the wedding. You know that I have long depended upon you as my "right-hand man" — forsake me not on that occasion.

The event (Deo volente) is to transpire on the morning of Thursday, September 4th. You can therefore (if pinched for time) take the stage for Brooklyn on Wednesday morning, and return on Thursday.

Make my compliments to your lady. Tell her I hope to get as good a wife as she is — a better one is out of the question. I despair of making half as good a husband as she has got — but I will imitate him as closely as possible. Rely upon it, I will not be naughty or froward, but very docile and obedient. So much for matrimony.

You will have seen by the Liberator, that a grand attack by all the combined forces of colonization and slavery has lately been made upon Boston, in relation to the Maryland scheme of expatriation. They have met with a Waterloo defeat, and yet they fought *pugnis et calcibus* — with tooth and nails, and even horns. The Messrs. Breckinridge complained piteously of their treatment in Providence. Not a meeting-house could they obtain in that city! — Alas, "there's none so poor would do them reverence." [3] Even in this city, it was with the utmost difficulty they could find a place in which to exhibit those young humbugs, the two "African princes"! and their *emanci-*

pation scheme, which is the greatest humbug of all! They could get into no churches but the Methodist — not even into Park-Street! Now let them ask, with a sneer, what have abolitionists done?

I shall go to Brooklyn via Providence, accompanied by my aunt, and by friend Knapp and his sister. We shall start on Monday morning, Sept *1*, and tarry over night in P., and on Tuesday go to B.; returning via Worcester.

I am happy to learn that your venerable father has been to P. recently, and that his health was improved by the journey. Was any thing done to effect an anti-slavery union, according to friend Brown's desire? [4]

Can you read this very flippant scrawl? If so, you are qualified to be an editor of a work on hieroglyphics. You know, very well, that I *can* write better — but that for you there can be no increase of affection on the part of

Your loving friend and brother,

Wm. Lloyd Garrison.

Mr. G. W. Benson.

ALS: Garrison Papers, Boston Public Library; extract printed in *Life*, I, 450.

1. Garrison adapts Shakespeare, *Midsummer-Night's Dream*, I, ii, 86.
2. This expression seems to have been used first by Fanny Burney in *Evelina*, Letter 82.
3. Garrison adapts Shakespeare, *Julius Caesar*, III, ii, 125.
4. Garrison apparently refers to a scheme conceived but never implemented by Moses Brown.

170

TO HELEN E. BENSON

Boston, August 18, 1834.

My blooming Rose:

It seems, then, that Prudence Crandall is no more! —

This will be handed to you by Mrs. Philleo, who has taken her place, and who resembles her in all things precisely.

On Thursday morning last, on my regular excursion to the cottage, who should I see approaching me but the Rev. Mr. Philleo, with Miss Prudence Crandall — no, no, *Mrs.* Philleo on one arm, and *Miss* Philleo on the other! — [1] What — thought I — is it possible that the deed has been done? that the twain have become one? that the Gordian knot has been tied? that the hymeneal yoke has been put on? that the maiden has been transformed into a wife, and the widower into a husband?

It was even so!

And so, my dear, they have got the start of us by almost a month!

Our salutations being ended, they let me into the secret of their union, and told me that they were compelled to come to Brooklyn to be married, as the Canterbury parson was afraid to make them husband and wife. It was not the fear of God, but of Andrew T. Judson, that deterred him.

They left Brooklyn somewhat hastily for this city, as they had some expectation that new writs would be issued by the court then sitting.

I could not congratulate them upon their union, but I could, and did, wish them much happiness. The bride looked smilingly — the bridegroom manifested a complacent spirit — and the young miss betrayed symptoms of hilarity.

"To-morrow," said I, "you must go and see my cottage in the woods." "Agreed," said they — and so we parted.

As I left them, I felt disposed to say with Peter Pindar —

"O Matrimony! thou art like

　　To Jeremiah's figs:

The good were very good — the bad

　　Too sour to give the pigs." [2]

But I will not apply this either relatively, invidiously, or prophetically, to the new couple. Joy and peace and prosperity be with them through life! I cannot wish them any thing less — it would be folly to wish them any thing more.

In the morning, on Friday, they visited the cottage, and expressed themselves highly gratified at its appearance and location. Mrs. P. thought it could not fail to please you. It is true, every thing now is in its prime, and therefore one can hardly form a true opinion of its suitableness.

Yesterday afternoon, and in the evening, Mr. Philleo preached to our colored brethren in their meeting-house. Both sermons were very good, and apparently very sincere. I am more and more puzzled to determine accurately his real character. He may be an eccentric man — a covetous man — and, occasionally, an erring man, in trivial matters; but I cannot think he is habitually a bad man.

This morning they leave for Canterbury. When I commenced this letter, I intended to send it by Mrs. P.; but as they may be detained by the way unexpectedly, I have concluded to send it by the mail, that you may be sure to receive it on Wednesday.

On Friday evening, that mammoth body of flesh — that queer retailer of excellent jokes — that huge personification of good humor — that unconquerable disturber of the hidden things of antiquity — videlicet, Joshua Coffin, came into my office smiling up to his eyes, and soon flooded me with a river of talk. Thinking that he was with you in B., and supposing that he would return to Philadelphia, (where he has been located for a year past,) without coming to this city, I should have doubted his bodily presence, had not flesh and blood abundantly confirmed it. No ghost was ever a thousandth part so lusty. There could be no mistake: and really I was happy to see him again; for with all his oddities, he is a tender-hearted and obliging creature, full of the milk of human kindness, and possesses talent and very considerable intelligence.

I find that, so far as our baggage is concerned, very little will be gained by taking a carriage, as it is not calculated for carrying large or heavy trunks. I now propose to go to Brooklyn in chaises, as I wrote you in my last; and then let Miss Chace and Aunt Charlotte go in one of them with us to Worcester, &c. My friend Knapp and his sister will take the stage from Brooklyn to Providence, and thus see our trunks safely conveyed to Boston. It happens, quite fortunately, that the stage goes down to P. on the day of our proposed union; so that they can reach Roxbury on Friday noon, and be in advance of us a few hours, and have things in preparation for us on our arrival. I hope this arrangement will prove as agreeable to you, as it will to friend K. and his sister.

All things being well, we shall probably arrive in Brooklyn about 3 or 4 o'clock in the afternoon of Tuesday, Sept. 2. Monday night we shall tarry in Providence.

I have purchased some of the larger articles of tin ware. You can, if you think proper, buy a few small ones; but every thing is so easily obtained here, at a moment's notice, that perhaps it will be hardly necessary to encumber yourself with them, unless you have plenty of spare room in your trunk.

What hour on Thursday morning have you selected for the wedding? You will remember that we shall have forty miles to ride after it is consummated, on that day; and it is desirable that we should arrive in Worcester before dark. If it should take place at 9 o'clock, we should be enabled probably to leave as early as 11, and this would make our arrival in W. seasonable. It would be preferable to start even as early as 10 o'clock. But you will make the arrangements to suit yourself.

I was very much gratified to learn from Mr. Coffin, that my much esteemed friend Lydia White, from Philadelphia, was in Canterbury at the school when he left. I hope she has made you a visit, as I have dwelt upon her merits to you, and as I am sure you will be pleased with her unobtrusive manners, her pure spirit, her generous disposition, and her noble benevolence. She is almost the first female pioneer in the anti-slavery cause in this country; and by her efforts to sustain a

free labor goods store, — efforts which never will be fully appreciated on earth, — she deserves to take a high rank in the annals of
female philanthropy.

My dear friend May's "long letter" has not yet been received. As
every thing that comes from his pen is pure gold, I shall be a great
loser if it do not come to hand.

I have concluded to burn wood, instead of coal, in the house the approaching winter. If I mistake not, you are more partial to a wood
than to a coal fire.

I envy you and dear Mary for your visit to Dr. Green: especially
if it was as agreeable as the one we enjoyed there together.[3] Did you
have any accident by the way?

On Thursday, Boston and its vicinity will be again in full commo-
tion. Mr. Durant is to make another visit to the upper world in his
balloon. It is in vain for me to wish that you might be here to witness
it.

You have doubtless seen by the papers, what terrible transactions
have taken place recently in Charlestown by the mob.[4] Our city has
been almost in a state of civil war — but the public mind is becoming
more tranquil. The news from Philadelphia is, that the mob in that
city have destroyed two meeting-houses, and about forty dwelling-
houses, belonging to the colored people! — One colored man was
killed, and several severely wounded. These things give hope and
courage to

Your unblenching lover,

Wm. Lloyd Garrison.

ALS: Villard Papers, Harvard College Library.

1. By a previous marriage Calvin Philleo had a daughter Elizabeth, who was
soon to die of consumption.
2. Garrison quotes from John Wolcot, *The Works of Peter Pindar*, "Orson and
Ellen; a Legendary Tale," canto 2.
3. Rowland W. Greene.
4. A riot occurred in Charlestown, Massachusetts, on August 17; for descriptions of it see *The Liberator*, August 23, 30, 1834.

171

TO GEORGE W. BENSON

Boston, Aug. 21, 1834.

My dear George:

It is midnight. The two last days have been stormy, so that the
Genius of Heat has gone to other climes, and that arch destroyer Cold
has taken his place. To-day, Mr. Durant was to have made his second

ascension, but the rain said, "Nay," and the clouds looked glum; and the excursion was postponed to Monday. It is thus that the weather keeps down body and soul. Very well: he who never ascends, will never break his neck by a fall. Besides, you know what the poet says —

"Ah! who can think how hard it is to climb?" [1]

The battlements of the sky are not so easily scaled. To get over them, it is clear that a man must be blown up "sky high" — i.e. by gas. Having built no castles in the air, — not even a cottage, — you will not catch me rambling in the fields of Space, at the risk of being necessitated to sleep upon nothing at all. In olden times, — the good old days of witchcraft, — they used to hang people for riding in the air upon broomsticks. Ought we not to hang Durant? To be sure, a balloon is a more respectable mode of conveyance than a broomstick — but it is no worse to ride in a wagon than in a coach. Every one to his taste.

But a better object bursts at this moment upon my sight. The moon is looking down upon me with a full and fair countenance from her throne of light, and challenges my admiration, as a beautiful woman always does. I like her car infinitely better than Durant's. She will descend towards daylight, and then her husband the Sun will take a trip.

I began this, not as a letter but as a note, to be handed to you by my esteemed friend, the Rev. Mr. Frost of Oneida Institute, with whom, I presume, you are slightly acquainted.[2] He has done our cause some service within the last two months by his lectures, and therefore deserves good treatment at the hands of abolitionists. Through his influence, many colonizationists have been sadly *Frost* bitten, and nothing but an abolition poultice could cure them.

In a fortnight from to-day, comes the consummation of my desires. I shall no longer herd with bachelors. A single life is indisputably an odd life; and, therefore, by taking one unto myself, I make things even. In this, I but imitate your example.

Hymen has substituted Mrs. Philleo for Prudence Crandall. What do you think of the transformation?

But here, dear George, I must pause —

Weary with toil, I haste me to my bed —
The dear repose for limbs with travel tired;" [3]

but whether vigorous or weary, whether waking or sleeping, whether standing or prone, whether late or early, I am, in all sincerity and affection,

Yours, ever,

Wm. Lloyd Garrison.

P.S. My best remembrances to your lady, and to Mr. and Mrs. Anthony.

Mr. G. W. Benson.

ALS: Garrison Papers, Boston Public Library.

1. James Beattie, *The Minstrel*, I, stanza 1.
2. John Frost had been since 1831 the minister of the Presbyterian church at Whitesborough, New York; he was also one of the founders of Oneida Institute.
3. Shakespeare, Sonnet XXVII, lines 1-2.

172

TO HELEN E. BENSON

Boston, August 23, 1834.

My dear Helen:

I may properly call your last letter, a beautiful *boquet* of friendship and love,[1] I prize it the more highly, as the flowers will not perish with the summer. They will survive the storms of autumn, and the cold of winter, even. The lily, transmitted by my estimable friend Lydia White, is exceedingly delicate and graceful. My dear May's amaranth is very precious. Henry's pinks are truly fragrant and pretty. Of course, the roses and "sweet Williams" from your hand are peculiarly acceptable.

I confess, on opening your letter, I was somewhat startled to see so many different chirographers, as it at once led me to fear that you were ill; and I could almost fancy that each epistle was a bulletin of your health. These feelings, however, were only momentary, as I quickly discovered your own familiar writing on the last page.

It gives me great pleasure to know that my friend L. W. is really in Brooklyn; for I assured her in Philadelphia that she would find congenial spirits among you, and be heartily welcomed by you all. In reply to her inquiry, "Can't you gratify your friends in Philadelphia with a visit this fall or winter?" I would not positively answer in the negative, nor do I hardly dare to hold out any encouragement. I am really anxious that you should see that beautiful city, and become acquainted with those dear friends; and therefore desire to seize the first convenient opportunity to make them a visit. If Lydia can be at our wedding, it will be very gratifying to me.

By informing our beloved May that the manuscripts of the arguments in Miss Crandall's case were duly received, you will relieve his mind of much anxiety. We shall strive to be expeditious in getting the pamphlet to press.

The Canterbury crew, it seems, are still implacable. Mr. Burleigh is now their victim — no, not exactly their victim, for, though he is prosecuted, they have not yet triumphed over him. Brooklyn will soon get to be famous for its law-suits. Five upon one, as in my own case, are four too many.

If you should happen to see Miss Lee, you may tell her that her brother is at present employed in my office.

I ought to have dated this letter at Freedom's Cottage, as I am sitting in the front parlor on the sofa, with my dear little kitten sweetly slumbering by my side. She has already developed many excellent traits — being affectionate, sagacious, neat and playful. Where she came from I do not know: her birthplace is quite a mystery. What towns or cities will contend for the honor of it after her demise, time must determine. The controversy will wax hottest between Roxbury and Boston.

Dear Helen, you ought not to be absent on a day so magnificently fine as this. It is the very carnival of Nature — "and every sense and every heart is joy." [2] Ah! at least ten days must elapse before we shall see each other — but you know they are growing shorter and shorter, and this must be our consolation. To be sure, the nights expand as much as the days contract; so that on the whole we gain nothing, except we take an Irish measure. Nevertheless, they are certainly diminishing in number, if not in duration. Ten days only! Leap, my heart, for joy! Why, it seems but as yesterday since we were counting *months* that must elapse before our union. Next, we were enabled to enumerate weeks. Now, we are marking days. Presently, we shall be numbering hours — then minutes — and then comes the consummation of our hopes!

> "Fly swifter round, ye wheels of time,
> And bring the welcome day!" [3]

I am afraid Mrs. Philleo's description of the cottage will raise your expectations too high. My mind will not be at ease, on the score of its location and fitness, until you examine it. It is not to be expected that a residence here will be so agreeable in the winter as in summer; and hence I could wish it were the spring, instead of the fall of the year. It is well that human happiness does not depend essentially upon external objects either of earth or sky. Some of the happiest days of my life were spent in a prison.

> " 'Tis home where'er the heart is,
> In sunshine or in shade." [4]

Our joy will spring from fountains of affection within us, which, mingling together, will make our stream of life pure and tranquil.

Bodily comfort and selfish complacency may be derived from meats and drinks, and an abundance of apparil: still it is a very trivial matter what we shall eat, or what we shall drink, or wherewithal we shall be clothed. It has been truly affirmed, that created good is always greater in the prospect than in the possession: while the heavenly bliss, like Solomon's glory and wisdom, appears still greater the nearer it is approached.

In to-day's Liberator, you will gather the particulars of the late dreadful assaults upon some of the colored inhabitants of Philadelphia.[5] It is somewhat difficult to decide who are most hated, or who are most in jeopardy, abolitionists or black people. Neither of them can claim popularity or safety; and there is a spirit abroad that would sacrifice them all in one great bloody hecatomb. We must endure these afflictions like good soldiers; for there are three notable reflections to comfort us. First, our warfare is only for a very limited period. Secondly, the cause which we espouse must surely obtain the victory, even though we may be defeated. Thirdly, if we are faithful unto death, there is a crown of life laid up for us in heaven. "He that has no long journey before him, but sits still in his own house, may escape the tempest, and hide himself from the storm; but he that sets out for another country cannot expect always to walk on the flowery champaign, or in the pleasant sunshine, but shall find a river to cross, and a mountain to climb — shall have darkness around him, and thunders roaring above him, the tempest attending his steps, and the storm dashing upon him — and perhaps enemies way-laying him. So it is with the traveller heavenward; for through much affliction, and many tribulations, we shall enter into the kingdom." [6]

I am to receive only one letter more from Helen Eliza Benson! — I am somewhat in the predicament of a person who courted a beautiful and accomplished lady for many years, and on being interrogated why he did not marry her, replied, 'True — I have resolved to do so repeatedly — but this is my grand difficulty: where shall I spend my evenings if I marry?" So, if *I* marry, how shall I get any more letters from H. E. Benson? I may go to the Post Office in vain. Well, I must make a bargain with Anna, and Mary, and Sarah, to supply your place. Mrs. Garrison or myself will endeavor to keep the weekly transmission of a letter to Brooklyn unbroken.

If I were certain that my friend Lydia White continued in Brooklyn or Canterbury, busy as I am, I would send her a letter; and I feel ashamed at my long silence.

This letter arriving on Monday will take you by surprise; but by writing thus early, I shall be able to send you one more — *the last* — a week hence. *The last!*

> "O, by that little word,
> How many thoughts are stirred, —
> That sister of the past." [7]

Of course, I shall not expect to receive your reply to this until Friday, as usual.

Anxious to obtain for our consumption, those articles which are not the productions of slave labor, I have bought of Charles Collins of New-York, who keeps a free goods store, one barrel of molasses, half a barrel of rice, half a barrel brown sugar, and half a barrel loaf and lump do.[8] A small portion of these I shall let my friend Bacon have, at his earnest request.[9]

If you have not sent the bundle to me from my Philadelphia friends, perhaps you had better keep it till I see you.

With your sweet voice return my thanks to all the letter-writers, and my best regards in addition. The public shall soon know that I am

Yours, indissolubly, through life,

Wm. Lloyd Garrison.

ALS: Villard Papers, Harvard College Library.

1. The letter written jointly by Helen and other Brooklyn friends has apparently not been preserved.
2. Not identified.
3. Not identified.
4. Not identified.
5. The riots in Philadelphia, resulting in the death of at least one Negro and the destruction of two Negro churches and some twenty-five houses, were among the many riots along the eastern seaboard occurring about this time. In the issue of *The Liberator* to which Garrison refers, riots were also reported in Charlestown, Massachusetts, and in New York City. Garrison blamed New York newspaper editors William Leete Stone and James Watson Webb for instigating the riots in their city.
6. Although in both form and substance, this quotation is reminiscent of Jeremy Taylor, search through his works has not revealed it.
7. Not identified.
8. Charles Collins has not been further identified. By "do." Garrison means "ditto."
9. Benjamin C. Bacon.

173

TO HELEN E. BENSON

Freedom's Cottage, ⎱
Roxbury, August 29, 1834. ⎰

Loveliest and dearest One:

My *first* letter to you was written with the feelings of an unacknowledged, unsuspected, yet sincere and ardent admirer. It was a telegraph of love, without its usual characters. How shall I write my *last?* Shall I fill it with fresh protestations of my attachment? No — for words are cheap, and you do not doubt my sincerity. Shall I fill it with promises to seek your happiness in all things during our sojourn together in this vale of tears? No — for this purpose is implied in seeking that connexion with you which death alone shall be able to destroy. Shall I fill it with visions of future bliss, as they arise in an exhuberant imagination? No — for "we know not what a day may bring forth," [1] and therefore it is equally unwise and dangerous to calculate upon earthly enjoyment.

The act of our union is soon to be consummated. Not even a week is to transpire, (if it be the will of God,) before we "twain shall be one" [2] one in affection, in interest, in destiny — one in joy and sorrow, in prosperity and adversity, in sickness and health, in life and death. New relations bring new duties, and multiply the obligations of life. A union, such as we have in view, is the most endearing, the most solemn, and the most responsible, which subsists between members of the human race. If I, my dear Helen, do not realize this truth in all its force, it is at least impressed upon my mind in deep and ineffaceable characters. That we shall be happy, I cannot doubt — for we do not make beauty, or opulence, or fame, or popularity, the basis of our happiness; and there is, I am satisfied, a simplicity of mind, and sweetness of disposition, and congeniality of spirit between us, that fit us to be one and indissoluble. That we shall be *perfectly* happy on earth, it is vain to expect — for this is not our home; and an exile from home — a heavenly home — must naturally have hours of sadness, and possess a restlessness of mind that can never be fully satisfied, until he catch the notes of angels, and mingle with the ransomed above — where never enter "the fearful, and unbelieving, and the abominable, and murderers, and whoremongers, and sorcerers, and idolaters, and liars" — "where there shall be no more curse" — "where there shall be no night, and no candle needed, nor light of the sun." [3]

Having our hopes of peace and joy on earth built upon the Rock of Ages, the mutable things of time will not be able to destroy them. Whatever may be our lot — whether reproach, or persecution, or poverty — we need not be unhappy, but may smile even in the midst of tears. Having fixed our hopes of eternal bliss upon the same immovable foundation, we may defy the combined assaults of earth and hell.

It behooves me to say, again and again, that I am deeply affected in view of your acceptance of me. The scorn and hatred of the world are levelled against me; — yet you vouchsafe to me your sweet love! I am every where branded as a madman, a fanatic, and a traitor; — yet you bestow upon me your sweet love! I am extensively regarded as cruel, boisterous, and repulsive; — yet you favor me with your sweet

love! I am doomed, by my devotion to a cause which is full of benevolence and sublimity, to receive an inadequate remuneration for my
labors, — so far as paltry dust is concerned; — yet you do not withhold
from me your sweet love! Thus I incur a debt of gratitude which I
can never repay; for time will steadily augment it, notwithstanding
the alacrity of my will to repay it.

> "All other fires are of the earth,
> And transient; — but of heavenly birth
> Is Love's first flame, which, howsoever,
> Fraud, power, woe, chance, or fate, may sever
> From its congenial source, must burn
> Unquenched, but in the funeral urn." [4]

Much as I love you, dear Helen, I do not think that even *you* could
make me give such proofs of my affection as are required in some
parts of our mundane world. In Greenland, for instance, virgin modesty requires that a girl be carried off by her suitor; nay, even dragged
by the hair; and when she is really in his hut, she runs away from
him several times, and at length perhaps compels him *to give a proof
of his affection, by cutting the soles of her feet* in several places, that
she may be obliged to sit still! Those who are baptized, now leave the
matter to the priest. The suitor explains his wish to him, and the girl
is called. After some indifferent questions, the clergyman says, "It
will soon be time for you to marry." "I will not marry." "That is a pity,
for I have a suitor for you." "Whom?" The clergyman names him.
"He is good for nothing — I will not have him." "Why not? — He is
young, a good seal hunter," &c. "I will not marry — I will not have
him." "Very well, I will not force you; I have, besides, another match
for him." — A pause. — The girl sighs — a tear comes into her eye —
and, at last, she whispers, "As you will, priest." "No, as you will; I
do not wish to persuade you." Here follows a deep sigh, then a half
audible "Yes," and the affair is settled. This kind of courtship would
suit neither of us, dear Helen.[5]

Your last letter was rendered peculiarly acceptable to me, as it
was put into my hands by our much esteemed and ever pleasant
friend Mr. Gray, with one from dear Anna and Mr. May. The retrospect that you have taken in it was natural, and the reflections candid and animating.

This afternoon I have been very busy in piling up wood in the barn,
and sawing and splitting it. It is excellent diversion, and good exercise.

To-morrow I expect the arrival of my aunt and Miss Knapp in
Boston. On Monday, at 12 o'clock, you will probably be perusing this
letter. They and my friend Knapp will at that hour be on the road

to Providence, in company with him who loves you more than words can tell, or fancy paint — that is to say,

Your truly obedient servant, and most affectionate lover,

Wm. Lloyd Garrison.

Miss Helen E. Benson.

P.S. I have been hesitating these two or three days past, whether to go to Brooklyn with my companions in chaises, or in a carry-all.[6] It is difficult and awkward to carry trunks with chaises, and I have therefore concluded to take a carry-all, which is a handsome and convenient vehicle, (for two horses,) and which will enable our esteemed friend Eliza and my aunt to be with us on the road. I hope this arrangement will be agreeable to you, as I presume it will to them. It is better to be together in stopping at taverns by the way, than in separate vehicles.

The hour at which our wedding shall take place, must be settled by you — perhaps as early as 9 o'clock, in view of the distance from Brooklyn to Worcester. It will be a source of mutual regret to us to quit "Friendship's Vale" in such haste. How I wish that Brooklyn was a part of Roxbury, that we might daily visit the abode of your dear parents! — I presume your bosom is at present the seat of conflicting emotions of joy and sadness, but I trust the former preponderate. Heaven's choicest blessings rest upon you! I sigh in bidding you adieu. I close this *last* letter with a kiss — with many kisses.

Saturday morning. — Mr. Gray has just called to see me, and says he shall not return until Monday after next. Next Saturday the balloon is to go up again, and there is to be a grand procession and a public oration on the death of La Fayette, and he wishes to be here. We shall see him on our return.

ALS: Villard Papers, Harvard College Library.

1. Proverbs 27.1, adapted.
2. Mark 10:8.
3. Revelation 21:8, 22:3, 5, adapted.
4. Not identified.
5. The source of Garrison's information about courtship customs in Greenland is Hans Egede Saabye, *Greenland, Being Extracts from a Journal* (London, 1818). The conversation and the description are quoted, with only a few changes in phraseology, from pages 129–130.
6. The carry-all, or "carriole," larger than a two-wheeled chaise, could carry up to four people.

174

TO ANNA E. BENSON

Freedom's Cottage,⎱
Roxbury, Sept. 7, 1834.⎰

Dear Anna:

But two days have passed since our return to the cottage, and yet we are settled down with as much quietude and intimacy, as if this had always been "home, sweet home," to us.

Our journey was made up of incidents, both bright and sombre, amusing and grave, accidental and natural. From Brooklyn to Worcester, we were blessed with as beautiful weather as man ever enjoyed. The monarch of Day threw aside his uncomely robes of mist at an early hour, and put on a regal vesture becoming one whose sway is universal. Scenes of exquisite beauty, far surpassing all that we have in Roxbury, constantly burst upon our view, presenting and blending the wildly grand and softly picturesque. It was a time of high romance to Nature and to us. Could we be otherwise than happy? At least, what emotions but those of joy and rapture could find a place in *my* bosom? She, for whose society I had so long sighed, with whom I had so long wished to be united, and upon whom my affections had so long rested, was by my side, not as a promised bride but as a wife indeed! We were journeying to a place and residence where we should see each other's person, and hear each other's voice, from earliest dawn to deepest night, from week to week, and from month to month, as long as a kind Providence should permit us to be together.

We arrived at Worcester about 6 o'clock in the evening. Aunt Charlotte was taken sick, with vomiting, soon after, but recovered during the night. Our dear friend Eliza was seized in a similar manner, but more violently. We were enabled to start for Boston in the morning, Eliza still continuing ill, but wishing not to tarry by the way. It rained steadily throughout the day, and we all got more or less wet, to the injury of some of our clothes, and not at all to the advancement of our health. Between Oxford and Worcester, I lost a bundle containing my coat, pantaloons and vest, with sundry manuscripts, and shall probably not recover it again. At Worcester, I left the whip that Henry gave to me — that I shall recover. One of our horses lost a shoe, and injured his foot, and both of them were much affected by the journey. Nevertheless, in despite of the difficulties and discouragements that attended us, arising from the storm, bad roads, lazy horses, &c. &c. we arrived in Roxbury on Friday evening, at half past 6 o'clock. Every thing was gloomy enough; but we had so much to attend to within doors, that we took little notice of what was transacting without. Yesterday, however, was a most brilliant day, and every thing looked charmingly. Dear Helen is much pleased with the cottage, and seems perfectly happy — that is to say, as happy as I am at this moment. Eliza has been attended by Dr. Windship,[1] and is now doing well.

Yesterday, Mr. Gray and Mrs. Cady called to see us in our little retreat — but they will go [2] you the particulars of their visit.[3]

I meant to have sent you a long epistle, but am obliged to close, abruptly and unexpectedly. You shall hear from us regularly. Come and see us soon. My best love to those whom I may now call father, mother, brother, and sisters — not forgetting Mary Burnett and Eunice, Mr. and Mrs. May.

In the midst of much happiness, I remain, as ever,

Your loving brother,

Wm. Lloyd Garrison.

Miss Anna E. Benson.

ALS: Garrison Papers, Boston Public Library; extract printed in Walter M. Merrill, "A Passionate Attachment: William Lloyd Garrison's Courtship of Helen Eliza Benson," *The New England Quarterly*, 29:202–203 (June 1956).

1. Charles William Windship (c. 1773–1852) was a 1793 graduate of Harvard College, who lived in Roxbury and practiced medicine in Boston for many years.

2. Garrison evidently means "give."

3. Garrison's callers were Frederick Gray and Margaret Livingston Cady, wife of the distinguished lawyer Daniel Cady and mother of Elizabeth Cady, who was to marry Henry B. Stanton.

175

TO GEORGE W. BENSON

Freedom's Cottage,⎱
Roxbury, Sept. 12, 1834.⎰

My dear George:

A year ago, I was just about half way across the Atlantic, between England and the United States, as little dreaming that I should be a married man within twelve months, as that I should occupy the chair of his holiness the Pope. At that time I knew nothing of Freedom's Cottage, and my acquaintance with Helen was too slight to authorise me to hope that a union for life might take place between us. It has been the most eventful year in my history. I have been the occasion of many uproars, and a continual disturber of the public peace. As soon as I landed, I turned the city of New-York upside down. Five thousand people turned out to see me tarred and feathered, but were disappointed. There was also a small hubbub in Boston on my arrival. The excitement passed away, but invective and calumny still followed me. By dint of some industry and much persuasion, I succeeded in inducing the abolitionists in New-York to join our little band in Boston, in calling a National Convention at Philadelphia. We met — and such a body of men, for zeal, firmness, integrity, benevolence and moral greatness, the world has rarely seen in a single assembly. Inscribed upon a Declaration which it was my exalted privilege to write, their names can perish only with the knowledge of the history of our times. A National Anti-Slavery was formed, which astonished the country by its novelty, and awed it by its boldness. In five months its first annual meeting was held in the identical city, in which, only seven antecedent months, abolitionists were in peril of their lives! — In ability, interest and solemnity, it took precedence of all the great religious celebrations which took place at the same time. During the same month, a New-England Anti-Slavery Convention was held in Boston, and so judicious were its measures, so eloquent its appeals, so unequivocal its resolutions, that it at once gave shape and character to the anti-slavery cause in this section of the Union. In the midst of all these mighty movements, I have wooed "a fair ladye," and won her — have thrown aside celibacy, and jumped, body and soul, into matrimony — have sunk the character of bachelor in that of husband — have settled down into domestic quietude, and repudiated all my roving desires — and have found that which I have long been yearning to find, a home, a wife, and a beautiful retreat from a turbulent city.

Here, then, conveniently remote and protectingly obscure from the great capital of our State, I am located in a cottage which I have long since ventured to designate by Freedom's appellation; for within its walls I have written much in defence of human liberty, and hope to write more. If my health should be mercifully preserved, and no unforeseen obstacles prevent, I hope to make the ensuing winter memorable for the aid I shall give to the anti-slavery cause; so that it shall be seen that matrimony, instead of hindering, rather advances my labors.

But a word as to our wedding. We did not give up the hope of seeing you present, until the last moment of delay. We knew how anxiously you desired to be there, to witness the surrendering of a beloved sister to the object of her choice; and though we yearned to see you, yet we rather commended the earnest solicitude and attentive watchfulness that kept you away. Less than an hour transpired from the assembling to the dispersing of the company — from the tying of the sacred knot to our departure from the valley. There was no precipitancy — no bustle — no confusion. The dear minister's heart was deeply affected, and almost too full for clear, unembarrassed utterance. His expressions of friendship for us both were ardent and tender — his parental and social admonitions valuable and timely — his wishes for our happiness large and multifarious. Rev. Mr. Frost was providentially with us, and manifested a lively interest in the solemn, yet joyous proceedings.

Having given our last reluctant adieu, we got into our carry-all as early as nine o'clock, and was soon out of the precincts of Brooklyn. An immense curtain of gloom for a time shrouded the sun from our view, but was soon drawn aside to usher in one of the brightest and loveliest days attendant upon the season. The ride from Brooklyn to Worcester, for wildness, beauty and opulence of scenery, was rapturous and romantic in the extreme. We reached the latter place about half past 6 o'clock in the evening. Soon after tea, my aunt and Eliza were seized with vomiting, and were quite ill during the night. In the morning, the former was nearly well, and the latter better. It began to rain as soon as we started, and it rained without abatement up to the moment of our arrival at the cottage, which was a little before dusk. Poor Eliza grew worse, and the next day required a physician, who attended her twice a day until Tuesday. She is now well, and says she loves cold water better than ever. Such a ride, at such a time, under such afflicting circumstances, was somewhat dispiriting — but being only a matrimonial episode, we all bore it very cheerfully, and looked forward to a brighter course and a fairer day.

Helen seems to be quite at home, and makes me happy with her love. She commends my taste in selecting the cottage for our residence, and so do Eliza and Abigail. We are now prepared to see our abolition friends, especially those from Providence and Brooklyn. We are anxious to hear of the safe delivery of your lady, that we may congratulate you as a father, and her as a mother, and that we may cherish the hope of seeing you shortly under our roof. Come and visit us as soon as practicable.

Accept my thanks for your hint respecting my trial in January, in your acceptable letter to Helen and myself. Let us make our epistolary interchanges regular and frequent. Express to your lady my lively solicitude for her safety, and believe me to be

Ever affectionately yours,

Wm. Lloyd Garrison.

☞ We are anticipating much pleasure from Mr. and Mrs. May's visit next week. Henry designs to be present at public anti-slavery meeting on the last Monday evening of the present month: — hope it will be convenient for you to attend. Perhaps we shall be interrupted in our meeting, and mobbed. I choose rather to be tarred and feathered than gagged, and mean, therefore, to lift up my voice on that occasion. The sooner the question is settled, — whe[ther] we are slaves or freemen, — the better. "Give me liberty, or give me death." [1]

ALS: Garrison Papers, Boston Public Library; printed partly in *Life*, I, 420–421. To this letter Helen added a postscript concerned with domestic details.

1. Patrick Henry, speech at the Virginia Convention, St. John's Episcopal Church, Richmond, Virginia, March 23, 1775.

176

TO SAMUEL J. MAY

Boston, Sept. 15, 1834.

My dear Coadjutor:

If I write in haste, my excuse must be that I am now a married man; if with less imagination and buoyancy than formerly, — I am a married man; if incoherently and disorderly, — I am a married man! And, remember, a portion of the blame attaches to you. Who broke up the ice of my celibacy, and plunged me into the river of matrimony? You! Who transformed me from a gay lover into a demure husband? You! Who took away my liberty, and put me into bondage with another? You! Who put such a noose around my neck, and tied such a knot, as to defy my industry and skill in emancipating myself? Who but Samuel J. May! Therefore, be this epistle brief or tedious — lively or dolorous — orderly or disorderly — elaborate or careless — you are not to criticise it condemningly; and so I write with impunity.

This pert introduction shows that I am not in a perturbed state of mind. It is too soon for me to chide you for what you have done. Until the honey-moon wanes and sets, there is a fair prospect that neither Helen nor myself will come down upon you for damages. Perhaps we shall not trouble you after that time — but *nous verrons*. Until I find that I have got a selfish, ill-tempered, and scolding wife, I shall thank you unceasingly for that kind piece of service which you rendered me on Thursday morning, September 4th — and for your good wishes, ardent expressions of affection, and seasonable admonitions, on that very memorable occasion.

My particular object in writing to you at this time is to say, that we (i. e. Helen and myself, for marriage makes us imperial,) are waiting with much solicitude for the arrival of Mr. and Mrs. May, with their dear little children, who have promised (with what sanctity I know not) to make us something more than a flying visit. "Come, for all things are now ready." [1] See to it that they come speedily. If they are Grahamites, we have a fine spring of water in our cellar, and plenty of Graham flour up stairs.[2] If they have an affection for coffee or tea, we have both. If they love retirement, we are in the midst of it. If they have an eye for natural scenery, we will show them as pretty a prospect as one could desire to see. Do they wish to be contiguous to the city, yet not implicated in its follies and fashions? Then they will assuredly come to "Freedom's Cottage."

At the quarterly meeting of our Anti-Slavery Society, on the 29th instant, we shall expect to hear your melodious voice lifted up strongly in behalf of suffering humanity. It is my intention to speak on that occasion; and I think it behooves all who address the meeting to assume a high and manly tone, befitting those who are conscious that theirs is the cause of God — invincible, glorious, and holy — and that the hour is come when we are to determine, whether this a land of worse than absolute despotism — whether we ourselves are slaves or freemen. — Possibly we may be disturbed in our meeting — but are we to be frightened either by prospective or real clamor and violence? Not if we are patriots or christians.

On the first of October, an anti-slavery convention for the county of Middlesex is to be held at Groton, and I am in some measure pledged to be present. Dr. Farnsworth, one of the most active, reputable, and influential among the inhabitants of Groton, was in my office on Saturday, and said he should write to you immediately, to attend the convention. He is *extremely* anxious to secure your services, and he *besought* me to *beseech* you to this effect. I hope we shall be able to go in company together. The occasion may be styled a great one, and I think it cannot fail of proving an interesting one. Middlesex is one of the first counties in the Commonwealth.

I gave not the slightest heed to the calumnious gossip against old Dr. Windship. As for the young Dr., he is a singularly agreeable and accomplished gentleman, and has won the esteem of us all.[3] On Saturday, all our family, to wit, Mr and Mrs. Garrison, Miss Eliza, Miss Abigail, and Mr. Knapp, went with the Dr. and his lady, (quite an affable lady,) to see the balloon ascension of Mr. Durant. It was so transcendantly beautiful that I shall not attempt to describe it.

It seems that the ruffians of Canterbury, have been again at their dirty work, and Miss Crandall's school is broken up! Well, shame on us, abolitionists, if we d[o] not, on all suitable occasions, make the facts of this case to tingle in the ears of the people! — I do not wonder that you felt so mortified and indignant in addressing the persecuted scholars, and telling them that they had better return home. In your affliction and displeasure deeply shares

Your admiring and grateful friend,

Wm. Lloyd Garrison.

☞ I would strongly dissuade you from making an appeal to the Canterburians. Why cast pearls before swine? [4] Why attempt to reason with beasts?

The proceedings of the N. E. A. S. Convention are all printed, and the sheets are now in the hands of the binder.[5]

The pamphlet containing Miss Crandall's trial will be completed in the course of a fortnight — probably.

I have not yet seen the last Unionist, and, consequently, cannot remark upon your Annual Report. I am sure it is a good one.

ALS: Garrison Papers, Boston Public Library. Helen added a postscript to this letter, telling the Mays how much she was looking forward to their planned visit.

1. Luke 14:17.
2. "Grahamites" were followers of Sylvester Graham (1794–1851), a Presbyterian minister turned reformer, who lectured extensively on health benefits to accrue from the use of coarse whole-wheat flour, cold water, cold showers, hard mattresses, and general cheerfulness, especially at meals. He had sufficient influence so that millers packaged Graham flour, and Graham boarding houses sprang up around the country.
3. This is probably Charles May Windship (d. 1865), the son of Dr. Charles William Windship. The younger man received an M.D. from Harvard Medical School in 1829.
4. Garrison alludes to Matthew 7:6.
5. A number of reports of the convention and of its various committees had been printed earlier in *The Liberator* (see the issues for May 31, June 7, 28, and July 19, 1834).

177

TO ANNA E. BENSON

Freedom's Cottage,⎱
Roxbury, Oct. 9, 1834.⎰

My dear Anna:

It is with a confused head, and a debilitated body, that I venture to seize my pen, for the purpose of making, at this late hour, at least a hasty acknowledgment of your *very* interesting letter, and of my remissness in answering it. In my letter to father, I have stated some of the causes which have prevented my writing until now; and I need not, therefore, occupy any portion of this sheet in detailing them. Great and unfeigned would be my lamentation if I could suppose, for one moment, that my silence had been construed by you into an indifference to your epistles, or into any abatement of my love for all who reside in Friendship's Valley. It is true, she who was peculiarly endeared to me, and who is even more so than ever, is no longer one of your number, but is with me constantly to cheer and strengthen me; but still my thoughts are hovering daily around your family circle, and I yearn as a son and a brother to be once more in your midst.

Your letter breathes a somewhat melancholy strain. Helen, on reading it, retired to her chamber and wept. There is a bereavement mutually felt by you both, and why should not relief be obtained in tears? If it were the grief of guilt, it would be insupportable; but it flows from the fountain of affection, and therefore, though it may temporarily drown the heart, yet it cannot destroy the life. I have, dear Anna, a remedy to propose, that shall cure you both. You mourn because of separation — of course, to be in each other's society again will effect an instant cure, *pro tempore* at least. Now, to bring gladness to your heart, and joy to our own, I beseech you, by all that is moving in eloquence, or importunate in weeping affection, to make us a visit immediately, in company with Henry, and also, if practicable, with Mary or Sarah. Next week we expect to be wholly alone. Eliza Chace has gone home, and I cannot think of even going into the city, and leaving Helen alone. She needs a female companion — and none can so well supply the vacancy that is now felt, as yourself. Surely, then, dear sister, if health permit, you will come. Do you wish for retirement? Here you will find it, even more completely than at home. With the exception of Mr. and Mrs. May's visit, and the presence of Mr. Thompson's [1] family, we have had scarcely half a dozen visitors since we came home: and as winter approaches, the more secure are we becoming from them. I feel the more anxious to have you come, because Helen is so sanguine that you will be delighted with the spot. Should you make up your mind to come, do not come for a week, or a fortnight, or a month, but for all winter; but if you cannot tarry so long, at all events come.

I have been married almost five weeks, and I am a warmer friend to matrimony than ever. "But," peradventure one may say, "the honeymoon is scarcely set, and therefore you decide too hastily." Very well — five months hence, if my life be spared, you shall have the fruits of my experience; and if five months be too short a period for a trial, why then, wait till five years shall have elapsed, and I will make a full and free confession.

I find that I have not calculated too largely upon the excellent traits that abound in the character of my dear wife. Her disposition is certainly remarkable — so uniformly placid, so generous and disinterested, so susceptible and obliging, so kind and attentive. Not to love and cherish her would argue, on my part, a most selfish and grovelling spirit.

I cannot give you a much stronger proof of my esteem than in scribbling this letter, at the present moment, unfit as I feel to be absent from my bed. I have so long enjoyed uninterrupted health, as to have grown, I fear, almost forgetful of the obligations which I owe to my heavenly Parent. Now I can enter fully into the feelings of the poet, and exclaim —

> "O, who can speak the vigorous joys of health?
> Unclogg'd the body, unobscured the mind;
> The morning rises gay; with pleasing stealth,
> The temperate evening falls serene and kind:
> In health the wiser brutes true gladness find." [2]

I hope your health is better than my own — unless, being ill, you are learning as profitable a lesson of resignation and thankfulness as I am, and then I am sure you will not regr[et be]ing ill.

I can hardly realise, as yet, that I am a married man, although I have one of the best wives in the wide world. When I was a boy, a married man (no matter what might be his age) seemed to me to have reached the *ultima thule* of life; but I feel as young as ever. It is probably one of the besetting sins of age to imagine itself still young, even to the verge of three score years and ten. We carry the delusion with us, from year to year, that whatever advances Time makes, we make none. Let us remember, always, that

"That life is long which answers life's great end," [3] and that only. It is, after all, a matter of little consequence, either to the world or ourselves, whether we die at thirty or fifty, at seventy or ninety. Five or six thousand years have rolled over the world — and what are they but a speck?

Winter is stealthily drawing near. He will scatter the leaves of the forest, and congeal rill and river with his icy breath — but he never will be able to extinguish that flame of affection which is cherished for you in the breast of

Your admiring brother,

Wm. Lloyd Garrison.

Miss Anna E. Benson

ALS: Garrison Papers, Boston Public Library.

1. George Thompson's.
2. James Thomson, *The Castle of Indolence*, Canto II, stanza lvi, lines 1–5.
3. Edward Young, *Night Thoughts*, "Night V," line 773.

178

TO AMOS A. PHELPS

Freedom's Cottage,⎤
Roxbury, Oct. 11, 1834.⎦

My dear and indefatigable Coadjutor:

This, I trust, will be put into your hands by one whose name and fame, and talents and services, have long since thundered across the Atlantic, and caused our hearts to beat high with joyful expectation at his coming — who has been triumphantly borne upon the shoulders of patriotic ardor and christian philanthropy from one end of the British kingdom to the other — whose appeals in behalf of 800,000 slaves in the British Colonies have rung from side to side, and electrified millions who were slumbering in the lap of moral death — and who has come hither to make one of a despised and persecuted band, who are chiefly known and estimated as firebrands, fanatics, and madmen! Need I write his name? Already you have given George Thompson the right hand of fellowship; for I am sure that he has not waited until you shall have read this letter, without making himself known.

Last week, a very interesting Convention was held in Groton, at which Prof. Wright, Mr. May, Mr. Thompson, myself, &c. were present.[1] Since my return, I have been quite unwell, having had an attack of the cholic and dysentery, which has weakened me very much. Although appointed a delegate to the Augusta Convention, it will not be practicable for me to attend. I regret this the more, inasmuch as it would be exceedingly gratifying to me to introduce Mr. Thompson to the Convention, with all the gratitude and admiration I feel in view of his eminent merits. Be the pleasing task yours. If practicable, get a resolution passed in favor of his mission, and commending him to private hospitality and public attention. And here one word as to *hospitality.* I hope that wherever he travels, he will in no case be necessitated to "put up" at taverns and hotels, as in such houses he will always be a signal mark for the shafts of opposition and insult, and as the least our abolition brethren can do is to give him a cordial reception at their own homes. Besides, as he has not come among us to receive one farthing of our money, we ought to make the burden as light for him and our English brethren as possible. These hints are wholly spontaneous on my part, neither known to, nor in any manner suggested by Mr. T.

I anticipate a brave, dextrous, and full discussion at the Convention. It is evidently the wish of the colonization scribes and pharisees, — taking the Christian Mirror [2] for an index, — to consider themselves, by a little jesuitical twisting, as included in the call of the meeting, and to *outvote*, if possible, the abolitionists, and make the whole affair an abortion. They neither mean to go ahead, nor to come up to your mark; and they dare not remain a long distance behind. Some of them are evidently under strong conviction, but pride and unbelief (the sinner's last refuges) prevent them from throwing down the weapons of their rebellion. As far as strict obedience to God and equal justice to man will permit, be placable and conciliatory — but do not give up one jot or tittle of principle, nor keep any thing back, merely for the sake of *conciliation*. You will doubtless have much sophistry and chicanery to contend with — but I fear not the issue in the hands of such men as Thompson, Pomroy, Fessenden, Shepard, and yourself. Let Thompson have a full swing, especially at the cavillers an[d] intermeddlers, if there be any. He always does nob[ly] when he has opposition — violent opposition. I pity the man who has him as an antagonist. Again I say, *let him have a full swing.*

The genuine and uncompromising character of the Convention would be indisputably settled, if you can get the Declaration of the National Convention read and adopted. Try it — it is a good touch-stone — any standard that is lower will be good for nothing.

Have something said, resolved, and *done*, respecting slavery in the District of Columbia. A petition should be agreed upon, and circulated throughout the State, immediately.

By all means, let the State Society be made auxiliary to the National. It is avowedly the intention of the enemy to "divide and conquer" — but let us remember that "united we stand,"[3] and that in union only, is there strength. Let whatever is done, be well done.

How bitter and malignant are the feelings of my enemies toward me! But I trust I can say, in all sincerity and truth, "The Lord is my portion for ever."[4] The editor of the Mirror is growing "exceedingly mad" against me, and seems determined to make me infamous. I cannot help smiling, and feeling very complacent, when such an opponent upbraids me with retarding the progress of the abolition cause!! It is not for me to say how much I have accomplished, but I remember that four or five years ago, there were scarcely as many individuals in the nation who were ready to endorse my principles, and now there are thousands — perhaps tens of thousands. Wonderful, indeed, is the change. Greater success it would be dangerous even for an angel to obtain, lest it might "exalt him above measure."[5] O, may I ever be as humble as God is glorious, and ascribe to him all the praise. Let this be my epitaph — *He never sought panegyric, nor feared obloquy.*

I shall probably send a letter to you by mail at Augusta, to be read at the Convention.

The God of Israel strengthen and bless you, my brother.
Yours, affectionately,

Wm. Lloyd Garrison.

Rev. A. A. Phelps.

ALS: Phelps Papers, Boston Public Library.

1. Of the names mentioned only Elizur Wright, Jr. (1804–1885), remains to be identified. He was a Yale graduate who had taught at Groton Academy, Massachusetts, and at Western Reserve College, Hudson, Ohio. In 1833, under the influence of Theodore D. Weld, he left Ohio and went to New York City to become first the secretary of the New York Anti-Slavery Society and later the corresponding secretary of the American Anti-Slavery Society. In the later 1830's he became one of Garrison's opponents and a leader of the New Organization, whose official organ, the *Massachusetts Abolitionist*, he edited in 1839.

2. Published in Portland, Maine, since 1822.

3. Garrison quotes two maxims, one usually attributed to Machiavelli, the other to Aesop.

4. Garrison alludes to Psalms 119:57.

5. Garrison perhaps adapts Exodus 15:2.

179

TO ANNA E. BENSON

[October (?), 1834.[1]]
Freedom's Cottage.

Dear Anna:

Whether Helen is willing to confess her remissness or not, I will confess mine. If my affection for my pen was a thousandth part as strong as it is for you and the rest of the dear friends in your quiet valley, the post office revenue would be vastly augmented, and whole reams of letters, very closely written, would be forwarded to you in tedious and formidable bundles. But I dislike it, as you well know, hugely — and this aversion is constantly getting me into difficulty, for it makes me hug that naughty and subtle thief Procrastination, with the fondness of a brother. In this respect, I am as bad as a slaveholder — I am the enemy of the wretch who robs me of my time, in the *abstract*; but *practically*, he and I live on terms of excellent fellowship.

Your letter is as gladdening to us as a choral strain of music in the hush of night, or the first song of the bird of Spring. In your promise to visit us, — in company with Henry and Sarah, — you have opened a fountain of delight quite refreshing to our spirits. Here we are almost completely isolated from the world — recluses of the most rigid order. Helen bears the solitariness of her situation with admirable contentment; but she certainly needs at least one female companion, especially in my absence. There is no companion like a sister; and your presence will be equal to a daily sip of elixir vitae, in animating her spirits and diversifying her employment. She has given me a fine proof of the deep attachment which she cherishes for me, in being so cheerful and happy in her seclusion. You will also show, in a signal manner, your attachment for us both, in leaving the cheerful fire-side of "home, sweet home," and coming to reside awhile with us. Be assured that I know how to appreciate such an act of kindness.

Since my marriage, and occupancy of this cottage, I have been quite a *home-body*. Helen hardly gives me credit enough, when she says that I am at home *forenoons*; for morning, noon, and night, I am generally to be found here, poring over my editorial budget, or scribbling letters to friends, or reading newspapers or books, by way of divertisement. Mr. Knapp is indeed very kind to spare me so much from the office — but my friends in the city would be glad to see me oftener. I should be equally pleased to see them frequently — I love not them the less, but Helen and home more.

You may say to Mrs. May, that next to the pleasure we experienced in having her company, is the pleasure we feel in learning that the visit was very agreeable to her. She knows, assuredly, that she and her dear husband will always be welcome guests at Freedom's Cottage, or at any other place which we may hereafter occupy.

Father has my sympathy and tenderest solicitude in his present ill-state of health. Age has naturally its maladies; but a life of temperance and regularity, such as he has led, is able to meet them victoriously for a long period. To the good man, sickness is not a calamity, nay, it makes earth worthless, and heaven precious: it clearly reveals the vanity of terrestrial things, and makes the christian anxious to depart and be with Christ, "which is far better." [2]

With your cheering epistle, I received a budget from other esteemed friends — one from Mr. May, another from Mr. Prentice, of Providence, a third from James Scott, and a fourth from Mr. Parrish. On the day preceding, a long letter was also received from George. Can we be otherwise than happy, with such tokens of friendship in our hands? But when the *living* epistles come — Anna, Sarah, and Henry — we shall be peculiarly honored and gratified. Love to mother, Mary, and all the household. My name is still as unchangeable as my affection.

Wm. Lloyd Garrison.

ALS: Garrison Papers, Boston Public Library.

1. The date is supplied, with the question mark, apparently in the hand of Wendell Phillips Garrison.
2. Philippians 1:23.

180

TO GEORGE W. BENSON

[November 1, 1834.]

My dear George —

If, agreeably to the suggestion of our brave and talented coadjutor on the preceding leaf, you will postpone, or rather adjourn, (for you can of course hold a meeting, transact business, and then adjourn,) your annual meeting for a few days, I will endeavor to attend with Mr. Thompson, although you must allow me to decline making any speech or speeches, as neither Mr. T. nor the anti-slavery cause will need my feeble advocacy or assistance on that occasion. Nevertheless, as a servant who is willing to be advised, and even commanded, I trust I shall shrink from no task which you and my brethren in Providence may be disposed to require at my hands. I have [b]een invited to attend the State Convention in New-Hampshire with Mr. Thompson, but cannot say at present whether I shall be able to comply with the invitation. Next to seeing the Sea Serpent and the newly imported Chinese female,[1] the people of the Granite State are anxious to get a glimpse at me — "monstrum horrendum," &c. Shall I go and terrify their minds, while I appease their curiosity?

Your letter to Helen gave us both unmingled pleasure. We congratulate you and your lady upon the precious gift which God has recently put into your hands.[2] Cherish and regard it as you do your own souls. We long to see and embrace it. Bestow a thousand kisses upon it for us both. In the course of this week, we expect to see you at our cottage, in company with Henry, Sarah and Anna. Bring Catharine[3] with you; if practicable. But ☞ do not fail to come yourself. We are well and happy.

Yours, unreservedly,

Wm. Lloyd Garrison.

ALS: Anti-Slavery Letters to Wm. Lloyd Garrison and Others, Boston Public Library. Garrison appended his message to Benson to Thompson's letter of November 1.

1. Doubtless referring to curiosities commonly exhibited in popular museums of the day.
2. Garrison refers to George W. Benson's new daughter, Anna Elizabeth.
3. George's wife.

181

TO ANNA E. BENSON

[November 9 (?), 1834.][1]

Dear Anna —

As Helen has made me promise not to read *her* part of this letter, I know not what she has written; but I presume she has expressed much regret on learning from Mr. Anthony, (who gratified us with a visit on Friday,) that it is probable you and Sarah will not be able to come to Freedom's Cottage under two or three weeks. In the midst of our disappointment, however, it is highly exhilarating to our spirits to think that you will come; for the time-honored adage, "Better late than never," applies in this instance with peculiar propriety. Of course, we are impatient to see you, and therefore deprecate delay; but still, you are coming, and this is pleasure indeed.

It seems to me as if I did nothing but neglect you all, and then make apologies. Why do I purpose to do so much, and yet accomplish so little? When I took my dear Helen from your household, I was bound, by all filial and brotherly ties, to make at least the petty compensation of sending to some one of you one letter a week. This was my intention — but have I fulfilled it? Well — forgive my remissness, inasmuch as you need no assurance that it has not arisen from any want of interest or affection.

I am truly happy in my new situation, and not less so because Helen expresses so much happiness herself. What is usually called "the honeymoon," is, I suppose, past with us, so far as a certain space of time is concerned, but our [love][2] is as pure as ever, and even more fervent. I have no fears that I shall ever have occasion to regret my choice; and I trust "my better half" will never need to repent of hers.

Have we not had a beautiful autumn? Winter is approaching with a milder aspect than usual, and, although he is not so beautiful as his predecessor, yet he is by no means an unwelcome guest to me.

Assure all the family of my unabated love, and believe me to be
Ever yours.

Wm. Lloyd Garrison.

ALS: Garrison Papers, Boston Public Library.

1. The date is supplied, with the question mark, apparently in the hand of Wendell Phillips Garrison.
2. The substantive "love" is omitted by Garrison and supplied by the editor.

182

TO THE COLORED INHABITANTS OF BOSTON

[Boston, December 18, 1834.]

At the late election in Massachusetts, for Governor, Lieutenant Governor, Senators, and Members of Congress, I regretted to perceive an advertisement in the daily newspapers, calling upon all the colored voters of Boston to rally on the side of the Whigs, and to meet preparatory to the election to take measures for insuring the success of JOHN DAVIS, SAMUEL T. ARMSTRONG, and ABBOTT LAWRENCE.[1] A meeting was accordingly held by you, which, I understand, was very fully attended, and at which, moreover, addresses were made by several white gentlemen, as well as by some of your own number, all in opposition to the Jackson administration, and all, of course, in favor of the Whig ticket. Strong approbatory resolutions were passed in favor of the gentlemen above named, which were published in some of the daily papers; and to secure a full vote, the precaution was taken to get those who were present to sign their names, by way of a pledge, that they would go with the Whigs. This movement, I am sure, was made by you with other and better motives than those which actuated the white voters: I have no doubt that you meant to act wisely for yourselves, and, indirectly at least, to advance that sacred cause which we deem to be paramount to all others, — the cause of our enslaved and bleeding brethren. I think you committed an error — I think you were misled, unintentionally, by those who you have every reason to believe are truly your well wishers. I am sorry that any of your white friends, in their zeal for the Whig cause, went so far as to attend your meeting, and make use of their influence (arising from the gratitude which you naturally feel toward those who are vindicating your rights before the nation) to secure your suffrages for their favorite candidates. It was surely a most impolitic step, which ought not to have been taken, and which, I trust, you will not be induced to take again, until you are placed in other circumstances. This I shall briefly attempt to prove, I hope to your entire conviction, and to their satisfaction.

You will bear me witness, my colored fellow-citizens, that ever since I espoused your cause as an injured and down-trodden people, I have scrupulously refrained from attempting to bias any of your minds on any religious or political points. I have very seldom attended any of your special meetings, and then only by express and urgent solicitation. My delicacy of feeling has even been carried to an extreme; for, aware that you place great (I fear too much) reliance upon my judgment, and listen to my opinions with deference, I have trembled lest you should, in some degree, forget your own responsibilities, and make mine greater than I can sustain. I have felt that, in advising you, to be misled myself, would prove a calamity to us all. Hence, in my addresses delivered before you on various occasions, you are aware that I have confined myself to topics of practical importance — exhorting you to be industrious, frugal, temperate, honest, peaceable; to return good for evil; to aim at social, intellectual and moral improvement; to respect yourselves, that you might win the respect of others; to rely upon the promises of God for succor and protection; and to be 'followers of Christ as dear children,' being chiefly solicitous for that rest which remains for the people of God.

In addressing you at this time, I can say with real sincerity of heart, that I am not actuated in the slightest degree by any political bias. I belong to no party in particular, but to all parties in general — in other words, I am not deceived or influenced by *names*, but governed by *principles*. Ordinarily, I perceive little intelligence, and scarcely any conscience, or honesty, or fear of God, at the polls. The politics of this nation, at the present time, are corrupt, proscriptive, and even ferocious; and the leading politicians of all parties fail in their allegiance to heaven and to their country. With regard to *Jacksonism*, broadly so called, I cordially detest it in principle and in practice; nor do I think much better of its antagonist, *Whiggism*. The organs of each are marked for their slander, vituperation and baseness. Look, for example, at the Washington Globe and the New-Hampshire Patriot [2] — the N. York Commercial Advertiser and the Courier & Enquirer. It is scarcely possible for a cause to be a righteous one, in which such unprincipled papers are leaders. We do indeed need a *christian* party in politics — not made up of this or that sect or denomination, but of all who fear God and keep his commandments, and who sincerely desire to seek judgment and relieve the oppressed. I know it is the belief of many professedly good men, that they ought not to 'meddle' with politics; but they are cherishing a delusion, which, if it do not prove fatal to their own souls, may prove the destruction of their country.

Let me inquire of those to whom these remarks are particularly addressed — Why did you cast your votes for the Whig ticket, and array yourselves as partizans on that side? If the Whigs, as a party, are your friends, and the active, uncompromising enemies of slavery and colonization, then you acted wisely in supporting their ticket. Nobody can blame you for preferring those who are striving to remove your disabilities and burdens, to those who are inimical to your rights. Now, if there be a party which you should dread and oppose more than any other, it is THE WHIG PARTY. It is in close alliance with the south — with the friends of perpetual slavery — with nullification and misrule.

It is fierce, implacable, blood-thirsty, and purely despotic towards those who are seeking the immediate abolition of slavery, and your social and moral elevation. It has excited all the mobs which have sought to destroy the liberty of speech and of the press: in this seditious conduct, it is true, it has been cordially assisted by almost every other party, but its guilt is, *in setting the example.* Who caused the riots in New-York and Philadelphia, by which the lives of your advocates and of your colored brethren were put in imminent peril, and their houses and property destroyed? Those notable WHIG papers, the Courier and Enquirer, Commercial Advertiser, Philadelphia Inquirer, and the Daily Intelligencer! What is the language of another *Whig* paper, distinguished for its knavery, its cowardice, its ruffianism, its utter destitution of principle — the *Boston Commercial Gazette?* what, I ask, is its language, respecting me, and all who advocate your cause in this city? Why, that if we attempt to discuss the subject of slavery in public, we ought to receive A COAT OF TAR AND FEATHERS, *to have no protection for our lives and property, and to be given over to the 'tender mercies' of the mob!* Who are the leaders in the colonization crusade, which would banish you from your country, and cast you ruthlessly upon the shores of Africa? They are WHIGS, at the head of whom stands HENRY CLAY, the man who has dared to say to the American people, in his address before the Kentucky Colonization Society, — 'If the question were submitted, whether there should be immediate or *gradual* emancipation of all the slaves in the United States, *without their* REMOVAL *or* COLONIZATION, painful as it is to express the opinion, (!) I HAVE NO DOUBT THAT IT WOULD BE UNWISE TO EMANCIPATE THEM'! ! This is the *Whig,* too, who uttered this language at the first meeting of the American Colonization Society: 'He was himself a slaveholder; and *he considered that kind of property as inviolable as any other in the country. He would resist as soon, and with as much firmness, encroachments upon it, as he would encroachments upon any other property which he held.'* [3] In short, if the Whigs, *as a party,* get full dominion in this country, and continue to cherish the same malevolent and desperate spirit towards the cause of emancipaction as they have hitherto done, what is the prospect held out to you, my colored brethren, or to the manacled slaves at the south?

My reasons for believing that you erred in proclaiming yourselves Whigs, and voting for the Whig ticket, are these:

1st. John Davis and Samuel T. Armstrong are colonizationists; and you certainly do not mean *intentionally* to put into office, those who support a scheme which contemplates your removal to Africa.

2d. With regard to Abbott Lawrence, I respect him as an honorable man and an enterprising merchant; but he had no claim upon you for your votes, for his letter was not at all satisfactory, nor such an one as an abolitionist would have written. Moreover, there was another candidate in the field, who was and is your friend and advocate, known openly as such — a man of moral courage, and a *christian* — AMASA WALKER. I gave him my vote on the ground of humanity, justice, benevolence and religion; [4] and I think, as you valued your welfare, he ought to have received your votes. It is true, had you all voted for him, he would not have been elected; but your support, on that ground, would have told well for him and for you, and increased the probability of his success at another election. Besides, it is our duty to throw our votes wisely, even if we are sure of defeat. We must try again and again, until we succeed; for in this, as in every good work, we shall reap in due season, if we faint not.

3dly — *and this is the main point to which I wish to draw your attention* — By voting for the Whig ticket, you gained nothing, and risked much. The Whigs are not more friendly to you than the Jackson men — nay, they persecute you and your friends with peculiar bitterness. They are quite willing, on election day, to make a cat's-paw of you — quite willing that you should be a ladder upon which they may climb to office; and when they have reached the top, they will kick it down again. The misfortune, however, is, not that you do not conciliate them, but that you unavoidably, naturally and needlessly excite the ill-will and bad passions of all other parties. Why should you run a tilt against them, to your own injury? You have friends, as well as enemies, in every political party; and until you and your brethren throughout the country are completely emancipated and enfranchised, you will behave discreetly not to act as partisans in any case, unless the party with whom you co-operate are seeking to overthrow prejudice, and to break the iron yoke of bondage. It behooves you, as far as in you lies, not to give any new cause of resentment and dislike to your enemies; and, therefore, so long as you have nothing to gain in supporting a particular party, it is scarcely worth while for you to encounter the hatred of those who are arrayed against that party. Do you not perceive the force of these suggestions?

In conclusion, I will add, that I am glad, yea proud, to see that you are appreciating the importance of exercising that elective franchise which is secured to you by the Constitution of Massachusetts. By rallying at the polls, you show that you understand and duly estimate an important right, and you elevate yourselves in public estimation, if you do not suffer designing men to mislead you. In many cases, you will undoubtedly be led astray, in consequence of a want of correct information: but by consulting your *tried* friends, you will generally cast your votes into the right scale. When the various parties present their lists of candidates, I would advise you to examine them all minutely, and from them all select such names of persons as you know or believe are most kindly disposed towards you as a people. This is not an appeal to your selfishness, but the presentation of a duty which you owe to yourselves, and to your brethren elsewhere, whether bond or free.

The foregoing hints are calculated for general application, wherever colored men are allowed to vote, although they are written with special reference to you who reside in Boston. Trusting that they will be read and pondered by you all, and received as another token of my interest in your welfare, I remain, dear brethren,

Your steadfast friend and humble advocate,

Wm. Lloyd Garrison.

Boston, Dec. 18, 1834

Printed: *The Liberator*, December 20, 1834; extract printed in *The Liberator*, April 5, 1839.

1. Of the three Massachusetts Whigs mentioned, only Davis has previously been identified. Samuel T. Armstrong (1784–1850) was a successful Boston publisher of religious books. He was active in the Old South Church and the American Board of Commissioners for Foreign Missions. Briefly, he was to be governor of the state in 1835 when Governor Davis went to the Senate. He was subsequently to serve as mayor of Boston as well as state senator. Abbott Lawrence (1792–1855), leading Boston merchant of the day, had made a fortune importing English drygoods and was also selling domestic cottons and woolens. In 1845 he was to found the textile city that bore his name, and he was an early promoter of railroads. Garrison had explained in *The Liberator*, November 8, 1834, that although he did not question Lawrence's "fairness of integrity and benevolence of heart," his own candidate for Congress was Amasa Walker, who was "publicly known to be a thorough-going, uncompromising abolitionist."

2. Published in Concord.

3. Garrison refers to Clay's speech to the American Colonization Society at Frankfort, Kentucky, on December 17, 1829, and to his remarks made after introducing a motion at the second annual meeting of the American Colonization Society held in Washington at the chamber of the House of Representatives January 1, 1818. The passage quoted from those remarks is accurate; see James F. Hopkins, ed., *The Papers of Henry Clay* (Lexington, Kentucky, 1961), II, 420.

4. Called by Garrison's sons "the one political vote of his lifetime" (*Life*, I, 455).

183

TO UNKNOWN RECIPIENT

[Between January 25 and April 12, 1834.]

Dear Friend —

Phelp's Lectures, which are worth their weight in gold, we put to you at four dollars per dozen — they sell at retail 50 cents each, and are very cheap at that rate. Garrison's Trial is not yet printed. The New-York Eulogium on Wilberforce [1] I cannot find in the office, as Mr. Knapp is absent. I know not how many take the Abolitionist in Reading, but send 6 copies. The work is now discontinued. Blessings upon you for your zeal in the good cause!

Yours, in haste,

W. L. Garrison.

ALS: Villard Papers, Harvard College Library.

Although the exact date of this letter cannot be established, it was written between January 25 and April 12, 1834, since the former is the date of the first advertisement to appear in *The Liberator* for Amos A. Phelps, *Lectures on Slavery and its Remedy*, and April 12 is the date of the first advertisement for *A Brief Sketch of the Trial of William Lloyd Garrison, for an alleged Libel on Francis Todd of Newburyport, Mass.* [a reprint]. Nor is it possible to identify the recipient with any certainty, though one might speculate that he could be the agent for *The Liberator* in Reading. The lists of agents published in the issues of *The Liberator* during this period, however, do not list any representative in Reading. Conceivably, it could be Horace P. Wakefield, who, according to the report in *The Liberator* for December 21, 1833, was the delegate for Reading at an antislavery convention held at Philadelphia December 4–6 of that year.

1. Advertised in *The Liberator* January 4, 1834.

V YEAR OF VIOLENCE: 1835

V YEAR OF VIOLENCE: 1835

LESS THAN four weeks after the wedding of William Lloyd Garrison and Helen Benson, George Thompson landed in New York to begin his mission to the United States. His advent ushered in a year of American reaction to the anti-slavery agitation so violent that it must have amazed both Thompson and Garrison — partly by its contrast to the friendly reception Garrison had received in England the year before. Garrison's life vacillated between the idyllic existence with Helen in Roxbury and the Bensons at Brooklyn on the one hand and the dangerous world inhabited by Thompson on the other.

Garrison himself did not entirely avoid the animosity everywhere offered Thompson. He was burned in effigy in Charleston, South Carolina. In Boston, September 10, 1835, a gallows, labeled for both of them, was constructed in front of the house at 23 Brighton Street (a house which the Garrisons had recently rented to relieve Thompson of some of his difficulties by assuming a lease he had signed). And, most spectacularly, Garrison was mobbed and might have been killed during the riot on October 21, occasioned by a meeting of the Boston Female Anti-Slavery Society. Although Thompson had been announced as speaker when this meeting had originally been called for October 14, he was not present at this postponed gathering. Disappointed at not finding Thompson, the mob turned its wrath upon Garrison in his stead.

Following this violent outbreak, Helen Garrison went to Brooklyn to live out the remaining months of her first pregnancy, and Garrison alternated between Brooklyn and Boston.

184

TO GEORGE BENSON

Boston, Jan. 12, 1835.

Dear and respected Sir —

I am not sure whether I ought first to apologize for my silence, or to wish you and yours a happy New-Year; but I will do both in one sentence, candidly confessing, however, that apologies are seldom good for anything, and that wishes are equally unsubstantial and unproductive. For the last three weeks, my mind has been considerably depressed, and my time very much occupied. My dear Helen has been quite ill with an internal pain in the head, affecting the ear, which has deprived her of sleep for several nights in succession; but I am happy to state that she is now recovered, and that, for the first time in three weeks, she ventured to walk out yesterday. Dear Anna, too, has been affected by a cold, though somewhat slightly. Just as the influenza was leaving this vicinity, it took me by the throat, and treated me somewhat roughly — but I soon conquered it, and am now doing very well. So you see we have had a share of the afflictions which are prevalent in our wo-stricken world; and happy will it be for us if we can learn to profit thereby, for time and eternity. Sickness and death are no flatterers — they are rough but useful admonishers — they are terrible only in proportion to the guilt and impenitence of the objects whom they attack.

When we write to those whom we love, we are too apt, perhaps, to hope that every thing has gone smoothly with them; that they have had a cloudless sky, a bright sun, flowers without thorns in their path, and zephyrs playing around them; and that disease and adversity have not intruded upon their threshold. It is true, this hope springs from an amiable disposition, and the fondness of affection; but we may question its propriety, as it is commonly expressed, without qualification. Perhaps it is safer and wiser to hope, that, whatever may have been the lot of our friends, it may have been endured with christian submission and humility, and have wrought out the peaceable fruits of righteousness. There is but *one* Being in the universe, who sees the end from the beginning, and who can tell whether our friends need most to be chastised or prospered, to promote their eternal good. Let us leave all temporal arrangements in his hands, consecrating both body and soul to his adorable service.

As soon as I get through publishing some long documents I have on hand, I shall insert in the columns of the Liberator those seasonable and truly excellent extracts, contained in your last kind epistle, relating to infidelity. It seems to me that the necessity to "cry aloud, *and spare not*," [1] in regard to private and public transgressions, was never so great in this nation as at the present time. I am appalled at the daring front and rapid growth of atheism — lascivious, blasphemous, heaven-defying, God-rejecting atheism — in New-England and elsewhere; and especially, as the christianity of our times is so effeminate, calculating, timid, and corrupt. We must bring back again the triumphant and memorable days of martyrdom. We must have a race of men who will be bold for God, and open-mouthed and trumpet-tongued for his truth, in the face of death. This is a time for plain dealing with sin in every shape — but wo to the man who speaks the truth without admixture and without abatement! I verily believe that there is malice enough in this nation to crucify the Lord of glory, were he to come on earth at the present time as he came in the days of the Jews. My prayer to God is, that I may be kept from the fear and the wisdom of man, and be ready to lay down my life victoriously in his service, whenever it shall be necessary.

I am truly glad that my Canterbury persecutors have withdrawn their suits against me; for law-business is any thing but agreeable, and victory in it generally results in ruin. They have put me to an expense of nearly or quite $150, (including traveling expenses,) which they ought in justice to bear — this, of course, they will not do. However, I trust my anti-slavery brethren will help me to meet at least a portion of it. Friend Buffum thinks he can raise half of that sum in Philadelphia. I have to-day received Mr. Parrish's letter, containing a list of the expenses, which shall be answered immediately. I think he has manage[d] my case very discreetly and economically.

I suppose you have received the last two or thre[e] numbers of the Liberator quite irregularly. The truth is, we have been hesitating, whether to stop or proceed with it, in consequence of the non-payment of our numerous subscribers, and the faithlessness of a majority of our agents; and on Friday last, I went home to write my valedictory, and to advertise the world of the downfal of the Liberator! It was truly an afflicting period, and I felt as if I was about cutting off my right arm, or plucking out my right eye. Ascertaining my purpose, several of my anti-slavery brethren rallied together, and have resolved to sustain me and the paper if I will proceed: so, hereafter, I trust, you will get it regularly.

In a short time, the annual meeting of our Society [2] is to be held in this city. How it would rejoice my heart, and the hearts of dear Anna and Helen, and the hearts of our anti-slavery friends, to see you presiding on the occasion; but I suppose we can hardly cherish the pleasing anticipation, without a more than equal chance of being disappointed. We shall not, however, despair of welcoming you, and dear mother, and Mary, at our little cottage, in the course of the ensuing spring.

If my dear friend May has not told you, I will, that I have treated him shamefully — that I owe him an epistle of amazing length, very closely written — and that he bears it all kindly, *very* kindly. You may tell him, if you please, that we talk of removing him from Brooklyn to Boston, and making him General Agent and Secretary of the N. E. Anti-Slavery Society. Our Board of Managers will decide this matter to-morrow evening, and I am pretty certain that he will be chosen.[3] Salary, perhaps, one thousand dollars.

Henry desires me to say that he is well, and in good spirits. His presence is very cheering to Helen, Anna, and myself. We shall be completely happy when you all come to Roxbury.

Tender my warmest affections to her whom I may now call my mother — to sisters Mary and Sarah — and to those at Providence, as you write to them. Remember me also to Eunice and Mary Burnet. Mr. and Mrs. Gray, Mrs. May, and all the rest of the friends, are duly remembered in love. Dear Helen and Anna join in this transmission. I remain, a happy husband, and

Your dutiful son,

Wm. Lloyd Garrison.

G. Benson, Esq.

ALS: Villard Papers, Harvard College Library; extract printed in *Life*, I, 468.

1. Isaiah 58:1; Garrison adds the conjunction and the italics.
2. That is, the New England Anti-Slavery Society.
3. May was apparently not chosen, or at least did not accept the position Garrison describes.

185

TO GERRIT SMITH

[January 31, 1835.]

Sir —

Three letters have recently appeared from your pen, addressed to the Rev. Leonard Bacon of New-Haven — the first, in vindication of the doctrine of Immediate Emancipation; the second, both in condemnation and praise of the American Anti-Slavery Society; and the third, in defence of the American Colonization Society. Having copied them into the columns of the Liberator, without mutilation or abridgment, I proceed to review them with all fidelity and candor. Not only am I bound to do this, as the professed and admitted advocate of the colored population of the United States, but I think in the introduction to your first letter, you court such a review, if there be any thing erroneous or pernicious in what you have written. You say to Mr. Bacon —

'If there are errors in the doctrines and reasonings of these essays, *as not improbably there are*, your comments may expose them, and prevent their injurious effects.' [1]

I presume you do not wish to confine this liberty of examination to Mr. Bacon, but, having published your sentiments to the world, are willing to have them freely canvassed by the world, without fear and without partiality. Indeed, to suffer them to pass unheeded, awarding to them neither censure nor praise, would scarcely be respectful or decorous to one whose reputation as a philanthropist is so widely extended as your own. I think there are errors, gross errors, both in the 'doctrines' and 'reasonings' of your essays; and if I succeed in detecting and exposing them, you will have too much candor to be angry, and too much love of truth to cling tenaciously to manifest error. I have altogether misapprehended your character, if I err in this opinion.

You have not displayed either much boldness or wisdom, in applying to Mr. LEONARD BACON for correction and reproof. Such 'errors in doctrines and reasonings,' as you have committed, are among the less enormous ones which he is constantly promulgating throughout the length and breadth of the land. His comments upon your letters are calculated to weaken the good, and to strengthen the evil, that is contained in them. Instead of probing your wounds, he has covered them up to fester and mortify: instead of providing a remedy for moral contagion, he has made that contagion even more virulent. Sir, you have sought to be made whole at the hands of a quack; and be assured, that if you follow his advice and take his prescriptions, not a sound piece of flesh will be left in your body.

In these letters, I will be neither apologetical nor sycophantic. I must be personal, because it is impossible to arraign transgression without implicating the transgressor — personal, but not, I trust, in a bad sense; not unkind, not abusive, not uncharitable. I am accused of harboring ill-will towards certain individuals, because I have called them by name, and identified them before the public; but in the strength of innocence, I repel the accusation. There are occasions when the success of the impeachment depends upon personal identity; there are cases in which general accusations fail to reach individual guilt; and these happen often. Besides, it is far more manly to say, face to face, without circumlocution or equivocation, '*Thou* art the

437

man!'² than to deal in subtle insinuations and dark imputations. The Bible is full of severe, unsparing, *terrible* personalities: its doctrines are efficacious, only as they are personal: its rebukes, its commendations, its threatenings, its promises, its penalties, its rewards, are all personal. In this respect, it is a remarkable volume. Look at the language of the patriarchs and prophets, of Christ and the apostles! O, but the gift of inspiration was theirs! True — but this inspiration having defined the nature and traced the consequences of sin, and the commandments being plain, we are authorized to imitate the conduct of 'holy men of old,'³ in rebuking and warning those who are led into error. I hold it to be a sound maxim, that no man should cherish a principle of action, or pursue a course of conduct, of which he is ashamed to be accused before the universe: therefore, when a man is accused of wrong-doing, if he be innocent or feel that he is innocent, he will not get into a passion and give railing for railing, but will rather smile in conscious integrity, and be willing to examine himself afresh with unwonted scrutiny. Indignation, I grant, may occupy the breast almost at the same moment with the complacency of innocence. This is my own case exactly. My enemies call me 'a fanatic,' 'an incendiary,' 'a madman,' and 'a cut-throat;' and these terms, applied and confined to myself alone, excite my merriment, because I know that they are unjust: but when I reflect upon the malignant motives with which they are often uttered, and how they are intended and calculated, by making me a by-word and a hissing in the land, to render odious that great and holy cause which I am so feebly espousing, they excite within me feelings of strong moral displeasure. I then forgive — I *forget*, the injury done to my own character, and think only of the turpitude of him, who, having 'no flesh in his obdurate heart,'⁴ is striving to make me by his calumnies a curse, instead of a blessing, to a manacled and bleeding race.

If I had confined my denunciations to this or that individual, and selected him out as the special object of my reprehension; then, indeed, such a limited and petty warfare might have worn an aspect of personal malice. But whoever may hereafter collect my writings together, in order to form some estimate of my character, will, I trust, be able to testify, that I was no respecter of persons, but was uniform in my condemnation of corrupt principles, however high the source from which they emanated. In attacking the system of slavery, over what slaveholder have I thrown the mantle of innocence? Where is the man, in the extended ranks of colonization, whose fear or favor has deterred me from exposing his error? With Luther I am ready to admit, that 'almost all men condemn the tartness of my expressions;' but with him, 'I am of opinion, that God will have the deceits of men thus powerfully exposed; for I plainly perceive that those things which are softly dealt with in our corrupt age, give people but light concern, and are presently forgotten. *If I have exceeded the bounds of moderation, the monstrous turpitude of the times has transported me.* Nor do I transcend the example of Christ, who, having to do with people of like manners, called them sharply by their proper names — such as, an adulterous and perverse generation, a brood of vipers, hypocrites, children of the devil who could not escape the damnation of hell.' [5] Young as I am, I have lived long enough to arrive at a moral eminence, beneath which, as I gaze downward, the earth dwindles into nothingness. How, then, is it possible for me to be careful, in the prosecution of my labors, lest I offend certain great and popular men? The truth, that 'all flesh is grass,' [6] is too deeply impressed upon my heart, and realized with too clear a conviction, for me to care whether I am despised or honored in the estimation of men, who are soon to be cut down and to perish as the flowers of the field.

He who undertakes to reform the morals of the age, will find his situation any thing but a sinecure. He will be as sagely admonished of his improprieties of speech, as was the poet for his satires. Pope gives us the following instructive interview in one of his Dialogues:

> *Friend.* Yet none but you by name the guilty lash;
> Even Guthrie saves half Newgate by a dash.
> Spare then the person, and expose the vice.
> *Poet.* How! not condemn the sharper, but the dice?
> Come on then, Satire! general, unconfined,
> Spread thy broad wing, and souse on all the kind.
> Ye statesmen, priests, of one religion all!
> Ye tradesmen, vile, in army, court or hall!
> Ye reverend atheists —
>   *F.* Scandal! name them — Who?
> *P.* Why that's the thing you bid me not to do,
> Who starved a sister, who forswore a debt,
> I never named — the town's enquiring yet.
> The poisoning dame —
>   *F.* You mean —
>   *P.* I don't —
>   *F.* You do.
> *P.* See, now I keep the secret, and not you!
> The bribing statesman —
>   *F.* Hold, too high you go.
> *P.* The bribed elector —
>   *F.* There you stoop too low.
> *P.* I fain would please you, if I knew with what;
> Tell me, which knave is lawful game, which not?
> Must great offenders, once escaped the crown,
> Like royal harts, be never more run down?
> Admit your law to spare the knight requires,

As beasts of nature may we hunt the 'squires?
Suppose I censure — you know what I mean —
To save a bishop, may I name a dean?
F. A dean, sir? No — his fortune is not made;
You hurt a man that's rising in the trade.
P. If not the tradesman who sat up to-day,
Much less the 'prentice who to-morrow may.
Down, down, proud Satire! though a realm be
    spoiled,
Arraign no mightier thief than wretched Wild —
F. Yes, strike that Wild — I'll justify the blow.
P. Strike? Why, the man was hang'd ten years
    ago!

     ❖   ❖   ❖   ❖   ❖   ❖

Ask you, what provocation I have had?
The strong antipathy of good to bad.
When truth or virtue an affront endures,
Th' affront is mine, my friend, and shall be yours;
Mine, as a friend to every worthy mind;
And mine as man, who feels for all mankind.' [7]

Sir, I will not hide the fact; there are already, even in the abolition ranks, some who are too eager to secure men of influence on their side, at the expense of plain-spoken honesty; and this leads them to be cautious and politic in what they do and say. They are anxious to retain, if possible, GERRIT SMITH, because he is a wealthy, generous-hearted, indefatigable philanthropist; and they say in a whisper, 'Let him alone for the present — he is moving slowly but surely, and will be wholly on our side very soon, provided his letters are not replied to.' No, sir, I do not believe you are to be caught in this manner. If the numerous fallacies and contradictions in your essays are not faithfully pointed out to you, I am afraid you will be led to think that you have written in so able, coherent and straight-forward a manner, as to defy refutation, and thus you will complacently continue in error. If the more light that is thrown upon your path, only serves to make you seek more profound darkness, you are not so good a man as you have the reputation to be.

Sir, I am as anxious to see you a convert to anti-slavery doctrines, and a patron of the American Anti-Slavery Society, as my more prudent brethren; and my reasons are — because it is lamentable to see a good man in error — because you have done immense injury to our colored population, and are bound to make reparation — and because, when once enlisted under the genuine standard of liberty, you will make a brave and valuable soldier. But until you can come with clean hands and a clear vision, and without wincing at the charge of inconsistency, I hope you will stay just where you are — or, rather, that you will be less equivocal in your conduct. I am offended to see you put an abolition cockade upon your cap, and still wear a colonization uniform: both sides of the combatants must naturally suspect you.

I have not the honor to be personally acquainted with you; but, in despite of your silence on the subject of slavery, and your advocacy of the Colonization Society, I have for many years entertained an exalted opinion of your character as a philanthropist and a christian. In the Temperance cause, you have labored nobly — uncompromisingly — consistently. I, too, early enlisted in that cause, and received at least a modicum of the ridicule and abuse which were at that period showered upon 'cold water men' — and can therefore appreciate, to some extent, the importance and bravery of your efforts. You have liberally assisted the cause of pure and undefiled religion, with a zeal according to knowledge. So much I admit — and a better and broader panegyric I might bestow, peradventure, if I were called upon to vindicate your conduct, apart from the anti-slavery cause. It is because I esteem you so highly, that I mean to deal faithfully with you; for, in the weighty language of the celebrated O'Connell, 'the errors of great men are doubly enormous — enormous as they contradict the tenor of their lives; and enormous by the force of example, and the species of palliation which they afford to vulgar criminals, whose vices are unredeemed by one single virtue.' [8]

One of my charges against you is, that you have done immense injury to our colored population — unwittingly done it, I would fain believe. How? By giving your example, your wealth, your influence, your talents, your efforts, to the support of the American Colonization Society. You have been, and are at the present moment, one of the main pillars that support it. Now, if what is alleged against that Society be true — that it is the malignant slanderer of the free people of color, the enemy of immediate emancipation, the ally of slaveholders, the apologist of man-stealing, the cowardly and selfish persecutor of the colored race, &c. &c.; if these accusations are true, (and I affirm that they are true, and will prove them to be so before I conclude these letters,) then, inasmuch as you have been one of its principal supporters, and have proclaimed to the world that you still mean to support it, it follows that your mighty energies have only tended to degrade and enslave the colored population of this country, to injure the whole country itself, and to curse poor benighted Africa. Sir, it seems to me that you occupy a dreadful position. You may plead sincerity of purpose — but does this excuse your blindness? What matters it to the victims who lie writhing beneath the car of the colonization Juggernaut, whether you drag its ponderous wheels over their bodies as a hypocrite or a sincere devotee? When Saul was persecuting the saints unto strange cities, and slaughtering them in his fury, what consolation was it to them to know that he thought he was thereby doing God service?

441

Sincerity in wrong-doing will not wash away its guilt; and, sir, I see not how you can stand clear in this matter. Your school at Peterboro', for the education of colored youth, is truly benevolent; but all your good deeds cannot justify or cancel that unrighteous act which binds you to the Colonization Society. Sir, strong as you are, it is not in human strength, or eloquence, or devotion, or activity, or wealth, or subtlety, to sustain that Society; for God, and Truth, and Humanity, are against it, and it must fall.

Respectfully yours,

WM. LLOYD GARRISON.

Printed: *The Liberator*, January 31, 1835.

Gerrit Smith (1797–1874) was a wealthy, though sometimes impractical, philanthropist who had dedicated his life to benefiting mankind. He had given generously to churches, to theological schools, and to colleges. He had advocated many reforms: strict observance of the Sabbath, vegetarianism, anti-Masonry, peace, and temperance — opposing the use of both alcohol and tobacco. By the time of Garrison's letter Smith had become a familiar figure in the pages of *The Liberator* for his contributions to the American Colonization Society, for his support of a manual labor school (issues for January 25, February 15, and November 8, 1834), and especially for the three letters to Leonard Bacon, editor of the *Christian Spectator* (reprinted in the issues for December 20, 27, 1834, and January 24, 1835). During 1835 Garrison remained patient but critical of the rich westerner (see the issues for January 10, 24, 31, February 7, 28, March 7, May 9, June 13, September 19).

1. In this and the other three letters (187, 188, 189) to Gerrit Smith (dated February 7, 28, and March 7), Garrison quotes from all three of Smith's letters as well as from Smith's speech as printed in the *African Repository*, 6:357–364 (February 1831). He follows the text of the letters and of the speech closely, though he changes somewhat the order of the statements, omits at least one word, transposes two of the Latin words, modifies the punctuation and capitalization, and adds the italics and the material within the parentheses and brackets.

2. II Samuel 12:7.

3. Garrison seems to adapt Deuteronomy 19:14.

4. William Cowper, *The Task*, Book II, line 8, with the substitution of "his" for "man's."

5. A search through Luther's voluminous works has not revealed these particular quotations, though Luther frequently alludes to the violence of his own language and to having God on his side. Certainly there is justification for seeing parallels between Garrison and Luther: they were both reformers; both were considered milder in person than in their writings; both were imprisoned for their own protection; both used a prison term to perform significant work while confined; both were married happily, to shy and reserved young ladies; and both at times rejected and attacked persons who had been close associates and followers. In *The Liberator* Garrison occasionally compares himself to Luther (see the issues for January 28 and September 9, 1842). Garrison was especially pleased when Henry C. Wright and Dr. George B. Loring compared him to Luther (see *The Liberator*, February 9, 1849, and the letter to Francis Jackson Garrison, November 20, 1876).

6. I Peter 1:24.

7. Making two short omissions (lines 40–53 and 200–201) and one long one (lines 56–196), Garrison quotes lines 10–204 of Dialogue II of the "Epilogue to the Satires." He also omits "Sir" (line 13) and substitutes "sat" for "set" (line 36) and "shall" for "should" (line 200). As in an earlier quotation of line 13 from the same poem, Garrison again changes "damn" to "condemn."

8. The speech by O'Connell from which Garrison quotes has not been identified.

186

TO LOUISA LORING

Freedom's Cottage,
Jan. 31, 1835.

Dear Madam:

It was only a few days since, that I received the beautiful little box which I purchased of you at the very memorable Fair — all owing to the forgetfulness of my partner, Mr. Knapp, to whose care it was committed. On opening it, I found a very kind note from you, and also, as a present for the new year, a neatly made pair of slippers; in return for which, I send you my very hearty thanks. You will not deem this grateful acknowledgment inconsistent with my determination to tread your pretty gift *under my feet*: I hope to *stand* all the better for it in your estimation, and to *walk* more uprightly than ever.

You have been wondering, no doubt, at my silence; but again I must throw all the blame upon Mr. Knapp. It was by the merest accident, at last, that I ascertained that the box had been quietly reposing on one of the shelves at the Anti-Slavery Room, for the space of three weeks!

Since I saw you, Mrs. Garrison has been sadly afflicted by the gathering of an abscess in each of her ears. At times, the pain she endured was excruciating. For more than a week, she was deprived of sleep, and opiates seemed to have no effect upon her. She is now nearly recovered, and will be happy to make you a visit as soon as convenient. She joins with me in wishing health, prosperity and happiness to you and your estimable husband.[1]

Respectfully yours,

Wm. Lloyd Garrison.

Mrs. Louisa Loring.

ALS: Ellis Gray Loring Family Papers, Radcliffe College Library.
Louisa Gilman Loring (1797–1868) was the wife of Ellis Gray Loring and in her own right an ardent abolitionist and generous contributor to the cause. She gave not only money but also her own time and energy. She and her husband made their home a center for abolitionists and later for the care of fugitive slaves.

1. Ellis Gray Loring (1803–1858), in background an aristocratic Bostonian and by profession a lawyer, was an abolitionist by the time Garrison began to publish *The Liberator*. He was one of those influential in founding the New England Anti-Slavery Society, though he could not at that time subscribe to the doctrine of immediate emancipation. Through the years he gave decisive financial support to *The Liberator* and the cause; he was also active as an attorney in defending fugitive slaves.

1 8 7

TO GERRIT SMITH

[February 7, 1835.]

Sᴵʀ —

In the whole course of my readings, whether relating to literature or morals, I do not remember an instance, in which I have met with such glaring contradictions and startling inconsistencies in the writings of an intelligent and virtuous man, as appear in your recent anti-slavery and colonization essays. You deny your own assertions — refute your own positions — ridicule your own principles — and excel in the use of hard and violent language, in the same breath that gives utterance to your rebuke of those whom you accuse of uncharitableness. These fatal discrepancies are the more surprising, inasmuch as you must have written with more than ordinary anxiety, caution and labor; for you well knew that your essays would excite attention, and be critically examined by keen-sighted and watchful opponents. You have gone to the battle courageously, but without discretion or skill. I am glad that your errors lie on the surface, and are palpable to the eye. I am glad, because another man, less honest and more dextrous, would have mixed the arsenic with the wholesome food, instead of serving up each on a different dish, and thus poisoned an unsuspecting community.

Your first letter, or essay, (excepting one or two sentences,) and a portion of your second, obtain the assent of my understanding and the gratitude of my heart, being a manly and successful vindication of all the principles, doctrines and measures, that I have ever espoused or recommended in the anti-slavery cause, or that have ever been recognized by the advocates of immediate emancipation; and yet they are those which have been scouted in all the publications of the American Colonization Society, from the earliest period of its existence! — a Society which you, Sir, are still so infatuated as to patronize. You brand *slaveholding* by as terrible an epithet, and denounce *slave-holders*, indiscriminately, in as severe terms, as can be found on any page of the Liberator, or in any anti-slavery production of ancient or modern days; and yet you rebuke abolitionists for their *indiscriminate censure* of these very individuals, which, you assert, is stirring up angry feelings, and inflaming one portion of our common country against the other! You contend for immediate emancipation, because 'slaveholding' is *a sin — evil, and only evil, continually — a crime against the life of the soul — a giant sin — a soul-killing relation;* and yet you 'have no fellowship for the reckless spirit, that is ever ready to exclaim, — *Fiat justitia, ruat cœlum!*' [1] Dare you, as a Christian, reject this

444

motto? You call northern ministers who become slaveholding residents at the south, '*dumb dogs*,' and '*greedy dogs;*' and yet you pathetically talk of the unfortunate 'young Christian brother at the south, in whose inheritance [how mild] are his deceased father's servants, [servants! not *slaves!*] to whom he is aiming to do good on gospel principles, albeit he has not yet learned that those principles require him to dissolve the *new* [why not '*soul killing*'?] relation he bears toward them,' — a Christian, and yet ignorant that gospel principles require him to be an honest man, and to cease from the villany perpetrated by his father! If he may be excused, then why not all other slaveholders? Sir, here your language is deceitful, and your plea worthless. I do not blame the Christian brother, young or old, whose man-stealing parent bequeathes his victims to his charge; because he is not responsible for the act. But the moment he holds them as his property, however kindly he may treat them, he is a man-stealer, whom the apostle classes among 'murderers of fathers and murderers of mothers.' [2]

Sir, if your letters were thoroughly sound and consistent, they yet lack one of the marks of genuine repentance, namely, confession of error. You are an immediate emancipationist: when did you cease to be a gradualist? To whom, or to what are you indebted, for now viewing *slaveholding* as sinful and soul-killing in its relation? When did the scales drop from your eyes? By your letters, one ignorant of your former principles would suppose, that you had always cherished the views expressed in them. Is this honest? is it acting penitently? Why not acknowledge a radical change of opinion on this subject? I will tell you, Sir. You do not make confession, for two reasons — either because you are too proud to own your indebtedness to anti-slavery writings, or because you are not a genuine convert. I adopt the latter: like a thousand other men, your theory is better than your practice. You are for immediate emancipation in the abstract — not practically. Some 'young Christian brother at the south' must set aside the application of eternal truth, because *it is good* to have respect unto persons, and not to say to the thief, (because he is a Christian,) '*Thou* art the man!' [3] And before emancipation takes place, the north must *in equity* agree to buy all the slaves! — This, Sir, is your immediate emancipation.

You *ought* to acknowledge your conversion, if indeed you are converted, to abolition doctrines, because you have *publicly* erred in word and deed, and have led astray a great multitude whose faith is pinned upon your sleeve. I have before me the Fourteenth Annual Report of the American Colonization Society, in which I find reported a speech of GERRIT SMITH, of Peterboro', N. Y., delivered only three years ago at Washington. In that speech, are sentiments which I do not hesitate to call cruel and atrocious, and upon which I bestow all the abhorrence of my soul. There are also other sentiments which are alike ludicrous and false, particularly in reference to the foreign slave trade. For example:

'Whatever means may be employed, [in raising Africa from her degradation,] we maintain, must be such as to accomplish the abolition of the slave trade, or they will fail' — [true.] 'Experience teaches that no laws, no treaties stop it. . . . . To suppress this trade, it must be made *physically* impossible. We must line the Western coast of Africa with civilized settlements. . . . . Such are the means, *and the only means*, by which the slave trade can be abolished.'

'*Physically* impossible'! It cannot be done, so long as a market exists for slaves in this country. The remedy for the traffic is, to make it *morally* impossible; and this can be effected, only by destroying the market. The immediate abolition of slavery, must inevitably produce the immediate abolition of the slave trade; for when the Africans cannot be sold, no body will steal them for sale. The proposition is self-evident: but more on this point, in the progress of this review.

In this speech, Sir, you completely sustain one of my charges against the American Colonization Society — that it aims at the expulsion (or, if you prefer the word, removal) of the colored population of this country. You say:

'The *object* of the American Colonization Society is to *remove from our country to Africa*, our PRESENT and FUTURE free colored population.'

Again:

'Another reason is, ["that Providence calls on us to regenerate Africa,"] the *pressing* and *vital* importance of *relieving ourselves*, as soon as practicable, *from this most dangerous element in our population.*'

Again:

'But who are there to feel for our 2,000,000 blacks? — more than five-sixths of whom are in bondage, and the other sixth *incapable of freedom on our soil.*'

Again:

'Then will even such slaveholder be as willing as other slaveholders to aid *in returning our blacks to their father-land.*'

Again:

'The principle is almost as true in relation to our blacks, as it is to water. They cannot rise above their source (!) They cannot rise *in our esteem* above the level of the moral state of the land of their origin(!) — for we are ever associating them with that land, which is *their appropriate*, THEIR ONLY HOME.'

Again:

'How important is it, *as it respects our character abroad,*(*!*) that we hasten TO CLEAR OUR LAND OF OUR BLACK POPULATION'!

In other portions of your speech, you speak of the colored people as 'an evil,' 'a nuisance,' 'an *immeasurable* evil' — and yet you at the same time declare, 'that in our colored population, we have *most abundant materials,* and, from their acquaintance with our excellent institutions,(!) *better materials* than are to be found elsewhere, for colonists'! — and, to cap the climax of this extraordinary harangue, you gravely and approvingly adopt Mr. Clay's nonsensical and impudent assertion, that 'every emigrant to Africa is *a missionary,* going forth with his credentials in the holy cause of civilization and religion and free instituions'! [4] Surely, this is not 'the poetry of philanthropy,' but the insanity of prejudice. *Every emigrant a missionary!* — I shall say nothing here of the character of those who have gone to Liberia, excepting to quote two sentences from your third letter to Mr. Bacon: — 'As yet, Russwurm is the only liberally educated colored man in the colony; and he, unhappily, is not pious.[5] I presume that there are not *a dozen* persons in it of attainments in learning, equal to what is understood amongst us by a respectable common education.'

Again, you say, in your speech:

'So far from reproaching the South with the evil of her colored population, I admit that the North owes her redemption, not to a better morality, but to colder skies and a less fertile soil.'

And so, because the North would have been as bad as the South, had circumstances permitted — therefore, the South is not to be reproached for its dastardly and murderous treatment of its slave population!

Once more:

'The slaveholder, so far from having just cause to complain of the Colonization Society, has reason to *congratulate* himself, that in this institution a channel is opened up, in which the public feeling and public action can flow on, *without doing violence to his* RIGHTS. The closing of this channel might be calamitous to the slaveholder *beyond his conception;* for the stream of benevolence that now flows so innocently(!) in it, might then break out in forms even more *disastrous* than ABOLITION SOCIETIES, *and all their kindred and ill-judged measures.*'

Really, Sir, such language being on record against you in the organ of the Colonization Society, you must not wonder that I deem it needful for you to make a public recantation.

But more — you *go with the south* in its tyrannous expulsion of its manumitted slaves from its territory, and thus are guilty of an outrage upon humanity. This language is to be found in your speech — O, that it had never been uttered! O, that it might be blotted out forever!

'The severe legislation, (I will not say that, under all the circumstances, it is TOO SEVERE) — the severe legislation of the slave states, which drives their emancipated blacks into the free States, and scatters the nuisance there, attests that we have a share in this evil.'

Still more — startling as it will be to the community, it is a fact that you have palliated, if not justified, the enslavement and degradation of our whole colored population!! Is this hard language? Is it a libel upon your character? Let the world judge between us. I make another quotation from your speech, to sustain this allegation:

'How much more consistent and powerful would be our example, but for that population within our limits, whose condition, (NECESSARY condition I will not deny,) is so much at war with our institutions, and with that memorable declaration — that all men are created equal.'

Sir, I am willing to believe any thing, rather than that you are a lover of slavery, or the intentional enemy of the colored people. But language, like the foregoing, is inexcusable — it is horrid. Even this, I believe, you will now be willing to admit. You have been in darkness — the light is now blazing upon you, and you are *beginning* the work of repentance.

I now turn to your Letters. Here are parallel columns of doctrines and precepts, which nullify each other, and defy the casuistry of the world to reconcile. How uncompromising is your opposition to slavery! How severe, how vehement, is your denunciation of it! And yet how kindly you apologize for slaveholding! how opposed you are to immediate justice, lest the heavens should fall! and [how] *mild* are the terms which you bring against some of our most eminent abolitionists — you who so dislike the use of hard language! Now, look on *this* picture, and on *this!* [6] — One of them is perfect — the other, deformed.

GERRIT SMITH vs. GERRIT SMITH.
HARD LANGUAGE VS. SOFT AND HARD LANGUAGE

'I need not consume any time in describing slavery. It is *evil*, and only *evil*, CONTINUALLY. Nor need I be at the pains of defending the right, or elucidating the duty, of endeavoring to induce our countrymen to forsake the SIN of SLAVEHOLDING.'

'We are under the divine requirement to "rebuke in any wise our neighbor, and not to suffer SIN upon him." ' [7]

'These states [Maryland and Virginia] are largely engaged in the *nefarious* and HEAVEN-DEFYING work of raising slaves for the supply of

'Whilst I see nothing in the Mosaic code, or in any other part of the Bible, in favor of American slavery, I am free to admit, that I am not of the number of those who think that they find there an express command against slavery(!) Moreover, I believe that much harm is done in taking the ground, that the will of God is as *clearly* revealed against *slavery*, as it is in the decalogue against *theft* and *murder*(!) We have not, in this case, the 'ita lex scripta est,' with which to cut short all doubts and cavils, and to confound our opthe demand in the other slave states. * * Africa sold us her children; the privilege of doing so is now denied to her; and Maryland and Virginia have taken up and continued *her guilty work.*'

'We want the SIN of SLAVERY to cease *immediately*. We want *every master* to REPENT of it *immediately*, that not another one of them may die in it. We want the *wrongs* and *miseries* of the slave to cease NOW.'

'But the doctrine is, that we should leave slavery to work its own cure. . . . Good men, however, never use such language respecting any other SIN. . . . It goes to quiet the *slaveholder* in his SIN, and to confirm his grasp of his victims.'

'Masters become *more and more wedded to slavery*, under its continual creation of those circumstances and habits, which make the idea of its abolition so unwelcome to the *pampered slaveholder*, who has "lived in pleasure on the earth, and been wanton, and nourished his heart as in a day of slaughter."'

'For a long time, the MONSTER [slavery] hung so heavily upon the wheels of legislation, that the spirit of freedom and righteousness could hardly impel them forward.'

'Here, the slave is not permitted to be reached by any meliorating influence from abroad. The laws have put him in the exclusive keeping of those WHO SEEK TO PERPETUATE HIS SLAVERY. Plans are *continually* devised to exclude every ray of light from his mind, and to chain him down to his deplorable ignorance of the rights and duties of a man.'

'The plea of our slaveholders, when pressed with the duty of immediate emancipation, for a little more time in which to prepare their slaves for freedom, is founded in *delusion*, where it is not in FRAUD: for never was there a period when these slaveholders were *crimsoning* themselves so fast with the guilt of '*crime against the LIFE OF THE SOUL*

ponents, as we have in the case of offences prohibited by a positive law of God' (!)

'I see in that spirit, [the spirit of the anti-slavery association,] an admirable share of profound respect and holy zeal for the laws of God and the rights of man; but I also see in it no small share of *weak impatience*(!) for the accomplishment of its object, and of intolerance, FEROCIOUS intolerance, towards those who either disapprove of that object, or would pursue it by different means.'

'It is distressing, as it is amazing, to find, in the admitted periodicals of this association, such *virulent abuse* of many of the wisest and best men of our nation.'

'Another fault, of which I hope the Anti-Slavery Society will soon repent and get rid, is its *violent*, BITTER, and UNMEASURED *denunciation of the whole slaveholding portion of our countrymen*. Even the Declaration of the Anti-Slavery Society, calls EVERY American slaveholder a 'man stealer;' and calls him such too on the authority of cited passages in the holy scriptures. What warrant there is in these passages for the charge, I do not perceive. (!) Nor do I envy the optics, which find no difference between the case of a pirate, who runs down the poor negro on the coast of Africa to carry him into hopeless captivity, and that of *our young Christian brother at the South* in whose inheritance are his deceased father's *servants* [SLAVES,] *to whom he is aiming to do good on gospel principles*, albeit he has not yet learned, that these principles require him to dissolve the new ['the SOUL-KILLING'] relation he bears towards them; — a relation, it is true, that was unsought by him, and that *was forced upon him*, by the course of events and by the laws of his state (!!) — but still, a relation that cannot be continued by him innocently.

of man,' as NOW. Never have they been so industrious, as for the last few years, to *shut out the light of truth* from the minds of their slaves, and to withhold from them *all fitness for the responsibilities of freemen;* and never, we may add, has the rate of emancipation in this country *been slower than it has been for the last few years.* The *truth* is, that the great body of our slaveholders do not *mean* to have slavery disturbed in their day — either to disturb it themselves, or to let others disturb it. Their occasional wishes for the termination of slavery at some indefinite future period, have gone far to keep *their dark and feeble consciences at ease;* whilst the expression of these wishes has gone (alas! how far!) to silence the remonstrances of others against their SIN.'

'Their duty, which had before been told to them from northern presses and northern pulpits — but with the ineffectualness of all precepts coming from those *who hypocritically preach one thing,* AND PRACTISE ANOTHER — will now be drawn out in living characters before them.'

'It is not intended, as the alarm goes, to turn loose our slaves — but merely to turn them from their subjection to *individual* CAPRICE *and* TYRANNY, and to place them in subjection to the laws.'

'It is nevertheless true, that the North is as properly the theatre on which to begin operations for the destruction of southern slavery, as that ☞ the *sober* are the subjects among whom the *work of reforming the* DRUNKEN is to be commenced.'

'Even ministers of the gospel among these emigrants, not unfrequently pollute their holy calling, by associating with it the SOUL-KILLING RELATIONS *of the slaveholder,* and such as do so, instead of obeying the commandment to 'cry aloud, spare not — lift up thy voice

Call that pirate what you will; but before I can class him with the *virtuous man,* whose case I have here contrasted with his own, and see the one, as well as the other, to be deserving of the deeply reproachful epithet with which they are equally stigmatized by the Anti-Slavery Society, I must have parted entirely with my powers of discrimination.' (!!)

'This charge against our slaveholders *indiscriminately,* is but a specimen of what is to be found on hundreds and thousands of pages, that have been published by the Anti-Slavery Society about these slaveholders. That *much of the censure* which these pages cast on the South, *is in the face of truth and grossly extravagant,* will not be denied by the intelligent and candid; and it is evident, that the *mutual exasperation* between the North and the South, *which such censure produces,* not only unfits the North for profiting the South on the subject of slavery, but unfits the South for being profited on it from any quarter. And how much reason have we to fear, that this *angry feeling,* with which one portion of our common country is *inflamed against the other,* will eventually separate them under different governments! — Better this separation, however, would the *violent* and FANATICAL portion of our abolitionists say, than that slavery should continue in our land, another year.'

'The treatment of the American Bible Society to which I have alluded, shows very strikingly the *fanatical and headlong zeal* which characterises some of the leaders of the Anti-Slavery Society. These leaders not only charged the Bible Society with falsely professing to have supplied all the destitute of our country with the holy scriptures; but they strove to plunge that Society *into a controversy with the South,* (!) which a moment's reflec-

like a trumpet, and show my people their transgression' — are *all* DUMB DOGS, *that cannot bark,'* and not unfrequently has their taste of their profits of slaveholding made them 'GREEDY DOGS, *which can never have enough.'* Oh, had all the emigrants from the free to the slave states been careful to 'touch not the *unclean thing;'* and had they been faithful to rebuke with the more impressive language of their lives, if not permitted to do so with their lips, the GIANT SIN of those states; and had they, moreover, in secret places if not permitted to do so publicly, lifted up to heaven their hands unsoiled with this SIN,' &c.

'Let that *injustice* ['in not teaching, and even in not permitting the slave to be taught to read'] be shown in all its ENORMOUS WICKEDNESS.'

'Another ground which the anti-slavery press takes for charging the SIN *of slavery* on the Constitution is,' &c.

'That this objection should prevail amongst those slaveholders, who look on the negro as holding but *a mid-way place between man and the brute;* and amongst those also, who live *habitually unmindful* of the fact, that he and they have a common rank in the scale of existence is not surprising; and that some of our slaveholders *deliberately deny* that the negro is 'created in the image of God;' and that *most of them* seldom think of the dignity and responsibility of his being, and have, *continually,* need to be admonished of the truth, that he is *a man*(*!!*) — are propositions too obviously true to be gainsayed.'

'This respect [for Africa!!] will ere long be felt even by the *slaveholder himself;* and he will shrink from the SINFUL and *odious* relation which he bears to such a people'!!

COMMENT. Mr. Smith says 'that tion must have taught them would prove utterly destructive of that precious institution. That such a controversy would have followed the *mad attempt* of the Bible Society to supply with the holy Scriptures the '460,000 *families,'* [Oh, Mr. Smith, what a cruel sneer!] as it suits the *fancies,* not to say the *designs,* in this case, of these leaders to style our slave population, is beyond a doubt. But could these leaders have been so *weak*(*!!*) as to hope **that** the Bible Society might be prevailed upon to make this attempt? It seems to me, that they could not. Their object, in pressing this measure on the Society, was probably to furnish themselves, in the refusal of the Society, with *occasion for arousing against it that clamorous bigotry,* which they are so *industrious* and *impatient* to arouse against every individual who refuses to yield up his brow to be stamped with their peculiar type of Anti-Slavery(*!!*) Or, if they did indeed hope, that the Bible Society could be moved to undertake to supply those '460,000 *families'* [another christian sneer at the wretched condition of the slaves!] — &c. I have dwelt thus long on this incident principally to manifest *how unfit are the men, who laid this snare for the Bible Society,* to give tone and direction to the measures of the Anti-Slavery Society; and also how important it is, that they should be exchanged for men of a *considerate* and *prudent* spirit.'

'I have already adverted to the *gross error* in it, [the Declaration of the Anti-Slavery Convention,] which classes all American slaveholders with 'man-stealers.' A few lines farther on, it makes the declaration — 'that all those laws, which are now in force, admitting the right of slavery, are, therefore, before God, utterly null and void.' *This is the highest toned nullification we have met with.* The doctrine involved in

much harm is done in taking the ground, that the will of God is as clearly revealed against slavery, as it is in the decalogue against theft and murder,' &c. &c. &c. Indeed, Mr. Smith! Are not the eighth and tenth commandments *expressly* against slavery — against stealing or coveting a man's wages, property, person, wife, children, *or any thing that is his?* Is not the command, *Thou shalt love thy neighbor as thyself*, as *expressly* against slavery as it is possible for language to be? Is it true, Sir, that God has more clearly revealed his will in relation to a single item of slavery, viz. *theft*, than he has against that system which is an unmingled mass of impiety, adultery, robbery, incest, cruelty and murder? Is that crime which is so huge that you brand it as *soul-killing*, so obscurely condemned in the Bible as to be ascertained as a matter of inference?]

this declaration being once admitted, *there is no longer any binding authority in* HUMAN GOVERNMENT *and* HUMAN LAWS.' (!!)

'When we see this doctrine, that individual *caprice*(!!) may sport with and nullify our laws at pleasure, embodied in an instrument of so high, if not indeed conclusive, authority with the members of the Anti-Slavery Society, we are no longer surprised that its leaders should, in conformity with that doctrine, make their SEDITIOUS *and* INCENDIARY *appeals to the public mind.* This accounts for the fact that even the principal secretary of the Anti-Slavery Society did not scruple in publications under his own name to VILIFY *the Superior Court* and the Recorder of the city of New-York; to hold them up as in league with slaveholders; and, in a word, to attempt to bring the laws and constituted authorities of the land into contempt. Such, indeed, is his *disrespect* for these authorities and the due course of law, that he appeals to the people of the State of New-York from a judicial decision, respecting the collision of a law of that State with a law of Congress!' 'When he [Mr. Wright [8]] is again disposed to complain of the New-York mobs, let him remember his own persevering efforts in his 'Chronicles of Kidnapping in New-York,' to obstruct the administration of the laws, and to kindle *an irregular and factious opposition against them*; and let him pause to consider, whether the sin of these mobs does not, in some measure, lie at his own door.'

'If the right, [to abolish the '*nefarious* and *heaven-defying* slave-trade' at home] does unquestionably belong to Congress, who but the man that would consent to see our nation severed, *could ask for its exercise?*' (!!)

'They are not intelligent friends, but *very dangerous enemies of their*

country, who seek to build up political [constitutional] parties on geographical [moral] distinctions, and
to array one section of their country
against another, ['to deliver him that
is spoiled, out of the hands of the
spoiler!'] But how *monstrous* is it,
that a religious society should virtually avow this to be its purpose!'

You shall hear from me again speedily. — In the mean time, I remain,
　　Yours, watchfully,

WM. LLOYD GARRISON.

Printed: *The Liberator*, February 7, 1835.

1. Smith quotes the legal maxim often used by seventeenth- and eighteenth-century writers, as in the famous instance of William Murray, Earl of Mansfield, in the case of Rex vs. Wilkes (see Burrows, *King's Bench Reports*, IV, 2562).
2. Timothy 1:9.
3. II Samuel 12:7.
4 Garrison quotes directly from his own *Thoughts on African Colonization*, p. 156, where the passage from Clay's speech is slightly misquoted. Clay's sentence is: "Every emigrant to Africa is a missionary carrying with him credentials in the holy cause of civilization, religion, and free institutions" (*African Repository*, 2:344, January 1827).
5. John Brown Russwurm (1799–1851), son of a Negro mother and a white father, was educated in Canada and Maine. He was evidently the first American Negro college graduate, receiving a degree from Bowdoin in 1826. The following year he founded and edited one of the earliest Negro papers, *Freedom's Journal*. By 1829 he had settled in Liberia, acting as colonial secretary and editing the *Liberia Herald*. In 1836 he moved to nearby Maryland Colony, serving for the rest of his life as governor.
6. Garrison alludes to Shakespeare, *Hamlet*, III, iv, 53.
7. Like Garrison's biblical quotations, Smith's contain only minor inaccuracies, as in the passages in this letter from the following: Leviticus 19:17, James 5:5, Isaiah 58:1, II Corinthians 6:17, Jeremiah 21.12.
8. Elizur Wright, Jr.

188

TO GERRIT SMITH

[February 28, 1835.]

SIR —

In my second letter, I said that you had asserted and vindicated all the principles, doctrines and measures, that I had ever espoused or recommended in the anti-slavery cause. This statement I shall prove.

I. I began my public advocacy of the anti-slavery cause by assuming, as a fundamental truth, that slaveholding was in all cases sinful.[1]

You declare, that slavery 'is evil, and only evil continually.' You call it 'a soul-killing relation' — 'a giant sin' — 'enormous wickedness.'

In this we are agreed.

II. My next doctrine was, if slaveholding was sinful, then it ought to be immediately repented of, and abandoned forever. As a christian, I could make no other deduction from the postulate.

You 'want the sin of slavery to cease immediately, and every master to repent of it immediately, that not another one of them may die in it.' You 'want the wrongs and miseries of the slave to cease now.' Nay, such is the nature and magnitude of the evil to be abolished, that you boldly affirm — 'If it were *indisputably evident* that our slaves, by continuing in slavery fifty, or even but ten or *five* years longer, would be better prepared than they now are for the boon of freedom, I do not concede the right of prolonging their bondage *even for the sake of an advantage so great.* By such a concession, I might be sanctioning the abhorrent doctrine *of doing evil, that good may come.*' The *first step* in preparing the slave for freedom is *to strike off his chains* — is to abolish the *cause* of his unfitness for freedom.' 'Universal, immediate emancipation is what I desire' — it is 'palpably a *righteous* doctrine' — it is 'the *true* doctrine, and the doctrines opposed to it are *false*, and go in effect but to *perpetuate slavery.*'

In this, also, we are agreed.

III. In opposition to the constant assertion of the American Colonization Society, and of the public generally, that emancipation was going on at a rapid rate at the South — that the slaveholders were becoming more favorable to the abolition of slavery, and more humane in their treatment of the slaves; I affirmed, that it was a gross delusion — that emancipation was almost entirely at an end — that the planters were growing more wedded to slavery — that the condition of the slaves was increasingly miserable — and that the southern laws were legalizing and enforcing the darkest heathenism.

You affirm, (and I quote your words afresh, because the admission is all-important) —

'The plea of our slaveholders, when pressed with the duty of immediate emancipation, for a little more time in which to prepare their slaves for freedom, is founded in *delusion*, where it is not in FRAUD: for never was there a period when these slaveholders were *crimsoning* themselves so fast with the guilt of 'crime against the LIFE OF THE SOUL of man,' as NOW. Never have they been so industrious, as for the last few years, to *shut out the light of truth* from the minds of their slaves, and to withhold from them *all fitness for the responsibilities of freemen:* and never, we may add, has the rate of emancipation in this country *been slower than it has been for the last few years.* The *truth* is, that the great body of our slaveholders do not *mean* to have slavery disturbed in their day — either to disturb it themselves, or to let others disturb it. Their occasional wishes for the termination of slavery at some indefinite future period, have gone far to keep *their dark and feeble consciences at ease;* whilst the oppression of these wishes has gone (alas! how far!) to silence the remonstrances of others against their SIN.'

In this, moreover, we are agreed.

IV. I maintained that the spirit of emancipation must begin at the North, inasmuch as slavery could be overthrown only by the moral power of the nation, which indisputably was possessed by the North; inasmuch as slaves were held and the slave-trade was tolerated by the nation, in the District of Columbia and in the Territories, and they should first be purged by the people; and inasmuch as the North was aiding and abetting southern oppressors, and trampling into the dust its own colored population.

You declare, that 'however loudly Southern men may complain of Northern interference on this subject, and however Northern apologists for slavery may chime with them, it is nevertheless true, that the North is as properly the theatre on which to begin operations for the destruction of Southern slavery, as that *the sober are the subjects, among whom the work of reforming the drunken is to be commenced.* . . . Very much, therefore, are they in error, who would dissuade us from making anti-slavery efforts at the North, and would have us go to the South, and make them there.'

In this, too, we are agreed.

V. I defined immediate emancipation to consist in the annihilation of *property in man* — of that tremendous power, by which one man is now authorized and enabled to reduce his fellow man to the condition of the brute — to sell the husband from his wife in exchange for a horse — to tear the babe from the bosom of its mother — to pollute, degrade, and lacerate woman at his depraved will — to defraud the laborer of his hire — to darken and destroy the soul of the slave; in recognizing and treating the slaves as rational and accountable beings, for whom Christ died; in employing them as free laborers, and giving them their wives and children, and equitable wages; and in placing them under the control and protection of righteous laws, instead of irresponsible and despotic masters — not (as I have been falsely accused) *in turning them loose,* without law and without employment.

You say, 'it is not intended, as the alarm goes, to turn loose our slaves; but merely to turn them from their subjection to individual caprice and tyranny, and to place them in subjection to the laws — a subjection as much safer in all respects than the other, as it is more rational.' 'Were the claim of man to property in man this day expunged, the intelligent advocates of immediate emancipation would, with thankful and happy hearts, acknowledge that immediate emancipation had already arrived.'

In this, we are fully agreed.

But, sir, with that singular confusion of mind which pervades your essays, and which weakens if it does not paralyze every sound principle which you have advanced, you proceed to the use of indefinite, incoherent and contradictory language, in order as it were to quiet the ruffled frames of slaveholders, by converting immediate into gradual emancipation. In one breath, you would emancipate all the slaves *instanter*, even though it were *certain* that they would be better prepared for the boon of freedom than they are now, by continuing in slavery only *five* years longer; and in the next, you are for mitigation, not abolition — for gradual, not instant enfranchisement. Now you would have the wrongs and miseries of the slave to cease at once; and anon, you think 'it might be the part of wisdom and mercy not to release our slaves at once from their servitude,' but to leave 'many of the *abuses* that belong to the relation of master and slave to employ the correcting hand of time and the laws'!!! If I misinterpret or pervert your language, then I will hasten my own condemnation by quoting your words in parallel columns:

READ THIS!

'We want the SIN of SLAVERY to cease *immediately*. We want *every master* to REPENT of it *immediately*, that not another one of them may die in it. We want the *wrongs* and *miseries* of the slave to cease NOW.'

'The *first step* in preparing the slave for freedom is *to strike off his chains* — is to abolish the *cause* of his unfitness for freedom.'

'If it were made *indisputably evident* that our slaves, by continuing in slavery fifty, or even but ten or *five* years longer, would be better prepared than they now are for the boon of freedom, I do not concede the right ☞ *of prolonging their bondage*, EVEN FOR THE SAKE OF AN ADVANTAGE SO GREAT!'

AND THEN THIS!

'The intelligent advocates of immediate emancipation are even *willing to believe*, that, instead of an *instantaneous*, unqualified emancipation, it might be the part of *wisdom* and MERCY, *not to release our slaves from their* SERVITUDE, but to ☞ *prolong that servitude for years*, provided it be but so modified, as that the subjects of it be raised from chattels — from things — to men. *Although many of the* ABUSES that belonged to the relation of master and slave *would still* remain, to employ the correcting hand of time and the laws, yet, were the claim of man to property in man this day expunged from it,' &c. &c.

Sir, there may be no confusion, no contradiction, no giving or taking back again, in the foregoing extracts; but, in my judgment, they are not only opposite but irreconcilable. I do not understand this logic — I do not like such philanthropy. It seems that you *would not* prolong the servitude of the slaves even for five years, though sure of better preparing them for the enjoyment of liberty; and then that *you would* prolong their servitude *for years*, leaving them liable to many *abuses*, in order to give them this preparation! Now, I claim, with all due modesty, to be an 'intelligent advocate of immediate emancipation,' and I will speak in behalf of those who are at least as intelligent; and I say, that I do not know of one consistent and uncompromising abolitionist, who is willing to believe that, with certain modifications, 'it might be the part of wisdom and mercy, not to release our slaves at once from their servitude, but to prolong that servitude for years.' Ah! but there is a saving clause — an important proviso: 'provided it be but so modified, as that the subjects of it be raised from chattels — from things — to men.' In other words, servitude may be prolonged for a term of years, in the opinion of abolitionists, provided it be instantly annihilated! For, as soon as the slaves are changed or raised from *things* to *men,* there must of course be an end to their servitude. Property in slaves — the transformation by law of human beings into brutes — this is THE SOUL of slavery: annihilate that, and the monster instantly dies, and the carcass can never again show symptoms of vitality. After all, Sir, you are really not for modifying, but extinguishing the evil at once: yet, with marvellous inconsistency, you still seem willing to leave the slave subject to many abuses at the hands of his master, to be remedied at some future indefinite period! Have you, or I, any right to make such a stipulation with tyrants?

I am compelled, for want of room, to cut short the parallel I have endeavored to run between our doctrines. It shall be completed in my next letter.

Yours respectfully,

WM. LLOYD GARRISON.

Printed: *The Liberator*, February 28, 1835.

1. In this letter Garrison traces clearly and succinctly the gradual development of the fundamental tenets in his doctrine of abolition.

189

TO GERRIT SMITH

[March 7, 1835.]

Sir —

It seems that there is between us an entire agreement as to the following anti-slavery PRINCIPLES or DOCTRINES: that slaveholding is in all cases sinful — that it ought to be immediately abandoned — that the first step in preparing the slave for freedom is to strike off his chains — and that if it were evident that only by a short delay, he could be better prepared to receive the boon of liberty, still the slave ought to be a freeman NOW, because we are not authorized to do evil that good may come.

It is for advocating these doctrines, that my name is cast out as evil among men, and that I am branded as a visionary, a jacobin, and a

madman, even by that Society to which you cling with so much ten-
aciousness. But none of my opponents make you the object of their
ridicule or vilification, although your positions are as high, and your
denunciations as severe, as my own.

How shall we account for this difference of treatment? Is it because
you are rich, and I am poor? No — the cause is not proportionate to
the effect; for just principles are ever offensive to the wicked, whether
they are advocated by a king or a peasant; and if opulence gives *you*
this protection, why has it not also shielded one whose acts of benevolence and holiness shine as the stars of heaven, but who has subjected
himself to apostolic persecution and reproach? To whom can I allude
but to ARTHUR TAPPAN? The reason is this: I am known to mean just
what I say — to make no individual exceptions among a nation of transgressors, on account of perplexing circumstances — and to carry out my
principles in all their severity and power, without modification and
without abatement. You, Sir, on the contrary, are seen to walk un-
steadily — to retract every one of your principles — to denounce your
own doctrines — to ridicule your own admonitions: in fine, to mix up
what is really good in your letters with what is evil, so skilfully and
equally as to render nugatory all your prescriptions for the malady of
oppression: therefore it is that your letters fail to excite opposition,
and have fallen almost still-born from the press. They are not calculated to do the cause of righteousness any good, for transgressors will
resort to them as to a store-house of palliations and excuses, abhorring
that which is sound, but battening like flies upon the large and visible
taint of corruption which is spread throughout.

Agreeing then as we do, professedly, in the doctrines adverse to
slavery, are we agreed in the means and measures to be adopted for
its overthrow, and in the objects at which we aim?

The first great object which I desire to accomplish is, the IMMEDIATE
EMANCIPATION of two millions and a half of American SLAVES. Your
language is —

'What we insist should NOW be done for these fellow men, fellow
countrymen, *fellow Christians*, whose cause we are pleading, is, that the
power of their masters over them should *no longer* be virtually absolute,
and undistinguishable from that which they possess over their cattle. As
their fellow men, their fellow countrymen, and their *fellow Christians*, CAN
WE INSIST ON LESS? BEFORE GOD WE CANNOT.' . . . 'We want the
wrongs and miseries of the slave to cease NOW.'

The next great object at which I aim is, the education and equalization of the colored with the white population of this country, so that
the hue of the skin shall no longer be a badge of servitude and opprobrium, and the cord of caste shall be consumed to ashes. I wish to see

every man respected and elevated according to his merits and abilities, without any reference to his height, his bulk, or his complexion. I wish to give our black 'fellow countrymen and fellow Christians' all the advantages and all the privileges of citizenship, without let or hindrance.

I am happy to perceive that you approve of this object, and advocate its propriety and feasibility with great clearness and force; and I am sorry to perceive that this object is scorned and contemned by you, as being hopeless and undesirable!! — as I shall show hereafter. So much for your consistency!

In stating what you consider the best and only lawful *means* and *measures* to be used to promote immediate emancipation, I shall be merely recapitulating those alone which I advocate, and which are recommended in the Declaration of the Philadelphia Anti-Slavery Convention — a paper which you have attempted to impeach in the spirit, but without the ingenuity of a sophist, and which I shall vindicate in the progress of this review.

I. The doctrine of immediate emancipation is to be *commended* to the adoption of others.

'In the first place, let every person, who has adopted this doctrine, commend it to the adoption of others, in all the ways which the Providence of God affords him for doing so.'

II. It is to be made a topic of *conversation*.

'Let him make it a topic of *conversation*, wherever he can do so fitly.'

III. It is to be enforced through the medium of the *press*.

'If he write for the *press*, let him remember how great is the power of the press to propagate this doctrine.'

IV. It is to be pleaded in *public assemblies*, and from every *pulpit*.

'And if he be accustomed to exhort the *public assembly*, and especially from the *sacred desk*, let him raise his voice in behalf of immediate emancipation.'

V. It is to be propagated and enforced by anti-slavery societies.

'The friends of immediate emancipation all over the land, should form themselves into SOCIETIES for the furtherance of this doctrine.'

VI. It is to be carried out *practically*, as well as theoretically, by those who profess to adopt it. Prejudice is to be crucified — unequal and invidious laws to be repealed.

'In addition to speaking and writing for this doctrine, he must *live* in conformity with it; and to do so, the citizen of the United States is required *to treat the slave* of his country as a *man*, and — what is next in kindness to the slave himself — to treat the *free* person of the slave's despised *color* as a man.' . . . 'Let the white citizens of the free States resolve to accord to the negro the privileges of CITIZENSHIP, and that place in society to which his moral and intellectual worth entitles him.' . . . 'Let the slaveholders, who flock to the North for pleasure and for trade, find that the *unjust*, UNPHILOSOPHICAL, and UNCHRISTIAN distinctions, which still exist among men here *on account of their different complexions*, are obliterated; that all our laws, founded in these distinctions, are repealed; that we are no longer *guilty* of the American peculiarity of judging of the worth and claims of human beings by the tinge of their skin; that colored youth are no longer denied employment in our stores, and even in our workshops; and no longer excluded, as with rare exceptions they have been, from our academic schools; that, in a word, *we have entirely purged our hearts of those prejudices against the black, which have hitherto blighted his hopes, and kept him in the dust:* — let these Southern brethren witness such changes among us, and who can calculate the effect on their hearts and minds of this exemplification of humane and Christian principles?'

For urging to the same course of duty as is enforced in the foregoing extracts, abolitionists have excited popular indignation, (especially that of colonizationists) from one extremity of the country to the other — brought upon themselves, by way of *infinite* reproach, the name of *amalgamationists* — stirred up the wrath of seditious and blood-thirsty men, who have invaded the religious sanctity of their assemblies, injured the meeting-houses in which they worship, and burnt their property in the streets!! — Yet you, Mr. Smith, excite nobody's displeasure — are not hunted as a wild beast — are not stigmatized as the friend of amalgamation — and stir up no mobs! Pray, how shall we solve this mystery? It cannot be that you are more prudent and judicious, and less plain and unequivocal, than abolitionists, seeing that you fully adopt and avow their sentiments, and use precisely their language. No. The reason, in this instance, is precisely like that which I have given at the commencement of this letter: — It is because you blow hot and cold in the same breath; because you recommend a just course of action, and then discourage the unjust from walking in it; because you advance one step forward, and then take two backward; because you rave at times like one in a high fever; and these infirmities being seen by those whom I doubt not you sincerely desire to reform, they laugh at the impotency of your efforts, and feel pitiful rather than angry emotions arising in their breasts, as they peruse your marvellously incoherent and contradictory essays. You know, Sir, that in the cause of Temperance, he who advocates the doctrine of total abstinence, and yet is seen to drink his glass of wine or gin, is an instructer who only excites ridicule, and whose precepts are nullified by his practices. It seems to me that you are in a similar predicament, in relation to the cause of abolition. I will try to sustain my assertions, by comparing one part of your letters against another, without garbling and in all fairness.

The Declaration of the Anti-Slavery Convention maintains, 'that all those laws which are now in force, admitting the RIGHT of *slavery*, are, *before God*, utterly null and void.'[1] Upon which position you make the following extraordinary comment:

'THIS IS THE HIGHEST TONED NULLIFICATION WE HAVE MET WITH. The doctrine involved in this Declaration being once admitted, there is no longer any binding authority in human government and human laws'!!!

This comment is utterly perverse and fabulous, and it grants to tyrants and men-stealers all that they desire. It is thus that *you* 'NULLIFY' your own principles, and pour contempt upon your own doctrines. What, Sir! do you mean to affirm, 'that all those laws which are now in force, admitting the RIGHT OF SLAVERY,' i.e. the right of that which is 'evil, and only evil continually' — the right of perpetuating 'a soul-killing relation' — the right to 'shut out the light of truth from the minds of the slaves, and to withhold from them all fitness for the responsibilities of freemen' — the right to seize, retain, buy, exchange and sell, to plunder, debase and lacerate, our fellow-creatures — I say, do you mean to affirm, that these heathenish and diabolical enactments are, '*before* GOD,' [mark! not before *men*.] just and equitable, and ought to be obeyed? Such a doctrine is the 'highest toned' *blasphemy* against Almighty God. It is not, for one moment, to be credited, that you mean to advocate it: yet your *language*, according to the rules of just interpretation, is decidedly in favor of it — for the laws referred to certainly involve moral principles, and by the law of God are rendered either 'null and void,' or legitimate and obligatory. But more upon this point in a subsequent number. It is evident that a strong delusion fills your mind, which, in this particular instance, endangers your allegiance to the King of kings, and leads you to fall down and worship the bloody monster SLAVERY, because it has been formally set up by the American people! Sir, your attack upon Professor WRIGHT, of New-York, — one of the most devoted christians, one of the most consistent reformers, and one of the noblest philanthropists, of this or any other age, — is an outrage upon humanity, and a libel upon the christian religion. He has made no 'seditious and incendiary appeals to the public mind' — his appeals have always been addressed to the *consciences* and *understandings* of men. As one who feels that the precepts of Jesus Christ ought to be obeyed, he has declared that he cannot assist in capturing the runaway slave, and sending him back again into bondage, but he will succor and hide him if practicable; and he calls upon every man, who professes to fear God and love his neighbor as himself, to give no aid to tyrants in this matter. This is 'the head and front of his offending'[2] — and for doing so, you accuse him of *sedition!* — thus plainly avowing that you are ready to seize, or assist in seizing, the captive who has fled from his oppressor, and to shackle his limbs anew with the galling fetters of slavery! — Now, Sir, for my own part, — talk as you will of the Constitution, — I would just as cheerfully steal a native of Africa, and carry him across the Atlantic to the shambles at New-Orleans, as to abet the southern slaveholder in recovering his wandering slave.[3] If 'the laws and constituted authorities of the land' require me thus to aid the tyrant, then *I will not obey them* — then I will strenuously endeavor to bring them 'into contempt' — then *I will resist them,* not by physical violence, but by christian boldness and by moral endurance. Every slave given up by Massachusetts to the slave States *is kidnapped by the State;* and every man who assists in returning the slave *is a kidnapper.*

Again: The Declaration insists, that 'all persons of color, who possess the qualifications which are demanded of others, ought to be admitted forthwith to the enjoyment of the same privileges, and the exercise of the same prerogatives, as others.' If it mean that the slave should be a voter at the age of twenty-one years, and eligible to civil office (i.e. be placed precisely on a level with the most ignorant and abject white citizen, and you profess to admire 'the truly republican doctrine of universal suffrage,') then, you declare, the Anti-Slavery Society 'is seeking for a change, which, EVEN MORE THAN SLAVERY ITSELF,(!!) *would be fraught with mischief to the institutions of our country'!!* Yes, Sir, to place white and colored persons, who possess the same qualifications, upon the same level, would, in your estimation, be more disastrous then even slavery itself! And yet you are for liberty and equality! you are an abolitionist! you are for immediate emancipation! you are for instantly abolishing 'the *unjust, unphilosophical,* and *unchristian* distinctions which still exist among men here on account of their different complexions'! you are for having every abolitionist '*live* in conformity' with his profession! you are bold to declare that 'the citizen of the United States is required to treat the *slave* of his country as A MAN: and — what is next in kindness to the slave himself — to treat the *free* person of the slave's despised *color* as A MAN'! you maintain, 'that to the negro belong the RIGHTS, the attributes, and the immortal destiny of A MAN'! you desire THE PEOPLE to 'resolve to accord to him the *privileges of citizenship,* ☞ and that place in society *to which his moral and intellectual worth* ENTITLES *him'!!* — [the very doctrine, and almost the precise language of the Declaration!]

Again: You call upon the people of the free States, as a christian duty, to *purge their hearts* of all prejudice against our colored population, and to give them that which is just and equal — thus will they rebuke, and in all probability bring to repentance, the southern oppressors. And then you hold out the following *truly encouraging* and *most convincing* view of the subject, as if purposely to apologise for prejudice and slavery, and lull the nation to sleep!

'Will this people, even when slavery shall have ceased in our land, ever attain to that equality of privileges with the whites, which will make them contented to dwell in the same land, and under the same government with us? *We can hardly expect, that such justice will be accorded to them.* Taking human nature, as it is, and as history presents it, we may rather expect, that our unhappy brethren, who are in bonds, will pass from slavery, ONLY to BECOME THE OBJECTS OF GREATLY INCREASED JEALOUSY AND OF NEW PERSECUTIONS. The arrogance of caste will, I apprehend, be, as yet, but *partially* subdued.'

Furthermore — You make the following surprising declaration:

'The writer of these essays joined the Colonization Society in the spirit and with the objects of *an abolitionist*. In that spirit, and with those objects, he continues his connection with it.'

And then you eat your own words thus:

'I do solemnly affirm, that it never meddles with THE QUESTION OF SLAVERY, WITHOUT VIOLATING ITS CONSTITUTION'!!
'In my judgment, the Anti-Slavery Society IS BOUND TO MAINTAIN AN OPPOSITION to the Colonization Society. ☞ UNTIL IT SHALL HAVE CORRECTED THIS GRIEVOUS FAULT' — i. e. the fault of meddling with the question of emancipation!!!

Thus, Sir, I have attempted to group together a few of the numerous absurdities and contradictions which abound in your letters.

But here is an important concession, which must have filled the bosom of your friend, Mr. LEONARD BACON, with grief, if not sore displeasure:

'I think there is no room to doubt, that the Anti-Slavery Association (I speak of all Anti-Slavery Societies as constituting but one association) is destined to contribute *more largely than any other system* of means, to the subversion of American slavery.'
'The American Anti-Slavery Society IS TRULY, as well as *professedly,* a CHRISTIAN institution.'

Now, Mr. Smith, allow me to make a proposition: — For every sentence that you will quote from the African Repository and the official documents of the Colonization Society, approving of the anti-slavery MEANS, and MEASURES, and ASSOCIATIONS, which you espouse, I will bring a page from the same authority, denouncing them as wild, seditious and incendiary. Yet you are a colonizationist!

Respectfully yours,

WM. LLOYD GARRISON.

Printed: *The Liberator*, March 7, 1835.

1. Garrison quotes from the Declaration of Sentiments which he wrote for the American Anti-Slavery Society in December of 1833. This document is reprinted in *Life*, I, 408–412.

2. Shakespeare, *Othello*, I, iii, 80.

3. Garrison defends Elizur Wright, Jr., and the ideas he expressed in *Chronicles of Kidnapping in New York*.

190

TO HELEN E. GARRISON

New-York, March 13, 1835.

My dear Wife —

Half past 8 o'clock — just arrived in Babylon the great. Our passage was as tranquil as it was rapid. Brother Thompson and myself had all the conversation to ourselves, for nobody seemed disposed to have any thing to say to us — company rather small. Did not sleep remarkably well — had a variety of dreams — thought you and I had been to ride in a carry-all, with two horses — 'twas late at night — after letting you get out, away went the horses with me at full speed, and forty times at least I came within a hair's-breadth of losing my life. What was the final result, I do not remember — but how could one sleep comfortably under such circumstances?

This afternoon, the Executive Committee of the American Anti-Slavery Society will hold a special meeting, at which Mr. Thompson and your husband will be present. This will probably determine how long I shall remain here. Think of going on to Philadelphia with Mr. T. on Monday, where we shall be received, I am sure, most enthusiastically.

I am extremely happy in anticipating the happiness you will experience in visiting your warm-hearted, — shall I not say, *our* warm-hearted friends? — at Pleasant Valley — in the city of P. — and at Brooklyn. You are a prudent wife, else I would caution you to be careful of your health, as you will be somewhat more exposed than usual, in making your affectionate, not *fashionable*, calls.

Henry is as fresh and rosy as usual, but does not like New-York. I like him all the better for that. How, when, and where he is to travel, I do not know.

Remember me, as sincerely and kindly as possible, to all the friends.

Thompson says he will return with me to Brooklyn — but I think it is somewhat doubtful. They are calling for him every where.

Be assured that I am far happier with you than with all others — and therefore I shall hasten back without delay. I would enclose a thousand kisses, if I could put them into a tangible shape, and in so small a compass. Still, I am

Your faithful and loving husband,

Wm. Lloyd Garrison.

☞ Ask brother George to see if there is a letter for me at the Post Office. Perhaps Mr. K.[1] wrote to me there. If so, let it be sent to this city.

ALS: Garrison Papers, Boston Public Library.

1. Isaac Knapp.

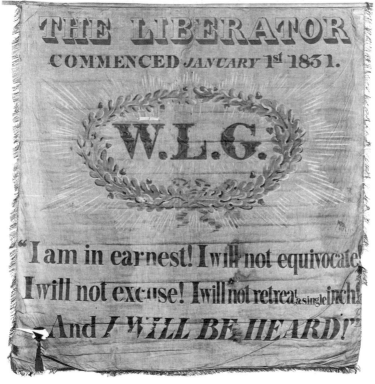

Banners used in antislavery demonstrations

Garrison, by Robert Douglass, about 1835

191

TO HELEN E. GARRISON

New-York, March 16, 1835.

My dear Wife:

A vacancy is in my heart, because I am away from you. Although I am in the midst of a populous city, and surrounded by friends of every complexion and condition; yet my thoughts encircle you continually, as dearer to me than any earthly object. Happily, the omnipresence of our God fills all space, and attends our footsteps whithersoever we go — we can commune directly with him, if not with each other, at all times and in all places. It is thus that we may rejoice in the infinitude of his love, and feast upon the banquet of heavenly munificence, roam as we may.

On Friday evening, the Executive Committee of the Am. Anti-Slavery Society assembled at the house of Mr. Lewis Tappan, at which meeting Mr. Thompson, Henry, and myself, were present.[1] It was a delightful, a soul-stirring interview. The peace, the disinterestedness, the integrity, the courage of Heaven, pervaded all our proceedings. The grand, the momentous question, proposed for our consideration, was, as to the propriety of sending a delegate or delegates to attend the anniversaries in London, in May next, to represent the anti-slavery cause of this country, and to augment and propel the tide of godlike sympathy and benevolence, which is fertilizing the hearts and bringing to maturity the hopes of the Christians of Great Britain. The mission was cordially and unanimously advocated by every one present: it was deemed to be of transcendant importance. Arthur Tappan was in the chair, and manifested a truly noble spirit. When the American Union caught him, "it caught a Tartar," and it will be glad to get rid of him; that our abolition friends in New-England may rely upon.[2]

We came unanimously to the conclusion, that two delegates should be sent to England, especially as several distinguished clerical colonizationists have already gone thither, who must be followed, confronted, and confounded — viz. Rev. Pres. Humphreys, Rev. Dr. Spring, Rev. R. J. Breckinridge, &c. &c.[3] But whom should we send? The vote was unanimous for Rev. Dr. Cox,[4] and Rev. Joshua Leavitt, editor of the N. Y. Evangelist. Both of these gentlemen were present, and gave us encouragement to hope that they would go. They will also visit France, and perhaps other parts of Europe, and form an alliance — one vast anti-slavery association — for the abolition of slavery and the slave trade throughout the world! God speed the mission!

On Saturday, I went over to Brooklyn, with Mr. Thompson, and was very hospitably entertained by Henry Ibbotson, a distinguished merchant of this city, recently of Sheffield, England, a gentleman who is as noted for his benevolence and moral excellence, as for his great wealth. He was led astray, for a time, in Sheffield, by Elliot Cresson, in relation to the Colonization Society, but is now its uncompromising foe.

Yesterday forenoon, I heard the Rev. Dr. Cox preach. His text embraced the eighth chapter of Romans. My soul was fed bountifully: it was a mighty effort for the cause of God. I took dinner at his brother's, the physician, one of my most enthusiastic friends, whose family is the loveliest of the lovely.[5] In the afternoon, I attended the Rev. T. S. Wright's church, with Mr. Ibbotson, Prof. Wright, Henry, and Mr. Thompson.[6] This is a colored church. The sermon was preached by Rev. Mr. Munroe, a colored minister — sound and even eloquent.[7] Mr. Thompson made the introductory prayer. After the sermon, I was invited to address the congregation, and did so — followed by Mr. Thompson. The effect, I believe, was good.

In the evening, I went to another colored church, and after the usual exercises were over, was requested to make some remarks to the audience. I made a brief address, and concluded the meeting with prayer.

To-day I expected to start with Thompson for Philadelphia, but we have concluded to wait until to-morrow. There is to be a large assemblage of highly respectable, wealthy and influential ladies at Dr. Cox's house this evening, and Mr. T. and myself have been invited to attend. Some of them, I understand, are somewhat prejudiced against your fanatical husband; but I am sanguine that an interview will reconcile us, — for you know my skill in winning female hearts.

How long I shall tarry in Philadelphia, or when I shall be in Brooklyn, I cannot precisely determine. I am all of a flutter to be with you *instanter*, and shall be expeditious in my movements. You may, if all be well, expect to see me by the middle of next week.

Many inquiries are made after your health, and my numerous friends are exceedingly anxious to see you.

You are now, I presume, in the paradise of home, happy in the love and smiles of your dear parents and sisters. May heavenly blessings rest upon you all, and the arm of Omnipotence shield you from danger! My individual remembrances to all.

Adieu, my love —

Your happy, yet sighing husband,

Wm. Lloyd Garrison.

ALS: Garrison Papers, Boston Public Library.

1. Lewis Tappan (1788–1873) was the brother of Arthur Tappan, abolitionist, and their careers were parallel. Lewis, however, resigned as corresponding secre-

tary of the American and Foreign Anti-Slavery Society in 1855, having gradually come to a more radical view. When he published the biography of his brother, *The Life of Arthur Tappan* (New York, 1870), his sympathetic treatment of Garrison indicated their reconciliation.

2. Garrison uses a common maxim of Greek origin to castigate the American Union for the Relief and Improvement of the Colored Race. The American Union had been founded the preceding January by sectarian colonizationists (most of them members of the Congregational church) who wished to modify the extreme views propounded by Garrison and both the New England and the American Anti-Slavery Societies.

3. Garrison groups together three colonizationists, all of them distinguished men. Heman Humphrey (1779–1861) — whose name Garrison misspells — from Connecticut and a Yale graduate, was a revivalist minister, a temperance worker, and the second president of Amherst College. Gardiner Spring (1785–1873), also a Yale graduate, was a former teacher and lawyer turned minister, the pastor of Brick Presbyterian Church on Beekman Street in New York City. Although long a sympathizer with the South and an opponent of the abolitionists, he committed himself to the Union cause during the war. Robert Jefferson Breckinridge has been identified in an earlier note.

4. Samuel Hanson Cox.

5. Abraham Liddon Cox (1799–1864), the physician, had been active in the American Anti-Slavery Society, having been one of the founders as well as the first recording secretary.

6. Elizur Wright, Jr., has been identified in a previous note. Henry Ibbotson (c. 1797–1849), formerly associated with the Globe Works in Sheffield, England, was at present a New York merchant engaged in the steel and cutlery trade. Theodore Sedgwick Wright (1797–1847), was a Negro born in Providence, Rhode Island. He had attended the Princeton Theological Seminary from 1825 to 1828 before being ordained in Albany in 1829. The next year he became the minister of the First Collegiate Church in New York City, a post he held until his death. In 1835 Wright was serving on the executive committee of the American Anti-Slavery Society.

7. Not identified.

192

TO HELEN E. GARRISON

Philadelphia, March 19, 1835.

My dear Wife:

You perceive that I am in the city, which, of all others, next to Boston, is my peculiar favorite. Of course, I am very happy, wanting only your dear presence to perfect my joy. The inquiries after your health, &c., and congratulations upon our union, are very numerous and particular. I would that you were here, not for my sake merely, but that you might participate in those rich tokens of love and kind fellowship, which are extended to me on the right hand and on the left. There are hundreds in this city who long to see and embrace you; but I am afraid that your natural diffidence would shrink from the thronged assemblies in which I mix. I am enjoying the hospitality of James Mott and family: in his abode dwells much of the disinterestedness, purity and peace of heaven.[1] His lady is certainly one of the most remarkable women I ever saw. She is a bold and fearless thinker, in the highest degree conscientious, of most amiable manners, and truly instructive in her conversation. Her husband is worthy of that sacred relation to her which he sustains, being distinguished for his goodness, benignity and philanthropy. Such a couple do not make it *very* difficult to comply with our Lord's admirable injunction — "Thou shalt love thy neighbor as thyself." [2]

Mr. Thompson is hospitably entertained by a highly esteemed orthodox Friend, Abraham L. Pennock.[3] Henry is located with my friend Robert Purvis. Happily, there is no other division between us, but that of bodily separation — our hearts are one.

On Monday evening, the party (of which I wrote in anticipation in my last letter) was convened at Dr. Cox's [4] house, composed of some of the most estimable men and women in the land. It was a delightful entertainment — beyond description pleasant. Mr. Thompson and myself were particularly favored with the kind attentions of all present — especially of the ladies — and we endeavored to reciprocate the kindness. How many were present I know not — perhaps fifty — but they were all prime abolitionists, and members either of the male or female anti-slavery society in N.Y. Of course, our tongues, eyes, limbs, and hearts were continually in motion. We separated about 11 o'clock. Henry, and Mr. and Mrs. Fuller of Boston, were of the party.[5]

Next morning, Rev. Dr. Cox, Mr. Campbell of Boston, Mr. Ibbotson, Mr. Thompson, Henry and myself, took passage in the steam-boat for Philadelphia.[6] Among the passengers on board were several slaveholders. Thompson and myself were soon identified, and a very long and earnest discussion ensued. I had a troop around me; Thompson another troop; Rev. Dr. Cox another troop; and Henry a fourth. Some writhed and gnashed upon us; some sneered; some ridiculed; some threatened; and some laughed. However, we argued all opposition down, although I cannot tell how many were converted. I know how many needed to be converted, not only to abolition doctrines, but to the doctrines of divine revelation generally. Practical infidelity, my dear Helen, abounds in our midst to a frightful extent. As a whole, the American people have no fear of God before their eyes. They assume the eternal prerogatives of Jehovah, and despise his law, and rebel against his authority. Miserable nation! who can foretel the judgments that are to come upon thee? Surely it behooves us all to pray, "O Lord, in wrath remember mercy!" [7]

Our Philadelphia brethren are quite joyous at our arrival. The knowledge that we are here has been communicated to the citizens by the newspapers, and there is quite a sensation felt throughout the community.

Last evening, Mr. Thompson gave a lecture in the Scotch Presbyterian Church, and spoke for about two hours. The notice was very hastily given, yet the house was crowded to overflowing, and very many could gain no admittance. Probably not less than one thousand persons were present. The discourse was solemn, pungent and powerful, and produced most evidently a favorable impression. Every body is buzzing about it to-day. Mr. T. will probably deliver another lecture to-morrow evening. How long we shall tarry here is uncertain — probably, however, till Monday. I shall not arrive in Brooklyn so soon as I expected, as I have much writing to do by way of epistles to England. It is quite probable that I shall tarry in New-York till the 1st of April, in order to see our friends, Rev. Dr. Cox and Rev. Joshua Leavitt, embark for Europe.[8] If so, I hope to see you in the course of the fortnight.

Now, do not think that I separate myself from you voluntarily. Circumstances compel me, (to aid the cause which we both so much cherish,) to tarry longer than I at first anticipated. Do you miss me, dear H.? Are you anxious for my return? Do the charms which dwell in Friendship's Valley exclude me from your thoughts? Ah! why do I ask these questions? Do I not know how warm, how sincere, how steadfast, is your attachment to me? Have you not given me bright and beautiful evidences of your love?

Still, though absent from me, I trust you are enjoying your visit, to complete satisfaction. It would give me great comfort and joy if I were to receive a letter from you. Will you not write to me at New-York, as soon as you receive this? I shall be troubled until I hear from you. Tell me of your health — declare your wishes — freely make your requests — and communicate whatever you may deem suitable and interesting.

Tell dear Anne, that, next to seeing my wife, I long to see her. How can we go back to Freedom's Cottage without her? I hope that painful necessity will not be imposed upon us.

I have not received any intelligence from Boston, and of course have none to communicate.

Tell brother May that I have just had a very pleasant interview with Rev. Mr. Furness, at Mrs. Mott's.[9] He heard Mr. T. last evening, and, on the whole, was quite delighted. I find he has an aversion to strong language, and I think he is not yet prepared "to go the whole." To-morrow we shall dine together.

Henry desires to send his love with mine to you, and father, mother, sisters, and all the household. He is much pleased with Philadelphia.

With increasing affection,

    Your poorer half,

                Wm. Lloyd Garrison.

ALS: Garrison Papers, Boston Public Library.

1. James Mott (1788–1868) had married Lucretia Coffin (1793–1880) in 1811. Both were birthright Quakers and of the liberal Hicksite branch after 1827. James Mott had prospered in the cotton commission business until 1830 when, at considerable financial loss, he transferred to the wool business in order to avoid even an indirect support of slavery. Both Motts were active not only in the cause of abolition but also in that of woman's rights.

2. Leviticus 19:18.

3. Abraham L. Pennock (1786–1868) was a Philadelphian who had grown prosperous in the wire business; his firm, Sellers and Pennock, supplied the United States government with a riveted hose and a riveted mailbag of his own invention. He was also an ardent abolitionist, whose country home in Lansdowne, Pennsylvania, was to be an underground station for fugitive slaves. George Thompson was apparently entertained at his town house at 12th and Market Streets in Philadelphia.

4. Abraham Liddon Cox.

5. The John E. Fullers were close friends of both Garrisons. They lived on Pitts Street, near the scene of the Boston mob of October 21, 1835, and Helen was to spend that difficult night at their house. In the early thirties Fuller was a Garrisonian, but, in protest against Garrison's dedication to multiple reforms, he was to join the New Organization during the schism of 1839–1840.

6. Mr. Campbell cannot be positively identified, but he may be John R. Campbell (or "Cambell," as his name is sometimes spelled), who appears in several Boston directories in the early thirties as a merchant selling shoes. It was John R. Campbell who helped Garrison at the time of the Boston mob (*Life*, II, 38).

7. Habakkuk 3:2, with an ellipsis following "O Lord."

8. Joshua Leavitt (1794–1873), after receiving two degrees from Yale, became a Congregational minister and subsequently distinguished himself as editor of three papers: the *Evangelist*, the *Emancipator*, the *Ballot Box*; and, for the last twenty-five years of his life, as assistant editor of the New York *Independent*.

9. William H. Furness (1802–1896), graduate of Harvard College and the Divinity School, had been the minister of the Unitarian church in Philadelphia since 1825. He was an ardent abolitionist and a distinguished scholar in the field of German literature.

193

TO HENRY E. BENSON

Brooklyn, March 30, 1835.

My dear Henry —

I regret to learn from Mr. Thompson, that our beloved coadjutors in the righteous cause of emancipation, Messrs. Cox [1] and Leavitt, will not be able to visit Europe this spring — consequently, it will not be necessary for me to visit New-York until the annual meeing in May.

We are all well and happy here, wanting only your presence to complete the gratification that we feel.

Last evening, Mr. T. gave an excellent address on slavery in Rev. Mr. Tillotson's meeting-house, to a tolerably large audience. [2]

To-morrow, Mr. May, Mr. Thompson, Helen and myself will leave for Providence, where we shall probably tarry until Thursday morning, and then start for Boston.

I feel rejoiced at the prospect of your being associated with Mr. May, in our anti-slavery office, after the annual meeting. Of course, if agreeable and convenient to you, Helen and myself desire to have you board with us.

Helen says that she and Mr. May conjointly addressed a letter to me at New-York, the day before I arrived here. Pray, do me the favor to call at the Post Office and take it out, with any others that may happen to be there for me, and keep them until I see you, or until a private opportunity offers to send them to me.

I suppose you are sighing to see New-England, especially a little spot near Providence, which shall be nameless, and one who shall also be nameless. Possess your soul in patience a little while longer.

We have a driving snow-storm this morning.

Ever yours,

Wm. Lloyd Garrison.

ALS: Garrison Papers, Boston Public Library.

1. Samuel Hanson Cox.

2. George J. Tillotson (1805–1888) had been a school teacher and studied both at Andover Theological Seminary and Yale Divinity School before being ordained in 1831 as the minister of the Trinitarian Congregational Church in Brooklyn, Connecticut. He was also active in various reforms.

194

TO HELEN E. GARRISON

Roxbury, May 4, 1835.

My dear Wife:

Mr. Knapp put your letter into my hands on Saturday afternoon, but I was then so absorbed in removing our furniture, that I was unable to sit down and pen a reply instanter. You shall have "ever so many" kisses for your promptness in writing, when I see you in Providence. I held the letter some time unopened in my hand, little dreaming that it was from her whom I am happy to call my wife, and who is equally happy in calling me her husband.

As household affairs are now of paramount interest to you, I commence with them. On Saturday, two loads of our goods were removed to our new house,[1] and to-day (Monday) three more loads, which took every thing away but the cat. — Not an article, thus far, has been either injured or broken. — I have been very busy to-day, in putting down the straw carpets in the chambers, which are now covered, and, having their appropriate furniture mostly arranged, they look very well. The carpeting fits to a charm — I have not had to cut a single piece for the three chambers. Whether the parlor will be as accommodating, I cannot tell, as I have not been able to measure it, in consequence of its being occupied with goods. The walls have been white-washed, the doors and fire-place painted, the vacuum in the attic boarded up, &c. &c. It is extremely doubtful, however, whether I shall be able to get all things in suitable order before I leave, as I am to be with you in Providence sooner than I anticipated, and in the mean time shall be occupied with my paper, and in sitting afresh for my portrait to Mr. Torrey, as he is confident he can make a good likeness, and is anxious to put it in the exhibition at the Atheneum Gallery.[2]

I am truly gratified that your ride to P. was so agreeable, nor am I at all jealous of the gallant old gentleman who paid you such marked attention. Blessings on him for his kindness, and especially because he is an abolitionist! Why did you not ascertain his name? Yea, why did you not give him to understand that he was talking to the wife of that most blood-thirsty and ferocious wretch, the "notorious" Garrison?

Dismiss your fears as to my health — it is perfectly good.

Agreeably to orders, I have destroyed sister Charlotte's letter to you, as also your own letter! Now, fail not to destroy this as soon as you have perused it, by way of equalization and reciprocity.

As to a servant girl, I will talk the matter over with you in P. Catharine [3] has promised to find me one, if possible, provided we want one. I think, with you, it would not be kind to take Eliza Jack from Charlotte at this critical period.[4] C's readiness to give her up deserves great commendation.

One word more with regard to our new house. Since staying in it, I have found this serious objection to it — that reading and conversation in the other part of the house, are very easily heard, and every movement seems to be as if we were living together with them in common. I do not fancy such proximity. But let us possess our souls in patience for a few months.

I think, with brother George, that it would be rather hazardous to defer leaving Roxbury for New-York till Monday, as a storm might on that day cause the loss of a trip, and of course the loss of the annual meeting; but I do not like the idea of arriving in N.Y. on Sabbath morning. So I shall leave Boston on Thursday noon, and take the steam-boat on Friday, so that I may be in the commercial emporium on Saturday — *Deo volente*. As I shall see you so speedily, I need not add any more — except to ask you to give my affectionate regards to all the family and other dear friends, and to say that I yearn to see and embrace you with still increasing affection.

Your devoted one,

Wm. Lloyd Garrison.

ALS: Garrison Papers, Boston Public Library.

1. 23 Brighton Street, Boston.
2. Manasseh Cutler Torrey (1807–1837), a pupil of Henry Inman, who worked principally in Salem, Massachusetts, first exhibited in the National Academy in 1833, becoming that year an associate member. Toward the end of 1835 his finished portrait of Garrison, said to have been a good likeness, was sent to Philadelphia to be engraved in mezzotint by John Sartain. The engraving was published in June 1836. A reproduction of the oil portrait is one of the illustrations in the current volume.
3. Wife of George W. Benson.
4. Charlotte Benson Anthony's maid, Eliza Jack, has not been further identified.

195

TO ISAAC KNAPP

New-York, Saturday, May 9, 1835.

MY DEAR PARTNER:

I arrived in this city at an early hour this morning — had a very quiet and favorable passage, and found in the boat quite a number of abolition brethren from the east, delegates to the annual meeting. No opponent ventured to peep or mutter. I have just seen Mr. Lyman, a delegate from Ohio, one of the noble band of students who left Lane Seminary for conscience' sake.[1] He attended the State Anti-Slavery Convention which was recently held in Zanesville, and brings with him its spirited proceedings in manuscript, to be published in pamphlet form in this city. I have barely time to copy the Declaration of Sentiment which was adopted by the Convention, and hope you will not fail to insert it in the next number of the Liberator. It is an uncommonly powerful production — its standard is as high as heaven, and its spirit full of holy resolution and uncompromising integrity. Mr. Birney and Mr. Stanton have just been addressing the Philadelphians, and are expected here this evening.[2] Of course, Mr. B. will be 'the observed of all observers.'[3] I trust we shall succeed in getting him to attend our New-England Convention. Our dear brethren Thompson and Phelps are also expected this evening from Albany. It is reported that their lectures have been very successful in that section. I shall try to send you something further for your next number.

In great haste, yours truly,

WM. LLOYD GARRISON.

Printed: *The Liberator*, May 16, 1835.

1. Huntington Lyman (1793–1900) entered Lane Seminary in 1833, where, along with Theodore D. Weld, Henry B. Stanton, and other students, he participated in February of 1834 in the famous antislavery debates, which affirmed the doctrine of immediate emancipation and attacked the American Colonization Society. When the students' antislavery work was repudiated by the board of the seminary, Lyman, Stanton, and other students left the school. Lyman transferred to the seminary at Oberlin and later became a famous antislavery lecturer and a minister in western New York state.

2. James G. Birney (1792–1857) was a wealthy southerner, a graduate of Princeton, and a lawyer, who sold his plantation, freed his slaves, and became, as a result of the influence of Weld, an active abolitionist. He remained enough of a lawyer, however, to be convinced that slavery must be abolished by constitutional means; two times he was the abolitionist candidate for President of the United States.

Henry B. Stanton (1805–1887), a lawyer, journalist, reformer, and like Lyman one of the Lane rebels of 1834, became an agent and a member of the executive committee of the American Anti-Slavery Society. He broke with Garrison in 1840 over the use of political action by abolitionists. This same year he married woman's rights leader Elizabeth Cady. Later in life he became a full-time journalist, first on the New York *Tribune* and then on the *Sun*.

3. This phrase from Shakespeare's *Hamlet* (III, i, 162) was one of Garrison's favorite quotations.

196

TO HELEN E. GARRISON

New-York, May 11, 1835.

My dear Wife —

Well — after all, we had a pleasant, safe and speedy passage to this city. There were so many abolitionists on board of the steam-boat, from various quarters, that we bore down all opposition, and not a single antagonist ventured to mutter, although a few had the curiosity to peep. We arrived in the morning as early as 3 o'clock, but did not land until about half past 5, being determined to tarry the whole night comfortably in the land of Nod. One of our brethren, Rev. Mr. Adams of Brunswick, Me., on waking up, found himself in as uncomfortable a predicament as I did a few weeks since at Norwich.[1] On looking for his trunk, lo, it had been carefully removed, whither no one could tell, but in all probability to Philadelphia. There is every reason to believe it was stolen, and therefore there is little hope of its recovery. Being a good man, he bears his loss quite philosophically; but, to be deprived of all clothing at this time, in the midst of so many anniversaries, when one must have more regard than usual to external appearance, is a severe trial of patience and resignation.

I am stopping at a fine hotel, (on the English plan,) directly opposite the Park, in the very heart of the city.[2] Every steam-boat, whether it comes from the east, or west, or north, or south, is freighted with "fanaticism" and "treason." The tide of holy sympathy and love is rolling in like an ocean, and a thousand hearts are leaping for joy as they are borne along upon the "sweet deluge," as Watts would call it. It will unquestionably be the strongest array of intellectual vigor and moral strength ever brought together in this country. The spirit of God seems to dwell richly with abolitionists.

Mr. Birney, the emancipated and emancipator, beloved and cherished so extensively, is here, "the observed of all observers."[3] I have already had considerable conversation with him, and am well pleased with his spirit and intelligence. He means to visit Providence and Boston — so, my dear, I hope you will have the pleasure of an introduction to him, and of hearing him plead the cause of the suffering and the dumb.

Every thing here is remarkably quiet — that is to say, there is no sign or token of opposition to our cause. The newspapers are dumb — and when "no voice or hideous hum"[4] comes forth from these oracles, it is difficult to get up an excitement. This state of things is marvellously different from that which presented itself a few months ago in this city.

Yesterday, Mr. Thompson preached before a colored congregation — Mr. Birney being present. In the evening, Beriah Green preached at the same place with great acceptance, from the text, "Remember them that are in bonds as bound with them."[5]

Henry looks well and happy. He has had a pleasant journey up the North River, and is very much pleased with Albany. He hopes soon to be in Brooklyn and Providence, but whether he will be able to return with me is uncertain — probably he will not. He has not yet fully determined about locating himself in Boston.

The colonizationists are to have a public meeting on Wednesday evening, when there will be plenty of hot shot thrown at us, as I understand they are preparing to give us a whole broadside. As we are immortal and invulnerable, they can neither kill nor wound us.

You may well suppose that my soul is full of joy and peace at this juncture. It is affecting and renovating to the mind, to see so much disinterestedness, so much well-tempered zeal, so much holy courage, so much attachment for truth, so much undissembled piety, and so much brotherly kindness and charity. — God is honored supremely in all our hearts — the spirit of prayer is poured out from our inmost souls — the poor, the despised and the down-trodden are remembered and defended — and every thing is sanctified and made precious.

With so many high responsibilities resting upon us — exerting so powerful an influence as we do upon this nation — and about planning and devising ways and means for the speedy redemption of a great multitude of captives — we need the wisdom that is from above — to examine carefully the motives that actuate us — to have a clear moral vision — to have believing and prayerful spirits — and to be strengthened and prospered by the petitions to heaven of those who are connected with us. Remember me in your private supplications, and remember us all.

I hope to be with you by Saturday evening. I feel anxious to learn your state of health, as I left you somewhat enfeebled in body. Professions of my love are needless. "Actions speak louder than words," [6] and these, I trust, have never been equivocal or cold. — We bear resignedly a brief separation here, if we can hope to be eternally together in bliss hereafter.

Proffer all the respect, veneration and affection of my soul to father and mother, and much love to dear Mary, Anne and Sarah, and esteem to all the rest of the household. In good health I remain,

Yours, indissolubly and happily,

Wm. Lloyd Garrison.

ALS: Garrison Papers, Boston Public Library.

1. George E. Adams (1801–1875), a graduate of Yale and of the seminary at Andover, had been professor of sacred literature at Bangor Theological Seminary before coming to Brunswick as minister of the First Parish Church.

2. Garrison probably refers to either Lovejoy's Hotel on Beekman Street or Park Row American Hotel, 229 Broadway, both of which were opposite City Hall Park.

3. Shakespeare, *Hamlet*, III, i, 162.

4. Milton, "On the Morning of Christ's Nativity," line 174.

5. Hebrews 13:3.

6. This maxim can be traced back to George Washington's *Social Maxims*.

197

TO HELEN E. GARRISON

Eastport, July 21, 1835.
Tuesday — noon.

My very dear, gentle and affectionate Wife:

I hasten to relieve your anxious mind, by informing you of our safe arrival at this port.[1] We left Boston harbor with a fair but moderate breeze, and soon tested the excellent speed of our packet by passing several vessels which had got under weigh some time before us. We mustered, altogether, as many as 16 or 18 passengers — three of them females — of whom a more minute account when we meet. During the first 24 hours, the breeze continued favorable, and the sea very gentle; so that on Sabbath evening, we had completed two-thirds of our passage, and had a pretty fair prospect of eating our breakfast next morning in Eastport! Before midnight, however, the wind died away, and we were becalmed until the afternoon, when a slight breeze sprung up, which was soon succeeded by a fog so dense as to prevent us seeing scarcely a rod from the vessel. Night was now approaching, and much anxiety was felt, as we were near the shore, but could not tell precisely our position. I was lying in a dozing mood in my birth, when I heard the cry of "Breakers!" To gain the deck was but the work of a moment. We were so near the breakers, that we could toss a biscuit upon them — the fog continuing thick and impenetrable. We had scarcely got through this difficulty, when we were saluted with the cry of "Rocks ahead!" And sure enough, our vessel was heading directly on to a towering mass of rocks, as ugly and terrific as a land-lubber would wish to see on a summer's day. At this moment, most providentially, the breeze increased in strength, and we were enabled barely to clear the reef: — but we saw a schooner, looking like a spectre in the fog, in a yet more perilous situation, and whether she got clear we do not know. However, as there was no gale, and the sea was comparatively calm, it is not probable that the lives of those on board would have been put in extreme peril, had either of the vessels struck — although the vessel itself might have been lost. Well — this, as you may suppose, was a serious moment. Aunt Charlotte was excessively alarmed, but the passengers generally behaved with commendable firmness. Now came the cry of "Land O!" and we found ourselves close under the bluff of West Quoddy head, looking like a beautiful heap of coral, piled up in most fantastic forms. As soon as we weathered this, we felt our danger to be past, and had now an almost certain chance of eating our supper (seeing we had been cheated out of our breakfast) in this place. Disappointment was again our lot. The fog became so dense as to defy all calculation in regard to our course, although our captain has no superior for skill or experience; but this playing blind man's buff under such circumstances is too puzzling for human foresight or success. We continued awhile to sail hap-hazard at a brisk pace, when all at once we found ourselves fast upon the flats — and after essaying in vain, for an hour or two, to get her off into deep water, we concluded to give the vessel and ourselves no further trouble during the night. As the tide left her, she of course fell over on one side, and our berths were far from being comfortable. Thus we lay, within only four miles of Eastport, and only 46 hours from Boston!

By day-break, the next morning, a boat came along-side; and as there was no prospect of getting the vessel off during the day, we concluded to charter this conveyance, to carry us to Eastport. So, putting our luggage into it, and all the passengers into the schooner's long-boat, we were rowed ashore to Lubec — thence we travelled half-a-mile on the sand, on foot, to the opposite shore — and from thence we were speedily conveyed to our desired haven, where we arrived about 7 o'clock, this morning, rejoicing to land once more upon terra firma. All last night I was afflicted with the tooth-ache, and all this morning have been almost frantic with it. The first thing to be done was to find a hotel — next, get up our trunks — next, for myself to get shaved (and I was shaved very neatly by a *woman*!) — next, get breakfast for aunt and myself, though I was in too much pain to enjoy it — next, put some peppermint upon lint into my tooth, and bathe the outside of my face with it — next, tie up my face with a handkerchief — next, get into bed, and try to get some sleep. After all this, the next thing in course, after reposing for two hours, was to get up, and write this letter to you. My tooth has grown more amicable, my nerves begin to be more steady, and my head is clearer.

Neither aunt nor myself was sea-sick enough on the passage to make us vomit, but enough to make us feel most disagreeably, and to spoil our appetite. On the whole, we have had a quick and favorable passage, and ought to be thankful to the Giver of all good gifts.

We have not had time to hunt up our relations, but shall commence our researches forthwith. From the window at which I sit, Deer Island is easily seen, upon which several of them reside. We shall go down to it to-morrow morning. From thence, we expect to go St. John, on Thursday, in the steam-boat; and from thence, tarrying a day or two at that place, to Annapolis and Granville where my aunt Nancy resides, in good circumstances.[2]

Be assured, dearest, that I shall use all despatch to return home. Luckily, perhaps, my means will not allow me to be long absent from you. I trust you are well — that sister Sarah is also, and happy — that Messrs. Knapp and Benson are safe guardians — and that all will go well with us, both at home and abroad.

Yours, with immeasurable love,

Wm. Lloyd Garrison.

☞ Aunt Charlotte sends her love to all the household, individually.

ALS: Garrison Papers, Boston Public Library.

1. Garrison and his aunt, Charlotte Lloyd Newell, were en route to New Brunswick to investigate a supposed inheritance from his mother's family.
2. Nancy Lloyd Delap was the sister of Garrison's mother.

1 9 8

TO HELEN E. GARRISON

Granville, July 25, 1835.

My sweet Helen:

A week ago this morning, I was by your side, making busy preparation to depart, and feeling all the regret in view of our separation that deep and unchanging affection could inspire. I am now at my journey's end, under the roof of my aunt Nancy, my mother's own sister, and truly a most worthy woman. It is twenty-five years in September since I was here; every thing is strange to me, although, from the sparseness of the population, there cannot have been many radical changes wrought since that time. I remember nothing distinctly, except the visits of the Indians to my aunt's house — especially do I remember the squaws who came with their little pappooses (babies) tied or slung upon their backs. These children of the forest have gradually melted almost entirely away — for the extermination of the weak and uncivilized has generally followed the presence and advancement of the white man.

Uncle and aunt were truly rejoiced to see us. The latter sobbed and wept like a child, for gladness of heart. We came upon them as those risen from the dead. They are living in very comfortable circumstances, owning two farms with a large stock of cattle. Last week, one of their daughters was married to a young man from Boston, whose appearance is agreeable, and who apparently possesses an intelligent mind. Although we were too late for the wedding, yet our congratulations come seasonably, and ours may be termed a wedding visit.

I have ascertained the facts in relation to the property left to aunt Charlotte and myself. The whole amount is trifling; but petty as it is, we shall have some difficulty in getting it, unless we engage in a lawsuit, which I cannot do. It seems that my grandmother bequeathed about sixty acres of land to her children, on Deer Island, about three miles below Eastport. This land has long been in the entire possession of my uncle Plato Lloyd,[1] of whom I wrote in a former letter. He has unjustly monopolised the whole of the land, although he has no right to any more of it than myself — that is to say, about ten acres, worth perhaps five hundred dollars only — for the soil is rocky and sterile generally, and the wood upon it of no great value. Uncle Plato promised aunt Charlotte that there should be an equitable settlement of the matter, but those who know him say that not the least reliance can be placed upon his word; so that our trip bids fair to be a bill of expense, unless we resort to compulsory measures to obtain our dues.

Under these circumstances, I shall shorten my visit, and make a rapid movement towards home. It is now Saturday: — here I must remain until Tuesday morning, when I shall take the steam-boat for St. John — from thence I shall start on Wednesday morning for Eastport, and take the packet of that evening for Boston — the same packet that I came in, viz. the schooner Boundary, Capt. Shackford.[2] So that I trust, my dear wife, I shall see you by Saturday evening — making only a fortnight from the hour of my departure. Indeed, it is somewhat probable that I shall arrive in Boston even in advance of this letter. Aunt Charlotte feels as if she must return with me — so you may expect us in company together.

My cousins Andrew and George Garrison, at St. Johns, gave me a very kind reception.[3] Both of them are married, and very likely men they are. I have two uncles residing up the St. Johns river,[4] but I am home-sick, and cannot therefore make them a visit. On Deer Island, I have about fifty-five different relations, and a multitude in other places.

Have you any objections, my dear, to my growing younger? I trow not. Well — it is a fact that I am not so old by one year as I have supposed myself to be. I thought I was born in the year 1804, but my aunt Catharine, who knows all about my birth, and is infallible as to these facts, says that I was born in December, 1805 — so that I am only 29 years old.[5] This is some compensation for my trip.

The health of aunt Charlotte and myself is excellent, but our faces present a fiery hue, being almost blistered by the wind and sun. My nose is as red as a toper's, so that I cannot easily pass for a cold water man. Fie upon the injustice of Phoebus!

How do you get along with your household affairs? — But I must ask you no questions, for you will not be able to answer them by letter. I shall hope for the best, and try to be prepared for the worst. I cherish some anxiety on account of your health, and long to know whether sister Sarah has recovered her own. May God bless and save you all! If I had the wings of an eagle, I would rise and soar away to you without an hour's delay; but I cannot travel any faster than the winds and waves can carry me. Adieu, my love!

Your affectionate husband,

Wm. Lloyd Garrison.
Eastport, July 29, 1835 —
Wednesday evening, 5 o'clock.

My Love — My arrangements, thus far, have corresponded with what I promise in another part of this sheet. Although this letter was written on Saturday at Granville, no mail has since left that place until the one that has come in company with myself — so I have brought it with me, and shall put it in the Post Office here to-night. The mail, however, does not start until Friday morning — so that the chance is still fair of my seeing you before this arrives in Boston. Aunt Charlotte has concluded to stay with aunt Nancy two or three weeks longer, before she returns. I left St. John this morning. Our packet (the Boundary) is ready to sail at any moment — but it now rains hard, and the wind is directly ahead. We shall probably leave to-morrow forenoon. — The cabin is full of passengers. I hope to spend the Sabbath with you, but fear we may be a week or more on our passage. Adieu!

W.L.G.

ALS: Garrison Papers, Boston Public Library.

1. Garrison's mother's brother.
2. John Shackford, Jr. (1781–1858) was the captain of his father's packet, the *Boundary*, known for some twenty years as the fastest vessel on the coastal run between Eastport and Boston.
3. Little is known about Garrison's paternal cousins, although Andrew and George were probably sons of Abijah's brother Nathan. Andrew Garrison (1805–1850), according to Francis Jackson Garrison (handwritten transcription of letter to Wendell Phillips Garrison, July 9, 1873, Villard Papers, Harvard College Library), was for some years a deputy sheriff and the editor of a paper at St. John, New Brunswick.
4. Silas and William Garrison.
5. Aunt Catharine was the sister of Plato Lloyd and of Garrison's mother. Although at this time Garrison accepted his aunt's opinion as infallible, he later questioned it and reverted to the earlier year as that of his birth (see his letter to Francis Jackson Garrison, April 23, 1867). The preponderant weight of evidence seems to be that he was born in 1805, but the day of his birth — whether December 10 or December 12 — is still not certain.

199

TO HELEN E. GARRISON

Eastport, July 31, 1835.⎫
Friday night. ⎭

My dear Love:

Although I sent you a letter by this morning's mail, informing you of my movements, yet as I am now detained contrary to my hopes and expectations, and knowing something of your anxiety on my account, duty and affection urge me to seize my pen once more, to bid you wait patiently for my arrival home, and not to argue from my delay that some disaster has happened unto me. Here I am in a most tiresome and vexatious situation, without friends or acquaintance, the place as dull as monotony can make it, and covered with the impending gloom of a perpetual fog, and my spirit in a high fever to fly to your dear presence. I came to this place on Wednesday evening, expecting to take the packet instantly, and hoping to be in Boston to attend the evening anniversary of the first of August — the greatest day in the history of human deliverance from slavery.[1] Well — the fog put an embargo upon the packet for that evening. On Thursday, all day and evening, it covered heaven, earth and sea, with its impenetrable veil, accompanied by showers of rain; the wind, moreover, was directly against us. This morning, for an hour or two, it was tolerably clear, and the wind fair though faint; but the fog soon came on as densely as ever, and the wind as suddenly turned against us. Thus was our hope of departure nipped in the bud. It is now almost midnight — Egyptian darkness that may be felt hovers around us — the rain is pouring heavily down — and the prospect of a fair wind and fair weather is as remote as ever. We may be detained here another week — the thought is insupportable.

I have scarcely ever been more miserable in my life. This place presents not one single attraction, and there is not a soul with whom I can commune. I am home-sick, dreadfully home-sick. Never did I long to see you more than at the present time. I send you a thousand kisses for each of your fair cheeks, and twice ten thousand for your pretty strawberry lips. O, my love, I pity you if our separation is as painful to you as it is to me. The agony of "hope deferred," [2] and the baffled expectation of love, prey heavily upon my heart. You are dear — very dear — almost *too* dear to me. Sometimes you have made me sorrowful, by expressing fears that you were not the one calculated to make me happy. Banish for ever from your mind, a thought so cruel and unjust. Where, in the wide world, can I find one more attentive, or loving, or devoted, or disinterested, or amiable, than yourself? Truly, our souls are one, and we will love constantly until death. — Dearest, I trust you are well — but think how wretched I must be, after so long a time, not to receive a single line either from you, or from Henry and my friend Isaac. If I could have received only half-a-dozen lines from your pen, they would have been as a cordial to my heart. * * * But here I will pause, and try to get some rest, and so fill up my sheet to-morrow. Good night, and may a guardian angel hover around you!

✿ ✿ ✿ ✿ ✿

Saturday morning — 7 o'clock.
I have passed a feverish night — sleep has failed to close my eyelids. You have absorbed all my thoughts, and upon your image I have gazed, "as on a jewel set in ghostly night." [3] The breakfast-bell is ringing, and I must arise, though much more fatigued than when I went to bed. How is the weather, and what is the prospect? I have reluctantly lifted my curtain, and my heart sinks within me. The same overshadowing and drizzly fog obscures every object at a few yards'

distance, and renders the scene truly dismal. I despair of our sailing to-day.

Half past 9 o'clock. — As soon as I had swallowed a hasty breakfast, I put on my cloak and hat, took my umbrella, and made a desperate sally out of doors, by way of a morning excursion — all in the fog. I have just returned from an indefinite stroll for about five miles, but see no appearance of fair weather. It is still fog — nothing but fog — which I now anathematize in the following

Misty-cal Lines.

> Or mud or mire, or marsh or bog,
> Is better than this drizzling fog.
> The BOUNDARY cannot sail — a clog
> Embargoes her — it is the fog.
> It gripes and binds like any cog
> In miller's wheel — tenacious fog!
> O [de]liver me from a mad-dog,
> And next — from this drear eastern fog!
> I like not to be flogg'd, or flog —
> As little do I like a fog.
> Hail, murrain, lice, and many a frog,
> Did Egypt plague — but not this fog!
> It blears and stupifies like grog —
> O, vile narcotic, muddling fog!
> In vain our eyes are all agog
> To see — we look in vain through fog.
> 'Tis obstinate as any hog —
> It will not budge an inch, this fog.
> Poor Patience keeps her easy jog
> No longer — how she scolds the fog!
> Better to have king Stork, or Log,
> Reign over us, than spectre Fog! —
> Call this not *East*-port more — transmog-
> Rify it thus — the *port of Fog!*

12 o'clock. — The sun is out! the fog is nearly dispersed! the wind is becoming more fair! and we now hope to sail after dinner! I tremble lest we may be again disappointed — and here I will pause, until afternoon come. ° ° °

1 o'clock. — The captain has just sent us up word, that we must be down by half past 1 — that is, as soon as we have eaten dinner. The prospect is now good of our getting a fair start. Blow propitiously, ye winds! Shine out, fair sun!

Now, my love, the load upon my heart lessens. O, how happy I shall be to return home in safety, and find all well as when I left!

I do not forget that this is the glorious 1st of August. Let the jubilee sound unto heaven! Glory be to God in the highest, because good will has been shown to down-trodden men! — O, that I could be at the meeting this evening in Boston!

Farewell — dearest —

Wm. Lloyd Garrison.

ALS: Garrison Papers, Boston Public Library.
1. Garrison refers to the date of emancipation in the British West Indies.
2. Proverbs 13:12.
3. The phrase as it stands has not been identified; possibly Garrison is echoing Shakespeare, *Romeo and Juliet* (I, v, 47–48): ". . . she hangs upon the cheek of night/As a rich jewel in an Ethiop's ear."

200

TO JOHN FARMER

Boston, Aug. 8, 1835.

Dear Sir:

My friend Wm. L. Chaplin, Esq. of Groton, informs me that he is about to make a short tour in New-Hampshire and Maine.[1] As he will probably visit Concord, I am anxious that he should enjoy the pleasure of your acquaintance; and when I tell you that he is not only a gentleman of the first respectability and a Christian, but also one of the most thorough-going, intelligent and zealous advocates of immediate and universal emancipation, I am certain you will gladly give him the right hand of fellowship, and a place in your confidence and esteem.

Yours, with much respect,

Wm. Lloyd Garrison.

John Farmer, Esq.

ALS: John Farmer Papers, New Hampshire Historical Society.
John Farmer (1789–1838), antiquarian, genealogist, and abolitionist, from Chelmsford, Massachusetts, had settled in Concord, New Hampshire, in 1821 to run an apothecary shop. For a number of years he was corresponding secretary of the New Hampshire Anti-Slavery Society.

1. William Lawrence Chaplin (1796–1871) of Groton, Massachusetts, was an enthusiastic abolitionist and subsequently was active in the Liberty party.

2 0 1

TO HENRY E. BENSON

Brooklyn, Aug. 24, 1835.

My dear Henry:

Our esteemed friends, Mr. and Mrs. Gray, leave Brooklyn this morning for Boston. If I had time, I would send an epistle regularly drawn up, instead of a hasty note. We are all on the tiptoe of expectation, and wait with great impatience for the arrival of the mail this forenoon. It may be, after all, that the Faneuil Hall meeting will prove any thing but satisfactory to the fiery spirits of the South, for they have already declared, that to *"rebuke"* the fanatics will effect nothing, and that they will be satisfied with nothing short of the suppression of anti-slavery presses by legal enactments or mobocratic violence.[1] As for ourselves, you know, we care not what course the enemy pursues — whether he threatens or rebukes, whether he is placable or furious, our cause is sure, and will go ahead.

The quietude of Brooklyn is refreshing to my spirit. It seems as if the moral elements had suddenly become hushed, and that violence, oppression and sin no longer abounded in our land. Would it were so indeed!

Next Thursday afternoon, the Windham County Anti-Slavery Society will hold a quarterly meeting at Pomfret, at which my presence is expected.

Ask brother Knapp to procure another bill of the types for which Mr. Parrish owes us, and send it on to me by the first opportunity. It is worth attending to immediately, for Mr. P. is liable to be removed at any moment.

Is puss drowned yet? If so, write me the particulars of the *cat*-astrope. Poor thing! in sincerity we will exclaim, "Requies-*cat* in pace."

Unless you and friend K. supply me pretty freely and very regularly with letters and papers, I shall not be able to content myself here long, away from the field of strife. I trust Mr. K. will examine all the papers carefully, and cut out of them every paragraph that meets his eyes relative to our subject.

Father's health and spirits are very good — much better than when I was here last. He even talks of making a trip to Boston, but he could hardly be persuaded to go on the rail-road. All the rest of the family are well.

Little Anna grows more and more interesting, and affords us all a great deal of amusement and pleasure.[2]

As much love as a letter can carry is sent to you by all in Friendship's Valley.

Take good care of yourself — the same advice to brother May, to whom give much love from me and all the household — ditto to brother Knapp.

We shall depend upon you for a letter quite frequently.

Yours, anxiously and affectionately,

Wm. Lloyd Garrison.

N.B. Send me New-York as well as Boston papers. Can you get me a copy of the Anti-Abolitionist? [3]

ALS: Garrison Papers, Boston Public Library; printed partly in *Life*, I, 515.

1. Garrison refers to the meeting held on August 21 for the purpose of expressing conservative Northern opposition to the abolitionists and their methods.

2. Anna Elizabeth Benson, George W. Benson's daughter.

3. Henry Benson may have found a copy of the "Anti-Abolitionist" to send to his brother-in-law, but the precise identity of that bibliographical item has eluded extensive search in leading American libraries, including not only the Boston Public and Harvard, but also the Library of Congress. It is a fact that the summer of 1835 was replete with agitation against the abolitionists. There were many meetings besides the one at Faneuil Hall. One was convened in Philadelphia, for instance, on the very day Garrison wrote this letter. The "Anti-Abolitionist" may have been an ephemeral publication — perhaps a circular or a broadside to be sent to editors of newspapers — resulting from the meeting in Boston.

202

TO HENRY E. BENSON AND ISAAC KNAPP

Brooklyn, Aug. 29, 1835.

Dear Henry and Isaac:

All continues well with us, here, as I trust it does with you and our friends in Boston. I thank you for the Atlas, containing all the Faneuil Hall speeches — they are all bad, but Sprague's is truly diabolical. I have sent you a letter to him for the next paper, and do not mean to spare him. Another letter — to Otis — I shall send by the next conveyance.[1] That meeting, with its speeches, will do our cause immense good — there can be no doubt of it.

I shall wait with much anxiety to receive the Liberator of this week. Hope you received all the editorial I sent for it.

Do not publish any of the Faneuil Hall speeches, as I shall review them all. I wish brother Thompson would prepare a reply to Sprague's murderous attack.[2]

I must write, once more, for 'squire Parrish's bill. Send it, I pray you.

Let me again suggest, that while I am here, you had better not put the paper to press until Friday. The delay will accommodate me essentially. Mrs. May returns on Tuesday — you may expect a budget by her.

Have you heard any thing further from "John Gerry, No. 20, Court-Street"?[3] I hope the letter was a hoax.

You must advise me when to return. I shall be ready to start at any moment, but enjoy myself much here. Every thing is beautiful to the eye, and grateful to the senses.

Write me as often as you can — for every scrap of intelligence is eagerly devoured.

What a tremendous fire in Charlestown![4] I should think it would divert public conversation from us, for a time at least.

What of our dear fellow laborers, Thompson and May? Love in abundance give to them on my account. Not a word do I yet hear from bro. Phelps — do you?

Yours, as ever,

Wm. Lloyd Garrison.

N.B. Set up the letter to Sprague in brevier, if practicable — as it will be read more easily. I should think it would be well to strike off an extra quantity of the next number, as it will probably excite some curiosity.

ALS: Garrison Papers, Boston Public Library; extracts printed in *Life*, I, 515–516.

1. Two long letters to Otis (208, 215) were printed in *The Liberator*, September 5 and 19.

2. Thompson apparently spent his time lecturing. It became Garrison's responsibility to reply to Peleg Sprague; see letter 203, to George W. Benson, August 29, 1835, and n. 1 thereon.

3. Garrison reports in his letter to Henry E. Benson on the first of September that "there is no such person as John Gerry."

4. The fire in Charlestown, Massachusetts, was reported in *The Liberator* of the same date as Garrison's letter; it burned between seventy and eighty wooden buildings, including houses, hotels, stores, and even a distillery, causing a total loss of between $150,000 and $200,000.

203

TO GEORGE W. BENSON

Brooklyn, Aug. 29, 1835.

Dear George —

You are the kindest of brothers — therefore it is that I trouble you with my packages for the Liberator, while I remain in Brooklyn. Please to send the accompanying bundle to-morrow. I should be extremely sorry to have it miscarry, as it contains a severe review of a portion of Sprague's speech at Faneuil Hall.[1]

I am heartily glad to learn that Burgess has lost his election. His speech was abominable.[2]

My visit here affords me a great deal of pleasure. If my enemies knew how happy I am, they would be more furious than ever.

Yours, affectionately,

Wm. Lloyd G——n.

ALS: Garrison Papers, Boston Public Library.

1. Garrison's review of Peleg Sprague's conservative speech attacking the abolitionists took the form of two long letters (209, 210) which appeared in *The Liberator* for September 5 and 12.

2. Tristam Burges (1770–1853), his name usually being spelled with one "s," had been teacher, lawyer, state legislator, and chief justice of the Rhode Island Supreme Court before being elected to Congress in 1825, as a representative from Providence. After serving for ten years, he was defeated for reelection primarily because he would not accept Clay's compromise on the tariff. Garrison refers to Burges' speech in Providence shortly before the election. At that time Burges made some comments on slavery, approving of abolition in the District of Columbia and labeling himself as a colonizationist. For Garrison's full comments on the speech see *The Liberator*, September 12, 1835.

204

TO HENRY E. BENSON

Brooklyn, Sept. 1, 1835.

My dear Henry —

I have only two or three minutes in which to say, that all the bundles and letters you have forwarded, have safely arrived. Ten thousand thanks for your attention and kindness. The letter from bro. Thompson was quite refreshing. Mrs. May goes this morning to Boston, via Worcester, in company with our esteemed friend Scarborough.[1] I regret that I have no editorial prepared to send by her, but shall send something by the Providence mail to-day noon — also more by the Worcester stage on Wednesday, which will be received on Thursday, I hope, in season for this week's paper. Hope the bundle containing my letter to Sprague has not miscarried. Thank you for paying such close attention to poor puss. Am pleased to learn that you and friend K. make such famous housekeepers. Success and happiness to all old bachelors! Feel rejoiced to learn there is no such person as John Gerry. We shall probably return to Boston in all next week. — All the dear domestic circle reciprocate your loving remembrances, and are all well.

Yours, ardently,

W.L.G.

ALS: Garrison Papers, Boston Public Library.

1. Garrison refers to one of his supporters, Philip Scarborough of Brooklyn, Connecticut, who was active in the Windham County Anti-Slavery Society.

2 0 5

TO GEORGE W. BENSON

Brooklyn, Sept. 1, 1835.

Dear George —

I send you another package of incendiary matter for the Liberator.[1] Hope it will prove hot enough to melt at least one chain, and burn up many bushels of chaff. If you can, send it in the morning, and request that it may be left without delay in Boston. In receiving bundles for me, and from me, you will be liable to some expense. Keep an account thereof, & I will settle it on my arrival in P——.[2] We shall probably remain here a week or ten days longer. Our enemies are working bravely to put down slavery — God grant they may succeed! Give my choicest affections to all my dear brethren in P.; I trust none of us will prove recreant to our God, our country, the cause of the slave, and the interests of mankind. The arm of the Almighty will be made bare in our defence.

Your grateful brother,

W.L.G.

ALS: Garrison Papers, Boston Public Library; extract in *Life*, I, 516.

1. Perhaps Garrison refers to his own long letters to Harrison Gray Otis and to Peleg Sprague (208, 209), which appeared in *The Liberator* for September 5.
2. Providence.

2 0 6

TO HENRY E. BENSON

Brooklyn, Sept. 3, 1835.

My dear Henry:

Your letter of Monday afternoon, addressed to "Geo. Benson," alias Wm. Lloyd Garrison, came this forenoon in the mail, accompanied by the Evangelist and the Republican Monitor, the latter a paper which I do not remember to have seen before, but which seems to be thoroughly imbued with the anti-slavery spirit.[1] The bundle of newspapers which you sent to P——[2] by D. L. Child, was not received to-day, and I am inclined to think he forgot to leave it, and so has carried it to New-York, and peradventure to England. All the other bundles alluded to in your letter have safely arrived, both by the way of Providence and Worcester. Your kind attention awakens strong feelings of gratitude in my heart. I thank you from the very bottom of it; for, cut off as I am here from society and the bustle of public life in a crowded city, the arrival of letters and papers is a time of thrilling interest to me. You deserve to have the freedom of the city of Boston bestowed upon you in due form.

The reading of your letter excited considerable pleasure and laughter on the part of our family circle. My wife was somewhat grave, and perhaps a little alarmed, on learning the entertainments which you have given, lest you may have forgotten to put down the crum-cloth, and thereby greased her gay carpet, for she has a lively remembrance of the porter which cousin Knapp spilt some weeks ago. However, I have comforted her as well as I could; as those who were willing to risk a mob, ought not to be afraid to trust a part of the household. She will probably send you a letter of warning to be careful, and then look out for yourselves if you go astray by design or accident! It makes my visit much more comfortable to learn that you are enjoying yourselves so famously. I am well aware of friend K's skill in cooking and taste in providing; and I presume you fulfil the duties of chamber-maid with becoming care and regularity.

Every line from you, assuring me of the continued safety and repose of dear Thompson, awakens thankfulness to God in my heart. I am rather sorry that he has concluded to visit Plymouth at present; for, though his personal risk may not be great, yet it is more than probably that if he attempts to speak, the meeting will be disturbed. There is yet too much fever, and too little rationality, in the public mind, either for him or any of us to make addresses to the patient without having him attempt to knock us down. Write — print — distribute — this we may do with profit to our cause. I am glad to learn from you, that the public curiosity still continues to thirst after our publications. Let it have a full supply — for, though we have not sown to the wind, hitherto, yet we are able to reap *in* the whirlwind.[3] The resolutions and speeches of our enemies will furnish us with an inexhaustible supply of arms and ammunition to carry on the war. I would not take a thousand dollars for those that were adopted and delivered in what was once the old Cradle of Liberty. By the bye, Bostonians have a strong patriotic attachment for Faneuil Hall; and we shall raise a blush of shame upon their cheeks, ere long, by dwelling continually upon the disgrace which has been cast upon it by a pro-slavery meeting.

Brother May's sickness and recovery call for condolence and gratulation. The intense action of his mind is almost too much for his body. Pure and devoted philanthropist! how heavy is the cross that he is called upon to bear! But, though scorned by men and even his own kindred, I believe he is contemplated by angels with admiration, and that God is his exceeding great reward.[4] May he be faithful unto death — hating, if necessary, both father and mother *for Christ's sake* — that he may receive a crown of glory in the presence of an assembled universe. I desire to receive further particulars respecting the reported mob at Haverhill. It is still my opinion, that we ought not to attempt holding *public* meetings at present; but we may be as active as we choose in distributing publications, and in seeking private interviews with those who are opposed to us, for the purpose of discussing the matter with them. Let our step be firm — our demeanor dignified — our speech just and fearless.

I did not attend the meeting at Pomfret, for on that afternoon I was engaged with Mary and Helen at Dr. Green's; [5] but we met Charles Burleigh on our return, who told us that he had been to P., but there was no meeting, no notice of it having, by mistake, been given out on the previous Sabbath. About half a dozen persons, however, met on the steps of the meeting-house, and had a social talk on the state of the times — among them was a young slaveholder from the south, who had come six or eight miles, expecting to hear me speak. He and Burleigh had a long conversation, and the latter riddled him through and through.

The news respecting the health and prowess of puss is absolutely exhilarating. "Well and bravely done!" as one of the New-York papers exclaimed, on learning that our petition for Faneuil Hall was rejected. He that is born to be hanged will never be drowned. I hope pussy's leg will not have a relapse.

You write nothing about brother James.[6] Has he yet sailed from Boston? and, if so, under what circumstances did he leave? My heart bleeds over him. God is merciful and long-suffering — and there lies all my hope of his complete restoration.

Mr. Parrish's bill arrived safely — but it will not be liquidated now, inasmuch as he wishes me to take the box of types with me on my return, and sell it for what it will fetch. It has not been opened since it was sent, and he has no opportunity here whatever to sell it. He will pay for whatever loss may ensue upon its sale.

"*Bother the whole concern!*" I don't wonder at this exclamation. Our books would have been a sore trial even for patient Job. The blame is ours — the trouble and mortication yours. But "don't give up the ship." [7]

I do hope that you will write to father [8] immediately. You can have no idea of his anxiety to receive a line from you — and to-day he was sadly disappointed to find the letter was not for him.

If you can, without too much trouble, (provided this reaches you in season,) I wish you would send a little package of papers, *with the Liberator of this week*, on Saturday morning by the Worcester cars —

in that case, I shall receive it on Saturday afternoon, instead of being necessitated to wait until Monday noon. No matter if you are not acquainted with any of the passengers. Enquire who among them is going through to Brooklyn or Norwich, and ask him to leave it with Mr. Bailey, the tavern-keeper in B.[9] — Direct it, as usual, to George Benson.

Our friend Mr. John Gray, and his wife and little one, leave to-day for Boston, via Providence. He thinks he shall tarry a month in B., so that he will be able to see you frequently, and give you a minute account of all the village transactions for the last three months, or for a longer period, if you desire.

Helen wishes you to make inquiries (with Mr. K.) for a good servant girl. We cannot return comfortably until we get one — but let us have a good one, or none.

I am glad Mr. K. consents to my absence, on condition that I am not deficient in editorial matter. It is a great relief to me to escape from the city at this season of the year.

I send a letter to your care for George Thompson. And having filled up my sheet, I must conclude with renewed expressions of brotherly love.

Wm. Lloyd Garrison.

ALS: Garrison Papers, Boston Public Library; extracts printed in *Life*, I, 516–517.

1. Garrison's mail consisted of a letter and two newspapers. The letter was addressed to his brother-in-law because George Thompson's visit to the United States had demonstrated that the better-known abolitionists were in physical danger and might be more safely addressed by more neutral pseudonyms. The *Republican Monitor* — also known as the Pittsfield *Sun* — had been published since 1800; the other paper was apparently the *Evangelist and Religious Review*, first published in New York in 1830.

2. Providence.

3. Garrison paraphrases Hosea 8:7.

4. Genesis 15:1, paraphrased.

5. Rowland Greene

6. James Holley Garrison (1801–1842) was the abolitionist's sailor brother, whose career first in the merchant marine and then in the navy was greatly hampered by his chronic alcoholism. Although virtually illiterate, he left as his memorial a frank and fascinating journal (see Walter M. Merrill, ed., *Behold Me Once More, the Confessions of James Holley Garrison*, Boston, 1954).

7. Although the phrase originated during the American Revolution, it was used also by Oliver Hazard Perry as the motto flown from the masthead of his flagship at the battle of Lake Erie.

8. The senior George Benson.

9. Mr. Bailey of Brooklyn has not been identified.

2 0 7

TO GEORGE W. BENSON

Brooklyn, Sept. 4, 1835.

My dear George:

This is a joyful day to me — for it is the anniversary of my marriage. A year ago, this morning, witnessed a solemn union of hands on the part of your dear Helen and myself: our hearts had been previously united. That year has sped its flight like an arrow; but its rapidity has not exceeded its bliss. My anticipations have been fully realized, and I have nothing to regret but my own unworthiness. In Helen I have found a loving, attentive and obedient wife — a pleasant and desirable companion — and a most disinterested and pure-minded creature. I am happy in believing, that she is not dissatisfied with her choice; that the seasons have rolled away not less pleasantly to her than to myself; that she loves me as deeply as one human being ought to love another; that, come weal or woe, applause or condemnation, preferment or persecution, she is ready to take her lot cheerfully with mine; and that she finds a state of wedlock —

"—— the highest bliss
Of Paradise, that has survived the fall." [1]

I did not marry her, expecting that she would assume a prominent station in the anti-slavery cause, but for domestic quietude and happiness. So completely absorbed am I in that cause, that it was undoubtedly wise in me to select as a partner one who, while her benevolent feelings were in unison with mine, was less immediately and entirely connected with it. I knew she was naturally diffident, and distrustful of her own ability to do all that her heart might prompt. She is one of those who prefer to toil unseen — to give by stealth — and to sacrifice in seclusion. By her unwearied attentions to my wants, her sympathetic regards, her perfect equanimity of mind, and her sweet and endearing manners, she is no trifling support to abolitionism, inasmuch as she lightens my labors, and enables me to find exquisite delight in the family circle, as an offset to public adversity. Long may we travel the journey of life together! and may Heaven at last be our eternal dwelling-place!

These things it is proper I should say to you — especially after the experiment of a year. I am sure they will give you pleasure, although they cannot be unexpected to you; for you have known Helen from her infancy, and always duly estimated her worth. She too loves you, if possible, with a more than sisterly attachment.

How wise, how benevolent, how invaluable, is the institution of marriage! Nature rejoices in it; purity closely allies itself to it; innocence beautifies it; joy attends it; and love crowns it. Break it down by violence or corruption, and the nations will become as Sodom and Gomorrah. It shuts the floodgates of pollution; it opens a fountain of virtue; it legitimates, preserves and dignifies its offspring. How endearing are its relations, how strong its ties, how sacred its obligations, how vast its responsibilities! What faithful husband can think, for one moment, of having the object of his love torn from his arms by the might of oppression, and not feel indignation and horror swelling like a swift inundation in his bosom? What affectionate wife can imagine the sale of her beloved partner at auction, as a beast is sold, without shuddering as if smitten by the icy hand of death? What obedient child can dwell, in thought, upon a violent separation from his parents, — a separation as perpetual as it is violent, — without execrating the spoiler? In this mirror, my dear George, how is the terrific image of the monster Slavery reflected! Should we not hate him with a perfect hatred! Can we be too earnest for his destruction? Is he a docile creature, that we should cherish him? Oh, my God, I thank thee that I am called, by thy good spirit, to wage a war of extermination against the dragon! Inflame thou my zeal yet more intensely — nerve thou my arm with augmented vigor — exalt my courage still higher by the aid of thine omnipotence! Violated chastity calls to the rescue; insulted honor demands redress; bleeding humanity shrieks for deliverance; manacled innocence invokes retribution! A cry is out upon the winds — it comes from a heart-broken mother just robbed of her sucking babe! A groan disturbs my midnight repose — it is the dying appeal of a lacerated, guiltless brother! A clank of chains sounds in my ear — it comes from the dungeon of oppression erected on a free soil! A peal of thunder shakes the land — it is the voice of God, saying — "Vengeance is *mine*! *I* will repay!" [2]

Your last letter — just received — is better than a lump of pure gold; it cheers and strengthens me, which gold can never do for its own sake. Tell my abolition brethren that I fully intend to return to Boston via Providence, for the purpose of communing with them. Their steadfastness is a proof that God is their hope and strength. There are many professed disciples of Christ, who, when zephyrs blow and the sun shines pleasantly, can *boldly* sing —

> "Though earth against my soul engage,
> And hellish darts be hurl'd —
> Still, I can smile at Satan's rage,
> And face a frowning world!" [3]

But let the light of heaven be eclipsed however slightly — let the wind begin to blow and the storm to rage, and you will find them, instead of being willing to "face a frowning *world*," actually afraid to face a D.D., or even the most cowardly wretch that preys upon his fellow-man! How many there are, who mock God and deny Christ in this shameless manner! This storm of persecution will sift us all, and remove from our cause the chaff that may have accumulated with the wheat. The fire which the emissaries and servants of the devil are kindling, will only consume the hay, wood and stubble — it cannot hurt that which is indestructable — thanks to the God of righteousness!

You are correct — those religious persons and papers that denounce our brother George Thompson as a foreigner, are virtually rebuking every foreign missionary who has been sent from our shores to evangelize a rebellious world; and they will find, ere long, that infidelity will meet and vanquish them with their own weapons. How evident it is that the love of God dwells not in their heart — that they do not really regard all mankind as their brethren — and that they belong in spirit to the ancient Pharisees!

I am not prepared fully to decide as to the expediency of calling a National Convention, but am rather inclined to think it inexpedient. Before the feverish excitement that now reigns in the public mind will have subsided, winter will be upon us. Such a Convention will not answer any good purpose *now* — and winter is too rugged a season in which to collect a large national meeting at any central point. Perhaps we had better work quietly, but *industriously*, until spring — but I am not *sure*.

How imminent is the danger that hovers about the persons of our friends George Thompson and Arthur Tappan! Rewards for the seizure of the latter are multiplying — in one place they offer three thousand dollars for his *ears* — a purse has been made up, *publicly*, of $20,000, in New-Orleans, for his person! — I, too, — I desire to bless God, am involved in almost equal peril. I have just received a letter written evidently by a friendly hand, in which I am apprised that "my life is sought after, and a reward of $20,000 has been offered for my head by six Mississipians." He says — "Beware of the assassin! May God protect you!" and signs himself "A Marylander, and a resident of Philadelphia." [4]

I fear that the times are too stormy for the Warren Baptist Association to march boldly up to the line of duty.[5]

Brother Stanton's success is animating information — and so is your proposal to organize a State Society in November.

Write as often as you can to father, for he watches the mail with astonishing interest, and is delighted to receive even but a hasty scrawl.

Give my love to Mr. and Mrs. Anthony, my dear friends the Chases, Mr. Prentice, &c.

Yours, in all truth and love,

Wm. Lloyd Garrison.

☞ As often as you can, send the packages by private conveyance.

ALS: Garrison Papers, Boston Public Library; extracts printed in *Life*, I, 423, 463, 517.

1. Garrison adapts William Cowper, *The Task*, Book III, lines 41–42.
2. Garrison adapts Hebrews 10:30.
3. Not identified.
4. This threat as alleged was only one of many such received during this period by Garrison and other abolitionists. Garrison was not alone in his willingness to face danger and martyrdom. Angelina E. Grimké, for instance, wrote to him, August 30, 1835: "O how earnestly have I desired, *not* that we may escape suffering, but that we may be willing to endure unto the end" (*The Liberator*, September 19, 1835).
5. Warren, Rhode Island, eight miles east of Providence and once the location of Brown University, was a Baptist center.

208

TO HARRISON GRAY OTIS

[September 5, 1835.]

Sir —

I have carefully read your speech against the abolitionists.[1] It leads me, involuntarily, to use the bold interrogation of the apostle: 'Where is the wise? where is the scribe? where is the disputer of this world? Hath not God made foolish the wisdom of this world?' In every great moral conflict, it is as manifest in modern, as it was in ancient times, that 'God hath chosen the foolish things of the world to confound the wise; and God hath chosen the weak things of the world to confound the things which are mighty; and base things of the world, and things which are despised, hath God chosen, yea, and things which are not, to bring to nought things that are' — for this grand and all-sufficient reason, 'that no flesh should glory in his presence.'[2]

In proceeding to review your speech, I am filled with sorrowful emotions. I remember how intimately associated is the name of OTIS with the revolutionary struggle that emancipated this nation from the thraldom of the mother country. You have dishonored that name — you have cast a stain of blood upon your reputation. You have presumed to lift up your voice, even in the very Cradle of Liberty,[3] in panegyric of the vilest 'brokers in the trade of blood,' in denunciation of the best friends of insulted freedom, and in support of 'A BARGAIN,' which, according to your own showing, is a loathsome compound of selfishness, oppression and villany. Well, therefore, in respect to yourself particularly, may I feel sad and indignant. Some of the earliest effusions of my pen were in earnest and generous defence of your character, against the calumnies of your political adversaries; for in one particular at least, there is a coincidence of suffering between us, — all manner of evil having been uttered against us, FALSELY.[4] It is my lot to be branded throughout this country as an agitator, a fanatic, an incendiary, and a madman. There is one epithet, I fervently desire to thank God, that has never been applied to me: — I have never been stigmatized as a *slaveholder*, or as *an apologist of slavery*. No — no! Bad as my traducers conceive me to be, they have never reduced me so low in the scale of humanity, nor so cruelly impeached my honesty, nor so aspersed my patriotism, as to bring so scandalous and degrading an accusation against me. As they have been *too conscientous* to throw that calumny upon my character, I cheerfully forgive them all the rest, and thank them for their magnanimity. On other occasions, Sir, I have been your advocate. With youthful ardor, I supported your nomination for the office of Governor of this Commonwealth. My maiden speech before a Boston audience was in your behalf, successfully urging the propriety of nominating you to represent this District on the floor of Congress.[5] I never doubted your attachment to the union of these States — I never believed you to be inimical to the rights of man. These disclosures I make, — not that I am any longer a politician, for I now view the politics of this country to be essentially corrupt and unholy, — but to show you that in my strictures, I am not actuated by any political grudge, and that my regard for principle is stronger than my partiality for persons. That you still love liberty, I do not deny. Liberty for whom? For the black as well as the white man? O no! For yourself, your children, and your white countrymen — for tyrants, but not for slaves — for the strong and powerful, but not for the weak and needy — for the rapacious and violent, but not for the guiltless and submissive! That you are still a patriot, I care not to dispute; but your patriotism excludes one-sixth portion of your countrymen from its embrace, and talks approvingly of making two millions and a half of your species, 'non-entities'! That you hate oppression, I cannot doubt; but it is not the oppression of the black man, but only of the white!

Sir, this great transgression of your life has been committed under circumstances of peculiar criminality. 'The frost of nearly three score years and ten' [6] is upon your head; — the hand of 'time and affliction' presses heavily upon you; — your 'days are nearly numbered;' [7] — and you will be soon called to stand at the tribunal of Him, who died to redeem as well the blackest as the whitest of our race! Yet, at this solemn period, you have not scrupled — nay, you have been ambitious, to lead and address an excited multitude, in vindication of all imaginable wickedness, embodied in one great system of crime and blood — to pander to the lusts and desires of the robbers of God and his poor — to consign over to the 'tender mercies' [8] of cruel task-masters, multitudes of guiltless men, women and children — and to denounce as 'an unlawful and dangerous association,' [9] a society whose only object is to bring this nation to repentance, through the truth as it is in Jesus! You have made a speech in public, (in your opinion, 'probably for the last time,') to prove the *innocence* of the people of the free States, because they have agreed to acquiesce in 'the claim of the South to consider their slaves [the rational, accountable creatures of God] as CYPHERS or NONENTITIES' — 'to seize and restore runaway slaves' — to allow the master to 'exercise all the political rights *of the slave,* and that he should be NOTHING' — and because on framing the Federal Constitution, the whole nation was licensed to pursue, for twenty years longer, the foreign slave-trade, which even *you* are compelled to designate as 'the abominable traffic!' 'Such,' you declare, 'is the bargain which we, THE PEOPLE OF THE UNITED STATES, have made with each other' — 'with our eyes open' — 'with a full knowledge of all the circumstances of the case, of all the inducements to make it, of all the objections that could be made against it!! ' — And then you have the infatuation or temerity to ask, 'In what age of the world, and among what people and States, was a compact ever made more *solemn* and SACRED?!!' Nay, you even dare to affirm, that 'every one of the people is bound to adhere to it!' for 'it speaks to every man's *understanding,* and ☞ *binds every man's conscience,* by all that is sacred in good faith, or sound in *good policy!!'* Really, Sir, in giving utterance to these profligate and atheistical sentiments, you must first have persuaded yourself that our fathers were the legitimate children of 'that man of sin, who opposeth and exalteth himself above all that is called God, or that is worshiped; so that he, as God, sitteth in the temple of God, *shewing himself that he is God.'* [10] For you talk as if, like the petty tyrant against whose authority they themselves rebelled, *'they could do no wrong,'* [11] and as if villany ceases to be villany when perpetrated by those who, having emancipated themselves from the *cords* of political injustice imposed upon them by the mother country, conspire to fasten *fetters of iron* upon the limbs of a large portion of their own countrymen, because of the complexion which the Almighty has been pleased to bestow upon them!

Sir, do you wish to put it within the power of impartial truth, after your death, to place upon your tomb-stone this awful inscription? If not, humble yourself before God, confess your sin, and lift up your voice in behalf of the perishing slave, as loudly as you have spoken in defence of his lordly master!

Here lies the body of

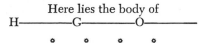

* * * *

Reader, weep at human inconsistency and frailty!
The last public act of his life,
A life conspicuous for many honorable traits,
Was an earnest defence of
THE RIGHTS OF TYRANTS AND SLAVE-MONGERS
To hold in bondage, as their property,
The bodies and souls of millions of his own countrymen!
This was made in
'THE OLD CRADLE OF LIBERTY,'
In the year of our Lord, 1835, and the fifty-ninth of the
Declaration of American Independence!
Pause, terrible Truth!
He has gone to the judgment seat of Christ!
'Inasmuch as ye did it not unto one of *the least* of these,
my brethren, ye did it not to me.' [12]

But, Sir, in justification of your conduct, you resort with pious alacrity to the Bible! The clergy make, proverbially, a wretched figure as politicians. But the climax of the ridiculous is attained only by politicians who enact the part of theologians! Here is a specimen of your scriptural knowledge — opposite to which I place a *very few* of the vast multitude of passages which may be adduced from holy writ in express 'prohibition of slavery.'

HARRISON GRAY OTIS,   *versus*   JEHOVAH OF HOSTS.

'Without pretensions to knowledge derived from biblical search, I cannot find in the Christian Scriptures *any prohibition of slavery*, and am warranted by the opinions of much better judges that *none such can be found*. And the probable cause for this silence is assigned by one eminent divine and denouncer of slavery, namely, that 'Christianity abstained from intermeddling with the civil institutions of any nation,' and that the 'discharging slaves from all obligation to obey their masters, which is the consequence of pronouncing slavery to be unlawful,' 'would have no better effect than to let loose one half of mankind upon the other.' The Saviour of the world gave no instructions to the twelve

He that stealeth a man, and selleth him, or if he be found in his hand, he shall surely be put to death. Exodus xxi. 16.

Ye shall not oppress one another. Lev. xxv. 14

The Lord will judge the fatherless and the oppressed, that the men of the earth may no more oppress. Ps. x. 18.

He shall break in pieces the oppressor. Ps. xxii. 4.

Envy thou not the oppressor, and choose none of his ways. Proverbs iii. 31.

Loose the bands of wickedness, undo the heavy burdens, let the oppressed go free, and break every yoke. Isaiah lviii. 6.

For the oppression of the poor,

or the seventy to interfere in the civil polity of States. His religion was intended for the heart of the individual. The command was to go and teach all nations — all nations that would receive them. But when not received, 'to shake off the dust of their feet.' Yet it cannot be imagined that he could regard the condition of slavery with complacency, though it prevailed among all civilized nations. He foresaw that the blessings of a divine morality and reformation of bad customs would advance in due time. But *he was not an immediatist*, and neither insisted or intended that 'every knee should bow and every tongue confess' [13] before the appointed time [! !] Why will the reverend abolitionists be wiser and more philanthropic than Christ and the Apostles!'

for the sighing of the needy, now will I arise, saith the Lord; I will set him in safety from him that puffeth at him. Ps. xii. 5.

Trust not in oppression, and become not vain in robbery. Ps. lxii. 10.

Seek judgment, relieve the oppressed, judge the fatherless, plead for the widow. Isaiah i. 17.

This is the city to be visited; she is wholly oppression in the midst of her. — Jeremiah vi. 6.

In thy skirts is found the blood of the souls of the poor innocents. ii. 34.

Thus saith the Lord, execute judgment in the morning, and deliver him that is spoiled out of the hand of the oppressor, lest my fury go out like fire, and burn that none can quench it, because of the evil of your doings. xxi. 12.

I will punish all that oppress them. xxx. 20.

I will come near to you to judgment; and I will be a swift witness against those that oppress the hireling in his wages, the widow, and the fatherless, and that turn aside the stranger from his right, and fear not me, saith the Lord of Hosts. Malachi iii. 5.

And the nation to whom they shall be in bondage will I judge, said God. Acts vii. 7.

Behold, the hire of the laborers which have reaped down your fields, which is of you kept back by fraud, crieth; and the cries of them which have reaped, are entered into the ears of the Lord of Sabaoth. James v. 4.

He that leadeth into captivity shall go into captivity. Rev. xiii. 10.

To bolster you up, you obtain the help of 'one eminent divine and *denouncer* of slavery,' (who he is you do not tell us,) who agrees with you exactly in opinion, that the Christian Scriptures do not prohibit slavery, although *he* denounces it in despite of these Scriptures! It is seldom that a politician wishes to be brought in close juxta-position with a clergyman, except to palliate political crime, and then indeed

they are hail-fellows! Your pious reference reminds me of another
that was made, for a similar purpose, by a Mr. Stanley, in the British
Parliament more than forty years ago, in opposition to the call of Mr.
Wilberforce, for the abolition of the slave-trade.[14] He said:

'A cry had been sounded forth, and from one end of the kingdom to the
other; *as if there had never been a slave from Adam to the present time.* But
it appeared to him to have been *the intention of Providence, from the very
beginning, that one set of men should be slaves to another.* This *truth* was
as old as it was universal. It was recognised in every history, under every
government, and in every religion. Nor did *the Christian religion itself,*
☞ if the comments of Dr. Halifax, Bishop of Gloucester, *on a passage in
St. Paul's epistle to the Corinthians,* were true, show more repugnance to
slavery *than any other!*' [15]

The above, Sir, is a mirror, in which you may contemplate your
features, and find them reflected perfectly.

Here I pause upon this point, that I may recur once more to the deep
degradation into which we are plunged, as a community, by our connexion with a merciless system. Sir, the fetters of slavery press heavily
upon the limbs of the descendants of the pilgrims. History has facts to
record upon its pages, respecting the conduct of Bostonians, that will
mantle the cheeks of posterity with indignation and shame. Among
them, the following will acquire perpetual conspicuity. Three months
ago, the New England Anti-Slavery Convention held its second annual
meeting in Boston.[16] It was composed of about three hundred members, representing a large share of the talent, respectability, patriotism
and piety of New England — among them, ministers of the various religious denominations — the most ardent friends of moral reform, of
temperance, of peace — and indisputably as quiet and orderly a body
of men as exist in the land, whose pole-star is principle, whose object is
liberty *with* righteousness, and whose refuge is Christ. It was soon
ascertained that not a meeting-house, or hall of any magnitude, could
be procured for the Convention, either as a favor or for money. In this
extremity a respectable petition was sent to the Mayor and Board of
Aldermen, containing one hundred and twenty names of legal voters,
as respectable and worthy as were ever presented to that Board, requesting the use of Faneuil Hall for that humane body. It was reasonably supposed, that of all places in which to plead for enslaved humanity, the old Cradle of Liberty would be most appropriate, and the
last to be closed against the advocates of universal freedom. But, as
you are aware, Sir, the petition was unanimously rejected! and the disgraceful fact was proclaimed to the world, with the highest exultation,
in the Boston and New York papers. It was styled 'an incendiary
request' — it was declared that to occupy the hall for this benevolent
purpose, 'would pollute it,' that 'such a contamination' would take from

it 'half the venerated sacredness of the place,' and that the meeting would only be 'a display of riotings and excess!!' The excellent, sedate, and devout men who came together in convention, were branded as 'the wretched plotters of mischief' — 'a disorganizing faction' — 'the fanatical banditti' — 'traitors' — 'ranters' — 'the basest organized band that had set itself seriously at work to dissolve the workmanship of our patriot fathers' — and as 'mad fanatics, who, if unchecked, will trample our freedom in the dust!!' The refusal of the Board of Aldermen was declared to be 'well and *bravely* done!' for 'the old temple of liberty must not be DESECRATED by admitting within its walls' those who actually believe that 'all men are created equal,' and that the oppression of our colored countrymen is a stain upon our national escutcheon!

Faneuil Hall may be used freely for all public convivialities — for toast-drinking to ebriety — for the delivery of political libels and squibs — for the maintenance of slavery and the security of domestic tyrants — and it is not desecrated; but to use it in the cause of oppressed millions of our own countrymen, in a series of strictly religious services, would contaminate it forever, and make the Cradle of Liberty become its coffin! — The SPIRIT OF SEVENTY-SIX shall yet rise from its ashes, and blot out that calumny! *The cause of the bleeding slaves shall yet be pleaded in Faneuil Hall*, in tones as thrilling, in language as stirring, in eloquence as irresistible as were ever heard within its walls! Even our WEBSTER may yet appear in it, as the voluntary, unpaid, undaunted advocate of manacled Americans; and his most numerous, most worthy, and most deeply wronged clients that he has ever had, will appear, and his best speech be made, on that occasion!

No! we have not yet been wholly subdued — we are not altogether servile. The FREE SPIRIT OF OUR FATHERS still walks unshackled, in pristine boldness and majesty, among us. Southern whips cannot conquer it — northern threats cannot terrify it. We must, we will speak out, as often, as plainly, as loudly, as we choose; and they who think to gag us, will find it an easier task to bind the ocean with a straw, or heave the Alleghany mountains into the sea. Our thoughts — opinions — voices — pens — the press — all *shall* be free as the air and the light of heaven; for, trusting in the God of freedom, we are resolved, that come what may — morally speaking —

> 'Living, we *will* be victorious,
> Or, dying, our deaths shall be glorious!' [17]

In the language of the great patriot O'CONNELL, we will turn toward the south, and each indignantly reply to its injunction to be silent —

'Why, I tell the American slave-owner that he SHALL NOT HAVE SILENCE! — for humble as I am, and feeble as my voice may be, yet deafening the sound of the westerly wave, and riding against the blast as thunder goes, it shall reach the rivers, the lakes, and the glens of America, telling the black man that the time for his emancipation has come, and the oppressor that the period of his injustice is about to terminate.' [18]

It is no time now to be silent — O, no!

> 'Where'er a wind is rushing,
> Where'er a stream is gushing,
> The swelling sounds are heard
> Of man to freeman calling,
> Of broken fetters falling,
> And, like the carol of a cageless bird,
> The bursting shout of Freedom's rallying word!' [19]

Sir, we believe that our cause is of God, and until he is dethroned, or until our accountability to him ceases, we never shall abandon it. Its light is as the morning sun. It rises sublimely to the zenith of heaven.

All weapons have failed to injure or retard it. Whether silence or contempt, whether slander or ridicule, whether threats or rewards, whether discussions or mobs, whether gags or padlocks, whether ecclesiastical anathemas or biblical sophisms, have been resorted to, they have only put up what they attempted to put down. God and his promises are with us — the wrongs and woes, the blessings and prayers, of the slaves are with us — the aspirations and gratitude of the free people of color are with us — the prayers of ministers and churches are beginning to be with us — the best consciences and intellects in our academical and theological institutions are enlisting with us — the most pious and devoted members of all denominations are with us — the truest partiots of all parties are with us — a vast multitude of anti-slavery associations are with us — the spirits of the departed dead of WILBERFORCE and SHARPE,[20] together with the wise philanthropists of Europe, are with us — Justice, Mercy, Righteousness, and impartial Love, are with us! And what else? The bloodless, peaceful and glorious consequences of the emancipation of eight hundred thousand slaves in the British dependencies are with us! What more do we want — what more can we have? Sir, we are resolved to consecrate ourselves anew to the work of man's redemption, having none but JEHOVAH for our strength and shield, our rock and refuge. No obstacles shall be too high for our faith to surmount — no dangers too formidable for our courage to encounter — no human authority too venerable for our reason and conscience to dispute. *Victory is as sure as that God reigns.* Man was not made to be a slave. True, the strife of freedom is just begun, but it will be short, and very glorious. We must toil, and sacrifice, and pray and venture much a little longer, as truly 'remembering those who are in bonds as bound with them.' [21] And when the conflict is over — when the little ones of Christ shall be chained and tasked no more — when woman shall be debased and flogged no more — when the infant shall be torn from the arms of its frantic mother no more — when the Bible, THE BIBLE, shall be banished no more; — and when the consummation of our hopes, and the desire of our eyes, shall come (as come it must) in the entire and everlasting emancipation, not only of all the slaves in our own land, but wherever a human being pines in bondage — when the thunders of a universal jubilee shall break upon our ears, and the acclamations of nations shall be like the noise of many waters — then will we, with genuine humility of soul, and true sincerity of speech, exclaim — 'Not unto us — not unto us — but unto thy name, O Lord, be all the glory, both now and forever!' [22]

I remain, Sir, the enemy of oppression, and your friend and well-wisher,

WM. LLOYD GARRISON.

Printed: *The Liberator*, September 5, 1835; printed partly in *Life*, I, 511–513.

1. Garrison printed Otis' speech in the same issue as his own letter.
2. The quotations are from I Corinthians 1:20, 27–29.
3. Faneuil Hall in Boston.
4. Garrison alludes to Matthew 5:11.
5. See letter 17 to the Boston *Courier*, July 12, 1827.
6. Psalms 90:10.
7. Originally a Chinese proverb, possibly here an adaptation of Psalms 90:12.
8. Luke 1:78.
9. This and the following quotations, from Otis' speech.
10. Garrison telescopes II Thessalonians 2:3–4.
11. Garrison evidently alludes to the British maxim, expressed by John Selden, Sir William Blackstone, and others, "The king can do no wrong."
12. Matthew 25:45.
13. Garrison telescopes Philippians 2:10 and 11.
14. John Stanley (1740–1799) was a member of a family prominent for many years in English political life. Like other Stanleys he had large holdings in the West Indies, and he was colonial agent for Nevis. The speech to which Garrison refers was delivered April 19, 1791. (See the description of it in *Cobbett's Parliamentary History of England*, London, 1806–1820, XXIX, column 315. The speech was also reported in the *Times*, April 20.) But, unfortunately, search through James Hansard, *Catalogue of Parliamentary Debates and Breviate of their Contents* (London, 1836) has not revealed the passage Garrison quotes.
15. Samuel Hallifax (1733–1790), who was Bishop of Gloucester and St. Asaph, was a scholar of considerable range, including the classics, Arabic, and mathematics among his specialities. After a distinguished career at Cambridge University, he became chaplain in ordinary to the king.
16. May 25.
17. Not identified.
18. Garrison quotes from O'Connell's speech at the anticolonization meeting at Exeter Hall in London, July 13, 1833; extracts from this speech, including the passage in question, are printed in *The Liberator*, September 7, 1849.
19. Not identified.
20. The Reverend James Sharpe, agent of the Wilberforce Settlement, Upper Canada.
21. Hebrews 13:3.
22. Garrison apparently runs together Psalms 115:1 and a liturgical ending.

2 0 9

TO PELEG SPRAGUE

[September 5, 1835.]

Sir —

Whatever respect I have cherished, hitherto, for your character as a patriot and a statesman, has fled on perusing your late speech in Faneuil Hall. In my opinion, there is not more of crime, or of moral turpitude, in firing a whole city, — in committing highway robbery or murder, — than in the delivery of such a speech, in such a place, on such an occasion, and under such circumstances. Nay, human barbarity towards your fellow creatures, or impiety towards heaven, can go no further. As far as one man *can* be answerable for all the horrors and blasphemies of American slavery, I believe you will be held responsible at the tribunal of the judgment day. I weep, I shudder, at your degradation. There seems to be no flesh in your heart. You are a *man* — and yet the eulogist of those monsters who are trampling your brother in the dust! You are a HUSBAND — a PARENT — and yet join in upholding a traffic and a system which ruthlessly sunder the holiest ties of life! You are an AMERICAN — and yet can look complacently, nay approvingly, upon the brutal enslavement of more than one-sixth portion of YOUR OWN COUNTRYMEN! — I was about to add, *You are a Christian* — but I dare not thus libel Christianity. 'He that saith he is in the light, and hateth his brother, is in darkness even until now.' 'If a man say, I love God, and hateth his brother, he is a liar. For he that loveth not his brother whom he hath seen, how can he love God whom he hath not seen?' 'Whosoever hateth his brother, is a murderer; and ye know that no murderer hath eternal life abiding in him.' [1] And what stronger evidence of hatred can be given, than is manifested in your defence of the heaven-usurped authority of American tyrants, — the sternest that have ever scourged our race, — 'the basest of the base, the most execrable of the exercrable'? [2] Such intelligent co-operation — such elaborate cruelty — such shameless abandonment of principle — are enough to chill the warm blood of humanity. May God grant you speedy repentance unto eternal life! I tell you, Sir, that you have dishonored your name, and tarnished your character, in the eyes of all genuine friends of human liberty. You have stopped your ears against the voice of God; you have steeled your heart to the cries of the poor and needy; you have dared to stand up even in THE OLD CRADLE OF LIBERTY,[3] and proffer the right hand of fellowship to traffickers in slaves and the souls of men; you have sought to base the pillars of your popularity upon the necks of down-trodden millions; and you have uttered sentiments which elicit thunders of applause from all that is loathsome in impurity, all that is hateful in revenge, all that is base in extortion, and all that is dastardly in *oppression*. Where are you, Sir? In amicable companionship and popular repute with thieves and adulterers; with slaveholders, slave dealers, and slave destroyers; with those who call the beings whom God created but a little lower than the angels, *things* and *chattels*; with the proscribers of the great chart of eternal life; with the rancorous enemies of the friends of universal emancipation; with the disturbers of the public peace; with the robbers of the public mail; with ruffians who insult, pollute and lacerate helpless women; and with conspirators against the lives and liberties of New-England citizens. *These facts are undeniable.* Talk not of more honorable associates, for no men deserve that epithet who throw the weight of their influence into the scale of oppression. Peradventure, you will ask, in due time, for the suffrages of Bostonians. Sir, we will remember you at the polls!

It was the desire of righteous Job, 'Oh that mine adversary had written a book!' [4] It is the earnest supplication of abolitionists, *Oh that our enemies would make speeches, and publish them in the newspapers!* Why, Sir, the Faneuil Hall meeting, though intended to strengthen the feeble hands and comfort the desponding hearts of southern taskmasters, will in the sequel prove of more benefit to our cause, than forty anti-slavery lectures and twice that number of tracts, prodigious as is their moral effect. It has already multiplied our converts, animated our zeal, and emboldened our spirit. Thus does the God of the oppressed sustain his veracity: 'He maketh the wrath of man to praise him, and the remainder of wrath he will restrain.' [5]

I mean to make your harangue, and the speeches of your associates, of signal use in the anti-slavery struggle. They are crowded with evidence of our national guilt, and clearly prove every allegation that has fallen from the lips of abolitionists — as shall be shown in the progress of this review. Upon your authority, henceforth, will I arraign the people of the free States — of New-England — of Massachusetts — as the abettors, upholders and guardians of as tyrannous a system as the sun has looked down upon since his creation. Upon your authority I will prove, that there is not a drop of blood extracted from the bodies, nor a tear which falls from the eyes, nor a groan which bursts from the bosoms of the heart-broken slaves, for which the north is not directly responsible. Sir, the more searchingly I investigate this great subject, the stronger is my conviction that hitherto I have erred — nay, that I have been alike unwise and partial, in declaiming so much against southern, and so little against northern criminality. I am not sure — especially since reading the speeches above alluded to — that, in the sight of God, (and it is of very little consequence how we stand in the sight of men,) there is not more guilt attaching to the people of the free States from the continuance of slavery, than to those of the slave States. At least, I am ready to affirm, *upon your authority*, that New-England is as really a slaveholding section of this republic as Georgia or South Carolina! If such evidence were wanted to sustain this tremendous accusation, I might stop to dilate upon the disgraceful fact, that the foundation of the slave system was laid by MASSACHUSETTS and Virginia — thus originated all the calamities, crimes and horrors which have attended it. I might show how, for thirty-two years after the Declaration of Independence was given to the world, New-England capital, New-England ships, and New-England men, were actively engaged in the foreign slave trade — engaged even up to the last moment that that traffic was legalized by Congress! I might resort to statistics to show how many villages were fired in Africa by New-England torches — how many natives were murdered by New-England swords and muskets — how many victims were kidnapped by New-England rapacity and force — how many were suffocated in the holes of New-England ships on the Middle Passage, and thrown to the sharks — how many perished before they became acclimated, how many were plundered and debased all their days, upon New-England territory — and how many were sent to the southern markets in New-England vessels. They who participated in these damning crimes have gone to the judgment seat of Christ, accompanied by their victims as swift witnesses against them. The present generation are not responsible for the acts of their fathers. It is with present, not past guilt, it is with actual, not past transgression, that we have to do in the present controversy. My accusation — *upon your authority, Sir* — is made to-day, is to be applied to-day, and refers to transgressors living to-day, in Boston as well as in New-Orleans.

Yet — marvellous enough, Mr. Sprague — you affect to think that abolitionists are cravens, laboring in the wrong section of the Union. You affirm of them and their doctrine, that 'we must do right, regardless of consequences' —

'They insist that it is right that they should urge their doctrines for the conviction of the South. Ask them why they do not go and preach them there, where they most desire to make converts? They reply, Why! we should be in danger of our lives! Then they begin to think of consequences. So that the practical result of that proposition, which sounds so well in the abstract, is, that they are to go on regardless of consequences to *others*, but not without a due regard to *themselves.*' [6]

Sir, there may be wit, but there is little truth, in the above extract. To do right, is always to regard consequences, both to ourselves and to others. Since you are pleased to banter us for prosecuting our labors at the north, I will take for my text the interrogation that is so constantly, either by ignorance or impudence, propounded to us. It is this:

'Why don't you go to the South?'

I proudly answer — Not because we are afraid to go there. Not because we are not prepared for danger, persecution, outrage and death. Not because the dungeon or the halter, the rack or the stake, appals us. Yet the question is sneeringly put, and sometimes with murder evidently in the heart, as if we were deficient in fortitude and courage, and all our seeming boldness. 'O, forsooth! it is very safe and convenient for Mr. Garrison to denounce the holders of slaves a thousand miles off, in Boston. A great deal of heroism is required to do this! But he is very careful to keep out of the slave States. Why don't he go to the South? Let him go there and denounce slavery, and we will then believe that he is sincere.' This is the language which is constantly uttered — by men, too, permit me to say, who have never peculiarly signalized themselves in any hazardous enterprise, whether moral or physical. I am vain enough to believe that those who bring this charge of cowardice against me, do not doubt my readiness to go wherever duty requires. Will they give me no credit for having published an anti-slavery publication in Maryland, as long as it could be sustained by a meagre patronage? — a publication in which my denunciations of slavery and slaveholders were as severe as any to be found in the Liberator. Did my spirit quail under my imprisonment in a southern cell, for denouncing the domestic slave trade? And is it indeed true, that I am hazarding neither my safety nor my life, in my advocacy of freedom in Boston? Has no endurance, no unusual courage, been required to oppose all classes of society, and to sustain the odium, derision and hatred of a slaveholding nation? Is it nothing to have large rewards offered by a southern legislature, and by private combinations, for my seizure and destruction? Sir, slaveholders and their apologists may call me a fanatic — they may call me a madman, or an incendiary, or an agitator, and believe me to be such; but to call me a coward — that is an epithet which they have too much good sense to believe is applicable to me, although they have so small a modicum of conscience as to resort to it. The southern oppressors themselves regard me in any other light than that of a craven: all the trembling, and shrinking, and alarm, is felt and manifested on their part — not on mine. I may be rash — I may be obstinate — but I fear no man, or body of men. In this vindication of myself, I am simply vindicating every other abolitionist who is publicly engaged in this cause.

'Why don't you go to the South?'

Why, Sir, when we denounce the tyranny exercised over the mis-

erable Poles, do we not go into the dominions of the Russian autocrat, and beard him to his face? Why not go to Constantinople, and
protest against the oppression of the Greeks? Why assail the despotic
governments of Europe here in the United States? — Why, then,
should we go into the slaveholding States, to assail their towering
wickedness, at a time when we are sure that we should be gagged,
or imprisoned, or put to death, if we went thither? Why rashly throw
ourselves into the ocean, or commit ourselves to the flames, or cast
ourselves into the jaws of the lion? Understand me, Sir. I do not mean
to say, that even the *certainty* of destruction is in itself, a valid reason for our refusing to go to the South, — for we are bound to take
up any cross, or incur any peril, in the discharge of our duty to God
and our suffering brother. Prove to me that it is imperatively my
duty, in view of all the circumstances of the case, to locate myself
among slaveholders, and I will not hesitate to do so, even (to borrow
the strong language of Martin Luther) though every tile upon their
houses were a devil.[7] Moral courage — duty — self-consecration — all
have their proper limits. When He who knew no fear — the immaculate Redeemer — saw that his enemies intended to cast him down
from the brow of a hill, he prudently withdrew from their midst.
When he sent forth his apostles, he said unto them, 'When they persecute you in one city, flee ye into another.'[8] Was there any cowardice in this conduct, or in this advice?

'*Why don't you go to the South?*'

If we *should* go there, and fall — as fall we certainly should —
martyrs to our zeal, our enemies would still call us, what we then
should deserve to be called, *fanatics* and *madmen*. Pointing at our
mangled bodies, they would commence their derisions afresh. 'Poor
fools!' they would exclaim — 'insane enthusiasts! thus to rush into the
cage of the tiger, with the certain knowledge that he would tear
them in pieces!' And this, Sir, would be the eulogy which they would
pronounce over us!

'*Why don't you go to the South?*'

Because it is essential that the beam should first be cast out of
the eyes of the people of the free States, before they attempt to cast
out the mote in the eyes of the people of the slave States. Because
they who denounce fraud, and cruelty, and oppression, should first
become honest, and merciful, and free, themselves. 'Thou that sayest, a man should not steal — dost thou steal?' Thou that preachest,
a man should not be a slaveholder — art thou a slaveholder? 'Physician, heal thyself!'[9]

'*Why don't you go to the South?*'

Have I answered the question satisfactorily? If not, Sir, you will help me to additional reasons for our staying here at the North, in my answer to another question which is iterated on all occasions — viz.

'What have *we* to do with Southern slavery?'

This question is put, sometimes with reference to legislation — at others, it refers to moral obligations. I answer, then, that WE, THE PEOPLE OF THE UNITED STATES, have legislated on the subject of slavery, and we have a right to legislate upon it, within certain limits. As to our moral obligation, it belongs to our nature, and is a part of our accountability, of which neither time nor distance, neither climate nor location, neither republican nor monarchical government, can divest us. Let there be but one slave on the face of the globe — let him stand on one extremity of the globe, and place me on the other — let every people, and tribe, and clime, and nation, stand as barriers between him and myself: still, I am bound to sympathize with him — to pray, and toil, and plead for his deliverance — to make known his wrongs, and vindicate his rights. It may not be in my power, it may not be my duty, directly to emancipate him; for the power rests in the hands of the tyrant who keeps him in chains, and it is his duty to break them asunder. But it matters not, except to demand an increase of zeal and activity, if every interposing tribe or nation, if the whole world is to be changed, before that solitary slave can go free. Then I will begin with him who stands next by my side, and with my associates, and with my country; and if the impulse must be sent by proxy, if every man, woman and child must be abolitionised by detail, before the captive can be disenthralled, I am nevertheless bound to commence the work, if no others will, and to co-operate with them if they have begun it. Why? Because he is my neighbor, though occupying the remotest point of the earth; and I am charged by the Lamb of God, the judge of quick and dead, to love my neighbor as myself. Because he is my brother, for whom Christ died; and if Christ estimated him so highly as to die for him, then, surely, he is an object worthy of my sympathy and regard. Because by his enslavement, man is no longer recognised as *man*, but as a *brute*, and *our whole species is degraded*. Because by it the laws of nature and of spirit are violated, the moral government of the universe is rebelled against, and God is insulted and dethroned, by the usurpation of his power and authority. Because by it an example is set, which, if passively submitted to, *may lead to the enslavement of others* — of a community — of a people — of myself. *Enslave but a single human being, and the liberty of the world is put in peril.* Nay, all the slavery that exists — all the tyranny of past ages — originated from a single act of oppression, committed upon some helpless and degraded being. Hence it is, that whether I contemplate slavery singly or in the aggregate, my soul kindles within me — the entire man is moved with indignation and abhorrence — I cannot pause, I cannot slumber — I am ready for attack, and will admit of no truce, and of no compromise. The war is a war of extermination; and I will perish before an inch shall be surrendered, seeing that the liberties of mankind, the happiness and harmony of the universe, and the authority and majesty of Almighty God, are involved in the issue. Hence it is, that I adopt the language of Fisher Ames:

'This, sirs, is a cause, that would be dishonored and betrayed, if I contented myself with appealing only to the understanding. It is too cold, and its processes are too slow for the occasion. I desire to thank God, that, since he has given me an intellect so fallible, he has impressed upon me an instinct that is sure. On a question of *shame and honor*, reasoning is sometimes useless, and worse. I feel the decision in my pulse: if it throws no light upon the brain, it kindles a fire at the heart.' [10]

If, Sir, I am again asked, 'What have *we* to do with slavery?' I answer by a retort — 'What have we to do with heathenism?' And yet —

'From Greenland's icy mountains,
To India's coral strand' — [11]

from frozen Labrador to the sunny plains of Palestine — from the rivers to the ends of the earth — from the rising of the sun to its going down — our missionary line is extended and we are continually sending out fresh troops to invade the dominions, and destroy the supremacy of the Man of Sin, and of the false Prophet — and Juggernaut is tottering to his fall; *we are disregarding institutions and laws, customs and ceremonies, governments and rulers, prohibitions and penalties;* we are setting 'a man at variance against his father, and the daughter against her mother, and the daughter-in-law against her mother-in-law;' [12] and we make a man's foes to be they of his own household; we are troubling the peace of Africa, of Asia, of the isles of the sea, and are mightily energizing to turn the world upside down — *for Christ's sake* — that He may come whose right it is to reign.

What have we to do with intemperance in England and France? And yet, Sir, we sent out to those countries the Apostle of Temperance, to scatter light, to reveal iniquity, to prick the consciences of men, to preach of righteousness, temperance, and a judgment to come — and to sow the seeds of holy strife between the distillers, the importers, the rum-sellers and the rum-drinkers, on the one hand, in those countries, and the friends of sobriety, mercy and good-will, on the other. All Europe is now warmly engaged in the conflict, and the issue must be glorious.

What have *we* to do with southern slavery? What has *England* to do with it? And yet, a few years since, the American Colonization Society (of which, Mr. Sprague, you are a champion,) sent out an agent to that country, to procure the charities of her philanthropists, in order to undermine and abolish American slavery — this being the great object of the Society, as stated to the British public by that Agent. Now, if *Old* England may meddle with this 'delicate' subject, surely *New*-England may venture to do so likewise. If that which is remote, is or ought to be interested in the abolition of American slavery, how much more that which is near!

I rejoice — join with me in this exultation, friends of freedom! friends of humanity! — I rejoice that old England did not meanly wrap herself up in the garb of indifference or selfishness, but acted in a manner worthy of her Christian renown. I am glad, and grateful, that she promptly responded to the call of the Agent of the American Colonization Society, *for assistance to put down American slavery;* and I honor her wisdom and discernment *in refusing to trust that Agent and his Society,* and in sending out to our aid *one whom she could trust* — one who was signally instrumental in bringing herself to repentance — one who has the confidence, and love, and admiration of her wisest and greatest and best of men and philanthropists — the self-sacrificing, the indefatigable, the courageous, the eloquent, the patriotic, the fearless THOMPSON! Sir, I shall come, in due course, to your scurrilous and ferocious attack upon the motives and designs of this devoted friend of God and man — an attack which is, upon the face of it, as malignant as the spirit of murder. GEORGE THOMPSON is the steadfast and sincere friend of this country, and will hereafter be ranked among her greatest benefactors. In respectability, Sir, he is your equal; and in eloquence and intellectual strength, (and I extol your abilities,) incomparably your superior.

Sir, what have we — what has Congress — to do with the oppression of the Greeks and Poles? And yet, as a people, how have we prayed for their deliverance! how warmly have we denounced Russia and Turkey! how cheerfully have we taxed ourselves to send food and raiment, men and money, banners and arms, in aid of the brave and struggling champions of liberty! how have we lifted up our voices to cheer them onward in the strife of blood! how have we taken them to our arms, when they were crushed and scattered abroad, and given them an asylum, and bound up their wounds, and comforted their souls! what speeches in their behalf have been made upon the floor of Congress! Now, Sir, have we so much to do with foreign, and nothing to do with domestic oppression? an oppression far more dreadful than that which the Greek or Pole has ever suffered!

What had the south to do with the *'three days'* in Paris — the

punishment of tyranny in France? [13] And yet, in honor of that san-
guinary event, the *patriotic* slaveholders of Baltimore, and Richmond,
and Charleston, got up bonfires, illuminated their dwellings, rung
the bells, fired cannon, formed processions, made orations, devoured
dinners, and ingurgitated toasts, even to ebriety!

What had Lafayette to do with the quarrel about liberty between
us and the mother country? Shall we apply to him the infamous
epithets which you have cast upon our *moral* Lafayette? Shall we
call him 'a foreign emissary,' 'a professed agitator,' and talk of his
'audacious interference'? Should he have been sent back to 'prostrate
the triple power of the Priesthood, the Aristocracy, and the Throne'?
Sir, will you answer these questions?

Here I might rest the argument. But, in a controversy like this, it
is well to make 'assurance doubly sure.' [14] In my next letter, we will
together descend to particulars, to show the guilty relations of the
north with slavery.

I remain, Sir, your faithful reviewer,

WM. LLOYD GARRISON.

Printed: *The Liberator*, September 5, 1835; printed partly in *Life*, I, 505–510.
Garrison published a rewritten and considerably expanded version of this letter in
Selections from the Writings and Speeches of William Lloyd Garrison (Boston,
1852), pp. 143–156.

1. As is frequently Garrison's practice when he wants to impress the recipient
with his erudition, he compiles a pastiche of quotations from the Bible; in this
instance I John 2:9, 4:20, 3:15.
2. Unidentified.
3. Faneuil Hall.
4. Job 32:35.
5. Psalms 76:10 (adapted).
6. Garrison printed Sprague's speech in the "Refuge of Oppression," *The
Liberator*, September 5, 1835.
7. Garrison alludes to the statement of the leader of the German Reformation
as he approached Worms on April 16, 1521.
8. Matthew 10:23.
9. Garrison adapts Romans 2:21 and Luke 4:23.
10. Garrison quotes accurately, adding his own italics, from Fisher Ames's
speech delivered in the House of Representatives on April 28, 1796 (Seth Ames,
ed., *Works of Fisher Ames with a Selection from his Speeches and Correspondence*,
Boston, 1854, II, 56).
11. Garrison quotes, with the change of a word, from a hymn written by Regi-
nald Heber in 1819, entitled "Before a Collection Made for the Society for the
Propagation of the Gospel."
12. Garrison adapts freely Micah 7:6.
13. Garrison refers to July 27–29, 1830, the days during which the revolution
in France culminated in the abdication of Charles X.
14. Shakespeare, *Macbeth*, IV, i, 83.

210

TO PELEG SPRAGUE

[September 12, 1835.]

Sir —

The language of the letter which I addressed to you, in the last Liberator, was sharp and condemnatory. I used it, not to irritate or offend you, but because I read, on good authority, that 'open rebuke is better than secret love,' and that 'faithful are the wounds of a friend.'[1] I stated that on the question of slavery, you were in very bad company, as well as connected with more honorable associates. In proof of this assertion, read the following paragraph which has just met my eye in the Richmond Whig, of August 27:

'*The Boston Meeting.* — We refer the reader with great pleasure to the proceedings at Boston, and to the brief sketches of the eloquent remarks of Messrs. Fletcher and Sprague.[2] The allusion of the latter distinguished gentleman to the fields of Concord and Lexington — his apostrophe to the likeness of Washington, and reminding his auditors of the time when the British foe was expelled from Boston by slaveholders, commanded by a slaveholder — presented a number of patriotic images sufficient we think to have softened the heart of Garrison himself towards the 'robbers and men stealers.''

Can you feel flattered by a panegyric from such a source? Is not the author of it distinguished alike for ferocity of spirit and moral lunacy, as it regards southern slavery? Does he not maintain, that the system is just, and worthy of perpetuity? that every postmaster ought to commit perjury, and plunder the mail of abolition documents? that it is proper to offer rewards, and form associations, for the abduction of northern abolitionists? that the north ought to destroy the liberty of speech and of the press, and shed innocent blood, in order to glut the appetite of the monster Slavery? that if the discussion of this subject is not prevented by force, there must be a dissolution of the Union? Of his audacity and wickedness, two small specimens shall suffice. He scouts the idea of meetings at the north — your Faneuil Hall meeting — to *rebuke* the advocates of justice — thus:

'What good will it do to rebuke them? There must be some *penalty*, some *law* of the States where they live, prohibiting their injuries to the Southern people, and *punishing* them for their infraction. Nothing short of it will cure the mischief or satisfy the South.'

Again:

'The people of the North *must* go to *hanging* these fanatical wretches, if they would not lose the benefit of Southern trade; and they *will* do it.

They know too well which side their bread is buttered on, ever to give up these advantages. Depend upon it, the northern people will never sacrifice their present lucrative trade with the south, *so long as the hanging of a few* THOUSANDS *will prevent it ! ! !*'

Now, Sir, let conscience and reason decide: what must be the character of your speech, to extort a panegyric from a creature so unprincipled, impudent and blood-thirsty as the editor of the Richmond Whig? What stronger evidence do you require of the unsoundness of your sentiments?

The Richmond Enquirer, too, is scarcely behind the Whig in fury and madness. One specimen shall suffice:

'We shall hereafter consider the propagation amongst us of incendiary doctrines, as an actual *levying of war* upon us, and shall govern ourselves accordingly. We do not mean to wait until the danger becomes too formidable for resistance — until the mine is ready for explosion — but will meet the evil at the threshold. The refusal of *the legislative authorities of the North* to act decisively, and to restrain their citizens from *acts of aggression on our peace*, will be considered as an *acquiescence in the outrages of which we complain*, and will be considered the signal for decisive measures of defence. We are sure we speak the almost universal Southern sentiment, when we repeat the remark, that *we can hold no fellowship, either political or social*, with those who let loose upon us incendiaries and cutthroats, or refuse to exert their legal powers in arresting the progress of the evil.'

Your speech commenced with the following concession to the rights of man and the claims of humanity:

'Mr. Sprague regarded slavery *as a great moral and political evil* — he had been early imbued with this sentiment, and all that he had seen and all that he had heard, had strengthened and deepened the conviction. *He deeply deplored its existence*, and from the very core and centre of his heart he prayed that our brethren of the South might see their own way clear, by their own free will, to effect its entire abolition. But it rested with them, and with them only.'

These sentiments, Sir, are precisely in accordance with those cherished by abolitionists, and printed in their 'incendiary' documents. They regard slavery as 'a great moral evil,' i. e. *a sin against God*, and they therefore maintain that, like every other *sin*, it ought to be immediately abandoned. They also regard it as 'a political evil,' and they call upon those whose right it is to vote in the South, to remedy it *immediately* — i. e. as soon as the first constitutional opportunity will allow them to do so. Of course, moral reformation may precede political. All that *they* see and hear, strengthens and deepens *their* conviction. *They* deeply deplore its existence, and *they* earnestly pray that their southern brethren may see their way clear, &c. as it rests

515

with them only. These are the 'incendiary doctrines,' which the Enquirer thinks ought to be restrained by the legislative authorities of
the north; for which the south 'can hold no fellowship, either political
or social,' with us; and the propagation of which will be considered
'as an actual levying of war' upon the south? Why, Sir, does not the
Enquirer offer a reward for your abduction? Oh — because there is
this remarkable difference between you and the abolitionists: You
blow hot and cold with the same breath — they do not. You eat your
own words — they do not. Yours is an *abstract*, theirs is a *practical*
dislike of slavery. You aim to please the oppressor, they to please God.
So abundantly do you atone for your 'seditious' exordium, before you
arrive at the conclusion of your speech, that the Enquirer indulges in
no objurgation, but, on the contrary, expresses its joy in the following
exulting strain — not indeed in reference to your remarks particularly,
but to the present aspect of public sentiment:

'*The North and the South.* — The ball is rolling on; and our Brethren
of the North are coming out, and speaking *trumpet-tongued* against the
Fanatics. We throw aside almost every thing else to give place to the
animated proceedings of the immense meetings in Boston, *Lynn, Bath*, and
Philadelphia. There is an unison in sentiment with the South, which we
hail with indescribable satisfaction. We were satisfied, that the great body
of the North was with us — but we wished it to come forth. And is it not
coming forth, in all the majesty of public opinion? They are coming forth
to undeceive the South about the putative numbers of the Incendiaries —
to give us *the right hand of fellowship* — to assure us of their respect for
the *rights*, and their sympathy with the *feelings*, of the South. It is thus
that the *Union will be preserved*. It is thus that the Chain may be brighted
and strengthened. Go on, Brethren of the North! Give us the full expression of your American and brotherly feelings. Teach the incendiaries
among yourselves, that the Union is not to be sported with, and that *you
will put them down* — and that you may also put down the clamors of those
heedless citizens among ourselves, who say that you are cold to the South —
that you are outnumbered by the Abolitionists — that you will quietly permit them to go on and plot our ruin — and that therefore we had better
dissolve the Union, which has been cemented by our mutual blood, and
which ought to be so dear to the heart of every American.
    What do the citizens of Boston tell us? that 'the numbers and influence
of these people have been greatly exaggerated' — What the people of Philadelphia? that 'the North is sound to the core, on the subject of slavery —
that the number of the Abolitionists is extremely limited' — The citizens of
Bath assure us of the same.'

Sir, are you not ashamed of your cause and your panegyrists?
    It may seem cruel to *disturb the satisfaction* of Mr. Ritchie,[3] by any
remarks upon his inflated article — but as he *disturbs our gravity*,
in boasting of 'the *immense* meetings in Lynn and Bath,' two pleasant
little villages, we may be allowed to retaliate, in good nature. To

balance the FOUR *pro*-slavery meetings which so completely dispel his fears, the abolitionists in various sections of New-England will probably hold, within three months, not less than FOUR HUNDRED *anti*-slavery meetings. But, says the Richmond veteran, 'teach them that you will *put them down.*' How? By argument, or by force? Both have been tried, and both have failed; and as to a resort to penal enactments for curbing the liberty of speech and of the press, in New-England — why, that is out of the question. But here is his consolation — 'the number of the abolitionists is extremely limited.' Why all this uproar, then, to put down nothing? And what guaranty has Mr. Ritchie, that the few will not increase, and ultimately become the many? Even you, Mr. Sprague, venture the assertion, 'that *the agitators here are few,* and that even the whole number of those who have permitted their names to be enrolled in these societies is small.' Perhaps this conviction furnishes the principal reason why you are found in opposition to them; for, to borrow the classical language of your admirer, the Richmond Whig, politicians 'know too well which side their bread is buttered on,' ever to be caught supporting the cause of moral reform in its unpopular stages. Let New-England become thoroughly abolitionised, and you, our distinguished opponents who now tower so loftily, will at once 'hide your diminished heads,' [4] and become the obsequious followers of public sentiment! Not one of you will be found in the minority! But, Sir, you deceive yourself, and therefore others, in estimating our numbers at so low a rate. It is true, we are far from constituting a majority, of the whole people; still, we are a very numerous, powerful and increasing association. We are rich in faith — strong in talent — unsurpassed in zeal — mighty in effort — victorious in conflict. We are never idle: our tongues, hands and feet, — our agents, pens and presses, — all are continually in motion. Remember, moreover, that it is only three or four years since the land was in a profound lethargy; that then a humble individual stood up alone in the field of strife; that the first anti-slavery society was not organized until the year 1832; and that the colonization dragon was first to be overcome before we could directly grapple with the slave system. Now look over the field, and count the number of standards, and measure the extended line of moral combatants, and behold the number of chiefs at the head of invincible squadrons! We now have an *American* Anti-Slavery Society; a *State* Society in Maine — another in New-Hampshire — another in Massachusetts — another in Vermont — another in Ohio — another in Kentucky; and two more are to be organized in October, namely, in New-York and Rhode Island. In addition to these, we have perhaps not less than *three hundred* auxiliary associations, each embracing from twenty to twelve hundred members. We have several presses and periodicals exclusively devoted to our cause, which are rapidly spreading our sentiments throughout the country; besides many newspapers, conducted by intelligent and independent men, that give us their hearty co-operation. Only two years ago, it was proclaimed, on the *honor* and *veracity* of the New-York daily papers, that the whole number of abolitionists in that city was only 'twenty-two men and two women' — but, ludicrous enough! to put them down, not less than five or six thousand persons assembled tumultuously together, and the victory was declared to be glorious and complete. The New-York Courier and Enquirer [5] issued a cheering bulletin, headed in staring capitals — 'THE AGITATORS DEFEATED! THE CONSTITUTION TRIUMPHANT!' It commenced in the following patriotic style:

'The citizens of New-York, ever true to the Constitution of the country, and determined to *put down* the desperate band of fanatics, &c. assembled in some thousands last evening, &c. to stamp the seal of disapprobation upon the *mad schemes* which the *ignorance of a few obscure individuals* had dared to throw before the public, &c. We rejoice that this opportunity has been presented to the inhabitants of our city to convince their Southern brethren, &c. &c.'

This was in October, 1833. In the ensuing spring, lo! there met together, in that very city, a mighty body of anti-slavery *delegates* from *societies* scattered all over the country! About once in every six months, the abolitionists are scattered to the winds of heaven by their *spasmodic* opponents, who rush upon them like a hurricane, fill the air with feathers, brickbats, and all sorts of argumentative missiles, and burn and destroy all before them! Semi-annually, too, the Constitution is triumphant! Still, the ghost of murdered Banquo 'will not down.' [6] In a short time, the abolitionists are seen in multitudinous array every where, marching from village to village, from city to city, and from State to State, augmenting their number at every step, and evidently invigorated by the respite from their labors which the storm enabled them to take. Once more, however, they have been utterly annihilated — and again has the Constitution been rescued from the hand of treason! It is more than probable, that the world will soon witness another miracle of restoration; for Truth, like our Saviour, may be scourged, and crucified, and buried — and the tomb may be sealed, and a watch set — but it has a divine energy in itself, that will burst the cerements of the grave, and reign triumphant over death. Nay, even the Courier and Enquirer begins already to despond! Hear it — 'It is dreadful to contemplate the short period of time which has elapsed since those abolitionists were a mere handful, to the MULTITUDE they have since become.' So, then, we derive from our opponents these instructive but paradoxical facts — that without numbers, we are multitudinous; that without power, we are sapping the foundation of the confederacy; that without a plan, we are hastening the abolition of slavery; and that without reason or talent, we are rapidly converting the nation!

Besides, Sir, the success of any great moral enterprise does not depend upon numbers. Slavery will be overthrown before a majority of all the people shall have called, voluntarily and on the score of principle, for its abolition. Ten righteous men would have saved Sodom. In a physical campaign, how often is a subordinate force victorious! What, Sir, is the promise to those who engage in a moral contest, that God may be glorified, and a rebellious world subdued? 'One shall chase a thousand, and two put ten thousand to flight.' [7] This has recently been fulfilled before our eyes, in the cause of temperance — and its faithfulness is continually verified in the strife of Christ with Satan. Cowardice, shame and irresolution are the treacherous companions of wickedness, and they readily yield to courage, virtue and integrity. The earliest infancy of Liberty causes the maturity of Tyranny to tremble, and the knees of the monster to smite together like those of 'Belshazzar, the king.' [8] Hence it is that we are led unwaveringly to believe, that as soon as the churches in our land will cleanse themselves from the pollutions of slavery, and bear a united testimony against it, the system must speedily fall — fall, not because they embrace a majority of the people, for they are in a lean minority, but because their example is mightier than an armed host. Hence, Sir, it is idle to sneer at us because we are less numerous than our opponents; for the same paltry *argument* might have been brought against the Temperance cause only six years ago. Sir, we may be branded with opprobrious epithets — we may be called 'agitators,' or 'fanatics,' or 'incendiaries' — but we deem it a very small thing to be judged of man's, and especially of a politician's judgment. Ours is that fanaticism which listens to the voice of God, which believes his promises and obeys his commandments, which remembers those in bonds as bound with them, which seeks the guidance of the Holy Ghost, which walks by faith and not by sight, which rejoices in tribulation, which overcomes the world. Ours is the agitation of humanity in view of cruelty — of virtue in opposition to pollution — of holiness against impiety. It is the agitation of thunder and lightning, to purify a corrupt atmosphere — of the storm, to give new vigor and freshness to field and forest. Ours is the incendiary spirit of truth, that burns up error — of freedom, that melts the fetters of the bondman — of impartial love, that warms every breast with the sacred fire of heaven. None but men of extraordinary moral courage and holy endurance could sustain, unflinchingly, a contest which requires such loss of reputation, such hazard of property and life, such anguish of body and soul, such painful collisions with parents and relations, with friends and neighbors. The risk that we run, the odium that we receive, the sacrifice that we make, and the persecution that we suffer, are the strongest evidence of the rectitude of our intentions, and the righteousness of our cause. We are constantly purified in the furnace of affliction, and the dross is taken away. Indeed, a perfect analogy is seen in the history of the abolition of the foreign slave-trade, as contrasted with the present anti-slavery struggle. The venerable CLARKSON, at the close of his instructive History,[9] makes the following remarkable statement — remarkable, because it exactly applies to the moral separation which is now taking place in our land on the great question of emancipation. He says, of the conflict in Great Britain —

'It has been useful, also, in the discrimination of moral character. In private life, it has enabled us to distinguish the virtuous from the more vicious part of the community. I have had occasion to know *many thousand persons* in the course of my travels on this subject; and I can truly say, that *the part which these took on this great question, was always a true criterion of their moral character.* It has shown the general philanthropist. It has unmasked the vicious, in spite of his pretension to virtue. It has afforded us the same knowledge in public life. *It has separated the moral statesman from the wicked politician.* It has shown us who, in the legislative and executive offices of our country, are fit to save, *and who to destroy a nation.*'

Sir, I will dwell no longer upon this point. What I intended only as incidental in this letter, constitutes its main part. It was my intention to depict, with your assistance, the bloody relations which the north sustains to the south, and to comment at some length upon the awful picture; but I must consign a large portion of my remarks to another epistle. The ground that you and your colleagues maintain is, that the free states are not involved in the guilt of slavery; that we have no right, morally, (for as to our political right, there is no difference of opinion,) to meddle with it; that the slave states alone are criminal, if there be any criminality attaching to the system; that the doctrine of immediate emancipation is impracticable and dangerous; and that the anti-slavery associations are unwarrantable and seditious. Abolitionists hold that the north and the south are alike involved in guilt, whether past, present or prospective; that therefore it is the right and the duty of the people every where, to seek the overthrow of slavery by moral means, and to wash the blood from their hands individually; that it is unjust and pharisaical for one portion of the country to say to another, — 'Stand by, for I am holier than thou;' [10] that the doctrine of immediate emancipation is the doctrine of common sense, common honesty, and the Bible; and that it is only by moral associations that deep-rooted evils can be eradicated. Here, then, we differ entirely.

To prove that the north neither upholds nor sanctions southern slavery, you adduce the following evidence:

1. 'The Constitution provides for the suppressing of insurrections; we should rally under the Constitution, we should respond to its call: nay, we should not wait for such a requisition, but on the instant should rush forward with fraternal emotions to defend our brethren from desolation and massacre.' That is, we have agreed to keep the slaves in bondage, and to crush or exterminate them if they should rise, as did our fathers, to obtain their freedom by violence: therefore, we are guiltless of the sin of oppression!

2. 'The Constitution recognizes and *provides for the continuance* of slavery:' therefore, we are not guilty!!

3. 'It does *sanction*, it does UPHOLD slavery'; therefore, we are not responsible!!!

4. 'Few parts of the Constitution were more carefully and deliberately weighed': therefore, we are sinless!!!!

This is your evidence of our innocence, Mr. Sprague! Mr. Otis adds his confirmation, thus:

5. 'The claim of the South to consider their slaves as *cyphers* or NONENTITIES is acquiesced in, and *confirmed* by the North': therefore, we are immaculate!!

6. We agreed to permit the South to carry on the foreign slave-trade — to plunder and desolate Africa — for the space of twenty years: therefore, we are innocent!!

7. We agree 'to seize and restore runaway slaves': therefore, we plead not guilty!!

8. We agree that 'the *master* shall, in reference to the constitution, exercise all the political rights of the *slave*, and that he should be *nothing*': therefore, we have nothing to do with slavery!!

Now, Sir, in presenting these facts to prove the innocence of the North, it seems to me that you must really believe that 'justice has fled to brutish beasts, and men have lost their reason.' [11] Or do you mean to mock us, as those who cannot discriminate between honesty and knavery — liberty and oppression? Why, Sir, I am filled with amazement. What would you think, if an associate of thieves should be arrested and brought up for trial, and, to prove his own and their innocence, should begin to specify what robberies they had perpetrated, what more they meant to effect, and what part each had to perform in plundering the community? You are a lawyer, Sir, and can readily decide how this testimony would operate. Your plea is just as rational: as well might the assassin bring the body of his victim into court, and brandish the reeking knife over his head, to prove that he ought not to be accused of murder!

But I run the following parallel, that the reader may see, at a glance, whether, in our alliance for the support of slavery, we are not fighting against God:

THE NATIONAL COMPACT   vs.   THE LORD ALMIGHTY!

PELEG SPRAGUE.

'It recognizes and provides for the continuance of the relation of master and slave; it further provides for the suppression of insurrections.'

'Every one who knows any thing of the history of the Constitution, knows that it could never have been formed, — that the Southern States would never have acceded to it for an instant, if it had not left to them the exclusive and *unmolested* treatment of *this terrible disease, this vital subject,* — their own domestic slavery.'

'The constitution is the supreme law of the land. *It does sanction, it does uphold slavery.'*

'With *slaveholders* they formed the Confederation, neither asking nor receiving any right to interfere in their domestic relations.'

'There is no pretence that the provisions [of the Constitution] in relation to it [slavery] were inserted by accidence or inadvertance. *Few parts of the Constitution were more carefully and deliberately weighed.'*

H. G. OTIS.

'The subject of slavery and the claims of the proprietors over their slaves must have been before them and considered *with great deliberation.* We find provision in those articles for apportioning the troops to be raised for the public service, among the free white inhabitants of the several states according to their numbers. In this article, the claim of

'When thou sawest a thief, then thou consentedst with him, and hast been partaker with adulterers.' Psalm i. 18.

'Shall the throne of iniquity have fellowship with thee, which frameth mischief by a law?' Ps. xciv. 20.

'Wo unto them that decree unrighteous decrees, and that write grievousness which they have prescribed; to turn aside the needy from judgment, and to take away the right from the poor of my people, that widows may be their prey, and that they may rob the fatherless!' Isaiah x. 1,2.

'They commit adultery, and walk in lies: they strengthen also the hands of evil-doers, that none doth return from his wickedness: they are all of them unto me as Sodom, and all the inhabitants thereof as Gomorrah.' Isa. xxiii. 14.

'Therefore, thus saith the Lord: Ye have not hearkened unto me, in proclaiming liberty, every one to his brother, and every man to his neighbor: behold, I proclaim a liberty for **you, saith the** Lord, to the sword, to the pestilence, and to the famine.' Jer. xxxiv. 17.

'Wherefore hear the word of the Lord, ye scornful men, that rule this people. Because ye have said, We have made a covenant with death, and with hell are we at agreement: when the overflowing scourge shall pass through, it shall not come unto us: for we have made lies our refuge, and under falsehood have we

the South to consider their *slaves* as CYPHERS or NONENTITIES *is acquiesced in and confirmed by the North.* Here was no surprise, no misunderstanding, no concealment of facts or of claims.'

'That this topic in all its bearings was presented and *examined* when the federal constitution was being formed, is known to all acquainted with the history of those times, and may be conclusively inferred from the instrument itself. So far were the Northern States from assuming any pretension to regulate the *interior economy* [*!!*] of the Southern, that they were *compelled* to exempt them for ten [twenty] years from the general operation of the laws regulating commerce, and allow the importation of slaves during that period. This constitutes a most important feature of the federal compact. It would alone be decisive on the subject.'

'Another clause in the Constitution is a contract on the part of the non-slaveholding States to seize and restore runaway slaves. Lastly, it was agreed by the clause apportioning representatives, that the master should, in reference to the constitution, exercise all the political rights of the slave, and that he should be nothing. Such, Fellow-Citizens, is the bargain which we, the people of the United States, have made with each other. In what age of the world, and among what people and States was a compact ever made more solemn and sacred? [*!!!*] It is plain and perspicuous. It was made with our eyes open; with a full knowledge of all the circumstances of the case, of all the inducements to make it, of all the objections that could be made against it. Every one of the people is bound to adhere to it. Every man who holds office has sworn to support it, and is perjured when by any appliance, direct, or indirect, he at-

hid ourselves. Therefore, thus saith the Lord God, judgment will I lay to the line, and righteousness to the plummet: and the hail shall sweep away the refuge of lies, and the waters shall overflow the hiding place. And your covenant with death shall be disannulled, and your agreement with hell shall not stand; when the overflowing scourge shall pass through, then shall ye be trodden down by it.' — Isaiah xxviii. 14, 15, 16, 17, 18.

'Take counsel, execute judgment; make thy shadow as the night in the midst of the noon-day; hide the outcasts; bewray not him that wandereth. Let mine outcasts dwell with thee; be thou a covert to them from the face of the spoiler.' Is. xvi. 3, 4.

'Thou shouldest not have looked on their affliction in the day of their calamity, nor have laid hands on their substance in the day of their calamity; neither shouldest thou have stood in the cross-way, to cut off those of his that did escape; neither shouldest thou have delivered up those of his that did remain in the day of distress. As thou hast done, it shall be done unto thee: thy reward shall return upon thine own head.' Obadiah i. 13, 14, 15.

'Thou shalt not deliver unto his master the servant which is escaped from his master unto thee: he shall dwell with thee, even among you in that place which he shall choose in one of thy gates where it liketh him best: thou shalt not oppress him.' Deut. xxiii. 15, 16.

'Thus saith the Lord: Execute ye judgment and righteousness, and deliver the spoiled out of the hand of the oppressor: and do no wrong, do no violence to the stranger, the fatherless, nor the widow, neither shed innocent blood.' Jer. xxii. 3.

'And the same day Pilate and

tempts to annul its provisions. It speaks to every man's understanding, and binds every man's conscience by all that is sacred in good faith, or sound in good policy.'

RICHARD FLETCHER.

'Slavery is no worse now than it was when we formed the Union with them. We then agreed to it. They came into the Union on that agreement.'

'The Constitution left the subject just as it found it. This was no mistake or accident; — it was fully understood and agreed. We formed our compact with the South understandingly and intentionally upon this principle. Each State retained to itself the exclusive right over the subject. We pledged our solemn faith that we would not infringe this right. Upon this ground we understandingly bound ourselves to the compact, and connected our fate with the South in a sacred union.'

THE PREAMBLE.

'By that sacred compact, which constitutes the American Union one nation, the rights and jurisdiction of the Southern States were recognized and confirmed by all the rest. The actual state of their social relations was the basis of that compact; and we disclaim the right, and disbelieve the policy, and condemn the injustice of *all* efforts to impair or disturb solemn obligations thus imposed upon ourselves by our free act, with a full knowledge of their nature and, bearing upon the political system.

Herod were made friends together.' Luke xxiii. 12.

'Be not partakers of other men's sins.' — PAUL.

'With the same measure that ye mete, it shall be measured to you again.' — Luke vi. 38.

'Whether it be right in the sight of God to hearken unto men more than unto God, judge ye.' Acts iv. 19.

Oh, Sir, when has a nation sinned so perversely, against so much light, so deliberately, so understandingly, as our own? Say not, as did transgressors of old, 'We are delivered to do all these abominations.' [12] The world must see, that we have planted the pillars of our liberty upon the necks of millions of our own countrymen; that, to accommodate ourselves, we have wickedly sacrificed the rights and happiness, the time and talents, the bodies and souls of an immense multitude of our fellow creatures, who are guilty of no crime! We must put away the unclean thing from our midst — it is a curse and contagion — it is fast hurrying us to ruin. 'God is just, and his justice will not sleep forever.' [13] Now that his judgments are yet kept back — now that space for repentance is yet mercifully granted unto us — let us abase ourselves as did the inhabitants of Nineveh; let us bring forth fruits meet for repentance; let us cease to do evil and learn to do well; and joy and peace will reign throughout our borders — the devourer will be rebuked for our sakes — and the Lord of hosts will open the window of heaven, and pour upon us a blessing that there shall not be room enough to receive it.

Yours, imploringly,

WM. LLOYD GARRISON.

Printed: *The Liberator*, September 12, 1835.

1. Proverbs 27:5, 6.
2. Richard Fletcher (1788–1869), a graduate of Dartmouth College and a law student of Daniel Webster, was himself one of the most distinguished trial lawyers in Boston. Although at the time of Garrison's letter Fletcher, along with Sprague and Otis, had attacked the abolitionists, later as a member of Congress he strongly favored the abolition of slavery in the District of Columbia and the elimination of the interstate slave trade.
3. Thomas Ritchie, owner of the Richmond *Enquirer*.
4. Garrison adapts Milton, *Paradise Lost*, IV, 35.
5. One of the largest, most conservative, and most influential of northern dailies.
6. Garrison alludes to Shakespeare's *Macbeth*, IV, i, 112.
7. Deuteronomy 32:30.
8. Daniel 5:1 or 30.
9. *The History of the Rise, Progress, and Accomplishment of the Abolition of the African Slave-Trade by the British Parliament* (London, 1808).
10. Garrison adapts Isaiah 65:5.
11. Garrison adapts Shakespeare, *Julius Caesar*, III, ii, 109–110.
12. Jeremiah 7:10.
13. Garrison quotes, somewhat inaccurately, Jefferson, *Notes on the State of Virginia*, Query XVIII (Trenton, 1803).

211

TO HENRY E. BENSON

Brooklyn, Sept. 12, 1835.

Dear Henry —

You cheer me like the sun, and are as faithful. Not a package has yet been lost. This afternoon I hope to receive the Liberator. I send some communications for brother Knapp, and will forward some editorial on Monday.

Bro. Thompson had a narrow escape at Concord.[1] Let him still trust in God — these things cannot last long — but while they do last, we had better not attempt to lecture. I think our first public meeting in Boston ought to be with reference, exclusively, to the abolition of slavery in the District of Columbia. Love that cannot be measured I send to bros May & Thompson.

I shall not be in Boston so early as I anticipated — not till week after next, as dear George is coming up next Saturday, and the family wish me to remain.

Helen is filled with anxiety and alarm on my account. She trembles when she thinks of our returning to Boston — probably there is less danger than she imagines.

As you send me the news, I have none to communicate. We are as quiet here as monotony can make it; but my time passes pleasantly and rapidly.

Hope bro. Knapp has fully recovered his health. Why don't he send me a scrawl? It is hardly fair to throw all the writing upon you. But I know his repugnance to the quill — and he knows mine. (Aside.)

I am glad you retained the manuscript from S. Carolina, respecting Mr. Woodbury. Let it be published, together with Mr. W's speech, & the pieces accompanying it, in the next paper, if practicable.[2]

Wishing you and all the brethren the consolations and blessings of heaven, I remain, in the bonds of brotherly love,

Yours,

W. L. G.

I shall notice J. F. Otis, in a *brief* editorial.[3] Let nothing be set up about him except what I shall send. It is a very small affair. Forward his bill, to him.

ALS: Garrison Papers, Boston Public Library; extracts printed in *Life*, I, 518–519.

1. On his tour of New Hampshire, after having spoken in Plymouth, Thompson was staying in Concord. The house in which he lodged was attacked, and Whittier and others, being mistaken for Thompson, were assaulted in the streets, though not hurt.

2. Garrison refers (see *Life*, I, 517) to a letter mailed from Pocotaligo, South Carolina, by W. Ferguson Hutson, secretary of the Vigilance Committee of Prince William's Parish, which was addressed to and attacked Levi Woodbury (1789–1851). Woodbury was one of New Hampshire's most distinguished citizens. A lawyer by profession, he had been governor, United States senator, and secretary of the navy under Jackson. On the slavery issue he was a moderate who, though he believed slavery to be wrong, thought laws supporting it must be obeyed. Apparently neither the letter nor Woodbury's speech was printed in *The Liberator*.

3. Garrison's bitter editorial on James F. Otis, a young lawyer from Portland, Maine, who, after a trip to Virginia, had become conservative on the abolition question, appeared in the issue for September 19. Garrison assured him that his name, as requested, would be expunged from the list of signers of the Declaration of Sentiments of the American Anti-Slavery Society.

2 1 2

TO GEORGE W. BENSON

Brooklyn, Sept. 12, 1835.

My dear George:

I have concluded to abide under the family roof until you come ——
that is to say, until Saturday next and a few subsequent days. It will
greatly refresh my spirit to see your countenance and hear your voice
once more.

Rumor is very busy in disposing of the persons of abolitionists.
One day, she sends Arthur and Lewis Tappan across the Atlantic as
fast as the winds and waves can carry them. On the next, she puts
you into Providence jail, at the suggestion of your friends, for safe
keeping from your enemies. Thompson she transports to Pittsburgh;
and she says I am here because I dare not go back to Boston. It is
thus we relieve the tediousness and monotony of those who have
nothing to do but to scandalize and gossip.

I have just received a letter from brother May, written immediately after his meeting was broken up by a shower of brickbats, &c.
in Haverhill. By the tone of it you would suppose he had done something better than making a fortune. He manifests a lofty spirit and
indomitable courage.

Our brother Thompson had a narrow escape from the mob at Concord, and Whittier was pelted with mud and stones, but he escaped
bodily damage. His soul, being intangible, laughed at the salutation.

That some of us will be assassinated or abducted, seems more than
probable but there is much apparent, without any real danger.
There is a whole eternity of consolation in this assurance he who
loses his life for Christ's sake shall find it. "To die is gain." [1]

"The soul, secured in her existence, smiles

At the drawn dagger, and defies its point." [2]

Angelina E. Grimke, sister of the lamented Grimke, has sent me a
soul-thrilling epistle, in which, with a spirit worthy of the best days
of martyrdom, she says — "A *hope* gleams across my mind, that *our*
blood will be spilt, instead of the slaveholders'; *our* lives will be
taken, and theirs spared." [3] Is not this Christ-like?

The southern clergy are openly abandoning their God, and bowing down to Satan, the prince of men-stealers. They are indeed
"greedy dogs, and dumb dogs that cannot bark," [4] except at abolitionists. They will not frighten you, nor

Your brother,

W. L. G.

ALS: Garrison Papers, Boston Public Library; printed partly in *Life*, I, 517–518.

1. Philippians 1:21.
2. Addison, *Cato*, V, i, 25.
3. Angelina E. Grimké (1805–1879), from an aristocratic slaveholding family in Charleston, South Carolina, became a Quaker and one of the most effective orators in the cause of abolition and of woman's rights. In 1838 she married Theodore Dwight Weld (see letter 228, n. 2). Her brother, Thomas Smith Grimké (1786–1834), was a graduate of Yale and an eminent attorney and state senator in South Carolina, as well as an ardent reformer. He died in 1834, en route to Columbus, Ohio, where he was buried. (Angelina Grimké's letter was printed in *The Liberator*, September 19, 1835.)
4. Garrison quotes, almost accurately, from an anonymous poem used as the subscription to Chapter V of Sir Walter Scott's *The Monastery*.

213

TO HENRY E. BENSON

Brooklyn — [Sept. 15] [1]
Tuesday Morning — 1835.

Dear Henry —

Your letter, per mail yesterday, informs me that a hanging apparatus was left at Brighton-street house, 23, *by* somebody *for* somebody or bodies. Quite a significant and expressive affair. They who brought the gallows, I presume, have had all the alarm and terror of the act. Am truly rejoiced to hear that you are all safe and in good spirits — but pray, be *very* careful all of you, especially about venturing out late at night. I yearn to see dear Thompson, and beseech him to look well to his movements for the present. Father seems to be quite alarmed for your safety, since reading your letter.

I send, now, all the editorial for this week, except the conclusion of Otis's Letter,[2] which I shall endeavor to forward this afternoon, via Providence.

Was much pleased with the correctness of Saturday's paper, and have no *Errata* to send.

We shall not return until next week.

Am very sorry that you and bro. Knapp did not secure the gallows, for our anti-slavery museum — or was it too large and cumbrous for that purpose?

Hear nothing respecting Mr. and Mrs. Child. Have they sailed yet for England?

To think of the pelting of our good Quaker brother John G. Whittier! What! has it come to this, that a Quaker garb gives no protection from the mob! Shades of George Fox and William Penn, arise![3]

Who wrote the communication, signed "Truth"? It is excellent.

I anticipate much pleasure on seeing the face of dear brother George. Rumor has said, that he has been put in Providence jail for safe keeping by his friends!!! [4]

In great haste, I remain,

Your much obliged brother,

Wm. L. G.

☞ Just as I thought on Saturday — that the failure was on account of oversleeping. No matter.

ALS: Garrison Papers, Boston Public Library.

1. This date is supplied probably in the hand of Wendell Phillips Garrison.
2. Letter 215, to Harrison Gray Otis, September 19, 1835.
3. Garrison links Whittier with early Quakers George Fox (1624–1691) and William Penn (1644–1718), who had also suffered for a cause.
4. It must have been merely a rumor, for there seems to be no evidence that George W. Benson was imprisoned. See, for instance, letter 212, to George W. Benson, September 12.

214

TO GEORGE W. BENSON

Brooklyn —

Thursday Morning [Sept. 17, 1835].[1]

Brother George:

Jail or no jail, we are expecting to see you in Brooklyn to-morrow noon, or on Saturday at farthest. Will you please to leave directions with my friend William M. Chace, respecting the packages that I may send to him for Boston, or that Henry may send to Providence for Brooklyn? I shall expect a bundle on your arrival here. So far, nothing has been lost, of all the letters and papers that have been forwarded to me.

I suppose you have heard of the presentation of a stout gallows to me, at 23, Brighton-Street, Boston, by order of Judge Lynch.[2] It was destroyed by the city authorities. I regret that it was not preserved for our Anti-Slavery Museum. Thompson has presented a brickbat to it, but this would have been a more substantial curiosity.

The slave States continue to be excessively agitated. They appear to have organized Vigilance Committee and Lynch Clubs in various places. The most daring propositions are made in the open face of heaven for the abduction of Arthur Tappan, George Thompson and myself. Public and private appropriations of money, to a large amount, are made for our seizure. Our preservation is remarkable. I presume that our principle cities will be visited by assassins, legalized by the

"State Rights" Government to destroy us. It matters not. To the obedient, death is no calamity. If we perish, our loss will but hasten the destruction of slavery more certainly. My mind is full of peace — I know what it is to rejoice in tribulation.

The two rival political parties, Whigs and Jacksonians or Van Buren men, are striving to see who will show the most hatred towards us, and do us the most injury, in order to win southern votes. They are all ferocious and unprincipled, caring not for God — truth — honesty — or justice.

You will be delighted to see your little darling babe.[3] She is certainly the most attractive infant I have ever seen. I love her almost as much as if she was my own.

Should you see the colored girl who is to live with us, you may tell her that we shall be in Providence next week.

Hoping that you will come to-morrow, I forbear writing more — and remain, under all circumstances,

Your much attached brother,

W. L. G.

ALS: Garrison Papers, Boston Public Library; printed partly in *Life*, I, 519–520. At the bottom of the second sheet of this letter is a brief note from George W. Benson to Garrison.

1. This date is supplied on the manuscript in the hand of Wendell Phillips Garrison.

2. Garrison makes the first of several references to the symbolic judge who is supposed to have ordered the gallows erected and in other ways to have opposed the abolitionists.

3. Anna Elizabeth Benson.

215

TO HARRISON GRAY OTIS

[September 19, 1835.]

Sir —

I am very sure that your knowledge of abolitionists and their writings is quite imperfect, and derived from popular calumny rather than from calm and deliberate examination: indeed, you frankly declare that you 'know nothing of them.' In one breath you affect great liberality towards us, and affirm that you 'make no personal allusions, and impeach no man's motives.' In the next — for 'error is fated to run crooked' — you brand us as 'a dangerous, most dangerous association,' 'an *unlawful* association,' 'hostile to the spirit and letter of the constitution of the Union,' '*designing* to trench upon its provisions by *overt* acts,' 'revolutionary,' 'inflammatory,' 'combining to spread disaffection in other states, and poison the sweet fountains of domestic safety and comfort,' &c. &c. All this, Sir, is extremely charitable and consistent, from the lips of one who complains of our sweeping censures and severe allegations! It is not personal — it is no impeachment of motives — O, no! It is honey and the honey-comb: it only means, in good plain English, that we are very honest, well-meaning traitors, who contemplate no mischief, but whose sole object is to destroy the Union, and spread disaffection throughout the land! Allow me to test the value of your charitable abstinence, by arraying

MR. OTIS	*versus*	MR. OTIS.

'In speaking of these [the anti-slavery] associations, I rely entirely upon the account they give of themselves and their objects. *I make no personal allusions, and impeach no man's motives.*'

'Almost all the epithets of vituperation which our language affords have been applied to the slaveholders or their principles: as if the feelings of such persons could be propitiated by *an affected distinction between a condemnation of the individual and his principles!*' [1]

Greek against Greek, and both are slain! It seems that your charity for our motives is but another name for affectation or hypocrisy. As for our accusations against slaveholders, they are precisely such as the Bible authorizes; and we cannot but feel confirmed in our belief of their applicability, when we perceive so powerful a mind as your own unable to rebut one of them! Positive assertion without proof, wholesale crimination without cause, and impassioned declamation without reason, constitute the whole of your harangue: it does not contain one argument. Ah! who *can* argue against the rights of man and the blessings of liberty? Are they not self-evident?

Here is another specimen of your moral acuteness and ingenious discrimination:

'Happily for our country, there is no disposition in the people of this community, nor I believe of any of our cities or towns, *to sustain a public discussion of a question* pregnant with these fatal consequences. But the time has arrived which makes it *the part of wisdom and safety to look at this question* in the distance, and forestall its approach — to satisfy ourselves and others that it ought never to be entertained, *except in the exercise and expression of individual judgment and opinion* — and that every effort intended to propagate a general sentiment favorable to the immediate abolition of slavery, is of forbidding aspect and ruinous tendency.'

This is contradictory and indefinite enough. If there be no disposition to sustain a public discussion of this question, how came you and the multitude to assemble in Faneuil Hall to discuss it? And why are similar meetings called in various sections of New England? The solution of the problem is, that there is no disposition to sustain a *free* and *fair* discussion, but only a discussion of one side of the question — that which is favorable to slavery. And why this unwillingness? Because it is clearly perceived, that free and unobstructed discussion will speedily change public sentiment in this country, as it did in Great Britain, and effect the abolition of slavery forever! What is the language of one of the most unprincipled and bloodthirsty newspapers in the land — the Boston Commercial Gazette [2] — your eulogist!

'*Free discussion* on the subject of slavery! Ay, as Petruchio says, 'there's the villany.' [3] The mischief all lies in a nutshell. *A free discussion on this subject leads at once to* ABOLITION *and* EMANCIPATION.'

Precious confession! too true and too important to be forgotten by the friends of human freedom! Yes, Sir, to uphold slavery in our midst, you must destroy THE LIBERTY OF THE PRESS, and put GAGS into the mouths of all your fellow citizens — or be content to see the chains of despotism shivered by the hammer, and melted by the fire of truth. 'Is not my word like a fire? saith the Lord; and like a hammer that breaketh the rock in pieces?' 'Speak unto all the cities, *all the words* that I command thee to speak unto them; DIMINISH NOT A WORD: if so be they will hearken, and turn every man from his evil way, that I may repent me of the evil which I purpose to do unto them because of the evil of their doings.' [4]

The oppressors at the south are aware, that, as surely as the light of morning disperses the darkness of night, so surely will *free discussion* put an end to slavery. What, then, do they demand of the people of New England? Not merely to hold public meetings, and denounce abolitionists; but they call upon them, unblushingly and expressly, to pass LAWS PROHIBITING THE FREEDOM OF SPEECH AND OF THE PRESS on the subject of southern slavery!! and if they refuse thus to make themselves speechless, — if they refuse to shackle and destroy that which is the palladium of their own liberty, — then these insatiate and haughty tyrants threaten to rebel against the Union! When Mr. Ritchie of the Richmond Enquirer, — that windy, self-conceited and cowardly braggadocio, — first read the proceedings of the Faneuil Hall meeting, he was elevated to ecstacy, for he persuaded himself that the SPIRIT OF TRUTH AND LIBERTY was actually dead and buried. His blissful reverie was almost instantly broken, as if by a frightful apparition, and he now says of that meeting —

'We shall, however, *expect something more substantial;* we shall look for a cessation of the issue of incendiary papers altogether, or for high penalties upon the circulators of them within our limits. If it be consistent with the right of discussion, *to impose restrictions upon the press in the North*, surely it cannot be asking too much to insist upon the *infliction of punishment upon those who mail them* for offices within the slaveholding states, or who transmit them in any other way.'

The tone of the Richmond Whig is still more imperial:

'The South *asks no sympathy or professions,* and needs no aid in respect to its slaves. It is competent to protect itself, even from neighborhood surprise and massacre, while its vigilance is awakened. *There is no remedy but one — abate the incendiary journals,* as the exciters of bloodshed and disunion. It is evident that *a thousand meetings will produce no permanent good.* Fanaticism is made of sterner stuff than to be checked or intimidated by a preamble or a string of resolutions, however strongly conceived or eloquently expressed. They have dared too much already to be removed by scarecrows. It is no less than a question of Union or Disunion, and stronger means must be applied. We reiterate to the North — *put a stop to this system of disgraceful and unmerited national destruction. What stops short of that, fails to give redress for past injuries, or security against future. Tell us not of sympathy, regret, etc; if you cannot reach the vile slanderers, say nothing.'*

This is the kind of *compensation* that southern masters give to their servants and slaves, whether at the North or the South. At their bidding, you and your associates have bowed the neck and bent the knee — you have bound yourselves ignobly to their chariot wheels — you have covered yourselves with the filth of slavery, that they might not be offended at the purity of your aspect: but because you cannot effect impossibilities — because you are unable to make others as servile, polluted and obsequious as yourselves — because, in short, the vigor of the bow has not equalled the venom of the shaft, and Liberty still lives — they spurn you with ineffable contempt, repel even your own slavishness, and threaten a terrible punishment! A very suitable reward.

You say it is happy for our country, that there is no disposition among the people to sustain a public discussion of the slave question. Why, then, in the very next sentence, do you contradict yourself by saying that 'the time has arrived which makes it the part of WISDOM to look at this question — to satisfy ourselves and others,' &c.? How can we look at it without examining it? and how can we satisfy ourselves and others, without first privately and publicly discussing it? You allow us to exercise and express our individual judgment and opinion: but, in so doing, you increase the exasperation of the south, and controvert a doctrine which it holds to be fundamentally important. Upon what authority, Sir, do you forbid our *publicly* discussing the subject of slavery, or any other, whether it relates to the affairs of the southern states, or to those of the Autocrat of Russia? You are well aware that the people of New England are not particularly fond of *secret* discussions: hence arose that strong hostility to the Hartford Convention, of which you were a member. Be assured, Sir, if we discuss the subject at all, the South prefers to *hear* what we *say*, and *see* what we are *doing*.

You say, the people ought to satisfy themselves 'that every effort intended to propagate a general sentiment favorable to the immediate abolition of slavery, is of forbidding aspect and ruinous tendency.' We think so, too; and therefore we call upon them to read, reflect and talk upon the subject — to '*satisfy*' themselves, not by taking the *ipse dixit* even of Harrison Gray Otis — not by hurling brickbats at the heads, or tarring and feathering the persons, of those whose sentiments do not accord with theirs — not by lynching their opponents — not by preventing free discussion, or closing their eyes, or shutting their ears — not by conspiring to seize and destroy private property, or to abduct or assassinate the advocates of universal emancipation — but by examining evidence, seeking light, listening patiently and candidly to both sides and all sides of the question — by loving their neighbors as themselves, and remembering those in bonds as bound with them — by hearkening to the voice of God, rather than to the voice of the oppressor or any of his apologists. All this supposes, and necessarily involves, action — excitement — discussion — association. Such a course, the south clearly perceives, would lead to abolition; for, as far as it has been pursued, it has resulted in a radical change of views and principles, subversive of slavery, and destructive to prejudice. Hence our southern masters tell us that we shall not argue the right of slavery, nor question the validity of their title to their slaves. The language of a public meeting in Norfolk is, — 'When asked by what right we retain this class of our population in bondage, we shall, like the chivalry of Scotland, on a similar occasion, (!) POINT TO OUR SWORDS. We shall scorn to render any other reply.' [5] It is obvious that they can make no other answer. If they could adduce a single good argument in support of their unrighteous conduct, they would never point to their swords. Now, inasmuch as the slave-system cannot bear investigation, any more than could the foreign slave-trade, it is certain that FREE DISCUSSION will destroy the one as it did the other. We have already grappled with the consciences of many anxious and inquiring slave masters, and our seed is falling upon good ground even in the south. The power of truth is beginning to be felt in that section of the country, and the advocates of slavery tremble in view of this encouraging fact. Read the following important confession of Duff Green, the editor of the Washington Telegraph: [6]

'We hold that our sole reliance is on ourselves; that we have most to fear *from the gradual operation on public opinion among ourselves*, and that those are the most insidious and dangerous invaders of our rights and interests, who, coming to us in the guise of friendship, endeavor to persuade us that slavery is a sin, a curse, an evil. It is not true that the south sleeps on a volcano — that we are afraid to go to bed at night — that we are fearful of murder and pillage. Our greatest cause of apprehension is *from the operation of the morbid sensibility* (!) *which appeals to the con-sciences* (!) *of our own people,* and would make them the voluntary in-struments of their own ruin' (!) — i.e. would make them voluntarily give up their impious claims upon their victims, undo every burden, and let the oppressed go free!'

You have just discovered 'that an association has been formed in a neighboring State, for the avowed purpose of effecting the imme-diate abolition of slavery.' In a neighboring State! Why, Sir, you seem to be ignorant of the fact, that Massachusetts is swarming with anti-slavery societies! She has State — county — town and village associa-tions, all harmoniously co-operating together, and all exerting a pow-erful moral influence upon the public mind, in deep and lasting op-position to southern slavery. These are multiplying in all parts of the Commonwealth.

You give the following singular reasons for branding them as a dangerous association:

1. 'Their number is at present comparatively small and insignifi-cant.' This proves nothing against them. If they are insignificant, then they are not dangerous. You venture to assail them because you believe them to be few!

2. 'Their printed constitution and proceedings, seen by me only within a few days, frankly develope their desire to establish auxiliary societies in every state and municipality, and to enlist in the service of the cause man, woman and child.' Well, Sir, there is no disguise — nothing of treason in this design. The same grave charge may be urged against the Bible, Tract, Missionary, Peace and Temperance Societies: they all aim to convert the nation. Yet, with extraordinary fatuity you say — 'This simple statement shows it to be a dangerous association'! That is to say, a society is dangerous because it is small, and because it means to enlist, if possible, every man, woman and child in its enterprise! Demonstration itself! 'A Daniel come to judg-ment — yea, a Daniel!' [7]

After this summary examination and conviction, you venture to allude to PRINCIPLES. Thus you reverse the order of things; what should be first, you put last, and vice versa; for a foundation you wisely take nothing, and for a pinnacle you hoist up the corner-stone! Surely, Sir, the Anti-Slavery Society must be judged by its principles — not by the number of its members; yet, before you come to these, you think that you have shown it to be dangerous! Then you pro-ceed:

'A very rapid exposition of the tendency of their principles will prove them to be not only imminently dangerous, but hostile to the spirit and letter of the constitution of the Union.'

Now, Sir, so rapid is your exposition, that you only darken counsel by words without knowledge. Abolitionists have three fundamental principles:

1. A man is a man, and not a chattel.

2. Hence, he cannot be the property of another.

3. Hence, that which makes him a chattel is unnatural, monstrous and unholy, and ought to be immediately destroyed.

You have not, in any part of your speech, attempted to refute either of these postulates, by any appeal to reason, analogy, or justice. Their soundness is self-evident: the wayfaring man, though a fool, understands them. Until you show them to be false, you can never prove them to be either slightly or imminently dangerous to the constitution of the Union, or to the interests and safety of the planters, or to any good thing.

WM. LLOYD GARRISON.

Printed: *The Liberator*, September 19, 1835.

1. The Otis passages to be found in this letter are quoted, for the most part accurately, from the speech printed in *The Liberator* for September 5, 1835.

2. Printed between 1795 and 1840.

3. Shakespeare, *Taming of the Shrew*, IV, iii, 145.

4. Jeremiah 23:29, 26:2–3.

5. Garrison doubtless quotes from a Norfolk paper. He often reprints in *The Liberator*'s "Refuge of Oppression" accounts of such meetings, though he apparently did not use this particular one.

6. Duff Green (1791–1875), of Kentucky and later Missouri, was one of the great industrial magnates of the day. He was involved in stage coaches, canals, railroads, mining, and land speculation. Politically, he stood for state's rights and the mutuality of interests between the South and the West. Since 1825 he had owned the *United States Telegraph*. Although he was neither a slaveholder nor a secessionist, he was to side with the South during the Civil War.

7. Shakespeare, *The Merchant of Venice*, IV, i, 223.

216

TO HENRY E. BENSON

Brooklyn, Sept. 19 — [1835,][1]

Saturday noon.

My dear and attentive Brother:

I give you but very brief notes for your long and crowded epistles; but, in a village like this, a circumstance that is worth relating does not often occur. Your letter of the 16th, with a bundle of papers, was brought here yesterday by brother George. I have gone over their contents minutely, and now send the fruits of my *scissors*. Friend K. will be puzzled to know how to meet such a rush of matter in the best way — but in another week I will relieve him. Let all these, with the other selections, be most carefully preserved. Let the last page — except poetry column — be filled up with the pieces *favorable* to our side, especially those which come from papers *not* abolition, as they will have more weight than others. Of course, the first page may be filled with the "Refuge." As it is difficult to dispose of long articles, let the shortest have the precedence as a general rule. We will not insert the whole proceedings of any other public meetings than those already published — I will make a synopsis of them all. Those pieces which tell of new outrages at the South, and of the designs of the southerners, should be promptly inserted.

I am refreshed again to hear of bro. Thompson's safety. *You did not send the letter that he left for me.*

Your indignation at the exhibition of that poor old piece of mortality in the shape of Joice Heth, is just and generous.[2]

Thank you for the Couriers. That long letter to Otis, &c. is excellent — but we have no room for it in our columns. It will *tell* for our cause.

The independence manifested by the N.Y. Post is as rare as it was unexpected. George tells me that there will be quite a number of abolition subscribers for the Post in Prov. & elsewhere.

I shall not be greatly disappointed if the Liberator be not received this afternoon — still, I will *hope.*

Young Hinckley is here from Amherst, during the vacation.[3] He says we have some excellent materials there in the institution. Colonization is dead — dead — dead.

Mary goes to Providence to-day, to make her usual autumnal visit among her Quaker friends, &c. She will probably make us a visit in Boston before she returns to Brooklyn.

Bro. George looks in fine health, and talks like a conqueror. He thinks these are animating and encouraging times for abolitionists. He will return on Tuesday, *unless* he can be induced to stay until Thursday, which is very problematical. I shall leave on Thursday for Providence, and, if all be well, be in Boston by Saturday noon.

Hope bro. Knapp has enjoyed his visit to N.[4] as highly as I have mine to B.

The family are all well, and quite happy. We speak of you frequently, and long to have your presence.

☞ Let the *last* bundle you send me to Brooklyn come by the Prov. stage to Brooklyn on Wednesday, as on Thursday I shall leave this place. If it is convenient, you may send me a package while I am in P. — i.e. until Saturday morning.

Yours, gratefully,

W.L.G.

☞ Tell friend K. to be careful not to insert any articles twice, as there is some danger among so many.

ALS: Garrison Papers, Boston Public Library; extract printed in *Life*, I, 521–522.

1. The year is supplied on the manuscript probably in the hand of Wendell Phillips Garrison.
2. The elderly and toothless Joice Heth (died 1836) was the first of P. T. Barnum's successful attractions. The young showman had first exhibited her in New York in August of 1835 as the 161-year-old nurse of George Washington. When an autopsy following her death showed that she had been only about eighty, Barnum wrote a series of newspaper articles explaining how he had been imposed upon and secured by this second hoax invaluable publicity.
3. Albert Hinckley (1811–1864), of Plainfield, Connecticut, was a member of the Amherst class of 1838, though he never graduated.
4. Presumably Newburyport.

217

TO GEORGE W. BENSON

Boston, Oct. 2, 1835.

My dear George —

I am a very naughty young man, truly. — Where is the call of the Convention that I promised to write and send to you on Tuesday? Ay, echo answers — Where? But when the head is all confusion, and one's hands are full, what can he do or say? I have not got regulated yet, since my return from rusticating in the country, and I already begin to sigh for the quietude and (selfish ease will out) *irresponsibleness* of Friendship's Valley. But I felt relieved, in regard to your conventional notice, as soon as I saw brother Stanton, whom it is always refreshing to see; for he told me that bro. Goodell [1] was still with you, and I knew he would use his pen very readily, if requested.

Boston is beginning to sink into apathy. The reaction has come rapidly, but we are trying to get the steam up again. We have held two public meetings, which were well attended, and all went off quietly.

I miss your dear little babe exceedingly — nay, do I not miss you all? But separation on earth is the lot of others as well as of

Your affectionate brother,

W.L.G.

ALS: Garrison Papers, Boston Public Library.

1. William Goodell.

2 1 8

TO GEORGE BENSON

Boston, Oct. 21, 1835.

Dear and venerable Sir:

A living epistle is so much more valuable than a dead one, as almost to render the latter altogether needless. — That living epistle will be your own dear son Henry, whom we send to-day, as the representative of our happy and peaceful household, on a visit to the Valley of Friendship at Brooklyn. There is no topic that can interest you particularly, no piece of household or domestic information, no transaction of our friends or our enemies, which he will not be able minutely to communicate, or upon which he cannot enlarge with edification and interest. It will, therefore, be useless for me to travel over the same ground in this letter.

The period of rest (I wish, for his own sake, it were longer,) which he intends to take, is much needed by his body and mind; for his duties have been very arduous at the office, and his industry and un-remitted zeal proportionate. In the midst of the great equinoctial storm which has raged all over the land, (of course I speak figuratively,) he has stood like the pine of Clan Alpine —

"Moor'd on the rifted rock,
Proof to the tempest's shock;
The broader 'tis rooted, the firmer it grows." [1]

May health, and peace, and joy, go with him; may his visit prove as delightful as was mine; and may his presence be as cheering to you all, as is the morning light to those who watch impatiently for its coming. His absence from us will make a void in our little family circle, which will be severely felt; but we give him up, for a time, with cheerful resignation, that you may be gladdened by his company.

Henry will be somewhat disappointed in not meeting brother George at Brooklyn, although he will probably see him at Providence. Perhaps it is well that they visit you alternately, as one will supply the absence of the other.

My health has been extremely good since I left Brooklyn, for which, as well as for other mercies, continual gratitude is due to God. My mind is in a peaceful and happy frame; for faith, and hope, and love, make it their abode. I desire to cease wholly from man, and to rely upon nothing but the promises of Him who cannot lie. Oh, what insanity marks the conduct of those, who, professing to believe in the existence of a God, and in the authenticity of a divine revelation, do nevertheless live without His fear before their eyes, but consult that fear of man which brings a snare! How is Christ wounded in the house of his professed friends! What a mean, dwarfish, corrupt, partial, limited, oppressive Christianity is that which generally prevails in our land! How it takes tithes, with all care and exactitude, of mint, cummin and annise, but neglects judgment, mercy and faith! How basely it cringes to the powerful! how swiftly it runs from danger! how, in the hour of trial, like treacherous Peter, it curses and swears, and denies all knowledge of Christ! how amicable are its relations with Belial! [2] how self-approvingly it transforms the image of God into an image like unto a beast, and buys and sells for gold, or exchanges for mules and swine, the souls for whose redemption the Son of God came down from heaven! how it relies for safety upon fortifications, and naval ships, and an armed host, and rushes to the bloody strife to avenge the sligh[t]est insult offered to its *dignity!*

The spirit of the Lord is now striving mightily with this nation, and the nation is striving as mightily to quench it; and in doing so, it is revealing to the eyes of an astonished world an amount of depravity and heathenism, that makes the name of our Christianity a reproach. Nevertheless, let the worst appear; let not one sin be covered up; let the number of the rebels, and the extent of the rebellion, fully appear; let all that is dangerous, or hypocritical, or unjust, among us, be proclaimed upon the house-tops; and then the genuine disciples of Christ will be able skilfully and understandingly to carry on the war. A large[r] number than Gideon had is left to us, and the same omnipotent arm is ready to be bared in our defence.

Not having received any letters from you since I left B., I hope to be favored with one when Henry returns. It was my intention to write to sister Sarah or Anna by this opportunity, but the chaise is now at the door, and the moment of separation has come. My dear wife has written to Anna, whom we confidently expect will come to Boston with Henry. Assure all at home of my constant remembrance and increasing love; and give my kind regards to Mr. and Mrs. Gray, Dr. Huntington and Dr. Whitcomb, and all my anti-slavery friends, both male and female, who call at your house.[3]

Trusting it may be the will of heaven to preserve your valuable life very many years longer, I remain with all fidelity and affection,
    Your dutiful son,

Wm. Lloyd Garrison.

ALS: Garrison Papers, Boston Public Library; extract printed in *Life*, II, 8.

1. Garrison quotes inaccurately Scott, "Boat Song," lines 15–17.

2. As Garrison used the term, Belial is the personification of evil and wickedness, resembling Milton's fallen angel of that name in *Paradise Lost*. Numerous Old Testament usages point to the Hebrew derivation meaning worthless, without value, unprofitable.

3. In addition to the John Grays, Garrison mentions two doctors who were living and apparently practicing in Brooklyn, Thomas Huntington (1793–1867) and James Bigelow Whitcomb (1804–1880). Dr. Huntington, a physician by profession, served as treasurer of the Windham County Peace Society and was an evangelist associated with the Baptist church. Dr. Whitcomb, a graduate of the Medical School of Maine, was primarily concerned with medical practice, though he was probably also a reformer. (See Ellen Larned, *History of Windham County, Connecticut*, Worcester, Massachusetts, 1880, II, and the *General Catalogue of Bowdoin College and the Medical School of Maine, 1794–1912*, p. 322.)

219

TO SAMUEL E. SEWALL

Brooklyn, Oct. 24, 1835.

My early, kind and faithful friend:

I have just written to my partner, Mr. Knapp, a hasty account of my exit from the jail in Leverett-st. and arrival in this village, under the roof of my venerable father-in-law.[1] He may communicate it to you and to others. Suffice it to say, that all is well with me, both in body and in mind, except that I am extremely anxious to learn what has transpired since I left. My obligations to you for your manifold kindnesses exceed, I fear, human ability to repay; but God, in whose cause you have acted, will bless you and yours abundantly. Our "recompense of reward," if not found upon the earth, will be obtained in heaven, provided we are actuated by that divine charity of which the apostle speaks, and without which we are as tinkling brass.[2] I speak the express language of my soul when I say, that I would rather have the peril and outrage through which I have passed, than such a reception as Lafayette received,[3] comparing the motives and objects of those who engaged in the general excitement. Give me brickbats in the cause of God, to wedges of gold in the cause of sin.

I write to you, not only to render thanks on the part of Mrs. G. and myself, but to ask your advice, particularly — as well as that of other friends generally — as to the course it will be just and dutiful for me to pursue. Probably you have all had frequent consultations together, and have come to some definite conclusions. It seems to me that we ought to resolve that the Liberator, despite all opposition, shall continue to be printed — and printed, too, in Boston. Whether it is necessary for me to abide in the city, is a question of lawful expediency. Should I remain here, I shall unquestionably be able to write much more copiously and promptly for the paper than I can in Boston, with the cares of a household upon me, and with almost ceaseless interruptions. Besides, the expense of boarding here will not be half so great as that of housekeeping in Boston. However, I am willing to take the advice of my friends, and desire that it may be given without reserve.[4]

As to our dear brother Thompson, I am feverish to learn how he is now situated, what are his views and feelings, and what is to be done publicly, respecting his case. How thankful am I that the mob seized me, and that he was safe with his family! Will it not be dangerous for him to appear in the streets of Boston, even in broad daylight, at present? Ask him to communicate with me directly.

To-night, I expect to hear some tidings from Utica.[5] Perhaps a worse affair has happened than any one anticipates.

If you can get time, pray write to me on Monday. Every item of intelligence will be truly acceptable. Let me know how the Mayor and Aldermen are disposed to act. Have any of the rioters been arrested? Would it not be well to suggest, through the medium of the Daily Advertiser, the propriety of calling a public meeting at Faneuil Hall, to denounce the transaction of the present week, and to protect citizens in the right of free discussion?[6] Or is ours, indeed, a city of mobocrats and tyrants?

I hope the friends will countenance, advise and assist Mr. Knapp — for he has now a heavy load of care and responsibility resting upon him. If the presence of Henry is needed, he will return as soon as he is apprised of the fact.

Freighting this hasty scrawl with grateful and affectionate remembrances to all my kind friends, and renewing the acknowledgments of my numerous obligations to you, I remain, as hitherto, the undaunted advocate of the perishing slave, and

Your steadfast friend and admirer,

Wm. Lloyd Garrison.

S. E. Sewall, Esq.

ALS: William L. Garrison Collection, Massachusetts Historical Society.

1. Garrison refers to the rather spectacular events of October 21 and to his flight to Brooklyn, Connecticut. Bostonians had anticipated with some excitement a meeting of the Female Anti-Slavery Society, scheduled for October 14, at which George Thompson was to be the principal speaker. But there had been sufficient agitation against Thompson to convince the abolitionists that the meeting should be postponed until the twenty-first, and that Garrison rather than Thompson should speak. In spite of the change, however, excitement had continued to build. A mob gathered around Congress Hall the day of the meeting and eventually seized Garrison, who offered no resistance and remained calm and brave. He might have been seriously injured or even killed but for the efforts of the mayor, the police, and a few level-headed citizens who whisked him off to the Leverett Street Jail for protection. The next day, after the hearing, Garrison was advised to leave Boston. He and Helen, who was soon to give birth to their first child, went promptly to her family in Connecticut.

2. Garrison alludes to I Corinthians 13:1.

3. During his triumphant tour of 1824.

4. Sewall answered Garrison's letter on October 27 (see *Life*, II, 42–43),

agreeing that all considered it would be better for Garrison to remain at present in Brooklyn. Sewall regretted the public's apparent approval of the recent mob as well as the city's reluctance to prosecute the leading rioters.

5. It was reported in *The Liberator* for October 31 that at Utica the anti-slavery convention had not been disturbed by any real violence.

6. The Boston *Daily Advertiser* took a position similar to that of nearly all Boston papers and of many city officials, that the real cause of the mob was the abolitionists' insistence upon holding meetings in spite of hostile public sentiment.

---

2 2 0

TO GEORGE W. BENSON

Brooklyn, Oct. 26, 1835.

My dear brother-in-law:

Henry has just finished the perusal of your truly interesting letter of yesterday, giving all the information that we have yet received, respecting the tumultuous proceedings at Utica. I am ready to leap joyfully into the air, on learning that our abolition brethren in the State of New-York, to the number of four hundred, went with christian manliness to Utica, willing to encounter every peril rather than be driven from their high and holy purpose. What is the fear of man in competition with the fear of God? Yea, what is brute violence in opposition to the might and majesty of a regenerated soul? "Why do the heathen rage?" "He that sitteth in the heavens shall laugh." [1]

Accept a brother's gratitude for your consoling letter of Friday last, and for your swift visit to Boston, that you might minister to me in my necessities. Your disappointment in passing me on the road is the measure of my own; but perhaps it was better that you should miss me, seeing you was enabled to give some timely advice to our friends in Boston, and to make some important arrangements for the publication of the last Liberator. We arrived safely under the paternal roof in Brooklyn, and were received joyfully with tears by all the household. Helen is well and in good spirits; and as for myself, I am as sound in body, and as cheerful in mind, as at any time of my life.

It were needless for me to detail the dastardly and riotous proceedings of Wednesday afternoon last in Boston, because you undoubtedly have received correct information respecting them — not from the Boston papers, for they garble and embellish, but from our friends Burleigh, Whittier, and others. Suffice it to say, that my life was almost miraculously saved; that, imminent as I felt the peril to be, my mind was placid and undisturbed throughout the trying scene; that my faith in the promises of God was as steadfast as his throne; that the prospect of a violent and dreadful end failed to excite within me one emotion of fear; and that I reposed as calmly in my prison-cell as if no uproar had happened, excepting an occasional throb of anxiety in regard to my dear wife.

Here I must abruptly stop — for Mr. Taylor [2] is at the door. I have not had a syllable of intelligence from Boston. More to-morrow.

Yours, with unquenchable love,

Wm. Lloyd Garrison.

ALS: Garrison Papers, Boston Public Library.

1. Psalms 2:1, 4.
2. Unidentified.

221

TO ISAAC KNAPP

Brooklyn, Oct. 28, 1835.
Wednesday morning.

My dear partner in the joys and honors of persecution:

I wrote a few hasty lines to you by yesterday's mail, stating that no intelligence had reached me from Boston since my departure. Last evening, however, I was overwhelmed with joy on receiving, by the kindness of Mr. Howard, a huge bundle of newspapers and a letter from you, and also one from friend Burleigh for brother Henry.[1] I sat up till 2 o'clock this morning, devouring the contents of the whole mass, and went to bed without feeling any fatigue, and have risen this morning with a cheerful heart. I shall now be able to drive my editorial quill somewhat freely.

After perusing your affectionate letter, the Liberator of Saturday came next in course. It gave me unalloyed satisfaction, as I think it is one of the best numbers we have ever published. Friend Burleigh's article, respecting the riot, is most admirably and graphically written, and I have scarcely any thing to add to it. However, as something on the subject will naturally be expected from my pen, I shall make a simple statement of my seizure, committal to jail, &c. Accordingly, I have commenced it, and now send you the introduction. Altogether, it is probable that it will be somewhat protracted, though I hope not tedious. I also send you for conspicuous publication, the excellent letter written by dear Thompson, (of whom, by the way, you write nothing,) which may answer a good purpose for him at the present time.

It seems to me that my presence in Boston is indispensable, on many accounts. — Something must be done to sustain the Liberator, immediately, or how can it survive beyond the present volume?

Something must be done, too, respecting the case of bro. Thompson. Then, as I am to break up housekeeping, it is proper that I should be present to give directions with regard to the disposal of things. Besides, I do not wish the charge to be made, that I have been driven out of Boston, and dare not return. Unless you and the friends interpose a positive *veto*, therefore, I shall probably be in Boston on Saturday evening, via Worcester. Henry and sister Anna will reach the city probably on Monday evening next.

Shall I come, or shall I not? I wish to be governed by your advice and the appearance of things in the city — but my desire is to be with you a few days.

If you see Mr. Vinal, tell him that I shall give up the lease immediately — i.e. as soon as I can remove my furniture.[2]

I dread to put up my things at auction, as the sacrifice must be great. But what else can I do?

You are right in surmising, that there is a determination on the part of the city authorities to put down the anti-slavery cause in Boston, although they talk smoothly and make fair professions. They are not to be trusted. Old birds are not caught with chaff.

Probably you will be hindered in getting out the next Liberator, in consequence of being deprived of an office. Well, impossibilities must not be expected of us by our subscribers.

Give my very best thanks to friend Burleigh for his editorials, and ask him to write for this week's paper as much as he can, until I get regulated.

Who wrote the Sonnet addressed to me? It is a fine one.

Write to me immediately, so that I may hear from you by Friday's mail, and govern my course accordingly. I shall send you the rest of my story to-morrow. Make such selections as you think best. Publish as much of the Utica Convention and uproar as you deem interesting.

Has my lost hat yet been found? I left my cloak at the Anti-Slavery Office — is it safe? Do not suffer my anti-slavery articles, at home, to be scattered. Hope Whittier will write something apropos respecting the Boston riot. My Helen is in good health and so am I.

Yours, truly,

Wm. Lloyd Garrison.

☞ Keep me supplied with letters and newspapers as regularly as you can. Be sure to let me hear from you or Burleigh on Friday.

ALS: Garrison Papers, Boston Public Library; printed partly in *Life*, II, 44–46.

1. Mr. Howard has been identified only as from Brooklyn, Connecticut.
2. Nathaniel Vinal, a Boston grain merchant who did business at Vinal's wharf and lived on Portland Street, was apparently Garrison's landlord for the house at 23 Brighton Street.

222

TO HELEN E. GARRISON

Boston, Nov. 4, 1835.

My dear Wife:

With all the speed, attention and ardor of a *lover*, (and that, you know, for a *husband* to say is something unusual,) I seize my pen to inform you of my safe arrival in Boston, this evening — say, one hour ago. Of course, as it was somewhat dark when I arrived, it is not yet known by my mobocratic friends that I am here.

Father, I presume, will tell you, in his epistle, of the pleasant and comfortable ride that we had from Brooklyn to Providence. He seemed to be as little fatigued as myself at the end of the journey. We were both exceedingly disappointed at the absence of brother George. I saw, however, William Chace, his father, Mr. Stanton, Mr. Goodell, and many other of our abolition brethren — and I need not add, that we had a joyous meeting together.

In the course of the forenoon, I took father over to friend Brown's, in a chaise, and there we had a real old-fashioned greeting. Friend Moses never manifested before so much gladness to see me. After chatting with him about half an hour, we reluctantly took leave of him. The more I see of him, the more I regard him with wonder, delight and satisfaction.

I rode to Boston in one of the open cars, filled with the "common people," and thus saved 50 cents — no trifling sum in these days of penury and persecution. I do not know that I was recognised on the way.

Instead of ordering the coachman to drive me to No. 23, Brighton-Street, I thought it most prudent to be set down at friend Fuller's.[1] Was just in season to eat supper there, though he and his wife had gone to Newton. After tea, friend Tillson took my arm, and we sallied out into the street — for my home, or rather the place that was once *our* home.[2] But we took another route — for he communicated a *secret* to me — viz. that our noble and persecuted brother Geo. Thompson was staying at friend Southwick's, (unknown even to the abolition friends generally,) and thither we went to see him.[3] Found him in good health and spirits. After mutual gratulations, and a rapid conversation, though brief — I said, "Give me a sheet of paper, ink and a pen, for I must not fail to send a line to my anxious wife by to-night's mail." Just at that moment, Henry and friend Burleigh burst into the room, and then Mrs. Grew, Miss Sullivan, and Miss Parker.[4] What a collection of raving fanatics and dangerous incendiaries! A happy meeting this!

I have left them all below, for a few moments, to scribble these few imperfect and scarcely legible lines, which Henry will take to the Post Office immediately.

Now, my dear wife, disburden your mind of uneasiness as much as possible, on my account. Be assured I will not *needlessly* run into danger, but shall use all *proper* precaution for my safety. I feel excellently well, both in body and mind. All the dear ladies, with Henry, Thompson and Burleigh, send the best remembrances to you. Mr. Knapp I have not yet seen, but shall probably see him this evening. Do not yet know where I shall sleep to-night — probably here or at bro. Fuller's.

Give a brother's love for me to dear sisters Sarah and Anne, also to Catharine [5] — and kiss her dearly little babe daily for me until my return. A son's affection I send to dear mother. Shall return with all despatch.

Yours, with inexpressible love,

Wm. Lloyd Garrison.

ALS: Garrison Papers, Boston Public Library; printed partly in *Life*, II, 46–47.

1. John E. Fuller lived on nearby Pitts Street.
2. Joseph Tillson was a young man who did odd jobs about the antislavery office. When Henry E. Benson was ill, the board of managers elected Tillson to take his place as secretary and agent of the Massachusetts Anti-Slavery Society, so that he could officially be the general factotum. (See Garrison's letter to his wife, June 1, 1836.)
3. Joseph Southwick (1791–1866), husband of the more famous Thankful Hussey Southwick (see letter 224, n. 2), was of Quaker stock and one of the signers of the Declaration of Sentiments of the American Anti-Slavery Society. Currently, he was the president of the Massachusetts Anti-Slavery Society. In later years he was to disagree with Garrison concerning disunion.
4. In addition to the familiar Henry E. Benson and Charles C. Burleigh, Garrison mentions Anna Grew and Catherine M. Sullivan, who have not been further identified, and Mary S. Parker (c. 1802–1841). Miss Parker, an active abolitionist, ran a boarding house in Boston at 5 Hayward Place, where the Mays, the Garrisons, and other abolitionists lived from time to time. Her house was a favorite gathering place for those active in the cause. Miss Parker was president of the Boston Female Anti-Slavery Society and chairman of the meeting on the day Garrison was mobbed.
5. George W. Benson's wife.

223

TO HELEN E. GARRISON

23, Brighton-Street,
Saturday afternoon, Nov. 7, 1835.

My dear Wife:

You perceive that I write in the house that we fondly expected to call our home, in which we have spent so many happy hours, but which can be our home no longer. Every thing looks, if possible, *more* than natural — at least, seems dearer to me than ever. The carpets — tables — chairs — sofa — looking-glasses — &c. &c. seem almost to have found a tongue, to welcome my return, and to congratulate me upon my escape out of the jaws of the lion. The clock ticks an emphatical and sonorous welcome. As for puss, she finds it a difficult matter, even with all her purring and playing, to express her joy. Then to pass to the reception which I receive at the hands of my friends: it is so kind, and sympathetic, and joyful, that one might almost covet to be mobbed, to obtain such a return. One anonymous individual has made me a present of forty-five dollars, which comes most seasonably.

I wrote to you on the evening of my arrival, at the house of my esteemed friend Southwick. That night I slept at home, in our chamber — and as you were absent, I permitted puss to occupy the *outside* of the bed, as a substitute. We reposed very lovingly until morning, without any alarm from mobs without, or disturbance from rats within. Mr. Knapp rose as regularly and as early to prepare breakfast, as if he were hired "help" — and, Henry completing the trio — nay, Mr. Burleigh made a fourth companion — we sat down and partook of a very comfortable entertainment.

In the course of the forenoon, Christiana [1] came to the house, to whom I gave your letters and instructions. She remained with Mr. and Mrs. York only a few days, as they soon left the city, and had since been doing house work for Mrs. Robinson, but had now quit, as Mrs. R. was somewhat difficult to please, her cooking being complicated and laborious. [2] Christiana was highly rejoiced to see me, and inquired after you with much affection. She has since been staying here, cleaning the house, (for it is quite dusty if not dirty,) packing up your things, providing meals for us, &c. She will stay here until the things are removed: in the mean time, I am endeavoring to find her a suitable place, for she thinks she should rather prefer to pass the winter in Boston, than to return to Providence. She says she will take your wrapper (or gown) at the price you mention, — $12, — provided you will wait until she can earn the money. I have told her that she need not give herself any uneasiness on that score — have I done right?

Well — after breakfast on Thursday morning, I sallied out into the streets, to see and to be seen — "the observed of all observers" [3] — peradventure. After all, I did not prove to be so great a curiosity as I had anticipated: very few stared at me, or seemed to know me, notwithstanding the previous exhibition of my self to four or five thousand "gentlemen of property and standing from all parts of the city."

I went directly to the Anti-Slavery rooms, (having no printing-office that I could first visit,) and there busied myself some time in shaking hands with various friends, answering inquiries, and asking questions. In a short time, a long procession marched by the office, with a band of music in full blast, and followed by a squad of spectators; and what do you think they had with them? It was a large board, on which were drawn two figures, quite conspicuously — viz. George Thompson and a black woman. Over the head of Thompson were the words, "The Foreign Emissary" — and the black woman asking him, "When are we going to have another meeting, brother Thompson?" It is fortunate, perhaps, that this company did not know that I was then in the Anti-Slavery office — else they might have stopped in front of it, made a demonstration of contempt, and excited another uproar. In this shameless manner they paraded through the streets until they were satisfied, and then went out of the city to make a target of Mr. T. and his sable companion. The city authorities made not the slightest attempt to interfere. As it was possible that our house might be disturbed that night, I slept at Mr. Fuller's, and last night at Mr. Southwick's; but every thing has been perfectly quiet in the city — and, although I have walked freely in all parts of Boston, yet no one has insulted me, or called for any manifestation of displeasure. Nay, many talk of putting me on the list of representatives to the Legislature, to be chosen on Monday next. There is a strong reaction already in our favor — and the news from the interior is most encouraging.

Mr. May has not yet returned to this city, but is laboring acceptably in Vermont, notwithstanding he was mobbed at Montpelier. I am ashamed to say that I have not yet seen Mrs. May — but Henry was at Miss Parker's last evening, and says she was in good health and spirits.

Mr. Thompson will probably sail for England in the course of a fortnight — but this must be kept private. Mrs. T. is going to make a visit to her sister in Baltimore, and will follow her husband in the course of a month or two. Louisa and Amelia will remain in Boston until her return from Baltimore.[4] Margaret[5] has now left her. Thus we are to lose our eloquent and devoted brother — but he will still labor for us in England. Heaven's choicest blessings go with him and his! It will be almost like tearing myself in twain when he departs. You will see an excellent letter from his pen in the Liberator of Saturday,[6] accompanying my story of the riot. It will be read with interest and admiration.

I have seen the Misses Weston, and they speak of you in the kindest terms.[7] On asking them, where I could get a room to store our furniture, they said that they occupied a large house, with scarcely any thing in it, and I might fill it if I chose. Accordingly, I shall move the things there next week, excepting such as Henry and Knapp may want to furnish their room. (By the way, they have not yet determined where to board.) The Westons will take excellent care of our goods. Hope this arrangement will please you.

We cannot sell our furniture hastily, now, without making a large sacrifice — and it would be blazoned over the land if it were known that we had put it up at auction. I suppose the beds and bedding had better be sent with the rest of the articles.

Aunt Charlotte has had to leave Rev. Mr. Young's in consequence of sickness, and is now with one of her cousins.[8]

At the expiration of ten or twelve days, (not sooner,) I may have the exquisite delight to see you, and father and mother, and dear Anna and Sarah — till then, and always, I remain,

Yours, in the dearest ties,

Wm. Lloyd Garrison.

☞ Tell Mr. Gray that I promptly left Frederick's letter, but did not see him. Saw Mrs. Gray and her little babe.[9] They are all well. Write to me by Tuesday's mail.

ALS: Garrison Papers, Boston Public Library; printed partly in *Life*, II, 47–48.

1. A servant not otherwise identified.

2. Mr. and Mrs. York have not been identified. Mrs. Robinson is probably Rachel Gilpin Robinson (1799–1862) of an old and distinguished New York City family and the wife of Rowland T. Robinson of W. Eaton and Company. Although the Robinsons farmed in Ferrisburg, Vermont, they lived for intervals in Boston. They were active abolitionists, their house in Vermont being a station on the underground railroad. (See the *Robinson Genealogy*, XI, and Hiram Carleton, *Genealogical and Family History of the State of Vermont*, New York, 1903, II, 103.)

3. Shakespeare, *Hamlet*, III, i, 162.

4. Louisa and the infant Amelia Thompson accompanied their parents to the United States (C. Duncan Rice, "The Anti-Slavery Mission of George Thompson to the United States, 1834–1835," *Journal of American Studies*, London, England, 2:21, April 1968).

5. Presumably a servant brought from Britain by the Thompsons.

6. November 7.

7. Garrison refers to two of the five Weston sisters, Caroline (1808–1882) and Anne Warren (born 1812). Although not so well known and so influential as their older sister Maria Weston Chapman, they were ardent abolitionists who expressed their sentiments in many poems and articles in the antislavery annual *The Liberty Bell*. The Weston sisters kept a school in a house on Boylston Street (site of the present Boston Public Library); it was probably to this house that Garrison was planning to move his furniture.

8. Apparently Charlotte Newell was living with a family in Lowell; the Reverend Mr. Young has not been identified.

9. Mr. Gray is John Gray of Brooklyn, Frederick is his son in Boston, and Mrs. Gray is the son's wife.

2 2 4

TO HELEN E. GARRISON

Boston, Nov. 9, 1835.

My dear Wife:

Yesterday (Sabbath) forenoon, I concluded not to go to church, because, to confess the truth, I had not replaced my torn pantaloons,[1] and as the weather was too warm to justify the wearing of a cloak. About eleven o'clock, one of Mrs. Southwick's daughters came down to our house, and gave me the startling information that my dear friend Thompson would leave the country in the course of an hour — that he was going to sail in a packet for St. John — and that he wished to see me immediately.[2] Of course, I went in all haste and with much trepidation; for the idea of separating from him — perhaps till the close of life — filled my soul with anguish. I found his wife in tears; she could not go with him, and no doubt felt somewhat unhappy. She is to visit her sister at Baltimore, and will then sail for England. My heart swells with sorrow, my cheeks burn with indignation, when I think of the treatment which Thompson has received at the hands of the people of this country. If he were a murderer, or parricide, he could not be treated more shamefully than he has been. To think of his being in danger of assassination, even in broad daylight — nay, even in the streets of Boston! Shame — infamy upon the city! But I have no time to moralise — you will feel deeply, without the aid of my comments. Suffice it to say, Mr. Chapman took Mr. T. down to the wharf in a carriage, saw him safely on board the packet, and the vessel move down the harbor.[3] So we trust he is now on his way to a place of safety and rest. From St. John he will sail for England. Mr. Knapp will probably go down to him, to convey his baggage safely.

Our election, to-day, has passed off quietly. Several votes have been cast for me, but how many is not yet known.[4] We have not been disturbed at the house, and I walk through the city without receiving any insult.

I have no lamp — and it is so dark (I am writing at the office) that I cannot see to write more. I am in very good health and spirits, and hope you and the rest of the household are in a similar condition.

Adieu! Ever yours,

W. L. Garrison.

P.S. I am now at the house, and have broken open the letter to enjoin secrecy upon you and the rest of the family, respecting Thompson's departure. — Here, in Boston, we shall say nothing about it, for the present.

Brother George has just written to me, giving me the agreeable information of his visit to Brooklyn, and kindly advising as to the disposal of our furniture. As our friend[s], the Westons, can accommodate it all, and will take good care of it, we shall have no difficulty on this score. At the first favorable moment, we shall attempt to sell it.

Saw Mrs. May to-day, who told me she presumed Mr. May was in Brooklyn, and would probably be here in a few days. She looks well, is cheerful, and seems undaunted, notwithstanding the perils of the times.

New subscribers to the Liberator still continue to come in — not less than a dozen to-day. Am much obliged to the mob.

If I should not get a letter from you on Wednesday, shall be very much disappointed.

ALS: Garrison Papers, Boston Public Library; printed partly in *Life*, II, 49–50.

1. Part of the suit destroyed by the Boston mob on October 21.
2. Garrison evidently refers to Sarah Southwick (born 1821), daughter of Joseph and Thankful Hussey Southwick (1792–1867). Mrs. Southwick, from a Quaker family of Portland, Maine, was the sister-in-law of both Isaac and Nathan Winslow. She was an energetic Garrisonian abolitionist during the thirties and forties. Immediately before his departure from the United States, she was Thompson's hostess.
3. Henry G. Chapman (1804–1842) was a Boston merchant and abolitionist. Although his wife, Maria Weston Chapman, played the more prominent role in the cause, he also was an active reformer and fund raiser.
4. Garrison inadvertently became a write-in candidate for the state legislature as a result of the publicity he had received during the mobbing on October 21. (See letter 223, to Helen, November 7, 1835, and letter 225, November 11.)

225

TO HELEN E. GARRISON

Boston, Nov. 11, 1835.

My dear Wife:

I sit down to write my *fourth* letter to you, since we parted — but not a syllable of intelligence comes from you! Ah! have I not reason to scold you a little, if I only knew how? How shall I interpret your silence? Shall I imagine you as saying — "I don't love him at all — I am glad he is as far removed from me as Boston. Why don't he go down to Eastport? I wish he would not pester me with his scrawls. What do I care whether he is sick or well, safe or in danger, sorrowful or happy? It is true, he is my husband — but why does he wish to hear from me on that account? Surely, fourteen months after marriage, it is idle to feel any throb of affection — any emotion of love!

Am I not the "better half"? Then he is not my equal — and being inferior, I will not put myself on a level with him. Nay, what ought he to expect from me? Has he not been mobbed — ignominously dragged through the streets — shut up in prison? Did he not cause me to be "turned out of house and home," and to find shelter in another State?" No, my love, these are not your sentiments — how dearly you love me, I know full well; still, where is my letter? Here I have been sitting for the space of two hours, most impatiently, waiting for the arrival of the Providence mail — it has come — to me in vain. Where is my letter?

It is now just three weeks ago, this afternoon, since the mob were assembled in front of the Anti-Slavery Office to tar-and-feather G. T. or myself. Here I am writing in the very room, and at the same desk; it is now raining heavily; the deluge would have been quite *apropos* in the time of the mob. "The respectable and influential" broadcloth rioters would have fled like a drove of sheep before this rain-storm; for they cannot easily face anything but sunshine and fair weather. A cold bath would have cooled their patriotism for the time being.

We have not had any tidings from G. T. since he left, but shall be expecting letters daily. Mrs. T. came to our house yesterday, and packed up and removed all her things — household furniture and all. How soon she will go to New-York, I do not know — probably in a few days. She is still remaining at Mrs. Southwick's, with all her children.

Last evening, we had a large meeting of select friends at Mr. Fuller's house, to take Mr. T.'s case into consideration. We came to the conclusion that he ought not to make any disclosures respecting the Marshall and Dale affair — but evidence must be obtained from London.[1] We also agreed to defray Mr. and Mrs. Thompson's expenses to England. It is not yet certain whether friend Knapp or Henry will go down to St. John. — Henry seems to think the trip might be advantageous to his health, as well as gratifying to his feelings.

To-day I fully expected to commence moving our furniture, but the rain has prevented. I long to get through with the job, and to be reposing in quietude at Brooklyn. Within a week, perhaps, if I am spared, I may enjoy this sweet satisfaction — and then, adieu to Boston! I hope I am not growing misanthropic — but my desire to be away from the many, and present with the few, increases daily. So, do not think I shall not be contented to pass the winter in Friendship's Valley. — Why, such a thought would be a libel upon sisters Sarah and Anna and Mary, and father and mother, and John Gray and his wife, and Dr. Huntington and his wife, and Mr. Williams and his wife, and Dr. Whitcomb and his wife, and Mr. Geers and his wife, and Eunice and Susan — and kittens and all! [2]

Brother May is expected home this evening — but where he is we really do not know. I shall be disposed to utter some lamentations, if he has not visited Brooklyn.

Christiana is still at the house — but puss has gone off on a strolling excursion, and perhaps has fallen into the hands of Judge Lynch.

I met Henry Clark a day or two since, and interchanged a few words with him.[3] Now that the excitement is over, I presume he feels ashamed of his treatment of a distressed woman — my wife. Let us forgive him cheerfully, as we ourselves hope to be forgiven above.

Abbe is now with Mrs. Lovering, in Roxbury, and will stay three or four weeks there.[4] She has written several notes to friend Knapp, and one to Henry, desiring to see him to-morrow evening. It seems to me that she loves Mr. K. too well to give him up.

Your husband is not yet very popular in Boston. As a candidate for the Legislature, he received only about seventy or eighty votes. Never mind — honors will come thick and fast enough upon him by and by. Don't be proud at the prospect!

I have not yet been out to Roxbury — nor seen whether Mr. Vinal [5] will allow me to give up the lease of the house — nor done many other things that ought to have been done.

With choice and endearing remembrances to all at home, and a lover's affection for you, I remain,

Your dutiful partner,

Wm. Lloyd Garrison.

ALS: Garrison Papers, Boston Public Library.

1. Garrison refers to a crime Thompson had committed in 1829. (See his letter to Angelina G. Weld, June 15, 1839, Gilbert H. Barnes and Dwight L. Dumond, editors, *Letters of Theodore Dwight Weld, Angelina Grimké Weld, and Sarah Grimké, 1822–1844*, New York, 1934, II, 774–777.) Thompson had embezzled £80 from his employers (presumably Marshall and Dale). In 1831 he was married, became active in the antislavery movement, and entered into an agreement to repay his former employers. By the time of his trip to the United States in 1834, he had a full receipt for the original debt, though he later expressed further repentance by continuing payment up to £150. For a full discussion of this episode see C. Duncan Rice, "The Anti-Slavery Mission of George Thompson to the United States, 1834–1835," *Journal of American Studies*, London, England, 2:25–26 (April 1968).

2. Garrison includes in the Benson circle, in addition to those already familiar, the names of the Herbert Williamses and the W. D. Geerses — both apparently farm families living in the vicinity of Brooklyn. (See letter 232, to Samuel J. May, December 5, 1835, and letter 228, to George W. Benson, November 27, 1835, as well as *The Liberator* for September 29, 1832, where W. D. Geers is listed among the correspondents whose letter has reached the office from Providence the preceding week.) Like Eunice, Susan was probably a servant in the Benson household.

3. Henry Clark, an acquaintance of the Garrisons, was presumably a member

of the "gentlemanly" mob that attacked Garrison on October 21. He was perhaps the one who rather rudely turned Helen Garrison back when she tried to attend the meeting of the Boston Female Anti-Slavery Society. (See letter 226, to Helen, November 14, for another reference to Henry Clark.)

4. Abbe ("Abbie" or "Abby," usual spelling) is Henry Clark's sister; Mrs. Lovering has not been identified.

5. Nathaniel Vinal.

226

TO HELEN E. GARRISON

Boston, Nov. 14, 1835.

My dear Wife:

I recal nearly all the first page of my last letter. It seems that you were neither dilatory nor forgetful, but a prompt and affectionate woman. Your letter, however, did not reach me so soon by Mr. May, by twenty-four hours, as it would have done by regular course of mail. So, hereafter, I shall put a *veto* upon him as a mail-carrier between Brooklyn and Boston. — Still, I am very much obliged to him, as he brought the letter without charging any postage!

Well — I expected it. Expected what? Why, a gentle scolding for speaking of Mrs. Garrison's "delicate" state of health, in the Liberator.[1] My dear wife is much more sensitive than the Queen of England, in a matter like this. But necessity was laid upon me thus to write, in order to exculpate myself from the base charge of cowardice, preferred against me by the newspaper press. I beg your pardon — or, rather, it is the duty of the mob to ask pardon of us both, for reducing us to such a dilemma. When I see you, I will kiss you, and make it all up. When will that be? Not as soon, perhaps, as you expect, or I could desire; for I have many things to occupy me, and a long trip to take, before I can be permitted to see Grey Mare Hill, or John Grey's house.[2] In the first place, we have had all kinds of weather but the right kind for moving household goods — and therefore my despatch has been nothing but delay. Yesterday, however, there was something like a rational pause in the elements, of which I took advantage, and removed a large portion of the furniture. On Monday, I hope to get the remainder removed, and thus effect a double removal, to wit, of the goods from the house, and of trouble from my mind. Mrs. May will have the use of our sofa, pier glass, and rocking-chair — the last, you know, is in a crippled state, but may prove serviceable in teaching a lesson of patience. The clock, Clarkson's Portrait, and the First of August,[3] I shall send to the Anti-Slavery Office. The Westons[4] have agreed to take charge of puss, (though she, or more truly *he*, has again decamped,) — and what is better, they have agreed to hire Christiana, who has been to see them, and agreed upon the terms. I think it will be an excellent place for her — don't you? As to our house, I have not seen Mr. Vinal, and shall no doubt have to pay rent for it until he can let it. Was ever married man more unfortunate with houses? Four times within sixteen months have I removed my furniture, and we have the authority of Benjamin Franklin for saying that three removals are as bad as a fire; so that I have had one fire and a third![5] — By the way, speaking of house-rent — I have got mine from my Roxbury tenant, promptly — and I have paid it all over, and more too, to Miss Sumner. The Sumners were, as usual, quite polite and chatty — they inquired particularly after Mrs. Garrison, and hoped she would visit them — declared that I was too good a man to be mobbed — &c. &c.[6] Am I?

I have visited Dr. Windship's, and seen him and his wife. They are well, and had many kind things to say about you. They hope we shall come to Roxbury again. I forgot to ask them whether they would insure us against mobs.

Now, about my trip. I don't wish to take it, but I must. It is to New-York — to settle the embezzlement case of brother Thompson, by consulting the Executive Committee of the American Anti-Slavery Society, so as to determine upon the manner of vindicating his character. I go by appointment, and at the earnest request, of our Board. It shall be my earnest endeavor to reach Brooklyn on Saturday — but I may be detained longer. It is hard to be separated, dearest, even for a few days, under the happiest circumstances. Ought we not then to pity the poor slaves?

While I talk of going south, brother Henry has gone east. Mr. May and I have just bade adieu to him at the wharf. He sails in a packet for Eastport, and will go from thence in a steam-boat to St. John, carrying with him brother Thompson's trunks and boxes. I hope his trip will be healthful and prosperous. He will probably be absent two or three weeks. Our friends have sent by him a large number of kind letters for Mr. T. Mrs. T. is still remaining at Mrs. Southwick's, but will leave for New York next week.

I am glad that Abby Clark has written to you, and that you have so kindly replied to her. Henry visited her at Mrs. Lovering's on Thursday evening. She expressed much sorrow because you were treated so coldly by her brother,[7] and seemed to be sad because Mr. Knapp had not replied to her notes.

This, I suppose, will find dear brother George in Brooklyn. How we have dodged each other since the riot! As I expect to return by the way of Norwich or Hartford, it is not probable that I shall see him for some time. He knows I love him and his.

What a change in the weather! It is not quite so cold as Greenland — but cold enough to force me to put on my robin and drawers.[8]

Our city is quiet enough. The piece in the Liberator, to-day, respecting the Mayor, will probably make some talk. The ladies hold their meeting at Francis Jackson's house, next week.[9] O'Connell, in his speech, calls our pro-slavery mobocrats, "two-legged wolves."

Love to father, mother, brother and sisters, &c. and believe me, with unabated affection,

Your devoted husband,

W. L. G.

ALS: Garrison Papers, Boston Public Library; extracts printed in *Life*, II, 50–51.

1. In his description of the events of October 21 (*The Liberator*, November 7), Garrison gave "the delicate state of Mrs. Garrison's health" as one of the chief reasons for his leaving Boston after he was released from the protective custody of the jail.

2. Garrison apparently modifies the spelling of John "Gray" to equate it with the spelling of the name of the hill.

3. Some memento for the emancipation of the slaves in the British West Indies.

4. Anne W. and Caroline Weston.

5. Garrison alludes to the famous aphorism from *Poor Richard's Almanac* (1757).

6. Garrison was apparently collecting rent on the sublease of the house he had formerly occupied in Roxbury. He refers, it would seem, to payment for some favor done him by Miss Sumner, sister of Charles Sumner and daughter of Charles Pinckney Sumner (1776–1839), the sheriff of Suffolk County. The elder Sumner was an abolitionist who favored integration of the schools and even legalizing interracial marriage. He had been especially polite and kind to Garrison on October 21 (*Life*, II, 29).

7. Apparently referring to the meeting described in letter 225, to Helen, November 11.

8. A robin is a flannel undershirt.

9. Francis Jackson (1789–1861) was a prominent Unitarian, associated with John Pierpont and Theodore Parker. After he had opened his home to the Boston Female Anti-Slavery Society, he became a close friend of Garrison's, supporting his policies and his projects throughout his life. He also served many years as president of the Massachusetts Anti-Slavery Society and vice-president of the American Anti-Slavery Society.

227

TO ISAAC KNAPP

Providence, Nov. 19, 1835.

My dear Knapp:

I arrived here safely last evening, a few minutes past 5, having experienced less fatigue than on any previous journey. Very little conversation was made by any of the passengers, for it is much more difficult to make one's self heard in a rail-car than in a stage-coach. There were two ladies in our car — one a fat dowager-looking female — the other younger and less corpulent — probably mother and daughter. As we were stopping a few moments at Canton, a gentleman somewhat jocosely expressed his surprise to them, that they had not waited and attended the Ladies' Anti-Slavery meeting that afternoon. "Oh," said they, quite emphatically, "we are not anti-slavery." I wanted to say to them — but the fear of being thought impertinent kept me from intruding upon their conversation — "What! not anti-slavery? Do you mean to say that you are in favor of slavery? Or what do you mean? If you are not anti-slavery, then you are for concubinage, pollution, robbery, cruelty; then you are for making merchandize of God's image, for setting aside the forms and obligations of marriage, for darkening the human intellect, and debasing the soul. Certainly, you must be either very ignorant or very inhuman." Not anti-slavery! How it sounds in the ears of a genuine republican! How the Autocrat of Russia would exult to hear such a sentiment from the lips of American women! There are those, however, — thanks be to God, — who *are* anti-slavery — high-souled, intellectual, courageous, devout females, and I long to know how their meeting, yesterday, went off — whether any disturbance was made, and how many were present — &c. &c.

Our Providence friends are decidedly of opinion, that we ought to publish Mr. Phelps's letter, respecting the Kaufman affair, either by itself, or appended in a note to our forth-coming vindication of Mr. Thompson's character. I think so too — for it is surprising to learn, how extensively Kaufman's unfounded and ridiculous accusation obtains credence. As to Professor Gregg's statement, as it was written without his having seen Kaufman's letter, I do not think we are called upon to publish it — nor, indeed, are we obligated to publish Phelps's, but that is so explicit and so positive, it ought to be given to the public without delay.[1]

The pro-slavery meeting in this city is universally regarded as a complete failure, and has operated visibly and decidedly in favor of our cause.[2] Already, four hundred excellent names, from twenty of the thirty towns in the State, have been obtained to the call for the State A. S. Convention in February — and brother George is sanguine that the list will rise as high as seven hundred! This will beat the Utica call, of the empire State of New-York, by nearly one half! Well done Rhode-Island! no longer little, but great! But this is *sub rosa.*

George was rejoiced to get the bundle I brought. He thinks it probable more may be wanted, and will let you know speedily.

To-morrow morning, I shall leave for Brooklyn. Give my kind regards to Mrs. Thompson, and to the rest of the friends — and believe
me

Ever your affectionate friend,

Wm. Lloyd Garrison.

Mr. Isaac Knapp.

N.B. There is an allusion in Mr. May's vindication of Mr. T.,
which, on reflection, I think ought not to be made. It is where we
make the confession, that "Mr. T. has made an explanation of the
affair to us." I do not think we ought to say so — for the public will
eagerly demand of us, what was his explanation? It will not satisfy
them to say — "It will not be regarded, if we give it." The best way is
to say nothing, directly or indirectly, about it — it is enough that we
refer the whole matter to those who sent Mr. T. out to us. I hope
this suggestion will be duly considered by the Board.[3]

If this arrives seasonably, put the following items [4] in the Liberator,
unless you have something to the same purport already in type:

ALS: Garrison Papers, Boston Public Library.

1. Garrison printed in *The Liberator*, December 5, 1835, letters from Gregg
and Phelps as well as his own farewell eulogy to Thompson. Abram Kaufman
(1811–1839), at this time a student at Andover Theological Seminary and subsequently an assistant minister at St. Philip's Episcopal Church in Charleston,
South Carolina, reported that during his visit to Andover Thompson had said:
"If we taught the slaves to do what they ought, we would tell every one of them
to cut their masters' throats." Jarvis Gregg (1808–1836), formerly a teacher in
the Boston public schools and a tutor at Dartmouth College and currently a student at Andover, heard the conversation between Thompson and Kaufman and
modified Kaufman's version of it, though he admitted that Thompson had made
statements that could be misconstrued and could hurt the cause. Amos A. Phelps,
however, denied that Thompson had made any such statements as those attributed
to him by Kaufman. The official position expressed later (*Life*, II, 4) by Garrison's
sons was that Thompson was arguing "that if it was ever right to rise forcibly
against oppressors, the slaves had that right."

2. This meeting was apparently not reported in *The Liberator*.

3. The vindication to which Garrison refers was printed as an official statement of the Massachusetts Anti-Slavery Society, signed by Samuel J. May as
Secretary, in *The Liberator*, December 5. It recounted the many honors Thompson had accumulated in Great Britain and described his outstanding service in
the cause during the year in this country. The final paragraph was concerned
with Thompson's private character. The sentence Garrison objected to seems to
have been revised as follows: "As yet we have had no opportunity to obtain an
explanation of this affair, from any other one than the accused. . . . We can
only assure our fellow citizens that *we* are still persuaded our confidence in him
has not been misplaced; nor our attachment to him undeservedly bestowed."

4. The items Garrison supplied have been cut off the bottom of the sheet.

2 2 8

TO GEORGE W. BENSON

Brooklyn, Nov. 27, 1835.

My dear George:

I have returned the gift of my kind friend Carpenter [1] with a note of thanks. The Vest is lacking in length and breadth, and, of course, does not fit me. I hope he will not give himself any trouble about another, although it is just such a present as would be useful to me this winter.

A letter from friend Burleigh, at the Anti-Slavery Rooms, informs me that letters had just been received from Henry and Thompson. Both arrived safely, and had good passages. Henry was only 36 hours in going from Boston to Eastport. Thompson had a pretty rough time, and if they had been an hour later, he thinks the vessel would have been exposed to imminent danger from a severe gale that suddenly sprung up. Mrs. T. was to sail from New-York for Liverpool in the packet of the 24th inst. We may now be looking daily for the return of brother Henry, with a budget of intelligence from our banished friend. What a mighty void is created by the return of G.T.! It is like the loss of a general to an army, whose presence gave inspiration and courage to the humblest soldier. — Who now shall go forth to argue our cause in public, with subtle sophists and insolent scoffers? It is true, we have the lion-hearted, invincible Weld at the West, and our strong and indefatigable brother Stanton in Rhode-Island; but the withdrawal of Thompson seems like the loss of many agents.[2] It is more than probable that "we ne'er shall look upon his like again." [3] Especially will his loss be felt, as we have so few in our ranks who are qualified to rouse, enlighten and electrify an audience. I cannot help cherishing the hope, that a change in public sentiment will render his return to this country desirable next fall.

Yesterday throughout this State, (perhaps in all Rhode Island, I know not,) by proclamation of the Governor, there was an immense slaughter among the turkeys, geese and chickens, who were destroyed by the jaw-bones of the people without the slightest remorse — nay, with evident satisfaction. It fell to my lot to carve not less than three chickens, "all in a row," which had been systematically roasted at a slow fire — a fourth one I spared from dissection until to-day. Sad havoc, too, was made among innocent pies, (potato, mince, apple, and all their relations,) and unoffending puddings. Although you are of a tender disposition, we regretted that you could not make one among our little family circle, and take part in the destructive exercises of the day. Almost every body got punished, more or less, for slaying and eating so pitilessly; for the conglomerated fragments of fowls and puddings and pies, which were ravenously swallowed, soon united in getting up an insurrection in the stomach, and peace was not restored until good digestion waited on appetite. By the way — looking at the thing in its true light, this custom of appointing one day in the year to be specially thankful for the good gifts of God is an absurdity, tending, I think, to keep up the notion that it is not very material whether we are particularly thankful or not, during the remainder of the year. The appointment, too, of a thanksgiving by a civil officer, is strictly a union of Church and State. I am growing more and more hostile to outward forms and ceremonies and observances, as a religious duty, and trust I am more and more appreciating the nature and enjoying the privileges of that liberty wherewith the obedient soul is made free. How can a people fast or be thankful at the bidding or request of any man or body of men?

Gerrit Smith has at last waived all his scruples, and joined our ranks. No doubt you have seen his letter in the Emancipator. You perceive he boggles a little at some of us and our measures, but never mind — he will soon be as rampant as any of us. We must remember that he has been our antagonist, and that he constituted one of the main pillars of the Colonization Society. Whether he has wholly swung clear of that Society does not appear; indeed, he does not allude to it. But as he declared in his speech at Peterboro', that he could go with us even in our most odious sentiments, and as he has now connected himself with a Society which aims to destroy his long cherished scheme, he must be strangely inconsistent if he can still support the Colonization Society. He certainly deserves much credit for the christian manliness and magnanimity which he manifests in joining our ranks at this perilous crisis. So much for the mob at Utica! [4]

I wish you would procure, and send by the first convenient opportunity, a steel-busk, as flexible as possible, for Helen. You may also send me a shirt collar of as good pattern as you can find at the stores, to serve as a model in the alteration of my present collars. Charge the same, and I will settle accounts when we meet, or sooner.

As yet, I feel very happily situated here, and have no desire to return to Boston. What I most need are method and diligence with my pen.

Mr. Geers talks of taking a load of pork to your market on Monday or Tuesday, should the weather prove favorable.

We are all well, and desire to be affectionately remembered to your wife, sister Mary, Mr. and Mrs. Anthony, Mr. and Mrs. Chace, &c. Yours, in the bonds of brotherly love,

W. L. Garrison.

ALS: Garrison Papers, Boston Public Library; printed partly in *Life*, II, 51–52.

1. Not identified.

2. Henry B. Stanton has been identified before, but not Theodore Dwight Weld (1803–1895), who, though he came originally from Connecticut, had made his reputation in New York state. His interest in reform was first whetted by retired British army officer Captain Charles Stuart, then principal of Utica Academy, and later by Presbyterian revivalist Charles G. Finney. By 1830 he was a dedicated abolitionist, and he became extraordinarily effective not only as an antislavery lecturer but also in converting to the cause a series of outstanding men, including Arthur and Lewis Tappan, James G. Birney, Elizur Wright, Jr., Harriet and Henry Ward Beecher. Weld, his converts, and the agents he trained had by 1835 been extraordinarily successful in abolitionizing New York and the West. In 1838 he married one of the most distinguished of the agents, Angelina E. Grimké of South Carolina. His most famous tract, *American Slavery As It Is* (New York, 1839), was eventually to be an important source for *Uncle Tom's Cabin.*

3. Garrison adapts Shakespeare, *Hamlet*, I, ii, 188.

4. An antislavery convention in Utica, New York, had assembled on October 17 and reconvened on the twenty-first. When it was disrupted by unruly mobs, Gerrit Smith had invited the abolitionists to transfer their meeting to his home town of Peterboro (see *The Liberator*, October 31, November 14, 28, 1835). Smith's generous action constituted his initiation into the group of Garrisonian abolitionists. Although in subsequent years Smith and Garrison were to differ regarding the use of political action, Smith becoming one of the founders of the Liberty party, they continued to respect each other.

229

TO MARY BENSON

Brooklyn, Nov. 27, 1835.

My dear sister Mary:

Yesterday we kept Thanksgiving, in company with the good and bad people of Connecticut, to the extermination of sundry chickens, pies and puddings, with the usual accompaniments of nuts, apples, &c. &c. It is, to be sure, quite an absurdity, that we should mourn or rejoice — fast or gluttonise, at the appointment of a civil officer of State: but so we do. This is one of our modes of being religious — of manifesting our obedience, if not to God, at least to the Governor; and thus we tread closely in the footsteps of the ancient Jews. We agree to fast once a year, and to be thankful once a year, whenever March or November arrives; provided a Proclamation comes forth from head quarters — not otherwise; and what amount of food we lose by our fasting, we are quite sure to recover by our thanksgiving.[1] These are ancient customs, and will not readily be abandoned: but they are just as obligatory as the call of a town-crier to an auction. What then? Is it not good to fast? Certainly, when the body needs it, and the soul assents to it; and body and soul must determine upon the proper time and the best mode — not the Chief Magistrate of the State. Ought we not to be thankful? Most assuredly. But when? Late in November, or early in December? Nay, but at all times and all seasons. But when the harvest is gathered in, ought we not to be specially thankful. I think not. I think our hearts should respond to the language of Habakkuk: "Although the fig-tree shall not blossom, neither shall fruit be in the vines: the labor of the olive shall fail, and the fields shall yield no meat; the flock shall be cut off from the fold, and there shall be no herd in the stalls: yet I will rejoice in the Lord, I will joy in the God of my salvation."[2] There is great danger that if we are thankful only when we are full or prosperous, ours is merely the gratitude of selfishness. Patient Job could exclaim, in the hour of utter calamity — "The Lord gave, and the Lord hath taken away: blessed be the name of the Lord."[3]

It would be treason, you know, and perhaps contrary to the Constitution,(!) to utter these sentiments aloud, respecting these time-honored observances; so, mind — they are only privately whispered into your ear, to be used very discreetly!

Two weeks more will complete my thirtieth year. My past labors, I trust, have not been wholly useless to my country and the world; yet they are sadly deficient in amount and value. You know my antipathy to the pen, and my want of method and despatch. I am plundered constantly by that most artful and dextrous of all thieves, the thief Procrastination. However, if my health be spared this winter, and I remain located in Brooklyn, away from intrusion and household care, I hope to write more, and write better, than I have yet done in any one season. Much as my mind is absorbed in the anti-slavery cause, there are other great subjects that frequently occupy my thoughts, upon which much light remains to be thrown, and which are of the utmost importance to the temporal and eternal welfare of man. As to the Peace question, I am more and more convinced, that it is the duty of the followers of Christ to suffer themselves to be defrauded, calumniated and barbarously treated, without resorting either to their own physical energies, or to the force of human law, for restitution or punishment. It is a difficult lesson to learn.

As you are now moving among the Friends, I hope you will be instrumental in stirring up their zeal and sympathy in behalf of the crushed and perishing slaves. They are a body whose great leading, fundamental principles are more in harmony with mine than those of any other; and therefore I feel peculiarly desirous that they should meet the opposing hosts of oppression in this country, as did their brethren in Great Britain. Certainly, it is not enough that we are not slaveholders, or that we have emancipated our slaves, or that we occasionally bear the testimony of a few words against so awful and heathenish a system of bondage as we are nourishing in our midst. In the days of John Woolman and Anthony Benezet, the Friends were wonderfully alive to the sufferings of the poor guiltless slaves, when these victims were comparatively few in number.[4] Surely, now that from thousands they have increased to millions, and their oppressors grow more and more cruel and obdurate, the Friends ought not to let the example of their ancient predecessors be lost upon them. There are many devout and resolute spirits, I rejoice to know, who feel and act with pristine boldness and vigor among them: but my prayer is, that not one, or ten, or a hundred, but *all* be quickened in this benevolent work.

Gerrit Smith has sacrificed his prejudices and objections, and openly joined himself to the Anti-Slavery Society. He has chosen the darkest and most perilous hour in which to give in his adhesion, and thus manifested great christian manliness and a truly self-sacrificing spirit.

Harriet Martineau, the distinguished authoress from England, has also shown true moral courage in attending the meeting of the Boston Female Anti-Slavery Society, and avowing her approval of its principles.[5]

When you see our venerable friend Moses Brown —
"Who stands with all his shining garments on,
Dress'd for the flight, and ready to be gone" — [6]
convey to him the expressions of my sincere affection and high respect. Truly, not in vain has he lived: he has done much by his example and efforts to repair the moral ruins of a sin-destroyed world. I could hope, submissively, that he might be permitted to live to see the year of jubilee in this country for the whole slave population, which, I trust, is not far distant.

The state of your father's health is comfortable: all the rest of the family are well and happy. Brooklyn, at present, presents a dreary aspect; for the transition of Nature's countenance in winter is as repulsive, as it is glorious in spring and summer. However, I am far, very far from being homesick. My dear Helen would make any spot agreeable to me; but, aside from her company, to be surrounded by such kind parents and sisters is happiness enough. The cold weather sensibly affects us all — but it cannot chill the affection of

Your friend and brother,

Wm. Lloyd Garrison.

ALS: Garrison Papers, Boston Public Library.

1. The custom of observing an annual fast day originated in Massachusetts during the latter part of the seventeenth century, its motive being to seek divine favor for the undertakings of the year, especially for the planting of the fields. The day was set by a proclamation of the governor, and the custom was not officially abolished until 1894.

2. Habakkuk 3:17–18.

3. Job 1:21.

4. Garrison mentions two of the leading Quakers of the eighteenth century, John Woolman (1720–1772) and Anthony Benezet (1713–1784), both of whom were reformers dedicated to abolition. Woolman's *Some Considerations on the Keeping of Negroes* (Philadelphia, 1754) and his famous *Journal* (Philadelphia, 1774) are classic works of antislavery literature. Benezet, who was Woolman's close friend, had his greatest influence on the abolition movement with the publication of *A Caution and Warning to Great Britain and Her Colonies on the Calamitous State of the Enslaved Negroes* (Philadelphia, 1766).

5. Harriet Martineau (1802–1876), sister of English philosopher and divine James Martineau, supported herself and acquired some reputation by writing moralistic tales, her first success being *Illustrations of Political Economy*, published in nine volumes (London, 1832–1834). Like Garrison she was attracted by almost anything controversial, including Unitarianism, abolitionism, mesmerism, and positivism. The meeting of the Boston Female Anti-Slavery Society adjourned from October 21 was finally reconvened on November 19; Garrison reported the meeting in *The Liberator* of the twenty-first.

6. Not identified.

230

TO GEORGE W. BENSON

Brooklyn, Nov. 30, 1835.

My dear George:

Two bouncing hogs have been summarily *lynched* to-day, by Geers and another man, and to-night they are to be sent to Providence, to be sold to and eaten by the "wealthy and respectable" mobocrats, if any such are to be found in your city. Grahamites and Jews vote them an abomination.

The bundle I forwarded to you on Saturday by the driver, I presume arrived safely, although your letter of yesterday, which we have just received, makes no mention of it — and probably it had not then been put into your hands.

All that I have received from Boston since I left, have been two small packages of newspapers through the Post Office. Henry is absent; and brother Knapp, you know, resembles me very closely in his habits of procrastination. — Indeed, I think he is rather worse than I am, in this respect. Where is my box of books — where my carpet — which he was to forward to your care without delay? Echo answers —

Where? I presume they are just where I left them — viz. at 23, Brighton-street, Boston.

To-day we have had a slight fall of snow, but the atmosphere looks heavy, as if it has some snow-drifts yet in reserve. Sleighs run easily — but there is not enough snow to authorise heavy teams to go upon runners. Although winter has begun somewhat early, I do not think we shall have so cold a one as we had last year.

The Liberator gets along tolerably well during my absence; but the proof-sheet is not read so critically as I could desire. Typographical blunders meet my eye rather too frequently. But it is a blundering world.

You see, some of us have got into a controversy about the conduct of the Boston Mayor, during the late riot by "men of property and standing from all parts of the city." [1] That he erred, all agree; that he erred *maliciously*, I do not believe; that he erred through a lack of firmness, and a deference to the respectability of the mob, is evident. It is urged in his defence, that he was stripped of all power — that he could not have commanded any force, &c.; but this is a mere assumption. One thing is certain — he was bound to read the Riot Act, and to call for support, even if he could not obtain it — but he did not do it.[2] However, I like to see this difference of sentiment respecting his conduct manfully expressed on the part of abolitionists, in a manner and with a freedom becoming independent men.

Accompanying this, is an excellently written epistle, both as to its composition and its penmanship, from Rachel Robinson, wife of Roland T. Robinson of Ferrisburgh, Vt. Your father feels desirous that sister Mary and friend Brown,[3] in particular, should peruse it. It is written in a delicate, tender, yet decisive spirit, and evinces a high degree of conscientiousness. Not a particle of the productions of slave labor, whether it be rice, sugar, coffee, cotton, molasses, tobacco or flour, is used in her family, and thus her practice corresponds admirably with her doctrine. But I cannot say that I have as yet arrived at clear satisfaction upon this point, so as to be able to meet the difficulties that cluster in our path.

Mr. Sabin [4] has started the rumor that the Liberator is to be printed in this village! and considerable oppugnation has been manifested, it is said, on the part of the "friends of the Constitution." They will not have it here — not they! This is very amusing, and serves to lessen the amount of melancholy in our sombre world. Think you, the dignity and self-importance of little villages are behind those of great cities? I tell you, nay. Did not Canterbury take the lead? And did not New-York, Philadelphia and Boston, obsequiously follow?

You must not calculate upon my being present at your State Convention in February. A crisis comes at or about that time to me and mine, which is of too much importance to allow me to be absent. It relates, you know, to a question of *domestic emancipation* — and let the south interfere, if it dares! [5] Be busy, my friend, thus early, in securing good speakers at your meeting; and see to it that upon your committees are placed the most substantial men.

We are still blessed with health and happiness at home. O, that our gratitude may keep pace with the good gifts of our bountiful Benefactor! We deserve no favors at his hands, and yet we are crowned with them continually!

Give tokens of our love to your dear wife and little one. We are glad to hear of Anna's progress. She will soon be a woman, and we old men, almost before we can dream of a change. But, no matter — time in his progress shall but increase and strengthen the affectionate regard of

Your admiring brother,

Wm. Lloyd Garrison.

N.B. An engraving of my portrait, by Torrey, will be made as soon as he sees any chance of disposing of copies enough to warrant the expense.[6] It will be skilfully done — price $1 a copy to subscribers — $1.50 to others. Would any of the friends in Providence like to procure it? It will be accompanied with certificates from May, Whittier, Knapp, &c. as to its accuracy.

ALS: Garrison Papers, Boston Public Library; printed partly in *Life*, II, 52–53.

1. See *The Liberator*, November 28, 1835. A generation later Mayor Theodore Lyman's conduct was still a sufficiently controversial subject for Theodore Lyman, III, to edit and publish *Papers Relating to the Garrison Mob* (Cambridge, Massachusetts, 1870).

2. In April of 1835 Massachusetts adopted a riot act which gave the mayor of a town the power to break up meetings of twelve or more armed men and meetings of thirty or more unarmed men. Rioters would be held responsible for any injuries incurred by officers discharging their duties, although officers were not responsible for similar injuries to civilians, even though they might only be spectators. Under the terms of the law, officials were instructed to obtain the assistance of the citizenry in discharging their duties.

3. Moses Brown.

4. Not otherwise identified.

5. George Thompson Garrison was born February 13, 1836.

6. In *The Liberator* for November 28 appeared an advertisement for a projected engraving of the Torrey portrait, provided there were a sufficient number of subscribers. See letter 194, to Helen E. Garrison, May 4, 1835, n.2.

231

TO HENRY E. BENSON

Brooklyn, Dec. 5, 1835.

My dear Henry:

Your safe arrival at Boston has removed a load of anxiety from all our minds, and filled us with joy. Your letters have been duly received, but you do not tell us how you like

"The sea — the sea — the foaming sea —
With the blue above, and the blue below": [1]

but I suspect you are something of my opinion, that one acre of ground is more to be coveted than two acres of water. How answer you? To be confined in a little vessel is to lose one's liberty and the power of locomotion — and this is to be in bondage, for the time being at least. Besides, immediate emancipation is out of the question: — it is nothing but gradualism, closely allied to colonizationism. Now the current of the sea is against you — anon, it is a dead calm — then follows a tempest — then comes a fog — then a head-wind — and, at last, the elements are propitious, and you are carried triumphantly into port. How emblematical of the great struggle in which we are engaged!

The Liberator was received yesterday, and its contents eagerly and critically perused.[2] Bro. Thompson's farewell letter is most happily conceived, and powerfully expressed, and well calculated to revive the hearts of our abolition brethren. With what alarm and fury will our enemies read his promise to expose their baseness and cruelty before the people of Great Britain — even to call them by name! He will hardly be safe from their murderous designs, even with the Atlantic rolling between. How earnestly do I desire that he may have a safe voyage, and that all those vitally important materials which he has so industriously accumulated may also obtain a safe conveyance!

What said cousin Andrew [3] to you? And how did you fancy St. John? For what port did Thompson embark? Did you meet with any opponents on the way?

There are a few bills of mine to be settled as soon as you can command the money — Vinal's for rent, Messer's for groceries, the butcher's, the milkman's, (a small one,) the bill for the wood, and the taylor's bill — the last I am somewhat anxious to have paid without delay, as he has sent for his money repeatedly, and was promised punctual payment.[4] Here my expenses are small, and I shall call upon you, from time to time, for very little more than enough to pay our board-bill; so that I shall not be so heavy a burden upon you and bro. Knapp, as I have been heretofore. I believe I owe no other bills than those enumerated above, except such as Knapp and myself are jointly responsible for, and these relate to the paper.

How many new subscribers has the Liberator received since the riot up to the present time? and what is proposed as to its continuance another year? I wish it could be enlarged, *safely* — but it would be hazardous to make the experiment. The engraving we will lay aside, and substitute a plain head — The Liberator. This alteration will admit of more reading in the paper. Let the present motto remain — we cannot have a better, although I made it. There's egotism for you!

I long to hear that friend Knapp has succeeded in hiring a printing-office, especially as the year is so near its close; for I know it must be exceedingly vexatious to be under the necessity of resorting to other printing establishments.

I send a letter to your care for bro. H. C. Wright, which I wish him to receive as soon as convenient.[5] He is a valuable acquisition to our cause — a fearless, uncompromising and zealous christian.

It strengthens and animates me to hear that bro. Phelps [6] is to remain in Boston. You know how highly I appreciate his worth, and what unwavering confidence I place in his judgment, integrity and devotion. His presence, with bro. Wright's co-operation, will make my absence from the city more excusable.

Our anxiety for your welfare, I presume, was met by a correspondent anxiety on your part for ours. We have all reason to be exceedingly grateful to God, for the full enjoyment of health, and the high degree of happiness, that we have had since you left us. Much as I love Boston, and much as I long to see you all, I am quite attached to this quiet village, and do not feel at all home-sick.

I perceive by the Christian Register,[7] that Dr. Channing has at last given publicity to his thoughts on slavery.[8] Send me the work in the next bundle of papers, for I am anxious to review it. The extract from it in the Register is singularly weak and inconclusive — but I suppose it is the most rotten spot in the volume, else Prof. Willard would have not have quoted it as the soundest.[9]

Once a week, either by the way of Worcester or Providence, I wish you would send me all the mail papers that may have accumulated upon your hands, and all the letters, communications, &c. which it is necessary that I should see. Send the bundle so that it may arrive in Brooklyn every Friday. Every Saturday evening, you may put into the mail the Evangelist, Recorder, Vt. Chronicle, Ch. Mirror, Ch. Register, and other papers that may be specially interesting — not exceeding a dozen.[10]

So, it seems, because I suffered a communication to go into the Liberator, reprimanding the Mayor [11] for his pusillanimous conduct, our friend E. M. P. Wells has captiously ordered his paper to be stopped. Very well — "Good by." The pretext is most ridiculous. See what it is to have respect unto persons! Surely, "An Abolitionist," and "Another Abolitionist," — two against one, — ought to atone for the essay of "Hancock." [12] I am disgusted with this squeamish regard for Mr. Lyman, and think it very unwise, as well as positively criminal, for any to attempt to exonerate him from blame.

Winter has come early. In this quarter, although there is not much snow, yet the sleighing is capital. On Thursday afternoon, Anne, Sarah, Helen and myself, (a crowded and heavy load I assure you,) took a sleigh-ride to Pomfret, and made a call upon Capt. Allen's family.[13] We enjoyed ourselves right merrily. To-day it is snowing again.

Give my best remembrances to all the brethren, and believe me ever

Yours in love,

Wm. Lloyd Garrison.

ALS: Garrison Papers, Boston Public Library; printed partly in *Life*, II, 53–55.

1. Garrison adapts Barry Cornwall (Bryan Waller Procter), "The Sea," combining a line from the first stanza with one from the second.

2. Garrison refers to a copy of *The Liberator* for December 5 which had been sent to him in advance of publication. George Thompson's letter was printed in this issue.

3. Andrew Garrison.

4. Nathaniel Vinal has already been identified. The grocer was Stillman Messer, who kept a grocery in Poplar Street. The others have not been identified.

5. Henry Clarke Wright (1797–1870), from Sharon, Connecticut, a hatmaker turned minister and licensed to preach in 1823, joined the New England Anti-Slavery Society in May 1835 and met Garrison in November. He was thereafter to be Garrison's loyal associate in virtually all reforms. He was a voluminous writer whose almost pathological fondness for children resulted in a number of antislavery works for juveniles and whose correspondence for *The Liberator* was so extensive that he was to write under many pseudonyms ("Hancock," "Law," "Wickliffe," "Cato," "Justice") as well as his own name.

6. Amos A. Phelps.

7. *Christian Register and* (Boston) *Observer*, an official Unitarian organ.

8. This is Garrison's first reference to William Ellery Channing's small book *Slavery* (Boston, 1835), which was in effect Channing's answer to Garrison's letter of January 20, 1834.

9. Sidney Willard (1780–1856), son of the former president of Harvard College, was himself a Harvard graduate and former librarian as well as professor of Hebrew and Oriental languages there. Between 1831 and 1833 he had edited the *American Monthly Review*. Currently he was serving as state senator; he was also an active member of the short-lived Cambridge Anti-Slavery Society, which survived for about a year (1834–1835) in opposition to Garrison and the New England Anti-Slavery Society.

10. Garrison names, in effect, the opposition press: the *Evangelist and Religious Review*, New York City; the Boston *Recorder*; the *Vermont Chronicle*, St. Johns-

bury; the *Christian Mirror*, Portland, Maine; and the *Christian Register and* (Boston) *Observer*.

11. Theodore Lyman, Jr.

12. Garrison refers to an article by Henry C. Wright attacking Mayor Lyman for his failure to control the Boston mob on October 21 and to two replies defending Lyman (one signed "AN ABOLITIONIST" and the other, "ANOTHER ABOLITIONIST"), which appeared in *The Liberator* for November 14, 21, and 28.

13. Daniel Allen (1763–1844) lived with his wife Betsey (1776–1845) in Pomfret, Connecticut; his two children had died some years before.

232

TO SAMUEL J. MAY

Brooklyn, Dec. 5, 1835.

Dear brother May:

I have made inquiries of Mr. Gray,[1] respecting your father's clock. He was quite surprised to hear, that, after all his care and anxiety about its safe conveyance, it had not arrived in Boston. For many weeks, he made the most strenuous efforts to get it conveyed to Providence, but in vain — for two reasons, first, on account of its bulk, and secondly, because all who were going to Providence had full loads, and could take no extra freight. About a month since, he forwarded it in a box to Norwich, to the care of Backus & Norton, to be sent to Boston by one of the Norwich packets.[2] It was directed to your father in a very legible and particular manner. Mr. Gray will probably send to Norwich immediately, to ascertain the cause of its detention. He says the clock has caused him not a little trouble and anxiety, and he wishes your father to give him credit for having endeavored to comply with his request without delay.

I have just read the scandalous attack upon Miss Martineau, in the Daily Advertiser, to which you refer in your letter.[3] It will confirm her in the faith, for it is too passionate to convince or alarm a steadfast and enlightened mind like hers. To think that the Advertiser has at last become so vulgar and malignant as to quote with deference and strong approval the vile slang of the Courier and Enquirer! Mr. Hale has lately had a failure in his pecuniary matters, and he now seems to be zealous to become a bankrupt in his editorial character as soon as possible.[4] We ought not to be surprised, however, that the attendance of Miss Martineau at the anti-slavery meeting creates a stir among our opponents, for it is as if a thunderbolt had fallen upon their heads. I believe, could they have foreseen this event, to prevent its occurrence they would have permitted even George Thompson to address the ladies without interruption, and have chosen to sacrifice the honor and glory accruing from a mobocratic victory. It is thus that the wicked are taken in their own craftiness, and the counsels of the froward are carried headlong. Surely, it [is] better to trust in the Lord, than to put confidence in princes.

Well, it is announced that the great Dr. Channing has published his thoughts upon the subject of slavery! Of course, we must now all fall back, and "hide our diminished heads." [5] The work I will not condemn until I peruse it; but I do not believe it is superior either in argument or eloquence to many of our own publications. However, I am heartily glad that he is now committed upon this subject; for, however cautiously and tenderly he may have handled it, if he does not soon have a southern hornet's nest about his ears, then it will be because hornets have respect unto the persons of men! They will sting him unmercifully, and he will suffer greatly if he is not provided in advance with the genuine abolition panacea. N.B. Mr. Gray has just loaned me the Christian Register of to-day, and I have stopped to amuse myself with some namby-pamby, fiddle-faddle comments of Prof. Willard upon the Dr's new work. He says — "It ought to go into the hands of every slaveholder. It is *impossible* that he should repel such a view of the subject; *impossible* that any *bad passions* can be excited by it in the breast of any thinking, reasonable man"!! Oh! oh! indeed —

> "I am Sir Oracle, and when I speak,
> Let no dog ope his mouth!" [6]

The hosts of abolitionists in Great Britain and this country have spoken and written in vain — but now Dr. Channing speaks, listen, ye heavens! and give ear, oh earth! It was not in the power of Jesus Christ, but it is in the power of Dr. Channing, to rebuke sin and sinners, without exciting their "bad passions"! Wonderful!

If the extract from the work be a fair sample of the whole of it, it is weak and incoherent enough — indeed, that alone is enough to spoil a good book, especially a book upon moral reform. The Dr. says there are *slaveholders* who "deserve great praise." Why? Because they profess to "deplore and abhor the institution." So did all the slaveholders until they were compelled to tear off their hypocritical mask — and now they go in a body, synods, presbyteries, and all, in open advocacy of the bloody system! But the Dr.'s meritorious slaveholders "believe that partial emancipation, in the present condition of society, would bring unmixed evil on bond and free." So do all of them — slave-drivers, slave-traders, and slave-robbers! But these *good* souls further believe, that "they are bound to continue the *relation*, [what a nice, soft term!] until it shall be dissolved by comprehensive and systematic measures of the State"! "They are appalled by what seem to them the perils and difficulties of liberating multitudes, born and brought up to that condition"! Here is a mantle of charity, [?] broa[d e]nough to cover the sin of the world.

I hope uncommon pains will be taken by our abolition brethren to circulate large quantities of this week's Liberator, before the types are distributed. Bro. Thompson's letter is full of the majesty of truth and the power of love.[7] The defence of his character is most happily written, and together they ought to traverse the length and breadth of the land.

John Edward [8] is in good health. Herbert Williams has sold his farm to Paris Dyer of Providence, and will vacate it on the 1st of April next. Whether he will reside in the village, or leave the place, is at present doubtful. He and his family would be a great loss or a great acquisition to any place.

All our family are in the enjoyment of excellent health, and wish to be cordially remembered with much esteem to Mrs. May and yourself.

Pray let me hear from you frequently. Letters from any of my Boston friends will be truly acceptable.

In the bonds of love,
Yours, steadfastly,

Wm. Lloyd Garrison.

ALS: Garrison Papers, Boston Public Library; printed partly in *Life*, II, 56–58.

1. Apparently John Gray.

2. Backus and Norton was the partnership of Joseph Backus and Henry Barker Norton (1807 1891), which had been involved in the wholesale grocery business since 1827; Norton was to become a wealthy man and one of the chief benefactors of his town (Frances M. Caulkins, *History of Norwich, Connecticut*, 1866, and *Genealogical and Biographical Record of New London County, Connecticut*, Chicago, 1905).

3. The article to which Garrison refers classified Miss Martineau as a spy and incendiary like George Thompson and suggested that Americans should shut their doors to foreign and especially to female interference (see *The Liberator*, December 19).

4. Nathan Hale (1784 1863), nephew of the Nathan Hale who was hanged by the British during the Revolutionary War, was, if at times conservative, the highly educated editor of the Boston *Daily Advertiser*, who had owned the paper since 1814. He was one of the first editors who conceived the role of a newspaper to sway public opinion as well as to record facts; indeed, he introduced the editorial as a regular feature. Since he retained control of the paper until 1854, it would seem that the financial failure to which Garrison refers was temporary and perhaps wishful thinking on Garrison's part.

5. Garrison adapts Milton, *Paradise Lost*, IV, 35.

6. Garrison adapts Shakespeare, *The Merchant of Venice*, I, i, 93–94.

7. See letter 231, n. 2, to Henry E. Benson, December 5, 1835.

8. Possibly, like Herbert Williams and Paris Dyer, a farmer.

2 3 3

TO HENRY E. BENSON

Brooklyn, Dec. 10, 1835.

My dear Henry:

I have but a very few minutes left before the stage starts, and consequently have time for only a word or two.

Yesterday, sisters Sarah and Anna spent the day with me at Dr. Green's, and had a pleasant and profitable time. The Dr. gave me a communication from his pen, addressed to slaveholders, for insertion in the Liberator, which is herewith sent, and I wish it to be inserted next week.[1] On our arrival home in the evening, we found a large bundle of letters and papers from you, via Worcester, which made us almost *too* lively, for joy. Your letter was a capital one, and altogether too short, although it was a very long one.

I am glad that bro. Phelps is to labor for the regeneration of Connecticut. He is admirably qualified for the work in this State. True, it will be arduous — but what citadel of prejudice or oppression can withstand the artillery of truth, and "the sacramental host of God's elect"? [2]

If the colored people are to be put together, by an arbitrary rule, in the free church, then that church is no longer free nor christian.

I have read Channing's work. It abounds with useful truisms expressed in polished terms, but, as a whole, is an inflated, inconsistent and slanderous production. I would not give one dozen of Rankin's letters for one hundred copies of Channing's essay.[3]

You must apprise me, without delay, of the result of the meeting respecting the Liberator. If my presence is indispensably necessary in Boston, I will go on immediately; but, if not, I had rather not incur the loss of time and the cost of the journey, needlessly.

I regret to learn that the house in Brighton-street is still on my hands. The paying of a dollar a day for that which is of no use to me, makes me wince. You are welcome to the use of any of our things — and so is bro. Knapp, of course.

Am glad to hear of pussy's safe transportation.

I send you that part of Thomas Shipley's letter which you desire to see.

If Mrs. Thompson has gone to Baltimore on a visit, I fear she will not return in season for the packet of the 16th. Hope all the friends will write to Thompson by her. You must not fail to send him a letter, informing him of your safe return. Am glad you are to forward my likeness to him by Mrs. T.

Tell bro. Wright his letter was very acceptable. I shall review Channing speedily.

I wish bro. Knapp to take special care of all the pieces I send, and make a choice selection from my selections. On the first page of next paper, I wish him to put the extracts from McDuffie's message and those of the other Governors' which accompany this.[4] They form one complete picture.

He will find some poetry and miscellaneous articles among the lot. The letters and communications I want inserted as soon as possible.

Tell my esteemed friend Loring I will answer his letter, and comply with his request, in my next budget.

You can compliment me no longer about my neat penmanship, &c.; but, although I am in a prodigious hurry, yet I am, as ever,

Your affectionate and much obliged brother,

W. L. G.

ALS: Garrison Papers, Boston Public Library; printed partly in *Life*, II, 61–62.

1. Dr. Rowland W. Greene's address was duly published in *The Liberator*, December 19, under the pseudonym "Woolman."
2. Unidentified.
3. John Rankin (1793–1886) was the minister of the Presbyterian churches of Ripley and Strait Creek, Ohio, and the author of *Letters on American Slavery*, written in 1824, published serially in *The Liberator* in 1832, and in book form by Garrison and Knapp as early as 1833.
4. George McDuffie (1790–1851) was a member of Congress, a senator, and a governor of South Carolina; he was that state's most important politician immediately preceding Calhoun. Garrison refers to his message to the state legislature, extracts from which are reprinted in *The Liberator* for December 12; see letter 237, to Thomas Shipley, December 17, 1835.

234

TO HENRY E. BENSON

Brooklyn, Dec. 15, 1835.

Dear Henry:

I have not sent but little editorial matter, that more room may be allowed this week for communications. The Report of the Juvenile Society need not be inserted till next week.[1]

My good friend John Cutts Smith has sent me a letter, making proposals to take the Liberator and vigorously push its subscription list, on certain conditions — one of which is, that some abolition friend will loan him $2000 for fifteen months, taking certain good notes for security.[2] If this arrangement could be made, I should greatly rejoice; for I am confident that Mr. Smith would soon increase our subscribers to a very large number. But where to look for the man who will be willing to loan the above sum, I do not know. I am fully sensible of the disinterestedness and liberality of friend Smith's proposal, and believe his great object is to put the Liberator upon a firm foundation, and thereby advance our holy cause. What shall be done? For my dilemma is just the same as his.

I expected to receive a letter from you by Monday's mail, but none came; because if it is important that I should visit Boston, I wish to know it without delay, that I may hasten on, and return in haste, as it is important for sundry reasons which you understand, that I should be "on hand" in Brooklyn as much as possible until the 1st of February.[3] It is an important case of domestic emancipation, in which I feel a deep interest, trusting it will illustrate anew the safety of liberty.

The bundle of papers, via Worcester, was safely conveyed and put into my hands on Friday evening — and great was my surprise, as well as pleasure, to receive a copy of the Liberator. In my article on Mr. Cheever's sentence, you perceive I have broached my ultra doctrines respecting reliance upon the civil arm and appeals to the law.[4] Tracy will probably nibble at it, and perhaps start anew the cry of "French Jacobinism!" but so be it.[5] I am more and more convinced that the doctrine is inseparably connected with perfect christian obedience.

Yesterday forenoon, brother George popped into our house from Providence on his way to Plainfield to purchase a flock of sheep. On his return in the evening in a sleigh, he was met by a tornado which gave him and his horse a thorough peppering, and almost lynched them both. He staid all night with us, and left us on his return this morning after breakfast, in fine health and spirits. He thinks it is not improbable that he may be in Boston next week, on his way to Brighton. He seems to be driving business at a great rate. The abolition cause, he says, is moving right onward, at a quick step, in Rhode-Island.

I shall miss having a complete file of the Liberator for this year, by way of reference.

Has my wallet been returned, with the letters? If not, friend Knapp must advertise it again.[6] Mr. Fuller thought he could identify the man who exchanged coats with me.

Keep a sharp look out for errors and blunders in the Liberator.

We are all well, and as happy and contented as kittens, of which none is more fond than

Your affectionate brother,

Wm. Lloyd Garrison.

ALS: Garrison Papers, Boston Public Library; extract printed in *Life*, II, 63.

1. The first annual report of the Providence Female Juvenile Anti-Slavery Society was printed in *The Liberator*, December 26, 1835.

2. John Cutts Smith (born John Smith Cutts), a Boston minister, was one of the founders of the New England Anti-Slavery Society in 1832. His plan for increasing the subscription list of *The Liberator* was apparently never effected. In the early forties Smith was to side with Knapp in a quarrel with Garrison.

3. Garrison is anticipating the birth of his first child; see letter 230, to George W. Benson, November 30, 1835, n. 5.

4. George B. Cheever (1807–1890), a graduate of Bowdoin College and Andover Seminary, was reformer as well as man of letters. Since 1833 he had been the minister of the Howard Street Congregational Church in Salem, Massachusetts. He had published in the Salem *Landmark* (reprinted in *The Liberator,* February 21, 1835) a brief satire, entitled "Inquire at Amos Giles' Distillery," which was interpreted by Deacon John Stone as an attack upon himself and his distillery. Considerable excitement followed: a mob destroyed the *Landmark* press, and Cheever was assaulted by the foreman of the distillery and sued for libel by Stone. Involved in the case were a number of illustrious men — Judge Lemuel Shaw on the bench, Attorney General James T. Austin for the prosecution, and Rufus Choate and Peleg Sprague for the defense. Ultimately Cheever was fined $1,000 and jailed for a month. Garrison followed the case closely in *The Liberator.* In the article to which he refers, printed December 12, he argues for the preeminence of biblical over legal morality; for other articles see also the issues for the following dates: February 14, 21, April 4, July 4, 11, December 26, 1835; February 13, March 12, 1836.

5. Joseph Tracy (1793–1874) was a Congregational minister, editor, and author. He became editor of the Vermont *Chronicle* in 1829, of the Boston *Recorder* in 1834, and of the New York *Observer* in 1835. For many years he was an active colonizationist, having been an officer of both the Massachusetts and the American societies. He also was largely responsible for founding the missionary Liberia College.

6. In the issue for November 21, 1835, had appeared the following: 🖙 The gentleman, who kindly exchanged coats with Mr. Garrison in prison, will oblige Mr. G. by leaving his wallet and letters which he forgot to take out of the pocket of the borrowed coat, at the Anti-Slavery Office, No. 46 Washington-street." Since no further advertisement was printed, we can perhaps assume that the wallet and letters were returned. Shortly before his death Garrison discovered that his benefactor had been Spencer Vinal, son of Nathaniel Vinal (see *Life,* II, 24).

235

TO AMOS A. PHELPS

Brooklyn, Dec. 16, 1835.

My dear brother Phelps:

Thanks for your Farmington epistle! I say to you, as the poet Gray's friend [1] said to him, — next to the pleasure of seeing you, is the pleasure of seeing your hand-writing; next to the pleasure of hearing you, is the pleasure of hearing from you. To-day, in this little village, — which is most emphatically "all out-doors," — it is "as cold as Greenland" — in other words, it is very, *very* cold, the mercury ranging several degrees below zero: but you shall have a hasty scrawl from me, nevertheless, if my fingers do not stiffen before I get through — for though the water, and the ink, and the oil, are disposed to congeal, yet I defy cold weather to ice the stream of my affection for you.

Connecticut has been let alone too long by us meddlesome and pestiferous abolitionists; and I am rejoiced to learn that you have resolved to commence operations in this Georgia of New-England — not having the fear of Canterbury before your eyes! Every now and then, there will be an Ephesian uproar to strengthen and animate you as you move along. Should I venture to give you any advice, it would be this: by all means, in the commencement, shun such places as New Haven, Hartford and Middletown — all the large cities and towns, until the country is revolutionized. Begin at the outskirts, and work your way as quietly as possible into the centre. It is in this manner that Rhode Island has been almost entirely conquered by bro. Stanton,[2] with scarcely a single tumult. He avoided Providence and Newport, and began with remote villages, and now more than five hundred substantial names, both morally and politically, have been obtained to the call for a State Convention in February. But you are an old counsellor, although a young man, and do not need any of my suggestions.

It makes me laugh (there is something, too, of ineffable contempt within me) to see the parade which some of our would-be abolitionists are making about the *little* book of the *great* Dr. Channing on slavery! The only portions of it which are of the least consequence or value, are the sheer *moral plagiarisms* which he has stolen from the writings of the abolitionists: the rest is a farrago of impertience, contradiction and defamation. Witness the ready credence which the Dr. gives, in the Appendix, to the ridiculous and mendacious charge of Kaufman[3] against Thompson! Our early prophecies are in process of swift fulfilment. We have blasted the rocks, decapitated the hills, filled up the valleys, and macadamised the road, and now the big folks are riding upon it in their coaches as proudly as if they had made it all — the cowardly and lazy drones! Not a pound of powder have they furnished — not a single drill made — not a single spade, shovel or pick-axe wielded — not a single farthing contributed, to make a highway of liberty. And now, forsooth, that the work is almost completed, they mean if possible to monopolize it all, and to transfer the credit of its design and completion to themselves! This is a little more daring and barefaced than some other attempts of the aristocracy to defraud and p[ro]scribe the hard working-men. If there had been a single spark of magnanimity in the bosom of Dr. Channing, could he have assumed our distinctive principles, in vindication of which we have suffered so much odium, without acknowledging that we had cherished them as the apple of eye, whatever may have been the inelegancies of our style, or the rashness of our zeal? I trow not.

What then? Are we jealous of rivalry, or covetous of applause? God forbid! It is of very little consequence who obtains the credit, provided the poor slaves are released from their servitude. But the apostolic in-junction is a good one: — "Render to all their dues"[4] — to the aboli-tionists the things which are the abolitionists' — &c. &c.

But the Dr. don't like our motto, "Immediate Emancipation": so don't our enemies. He wishes us to give it up: so do they. He is offended because we admit colored members into our anti-slavery societies: so are they. He thinks we are fanatics: they think so too. He advises us to disband our four or five hundred societies, and to act without concert: so do they. He believes that slaves may be properly retained in bondage, for their good: so do all the slaveholders. He con-demns us because we have sent our appeals and warnings to some of the southern oppressors: so do they. Turn to his chapter of "Explana-tions," and see what a nice distinction he draws between men's motives and their actions! How would such a rule work in our courts? Dear brother, don't fail most critically to review the book. No one can do so better than yourself. Strip the daw of his borrowed plumage.

So! Dr. Hawes is coming out — but he must "save his shins"![5] How humiliating it is to see so much hypocrisy, injustice and servility in the heart of a good man! All the D.D's. will be out very shortly, and they will all steal our principles and abuse us roundly by way of compen-sation. You will observe that "our strength is in Truth and God."[6] Human dignity cannot exalt our cause — human authority cannot add to its excellence. Still let us lean on the arm of Omnipotence, as we have hitherto done.

It is probable that our dear brother Thompson is now in England. Our enemies, I opine, will rue the day that they ever drove him out of this country. A voice will soon come thundering over the vast Atlantic, louder than the roar of its multitudinous waves.

Pray write again soon. Mrs. G. joins in sending affectionate re-membrance to you and yourself.

Yours, with christian love,

Wm. Lloyd Garrison.

ALS: Phelps Papers, Boston Public Library.
1. Richard West, who was also quoted in letter 154, to Helen, June 2, 1834.
2. Henry B. Stanton.
3. Abram Kaufman.
4. Romans 13:7.
5. Joel Hawes (1789–1867) was a minister of Hartford, Connecticut, and a moderate abolitionist. Phelps had written Garrison December 10 (*Life*, II, 62–63), describing his recent visit to Dr. Hawes, who reported that he had preached Thanksgiving Day as boldly on slavery as he dared and that he was going to publish the sermon. Phelps said "I hoped he would *if* it was orthodox. He said, O, yes, yes, he was true to the principles, but then he couldn't go exactly with *all* our movements; and intimated that he had taken some exceptions to them — just enough, to use his own expression, to 'save his shins.'"
6. Unidentified.

2 3 6

TO LEWIS TAPPAN

Brooklyn, Ct. Dec. 17, 1835.

My very dear friend:

Your favor is just received. I perceive it is dated Dec. 1st, but having been absent from Boston several weeks, it did not reach me until to-day. This will explain the cause of my silence.

In the midst of the Ephesian uproar in Boston, my soul was sustained alike by the promises of God, and the conviction that I should have the rich sympathies and prevailing supplications of all who truly pity the slave and hate oppression, and whose love for the Redeemer is paramount to all earthly considerations. I thank you for the sympathetic and congratulatory expressions contained in your letter. But I am anxious to forget what I then endured, and all that I have been called to suffer since I began to plead in behalf of my fettered countrymen, — excepting, indeed, to draw from it new motives of gratitude and obedience to God, — because it makes me blush to compare my lot with that of the early sufferers in the cause of truth and righteousness. I have not been called upon to wander about in sheep-skins and goatskins, or to hide in dens and caves of the earth. After all, dear friend, in these modern days, the burden of the cross is light, very light to bear. What one of us has endured the hardships, or run through the perils, of the apostle Paul? Our brother Dresser [1] has received *twenty* stripes, at the hands of "false brethren"; but of the Jews, five times did the apostle receive *forty* stripes save one, and thrice was he beaten with *rods*. Turn to the catalogue of perils through which he had to pass, and then hear him declare — "I take *pleasure* in infirmities, in reproaches, in necessities, in persecutions, in distresses"! — Why, Paul? Because these things are in themselves desirable, or because, like the stoic, you make a merit of the pride of endurance? O, no! but simply and exclusively "for Christ's sake"! "For we which live are *always* delivered unto death *for Jesus' sake*, that the life also of Jesus might be made manifest in our mortal flesh." [2]

You and your much-devoted brother have long been, and still are, and undoubtedly, for some time to come, must still be surrounded with perils, and liable to be abducted or murdered by blood-thirsty men. Marvellously have you been preserved in the midst of them all! I rejoice that you are thus *counted worthy* to suffer, although I pray that the sacrifice of your lives may never be needed. The *united* suffrages of the ungodly against a moral enterprise are very strong proofs that it is a righteous one, independent of all other evidence.

But I must refer to the business part of your letter. *Your impressions are correct*, respecting the arrangement that was made between us as to the books and the sum that I owed the Rev. Mr. Paul. I thought that at the time, immediately on my return to Boston, I sent you or your brother a letter, in which I acknowledged the receipt of $240, and authorised you to retain the remaining $200 in your hands, to liquidate Mr. Paul's loan to me. At least, I am quite confident that I wrote such a letter, but how it was sent I do not remember: it seems to have miscarried. However, I am glad an opportunity is now presented for a final settlement. Appended to this letter you will find the authority that you desire. It was exceedingly kind, and truly seasonable, in brother Paul to lend the money to me, so that I could return home without begging; and equally kind in you, and the Executive Committee, to make the purchase of books by way of adjustment and relief. — I feel too grateful to you all to resort to many words.[3] Please to inquire of Mr. Paul if he received a letter from me a few days since.

At last, the great little Dr. Channing has condescended to enlighten the world with a little book on slavery — and all the world is agog![4] Why, one copy of bro. Phelps's book, is worth a hundred of Channing's — and yet what a deference is paid to the latter! O, this cringing man-worship! it sickens me. Portions of the Dr's marvellous production, I grant are sound, excellent, and clearly expressed; but all these have been taken from the writings of the despised abolitionists, without the slightest credit, and are thus grand moral plagiarisms: the rest of it is made up of contradiction, defamation, and servility to popular opinion. Can any thing be more impertinent or more unmerited than his proscription of those who have digged and M'Adamised[5] the road, at great cost and labor, upon which he is now so grandly riding in his coach? And then, too, his *treasonably modest* suggestions — 1st. That we should [. . . ious] motto, "Immediate Emancipation"! 2d. [. . . .] disorganize our four or five hundred societies! 3d. That we ought never to have permitted our colored brethren to unite with us in our associations! 4th. That we have sinned in sending our publications into the southern States! — &c. &c. But, hush! Let every thing that hath breath praise the book, *as a whole,* for it was written by the great little Dr. Channing!

In the free States, our cause is sweeping every thing before it; and the time has gone by for men to manifest extraordinary courage or disinterestedness in espousing it. We shall constantly see "great men" coming in "at the death" of the monster slavery, now that we have given him a mortal wound. Let us beware how we trust or eulogise such men!

Desiring to be most affectionately and gratefully remembered to your brother, and to your estimable lady and family, I remain with all respect and fidelity,

Your truly obliged friend,

Wm. Lloyd Garrison.

Brooklyn, Ct. Dec. 17, 1835.

Lewis Tappan, Esq.

Dear Sir — Please pay to Rev. Nathl. Paul, or his order, the sum of £40 sterling, and charge the same to the acct. of

Yours truly,

Garrison & Knapp.

ALS: Lewis Tappan Papers, Library of Congress.

1. Amos Dresser (born 1812), of Mendon, Massachusetts, a Universalist minister and leader of the Restorationist sect.
2. II Corinthians 11:26, 12:10, 4:11.
3. Undoubtedly Garrison was dilatory in repaying the loan to Paul; but his manipulation of the available funds was naïve rather than shrewd as alleged by Gilbert H. Barnes (*The Antislavery Impulse*, New York, 1933, pp. 56–57) and John L. Thomas (*The Liberator, William Lloyd Garrison, a Biography*, Boston, 1963, p. 176).
4. Garrison refers to the publication of William Ellery Channing's 165-page book *Slavery* (Boston, 1835).
5. A process named for the Scot who invented it, John L. McAdam (1756–1836).

237

TO THOMAS SHIPLEY

Brooklyn, Ct. Dec. 17, 1835.

Esteemed friend Shipley:

Not having been in Boston at the time your welcome epistle was received, some days elapsed before I saw it, which will account in some measure for my silence. Although the mercury ranges several degrees below zero to-day, in this village, yet the warmth of my esteem and the ardor of my gratitude enable me to send you a few lines in the shape of a reply. Be assured that I am deeply affected in view of the sympathy and regard which some of my beloved friends in Philadelphia have recently manifested for me, especially on account of my ill treatment by an infuriated mob, a few weeks since. Among their names I was truly gratified to see that of Thomas Shipley, whose labors in the cause of bleeding humanity have been so indefatigable, so disinterested, and, in a multitude of cases so abundantly successful. I am young in the service — you are old; and if, since our acquaintance happily commenced, we have not always seen precisely alike as to the best mode of advancing the sacred cause of liberty, yet our principles have run *pari passu*, and our hearts beat spontaneously together. It is cheering to see that the unsophisticated disciples of Christ, and the true friends of emancipation, are beginning to see and feel and act alike, as it respects both principles and measures. They would have coalesced much earlier, had the same horrible developments of southern and northern sentiments, which now affright them by their enormity, been made at an earlier period. Now that it is proclaimed, from the high places of power, that "domestic slavery is the cornerstone of our republican edifice"; [1] now that the punishment of death is denounced against those who shall plead for emancipation, whether immediate or ultimate; now that the "self evident truths" of the Declaration of Independence are *religiously* declared to be mere "rhetorical flourishes"; now that Churches, and Presbyteries and Synods, are impiously voting that slavery is divinely sanctioned, and may properly be perpetuated; now that no man, however venerable in years, or high in station, or estimable in character, can openly plead the cause of more than two millions of stolen men, women and children, without losing his reputation, and subjecting himself to every species of insult, injury and peril; now that lawful and benevolent meetings are systematically broken up, or suppressed, by mobs headed by "respectable" and "honorable" men; now that guiltless citizens are seized ruthlessly, and with perfect impunity tarred and feathered, or beaten with stripes, or driven away by force, or *suspended upon gibbets*, and that a tempting price is put upon the heads of others; and, finally, now that there is a loud clamor for the passage of laws that shall deprive us of the liberty of speech and the liberty of the press: — I say, now that this is the state of the controversy, and this the condition of our country, and this the direful alternative that is presented to us, hereafter all "good men and true," all who fear God and hate covetousness, and all who love their country and their kind, will rally under a common standard, adopt common measures, and cherish common principles. As in the days of the early Christians, when fiercely proscribed and hunted, they became united in a common bond, as one man, because it was a common cause, and stopped their useless discussions about the eucharist, baptism, and outward forms and ceremonies; so now, we may no longer dwell upon minor points in combatting slavery, but are called by the exigencies of the times and the new aspect of the warfare to unite in one vast, unbroken phalanx, and settle the point without delay, whether God or Belial, Liberty or Slavery, Right or Wrong, Order or Anarchy, Life or Death, is to reign in and over this nation. Who will not, at such a crisis, and in so glorious a strife, come with swift alacrity to the help of the Lord, and of outraged humanity, against the mighty? We must crucify all our sectarian prejudices, and all our local and political jealousies, and combat right valiantly for God and Truth, counting not our characters, or property, or lives dear unto us: so shall we be conquerors, and more than conquerors, through Him who hath loved us, and given himself for us, for through Christ strengthening us we can do all things, even to the extermination of American slavery and prejudice!

I join with you in high commendation of the speech of Gerrit Smith before the Convention at Peterboro'.[2] It will be preserved and read when marble monuments are crumbling into dust. It is the rich, spontaneous, irresistible eloquence of nature — and nature is truth. It is the soul, speaking in ["]thoughts that breathe, and words that burn." [3] It is the impalpable, deathless spirit which our enemies are so insanely endeavoring to degrade and murder. As rationally might they attempt to stab, or brickbat, or tar-and-feather, or abduct the atmosphere!

Most cordially, too, do I agree with you in your views respecting the duty of procuring an amendment to our national Constitution — of that part of it which is wet with human blood, which requires the free States to send back into bondage those who escape from the lash and the chain. It makes us as a people, and as a State, the abettors of human degradation and soul-murder; and shall we not, if possible, by a constitutional process, blot out that bloody stain? The course of events during the present session of Congress will undoubtedly indicate what steps we may wisely take upon this subject. I like your suggestion, respecting the propriety of holding quarterly meetings of the Managers of the Parent Society, and will allude to it in the Liberator. It is quite refreshing to see friend Lundy and the Genius of Universal Emancipation again in the field together.[4] They are bullet-proof. Thou murderer Lynch, avaunt!

I am much obliged to friend —— for his donation, and also to you for your kind offer of hospitality to me and my dear wife. Both of us send affectionate greetings to you and your spouse and family.

Your much obliged friend,

Wm. Lloyd Garrison

N.B. I know not whether you intended the expression of sympathy of my Philadelphia friends, for publication in the Liberator. If not, do not blame *me*, as I was absent from the city, and did not see it until it appeared in print.

Rev. Dr. Channing has just published a sort of Ishmaelitish work on slavery. He modestly asks us to give up our watchword "Immediate Emancipation," to disband our societies, and to keep our publications away from the slaveholders! His book is an 18Mo.[5] of contradictions, and contains some unmerited defamation of abolitionists, although he confesses he has never attended one of their meetings nor heard one of their addresses! However, there are many eloquent and powerful passages in it.

Please give my most respectful and affectionate remembrances to my friends A. L. Pennock and family, James Mott and family, Dr. Parrish and family, Arnold Buffum and family, &c. &c. Also to Drs. Atlee, both young and old, with their families, and to Benjamin Lundy, whom I hope to see many times in the flesh.[6]

Handwritten transcription: Garrison Papers, Boston Public Library; extracts are printed in *Life*, II, 64–66.

1. Garrison quotes from Governor George McDuffie's message to the legislature of South Carolina, which is reprinted in *The Liberator*, December 12, 1835.

2. In the speech Smith aligned himself with the cause of antislavery and immediate emancipation. The speech is reprinted in *The Liberator*, November 14, 1835.

3. Thomas Gray, *The Progress of Poesy*, line 108.

4. Garrison reported in *The Liberator*, December 19, 1835, that Lundy "is once more . . . at his editorial post, as racy, bold and eloquent . . . as ever." Lundy continued editing the paper until his death in 1839.

5. Octodecimo.

6. Dr. Joseph Parrish (1779–1840), a physician involved in various medical charities and for many years on the staff of the Philadelphia Almshouse, had been president of the Pennsylvania Society for Promoting the Abolition of Slavery. Dr. E. P. Atlee has been identified previously; old Dr. Atlee is presumably his father.

238

TO SAMUEL J. MAY

Brooklyn, Dec. 26, 1835.

My dear Coadjutor:

How is it that you Brooklynites — to wit, Henry and yourself — make such miscalculations respecting the mails between this place and Boston? Yesterday (Friday) I received your favor of Tuesday, in which you request me to hurry back to the place where I had the honor of being mobbed and imprisoned a few weeks since, and in which Henry talks of going to New-York and Philadelphia this week, and says he must see me before he goes — thereby seeming to expect my arrival in Boston by Thursday or Friday evening. I can easily account for the mistake. As there are now two mails daily between Boston and Providence, you probably presumed that your letter would reach the latter place on Tuesday evening, and arrive in Brooklyn on Wednesday forenoon. But whatever may have been the cause of its delay, it did not come to hand until yesterday. As to-morrow is the Sabbath, I shall defer leaving for Boston until Monday, via Worcester.

This week has been the only long and dull one since I came to B. I have a good editorial reason to give for it — viz. the deprivation of letters and newspapers. Every Friday, I have received a large bundle via Worcester or Providence, which has told me how the multifarious affairs of this mundane sphere are going on — but no such bundle has come to hand this week, and, what is worse than all, none of the Liberator of last week have been received, either by myself or by any of the Brooklyn subscribers. Liken me, therefore, to a fish out of water — to a bird in a cage — to a hungry pauper without victuals — to a king-fisher that has lost his prey — to any thing, in short, that implies bereavement and uneasiness. And yet I warn you not to conclude, that my peace or happiness of mind depends upon a bundle of newspapers! especially, such newspapers as abound in our country! Let this unravel the paradox — I am an editor!

I am happy to learn that there is a disposition, on the part of the abolition brethren, to place the Liberator, if possible, in a better condition than it has been heretofore. Two or three things are certain. 1st. The debts of the Liberator ought to be liquidated. 2d. If they are not, it must of necessity be discontinued. 3d. The publishers are wholly unable to discharge the debts. Now it is for the friends of our cause to consider, whether this is one of those cases in which it is a gospel duty to "bear one another's burdens." [1] I presume if a frank statement, signed by a responsible committee, were drawn up and circulated among abolitionists in various parts of the country, the sum that is needed would readily be obtained.

Undoubtedly, now is a favorable time to increase the number of subscribers to the Liberator, more so than at any period since its commencement. Brother George expressed his belief, when he was here a short time since, that 500 subscribers might easily be procured in Rhode-Island — such has been the progress of abolitionism in that State for the last six months. Our indefatigable friend John Cutts Smith, should he put his shoulders to the wheels, would undoubtedly, for a time at least, give a rail-car velocity to anti-slavery vehicle; and I hope that we shall be able to make our arrangements with him accordingly. [2]

Whatever change is made, of course the feelings and desires of Mr. Knapp must be consulted as well as mine. Should he wish to contract for the printing of the paper, at the same rate as others print, he ought to have the preference. I am inclined to think that our friends, wholly ignorant as they are, generally, respecting the losses and crosses of every newspaper concern, more or less, hardly do us justice as to our past management. I admit that we have not been methodical or sharp in keeping our accounts; but we suffer much more from the negligence of our subscribers than from our own. We have not squandered or misapplied, but, on the contrary, as a whole, been careful of our means. Recollect that we have passed through a struggle of five years; that we commenced our paper without a single subscriber, and without a cent in our pockets; that we had very few subscribers for the first two years; that our patronage, even if all had punctually paid, has always been inadequate; that we have printed and circulated, at our own charge, a large amount of publications — tracts, pamphlets, circulars, and even books; and that we have had to encounter the losses inseparable from a newspaper establishment. Yet we are in arrears only about $2500. Remember, too, that of this sum, $800 are due to us from our subscribers in two places only, *for the present year*, (and you know that the accounts have been most accurately kept at the office,) viz. New-York and Philadelphia — places which we have relied upon as the two prominent pillars of our support! The few months in which the Unionist [3] was printed made a heavily losing concern of it, as you well know. How many religious and political papers have perished, (though supported by sectarian and political zeal,) since we started the Liberator, a paper of an Ishmaeltish character! — In establishing the Western Luminary, Cincinnati Journal, The Standard, &c. &c.[4] from five to ten thousand dollars were sunk. On the whole, therefore, I marvel that we have succeeded so well.

I thank you for your hints respecting Dr. Channing. I mean to be only as severe as truth and justice require. His book, as a whole, I do not like: it is entirely destitute of magnanimity, and it requires of us about as much, in fact, as do our southern opponents. Probably I shall not commence my review until the second edition appears.[5]

Mr. Gray [6] was very much relieved in his mind to hear of the safe arrival of the clock. I will bring the articles that you desire. Mr. Parrish has been very low during the present week, so that his demise was expected daily: he is now rather better.

Your remembrances of love are reciprocated by us all. Hoping to see you on Monday evening, or on Tuesday forenoon at furthest, I close with the assurances of my love and esteem.

Ever yours,

Wm. Lloyd Garrison.

ALS: Garrison Papers, Boston Public Library; printed partly in *Life*, II, 66–67.

1. Galatians 6:2.
2. Smith's proposal was apparently never implemented, though Garrison and Knapp ceased to be partners with the last issue of 1835. Knapp became the sole publisher and Garrison continued as editor (see the masthead of *The Liberator* for January 9, 1836).
3. Edited in Brooklyn, Connecticut, by Charles C. Burleigh.
4. The *Western Luminary* was published in Lexington, Kentucky, between 1824 and 1835, and the Cincinnati *Journal* was founded in 1828; the two papers

were combined in 1835 to form the Cincinnati *Journal and Western Luminary,* which was published until 1837. The *Standard* was printed in New York between 1827 and 1834.

5. Although there were comments on Channing's *Slavery* in many issues of *The Liberator* (see, for instance, December 12, 19, 26, 1835; January 2, 9, 16, 30, 1836), the review to which Garrison refers was postponed until after the publication of the second edition and appeared February 27, 1836.

6. Evidently John Gray.

239

TO HELEN E. GARRISON

Anti-Slavery Office,
Monday Evening, Dec. 28, 1835.

My dear Wife:

Without accident or detention, I have safely arrived in Boston, having been only eight hours on the journey. We accomplished the distance from Brooklyn to Worcester, (40 miles,) in less than five hours, including stoppages and the changing of horses! Thanks to an accommodating driver and a fine team! As the travelling was hard, the stage by its rumbling discouraged conversation — and so, very little was said, except between the young minister and Miss Putnam,[1] who conversed together with the zest and fluency of lovers. But, mind — I have not said that they love each other, or mean to be united together in wedlock, either according to the Episcopal fashion or any other; but unquestionably Shakspeare was right: "there are more things in heaven and earth, than are dreampt of in our philosophy."[2]

Dear brother Henry was at the depot, and clapped his hand upon my shoulder as soon as I put my foot upon the soil, giving me quite a brotherly welcome. We then rode to Miss Parker's,[3] (where I am to remain,) and were just in season to take tea. It was quite refreshing to see familiar faces once more. Mr. and Mrs. May sat at my right hand, propounding many questions about the Brooklynites, to which I responded as rapidly as possible. As soon as I had finished my supper, I came down to the office, and having first chatted a little with brother Henry and friend Knapp, then read the last Liberator, I have now seized my pen to write to one who is dearer to me than any other earthly object. I mean this shall reach you on Wednesday, if possible, because I know how you will appreciate my promptness.

Whether Mr. May will visit Brooklyn, I had no time to learn, but gave him the letters, which he read at the table, but made no remarks upon them. I do not think Mrs. May will feel willing to have him leave her at this time.

Brother Phelps [4] has been mobbed in Farmington. A large brick-bat was thrown through the window, almost with the velocity of a canon-ball, and narrowly missed his head. Had it struck him, undoubtedly he would have been killed on the spot. He went on with his lecture, however, and told the people he would not cease to plead the cause of enslaved humanity in that place, until either mob-law was put down, or he should fall a victim. The next evening his meeting was slightly disturbed, but the third evening he carried his point triumphantly. About twenty of the rioters have been arrested — all "men of cloth."

Rev. Mr. Grosvenor has been mobbed in Worcester county.[5]

Charles Stuart has been mobbed in the western part of the State of New-York. A brickbat struck him on the head, which made him senseless for a time — but as soon as he recovered, he began to plead for the suffering and dumb, until he was persuaded by a clergyman to desist.

Rev. George Storrs has been mobbed, (according to law,) in New-Hampshire.[6] In the midst of his prayer, he was arrested, and violently shaken, and carried before a Justice of the Peace, as a vagrant, idler and disturber of the peace ! ! by gentlemen, too ! ! But they could find nothing against him legally, and so he was dismissed.

These shameful transactions will doubtless be multiplied — but our safety and strength lie in an omnipotent arm. — "The Lord reigneth" [7] — we have no other, and desire no better consolation.

A sharp Review of Dr. Channing's book has just appeared, said to be from the pen of James T. Austin, the famous Attorney General in the case of Mr. Cheever.[8] Of course, I have not had time to read it.

The anti-slavery debate in Congress continued five days! Mr. Slade of Vt. spoke nobly.[9] They did not dare to reject the petitions, but laid them on the table. The southerners were very fierce.

I suppose very many will be disappointed in not seeing me at the Monthly Concert this evening — but I felt somewhat wearied, and preferred writing to you.

Already my brain whirls with excitement, so many things are said to me, and so many documents and papers remained to be examined.

If I continue writing any longer, I shall lose the mail; so I hastily conclude the worst scrawl I ever sent to you.

With the kindest remembrances to all the dear household, I remain in the bonds of love,

Your devoted husband,

Wm. Lloyd Garrison.

ALS: Garrison Papers, Boston Public Library; printed partly in *Life*, II, 67–68.

1. Possibly Caroline F. Putnam, friend of the family and later companion to abolitionist lecturer Sallie Holley; see the letter to Helen, October 10, 1853.

2. Shakespeare, *Hamlet*, I, v, 166.

3. Mary Parker.

4. Amos A. Phelps.

5. Cyrus P. Grosvenor.

6. George Storrs (1796–1879) was arrested in Northfield, New Hampshire, following a lecture on slavery. The justice of the peace sentenced him to three months of hard labor in the House of Correction, but the conviction was reversed on appeal.

7. Several possible biblical sources, including I Chronicles 16:31.

8. As mentioned in n. 4 of letter 234, to Henry E. Benson, December 15, 1835, James T. Austin (1784–1870) was the attorney general of Massachusetts, who tried the Reverend George B. Cheever for libel, insisting on a legalistic definition of morality. The review to which Garrison refers was printed in *The Liberator*, January 2, 1836. Garrison objected to this review almost as much as to Channing's book; see the issue for January 16 and "A Reviewer Reviewed," February 20.

9. William Slade (1786–1859) was elected to Congress in 1830 after a career as lawyer, editor, and state politician. Late in life he became governor of Vermont.

240

TO HELEN E. GARRISON

Boston, Dec. 30, 1835.

My dearest:

You see I commence another hasty letter to you; for, the fact is, when I was here before, you know I established the precedent (a most extraordinary one for me) of sending you something in the shape of an epistle by every mail. May it not seem an abatement of affection or interest, if I should now infract upon this rule? It is too late to repent.

My exilement from Boston, I find, has not weakened the attachment of my abolition brethren for me. Wherever I move, whatever faces I see among them, all is welcome — all is delight. "How do you do?" "Welcome back again!" "Where and how is your lady?" These and a hundred other things are said or asked continually. Great interest is felt in your welfare.

To-day has been the day for the Ladies' Fair — but not so bright and fair out of doors, as within doors.[1] The Fair was held at the house of Mr. Chapman's father, in Chauncey Place, in two large rooms. Perhaps there were not quite so many things prepared as last year, but the assortment was nevertheless various. There were several tables, as usual, which were under the superintendence of the Misses Weston, the Misses Ammidon, Miss Paul, Miss Chapman, Mrs. Sargeant, (who, by the way, spoke in the kindest manner of you,) and one or two other persons whom I did not know.[2] I bought a few things, and had one or two presents for Mrs. Garrison. The fair will be continued to-morrow, but I do not think the proceeds will equal the sales of last year. Every thing has been conducted in a pleasing manner. Friend Whittier's and Thompson's portraits were hung up to observation — mine has gone on to Philadelphia to be engraved.

Henry, Knapp and myself sleep (all in a row) in the office, in good style and fine fellowship — one of us upon a sofa-bedstead, and two upon settees, which are not quite so soft, to be sure, as ours at Brooklyn. I have had invitations to stay with friends Fuller, Southwick and Shattuck,[3] and at Miss Parker's, but prefer to be independent.

The arrangements for the Liberator are not yet definitely made, but I think all past affairs will soon be settled.

Our friend Sewall's *"intended,"* Miss Winslow, is now in the city, and was at the fair to-day, with two sparkling eyes and a pleasant countenance.[4] How soon the marriage knot is to be tied, I cannot find out. Don't you think they are unwise not to hasten matters?

I have not yet seen Christiana, or Mr. Gray — this confession is to my condemnation; but to-morrow, if I am spared, I will visit both. The Westons like C——a very much — but not the cat.

This evening I took tea at Mr. Loring's.[5] He has been somewhat ill, but is now better, though still feeble. His amiable wife was at the fair, selling and buying, and giving away, with her characteristic assiduity and liberality. Both of them were very kind in their inquiries after my wife.

This forenoon, bro. May and myself, by express invitation, visited Miss Martineau, at Mr. Gannett's house.[6] The interview was very agreeable and satisfactory to me. She is a fine woman.

All are regretting that I cannot prolong my visit until after the 20th of January, so that I might be present at the annual meeting of our Society — but I tell them I cannot, for many reasons too numerous to particularize.

I shall despatch matters as fast as possible, so as to make my absence comparatively. In the mean time, I remain, with increasing love for you and the dear family,

Your devoted husband,

Wm. Lloyd Garrison.

ALS: Garrison Papers, Boston Public Library; printed partly in *Life*, II, 68–69.

1. Garrison describes the second antislavery fair, which was to become an annual and increasingly important fund-raising event for more than twenty years. In 1834 it had raised $300 for the New England Anti-Slavery Society, and it was to raise $350 at Warren Weston's house in the current year. Subsequent versions of the bazaar, as it was called by 1845, were to raise for the Massachusetts Anti-Slavery Society as much as $5,250 in 1856. Following that year the National Anti-

Slavery Subscription took the place of the bazaar, raising a maximum of $6,117.02 in 1859. During the war this type of fund-raising venture became less successful.

2. Apart from the Westons relatively little is known about these young ladies who were active in the fairs and in the Boston Female Anti-Slavery Society. The Misses Ammidon, daughters of Philip Ammidon of Boston (born 1774), are Melani (born 1809), who later married the Reverend Joseph Parker of Boston, and Silvia (born 1814), who was to marry the Reverend Henry Parker. Miss Paul is Susan Paul (c. 1809–1841), the daughter of the Reverend Thomas Paul, who had been until his death in 1831 pastor of the African Baptist Church on Belknap Street; she was by profession a teacher (see *The Liberator*, April 23, 1841). Miss Chapman is Anne Green Chapman (c. 1802–1837), a daughter of Henry G. Chapman and one of those ladies who attended the famous meeting of the Boston Female Anti-Slavery Society on October 21, 1835. At her death she left generous bequests to both the Boston Female and the American Anti-Slavery Societies; Garrison eulogized her in verse printed in *The Liberty Bell* for 1839. Mrs. Sargeant is perhaps intended to be *Miss* Henrietta Sargant (the usual spelling), who was on many occasions hospitable to the Garrisons and who became their increasingly good friend.

3. Although identification is far from certain, this might be George Cheyne Shattuck (1783–1854), from a distinguished Boston family and one of the leading doctors of the day; he was also noted as a philanthropist.

4. Louisa M. Winslow (1814–1850), the daughter of Nathan Winslow of Portland, Maine, was to marry Samuel E. Sewall in 1836.

5. Ellis Gray Loring's.

6. Ezra Stiles Gannett (1801–1871), a colleague of Dr. Channing's, was moderate in his antislavery views and, therefore, somewhat hostile to Garrison.

Index of Recipients
Index of Names

Index of Letter Recipients

Index of Names

The following abbreviations are used: AA-SS, American Anti-Slavery Society; MA-SS, Massachusetts Anti-Slavery Society; NEA-SS, New England Anti-Slavery Society; WLG, William Lloyd Garrison.